"A fabulous piece of scholarship. This book will open a whole new chapter in our study of Vietnam."
　　　　—Tom Clancy

"Thoroughly researched, clearly written and forcefully argued."
　　　　—Brian VanDeMark, author of *Into the Quagmire*; *Los Angeles Times Book Review*

"H. R. McMaster's new *Dereliction of Duty* stands out as a particularly well-documented, searing indictment of the civilian and military leadership. This is the clearest and most cogent argument as to the basic causes of the disaster."
　　　　—Edward M. Coffman, author of *The War to End All Wars* and *The Old Army*

"Brilliant . . . a penetrating analysis."
　　　　—*San Francisco Chronicle*

"Invaluable . . . a most readable, yet meticulously documented history."
　　　　—Col. Harry G. Summers Jr., U.S. Army (retired), author of *On Strategy: A Critical Analysis of the Vietnam War* and editor of *Vietnam* magazine

"McMaster's book has drawn high praise from experts. . . . His dogged research unearthed thousands of pages of material denied other historians and writers."
　　　　—Ed Offley, *Seattle Post Intelligencer*

"A chilling indictment. . . . There have been many books on the Vietnam War, but none that examines so closely and intensively how Lyndon Johnson, Robert McNamara, and Maxwell Taylor systematically conspired to prevent the Joint Chiefs of Staff from performing their duty."
　　　　—Michael Barone, author of *Our Country: The Shaping of America from Roosevelt to Reagan*

"Red hot. . . . Brilliantly shows how the American people were conned."
　　　　—Col. David H. Hackworth, U.S. Army (retired), *New York Times* bestselling coauthor of *About Face*; *Newsweek*

"H. R. McMaster's incisive and brilliantly researched analysis demonstrates conclusively that when Robert S. McNamara said, in his belated apologia, that he had been 'wrong, terribly wrong,' he still didn't have it right. What he should have said was that he and his crowd had been 'incompetent, terribly incompetent,' and 'deceitful, terribly deceitful.'"

    —Lewis Sorley, author of *Thunderbolt: General Creighton Abrams and the Army of His Times*

"It's stunning. . . . Go get *Dereliction of Duty*, a blistering and scholarly exposé."

    —Rush Limbaugh

"The hottest book among some top brass in the Pentagon is *Dereliction of Duty*."

    —*Wall Street Journal*

"H. R. McMaster, in his book *Dereliction of Duty*, has done what other historians might have done, but didn't. . . . His research was thorough and organized. McMaster's conclusions are equally impressive."

    —Lt. Gen. Victor H. Krulak, U.S. Marine Corps, *Marine Corps Gazette*

"In addition to being an absorbing and provocative account of an extraordinarily painful episode in our nation's history, *Dereliction of Duty* addresses vital and difficult questions about senior officers' responsibilities to the Constitution, the president, Congress and their services. . . . *Dereliction of Duty* is an important Vietnam book that is well worth reading."

    —Lt. Col. Alan C. Cate, U.S. Army Command and General Staff College, *Military Review*

"Compelling . . . scathing . . . tightly reasoned, well-referenced . . . excellent . . . provocative."

    —Dr. Paul F. Braim (Colonel, U.S. Army, retired), *Parameters*

"Controversial . . . provocative . . . disturbing. . . . McMaster succeeds admirably. . . . *Dereliction of Duty* is a scathing indictment of senior military leadership . . . [and] a major contribution to the historiography of the conflict."
—Col. Cole C. Kingseed, U.S. Army, *Army* magazine

"A meticulously researched blockbuster of a book."
—Lt. Gen. John H. Cushman, U.S. Army (retired), *Proceedings*

"*Dereliction of Duty* is a searing indictment. . . . Today's military leaders should read the book and look forward to McMaster's next one."
—Dr. Steven Metz, Henry L. Stimson Professor of Military Studies, U.S. Army War College, *Parameters*

"If those who forget the past are condemned to repeat it, then H. R. McMaster has done the Pentagon and the nation a favor. . . . He has good advice for readers, especially high ranking military ones. . . . Like all good history books, it unlocks the past and guides an understanding of the present."
—Ernest Blazar, Pentagon correspondent, *Washington Times*

"Major McMaster has written an important, well-researched, provocative book. . . . He has done his part to help us learn from history."
—Brig. Gen. Douglas Kinnard, U.S. Army (retired), Ph.D., Emeritus Professor of Political Science, University of Vermont, and author of *The War Managers*; *Parameters*

"A book to boggle your mind with new revelations of ineptness, duplicity, and arrogance amongst the senior-most officials of the United States. . . . McMaster pastes all the puzzle pieces together to reveal a plot Shakespearean in its proportions. . . . McMaster's scholarship and presentation is exemplary in *Dereliction of Duty*. . . . The author's arguments are coherent and convincing and important to the historical record."
—Peter Arnett, *Washington Monthly*

"Four star generals do not normally consult the writings of junior field grade officers for advice about career decisions. But it was widely reported that when Air Force Chief of Staff General Ronald Fogelman decided to resign in 1997, he did so at least in part on the basis of a careful reading of H. R. McMaster's *Dereliction of Duty*.

"McMaster has written a scathing indictment of America's civilian and military leadership during the early phases of the Vietnam war, and he speaks . . . with unique moral authority. . . . McMaster earned his moral authority under fire. . . . By virtue of his actions [in the Gulf War], McMaster became a hero.

"[McMaster] speaks with unusual authority as a symbol of the confident young veterans of the Gulf. His call to his leaders to hold themselves to high standards of professional integrity is, therefore, an important one. No wonder, then, that General Fogelman, himself an acute student of history, would pay close attention to work that on nearly every page excoriates his predecessors for their unwillingness to speak and act as their positions required.

"Recently, the chairman of the Joint Chiefs of Staff, General Henry Shelton, invited Major McMaster to lecture to the most senior generals in the American military about his book."
> —Eliot Cohen, professor of strategic studies of
> The Johns Hopkins University School of Advanced
> International Studies, *National Interest Magazine*

"[A] provocative account . . . interesting and important . . . painstaking and eloquent. . . . It is an unanswerable indictment of the inattentiveness and deceitfulness of the Johnson Administration and the arrogance and hubris of McNamara's band in the Pentagon."
> —Michael Desch, *Orbis*

"In late 1997, the *New York Times* ran an article about the resignation of Air Force Chief of Staff Gen. Ronald Fogleman. . . . The *Times* stated that his decision to retire had been influenced by a book then newly released, titled *Dereliction of Duty*. . . . [That book] is destined to become one of the most controversial volumes on the greatest military debacle in American history."
> —Edward Shapiro, professor of history at
> Seton Hall University, author of *The World and I*

"Thoroughly researched and fascinating. . . . McMaster has done an admirable job . . . with intelligence and control and fairness."
> —*American Historical Review*

"*Dereliction of Duty* . . . has achieved a cult following."
> —*The New Republic*

"Well-written and full of enlightening new details, *Dereliction of Duty* adds significantly to the historical record of a great national failure."

—Arnold R. Isaacs, *Washington Post Book World*

"Carefully researched and vividly narrated, H. R. McMaster's book adds a new and disturbing dimension to an understanding of the decisions that propelled us into the Vietnam War. It should be read by anyone interested in the origins of one of the great tragedies in American history."

—Stanley Karnow, Pulitzer Prize–winning author of
Vietnam: A History

"A book to boggle your mind with new revelations of ineptness, duplicity, and arrogance among the senior-most officials of the United States . . . McMaster's scholarship and presentation is exemplary in *Dereliction of Duty*. . . . The author's arguments are coherent and convincing and important to the historical record."

—Peter Arnett, *Washington Monthly*

"An outstanding example of historical research, interpretation, scholarship, and fair-minded analysis."
—Donald Kagan, Bass Professor of History, Classics, and Western
Civilization, Yale University, and author of *On the Origins of War*

"Superbly researched, play-by-play, riveting inside story of the genesis of the American War in Vietnam. Assorted firepower explodes on every page."

—Lt. General Harold G. Moore, U.S. Army (retired),
coauthor of the *New York Times* bestseller
We Were Soldiers Once . . . and Young

Dereliction of Duty

Lyndon Johnson, Robert McNamara,
the Joint Chiefs of Staff, and the Lies
That Led to Vietnam

H. R. McMaster

HARPER  PERENNIAL

NEW YORK • LONDON • TORONTO • SYDNEY • NEW DELHI • AUCKLAND

First HarperPerennial edition published 1998; reissued in 2017.

Designed by Elina D. Nudelman

The Library of Congress has catalogued the hardcover edition as follows:

McMaster, H. R., 1962–
    Dereliction of duty : Lyndon Johnson, Robert McNamara, the Joint Chiefs of Staff, and the lies that led to Vietnam / H. R. McMaster.—1st ed.
        p.   cm.
    Includes bibliographical references and index.
    ISBN 0-06-018795-6
    1. Vietnamese Conflict, 1961–1975—United States.   2. United States—Politics and government—1963–1969.   3. Johnson, Lyndon B. (Lyndon Baines), 1908–1973. I. Title.
DS558.M43   1997
959.704′3373—dc21   97-5152

ISBN 978-0-06-092908-4 (pbk.)

22 23 24 25 26 LBC 41 40 39 38 37

For Katie

Contents

Photographs follow page 254.

Preface

Despite scores of books on the subject, the why and how of direct U.S. intervention in the Vietnam War remains unclear. The war continues to capture the public interest in part because, looking back, its cost seems exorbitant—and would seem so even if the United States had "won." The war took the lives of fifty-eight thousand Americans and well over one million Vietnamese. It left Vietnam in ruins and consumed billions of American dollars, nearly wrecking the American economy. Vietnam divided American society and inflicted on the United States one of the greatest political traumas since the Civil War. Indeed, the war's legacies proved to be as profound as the war was traumatic. It led Americans to question the integrity of their government as never before. Thirty years later, after the end of the Cold War, the shadow of the American experience in Vietnam still hangs heavy over American foreign and military policy, and over American society.[1]

It would be impossible for an Army lieutenant, obtaining his commission in 1984, not to be concerned with the experience of the Vietnam War. I thought that to better prepare myself to lead soldiers in combat it was important to learn from the experiences of others, and the most recent U.S. war seemed as good a starting place as any. I read personal accounts written by junior officers, but found to my surprise that the Army I entered barely spoke of Vietnam. The emotions connected with sacrifices made in a lost war ran too deep to permit the veterans of that conflict to dwell on their experiences. Those who had remained in uniform seemed eager to forget and had turned their energies and talents toward building an organization capable of fighting and winning the next war. In 1991, as commander of an armored cavalry troop in the Persian Gulf War, it was clear to me that our unit's experience was dramatically different from the Vietnam accounts that I had read. The ease with which we could connect our combat mission to strategic objectives that seemed clear and attainable contrasted starkly with combat actions in Vietnam, which seemed to achieve nothing beyond adding more enemy dead to the weekly body count.[2] I wondered how and why Vietnam had become an American war—a war in which men fought and died without a clear idea of how their actions and sacrifices were contributing to an end of the conflict. When I arrived at Chapel Hill, North Carolina, in 1992 to begin my graduate work in American history, I began to seek answers to those questions.

I discovered that the military's role in Vietnam decision making was little understood and largely overlooked.[3] By law the Joint Chiefs of Staff were the "principal military advisers to the President, the National Security Council, and the Secretary of Defense."[4] That was not the role of the Joint Chiefs of Staff (JCS) during the escalation of the Vietnam War. It became clear to me that I would need to understand the role of the president, his principal civilian advisers, and the JCS in the decision-making process.

The timing was right. Recently declassified documents, newly opened manuscript collections, and the release of the official history of the JCS during the Vietnam War shed new light on the subject. I gained access to thousands of documents that had previously been unavailable to researchers and historians. Interviews with those close to the decision-making process, taped meetings and telephone conversations, and oral histories and memoirs of top civilian and military officials who served during this period placed the documentary record in the context of personalities and advisory relationships. The discoveries astonished me, and I felt compelled to share them with others.

Any interpretation of direct American intervention in the Vietnam

War must address the question of responsibility for one of the greatest American foreign policy disasters of the twentieth century. Assessing blame for the disaster in Vietnam, however, is beside the point. Much more important is to determine how and why key decisions were made, decisions that involved the United States in a war that it could not win at a politically acceptable level of commitment.

Acknowledgments

This work has benefited, directly and indirectly, from the assistance of many. At its inception in 1992, the advice of Dr. Herbert Schandler; Col. Charles Brower, USA; and Col. Cole Kingseed, USA, proved invaluable. Joseph Galloway, through his example and friendship, was and remains a great inspiration to me. I want to express my thanks to those who read and commented on earlier versions of the manuscript, including Professor George Herring; Professor John Gates; Professor Donald Kagan; Gen. Frederick Franks, USA (Ret.); Lt. Gen. Julius Becton, USA (Ret.); Tom Clancy; Gen. William Y. Smith, USAF (Ret.); Maj. Gen. Perry Smith, USAF (Ret.); Maj. Gen. Harry Jenkins, USMC (Ret.); Cmdr. Thomas Buell, USN (Ret.); Ambassador Bui Diem; Col. Douglas MACgregor, USA; Maj. Toby Green, USA; Peter Braestrup; Dr. Michael Pearlman; Mark Rader; Fred Griffin; Pierce O'Donnell; Dr. Ronald Glasser; J. Peter Findlen; William Coyle, Jr.; Margaret Herbert; Justice John K. Trotter; and Kevin Trotter. I am particularly indebted to the professors of the University of North Carolina at Chapel Hill and Duke University who guided and encouraged me throughout the effort; especially Richard Kohn, Michael Hunt,

Don Higginbotham, Tami Davis Biddle, Alex Roland, Terry Sullivan, and Lt. Col. Mark Clodfelter, USAF. Dr. Fred Logevall of the University of California at Santa Barbara, who was completing a book on the international aspects of the Americanization of the war, was a sympathetic listener and thoughtful critic. My friend Dr. Lewis Sorley gave valuable editorial advice. He and his wife, Ginny, provided encouragement throughout, as well as lodging during my research visits to the Washington area. I also benefited from the first-rate editorial guidance of Buz Wyeth and Susan H. Llewellyn at HarperCollins.

I could not have asked for a better environment in which to write this book than that provided by the Department of History at the United States Military Academy. Although I am indebted to all my colleagues, I would like to acknowledge in particular the assistance of Col. Charles Brower, Lt. Col. David Fautua, Maj. Kevin Farrell, Professor Eugenia Kiesling, and Professor Cliff Rogers. During the final preparation of the manuscript, my good friends Professor Fred Kagan and his wife, Kim, gave generously of their time to help with typing and editing. They not only made it possible for me to meet deadlines and enhanced the appearance and clarity of the manuscript, but they were a source of moral support. Lisa and Tom Cornell and their children, Jane and Matt, contributed to the effort by spending many a weekend and evening with my family while I was absorbed in the process of writing. Melissa Mills and Carla Majors enabled me to discharge my teaching and administrative duties efficiently so that I could devote more time after hours to writing. I am indebted as well to my students at West Point and Mount Saint Mary's College of Newburgh, New York, with whom I shared the experience of historical inquiry and discovery.

I want to thank the many archivists and historians who made researching and writing this book both efficient and enjoyable; especially Regina Greenwell, Ted Gittinger, Jeremy Duvall, Linda Hanson, Phillip Scott, and Allen Fisher at the Lyndon Baines Johnson Library in Austin, Texas; Susan Lemke and Tina Lavato at the National Defense University Library in Washington, D.C.; Dr. Richard Sommers, David Keogh, and Pamela Cheney at the U.S. Army Institute for Military History in Carlisle Barracks, Pennsylvania; Fred Graboske, Benis Frank, and Brig. Gen. Edwin Simmons, USMC (Ret.), at the Marine Corps Historical Center in Washington; Drs. Ed Marolda and Jeffrey Barlow at the Navy Historical Center in Washington; Drs. Cary Conn and Tim Nenninger at the National Archives; and Vincent Demma and Joel Meyerson at the U.S. Army Center of Military History in Washington. Dr. Walter Poole at the Joint History Office in Washington gave the manuscript a critical reading and provided me with valuable comments and suggestions. Librarians at the United States Military Academy library—Paul Nergelovic, Margaret Tackett, and Dean Hough—provided research assistance and gave me much-needed space to organize the vast amount of materials that I had collected.

The work benefited from those who granted interviews and offered advice and assistance, including Dr. Walt Rostow; Gen. William Westmoreland, USA (Ret.); Gen. Andrew Goodpaster, USA (Ret.); Gen. Bernard Rogers, USA (Ret.); Lt. Gen. Victor Krulak, USMC (Ret.); Maj. Gen. Edwin Simmons, USMC (Ret.); Brig. Gen. Theodore Mataxis, USA (Ret.); and Brig. Gen. John Johns, USA (Ret.). Former Commandant of the Marine Corps Gen. Wallace Greene granted me generous access to his personal papers.

The Marine Corps Historical Foundation in Washington supported the project with its 1995 General Lemuel C. Shepherd, Jr., Fellowship. I received early assistance from the Lyndon Baines Johnson Foundation and the United States Military Academy Faculty Development Fund.

■

My family made what could have been an arduous task a most enjoyable and fulfilling experience. My mother, Marie C. McMaster, a dedicated and brilliant educator, instilled in me an appreciation for history and a desire to teach and write. Although I knew that she was not the most objective reader, I could always count on my mom for an encouraging review of the manuscript. She and my father, Herbert R. McMaster, have remained a great source of strength. My sister and best friend, Letitia McMaster, gave critical assistance when I needed it most. This book would have remained an unfulfilled aspiration without the love and support of my wife, Katie. She shouldered the vast majority of parental responsibilities during the four years of researching and writing. My beautiful daughters, Katharine, Colleen, and Caragh, inspired me to work efficiently so that I could spend more time with them on the playground, on the soccer field, and reading bedtime stories. When I felt under pressure to complete a chapter or to synthesize a particularly vexing array of evidence, their smiling faces helped to keep the project in proper perspective.

Of course, any errors or shortcomings that remain are mine alone. The views presented herein are also mine alone and do not necessarily represent the views of the Department of Defense or its components, including the United States Military Academy and the United States Army Command and General Staff College.

Abbreviations

ARVN	Army of the Republic of Vietnam
BLT	Marine battalion landing team
CIA	Central Intelligence Agency
CINCPAC	Commander in Chief, Pacific Command
CNO	Chief of Naval Operations
DCI	Director of Central Intelligence
DESOTO patrols	code name for U.S. Navy destroyer patrols in the Gulf of Tonkin
DMZ	demilitarized zone
DOD	Department of Defense
DRV	Democratic Republic of Vietnam [North Vietnam]
FRUS	*Foreign Relations of the United States*

GVN	Government of [South] Vietnam
ISA	International Security Affairs Division, Department of Defense
JCS	Joint Chiefs of Staff
MACV	Military Assistance Command, Vietnam
MAROPS	Maritime Operations
MIG	Soviet-made jet fighter aircraft
NSAM	National Security Action Memorandum
NSC	National Security Council
NVN	North Vietnam
OPLAN	Operations Plan
OSD	Office of the Secretary of Defense
RVN	Republic of Vietnam [South Vietnam]
SAC	Strategic Air Command
SAM	Surface-to-Air Missile
SEACOORD	Coordinating Committee for U.S. Mission Southeast Asia
SEATO	Southeast Asia Treaty Organization
SECDEF	Secretary of Defense
SNIE	Special National Intelligence Estimate
SVN	South Vietnam
VC	Viet Cong

Dereliction of Duty

1
The New Frontiersmen and the Old Guard

1961–October 1962

Allowing for reasonable exceptions and a wide latitude of variation, the typical New Frontiersman is about 46 years old, highly energetic, distinctly articulate and refreshingly idealistic. In short, he has much in common with the man the American people have chosen as their President.

—M. B. SCHNAPPER, 1961[1]

The disaster of the Vietnam War would dominate America's memory of a decade that began with great promise. In the 1960 presidential election, John F. Kennedy narrowly defeated Dwight Eisenhower's vice president, Richard Nixon. Despite a narrow margin of victory, the new president exuded confidence. His clarion call, "Let us begin anew," evoked the prospect of a new era of prosperity and opportunity.[2] Although he was only five years younger than Nixon, Kennedy at forty-three seemed youthful and vigorous compared to his opponent and the "old timers" of Eisenhower's administration. A witty, attractive man, Kennedy was a World War II hero and Pulitzer Prize winning author who had gained considerable political experience as a congressman and senator. His rhetoric exhorted America's youth to "pay any price" and "bear any burden" to extend the virtues of their country to the rest of the world.[3] The idealism that Kennedy seemed to personify

1

would be lost in a place that, in 1960, was of little interest or significance to Americans.

■

A campaign issue that Kennedy had taken up with some vigor was that of the need for reform in national defense strategy and the management of the Department of Defense. Truman administration Defense Secretary Robert Lovett advised Kennedy that reform in the Pentagon would be "painful" but was "long overdue." He told him that his defense secretary should be "an analytical statistician who can . . . tear out the overlap, the empire building."[4] Lovett urged the president-elect to consider the forty-four-year-old president of the Ford Motor Company, Robert Strange McNamara, for the job.

When World War II began, Robert McNamara was serving on the business faculty at Harvard University, teaching the application of statistical analysis to management problems. Initially disqualified from military service because of his inability to pass an eye examination, he became a consultant to the War Department to develop statistical controls within the Army Air Corps supply system. After spending the first year of the war teaching at the Army Air Forces Statistical Control Officers School, McNamara requested an assignment to the Eighth Air Force in England. McNamara arrived in England in February 1943 and, after three weeks, sought a commission as a captain. The professor-turned-military-officer became part of a traveling statistical control group that analyzed maintenance, logistics, and operational problems in England, India, China, and the Pacific. McNamara often met resistance from military officers who discounted his new methods. A lieutenant colonel in 1945, he left the Army an ardent believer in the need for statistical management and control over military organizations.[5]

After World War II, McNamara, with several of his Army Air Corps statistician colleagues, joined Ford. They were known collectively as the Whiz Kids, a term later associated with the young analysts McNamara brought with him to the Pentagon. At Ford, McNamara preferred the academic milieu of Ann Arbor to the corporate culture of suburban Detroit. His drive, ambition, and analytical talents led to his appointment, in November 1960, as the first company president who was not a member of the Ford family. One month later R. Sargent Shriver, John F. Kennedy's brother-in-law, visited McNamara on behalf of the president-elect. Although he intended to remain at Ford, McNamara agreed to fly to meet Kennedy.[6]

Among the qualities that Kennedy admired was self-assurance. During his second meeting with Kennedy, McNamara surprised the president-elect and his brother Robert with his assertiveness. He handed Jack Kennedy a contract stipulating that he be given free rein over appointments in the Department of Defense and not be expected to engage in purely social events. Kennedy read the document and passed it, unsigned, to his brother.[7] McNamara seemed the man for the job. The Kennedy brothers swept McNamara out the front door of the brick Georgetown house and introduced the secretary of defense–designate to the bevy of reporters waiting outside in the freezing cold.

Kennedy worried most over the appointment of a secretary of state. Reluctant to alienate any of his key Democratic constituencies, he settled on everyone's second choice, Dean Rusk. Rusk, a former Rhodes scholar from Georgia, was a professor of government and dean of faculty at Mills College in California, when, in 1940, he was ordered into active military service as an Army captain. He served initially in Washington as an intelligence analyst. With the advent of American involvement in World War II, Rusk left the capital for the headquarters of the China, Burma, and India theater of operations. The quality of the cables that the young staff officer sent to the War Department caught the eye of Army Chief of Staff George C. Marshall. General Marshall summoned Rusk to Washington, where he joined Col. George A. Lincoln's Strategy and Policy Group to help develop long-range politico-military contingency plans. In 1946 Rusk joined the State Department and, in 1950, became Secretary of State Dean Acheson's assistant for Far Eastern affairs. In 1952 he left the State Department to head the Rockefeller Foundation. During his years of government service, Rusk built a solid reputation for loyalty and trustworthiness within the Democratic establishment. The unprepossessing, introspective Rusk provided a conspicuous contrast to the confident, assertive McNamara. Lovett and Acheson had recommended Rusk enthusiastically, and, after a brief interview, Kennedy decided to appoint him.[8]

Kennedy had considered McGeorge Bundy for secretary of state, but concluded that he was too young. In 1953, Bundy, at thirty-four, was appointed dean of Harvard University's Faculty of Arts and Sciences. His formative years were spent in the best schools of the Northeast—Groton,

Yale, Harvard—and in association with some of the most influential people in the twentieth-century United States. He assisted Henry Stimson (William Howard Taft's secretary of war, Herbert Hoover's secretary of state, and Franklin Roosevelt's secretary of war) in the preparation of his memoirs. He also helped Dean Acheson prepare a collection of his personal papers for publication. Bundy was known for an abruptness and imperious demeanor with those he considered his intellectual inferiors, but he could also be effusive and engaging in a social setting.[9] Kennedy chose him as special assistant for national security affairs (usually called national security adviser).

Kennedy placed a premium on academic qualifications and superior intellect. McNamara, Rusk, and Bundy all shared distinguished academic backgrounds. Moreover Kennedy wanted men who shared his broad interests and could engage in wide-ranging, informal discussions. Perhaps the most important determining factor of each man's relative influence would be his ability to establish a close personal rapport with the president. Rusk, who preferred established procedures and protocol, had difficulty adjusting to the president's freewheeling style. Socially he remained distant from the president and was the only senior official Kennedy did not address by his first name. McNamara and Bundy would prove more adept at securing the president's confidence and affection.[10]

■

The president's personal style influenced the way he structured the White House staff to handle national security decision making. Having no experience as an executive, Kennedy was unaccustomed to operating at the head of a large staff organization. He regarded Eisenhower's National Security Council (NSC) structure as cumbersome and unnecessary. Immediately after taking office, he eliminated the substructure of the NSC by abolishing its two major committees: the Planning Board and the Operations Coordinating Board (OCB). Kennedy resolved not to use the NSC except for the pro forma consultation required by the National Security Act of 1947. In place of the formal Eisenhower system, Kennedy relied on an ad hoc, collegial style of decision making in national security and foreign affairs. He formed task forces to analyze particular problems and met irregularly with an "inner club" of his most trusted advisers to discuss problems informally and weigh the advantages and disadvantages of potential courses of action.[11]

Kennedy's dismantling of the NSC apparatus diminished the voice of the Joint Chiefs of Staff (JCS) in national security matters. Under Eisenhower military officers connected with the JCS were assigned to the Planning Board and the OCB. Through these representatives, the JCS could place items important to the military on the NSC agenda. During NSC meetings Eisenhower considered differing opinions and made decisions with all the Chiefs in attendance. Kennedy's structural changes, his practice of consulting frankly with only his closest advisers, and his use of larger forums to validate decisions already made would transcend his own administration and continue as a prominent feature of Vietnam decision making under Lyndon Johnson. Under the Kennedy-Johnson system, the Joint Chiefs lost the direct access to the president, and thus the real influence on decision making, that the Eisenhower NSC structure had provided.[12]

Diminished JCS access to the president reflected Kennedy's opinion of his senior military advisers. Kennedy and the young New Frontiersmen of his administration viewed the Eisenhower JCS with suspicion. Against the backdrop of Kennedy's efforts to reform the Defense Department, and under the strain of foreign policy crises, a relationship of mutual distrust between senior military and civilian officials would develop. Two months after Kennedy assumed the presidency, tension between the New Frontiersmen and the Old Guard escalated over a foreign policy blunder in the Caribbean. The Old Guard in the Pentagon were soon relegated to a position of little influence.

■

The Bay of Pigs shattered the sense of euphoria and hopeful aspiration that surrounded the New Frontiersmen during their first months in Washington.[13] In early 1960 the Eisenhower administration had authorized the Central Intelligence Agency (CIA) to form, arm, and train a Cuban exile force for the purpose of overthrowing Fidel Castro's government in Cuba. When Kennedy took office, a brigade of approximately fifteen hundred men located in secret Guatemalan bases comprised this "Army of Liberation." Embarrassed by the anti-Castro training camps, President Miguel Ydigoras Fuentes asked Kennedy to have the force removed from Guatemalan soil by the end of April. Faced with the choice of using or losing the exile brigade, the president approved a plan designed to support the invasion while preserving his ability to deny U.S. involvement.[14]

After dark on April 16, 1961, the invasion force set out for the Bay of Pigs, Cuba. The invaders soon discovered that their American destroyer escort would not accompany them after they moved to within twenty miles of their homeland. Any hopes of gaining surprise were futile: The Kennedy administration had failed in its attempts to suppress news articles that revealed the plan for a U.S.-sponsored invasion, and the invasion was a hot topic of conversation on the streets of Havana. Castro was awakened at 1:00 A.M. on April 17 with the news of the brigade's arrival. Unmarked antiquated planes attacked the Cuban Air Force base but failed to destroy many of Castro's fighters. Denied American air cover, the ships supporting the landing force were either sunk or fled from the area. Castro's jet fighters attacked the exile brigade from above as his ground forces began pushing them back to the sea. The "liberators" were running out of ammunition. On April 18 Kennedy, with the support of Secretary of Defense McNamara, fended off requests from the Joint Chiefs and others to provide direct American support to the besieged brigade. The next day, in the face of incessant attacks, the abandoned exile force surrendered. Of the approximately thirteen hundred men who actually reached the beaches, almost twelve hundred were taken prisoner and about one hundred were killed in action.[15]

John Kennedy had not considered the consequences of going forward with the Bay of Pigs invasion. The president's informal style and structure of decision making did not allow for a systematic review of the planned invasion of Cuba. Under Eisenhower a White House intelligence office closely monitored CIA plans and operations. Eisenhower had approved only planning and preparation for the invasion. When Kennedy abolished the intelligence office of the OCB, he impeded his staff's ability to gain familiarity with and take control of the Eisenhower administration's policies and programs. The CIA was able, therefore, to present the plan for the invasion as a decision already made by Kennedy's predecessor.[16]

Although the president took public responsibility for the Bay of Pigs failure, he placed a large measure of blame for the disaster on poor military advice from the Joint Chiefs of Staff. He thought that his senior military advisers should have been more assertive with their doubts about the operation's chances for success.[17] For their part the JCS believed that Kennedy's ire was misdirected. The president consulted the JCS only after he had made the decision to launch the invasion. The military services had provided personnel on special assignment to the CIA, but remained unaware of their activities. The Chiefs were skeptical about the operation's chances of success and stated that the landing could only succeed if the landing force controlled the air. They blamed the president for not consulting them earlier and thought his decision to leave the landing force stranded on the beach reprehensible.[18] The Bay of Pigs debacle not only exacerbated mutual distrust between the president and his senior military officers but spurred an intense desire on the part of John Kennedy to overthrow the Castro regime.[19]

■

Meanwhile another foreign policy challenge had developed in Laos—a landlocked nation in Southeast Asia positioned among China, Cambodia, Thailand, North Vietnam, and South Vietnam. In its effort to deny control of the country to Pathet Lao communist guerrillas, the Eisenhower administration had alternately provided military assistance to, and acted to weaken, the Lao government in Vientiane. When Kennedy took office in January 1961, the Pathet Lao had seized key objectives on the strategically vital Plain of Jars and threatened the fragile American-supported government of Prince Boun Oum. By late April the president was considering U.S. military intervention.

Smarting from what they believed had been unfair criticism after the Bay of Pigs, the Chiefs were determined that any commitment of U.S. military force not suffer from the indecision and lack of firepower that had been evident in the abortive Cuban invasion. They told Kennedy unambiguously that military action in Laos could involve the United States in a large-scale land war in Southeast Asia and might escalate into a confrontation with China. They recommended that if any troops were deployed, they should arrive in a strength of at least sixty thousand men.[20] Army general Lyman Lemnitzer, chairman of the Joint Chiefs of Staff, and Army Chief of Staff George H. Decker warned Kennedy not to take action unless he was prepared to use nuclear weapons to "guarantee victory."[21] A military commitment in Laos reminded Lemnitzer and Decker of the same sort of limited, costly, protracted commitment that the generals had experienced in Korea. After a meeting at the State Department on Laos, Rusk asked Lemnitzer, "Lem, do you think we can get the 101st [Airborne Infantry Division] in there?" The general responded, "We can get it in all right. It's getting it out that I'm worried about."[22]

During the Laotian crisis, the president was again dissatisfied with the advice of the Joint Chiefs, whose thinking he regarded as outmoded and unimaginative. He found the JCS estimate of the number of troops needed excessive and ordered only ten thousand Marines, then stationed in Japan, to prepare for deployment to Laos. He believed that strategic options in military affairs should give him more flexibility than a stark choice between inaction and large-scale commitment. Meanwhile preparations for the deployment of the Marines, coupled with diplomatic activity, seemed to have a positive effect on Moscow's attitude toward the Laotian problem.[23] Eventually Soviet premier Nikita Khrushchev agreed to negotiations aimed at developing a neutral Laos.

The May 1961 international conference on Laos assembled in Geneva and lasted until July of the following year. The U.S. government considered the outcome less than favorable.[24] The diplomatic settlement left the Pathet Lao in control of roughly the eastern half of the country, a region that North Vietnam used to supply and reinforce the Viet Cong insurgents in their fight against the American-backed South Vietnamese regime.[25] The unfavorable Laotian settlement, combined with the apparent connection between American threats of Marine deployment and Soviet willingness to negotiate, reinforced Kennedy's opinion that JCS advice was of limited value and heightened the distrust between the president and his senior military advisers.[26]

The New Frontiersmen were men of action, and the Chiefs' reluctance to take military action short of a large-scale deployment upset them. Assistant Secretary of State Roger Hilsman and White House Assistant Michael Forrestal, son of the late secretary of defense, thought that the military had gone "soft." With respect to Laos, they "beat their chests until it comes time to do some fighting and then they start backing down," Hilsman wrote in 1962.[27]

Because the front line against Communism had not been drawn in Laos, South Vietnam would become the principal focus of U.S. policy in Southeast Asia. Under those circumstances Kennedy brought into his administration a man who would exert great influence over two presidents' decisions to escalate American involvement in Vietnam.

■

Reeling from the wave of public criticism following the Bay of Pigs and aware of his increasingly troubled relationship with the JCS, Kennedy told his staff that he needed someone to be "my advisor to see that I am not making a dumb mistake as Commander in Chief."[28] To provide him with military advice and to coordinate the efforts of the White House staff, Defense Department, and intelligence agencies, the besieged president looked to former Army Chief of Staff Maxwell Davenport Taylor.

Max Taylor seemed the model of the soldier-statesman. Inspired by his Confederate grandfather's Civil War tales, Taylor pursued a military career with great enthusiasm from an early age. When his sixth-grade teacher asked him to name his professional ambition, the young Taylor wrote "major general." Twelve years later he graduated fourth in the West Point class of 1922. A talented linguist, Taylor later returned to the Military Academy to teach Spanish and French. During assignments in China and Japan, he became proficient in Japanese.[29] It was, in part, his reputation as both a warrior and a scholar that made the general attractive to Kennedy.

Taylor earned a reputation as a successful combat commander during World War II. He began the war on General Marshall's secretariat, but soon rose to command the 101st Airborne Division in Europe. He returned to Asia in 1953 to lead the Eighth Army in the closing months of the Korean War.

In 1955, when Army Chief of Staff Matthew Ridgway retired without a second two-year term because of his unhappy relations with the Eisenhower administration, Taylor was named his successor.[30] Like Ridgway, Taylor soon became frustrated by his inability to persuade the president or his indecisive secretary of defense, Charles Wilson, that a larger and more capable Army was vital to America's national security.[31] Taylor served a full four years but retired eighteen months before Eisenhower relinquished the presidency to John F. Kennedy. The fifty-eight-year-old had been a general officer for sixteen years. When he retired, Taylor was "thoroughly fed up with the Pentagon and . . . its ways."[32]

Taylor's frustration stemmed in part from Eisenhower's subordination of military policy to domestic economic priorities. Eisenhower believed that the United States, engaged in protracted competition with the Soviet Union, had to husband American economic strength as the basis for prevailing in the Cold War.[33] When the fighting in Korea ended on July 26, 1953, the president developed a lower-cost strategy for national defense, the "new look." The new look rejected Ridgway's and Taylor's arguments that American military forces must remain "balanced" in size or configuration with those of the Soviet Union and relied instead on the military doctrine of "massive retaliation." To maintain a credible deterrent against Communist aggression, massive retaliation gave top priority in the defense budget to the Air Force and nuclear weaponry. Under the new look, the Army dropped from twenty to fourteen divisions (a reduction of nearly five hundred thousand soldiers) while the Air Force expanded from 115 to 137 wings and added thirty thousand airmen.[34] To achieve economy as well as security in national defense, the new look sought to combine the threat of nuclear force with alliances, ready reserves, and psychological and covert operations.[35] On January 12, 1954, Secretary of State John Foster Dulles announced in a speech before the Council on Foreign Relations that the administration would "depend primarily on a great capacity to retaliate instantly" to achieve a "maximum deterrent at a bearable cost."[36] In addition to his desire to cut costs, the lesson of the Korean War—that the American public would not support a protracted, limited conflict in a distant land—weighed heavily on Eisenhower.[37]

In contrast to Eisenhower, Kennedy had been sympathetic to Taylor's argument that massive retaliation be supplanted with a military doctrine of "flexible response." In *The Uncertain Trumpet*, a scathing critique of Ike's defense policy published soon after the Army Chief's retirement, Taylor called for "the unqualified renunciation" of the doctrine of massive retaliation. He wrote that reliance on the threat of "blasting [our enemies] from the face of the earth with atomic bombing if they commit aggression against us or our friends . . . offers no alternative other than reciprocal suicide or retreat." His proposed military strategy of flexible response would "give multiple choices to our political leaders" and allow them to "cope with threats of many gradations, extending from subversive insurgency . . . to limited war—conventional or nuclear—and finally to unlimited nuclear war." To rebuild its ability to fight conventional wars, Taylor argued that the United States had to expand and reinforce its ground forces overseas and create a robust strategic reserve of ground and air forces on its own soil.[38]

Kennedy became enamored of Maxwell Taylor's ideas. Two weeks before declaring his candidacy for the presidency, Kennedy wrote to Evan Thomas, Maxwell Taylor's editor, with an assessment of *The Uncertain Trumpet*. The book had persuaded Kennedy that "we have not brought our conventional war capabilities into line with the necessities." The senator thought that Taylor's critique of American defense policy and structure deserved "reading by every American."[39] It was Kennedy's and Taylor's first contact in what would become a relationship of mutual respect and great affection. Taylor's ideas were evident in Kennedy's first presidential address on defense policy, in which he stated that "any potential aggressor contemplating an attack on any part of the free world with any kind of weapons, conventional or nuclear, must know that our response will be suitable, selective, swift, and effective."[40] Taylor would help Kennedy effect a doctrinal shift that influenced deepening U.S. involvement in Vietnam. But first Kennedy needed Taylor to redress the balance of the president's troubled relationship with the Joint Chiefs of Staff.

On April 21 President Kennedy telephoned Taylor, who had just taken over as president of the recently opened Lincoln Center performing arts complex in New York City. Distraught over the Bay of Pigs, Kennedy asked Taylor to come to Washington immediately for consultation. Nine weeks later Taylor returned to active military duty to take an unprecedented White House position as "Military Representative of the President." The president outlined his duties:

> 1: The Military Representative is a staff officer to advise and assist the President with regard to those military matters that reach him as Commander-in-Chief of the Armed Forces. The Military Representative is not interposed between the President and any of his statutory advisors or advisory bodies such as the Secretary of Defense, JCS or the NSC but maintains close liaison with them and is prepared to give his personal views to assist the President in reaching decisions. He is available to represent the President when the latter desires senior military representation at home or abroad.

> 2: The Military Representative has an analogous function of advice and assistance in the field of intelligence. He is not interposed between the President and the DCI [Director of Central Intelligence] or the intelligence community but

watches the functioning of the intelligence apparatus of the government to assure that it meets the present and future needs of the President.

3: In the so-called Cold War planning and action, the Military Representative will check on the use of our military and intelligence assets and verify the effectiveness of their integration and employment.

4: The Military Representative has no command authority except within his own office. He may, however, call directly on any department or agency of the government for information necessary for the discharge of his responsibilities.[41]

Qualifications in the text reflected Kennedy's desire to avoid criticism from the JCS and members of Congress who might view the position as an infringement on the statutory responsibilities of the Joint Chiefs.

The Joint Chiefs had reason to believe that Taylor would assert himself in areas that had been the sole responsibility of the JCS. Taylor's experience as Army chief of staff led him to recommend radical reform in the JCS organization. He had left the Eisenhower administration exhausted from "well nigh continuous conflict" with his civilian leaders and fellow officers of the Joint Chiefs.[42]

Taylor's difficult experience stemmed, in part, from the institutional conflict endemic in American democratic government. After World War II questions of defense policy figured prominently in the continuing power struggle between the executive branch and Congress. Dissent from members of the Joint Chiefs could weaken the president's position with the legislature and undermine an administration's policy decisions. Although Eisenhower had described the Chiefs' statutory right to appeal to Congress as "legalized insubordination," Taylor disapproved of the president's expectation that military officers mold their advice to the views and feelings of superiors and accept public responsibility for policy decisions that they opposed. Taylor thought that Eisenhower was obsessed with "loyalty and teamplay," and castigated him for creating an environment in which members of the administration pressured the JCS to accept a "preconceived politico-military line." In Taylor's view the military's "ultimate loyalty" to the Constitution and the people, as embodied by their congressional representatives, outweighed personal fealty to the commander in chief. He believed that Congress and the public should be aware of the dissenting views of the nation's top military leaders.[43] However, Taylor revised his opinions on the proper relationship between the military and the commander in chief when he returned to government service under Kennedy.

The formation of the Joint Chiefs of Staff reflected the tension between the need to integrate military advice into the national security policy process and the desire to retain civilian control over the defense establishment. In January 1942 President Franklin D. Roosevelt had established the JCS to satisfy the exigencies of America's newly formed military alliance with Great Britain. During World War II the JCS planned and directed U.S. military strategy, managed matériel and manpower, and coordinated among the nation's military allies. In 1944 Congress began hearings on postwar defense organization and examined the issue in earnest after the war.[44] After a two-year debate, Congress passed the National Security Act of 1947 to "provide a comprehensive program for the future security of the United States." The act and its amendments in 1949 established the CIA, created the NSC to coordinate policy for the president, and created a loose confederation of the armed services under the Office of the Secretary of Defense (OSD). The new Department of Defense consisted of OSD, the JCS, and the military departments of the Army, Navy, and Air Force (the Marine Corps remained within the Department of the Navy). The act, which was essentially a compromise between Army and Navy proposals, shifted responsibility away from individual service secretaries and gave OSD authority over the "national military establishment." The legislation stipulated that the full-time members of the JCS include a chairman and the military heads of the Army, Navy, and Air Force. The commandant of the Marine Corps would vote only on matters directly affecting his service. Congress provided the JCS with a staff to aid the Chiefs in their advisory and executive functions.[45]

Congress designated the Joint Chiefs as the "principal military advisors" to the president, the National Security Council, and the secretary of defense.[46] The legislators concluded that the most senior professional officers from each of the services could offer the best military advice to the "national command authority." Testifying before the Senate Committee on Naval Affairs on May 1, 1946, Secretary of the Navy James V. Forrestal argued that reliance on "a single military genius" would risk "mistakes of judgment." Meeting together, each Chief would have to "justify his case before a group of intelligent partners."[47] Congress was persuaded that the JCS, meeting together as a corporate body, comprised the best forum from which to obtain military advice.

However, interservice competition for scarce resources impinged on the Chiefs' ability to cooperate in the interest of national security. Differences among the Chiefs centered on the definition of "roles and missions" of the services. The way the Chiefs defined roles and missions determined force size and structure and the research, development, and procurement of new weapons systems. Conflicts between the services led to inefficiency and redundancy. During his second term as president, Dwight Eisenhower grew increasingly concerned that, if the Chiefs did not cooperate, transcending narrow service views, civilians less familiar with the complexities of warfare, such as the secretary of defense, might assume the Chiefs' responsibilities.[48]

Eisenhower sought a structural solution to the problems of service parochialism and inefficiency. The Defense Reorganization Act of 1958 aimed to centralize control over the services, remove redundancies, streamline command channels, and provide for tighter civilian control at the Pentagon. Although Congress expected the act to affirm JCS responsibility to provide military advice and plan military operations within unified commands (geographical commands that included forces from all four services), the law permitted the OSD to share the Chiefs' advisory role and removed the JCS from the chain of command that ran from the president to the commanders in the field. The secretary of defense would direct the unified commands while the Joint Chiefs performed executive functions, such as translating guidance from the secretary into military orders and directives. Although the Chiefs retained their charter as "principal military advisors," the wide latitude given to the secretary of defense to provide for more effective and efficient administration would permit a strong-willed secretary to concentrate power in his hands.[49] The erosion of the Chiefs' power and influence, which Eisenhower had predicted, was closer to becoming a reality. Centralization in the Department of Defense did nothing to attenuate interservice rivalry. Indeed, Eisenhower's defense policies intensified competition between the services.

In *The Uncertain Trumpet* Taylor advocated even greater centralization of JCS advisory responsibility. Deeply affected by conflict among the

Chiefs, Taylor wrote that he would "dissolve" the organization and replace it with a single defense chief of staff, who, as the senior military officer of the U.S. government, would report directly to the secretary of defense and the president. Taylor recognized that pressures from within the military services colored the advice of JCS members. If a chief were seen as abandoning that service's interest, he risked losing all credibility and respect. Taylor's plan called for an advisory body, independent of the military services, called the Supreme Military Council. The council would consist of senior officers from each of the services who were either retired or on their last tour of duty.[50]

■

Aware of Taylor's views, the JCS chairman, General Lemnitzer, had been less than enthusiastic about Taylor's appointment as military representative of the president, and Kennedy moved to defuse potential criticism from the Pentagon. Brig. Gen. Chester "Ted" Clifton, the president's military assistant, telephoned McNamara's military assistant to discuss the formal announcement of the president's decision to place Maxwell Taylor on the White House staff. Clifton observed that Taylor's duties would be "laid out very carefully" so that members of Congress and the press sympathetic to the JCS would not deem Taylor a usurper of the Joint Chiefs' advisory responsibilities. The White House statement would say only that the matter had been "discussed" with the secretary of defense and the joint chiefs of staff. The president directed, however, that General Lemnitzer attend the formal announcement and "stand by to come out with a hurrah." Kennedy also indicated his expectation that Secretary McNamara publicly convey his enthusiasm in some fashion.[51]

The president privately acknowledged that Taylor's responsibilities could easily have been performed by the Pentagon's senior military men.[52] He was not only dissatisfied with the Joint Chiefs' advice but also frustrated by his inability to establish with them the kind of friendly rapport that he enjoyed with the rest of his staff and with many of his cabinet officials. To Kennedy generals and admirals were too formal, traditional, and unimaginative. Bundy confided to Taylor's principal assistant that Kennedy "would never feel really secure" about the military until "young generals of his own generation in whom he has confidence" filled the top uniformed positions in the defense establishment. Bundy knew that it was important to Kennedy that the top military men be able to "conduct a conversation" with the president to give him a "feeling of confidence and reassurance."⁵³ Taylor would strive to satisfy the president's need. Kennedy's new personal adviser found the president "an amazingly attractive man—intelligent with a ready wit, personal charm, an ability to inspire loyalty in the people around him." He soon cultivated a warm friendship with the president and his family.⁵⁴

Taylor knew that the Chiefs and the secretary of defense viewed him as a competing voice in national security issues. The retired general moved to head off potential animosities and assured his old friend Lemnitzer that he would be more of an ally than a source of competition. He told Lemnitzer that his "close personal relations with the President and his entourage" would help to ensure that the Chiefs' advice reached the president.⁵⁵

When he arrived in Washington on April 22, Taylor's first responsibility was to conduct an investigation of the decision to mount the Bay of Pigs invasion. Although he concluded that the Chiefs were "not directly responsible" for the misadventure, he criticized them for not warning the president more urgently of the dangers. When the administration sought military advice on narrow questions about the operation, the Chiefs gave competent answers but offered no overall assessment because "they hadn't been asked." Taylor concluded that relations between the commander in chief and the JCS had reached "crisis" level.⁵⁶

To address the problem he drafted a memorandum outlining what the president ought to expect from the Chiefs in the area of military advice. The memo ordered the JCS to initiate advice as well as respond to specific requests. Moreover the Chiefs should fit "military requirements into the overall context of any situation, recognizing that the most difficult problem in government is to combine all assets in a unified, effective pattern." The president used Taylor's memo as the basis for a meeting with the Chiefs on May 27, 1961. One month later he signed a slightly revised version, which he designated National Security Action Memorandum (NSAM) 55.⁵⁷

Taylor's memorandum revealed how much his few weeks' association with the Kennedy White House had changed his thinking about the advisory role of the JCS. When he left the Eisenhower administration, he believed that the Joint Chiefs should provide narrowly focused military advice with "limited, if any, attention to political or economic factors, since these components of national strategy had qualified spokesmen elsewhere in the governmental structure."[58] After witnessing the "crisis" that grew out of mutual dislike and distrust between the president and the Joint Chiefs, Taylor abandoned his previous view that the JCS should not "take into account the views and feelings of superiors," and supplanted it with an acknowledgment of "the importance of an intimate, easy relationship, born of friendship and mutual regard between the president and the Chiefs." He revised the conviction that he had held as Army chief of staff that the JCS should remain a "nonpolitical body" whose loyalty to the Constitution and the people superseded allegiance to any particular administration.[59]

■

When Taylor arrived in Washington, the Joint Chiefs were in the middle of scrambling to keep up with the new defense secretary's demands for information and quantitative justifications for existing policies and programs. President Kennedy had given McNamara thirty days to accomplish a complete review of defense policy and the organization of the Pentagon. McNamara was to develop a program to eliminate waste and inefficiency. Anxious to provide "active, imaginative, and decisive leadership" in the Department of Defense and abandon "the passive practice of simply refereeing the disputes of traditional and partisan [service] factions" that had characterized the efforts of Eisenhower's defense secretaries, the new secretary undertook a comprehensive analysis of his department.[60]

The Joint Chiefs were unable to respond to McNamara's demands fast enough, and their cumbersome administrative system exacerbated the administration's unfavorable opinion of them.[61] Any issue that came before the Chiefs first went to "action officers" of each of the services, who worked on a "flimsy" copy of the proposal. When the action officers reached consensus, they forwarded the issue on buff paper to experienced colonels called "planners." Each planner incorporated his service's position into the paper. The paper, now green in color, rose to the three-star operations deputies of each service, who, if in agreement with the position in the paper, acted for the Chiefs. If the operations deputies could not agree, or if the matter was of critical importance, the issue went before the Chiefs themselves. If the JCS could not reach a consensus opinion on the subject, the dissenting members prepared letters of nonconcurrence and forwarded them to the secretary of defense for decision.

The system, based on compromise at every level, often resulted in ambiguous, watered-down proposals.[62]

■

Interservice rivalry complicated an already cumbersome administrative system. Since the Air Force had become an independent service in 1947, the bickering over the organization and employment of military aviation, which had begun in the early 1920s, had worsened. Historian Earl Tilford, Jr., emphasized that the Air Force, "like an illegitimate child at a family reunion . . . felt less than comfortable with its origins, and all the more so since its primary reason for being was based on the unproven doctrine of strategic bombing."[63] The Marines constantly felt threatened by the Army. The Navy, Air Force, and Army each sought important roles within American nuclear strategy and continental defense. Each service feared that another might usurp its role and thereby undercut its structure, its ability to develop future weapons, and thus its ability to wage war. Split decisions in the JCS often resulted from one or more of the services challenging another's justification for the development or procurement of particular weapons.[64] This unhealthy competition often took on the character of an argument between selfish children and undercut further the credibility of the Joint Chiefs as an advisory body.

McNamara quickly lost patience with the Chiefs' unresponsiveness and squabbling. His answer to the mutually reinforcing problems of parochialism and administrative inefficiency became familiar: increased centralization in the OSD.[65] Kennedy gave his new secretary of defense carte blanche, and McNamara took advantage of it. Drawing on his experience with analytical methods and statistics, he forced new management techniques on a reluctant department. He brought in an army of bright young analysts to assist him, and used the wide latitude given the secretary of defense in the Defense Reorganization Act of 1958 to create a staff structure that mirrored military staff functions. Freed from dependence on the JCS for analysis, McNamara exerted civilian control over what had before been almost exclusively military prerogatives.[66]

■

McNamara's principal staff included young men such as Department of Defense General Counsel John McNaughton (a Harvard Law School professor who replaced Paul Nitze as assistant secretary of defense for international security affairs in 1963), Special Assistant Adam Yarmolinsky (a longtime Kennedy aide), Charles J. Hitch (former president of the University of California), and the man some referred to as the "chief whiz kid," Alain Enthoven, for whom McNamara created a new Office of Systems Analysis. The defense secretary gave his team "full backing," and the young civilians discharged their responsibilities and exerted their authority with vigor.[67]

McNamara's Whiz Kids were like-minded men who shared their leader's penchant for quantitative analysis and suspicion of proposals based solely on "military experience."[68] Many of them had worked in think tanks and research corporations, such as RAND, and they were eager to apply their techniques to the problems of the Defense Department. Taylor recalled that "cost-effectiveness charts appeared on all the walls, and a whole host of requests for information and advice flooded the JCS."[69] The two most important offices were Paul Nitze's International Security Affairs (ISA) and Alain Enthoven's Systems Analysis divisions.

Enthoven quickly became McNamara's point man in establishing firm civilian control over the Defense Department. His flair for quantitative analysis was exceeded only by his arrogance.[70] Enthoven held military experience in low regard and considered military men intellectually inferior. He likened leaving military decision making to the professional military to allowing welfare workers to develop national welfare programs. Enthoven suggested that military experience "can be a disadvantage because it discourages seeing the larger picture." He and many of his colleagues believed that most people in the Department of Defense simply tried to "advance their particular project or their service or their department." He was convinced that "there was little in the typical officer's early career that qualifies him to be a better strategic planner than . . . a graduate of the Harvard Business School." He used statistics to analyze defense programs and issues and then gave the secretary of defense and the president information needed to make decisions. Enthoven saw no limits to the applicability of his methods.[71]

McNamara's autocratic style and the condescending attitude of his young civilian assistants deeply disturbed the Joint Chiefs and other military officers in the Pentagon. The military viewed Enthoven and the rest of McNamara's staff as adversaries. Differences arose between the JCS and McNamara's office over new management techniques, the military budget, and weapons procurement. The officers resented the lack of respect for military experience among those whom they nicknamed derisively McNamara's "happy little hotdogs."[72] Air Force Chief of Staff Curtis LeMay recalled that McNamara's Whiz Kids were

> the most egotistical people that I ever saw in my life. They had no faith in the military; they had no respect for the military at all. They felt that the Harvard Business School method of solving problems would solve any problem in the world. . . . They were better than all the rest of us; otherwise they wouldn't have gotten their superior education, as they saw it.[73]

Although united in their vexation with McNamara and his staff, the Chiefs remained divided on substantive defense issues.[74]

McNamara, who had promised to act "decisively and effectively to accomplish . . . solution[s]," intervened to resolve issues of contention between the Chiefs. He battled with the Air Force and Navy over his plan to develop a fighter jet common to all the services, the notorious TFX.[75] His and Enthoven's belief that submarines and unmanned missiles were more efficient and effective nuclear deterrents than bombers ran afoul of the Air Force's traditional preference for piloted aircraft. McNamara's opposition to the B-70 bomber program soured his relations with the Air Force until Curtis LeMay retired in 1965.[76] The Army, neglected during the Eisenhower years, benefited from McNamara's belief in strong conventional forces to fight limited wars. In less than one and one-half years in office, McNamara added more than three hundred thousand troops to the Army.[77] Differences over defense allocations and structure diminished the Chiefs' influence relative to the defense secretary's civilian analysts.

The initiative that displeaseed all the services equally was McNamara's method for determining the military budget. Although each of the Chiefs opposed the new budget system, McNamara's requirement that each service prepare an unconstrained estimate based on perceived needs kept the Chiefs divided over how defense dollars should be allocated. After receiving uncoordinated service estimates, the Whiz Kids would make recommendations to McNamara on what he should retain and what he should cut from each of the proposals. The Joint Chiefs felt that they had no real influence over the budget process. Adm. David Lamar McDonald later accused McNamara of dishonesty for never admitting that there was in fact a real ceiling on the budget, and expressed his frustration that "the whiz kids . . . decided what we could get along without," cutting programs without explaining their decisions to the people who would "have to fight" with the weapons and equipment.[78]

Officers on Taylor's personal staff warned the general that the Kennedy administration was making a deliberate effort to minimize the military's influence over defense policy. Air Force major William Y. Smith had observed a "general trend to downgrade the influence of military leaders in the determination of policies." Part of the responsibility, Smith observed, rested with the Chiefs. Citing the inability of the Joint Chiefs to abandon their preoccupation with service interests, he predicted that unless they began to project their advice "outward and upward" and address policy concerns rather than narrow service interests, the prospect for harmonious civil-military relations would remain dim.[79] Taylor's principal assistant, Col. Julian Ewell, blamed the dominance of McNamara's civilian advisers for the weakening of the Chiefs' voice in issues of national security. He shared Bundy's view that no matter what the JCS did to improve their own operation, "the progressive tightening up of the McNamara regime might tend to cancel it out."[80]

Taylor discovered that McNamara often suppressed JCS advice in favor of the views of his civilian analysts. On several defense issues McNamara either failed to consult the JCS or did not forward their views to the White House. Taylor's staff reported that, in addition to McNamara's strict control over the JCS, greater centralization in the Kennedy White House prevented military advice from reaching the president. The president had increased his reliance on ad hoc gatherings of "principals" that usually included Bundy and McNamara. Informal committees with responsibility for particular issues conducted closed deliberations and often sent papers directly to the president. Ewell observed that loose associations of second-level officials in the White House and the Defense and State departments furthered their own defense agendas by working "across channels by personal contact" and calling on their associates who were "members of the club, and whom they [could] count on to agree with them." The members of Kennedy's inner circle protected their ideas with ideological fervor. The New Frontiersmen believed that to effect change they had to "ignore . . . the minor frictions involved in changing policy." Ewell found that a "moralistic approach" inspired Kennedy's closest advisers to make judgments "which the actual circumstances support only very tenuously."[81]

∎

Having concluded that the Joint Chiefs were more an impediment than an asset, Kennedy moved to replace the "holdover" chiefs of the Eisenhower administration with his own men, who would be less likely to resist his administration's defense policies.[82] JCS chairman Lemnitzer had taken an unequivocal position on Laos and believed that the United States should be prepared to use its full power before deciding to intervene anywhere.[83] Although Lemnitzer's advice may have been appropriate under Eisenhower's policy of massive retaliation, it was anathema to Kennedy's and Taylor's conception of flexible response. When Gen. Lauris Norstad, the North Atlantic Treaty Organization (NATO) commander, announced his intention to retire in September 1962, Kennedy designated Lemnitzer as Norstad's replacement in order to create a vacancy in the chairmanship. He then broke the traditional rotation between the Army, Navy, and Air Force and installed Taylor as the new chairman.[84] Taylor, who had ostensibly retired from military service four years before and had condemned Eisenhower for replacing the Chiefs in similar fashion, thus pushed aside Adm. George Anderson, who had assumed that he was next in line for the job.[85] Simultaneously, Kennedy and McNamara forced Army Chief of Staff Decker, who in April 1961 had told McNamara that "we cannot win a conventional war in Southeast Asia," to retire after only two years in the job.[86] McNamara, based on Taylor's recommendation, designated the deputy commander in chief of the European Command, Earle G. Wheeler, as Decker's replacement.[87] With his own man as chairman of the JCS, Kennedy would no longer need a "military representative." When Taylor moved across the Potomac River to the Pentagon, the president abolished the White House position.

On October 1, 1962, Taylor took over as chairman of the Joint Chiefs of Staff. He found the Chiefs, still embittered over what they regarded as Kennedy's unfair criticism in the wake of the Bay of Pigs, engaged in ongoing battles with civilian officials in the OSD. The Chiefs saw Taylor's selection as the imposition of a Kennedy man on an organization designed by law to give impartial military advice to the commander in chief.[88]

Taylor quickly cultivated a warm relationship with the man whom many of the military officers in the Pentagon deeply resented.[89] Taylor and McNamara found common ground in their belief in the need for administrative reform in the Pentagon, faith in the "flexible response" strategy, and utter devotion to their commander in chief. Like McNamara, Taylor concluded that the answer to problems of service rivalry and administrative inefficiency was increased centralization of power in the chairmanship and the OSD. Taylor had once lamented the indecisiveness of Eisenhower's defense secretaries, and he lauded McNamara for tackling the tough problems of the department.[90] The bond of respect between the two men was mutual. McNamara considered Taylor "one of the wisest, most intelligent military men ever to serve."[91] Much to the chagrin of the other Chiefs, Taylor and McNamara formed a partnership. Taylor's overwhelming influence with the secretary of defense and the president made opposition to his views futile.[92]

■

Historian Robert Divine observed that "Vietnam can only be understood in relation to the Cold War."[93] Indeed, Cold War crises during Kennedy's first months as president shaped advisory relationships within his administration and influenced his foreign policy decisions until his assassination in November 1963. Already predisposed to distrust the senior military officers he had inherited from the Eisenhower administration, the Bay of Pigs incident and Laotian crisis motivated the president to seek a changing of the guard in the Pentagon. After the Bay of Pigs, an unsatisfactory diplomatic settlement in Laos, confrontation with the Kremlin over divided Berlin, and Soviet premier Nikita Khrushchev's bullying rhetoric persuaded Kennedy that the United States needed to make its "power credible." "Vietnam," Kennedy concluded, "is the place."[94] Vietnam, however, loomed in the background while the New Frontiersmen confronted in the Caribbean what would become the best known of Kennedy's Cold War crises.

2
Havana and Hanoi
October 1962–November 1963

McNamara has proved a real find. Under the leadership of
"McNamara and his band" in the Defense Department, the
country has markedly improved its capacity to fight both
conventional and unconventional wars. No less important,
McNamara has asserted the authority of the civilian
Secretary of Defense over the entire military establishment. In an era when Americans are growingly alarmed by
the rise of the "garrison state," McNamara's achievement
may well stand out as the most important development of
the Kennedy era.

—WILLIAM E. LEUCHTENBURG, 1963[1]

On Taylor's first day as JCS chairman, he and his colleagues heard an
intelligence briefing about the possibility that Soviet ballistic missiles
were in Cuba. With the exception of Director of Central Intelligence
John McCone and some midlevel analysts, however, the administration
dismissed the possibility. With an eye toward the impending congressional
midterm elections, the president wanted to keep Cuba out of the lime-
light. The Bay of Pigs had left Kennedy and his Democratic Party vulnerable to accusations that they were "soft" on Communism. Critics charged
the young president with naïveté and, in a reference to the title of his
Pulitzer Prize–winning book, asserted that Kennedy was "all profile and no
courage." Republican senator Kenneth Keating of New York cited reports
of Soviet technicians and antiaircraft missiles entering Cuba and attacked
Kennedy as a "do nothing" president.[2] To defuse such criticisms, the
administration took the public stance that the Soviet buildup in Cuba was

defensive. Afraid of leaks, the president limited intelligence that indicated otherwise to the small circle of his most trusted advisers. On October 11, 1962, when Director of Central Intelligence (DCI) McCone brought Kennedy photographs of large crates thought to be Soviet-made IL-28 bombers, Kennedy asked that the information "be withheld at least until after the election."[3]

In fact, Kennedy was obsessed with Cuba and Fidel Castro. His administration was hard at work on a covert program, code-named Mongoose, to undermine the Cuban government, incite insurrection, and assassinate Castro. He viewed Castro as a reminder of the Bay of Pigs humiliation.[4] In November 1961 Attorney General Robert Kennedy told the "Special Group" charged with getting rid of Castro that "the Cuban problem carries top priority in the U.S. government," promising that "no time, money, effort or manpower is to be spared."[5] While the CIA planned to assassinate Castro and foment insurrection, the JCS planned a full-scale invasion of the island. Each of the services conducted extensive rehearsals for the invasion. The largest, Operation Swift-Strike, involved more than seventy-thousand men. In October 1962, as the Joint Chiefs refined their plans, Soviet soldiers, advisers, and military equipment poured into the island nation.[6]

As evidence of the presence of Soviet missiles in Cuba mounted, McNamara encouraged the JCS to plan not only for the destruction of the missiles but also for Castro's removal from power. The Chiefs, for their part, urged McNamara to gain Kennedy's approval for U-2 surveillance flights over Cuba to gain information about troop dispositions, landing beaches, airfields, and surface-to-air missile (SAM) sites.[7] Permission for the overflights, however, was not immediately forthcoming.

The Joint Chiefs had grown frustrated with what they regarded as the White House's obsession with the potential political costs of losing a surveillance aircraft over Cuba. Dean Rusk predicted an outcry from allies in the Americas and the United Nations. In deference to Rusk's concerns, the president authorized flights no closer than twenty-five miles from Cuba's shoreline. These peripheral reconnaissance missions were ineffective, as distance and camera angle blurred photos beyond utility. Meanwhile agent reports of Soviet missiles in Cuba began to arrive in Washington. Finally Kennedy authorized a U-2 overflight for October 14.[8]

As the administration sought confirmation of the missile sightings, the JCS edged toward a war footing, recommending mobilization of the 150,000 reserves that Congress had authorized several weeks earlier. The Air Force moved fighter aircraft to Florida and began stockpiling bombs, ammunition, and other supplies needed for attack. After the October 14 U-2 photographed the missiles, the Joint Chiefs thought military action against Cuba a certainty. They recommended a powerful air strike to destroy all significant military targets, a naval blockade to isolate Castro from outside support, and an invasion to ensure the eradication of the missile threat and the removal of Castro from power.[9]

On October 15, after the National Photographic Interpretation Center developed and studied the U-2 photographs, Kennedy gathered his most trusted advisers to analyze the situation and formulate a response to this challenge to U.S. national security. These men formed the Executive Committee (EXCOM) of the National Security Council and deliberated secretly to weigh political and military options. EXCOM included Attorney General Robert Kennedy, Secretary of State Rusk, Secretary of Defense McNamara, DCI McCone, Secretary of the Treasury Douglas Dillon, Special Assistant for National Security Affairs Bundy, Special Counsel Theodore Sorensen, Under Secretary of State George Ball, Deputy Under Secretary of State for Political Affairs U. Alexis Johnson, Assistant Secretary of State for Latin American Affairs Edwin Martin, Soviet expert Llewellyn Thompson, Deputy Secretary of Defense Roswell Gilpatric, Assistant Secretary of Defense for ISA Nitze, and JCS chairman Taylor. Although the group included McNamara's deputy and principal operational planner from OSD, Taylor was the only professional military officer who attended the meetings.[10]

On October 16 McNamara offered an alternative to the Chiefs' recommendations for a full-scale air strike, blockade, and invasion. He argued that the EXCOM had focused on a false choice between the all-out military solution and an exclusive reliance on diplomatic pressures. McNamara suggested that the United States blockade Cuba to search approaching ships and remove offensive weapons. The defense secretary based his "third category of action" on "overt military action of varying degrees of intensity" including a naval "quarantine," aerial overflights of the Caribbean island, and the mobilization of a large military force. McNamara was confident and articulate. He set the agenda for the discussions, persuading the EXCOM with what seemed reasoned judgment and cogent analysis.[11] Although the president's advisers had intially favored offensive military action against Cuba, a consensus soon formed around McNamara's proposal. In an evening meeting on October 18, President Kennedy told his advisers that he had rejected the first-strike option in favor of the blockade.[12]

The JCS resented being excluded from the EXCOM meetings.[13] Every evening during the crisis, Taylor found the Chiefs anxiously awaiting his return from the White House. They grilled him to ensure that he had accurately represented their recommendation to bomb the missile sites and follow the air strike quickly with a ground invasion of Cuba. Taylor requested that Kennedy invite the Joint Chiefs to the White House to allay their agitation over not being consulted directly. Having absorbed much of the blame for the Bay of Pigs, the Chiefs wanted to make unambiguous their position on the level of force required.[14] The decision in favor of a naval quarantine of Cuba, however, had already been made, and the president's October 19 meeting with the Chiefs was designed to keep them from opposing his decision rather than to solicit their advice.[15]

At the beginning of his meeting with the JCS, Kennedy suggested that an air and ground offensive against Cuba would alienate U.S. allies in Europe and precipitate Soviet retaliatory action against Berlin. The Chiefs, however, argued that a failure to act decisively in Cuba was even more likely to embolden the Soviets in Berlin and elsewhere. LeMay told the president repeatedly that he did not see "any other solution than direct military action." He argued that the blockade option would be "almost as bad as the appeasement [of Hitler] at Munich" and, he suggested, would encourage further Soviet aggression and result in the United States gradually drifting into war under unfavorable conditions. LeMay declared that if the president took strong action, the Soviets would be forced to back down and would not respond in Berlin or anywhere else. The other Chiefs reinforced LeMay's argument, describing a surprise air strike, blockade, and invasion as the "lowest-risk course of action." Taylor seemed to support his colleagues, arguing that "our strength in Berlin, our strength anywhere in the world is our credibility."[16] The Chiefs, however, suspected that Taylor did not really share their views and doubted that he was faithfully representing their position during EXCOM deliberations.[17]

The JCS concerns were well founded. Taylor had distanced himself from the JCS position. On October 27, three days after the naval quarantine of Cuba was in place, Taylor again presented the Chiefs' recommendation for air strikes followed by a ground invasion. Robert Kennedy, whose close friend Taylor had become, remarked sarcastically, "That was a surprise." After the laughter subsided, the meeting continued without further reference to the JCS position. Taylor later gave his "personal view," which was that forces should remain ready to invade, but the president "make no advance decision on that."[18] He expressed support for continuing the blockade as the first step in McNamara's proposed campaign of pressure aimed at coercing Khrushchev into withdrawing the missiles.[19]

In combination with Robert F. Kennedy's secret negotiations with the Soviet ambassador Anatoli Dobrynin, during which he discussed a quid pro quo arrangement involving the withdrawal of U.S. Jupiter missiles from Turkey, McNamara's plan for gradually intensifying military pressure, or "turning the screw," on the Soviets seemed to produce the desired result. The Soviets agreed to withdraw the missiles in exchange for a U.S. promise not to invade Cuba and a secret pledge to remove American intermediate-range missiles from Turkey. After the crisis President Kennedy told Arthur Schlesinger, Jr., a historian and White House aide, that it was "lucky for us" that Robert McNamara was at the helm in the Pentagon.[20]

Although Kennedy was pleased with McNamara, the deliberations increased his frustration with his military advisers. The crisis ended with Kennedy thinking that the Joint Chiefs were "mad" in their insistence on the use of military force.[21] On November 15, 1962, while discussing the JCS performance during the Cuban missile crisis, Kennedy vowed that "the first advice I'm going to give my successor is to watch the generals and to avoid feeling that just because they were military men their opinion[s] on military matters were worth a damn."[22] The Chiefs' persistence in recommending a full-scale attack appeared insensitive to political constraints and the dangers of nuclear confrontation with the Soviet Union.

The president's scorn, however, stemmed in part from a fundamental conflict in goals and objectives. He and his civilian advisers sought the more limited objective of removing the missiles, whereas the Chiefs viewed the missile crisis as an opportunity to satisfy the objectives of Operation Mongoose. McNamara had charged the Chiefs with planning for military action to rid Cuba of Castro, and, although the president had no intention of invading Cuba, he continued to encourage the JCS planning efforts. To prevent the Chiefs from complaining to his political opponents that he was "soft" on Castro and the Soviets, Kennedy preserved the impression that he was willing to consider overwhelming military intervention.[23] Without a common understanding of the objective of military force or of the limitations that the president considered necessary to avoid escalation, the JCS continued to recommend actions that Kennedy privately regarded as extreme. The divergent civilian and military views on American objectives during the Cuban missile crisis foreshadowed what would become a major obstacle to the development of a strategy for the Vietnam War.

Despite having declared "victory" in the missile crisis, the president was concerned that concessions to the Soviets would make him vulnerable to charges of appeasement and weakness. He kept secret his agreement to remove American missiles from Turkey, and told reporters to downplay the extent of the American victory. The president feared that boasts from Washington would incite the Soviet leader to reveal the missile bargain, made without consultation with NATO or the Turks.[24]

Although the president could rely on McNamara to tell the Congress that there was "absolutely no connection" between the removal of U.S. missiles from Turkey and the resolution of the missile crisis, the JCS posed a special problem.[25] To keep the Chiefs "on the team," Kennedy again invited them to the White House, where he lauded their advice and performance during the crisis. Recognizing the duplicitous nature of the president's praise, Chief of Naval Operations (CNO) Admiral Anderson remarked to his colleagues, "We have been had." Air Force Chief LeMay considered the missile trade and the fact that Soviet troops and non-nuclear weapons remained in Cuba "the greatest defeat in our history."[26] Air Force major William Y. Smith of General Taylor's personal staff recalled that the missile crisis left relations between the president's civilian and military advisers "more frayed than before."[27]

■

The missile crisis emboldened Secretary of Defense McNamara in the realm of strategic planning and enhanced his reputation as a level-headed adviser. As one of Taylor's White House staffers noted in February, the defense secretary was already "getting away from what was perhaps an early preoccupation with counting noses and beans" and had become more assertive in the area of military strategy and operations.[28] McNamara had gained confidence in these areas and no longer felt as though he needed military advice in developing strategic options. Suppressing the critical role of the missile trade-off in ending the crisis, he pointed to his military program of increasing pressure on the Soviet Union through overflights, mobilization, menacing troop deployments, and the blockade. In a 1987 interview McNamara admitted that he had been a novice in the area of strategy when he took over as secretary of defense. He surrounded himself with people who "knew a hell of a lot more" than he did about national security issues and learned from them. He was a good student, however, and "by the time of the Cuban missile crisis [his] views were pretty well fixed and [hadn't] changed to this day."[29] McNamara was proud of what he portrayed as a personal triumph during the Cuban missile crisis. When he turned his attention to Southeast Asia, he exuded confidence that he had gained in the Caribbean.

■

The defense secretary was determined to remove obstacles that might prevent him from assuming the role of chief strategist in the Pentagon. During the Cuban missile crisis, McNamara kept tight control over the ships, submarines, and aircraft enforcing the quarantine around Cuba to ensure that the demonstration of American resolve sent the proper message to the Soviets. He literally lived at the Pentagon between October 16 and 27 because he "feared that [the military] might not understand that this was a communications exercise, not a military operation." Admiral Anderson resented McNamara's intrusion into what he regarded as the Navy's responsibility and area of expertise. In "Flag Plot," the naval operations room, Anderson became irritated with McNamara's specific instructions on how to run the blockade. The admiral told McNamara that the Navy had been conducting blockades since the days of John Paul Jones and suggested that the defense secretary return to his office and let the Navy run the operation. McNamara rose from his chair and retorted that the operation was "not a blockade but a means of communication between Kennedy and Khrushchev," and ordered the admiral not to use force without his express permission. After demanding that Anderson acknowledge his command, McNamara left. The secretary, who had previously clashed with the recalcitrant admiral over the development of the TFX fighter and other defense issues, concluded that Anderson had left him with no option other than to have the admiral removed from the Joint Chiefs. Taylor supported McNamara in the altercation. To prevent Anderson from criticizing the administration after his retirement, President Kennedy waited until his first two-year term as CNO expired and then offered him the ambassadorship to Portugal. A few months after the Cuban missile crisis, Anderson left the naval service for the relative seclusion of the Iberian Peninsula.[30] To control military operations in times of crisis, the president and the defense secretary would need men on the JCS who would permit civilian oversight in areas that had been previously regarded as sacrosanct and free from civilian "interference." Kennedy had effected the early replacement of the JCS chairman, the Army chief of staff, and the CNO. He wanted to sack LeMay at the same time as Anderson, but McNamara warned that two simultaneous removals would be one too many.[31]

The desire to control military operations more closely at the civilian level in the OSD and in the White House coincided with advances in communications technology that made possible the detailed monitoring of military activities in faraway theaters. During the Cuban missile crisis, communications equipment established in the White House after the Bay of Pigs incident allowed the president to monitor and control military operations from his desk in the Oval Office.[32] The Defense Department installed high-volume communications and data display systems that let the White House Situation Room monitor closely the most technical aspects of military deployments and activities.[33] Rather than give the military the mission to enforce the blockade, McNamara and the president orchestrated the specific activities of U.S. ships.[34]

The Cuban missile crisis was the best known of the Cold War flare-ups that dominated the beginning of the Kennedy administration. The Cuban crisis of 1962 and the Berlin crisis of 1961 (during which the Soviet Union began to build the Berlin Wall and threatened to close off Western access to the divided city) were direct confrontations between the two superpowers. In 1961, however, Soviet premier Khrushchev announced a subtler form of conflict between his bloc and the West. He declared his support for Communist insurgents fighting wars of national liberation in the countries of the developing world. The crises in Laos in

1961 and the Congo from 1961 to 1963 (during which the United States in cooperation with the United Nations sent a military mission to prevent Soviet-supported insurgents from toppling a feeble national government) seemed to confirm his declaration.

After President Kennedy was forced to accept a compromise settlement in Laos, his interest in a strategy to counter Communist insurgencies in Southeast Asia and elsewhere was heightened.[35] The president read everything he could on the subject of "para-wars" and worked hard to gain a conceptual grasp of how best to meet this challenge. Kennedy told the graduating cadets of the West Point class of 1962: "If freedom is to be saved, we need a whole new kind of strategy, a wholly different kind of force, and a wholly different kind of training and commitment."[36] Despite the president's interest in this perceived threat to freedom, Kennedy had not developed a clear concept of how to combat Communist-sponsored insurgencies. Maj. William Y. Smith observed at the time that there existed a "lack of clarity" in counterinsurgency doctrine and a lack of coordination between agencies.[37]

■

South Vietnam had become the American test bed for counterinsurgency programs and techniques, and the Kennedy administration had dramatically increased economic and military aid to the American-backed government in Saigon. By the summer of 1963, 16,500 military advisers were in South Vietnam. Although Vietnam remained until 1963 a national security concern of tertiary interest, the U.S. imperative to contain Communism impelled American involvement in what would otherwise have been considered an insignificant place, unworthy of even the most cursory policy deliberations.

Before World War II, America had demonstrated no interest in Vietnam, a narrow, thousand-mile-long stretch of land on the Asian rim under the domination (along with Cambodia and Laos) of French colonialism. The U.S. government took notice, however, when Japanese troops landed there in 1940. Vietnam was important to the Japanese for access to China and as a stepping stone toward the oil-rich Dutch East Indies. Although native nationalists in Southeast Asia initially rallied to Japan, it soon became apparent to most of the Vietnamese people that the Japanese had come to oppress them and strip their land of food and resources. Millions would starve while the Japanese exported rice to their home islands. Ho Chi Minh, a Vietnamese patriot who had traveled the globe and was then living in Moscow, recognized that welcoming the Japanese as liberators was tantamount to "driv[ing] the tiger out the front door while letting the wolf in through the back." In 1941 Ho, disguised as a Chinese journalist, left Moscow and returned to his native land for the first time in thirty years.[38]

He appealed to Vietnamese nationalists and helped form and lead a resistance movement against the Japanese. Communist in ideology, Ho's Vietminh was the strongest of the nationalist groups seeking independence. In August 1945, after the defeat of Japan, the Vietminh filled the power vacuum, and on September 2 Ho declared Vietnam's independence.

Before his death, President Franklin D. Roosevelt had made self-determination part of his vision for the postwar world. Under the tutelage or "trusteeship" of the West, the Vietnamese and other "brown people of the East" would gradually gain their independence.[39] After World War II, Roosevelt's successor, Harry S. Truman, rejected trusteeship in favor of conciliating France and Europe. Despite Ho's attempts to emphasize his nationalistic aims over his Communist predilections, the United States watched passively as France moved to reclaim Indochina, first in the south, then in the north. In mid-December 1946 increasing tension between the French and Vietnamese nationalists gave way to direct military conflict, with the Vietminh leading the effort against the French.[40]

As the First Indochina War began, the fear of global Communism along with U.S. loyalty to its European allies impelled American support for the French. U.S. approval of French aims in Indochina was already an important element of building a European alliance against the Communist threat to Western Europe.[41] At the end of the 1940s, against the backdrop of the iron curtain's descent over Europe, the Soviet Union's successful explosion of an atomic device, and the Communist victory in China, the Truman administration concluded that Ho was part of a Soviet-sponsored, monolithic Communist movement.

The French, meanwhile, attempted to counter Ho's popularity and curry favor with the United States by creating a veneer of independence for Vietnam under Emperor Bao Dai's puppet government. Contrasts between the emperor and his competitor to the north were striking. Ho seemed to personify Vietnam's experience with French colonialism. His time in the West had left a deep impression on him, yet he retained his native identity and peasant appearance. He had studied and appropriated the ideas that had sparked revolutions in America and France in the eighteenth century as well as in Russia in 1917. Ho's reputation as a learned ascetic devoted to the Vietnamese people contrasted with Bao Dai's opulent affectations, philandering, and record of collaboration with the French and Japanese. Indeed, pro-French intentions were obvious. Bao Dai himself remarked: "What they call a Bao Dai solution turns out to be just a French solution."[42] Although some American officials predicted that the regime would collapse, Washington recognized Bao Dai's government in 1950 and began actively supporting the French in the war against the Vietminh. The outbreak of the Korean War in June highlighted the importance of containing Communism in Asia; American military and economic aid for the French increased.

Despite growing American support, the French effort in Vietnam faltered. The elusive, determined, and increasingly competent Vietminh, with the aid of equipment and supplies from Communist China, inflicted a series of defeats on the French. By 1952, French casualties in the war had exceeded ninety thousand. The Vietminh had lost even greater numbers of men, but by 1953 it was clear that they could outlast the French. The French people had begun to call the seemingly interminable conflict in the faraway forests and jungles of Indochina the "dirty war."

In early 1952, Truman's National Security Council postulated that "the loss of any of the countries of Southeast Asia to Communist aggression would have critical psychological, political and economic consequences." The objective of U.S. policy in the region was to prevent countries "from passing into the communist orbit, and to assist them to develop will and ability to resist communism from within and without."[43] It was the first clear articulation of the domino theory, the enduring rationale for fighting Communism in Southeast Asia. In 1953, as he sought to fulfill his election-year promise to end the stalemated and unpopular Korean War, President Dwight D. Eisenhower continued and expanded upon the Truman administration's support for the French in Indochina.

During the first months of 1954, the French military situation in Indochina grew desperate. When the French attempted to lure their enemy into a conventional confrontation, the Vietminh surrounded their garrison at Dien Bien Phu. By the end of March, it appeared as if only American military intervention could save them.

When JCS chairman Adm. Arthur Radford and Air Force Chief of Staff Nathan Twining advocated air strikes in support of the beleaguered French forces, Army Chief of Staff Matthew Ridgway dissented, and Marine Corps Commandant Lemuel Shepherd supported him, citing "no significant promise for success."[44] Predictions of an uncontrollable, futile military commitment in Vietnam combined with British reluctance and Franco-American difficulties to outweigh arguments for intervention. In April 1954 Eisenhower, unwilling to intervene "without allies and associates" in a war that "would absorb our troops by the division," denied a French request for direct military support.[45] Vietminh forces overran the French garrison on May 7. Only seventy-three of the more than 15,000 men at Dien Bien Phu escaped. Vietminh losses were estimated at 25,000. Ho, however, had told a French visitor at the outset of the conflict, "You can kill ten of my men for every one I kill of yours. But even at those odds, you will lose and I will win."[46]

The end for the French signaled a new beginning for the United States. In July 1954, the United States gave its oral endorsement to the Geneva Accords, which temporarily ended the hostilities in Vietnam. The agreement temporarily partitioned Vietnam into north and south, limited the introduction of foreign troops into the region, and called for general elections to unify the country by July 1956.

During the Geneva conference, Bao Dai appointed Ngo Dinh Diem, then living in Paris, as prime minister. As a young man, Diem had pursued a career as a politician and bureaucrat until he became frustrated with French colonial rule. He had long advocated Vietnamese independence, but rejected Ho's Communist vision. In 1945 the Vietminh held Diem prisoner for six months until, after a brief meeting with Ho, he was released. While in captivity, Diem learned that the Vietminh had murdered one of his five brothers, Khoi, and Khoi's son. A bachelor and devout Catholic, Diem left Vietnam and spent two years at the Maryknoll Seminary in Lakewood, New Jersey, before moving to Europe in 1953. Not long after his return to Vietnam as prime minister, Diem, with the assistance of his brother, Ngo Dinh Nhu, organized a referendum to oust Bao Dai. It was rigged; Diem received almost all of the votes and in several places the ballots for Diem exceeded the number of registered voters. Despite his undemocratic practices, Ngo Dinh Diem became America's ally in the fight against Communist domination in Southeast Asia. The CIA helped thwart several attempts to overthrow him and the Eisenhower administration pumped millions of dollars in economic and military aid into South Vietnam to prop up his fledgling government.

In 1956 the United States assumed full responsibility for training and equipping the Vietnamese Army and established a Military Assistance and Advisory Group (MAAG) in Saigon.[47] Meanwhile, the Eisenhower administration worked outside of the Geneva agreements to weaken Ho's North Vietnamese regime through psychological warfare and covert operations.[48] Diem, with the approval of the U.S. government, refused to hold the elections called for in the Geneva Accords, and the boundary between North and South Vietnam became another frontier that separated the "free world" from "world Communism."

In the late 1950s, it appeared that Diem had worked a miracle in South Vietnam. With the aid of the CIA and Catholics who had fled the North, Diem consolidated political control. He made the cover of *Time* magazine, and his American sponsors celebrated the apparent progress. The appearance of success, however, belied an approaching storm. Diem's aloof political style and his religion (Catholicism was a minority faith introduced by the French) prevented him from gaining real popular support. Personal loyalty overwhelmed competence as the principal criterion for appointments to high civilian or military posts. Most important, however, Diem had failed to eliminate Vietminh resistance, and Ho, preoccupied with economic difficulties and the consolidation of his own political power in the North, had not yet concentrated on his goal of unifying all of Vietnam under the control of Hanoi.

In 1959, as Kennedy began to organize his bid for the Democratic presidential nomination, Vietnamese Communists were responding to the directive of the Fifteenth Plenum of the Communist Party's Central Committee. In January the committee had declared,

> The fundamental path of development for the revolution in South Vietnam is that of violent struggle. Based on the concrete conditions and existing requirements of revolution, then, the road of violent struggle is: use the strength of the masses, with the political strength as the main factor, combined with military strength to a greater or lesser degree depending on the situation, in order to overthrow the ruling power of the imperialist and feudalist forces and build the revolutionary power of the people.[49]

Based on the premise that the unification of Vietnam under Hanoi's rule
had to be won in the minds of the people, the Vietnamese Communist
strategy of revolutionary war called for a shifting combination of political
and military action to obtain the loyalty of the people of the South.
During the 1960 presidential campaign, as Senator Kennedy and Vice
President Nixon debated issues that resonated more clearly with the
American electorate, the Diem government's counter-insurgency effort
was intensifying against a more active Viet Cong.

■

Although Kennedy was willing to send U.S. military "advisers" into
South Vietnam and mount covert operations in North Vietnam,
Cambodia, and Laos, he drew the line on U.S. combat units. The word
"adviser" implied that the South Vietnamese would do their own fighting. The introduction of American combat units risked transforming the
war into an American war, raising the specter of high U.S. casualties, and
fomenting congressional and public debate over administration policy.
On November 11, 1961, President Kennedy decided to commit U.S.
advisers to South Vietnam in excess of the number permitted in the
Geneva Accords of 1954. Kennedy believed that increased Viet Cong
activity in South Vietnam and Laos justified crossing that threshold. In
the following twenty months, the U.S. military presence in South
Vietnam ballooned without a deliberate examination of policy options.
Other issues and events, such as the civil rights movement and a series of
foreign policy crises, hit closer to home and overshadowed the increasing
U.S. involvement in Vietnam.[50] Although U.S. advisers were fighting
with South Vietnamese units and U.S. pilots were flying combat missions
in South Vietnam, Kennedy denied that Americans were involved in
combat, and Vietnam attracted little public or congressional attention.
Vietnam was far from front-page news and Americans still believed that
their government told them the truth.[51]

It seemed by early 1963 that the tripling of the American advisory effort
during the previous year had stabilized the situation in Vietnam. A year
before, the Diem government had initiated the Strategic Hamlet Program
involving the consolidation of much of the South Vietnamese rural populace into villages in which they theoretically remained insulated and
secure from Viet Cong activities and influence. Despite problems of mis-
management, the program, in combination with increased American mili-

tary support, caused the Viet Cong and their North Vietnamese sponsors considerable consternation.[52] American visitors to South Vietnam returned with optimistic reports. After a January visit to Vietnam, Earl Wheeler, by now Army chief of staff, reported: "We are winning slowly on the present thrust" and concluded that there was "no compelling reason to change" the current policy.[53] Periodic reports on the situation in South Vietnam from Gen. Paul D. Harkins, commander of Military Assistance Command, Vietnam (MACV), were similarly optimistic.

■

The outbreak of Buddhist uprisings in May 1963 against the government of the Catholic Diem, and Diem's brutal repression of the revolt, militated against these sanguine assessments. The United States failed to dissuade Diem and his brother, Ngo Dinh Nhu (head of the secret police), from taking drastic action against the Buddhists. On June 11 the first self-immolation by a Buddhist occurred. In August, Nhu's units invaded the main pagodas of Saigon, arrested bonzes (Buddhist clergymen), and inflicted great damage on the holy places. Vietnam hit the front pages of America's newspapers.

Officials within the Kennedy administration grew increasingly concerned as a significant portion of the South Vietnamese populace began to connect American support for the government with Nhu's obdurate callousness. The new ambassador to South Vietnam, Henry Cabot Lodge, cabled Secretary Rusk to inform him that "we have been hearing increasing comments from Vietnamese from many walks of life criticizing us to [the] effect that events of the past several days would not have been possible without U.S. equipment, and asking why [the] U.S. refrains from stopping" the brutality. Lodge went on to observe that many Vietnamese implied or stated overtly that the "Diem Government and [his] family must go."[54] William Bundy, McGeorge's older brother and McNamara's Deputy Assistant Secretary of Defense for International Security Affairs, recalled that, after mid-August 1963, the Kennedy administration became "more pre-occupied with Vietnam than at any previous time."[55]

For several weeks the president and his advisers had been debating options concerning the future of the Diem government. The JCS had agreed with former Ambassador Frederick Nolting that there was no viable alternative to Diem, and were unified in their position that the United States should do nothing to engineer a change in government in

South Vietnam. Members of Kennedy's inner circle, however, including Roger Hilsman, the Democratic Party's elder statesman Averell Harriman, and Michael Forrestal, thought that getting rid of Diem was the only alternative. True to a well-established pattern among members of the Kennedy administration, these men worked surreptitiously to advance their own solution to the problem. Hilsman teletyped a draft cable to the president's Cape Cod home that would instruct Ambassador Lodge to give Diem's and Nhu's military opponents "direct support" in an effort to replace them with "the best military and political personalities available." Because Hilsman sent the cable on a weekend during which the president's principal advisers were out of Washington, Kennedy approved its contents without considering fully its potential consequences.[56]

Initial contacts with South Vietnamese generals revealed that there was little in-country backing for an anti-Diem coup. In a meeting with the president on August 27, Nolting told Kennedy and his advisers that "military support for a coup did not now exist." Several days later Hilsman reported that contacts with two generals revealed "less support than anticipated." Lodge confirmed the lack of support for the coup within the South Vietnamese military, but cabled Rusk that "we are now launched on a course from which there is no respectable turning back: The overthrow of the Diem Government." The question of how involved the United States should become in inciting Diem's ouster incited heated debate in Washington. Both Taylor and McNamara voiced objections, but the president seemed unable to make a decision.[57]

Meanwhile Ambassador Lodge, convinced that Diem had to go, continued to explore the possibilities of a coup. Rusk blamed Diem's ineptitude and callous treatment of the Buddhists for the reversal of the "favorable developments of the first six months of this year when we were beginning to feel that a corner had been turned and that we would anticipate a successful conclusion." He gave Lodge a free hand as long as the ambassador minimized "the appearance of collusion with the Generals."[58] Certain that the "ship of state" in Vietnam was "slowly sinking," Lodge saw a "drastic change in government" as the only answer to the difficulties in South Vietnam.[59]

With plans to orchestrate a coup already well under way in Saigon, President Kennedy sent Taylor and Robert McNamara to Vietnam from September 23 to October 2 to produce "the best possible on-the-spot appraisal of the military and paramilitary effort to defeat the Viet Cong."

Members of the McNamara-Taylor mission were split between those agreeing with General Harkins's optimistic reports of progress and others who viewed the situation in South Vietnam more skeptically. Because the report had to be acceptable to the whole team and was prepared in a hurried manner, it was rife with contradictions and failed to reach useful conclusions. It acknowledged the problem of unrest in the cities, for example, but watered down the assessment by noting that considerable progress had been made in the countryside. To place additional pressure on Diem and give the American people the impression that the South Vietnamese were gaining the upper hand against the Viet Cong, Kennedy publicly announced a decision to withdraw one thousand U.S. advisers from South Vietnam by Christmas. At the same time he suggested that all American military advisers would be out of Vietnam by the end of 1965. The president also instructed Lodge to suspend portions of American aid to dissuade Diem from committing further acts of violence against the Buddhists.[60]

Kennedy failed to establish a clear policy toward the Diem government. McNamara and Taylor had recommended not encouraging a coup. Referring to his initial cable authorizing Lodge to conspire against Diem, Kennedy told George Ball on October 4: "we fucked that up." Despite his misgivings, however, Kennedy sent contradictory signals to Lodge, and the ambassador continued to undermine the South Vietnamese regime. On October 6 the president instructed Lodge to take "no initiative . . . to give any active covert encouragement to a coup." The next day, however, Lodge received instructions not to "thwart a change of government . . . to a new regime" if the alternative appeared viable.[61] On October 29 the president met with his advisers to discuss Diem's fate.

Taylor expressed frustration that Lodge was acting without the counsel of Harkins, who remained unaware of what the embassy and the CIA were doing. He felt that members of the administration were watching the coup preparations as if they were a "football game." Taylor, expressing the JCS view, warned that Diem's ouster would impede the war effort. McCone and Robert Kennedy voiced support for Taylor's position. Rusk, Harriman, Hilsman, and Forrestal, however, recommended going forward with the coup. The president seemed ambivalent. Advice from his brother and Taylor almost swayed him, but, at the end of the meeting, Kennedy declared indecisively that he would "discourage" a coup only if Lodge, on whom he depended to generate Republican support for his policy, shared Taylor's and Robert Kennedy's misgivings.[62] On October 31 McGeorge Bundy instructed Lodge that "once a coup under responsible leadership has begun . . . it is in the interest of the U.S. government that it should succeed."[63] Diem's fate was sealed.

The coup began just after noon Saigon time on November 1, and the generals notified their American coconspirators shortly thereafter. Several hours later Diem called Ambassador Lodge wanting to know the attitude of the U.S. government. Lodge pleaded ignorance and patronized the South Vietnamese leader with compliments on his courage and great contributions to his country. Diem hung up after telling the ambassador that he would try to reestablish order.[64]

■

November 1963 marked a turning point in the Vietnam War. The U.S. role in fomenting a change in the South Vietnamese government saddled the United States with responsibility for its successor. Instability in the South presented the Viet Cong and their North Vietnamese sponsors with an opportunity to exploit, and the deteriorating situation forced the United States to consider deepening its involvement in what had become a new war. An assassin's bullet, however, would bequeath those decisions to John Kennedy's vice president, Lyndon Johnson.

Along with the question of what to do about Vietnam, Lyndon Johnson inherited Kennedy's closest advisers and the relationships that had developed among them. The relationship between the JCS and those to whom they provided military advice had become one of deep distrust. The chairman, selected for his personal loyalty to the president, had forged a closer relationship with the secretary of defense than the one he enjoyed with his military colleagues. McNamara, emboldened in the realm of strategic planning, was poised to become the president's dominant adviser on military affairs. Convinced that military advice based on the objective of achieving victory was outmoded, even dangerous, he would use his talent for analysis and the experience of the Cuban missile crisis to develop a new concept for the use of American military power. John Kennedy bequeathed to Lyndon Johnson an advisory system that limited real influence to his inner circle and treated others, particularly the Joint Chiefs of Staff, more like a source of potential opposition than of useful advice.

3
New War, New Leader
November 1963–January 1964

The president is not a shapeless organism in a flood of novelties, but a man with a memory in a system with a history.

—JAMES DAVID BARBER, *THE PRESIDENTIAL CHARACTER*[1]

At 3:00 A.M. on November 1, 1963, a phone call from the National Military Command Center at the Pentagon awoke JCS chairman Taylor and informed him that the anticipated coup against South Vietnamese president Ngo Dinh Diem and his brother, Ngo Dinh Nhu, had begun at about noon Saigon time. Taylor dressed quickly and left his home at Fort Meyer, Virginia, for the Pentagon.[2] His trusted aide, Lt. Col. Bernard W. Rogers, met him at the office.[3] Rogers had organized the incoming cables concerning the Diem coup. Taylor read them before meeting with the Joint Chiefs to discuss the consequences of events unfolding in South Vietnam.[4]

Taylor's relationship with the Chiefs was mixed. He had spent a great deal of his time trying to reconcile differences of opinion between himself and Air Force Chief of Staff Curtis LeMay, whom he had antagonized with forceful attacks on the Air Force in *The Uncertain Trumpet*.[5] Taylor was not the only one who disagreed with LeMay's opinions, however. The general's impassioned recommendations of bombing as the definitive solution to military problems had earned him a reputation as a "loose cannon." Deputy Secretary of Defense Gilpatric told one of his assistants that President Kennedy "has kind of a fit when you mention LeMay." However, LeMay's combat and command records would have made removing him from the JCS controversial. When his first two-year term came to an end, Kennedy, rather than risk opposition from LeMay's supporters in Congress, extended his appointment for only one year, sending the general a clear message.[6]

Taylor had recently persuaded LeMay to support the September 1963 limited test ban treaty that restricted American and Soviet nuclear testing to underground explosions.[7] They had come to agreement, however, at the price of congeniality. LeMay was unable to conceal his animosity for Taylor and often felt like "letting him have one."[8] The bad feelings were mutual. Taylor regarded LeMay as politically naïve and believed that his appointment as Air Force chief of staff had been a "big mistake."[9] Traditional seating protocol at JCS meetings put LeMay at Taylor's immediate right. LeMay's bushy eyebrows, sagging jowls, and jutting jaw advertised an irascible personality. Aware of Taylor's aversion to tobacco smoke, he hung his ever-present long dark cigar out of the left side of his mouth and intentionally puffed the thick smoke in Taylor's direction. Both men were hard of hearing, and the resulting misunderstandings worsened the tension between them.[10]

Seated to LeMay's right at the short end of the table was Marine Corps Commandant David Shoup, the last remaining holdover from the Eisenhower administration. Before Taylor became chairman, the often-profane poker-playing Shoup had grown frustrated because Taylor's predecessor, General Lemnitzer, never directly questioned Secretary McNamara's controversial methods. Shoup, who had received the Medal of Honor for heroism on the Pacific island of Tarawa in World War II, planned to retire in January 1964 after a distinguished career. Considering his position on the Joint Chiefs tedious, the commandant gave priority to his duties as head of the Marine Corps. Although he attended JCS meetings only when issues directly affected the Corps, Vietnam was a subject on which the general possessed strong opinions. A trip to South Vietnam in 1962 confirmed his abiding conviction that the United States should "not, under any circumstances, get involved in land warfare in Southeast Asia."[11]

Disagreements among the Chiefs often reflected differences in their philosophies of war. LeMay, for example, felt that the United States should respond to security threats with massive retaliation from the air, whereas Shoup was against using military force at all unless U.S. vital interests were at stake.[12] Shoup based his philosophy on practical experience; to him the "lesson" of Korea was that the United States was not adept at fighting protracted limited wars.[13] In contrast to both of them, Taylor believed that the United States could take military action in Southeast Asia short of committing to war, and that fighting limited wars was essential to a strategy of flexible response, which would avoid the extremes: nuclear war or buckling to Communist aggression.[14] Accordingly he expressed frustration with those, like Shoup and LeMay, who refused for various reasons to support the shift in national security strategy to Taylor's concept of flexible response. In Taylor's view, LeMay typified the Air Force's blind preoccupation with the "preponderant use of air power." Taylor thought that Shoup and others who refused on principle to fight on the Asian mainland overemphasized the country's domestic political reaction to the Korean War and had an "American penchant for simple solutions" to complex problems.[15]

The Navy stayed aloof from the debate because the outcome of the discussion was less consequential for the Navy than for the Air Force or Army. A fixation on limited war was likely to cut into the Air Force's strategic nuclear force, just as Eisenhower's policy of massive retaliation had strengthened it at the Army's expense. The Navy, however, had succeeded in carving out a role independent from the contest. Adm. David McDonald, like the chiefs of naval operations (CNOs) before him, was interested primarily in maintaining America's global dominance at sea.[16]

Although the Navy was still angry over McNamara's removal of Anderson as CNO, his replacement, Admiral McDonald, had fared well during the Kennedy administration. In April 1963 McDonald was selected over twenty-eight more senior vice admirals for promotion to four-star rank and given command of all U.S. naval forces in the European theater of operations. McDonald had been in his new command less than one month when President Kennedy announced that he would appoint him CNO. McDonald was more adept politically than Anderson and, therefore, well suited to maintain the Navy's bargaining power within the government. He was not reluctant to make compromises to further the Navy's interest. When asked to expound on his personal philosophy, the admiral responded with an anecdote: "You know about the fellow who says, 'I'd rather be right than be President,' he never was President." McDonald valued the expediency of "giving in to something [he] knew was going to happen anyway."[17] His tact and political sensitivity contrasted sharply with the stubbornness of LeMay, across from whom he sat.

General Wheeler, the Army chief of staff, sat next to McDonald and across from Taylor. Wheeler was a "new type" of JCS member.[18] Unlike LeMay and Shoup, who mostly held command positions, Wheeler was primarily a staff officer who spent nearly half of his post–World War II career in Washington.[19] Like McDonald, Wheeler was particularly adept at working within the Washington bureaucratic maze and was talented at creating compromises between parties otherwise disinclined to reconcile their differences.[20] Taylor recommended to the administration that Wheeler be appointed Army chief of staff and knew that he could be counted upon for his loyalty and support. When, in January 1963, at the village of Ap Bac, the South Vietnamese Army suffered a costly defeat at the hands of a smaller Viet Cong force, Taylor sent Wheeler to Vietnam to investigate. Wheeler, who recognized that a negative assessment of South Vietnamese fighting ability might call into question the counterinsurgency effort for which Taylor had been largely responsible, helped damp down the controversy over the battle.[21]

■

Whatever their differences, the Chiefs had been united in their opposition to the Diem coup. Although Diem had handled the Buddhists roughly and the brutality of his brother Nhu was disquieting, the military officers viewed the war against the Viet Cong as the "major problem" in South Vietnam and thought that engineering a change in government after supporting Diem for so long would "invalidate" the U.S. effort in Vietnam. The Chiefs also did not think that anyone was capable of taking Diem's place.[22] They resented the administration's disregard for their advice and the secrecy under which the coup plotting had been carried out, referring to the coup scornfully as the "Asian Bay of Pigs."[23]

Nonetheless the coup gave the Chiefs time to consider the situation in South Vietnam. Reports brought into the meeting confirmed that a group of generals headed by Duong Van "Big" Minh, with support from the Saigon garrison, had attacked the presidential palace. When the Joint Chiefs began to discuss the probable character of Minh's leadership, one of them sarcastically remarked that other than being "weak, dumb, and lazy," Minh was well qualified for the South Vietnamese presidency. The Chiefs agreed that the situation in Vietnam was deteriorating.[24] The optimism of early 1963 was gone as the Chiefs contemplated the effect that the coup would have on the counterinsurgency effort. As the JCS meeting ended, the coup was still in progress.

Later that morning Kennedy learned Diem's and Nhu's fate. An aide informed the president that the former U.S. allies in the fight against Communism lay dead in the back of an American-made armored personnel carrier with bound hands and execution-style bullet wounds in the backs of their heads. The president was shocked. He had not realized that his failure to give clear instructions to Ambassador Lodge would have such unpleasant consequences halfway around the world.[25] Yet he felt no remorse for the death of the brothers. By November 2 Kennedy turned his thoughts to ensuring stability in South Vietnam and explaining the affair to the American people. Kennedy made it clear that deposing Diem was purely pragmatic. His immediate concern was that the new government have the will and capability to continue the fight against the Viet Cong. Afraid that the United States might "lose [its] entire position in Southeast Asia overnight,"[26] he told his advisers that "we need an effective government more than a 'pretty' government."[27] McNamara informed the president that U.S. forces were steaming toward Vietnam to deter the Viet Cong from taking advantage of the turmoil in Saigon.[28]

For his part McGeorge Bundy was relieved that the coup had finally been accomplished. He told the president and his closest advisers, "Now we have nothing to divide us."[29] Bundy's comment was unrealistically sanguine. Instead of fostering unity among agencies and individuals in the administration, the legacy of the Diem coup and assassination would inspire divisiveness and animosity. Although McNamara's forces did not disembark in South Vietnam immediately after the coup, American complicity in precipitating a violent change of government in South Vietnam paved the way for an expanding American military and political commitment to Diem's successor. Responding effectively to a deteriorating situation in South Vietnam, furthermore, would require close coordination between civilian and military officials. Rather than relieving tensions between the JCS and the Kennedy administration, the "Asian Bay of Pigs" exacerbated them and made cooperation even more difficult.

November 22, 1963, was Taylor's first day back from a whirlwind trip to Honolulu. He and Secretaries McNamara and Rusk had met with Ambassador Lodge, General Harkins, and others from Saigon to discuss the situation in Vietnam in the aftermath of the coup. Although it was still too early to assess the new government's viability, or the Communist reaction to the coup, Minh's hasty purge of old Diem officials removed expertise that would have helped the Saigon government to fight the Viet Cong.[30] Taylor left the conference pessimistic. His itinerary on the day he returned to Washington probably seemed more pleasant to him; he was to entertain the West German chief of staff and his successor-designate.[31]

As the Chiefs and their visitors finished their lunch in the chairman's dining room, President Kennedy's motorcade began its fateful journey from Love Field in Dallas. After lunch Taylor reclined on the couch in his office to take his customary afternoon nap. Before he could drift off to sleep, however, Bernard Rogers entered his office with the news that President Kennedy had been shot. Taylor called the Chiefs into his office and met briefly with McNamara to discuss the possible consequences of the shooting. He sent a message to U.S. commanders throughout the world urging them to increase their alertness. The Chiefs returned to the conference with the German officers. While seated in the meeting room, General Taylor received written confirmation of the president's death. He and the other Chiefs passed the message underneath the table so as not to interrupt the discussion. When the meeting was over, Taylor gave the news to the German officers. He recalled having rarely seen such "spontaneous grief."[32]

■

Approximately two hours after Kennedy was assassinated, Lyndon Baines Johnson was sworn in as president of the United States. Two days later, while the country mourned Kennedy's death, Johnson conferred with Ambassador Lodge, who had flown to Washington after the Honolulu conference. Johnson had just returned from an emotional memorial service for Kennedy in the Great Rotunda of the Capitol. Rusk, McNamara, Under Secretary of State George Ball, and DCI McCone joined the president and the ambassador in the White House. Lodge, who had engineered the coup, assessed the situation optimistically, but McCone disagreed with him. Johnson, reflecting on the contrasting appraisals, muttered, "We'll stand by our word, but I have misgivings. I feel like a fish that just grabbed a worm with a big hook in the middle of it."[33] The president's instructions to his advisers, however, emphasized continuity with Kennedy's policies. He told Lodge to tell Minh that he "can count on us" and pledged that he was "not going to be the president who saw Southeast Asia go the way China went."[34]

Johnson's support of the U.S. commitment to South Vietnam was unsurprising given his Cold War political experience. Remembering Republican attacks on the Democratic Party in the wake of President Truman's "loss" of China, he feared that another Communist victory on the mainland of Asia would destroy his nascent administration.[35] In 1961 he had taken a vice presidential tour of Southeast Asia, which, he told Kennedy, served to "sharpen and deepen" the basic convictions he had held before he left. He had concluded that "the battle against Communism must be joined in Southeast Asia with strength and determination to achieve success," and that there was "no alternative to United States leadership" in South Vietnam.[36]

Consistent with his decision to stress continuity during his sudden elevation to the presidency, Johnson asked the Kennedy team to remain with him. This decision was not particularly difficult because Johnson already held the secretaries of state and defense in high regard. Johnson sympathized with Rusk because he also had not been part of the Kennedy "inner circle." Kennedy had tasked Rusk with keeping Vice President Johnson abreast of international developments, and LBJ had deeply appreciated the secretary's diligence in discharging that duty. As vice president, Johnson had quickly recognized McNamara's talents. He once said of McNamara, "that man with the Sta-Comb hair is the best of the [Kennedy] lot."[37]

Many members of the administration who had great influence with President Kennedy, however, would hold far less sway with Johnson. Although the new president retained Kennedy's informal, ad hoc style of consultation with advisers, Johnson felt comfortable with different people and favored their views. Johnson had from the first rejected the advice of those who advocated the removal of Diem. In a meeting at the State Department on August 31, Vice President Johnson had told those arguing for the South Vietnamese president's removal that he had "never been sympathetic" with the idea, and recommended that the United States actually strengthen ties with the Diem regime.[38] After the coup he believed that the United States government had "killed" the man he once called the "Churchill of Asia." Johnson thought that Lodge had gotten "things screwed up good."[39] The president had little faith in the ambassador and his allies in the State Department.

On November 26, the day after President Kennedy's funeral, President Johnson approved NSAM 273, which affirmed the American commitment to "assist the [South Vietnamese] to win their contest against the externally directed and supported Communist conspiracy" and called for the prompt submission of plans for covert, cross-border operations against North Vietnam. In light of divisions in the Kennedy administration caused by the Diem affair, Johnson made it clear that he expected all members of his administration to "insure full unity of support for established U.S. policy in South Vietnam." He ordered officials to avoid criticizing officers in other departments and offices and to desist from dissension and infighting.[40]

On the same day General Taylor and the Chiefs wrote to their new president requesting the opportunity to "pay their respects and receive such guidance as he might wish to give them."[41] Johnson first met with the Chiefs three days later, on November 29. He primarily discussed cutting defense expenditures and asked the Chiefs to look for ways to save money. Taylor had his own agenda: He suggested to the president that military advice should transcend "purely military considerations" and recommended that Johnson adopt Kennedy's instructions to the Chiefs, as encapsulated in NSAM 55, to place military advice in a broader political and economic context. Johnson decided to retain those guidelines.[42]

Johnson's first meeting with the JCS betrayed his sense of insecurity as a new and unexpected president. A request Johnson made of the Chiefs at the end of the meeting illustrated this aspect of his character and revealed his attitude toward his military advisers. He asked each of the Chiefs to send him individual photographs of themselves so he could have them framed and put on his wall in the White House. He promised to look at the pictures often and think about his top military men.[43] Johnson thereby notified the Chiefs that he would be watching them symbolically and that he expected their unqualified support.

Johnson was a profoundly insecure man who craved and demanded affirmation. He was especially uncertain about his presidency because he had realized his lifelong dream not through his own efforts to gain the support of the American people but through the murder of his predecessor. He later told a biographer that he felt as if he was "illegitimate, a naked man with no presidential covering, a pretender to the throne, an illegal usurper." He feared those who were "waiting to knock me down before I could even begin to stand up." He was so frightened that he found his transition to the presidency "almost unbearable."[44]

Johnson's lack of self-confidence manifested itself in a reluctance to trust those around him. Reflecting on his service in the Johnson White House, McGeorge Bundy recalled,

> Johnson was worried about the unknown. He knew how many unknowns there were; he knew how complicated and uncertain life was. He knew that the only way to avoid failure was to put yourself on guard against it, and he was, in that sense, the wariest man about whom to trust that I have ever encountered.[45]

The new president's preoccupation with consensus and unity came from his insecurity and his consequent distrust of his advisers. At times he manifested a kind of paranoia about dissent.[46] His quest for reassurance and support, rather than wide-ranging debate on policy issues, would color Johnson's relationship with the Joint Chiefs and his other advisers and determine who exerted influence over American policy toward Vietnam.

Johnson especially distrusted his military advisers. His first contact with the military had come during his initial bid for the Senate in Texas in 1941. He seized on the issue of military preparedness to put a more conservative face on his campaign. Johnson hoped that his strong position on defense matters would mitigate his support for President Franklin D. Roosevelt's New Deal. His strategy failed, and he lost the election. After his defeat Johnson took a five-week leave from his office in the House of Representatives to fulfill his campaign promise to volunteer for military service.[47]

Serving in World War II helped Johnson advance his political career. After gaining a commission as a lieutenant commander in the U.S. Navy, he secured from President Roosevelt an assignment to the Pacific as part of a three-man observation team. One of Roosevelt's aides wrote in his diary that Johnson was anxious to be in a danger zone to enhance his appeal to the electorate. On June 9, 1942, Johnson got his wish. He rode on a B-26 bombing run from an airfield in New Guinea. While approaching the target area, Johnson's plane experienced a mechanical malfunction and came under attack from Japanese fighters. The pilot nursed the aircraft back to base and landed it smoothly on the runway. The plane to which Johnson had initially been assigned was not as fortunate and crashed into the ocean, killing the entire crew and one of his fellow observers, Lt. Col. Francis Stevens, who had taken Johnson's seat. The next day Johnson headed for home. During a brief stopover in Australia, Johnson and his surviving fellow observer met the commander of the Southwest Pacific Theater, Gen. Douglas MacArthur. MacArthur told Johnson that he was awarding him the Silver Star Medal for gallantry during his ride on the B-26 bomber. No other crew member, not even the pilot who landed the crippled plane, received a decoration. A week after his return to the United States, LBJ was out of uniform and back in the House of Representatives.[48]

Despite his limited experience, Johnson assumed the demeanor of a war-weary veteran. He told reporters of his "suicide mission" against the Japanese and "the harrowing flight home under fire." The press, caught up in the emotional fervor of the war, eagerly embraced his deliberate misrepresentation of his service in the South Pacific. Johnson told his rural Texas constituents that he was simply happy to have survived the ordeal. In December of 1942, when a reporter asked him if he had been in combat, Johnson replied, "Yes I was, I was out there in May, June, and part of July. We exchanged greetings [with the enemy] quite often. They [the Japanese] paid us very busy visits every day for a time." In Johnson's accounts enemy fire had "knocked out" the engine that had malfunctioned. He even told a reporter that the men with whom he had served in the 22nd Bomber Group had called him "Raider" Johnson. Although Johnson once told a journalist that he didn't deserve the Silver Star Medal and told a receptive audience that he had refused the honor, he arranged to have the medal bestowed upon him in public—several times.[49] His misrepresentation of his war experience for political benefit revealed a real propensity for lying. Both Lyndon Johnson's self-doubt and his willingness to forgo the truth would color his relationship with his principal military advisers and shape the way that the United States became more deeply involved in the Vietnam War.

After his stint in the Navy, Johnson lobbied vigorously on behalf of military preparedness. Rep. Carl Vinson, Chairman of the House Naval Affairs Committee, placed him at the head of a new subcommittee to investigate the progress of the war. Johnson's critical inquiries into Navy policy quickly earned him a reputation as a defense expert. He dealt with the Navy's senior officers daily, and he came to regard them as uninspired personalities who were often disorganized and ill informed. Vinson recalled that the Navy's inefficiency and proclivity to waste resources appalled Johnson. The large number of sailors assigned to clerical duty at Navy headquarters particularly incensed him.[50]

Lyndon Johnson leaped at roles that might enhance his popular appeal. In 1950, days after the United States sent troops to Korea, Johnson, now a freshman senator, urged Richard Russell, a Georgia Democrat who chaired the Senate Armed Services Committee, to establish for him a Defense Preparedness Subcommittee to investigate the American military's conduct of the Korean War. Johnson relished the publicity that he gained as "watchdog" over the military establishment and did not hesitate to criticize President Truman for rejecting JCS requests for an increase in U.S. air power. During the Korean War the senator criticized Truman's "makeshift mobilization," stating that "we are in a war but all our effort is seemingly directed toward staying out of the war that we are in already." Even as Johnson supported the military on those and other issues, however, he demonstrated his contempt for senior military officers. He was dismayed that high-ranking officers often appeared before his committee with disjointed, erroneous, and confused presentations. During a 1958 hearing Johnson told Army Lt. Gen. James Gavin, who was testifying about the resignation that he had tendered to Eisenhower, that his departure would leave "second raters" in charge of the Army.[51] Johnson brought with him to the presidency a low opinion of the nation's top military men and a long history of taking positions on military issues to enhance his political fortunes.

Johnson's distrust of the military was evident during his first weeks as president. Immediately after taking office he dismissed three of the four military aides who had served on McGeorge Bundy's staff because they "get in my way." After protest from the Pentagon reached Johnson through the White House staff, the president told Deputy Secretary of Defense Gilpatric to "tell the admiral and tell the general that if their little men like that believe they can pressure their Commander in Chief on what his strategy ought to be in war or what his decision ought to be in peace . . . they don't know their Commander in Chief." Johnson agreed with Gilpatric's observation that "they've got a lot to learn" and was miffed that the military never "paid one damn bit of attention" to him when he was vice president. He ordered the Chiefs to prevent Bundy's former aides from complaining to Congress or the press.[52] The former senator knew all too well how an ambitious politician might use military issues to attack the administration. Accordingly he would take great care to maintain the appearance, if not the reality, of close consultation with his military advisers.

■

After only one week in the Oval Office, Johnson set out to make political capital out of reforms in the Defense Department. Defense savings, he thought, would allow him to persuade members of Congress to support expensive domestic programs, and Johnson spent virtually all of December 2 on the phone with key representatives and senators extolling the virtues of his plan to cut defense spending. He explained to Sen. John McClellan how defense savings could fund increased domestic spending, and he told his old colleague Vinson that he "was not going to have any fat" in the defense budget. Other calls went out to Reps. Bill Dawson and Jack Brooks, and to Sen. John Stennis.[53] The president was staking a large portion of his political reputation on his ability to bring defense spending under control and was anxious to squeeze the most political value out of McNamara's reforms in the Pentagon.[54] He noted that McNamara had "already shown realized savings of one billion dollars" and promised to "save four billion more by fiscal year 1967."[55]

McNamara's desire to please the boss and the president's need for reassurance generated an immediate rapport between the two men. The president already held his defense secretary in high regard, and McNamara soon established himself as the most indispensable member of Johnson's cabinet. When Johnson called congressmen, he told them what a great job McNamara was doing in the Pentagon. A month after taking office, the president worried that he would have to report a cost overrun of $400 million in defense spending for fiscal 1964. McNamara, who had a knack for manipulating numbers, offered a solution. He volunteered to underestimate deliberately what moneys were spent for defense and later feign surprise when spending exceeded his department's forecast. The dependable McNamara saved the president from considerable embarrassment with Congress.[56] When necessary McNamara would disparage the military members of his department to protect Johnson's standing with the legislators. When Republican Rep. Gerald Ford confronted McNamara with charges that Navy yards had been withheld from a base closure list to protect Democratic constituencies, the defense secretary blamed incompetent naval officers for the omission. McNamara boasted to Johnson that he had deflected Ford's criticism by telling him that "the Navy didn't know their [sic] ass from a hole in the ground." The president expressed his gratitude to McNamara: "That's excellent. Excellent. Thank you very much."[57] Johnson praised McNamara to Sargent Shriver as the most "valuable" man in his administration. "He just gives you the answers and he gives you cooperation, and he's a can-do fellow."[58] Later, when the president wanted to conceal from the American public and Congress the costs of deepening American involvement in Vietnam, McNamara's can-do attitude and talent for manipulating numbers and people would prove indispensable.

■

General Taylor enjoyed close personal ties with President Kennedy and his family, but Johnson may have considered that a liability. The quality of their relationship was unclear at first. Taylor nevertheless needed the president's help to consolidate his power in the chairmanship and expand that position's prerogatives. Taylor thought that Congress should "dissolve the JCS" and replace it with a single "Defense Chief of Staff" and a "Supreme Military Council." The defense chief of staff would have "great authority" and report directly to the secretary of defense and the president.[59] Now that he was chairman, Taylor thought that he could become a de facto "defense chief of staff." In an effort to centralize authority, he gave his special assistant for policy, Maj. Gen. Andrew Goodpaster, formerly President Eisenhower's national security assistant, unprecedented responsibilities and latitude. Goodpaster became, in effect, a deputy chairman. Previously, in the absence of the chairman, the senior service chief presided over important sessions as acting chairman. When Taylor was out of town, Goodpaster, as his "deputy," attended White House and other high-level policy and planning sessions in place of another Chief. Taylor thereby retained more control over the advice that the JCS gave, and the service chiefs thus had less access to and influence with the president.[60] Taylor's initiative anticipated the creation of a vice chairman of the JCS, a structural reform that Congress mandated nearly twenty-five years later.

Taylor tried to formalize Goodpaster's position and make it permanent. He wanted him promoted to lieutenant general and his title changed to Assistant Chairman, Joint Chiefs of Staff, a maneuver that required considerable political support. In early December, Taylor sought the assistance of McGeorge Bundy and Sen. Richard Russell. Taylor sent Bundy a hand-carried letter stating that Goodpaster's promotion and change of title would "reflect the expanded activities and responsibilities of the position as it has developed with Andy the incumbent." Taylor anticipated "service grumbling that this is an enhancement of the position of the Chairman which should be resisted" and asked Bundy to solicit the president's support. In his letter to Senator Russell, Taylor downplayed the significance of the change, emphasizing the positive effect that it would have on administrative procedures within the JCS and implying that the Chiefs supported the initiative.[61]

The Chiefs, however, recognized Taylor's bid to expand his power, and they resisted it. Taylor initially appointed Goodpaster against their advice. In August 1962, when Kennedy first announced Taylor's appointment as chairman, the Navy and Air Force Chiefs suggested special assistants to him. Admiral Anderson recommended that Taylor select "a top-flight one starred officer of a service other than your own."[62] Instead Taylor chose Goodpaster, an Army two-star general. Although other chairmen had selected assistants from their own services, Taylor's rejection of the Chiefs' advice probably further fueled their desire to foil his latest bid to strengthen the chairmanship at their expense. LeMay, McDonald, and Shoup opposed Taylor, whose only support came from Wheeler. McDonald pointed out that Goodpaster's position would end the practice of the senior member of the Joint Chiefs filling in as acting chairman in the chairman's absence. Under fire from the Chiefs, Taylor changed the proposed title of Goodpaster's new position to Assistant *to the* Chairman without changing the broad definition of his duties.

In an effort to derail Taylor's proposal, one of the Chiefs (or a member of his close personal staff) leaked a story to Hanson Baldwin, the respected military correspondent of the *New York Times*, that detailed the Chiefs' dissatisfaction with the Goodpaster initiative.[63] The proposal was also brought to the attention of Carl Vinson, now chairman of the House

Armed Services Committee. The newspaper leak and surreptitious contact with the congressman deeply angered Taylor, and he admonished the Chiefs for what he regarded as an incident "without precedent." Although he had attempted to gain support for his initiative without the knowledge of his colleagues, he secured a pledge from the Chiefs to preserve the confidentiality of their exchanges in the future.[64]

On December 11, amid this controversy among his senior military advisers, President Johnson delivered a speech at the Pentagon to top civilian and military officials. He told the audience that he had "special confidence in General Taylor" and pledged his support for Taylor and all the Chiefs in "their efforts to discharge their duties more effectively." On the written copy of the address, the drafter alerted the president parenthetically that "this sentence is designed to give your personal support in a quiet but clear way to General Taylor in the Goodpaster matter." Johnson's support for Taylor's consolidation of advisory influence at the chairman's level would help satisfy the president's penchant for unity and consensus. Taylor would help keep the Chiefs from voicing dissent over administration policies while limiting JCS access to deliberations on sensitive issues. "We need unity across the board in the execution of the national security policies of the United States," Johnson told the Defense Department's top civilian and military officials. "My object . . . is a unified administration, and not a divided Pentagon. . . . We are bound together, you and I, not only by our oaths of office, but by the loyalty which underlies them." Not only did Johnson express support for Taylor's consolidation of influence at the chairman's level, but Johnson went on to pledge his unqualified backing for "Mr. McNamara and the men who work with him."[65] Taylor, no doubt grateful for the president's support, demonstrated the same loyalty to Johnson that he had shown Kennedy. The other Chiefs and the JCS as an institution were the losers in status, influence, and power. Although he would not assume the title, Goodpaster would continue to operate as de facto deputy chairman. As Lyndon Johnson confronted instability in Vietnam, Taylor's and McNamara's dominance over the JCS increased.

■

At the conclusion of his speech, Johnson designated "Communist subversion in South Vietnam" a matter of urgent priority. The president's closing remarks reflected a growing concern over increased Viet Cong activity and the unabated flow of arms and supplies from the North to the insurgents in the South through Laos and Cambodia.[66] During the first week in December, President Johnson had directed government officials to ask themselves each day what more they could do to contribute to the struggle in Vietnam.[67] Contradictory reports from the field and differences of opinion among key advisers, however, frustrated efforts in Washington to assess the situation accurately. As a result White House meetings on the issue were confused and lacked focus.[68] The situation in the American Embassy in Saigon was even worse. The two senior officers of the "Country Team" in Vietnam, General Harkins and Ambassador Lodge, who had worked at cross-purposes before the Diem coup, had become further estranged from each other.[69] Because information from the embassy was unreliable, Johnson asked Taylor and McNamara to visit South Vietnam to ascertain the true state of affairs there.

Taylor and McNamara departed for Saigon on December 18, 1963, and returned after two days in South Vietnam. Their habit of viewing their counterinsurgency program as a success, however, prevented them from making a realistic assessment. To support Kennedy's Vietnam policy, both men had a long background of suppressing bad news. The purpose of their last trip to South Vietnam, in September, was to "make [an] effective case with Congress for continued prosecution of the war effort" and Kennedy had cabled Lodge that he needed "ammunition I will get from an on-the-spot and authoritative military appraisal" to mislead the people's representatives.[70] Not surprisingly the report that McNamara and Taylor had filed upon their return omitted some of their more pessimistic findings. For example, they failed to report that the old, revered vice president Nguyen Ngoc Tho considered U.S. assistance "unintelligent" and thought that the Diem regime was alienating the people through brutal repression. Instead McNamara stated that the South Vietnamese military program had "made great progress" and that "we may all be proud of the effectiveness of the U.S. military advisory and support effort."[71] Taylor's and McNamara's willingness to render overly optimistic reports tailored to the president's domestic political concerns would make the JCS chairman and the defense secretary as valuable to LBJ as they had been to his predecessor. On their December visit McNamara and Taylor found it difficult to distance themselves from their previous assessments, and they could hardly gain a comprehensive appreciation for the situation during these brief trips, sixteen thousand miles back and forth, to Saigon.

Even so, McNamara and Taylor could not deny the deterioration of the situation in Vietnam in December. The tone of McNamara's report to the president was one of foreboding, and its predictions were pessimistic. McNamara wrote that "the situation is very disturbing," and "current trends, unless reversed in the next 2–3 months," are likely to lead to a "Communist controlled state." The new South Vietnamese government was unstable. McNamara also confirmed the friction within Lodge's Country Team. He attributed the troubled relations between Lodge and Harkins to the ambassador's ineptitude and propensity to act as a loner.[72]

Rather than accept some responsibility for the failure to report earlier the frailty of the counterinsurgency effort, McNamara blamed Harkins's overoptimistic reports. McNamara viewed military intelligence as a tool by which the services sought to justify greater resources, and he resolved to pay little attention to reports from Harkins's MACV.[73] To assess the situation in Vietnam, McNamara would rely on his own team of civilian analysts.

■

Before the Diem coup, no one figure in the Kennedy administration had dominated the development of plans for the American counterinsurgency effort. William Bundy recalled that there had been "no oracle on Vietnam."[74] McNamara, however, now began to take charge. He resolved on a complete review of the situation in Vietnam and took steps to reverse the downward trend. Although he acknowledged that "statistics received over the past year or more from the GVN officials and reported by the U.S. mission . . . were grossly in error," he firmly believed that tracking quantitative indices would give him a clear picture of how the war against the Viet Cong was going.[75] Despite MACV's protest that it was "impossible to measure progress in any meaningful way on a weekly basis," McNamara insisted on "Weekly Headway Reports" that included "measurable criteria" to help chart the progress of the war.[76] The very title of the report revealed his eagerness to demonstrate the South's improvement under his program.

McNamara began to do more than just gather information. Immediately after his return to Washington, the secretary of defense, bypassing the JCS, sent a cable directly to the Commander in Chief Pacific (CINCPAC), Adm. Harry Felt in Honolulu, suggesting that the Navy send a special operations team to counter infiltration in the vital Mekong Delta region.[77] McNamara believed that increased military activity on the part of the South Vietnamese, in conjunction with covert American assistance, would make "headway" in the fight against the Viet Cong.

Although McNamara favored gradually intensifying the military effort, the JCS questioned the value of limited, covert action. The Chiefs, in coordination with CINCPAC, had been evaluating plans for covert "hit-and-run" operations against North Vietnam since early 1963. In November, McNamara had directed MACV and the Saigon office of the CIA to develop a comprehensive program for plausibly deniable operations against the North.[78] LeMay questioned the usefulness of these "pinprick" operations and urged his colleagues to press the administration for permission to plan more resolute, overt military actions. After South Vietnam's deterioration became apparent, LeMay persuaded Marine Corps Commandant Shoup that bolder action was needed, and his arguments had made an impression on Wheeler and McDonald.[79] LeMay had another ally. Admiral Felt believed that even if nearly all of the targets included in OPLAN 34A, the name for a series of covert commando operations in and against North Vietnam, were attacked, these operations would have little effect on North Vietnam's determination to support the insurgents in the South.[80]

Others in the administration, however, did think that covert actions could gradually pressure North Vietnam into withdrawing its support for the Viet Cong. In a memo to the president on December 11, Michael Forrestal, special assistant to the president for Far Eastern affairs, recommended that Johnson "explore the possibility of larger-scale operations against selected targets in the North," aimed at getting "a practical reaction out of Hanoi." Forrestal suggested that he and others in the administration "work out a diplomatic scenario in which military pressure against the North would play a part." McNamara and Walt Rostow of the State Department's Policy Planning Committee shared Forrestal's enthusiasm for covert operations against North Vietnam.[81]

Despite LeMay's and Felt's reservations, the planning for covert operations continued. On December 21 Johnson ordered an interdepartmental group under Marine Corps lieutenant general Victor Krulak to study the

OPLAN and to "select from it" those targets the hitting of which would pose the "least risk" of being attributed to the United States.[82] Covert operations appealed to McNamara and the president because they appeared to be low-cost. U.S.-sponsored action against the North, however, represented a shift in the nature of the American commitment to the war. The formation of Krulak's committee bypassed the JCS and excluded the Chiefs from the planning process. LeMay recalled that "we in the military felt we were not in the decision-making process at all. Taylor might have been but we didn't agree with Taylor in most cases."[83]

■

The administration, meanwhile, had to forge unity and cooperation in the Country Team in Saigon. At the end of December, Taylor wrote a personal letter to Johnson stating that there could be no solution to the problem as long as Lodge remained ambassador. He doubted that anyone could work effectively with the impetuous Massachusetts patrician. He recommended that Johnson appoint a new ambassador with considerable military experience who could run the entire American effort in Vietnam, including military operations—qualifications strikingly similar to his own.[84] Johnson would not replace Lodge, however, until seven months later. The Republican ambassador and former political opponent of President Kennedy had been chosen to build bipartisan support for Kennedy's Vietnam policy. Ousting Lodge so soon after the Diem coup, going into a presidential election year, might prove politically damaging. His removal would have to appear to be a voluntary departure.

Because the administration was displeased with the Country Team, officials in Washington made Vietnam policy largely without its assistance. Johnson, ever fearful of disloyalty, favored the policies of those he trusted most. He would place exceptional trust in Robert McNamara. McNamara's personal philosophy complemented the president's preoccupation with loyalty; he believed that the government of a large and powerful state could not "operate effectively if those in charge of the departments of the government express disagreement with decisions of the established head of that government."[85] Despite their dissimilar backgrounds, the two men shared many of the same characteristics. Both exhibited an obsessive devotion to their work and neither hesitated to misrepresent the truth for the sake of political expediency.[86] On Christmas Day, President Johnson telephoned McNamara from his Texas ranch to convey his gratitude. He told the secretary that he was "one of the nicest things about this Christmas. You've made our year mighty comforting to know you're around. . . . There's no one in government that means more than you, and I just wanted to say that to you."[87]

■

As the president's relations with his key advisers solidified, the situation in Vietnam changed fundamentally. The Diem coup marked a turning point in the Vietnam War. The Strategic Hamlet Program was falling apart. By March the Viet Cong would control between 40 and 45 percent of the land of South Vietnam, up from less than 30 percent before the coup.[88] Addressing those difficulties effectively would require close and frank consultation between the country's political and military advisers. The civilian-military relationship, however, did not permit a candid assessment of the situation or evaluation of possible American actions designed to influence it. Tension among the Chiefs, and between them and the administration, would escalate as the situation in Vietnam deteriorated and the U.S. government developed plans for deepening American involvement in the war. Taylor would be more sensitive to the administration's needs than to his military colleagues' views. McNamara, having completed most of his administrative reforms in the Pentagon, had gained the new president's confidence and began to focus his analytical talents on developing a military strategy to shape and direct the American effort in Vietnam.

McNamara would dominate the policy-making process because of three mutually reinforcing factors: the Chiefs' ineffectiveness as an advisory group, Johnson's profound insecurity, and the president's related unwillingness to entertain divergent views on the subject of Vietnam. Above all President Johnson needed reassurance. He wanted advisers who would tell him what he wanted to hear, who would find solutions even if there were none to be found. Bearers of bad news or those who expressed views that ran counter to his priorities would hold little sway. McNamara could sense the president's desires and determined to do all that he could to fulfill them. He would become Lyndon Johnson's "oracle" for Vietnam.

4
Graduated Pressure
January–March 1964

We had seen the gradual application of force applied in
the Cuban Missile Crisis and had seen a very successful
result. We believed that, if this same gradual and
restrained application of force were applied in South
Vietnam, that one could expect the same result.

—CYRUS VANCE, 1970[1]

Robert S. McNamara and his principal assistants in the Department of
Defense, convinced that traditional military conceptions of the use of
force were irrelevant to contemporary strategic and political realities,
developed courses of action for Vietnam that reflected their experience
during the 1962 Cuban missile crisis (which molded their thinking on
strategy) and their predisposition toward quantitative analysis. In
McNamara's concept of "graduated pressure," the aim of force was not to
impose one's will on the enemy but to communicate with him. Gradually
intensifying military action would convey American resolve and thereby
convince an adversary to alter his behavior. Johnson found McNamara's
strategic concept particularly attractive because it would not jeopardize
his domestic political agenda. Although the presidential election was still
ten months away, he thought that mishandling Vietnam policy might easily cost him victory. He tried to use American involvement in Vietnam to

his advantage. He wanted to be seen as a "moderate" candidate, so he resolved to take only those actions in Vietnam that bolstered that image.

The president's deep distrust of his senior military officers manifested itself in exclusive advisory forums that limited JCS access to the president. In those forums Taylor deliberately misrepresented the Joint Chiefs' opinion and helped McNamara forge a consensus behind a fundamentally flawed strategic concept that permitted deepening American involvement in the war without consideration of its long-term costs and consequences.

■

During the last days of 1963, President Johnson was enjoying a holiday respite at his Texas ranch and pondering the challenges that he would face in the coming year. His deliberations on Vietnam since assuming the presidency had been brief and episodic. He had concerned himself primarily with his predecessor's stalled legislative program and his own domestic agenda.[2] On New Year's Eve, however, the president, in a letter to Duong Van Minh, chairman of the South Vietnamese Military Revolutionary Council, emphasized that the South Vietnamese must take primary responsibility for the war. While prodding General Minh to take more vigorous action against the Viet Cong insurgents, Johnson pledged to "maintain in Vietnam whatever American personnel and matériel are needed to assist you in achieving victory" and indicated that he was "pleased" with Minh's plans to intensify the counterinsurgency effort. Johnson's letter exuded hope and optimism. He concluded: "As the forces of your government become increasingly capable of dealing with this aggression, American military personnel can be progressively withdrawn."[3] However, Johnson sent a less auspicious telegram to Lodge, in which he called reports of antagonism between the president and the ambassador "nonsense" and instructed Lodge to "be alert and demanding in telling all of us in Washington how and what more we can do to help."[4]

The new commandant of the Marine Corps, Wallace Greene, urged his colleagues to provide their commander in chief with a comprehensive assessment of the situation in Vietnam. Greene was determined to take a more active role than his predecessor, General Shoup, in JCS policy deliberations. He had gained experience in national security affairs as a member of Eisenhower's NSC staff. Most important, he did not share

Shoup's misgivings about entering a land war in Asia. He soon joined Air Force Chief Curtis LeMay in urging a sharper American military response to North Vietnamese support for the Viet Cong.[5] The Chiefs were frustrated because the president's objective in Vietnam seemed ambiguous to them, even though the need to combat communism and "win" in Vietnam seemed very clear. Meeting on January 8, the JCS agreed on the need to exact a clear commitment from the president and the administration to "victory" in Vietnam. Without such a clear statement of purpose, they were unsure about what recommendations to make to the secretary of defense and the president about the next steps to take in the war.[6]

While lacking a clear understanding of the policy objective and an accurate assessment of the military situation, the Joint Chiefs set out to break down restrictions on the use of American military force and gain from the Johnson administration a firm commitment to see the war through to a positive result. On January 22, 1964, the JCS sent McNamara a memorandum on Vietnam and Southeast Asia that referenced NSAM 273 of November 26, 1963. Examined together, the two documents revealed a clear divergence in thinking between the president and his top military advisers. Although the NSAM had affirmed President Johnson's commitment to South Vietnam, it had emphasized that the American objective was to "assist the people of *that* country win *their* contest against the . . . Communist conspiracy."[7] The Joint Chiefs' memorandum, however, listed "victory" as the unqualified objective of American military force. Accordingly, it recommended that the United States "put aside many of the self-imposed restrictions which now limit our efforts, and undertake bolder actions which may embody greater risks." The Chiefs, arguing that limitations on military operations "tend to make the task in Vietnam more complex, more time consuming, and, in the end, more costly," recommended that a "more aggressive program" be approved immediately. That program would include overflights of Laos and Cambodia to acquire operational intelligence, bombing key North Vietnamese targets using U.S. resources (and assuming full responsibility for the attacks), and mining the sea approaches to North Vietnam. The Joint Chiefs argued that the United States was currently fighting the war on the enemy's terms, and warned that the United States would ultimately have to commit its own forces "in support of the combat action within South Vietnam" and "in direct actions against

North Vietnam."⁸ They sought the administration's permission to develop and execute plans designed to achieve outright victory.

The administration, however, had decided to commit only those forces necessary to keep South Vietnam from losing the war.⁹ Frank communication between the JCS and the president might have permitted a reconciliation of their divergent perspectives and lent coherence to Vietnam planning. The relationship between the commander in chief and his principal military advisers, however, did not permit a frank exchange of views. The Chiefs and the administration had started down divergent paths.

■

Four days after the Joint Chiefs sent their memo to McNamara, events in South Vietnam again brought that country to the urgent attention of the U.S. government. On January 30 at 4:00 A.M. Saigon time, tanks and infantrymen of the South Vietnamese Army quickly surrounded the Joint General Staff Headquarters and arrested General "Big" Minh and the key members of his government. South Vietnamese I Corps commanding general Nguyen Khanh, reacting to rumors that members of the Minh government were considering a "neutralization" agreement with North Vietnam, quickly seized power in a bloodless coup that took the U.S. Embassy completely by surprise. To avoid the embarrassment of having to recognize yet another successful perpetrator of a military coup, President Johnson decided not to acknowledge the change in government.

However, Johnson, like Kennedy before him, wanted the South to have a stable government capable of continuing the fight against the Viet Cong. Thus, one month after he penned his greeting to General Minh, Johnson drafted a letter to his new partner in the fight against Communism, General Khanh. He encouraged Khanh to intensify military actions against the Viet Cong and renewed his pledge to help "carry the war to the enemy and to increase the confidence of the Vietnamese people in their government." Ambassador Lodge visited Khanh to deliver the president's message and "make him understand that he would rise or fall in the [eyes of the] U.S. depending on his effectiveness in bringing victory."¹⁰ Johnson hoped to get the Vietnamese to fight more effectively and thereby avoid direct American intervention.

The Khanh coup dashed McGeorge Bundy's hope that, after the Diem coup, no issues would divide the administration. Divisions persisted and grew wider as the situation in Vietnam became more precarious. Indeed, the administration was receiving conflicting advice about what to do in Vietnam from numerous sources in Washington and Saigon. Bundy told the president that without "improvement in our organization here and in the field," the United States would have difficulty furthering its objectives in Southeast Asia. The conflict between Lodge and Harkins continued and hampered coordination between the embassy staff and the Military Assistance Command. The Defense Department regarded the office of Assistant Secretary of State for Far Eastern Affairs Hilsman with contempt because it had advocated the Diem coup. Special Assistant to the President for Far Eastern Affairs Forrestal recalled that the period was marked by a "two-tiered conflict" within the Department of Defense and "between that Department and the State Department." The president met with Bundy, McNamara, and Rusk over lunch on Tuesday, February 4, to discuss how to organize and better coordinate the government's effort in Vietnam.[11]

During the lunch the subject of replacing Lodge, suggested by Taylor in December, came up. The president and his guests agreed that Lodge was the principal impediment to a smooth-running Country Team in Saigon. Johnson, however, was reluctant to take the political risk of replacing the man whom John Kennedy had appointed to build bipartisan support for the administration's Vietnam policy. Bundy recommended instead accelerating the replacement of Harkins by Lt. Gen. William C. Westmoreland, who was serving as Harkins's deputy at General Taylor's recommendation.[12]

Taylor had first encountered "Westy" in Sicily during World War II. Lieutenant Colonel Westmoreland's confidence while commanding an artillery battalion supporting Taylor's paratroopers inspired the general to record the younger officer's name in his ever-present black notebook. When Taylor became army chief of staff in 1955, he appointed Westmoreland his secretary of the general staff. After promotion to major general, Westmoreland assumed command of the 101st Airborne Division, and in 1960 Taylor used his influence to secure for Westmoreland the superintendency of West Point.[13] In 1963 Taylor— knowing that the president and the secretary of defense wanted the perennially optimistic Harkins removed at the earliest opportunity— selected his protégé to be Harkins's deputy.[14]

McGeorge Bundy also recommended that the president create an ad hoc committee, including representatives from the principal agencies, to study the Vietnam problem, recommend solutions, and build consensus within his administration. The committee would give the president a source of information and analysis free from the infighting that had characterized the debate surrounding the Diem coup and its aftermath. Because the committee would represent all the agencies involved in Vietnam policy making, the effort would forge unity between different factions within the administration and end the bickering of the past several months. Ten days after the luncheon, the president ordered the formation of "a small committee for the management of U.S. policy and operations in South Vietnam." The president rejected Bundy's recommendation that his own man, Forrestal, serve as the committee's chair and instead named William Sullivan, a career diplomat from the Department of State.

Sullivan was a specialist in Far Eastern affairs who had served in Bangkok, Calcutta, and Tokyo. In 1961 he joined Harriman's delegation to the Geneva conference on Laos. Later, in December 1964, Sullivan would be appointed ambassador to Laos, a post from which he controlled the U.S. secret war to prevent North Vietnam from using that country as a supply route to the South. Forrestal and representatives from the Department of Defense, the CIA, and the Agency for International Development joined Sullivan's committee. The president ordered that "department appeal from Mr. Sullivan's decisions shall be kept at a minimum" in accordance with the principal purpose of the new council. He hoped that the committee would "permit an energetic, unified and skillful prosecution of the only war we face at present."[15]

The Chiefs sensed that the committee would further undercut their influence.[16] Five days after his appointment Sullivan met with the Joint Chiefs, and LeMay asked him why the committee had been formed. Sullivan emphasized that the president wanted "one place to look" for accountability, and indicated that it would be his neck if American policy failed to keep South Vietnam from falling to the Communists. Foreshadowing the tight control he would later exercise over military operations in Laos, Sullivan told the Chiefs that they did not have a monopoly on the ability to examine military options for Vietnam because no one had yet learned how to prosecute a counterinsurgency.[17]

Sullivan informed the JCS that the president had tasked him with considering options ranging from withdrawal to large-scale American intervention in the war. Subsequent comments in the meeting indicated, however, that Sullivan would genuinely explore only those options that included sharply limited military actions against the Viet Cong and North Vietnamese. His mission was not to study the possibility of expanded American military involvement but to determine "what changes in the [current] mix" of military and diplomatic actions were necessary. Taylor warned Sullivan that an advisory effort in the South coupled with "deniable" covert actions against North Vietnam would not hurt the enemy, but he admitted that he had "no idea" how much more effort would be required. General LeMay was more direct. He told Sullivan that the current policy would result in American involvement over "an indefinite period with no light in sight."[18]

Sullivan asked the generals how long they thought the United States could sustain the current policy. Taylor replied that the American people would not support it beyond the end of 1965. Sullivan, disagreeing, told the JCS that a military "presence" in Vietnam did not have to mean "heavy forces." The Chiefs' doubts about the current policy and about domestic support for a limited war fell on deaf ears, because Johnson had constrained Sullivan to consider one option only, whose consequences he need not explore because he had to support it. Forrestal recalled that Sullivan had already been given instructions to work on options involving the "slow, very slow, escalation" of bombing pressures against North Vietnam.[19] In contrast to the Chiefs' call for "increasingly bolder actions," Sullivan's committee developed a program of "measured pressures against North Vietnam."[20]

■

The formation of the Sullivan Committee did not quell pressures from within the administration to use American military force to improve the situation in Vietnam. Generals Greene and LeMay urged strong military intervention in the war. Greene believed that the time had come to "either pull out of South Vietnam or stay there and win." He told his colleagues that the Marine Corps position was that victory ought to "be pursued with the full concerted power of U.S. resources."[21] Greene went on a speaking tour of military staff colleges to persuade others that decisive action aimed at military victory would solve the Vietnam problem.[22]

Greene was frustrated that the Joint Chiefs had not formed a plan for the conduct of the war and ordered his staff to prepare a series of proposals, the most significant of which was a twenty-four-point plan calling for United States Marine Corps units to secure the coastal areas of South Vietnam in order to deny the Viet Cong access to a large percentage of the population. According to his operations officer, Lt. Gen. Henry Buse, it was based on an "enclave principle where you establish a bunch of beachheads . . . and protect them." Greene felt that America's chances of success in Vietnam would increase proportionally with the introduction of large numbers of Marines. Taylor, who considered Greene's plan parochial because it emphasized actions only by Marines, did not forward it to the Secretary of Defense or the president.[23]

Calls for more military force in Vietnam were not limited to the Joint Chiefs. Ambassador Lodge sent a cable to the president on February 20 recommending that "various pressures . . . be applied to North Viet Nam to cause them to cease and desist from their murderous intrusion into South Viet Nam."[24] The president met with Rusk, McNamara, Taylor, McCone, Under Secretary of State Ball, and members of the Sullivan Committee and instructed them to respond promptly and sympathetically to Lodge's cables to ensure that the ambassador did not become disaffected and entertain notions of public disagreement with the current policy.[25] The president sent Lodge a disarming cable telling the ambassador that he agreed with much of his assessment.[26] LBJ, however, concealed that he was pursuing a course in Washington that contradicted the recommendations of his representative in Saigon. To satisfy the ambassador's enthusiasm to expand American involvement, Johnson ordered that contingency planning be accelerated and decided to send Taylor and McNamara to Saigon in early March. He told Lodge that the men would review the ambassador's recommendations and other aspects of the counterinsurgency campaign and promised that "very soon thereafter" he would "make definite decisions."[27] He was more candid on the telephone with Rusk and McNamara. LBJ told Rusk that Lodge was "feeling sorry for himself and he's naturally a martyr." The president wanted the secretary to "build a record" of support for Lodge to make the ambassador believe that he is "Mr. God" and has the "maximum attention" of the government.[28] Johnson told McNamara, "Now I'm thinking politically. I'm not a military strategist, but I think as long as we got him there and he makes recommendations, we act on them."

Otherwise, Johnson feared, "we are caught with our britches down."[29]

Johnson met with the JCS on March 4. Greene and LeMay told the president pointedly that, once the nation embarked on a military course in Vietnam, it must carry it to success regardless of the cost. They saw only two options in Vietnam, "either get in or get out."[30] Johnson, however, was determined not to make a tough decision on Vietnam until after the 1964 presidential election, and Taylor helped him deflect LeMay and Greene. LBJ told the JCS,

> We haven't got any Congress that will go with us, and we haven't got any mothers that will go with us in the war. . . . I've got to win the election or Nixon or somebody else has . . . and then you can make a decision. . . . But in the meantime let's see if we can't find enough things to do . . . to keep them off base, and to stop this shipments [sic] that are coming in from Laos, and take a few selected targets to upset them a little bit without getting another Korean operation started.[31]

Taylor indicated that he too favored "progressive, selective air and naval attacks against North Vietnam" and, in contrast to Greene and LeMay's position, argued that such attacks would not lead to war.[32] Taylor had already revealed his sensitivity to the president's political concerns by drafting a letter for the president's signature to explain reasons for rejecting more resolute military action in Vietnam.[33]

Taylor discouraged his colleagues from forcefully voicing their doubts about applying incremental military pressure against the North. He had warned them that their new commander in chief does not like "split advice."[34] Less than a week before their meeting with the president, Taylor pressed the Chiefs to agree on a "broad outline" for the war. He said they must agree that a strong political base in the South be the first priority and discuss further military action in terms of gradually intensifying phases. Taylor exhorted the Chiefs to "leave open" the issue of "incremental attack versus hard blow" and advised them to be cautious about advertising air and sea actions alone to avoid charges of parochialism. He held out the prospect of mobilization if the situation in Vietnam worsened.[35] He succeeded in mollifying the JCS before the meeting with the president. McDonald and Wheeler did not support Greene and LeMay, and, after the meeting with the president, Taylor recorded "general agreement" with his proposal for measured, gradual action against the North.[36]

Despite Taylor's efforts, Johnson remained under pressure from Lodge, the JCS, and the press to clarify his Vietnam policy. The president feared that recent leaks to reporters from the military and members of his administration were making him "look like an ass."[37] At the March 4 meeting he expressed indignation over a recent newspaper article that revealed sentiment within the military for an expansion of the war, and he ordered the JCS to prevent such transgressions in the future. On the same day, Johnson telephoned Walt Rostow, the chairman of the state department's Policy Planning Committee, about a recent article in which Rostow was quoted. He questioned Rostow's loyalty to the administration and ordered him not to talk to the press at all.[38] LBJ thought the press were "anti-Johnson" and were making a "concerted move to discredit him."[39] He found a sympathetic listener in McNamara. McNamara told the president that the *New York Times* editorial page was "influenced by Zionists" who were trying to make him look like a "warmonger."[40]

The principal purpose of McNamara's forthcoming trip to Saigon would be to alleviate pressure on the president in connection with his Vietnam policy. To keep the JCS and other potential critics at bay, Johnson would need a consensus report. He told McGeorge Bundy that he did not want "anybody on this trip to come back with two different plans" and he was particularly concerned about the possibility that McCone might return with a dissenting opinion.[41] LBJ even suggested to McNamara that former Marine Corps commandant David Shoup join the trip to Saigon to lend additional military credibility to the defense secretary's report. Johnson thought that Shoup's Medal of Honor and military record would shield the administration from criticism. The recently retired general could "sit in the back room and you don't have to mess with him, but when he gets back here he can take the McNamara line and sit down . . . and say 'now here's the story.'"[42] Shoup, however, would not make the trip to Saigon. It would be up to McNamara and Taylor to do the president's bidding.

Consistent with the principal purpose of his trip, McNamara did not wait for his visit to Saigon to begin conceptualizing recommendations for the future course of America's involvement in Vietnam. He directed his International Security Affairs division, under John McNaughton, to develop a draft memorandum to "serve as an over-all vehicle for thought . . . and a framework for his report on his return." McNaughton and the newly appointed assistant secretary of state for Far Eastern affairs, William P. Bundy, incorporated the findings of the Sullivan Committee and guidance from McNamara into the memo. On March 5 William Bundy sent the memo to the members of McNamara's party.[43] The fact that the report was prepared before the team's visit indicated that neither McNamara nor Johnson intended to learn anything from the trip. In his instructions to the members of the mission, McNamara discouraged interim reports to any department or agency in Washington and forbade sending them without his approval. McNamara hoped that it would "be possible for all senior members of the party to concur in all significant points."[44]

On March 2 the secretary of defense met with the Joint Chiefs of Staff to discuss the impending mission to Saigon. McNamara promised the Chiefs that he would make a copy of the draft memorandum available to them for comment before it became government policy. He led them to believe that he had not yet taken a position on whether to embark on a course of incremental pressure against the North or to strike North Vietnam with a "hard blow." That same day, however, William Bundy was circulating his first draft, which called for planning retaliatory actions on a "tit for tat" basis and for the application of "graduated overt military pressure" on North Vietnam. Three days later Bundy's second draft went to the White House—before the Chiefs saw it. President Johnson read it with interest and asked to see it a second time on March 8, the first day of McNamara's "inquiry" in Vietnam.[45] The Chiefs did not receive a copy of the Draft Presidential Memorandum (DPM) until after McNamara and Taylor returned from Saigon on March 13.[46]

Traditional military experience mattered little to McNamara—even less in an era of nuclear deterrence and superpower competition.[47] Admiral McDonald recalled that the defense secretary once said, "Oh, let's stop doing it John Paul Jones' way. Can't you have an original thought for a change?" One of McNamara's assistants told the admiral, "I know you military fellows have always been taught to get in there with both feet and get it over with, but this is a different kind of war."[48] The military's unrealistically sanguine assessments of progress in Vietnam had heightened the defense secretary's doubts about the relevance of military experience to what he regarded as a novel kind of warfare. In keeping with McNamara's views, Taylor told the Chiefs on March 2 that the White House intended to use South Vietnam as a "laboratory, not only for this war, but for any insurgency."[49] McNamara became the principal

architect of the new strategy of graduated pressure, which he would test
in Vietnam.[50]

■

While in his estimation military experience was irrelevant to the new
kind of war, McNamara drew heavily upon his personal experience during the Cuban missile crisis. The rejection of JCS advice in October
1962 had led to the withdrawal of the offensive weapons without war. He
acknowledged that the missile crisis "was very influential in [his] decisions relating to Vietnam."[51] Indeed, U.S. Military Action Against North
Viet Nam—An Analysis, Annex A to the report that McNamara drafted
for the president in early March 1964, contained several direct references
to the Cuban missile crisis.[52]

Although McNamara believed that JCS advice was inapplicable, he
thought that the use of American military force was integral to the foreign
policy of the Cold War period. He viewed the North's support of the Viet
Cong as a manifestation of the Communists' unflagging support for wars
of national liberation and as a challenge to U.S. global interests.
Similarly, Secretary of State Dean Rusk thought that the administration
could not conceivably abandon Vietnam because the United States would
lose its prestige in the world.[53] Their assumptions and policies demanded
that the United States demonstrate resolve against Communist-backed
wars of national liberation, but they would ignore JCS advice while planning military action.

If the global reputation of the United States and U.S. desire to fight
the spread of Communism made withdrawal from Vietnam unacceptable,
weapons of mass destruction rendered policies that risked escalation to
nuclear confrontation unthinkable. McNamara thought that graduated
pressure offered a sensible compromise between those two options. He
concluded that the principal lesson of the Cuban missile crisis was that
graduated pressure provided a "firebreak between conventional conflict
and that situation of low probability but highly adverse consequences"
that could lead to nuclear war. Rusk, agreeing with McNamara, believed
that graduated pressure would never present "Peking or Moscow with
enough of a change in the situation to require them to make a major
decision . . . in terms of intervening in [Vietnam]." Rusk believed that
applying force in carefully controlled gradations would help to "limit the
war to Viet Nam."[54]

The reluctance of some of the Chiefs to embrace the evolving doctrine of graduated pressure diminished their influence with civilian officials, who adopted the new strategy with an almost religious zeal. LeMay and Greene particularly opposed the application of force for any purpose short of victory. Secretary of the Air Force Eugene Zuckert, who had been associated with that service since the early 1940s, recalled that, "On this Vietnam thing . . . the military, particularly General LeMay, just didn't understand gradualism. LeMay simplified the point where you had a war, you want to win the war. . . . He never could grasp the subtleties involved which might make you want to run it a different way."[55] LeMay knew that Taylor advocated the new strategy and lamented the fact that Army Chief of Staff Wheeler and, to some extent, Admiral McDonald supported the chairman.[56] To Taylor, graduated pressure may have seemed a logical outgrowth of the "flexible response" strategy that he and the Army had advocated as an alternative to Eisenhower's strategy of massive retaliation. Both concepts were based on a force structure capable of carrying out military options across all gradations of conflict. Whereas flexible response envisioned a clear decision to apply military force at a particular level, graduated pressure involved starting the application of force at a very low level and gradually increasing it in scale and intensity. Whereas the traditional objective of imposing one's will on the enemy still pertained to flexible response, graduated pressure aimed to affect the enemy's calculation of interests. Due to ambiguities in both strategic concepts, and to the evolving nature of graduated pressure, however, distinctions between the two were difficult to discern.

McNamara deceived the Joint Chiefs of Staff, concealing his position from them until they could neither oppose his recommendations nor offer a cogent alternative. The Chiefs were vulnerable to McNamara's tactics because they remained divided on the issue and because the defense secretary could count on delays caused by the cumbersome JCS administrative and decision-making system. McNamara had only the most trusted members of his staff develop strategic options for Vietnam and revealed his position only after he was assured that his view had made it to the president uncontested. Deputy Assistant Secretary Arthur W. Barber of ISA recalled that his boss, John McNaughton, "almost seemed to adopt many of the LBJ manners . . . hiding his direction, talking with many people, and then popping out with an announcement."[57] To maintain his predominant influence over Johnson, McNamara sent draft memorandume to the president before the Joint Chiefs had an opportunity to comment.

■

During their trip to Saigon from March 8 to 12, McNamara and Taylor found the Khanh government besieged. The level of Viet Cong activity had risen sharply, and the government was losing control of rural areas. "The enemy was clearly making the most out of the political turbulence and reduced military effectiveness resulting from the November and January coups," General Taylor recalled.

The political structure linking the central government to the provinces had virtually disappeared. Thirty-five of the forty-one province chiefs were new appointees, and most of the senior military commands had changed twice since the previous October. The desertion rate in the South Vietnamese forces was high and increasing, while confidence in their ability to provide security was decreasing proportionally throughout the countryside. There was corresponding evidence of a growth of strength on the part of the Viet Cong derived from local recruiting and added assistance in equipment from North Vietnam.[58] When he returned McNamara revised his DPM and sent it to the White House.

McNamara's memo contained the intellectual foundation for further American involvement in the Vietnam War. He listed alternative courses of action, including direct military action against North Vietnam, that could be planned in greater detail during the eight months before the election in November 1964. He divided future actions into three categories: border control operations, retaliatory actions, and graduated overt military actions by South Vietnamese and U.S. forces against North Vietnam. The military pressure would aim to convince Hanoi to stop supporting the Viet Cong. Border control actions included expanding patrols into Laos and North Vietnam, and South Vietnamese air and ground strikes against selected targets in Laos. Retaliatory actions could escalate gradually from reconnaissance flights over North Vietnam to bombing strikes against North Vietnamese targets and mining North Vietnamese ports. McNamara contended that the program of graduated pressure would have to be calculated carefully to minimize the risk of escalation and avoid domestic and international political opposition to widening the war. He recommended against the initiation of overt attacks against the North and urged the president to take only those actions aimed at intensifying the American advisory and assistance effort.[59] McNamara's concept of the use of force appealed to Johnson's desire to avoid deepening American involvement in Vietnam until after the election.

On the morning of March 14, the Joint Chiefs met to discuss the McNamara memo, which they had first received the day before. Greene had already commented on it, noting that "half-measures won't win in South Vietnam."[60] Army Chief of Staff Wheeler stated that the actions included in the memo were inadequate to win the war. Admiral McDonald agreed that the paper did "not go far enough" and asserted that the United States must take "stronger action." He argued that the administration should give immediate approval for "hot pursuit" of Viet Cong guerrillas into Cambodia, and he called for more rapid retaliation against North Vietnam in response to Viet Cong actions in South Vietnam. Taylor defended McNamara's provision allowing seventy-two hours before retaliation on the grounds that the United States needed to decide what targets were appropriate for a "tit for tat" response. McDonald also suggested that U.S. dependents (family members of military and civilian officials) be withdrawn from Vietnam. Taylor asked McDonald incredulously if he wanted to "make Saigon look like a war capital." LeMay and McDonald answered emphatically, "Yes." McDonald observed that Vietnam is an "active war area" and contended that American forces should set a determined example for their South Vietnamese allies. He concluded that the memo must be "strengthened" by including options such as hot pursuit, stronger military action in the strategically vital Mekong Delta region, and high- and low-level aerial reconnaissance of Viet Cong sanctuaries and lines of communication outside South Vietnam. Greene agreed with McDonald and again emphasized the need for a comprehensive military estimate of the situation to determine what U.S. military action was required. Greene then provided his own estimate, in which he again recommended the introduction of Marines into enclaves in South Vietnam. LeMay agreed with McDonald and Greene that the McNamara paper did not go far enough. He discounted McNamara's argument for postponing action against the North until the political situation stabilized in the South because he doubted that a stable political base in the South was possible without taking overt military action against the North. He argued ardently that the United States should initiate attacks against the North "now" and predicted that the American people would be behind strong action. Even the usually unimpassioned Wheeler put Taylor on notice that he would not be a party to proposals suggesting that American objectives in Vietnam could be achieved "with mirrors." LeMay, who believed that Taylor and McNamara did not adequately represent the Chiefs' views to the president, wanted a JCS memo that outlined their concerns to go directly to the commander in chief.[61]

Taylor did not support LeMay's recommendation and kept the JCS position on the McNamara memo from President Johnson. Later that day Taylor sent a memorandum to the secretary of defense that ostensibly represented the JCS commentary on the McNamara memo, but did so only superficially. Taylor hedged the JCS's recommendations in ambiguous language. He stated that the Chiefs did "not believe that the recommended program . . . will be sufficient to turn the tide against the Viet Cong in South Vietnam without positive action being taken against the Hanoi Government at an early date." Although he noted that the Chiefs had suggested the "kind of action" that they had "in mind" in a prior memo, Taylor left room for a broad interpretation of what the Chiefs meant by "positive action." He then explained that the Chiefs disagreed with the specific recommendations of McNamara's proposal on the issues of hot pursuit and reaction time for retaliatory strikes. Taylor did not mention, however, the Chiefs' reservations concerning the key premises and recommendations of the McNamara paper. He also obscured their general assessment that McNamara's program would not obtain the desired results.[62] McNamara prevented even Taylor's toned-down memo from reaching the president and the NSC.

On March 17 the president met with the NSC to discuss the McNamara report; Taylor was the only military representative in attendance.[63] Secretary McNamara said that his paper spoke for itself and deferred to his general to "present the military actions discussed in the report." Instead of emphasizing the Chiefs' assessment that more resolute military action was necessary, Taylor stressed the risks of escalation posed by even the most limited actions against North Vietnam. He baldly stated that the Chiefs "supported the McNamara report." According to Taylor the Chiefs mainly criticized the length of the reaction time allowed for retaliatory strikes and recommended changing this from seventy-two to twenty-four hours (Admiral McDonald had actually said that the reaction time should be "three hours not three days"). McNamara interjected that "each Department and Agency concurs with the recommendations which fall in its area of responsibility." The president, evidently pleased with the apparent unanimity behind the paper, said that he understood that even Ambassador Lodge approved the report. Johnson said that the ambassador could be "told lies in the area of unfinished business [that is, the ambassador's appeals for direct American military action against North Vietnam]" to quell his concerns. To allay the president's worry that Vietnam might become an issue before the election, McNamara reported confidently that no supplemental budget request would be necessary to take the actions outlined in his report. McNamara, like Taylor, feigned sensitivity to JCS concerns by graciously agreeing to have the Chiefs study the proposal to reduce the seventy-two-hour delay prior to retaliation.

To make sure that he understood McNamara's analysis, President Johnson asked him whether "his program would reverse the current trends in South Vietnam." McNamara, disregarding the Chiefs' warning that his program would be insufficient to "turn the tide" against the Viet Cong, predicted with unqualified confidence that, if the government carried out his proposals energetically, the Khanh regime could stop the situation from deteriorating further and, within four to six months, begin to improve it. General Taylor noted weakly that "the Chiefs believed the proposed program was *acceptable* but it *may* not be sufficient to save the situation in Vietnam." He said that the Chiefs felt that action against North Vietnam "*might* be necessary" to make the program work. In case Taylor's distortion of the Chiefs' position was not sufficient to defuse potential challenges to graduated pressure, McNamara quickly added that Khanh was opposed to taking the war to North Vietnam because the South Vietnamese leader's political base was insecure. That was not Khanh's genuine feeling, but a concession that McNamara brokered in Saigon to suppress Khanh's calls for decisive military action against North Vietnam.[64]

McNamara was persuasive. Johnson told the men gathered in the Cabinet Room that they were "following the only realistic alternative." The defense secretary's ebullient confidence, untempered by the Chiefs' pessimistic assessment, was contagious. Johnson proclaimed that the McNamara plan would "have the maximum effectiveness with the minimum loss." McNamara's strategy of graduated pressure seemed not only to reconcile the administration's need to intervene against Communist insurgents with its need to minimize the risk of escalation, but it also reconciled Johnson's desire to get elected with his need to address the difficult situation in South Vietnam. The president concluded the meeting by noting that the McNamara proposal did not rule out further action later if the situation did not "improve as we expected." Lyndon Johnson looked around the room and asked whether there were any objections to the McNamara paper. There were none.

■

Meanwhile top civilian advisers had to rely on rumors to determine what the president's "principal military advisors" thought about plans for American military intervention in the Vietnam War. While Johnson was meeting with the NSC in the Cabinet Room, recently promoted Air Force lieutenant colonel William Y. Smith wrote a memo for his boss, McGeorge Bundy, to inform him that the JCS did not support the McNamara plan. After agonizing over whether or not to forward it, Smith concluded that his observations might help avert developments "that in the long run could do no one any good." He opened the memo with the following passage:

> I believe you will be interested in certain attitudes in the Pentagon concerning Vietnam. These still small but growing undercurrents seem to have been given extra momentum by the McNamara trip report. I am not supposed to know a lot of this but here it goes.[65]

Smith wrote that he had learned from corridor conversations in the Pentagon that the JCS had become pessimistic about conditions in Vietnam and believed that only "strong and forthright action" could save the American position. He reported "some feeling" that the "moderate actions proposed by Secretary McNamara do not correspond to the desperate situation the report depicts"; indeed, McDonald made this comment in the Chiefs' March 14 meeting. The Chiefs also believed that strong action would not be taken because advisers close to the president, such as Taylor and McNamara, were telling him that he should make decisions based on his chances for reelection rather than the "national interest." The Chiefs believed that Taylor's and McNamara's loyalty to Johnson prevented them from telling him that only forceful action could influence the situation in South Vietnam. Smith recommended that the administration "go out of the way to defuse any incipient beliefs that Vietnam is becoming a political football," and noted that Lyndon Johnson would be the big loser if it did.[66]

After collecting his thoughts on the potential political ramifications of open conflict between the president and the Joint Chiefs, Smith wrote a second memo. He warned that Vietnam could become the "missile gap issue of the '64 campaign." In 1960 presidential candidate Kennedy attacked Eisenhower for allowing the Soviet Union to obtain a prepon-derance of power over the United States in nuclear missiles. The charge was unfounded, as the United States actually possessed an overwhelming superiority in that area. Smith recommended that the president discuss the Vietnam problem with former presidents to give the policy a biparti-san flavor and to ensure that "key opinion makers in and out of the administration were on-board in support of the administration's policies." Smith warned that finessing a crisis situation for eight months would be difficult and noted that, if the president took forthright action, the public would support his decision. Smith urged the administration to take steps to raise the level of discourse on Vietnam policy above a partisan politi-cal preoccupation with the presidential campaign.[67]

Two days later the president's military assistant, Brig. Gen. Chester Clifton, corroborated the Joint Chiefs' frustration. Clifton reported to McGeorge Bundy that a "usually reliable source" had divulged the Chiefs' assessment that the McNamara program fell well short of the minimum level of force needed in Vietnam. Clifton said that Taylor was the only member of the JCS satisfied with the McNamara plan, and he related the Chiefs' opinion that the United States must take action to interdict supply lines connecting the Viet Cong to support from the North. He told Bundy that one of the Chiefs had likened the level of force that McNamara supported to that used at the Bay of Pigs. Clifton recommended that, if the other Chiefs felt the same way, the president should "be informed that some military advice would indicate that the present plans are insufficient."[68]

After reading Smith's memoranda with "great interest," Forrestal wrote to McGeorge Bundy to offer "additional evidence" that the Joint Chiefs were disaffected. He said that Sullivan, when he met with the Chiefs in early February, was surprised by the "vehemence of opinion in the JCS for strong overt U.S. action against the North." Sullivan recalled that Admiral McDonald had been particularly adamant, but the other Chiefs seemed to support his views. Sullivan told Forrestal that military officers in MACV and on his own committee had severely criticized McNamara's report. Forrestal suggested that, to avert a public dispute with the JCS, the president should avoid "too flat an impression that we have stopped thinking about all the possibilities." The administration should emphasize that actions against the North are "constantly being reviewed by Defense and State to see if further actions need to be taken."[69] If the JCS could be convinced that no important or final decision had been taken, the veneer of continuing consultation and evaluation might forestall open conflict and dissent.

Taylor learned about the grumblings that had reached the White House staff.[70] He met with the Chiefs on March 20 and asked them pointedly whether they were prepared to go to the secretary of defense immediately with more recommendations. He pressed them: "What are the Chiefs prepared to recommend?" Taylor instructed them to "bear in mind that the president has said that the in-country program must be solidified before any other actions are taken."[71] The Chiefs withdrew from the meeting without deciding to confront directly their differences with McNamara over his plan for Vietnam. Taylor's and McNamara's delaying tactics had worked. Although the Chiefs disagreed with McNamara's program, McDonald and Wheeler indicated their reluctance to challenge a policy decision already made "at the highest level."[72]

Taylor had again suppressed direct opposition to McNamara's policy. This suppression would soon become outright circumvention, and Taylor and McNamara worked together to use the divisions among the Chiefs against them. In January 1964, when the Chiefs could not reach a consensus over roles and missions for the armed services, Taylor hand-picked a group of staff officers from each of the services to prepare a proposal independent from them. When Taylor brought the report up to McNamara's office, the secretary said, "If you say it's good, I'll sign it right now." Taylor told McNamara that several people knew that he had just completed the study and recommended that the defense secretary leave it in his desk drawer for a while to give the impression that he had read it in detail. The roles and missions report did not see the light of day until McNamara signed it weeks later.[73] In March McNamara took steps to squelch Air Force calls for a new manned bomber. He told LBJ that he was issuing a statement signed by Secretary of the Navy Nitze and Adm. McDonald claiming that "it doesn't make any difference whether the Air Force's missiles or bombers are reliable, that the Navy can win the war alone. . . ." LBJ responded, "Won't that start a fight between them?" McNamara, chuckling, replied,

Well, that's what I'd rather like to do. Divide and conquer is a pretty
good rule in this situation. And to be quite frank, I've tried to do that
in the last couple of weeks and it's coming along pretty well. . . . [74]

The Chiefs' inability to overcome the service parochialism that had
plagued the JCS organization since its inception undercut their legiti-
macy and made them vulnerable to Taylor's and McNamara's tactics. The
administration could not seriously evaluate proposals from a service chief
that relied almost exclusively on the resources of his particular service.
As has been mentioned, General Greene thought that the Marine Corps
was ideally suited for occupying Vietnam's seaboard and proposed that it
establish secure enclaves along the coast. LeMay remained a zealot for air
power.[75] McDonald emphasized mining ports, riverine patrols in the
Mekong Delta, and using Navy aircraft to conduct reconnaissance and
air strikes. The exception was General Wheeler. Because the Army was
larger and more central to defense strategy than it had been under
Eisenhower, and because Wheeler owed his position to Taylor, the new
Army chief was predisposed to support the administration's policy.

Interservice rivalry also played a prominent role in the consideration
of key personnel assignments. As they were attempting to provide advice
on Vietnam, the Chiefs were in the middle of arguing over who should
become Westmoreland's chief of staff. LeMay, arguing that the "Air Force
is not properly represented among the three senior positions" in MACV,
strongly recommended that an Air Force officer be assigned the job.
Taylor and Wheeler argued that Westmoreland, who preferred Army
major general Richard G. Stilwell, should choose his own man.
Anderson and Greene agreed on Stilwell but, as "a matter of principle,"
expressed anxiety that Army officers filled the three top military positions in Saigon. McNamara, forced to resolve the squabble, supported
Taylor's recommendation that Stilwell get the job.[76]

The Chiefs had another heated exchange over who would succeed
Admiral Felt as CINCPAC. Pacific Command was the headquarters
through which orders and communications flowed between Washington
and MACV. On February 20 the Chiefs ranked the candidates from each
of the three services, and Taylor tallied the score. The winner was Air
Force general Jacob E. Smart. Admiral McDonald was dismayed that a
command that had always been under Navy control, in the Navy's most
important traditional theater of operations, might shift to another ser-

vice. He was especially astonished that, given their traditional partnership, the commandant of the Marine Corps voted against him in this matter of great importance to him and the Department of the Navy. Greene felt that General Smart was the best man for the job. Admiral McDonald and General Greene exchanged bitter words over the phone immediately after the meeting. McDonald threatened to repay Greene in kind on issues important to the Marine Corps. The controversy between Greene and McDonald created a lasting and deeply felt animosity between them. After he talked to Greene, McDonald went directly to McNamara's office to plead his case. McNamara listened and, on the same day, supported McDonald by selecting Admiral Ulysses S. "Oley" Sharp for the post.[77] But McNamara's intervention on behalf of the Navy had a price—McDonald, who had hitherto opposed McNamara's plans, no longer objected to them outside JCS meetings.

Each Chief's desire to further his own service's agenda hampered their collective ability to provide military advice. After gaining McNamara's support in the CINCPAC dispute, McDonald felt indebted to him. McDonald had regarded the CINCPAC issue as a "test of his mettle," and he was striving to protect his credibility with the officers and sailors of the Navy. Losing CINCPAC might have caused the Navy to lose faith in its chief of naval operations (CNO). McDonald also felt himself indebted to civilian officials in the Pentagon for instituting a new policy that allowed "the wife of every Naval officer who attains the rank of three stars or more [to] christen a United States Navy ship."[78]

The controversy over the CINCPAC replacement explained why Admiral McDonald voiced his dislike of McNamara's plan in JCS meetings, but balked at the opportunity to bring his objections forward to the secretary of defense or the president. The admiral was a pragmatist who believed that an officer who rises to high rank "must be guided by the conditions that exist at that particular time." McNamara's patronage made McDonald "obligated" to the secretary of defense for his support on matters that the Admiral regarded as "vital to the morale of the Navy."[79] McDonald's preoccupation with furthering the interests of his service impelled him to make concessions in what he regarded as less important areas to gain support (or at least acquiescence) on more vital issues.

The Chiefs desperately needed a leader to bring them together. Only the chairman could overcome their profound preoccupation with service interests. But Taylor, anxious to keep competing advice from the president, resolved to use the Chiefs' divisions to keep the policy-making initiative with McNamara and himself. Unable to work together in a productive manner, and with their advice silenced by the secretary of defense and the chairman, the Chiefs did not challenge McNamara's strategic concept for American military involvement in Vietnam.

■

The president, distrustful of his military advisers and preoccupied with achieving unity in his administration, sought to keep the Chiefs from opposing his Vietnam policy. Uninterested in the Chiefs' advice, but unwilling to risk their disaffection, Johnson preserved a facade of consultation, concealed the finality of his decisions on Vietnam policy, and promised that more forceful actions against the North might be taken in the future. Preoccupied with the election and committed to taking only the minimum action necessary to keep South Vietnam from going Communist, he depended on McNamara and Taylor to provide him with advice consistent with that overwhelming priority. The president got the military advice he wanted.

McNamara's strategy of graduated pressure seemed to "solve" the president's problem of not losing Vietnam while maintaining the image that he was reluctant to escalate the war. If the Chiefs had successfully pressed with the president their position that the United States needed to act forcefully to defeat the North, they might have forced a difficult choice between war and withdrawal from South Vietnam. Through their own actions as well as through the manipulation of Taylor and McNamara, the Chiefs missed their opportunity to influence the formulation of a strategic concept for Vietnam, and thereafter always found themselves in the difficult position of questioning a policy that the president had already approved. The intellectual foundation for deepening American involvement in Vietnam had been laid without the participation of the Joint Chiefs of Staff.

5
From Distrust to Deceit

March–July 1964

I don't object to it being called McNamara's war. I think it is a very important war and I am pleased to be identified with it and do whatever I can to win it.

—ROBERT S. MCNAMARA, 1964[1]

He who permits himself to tell a lie often finds it much easier to do it a second and third time, til at length it becomes habitual; he tells lies without attending to it, and truths without the world's believing him. This falsehood of the tongue leads to that of the heart, and in time depraves all its good dispositions.

—THOMAS JEFFERSON, 1785[2]

At the end of March, after the president had approved McNamara's strategy of graduated pressure, discontent within the Joint Chiefs of Staff bubbled to the surface. Suspecting that Taylor had misrepresented their views to the president, McDonald, Greene, and LeMay, on separate occasions, confidentially contacted the president's military aide, General Clifton. Clifton briefed the president on the information the Chiefs had given him, telling Johnson that he sensed a "potentially difficult and even dangerous situation in the Joint Chiefs of Staff" in connection with the McNamara plan of action for Vietnam. Although Clifton acknowledged that the Chiefs were "badly split" on what action to take, he explained that they agreed on the minimum measures that were necessary to improve the situation in South Vietnam. Unlike McNamara and Taylor, they did not think that political stability in South Vietnam was a prerequisite for attacking the North. LeMay and Greene, saying that the

French had failed to secure Vietnam with five hundred thousand men, believed that limited American military activities would be useless and urged that the war be expanded into the North. Because the first covert operations under OPLAN 34A had been a dismal failure, the Chiefs recommended sending American aircraft to bomb the petroleum supply center in North Vietnam. They argued that it was necessary to cut off supply lines in Laos and Cambodia and to pursue the Viet Cong across those borders.[3] The Chiefs expressed doubt that the "present holding action" would be sufficient and warned that the policy could lead to a major foreign policy failure.

Appealing to the president's concerns about the election, Clifton reported that the Chiefs called the graduated pressure policy the "Asian Bay of Pigs" and were carefully recording their dissent so that, this time, they could not be blamed in case of a disaster. He warned the president that LeMay's scheduled retirement presented an "inherent danger" for the president because the general "will be tempted to speak out on this matter especially when he feels that so much more should be done against the North Vietnamese sanctuary, and especially when he feels that this proposition hasn't been reviewed thoroughly and that all the Chiefs haven't had a chance to speak on the matter. . . ."[4] Clifton explained that LeMay, like any military professional, would not publicly challenge the policies of the government lest he undermine civil control over the military; once LeMay retired, however, the professional military ethic would no longer bind him and he would feel free to speak out against the administration.

Clifton also warned Johnson about potential political threats from Ambassador Lodge and General Harkins. The Chiefs felt that Harkins was "being made a patsy" and might speak out after retirement about his troubled relations with the ambassador. They believed that Lodge, who had not fully supported the "hold until November" strategy, might return to campaign against the president on the basis of Vietnam policy. According to Clifton, the Chiefs felt that Westmoreland had a malleable personality and would fare no better than Harkins.

The general offered a number of solutions to this "messy situation." He recommended that Johnson send a copy of the McNamara paper to each of the Chiefs to solicit their individual views on it, as well as to Ambassador Lodge and General Harkins to get them "signed on." To determine the feasibility of holding on until November, Clifton advised that Johnson demand from the Chiefs two estimates of the situation: one to determine the possibilities of success or failure before the election, and the other a long-range analysis based on the assumption that there would be no crisis before November. Clifton suggested that Johnson assign someone "tougher" than Westmoreland to MACV, and suggested that Harkins might be kept silent by reassigning him to another post or by offering him an ambassadorship. Clifton urged the president to meet informally with the Chiefs and invite them to bring their suggestions directly to his attention.

The implications of Clifton's memo forced Johnson to define his relationship with his top military advisers more precisely. He did not, however, honestly seek advice from the JCS, as Clifton had suggested, but rather solicited their opinions on aspects of Vietnam policy without intending to heed them, so that they would not voice their disagreement publicly. Most of all Johnson held open the option of more determined military actions to co-opt his military advisers, as Forrestal had recommended.[5] The president, who desired unity and feared dissent, instinctively treated his military advisers as a potential source of political opposition. Although his principal concern was the November election, he was unwilling to tell the Chiefs that he was basing his Vietnam decisions on his campaign strategy rather than on military considerations and foreign policy concerns.

■

The first problem that LBJ would tackle was what to do about Gen. Curtis LeMay, whom Air Force Secretary Eugene Zuckert described as a "thorn in the administration's side." While considering the General's reappointment in January 1964, Johnson asked outgoing Deputy Secretary of Defense Gilpatric to advise him about LeMay. Gilpatric, a New York attorney who had previously served as Under Secretary of the Air Force in the Truman administration, thought that LeMay "just wasn't cut out to be in the role of principal military advisor" and regretted that he was not a "strategist and thinker like General Taylor." He recommended that "some kind of mission be found for LeMay" to "keep him occupied and not making statements to the press," such as an inspection tour of U.S. and allied air bases overseas.[6] On January 28 Clifton suggested that LeMay might not be interested in the assignment and recommended instead that he serve as the president's consultant on the supersonic transport. General Taylor, eager to find a more pliant officer to serve as Air Force Chief, began to consider whom to recommend as LeMay's replacement and solicited General Lemnitzer's opinion of General John P. McConnell.[7] In early spring LeMay learned from Zuckert that McNamara was not recommending his reappointment because he could not get along with civilian officials in the Department of Defense. LeMay responded cavalierly, "I didn't expect anything different. What's your problem?"[8] However, the president's talk with Clifton at the end of March forced him to reconsider the "LeMay problem."

On April 3 LeMay attended a cocktail reception at the White House, at which President Johnson asked the general about his post-retirement plans. The president, perhaps remembering how Kennedy had removed Admiral Anderson, offered LeMay an ambassadorship. When LeMay told the president that he was not interested in such a position, Johnson asked LeMay to give him about ten days to make him another offer. Four days later the president informed LeMay that he would reappoint him as Air Force chief of staff for another year. Johnson knew that LeMay, who believed that "civilian control [of the military] is essential to a Democracy," would not publicly oppose the administration's policy as long as he remained in uniform.[9]

■

Johnson, meanwhile, drew his advisory circle even tighter as the election approached. He met with his closest advisers every Tuesday for lunch. The principal participants in this advisory and decision-making forum were Rusk, McGeorge Bundy, and McNamara. Beginning in 1964, these Tuesday lunches became councils in which the president discussed both foreign and domestic policy. The first luncheon was held on February 4, just eleven weeks after Johnson became president. Twenty more were held in the spring and summer of 1964. According to Walt Rostow, Tuesday lunches were the "heart" of the national security process, and "the only men present were those whose advice the president most wanted to hear." The agenda often included Vietnam and the election campaign together. No military officer, not even Taylor, was a regular member of this select group.[10]

The luncheon forum was designed to achieve consensus on major policy issues and, by its exclusivity, to prevent leaks of those discussions to Congress or the press.[11] White House special assistant Forrestal recalled:

There was a bad thing in this period. The government was extremely scared of itself. There was tremendous nervousness that if you expressed an opinion it might somehow leak out . . . and the president would be furious and everyone's head would be cut off. . . . It inhibited an exchange of information and prevented the president himself from getting a lot of the facts that he should have had.[12]

The advisers' desire to demonstrate unity inspired them to coordinate their positions before discussing them with Johnson. Rusk recalled that the president "disliked the role of refereeing among senior colleagues" and "wanted his senior advisers to come to conclusions that they themselves would reach if they were President." Rusk's previous experience in the Truman administration as liaison between the often opposed Secretary of State Dean Acheson and Secretary of Defense Louis Johnson convinced him that the two cabinet officials with primary responsibility for foreign affairs should harmonize their positions. According to Rusk, he and McNamara "almost never went to the president with a divided opinion. We took it upon ourselves to make a special effort to reach a common conclusion."[13] The men encouraged close contact between both departments at all levels. According to Walt Rostow, Bundy, McNamara, and Rusk "regarded themselves as kind of a family."[14] McNamara was the most assertive of the president's personal advisers, and his positions on the war dominated the discussions.[15]

The Tuesday lunches further isolated the JCS from the planning and decision-making process. Because the advice that Johnson received represented a coordinated position between the secretaries of state and defense, it was unlikely that the president or the other civilian advisers would question it. The president remained ignorant of the Chiefs' opinions, and the Chiefs remained ill-informed of the direction in which the administration's Vietnam policy was headed.

■

Because they were dissatisfied with McNamara's March report advocating graduated pressure, the JCS decided to organize a war game to test the assumptions that underlay this strategy.[16] Between April 6 and 9, the war games division of the Joint Chiefs of Staff conducted SIGMA I–64 to examine "what might be produced" if the Republic of Vietnam and the United States undertook a program of gradually increasing pressures against North Vietnam. Military officers were assigned political and military roles and "played" the United States, North Vietnam, and such third countries as China and the Soviet Union. The outcome of the game was eerily prophetic. In response to U.S. military action, North Vietnam and the Viet Cong raised the tempo of attacks in the South and conducted terrorist attacks on U.S. installations and personnel. The game's final report concluded that "a small expenditure of iron bombs" led the United States to commit sizable forces and funds to defeat the North, while the war in the South continued with less attention and fewer resources. The paper warned that the U.S. public and Congress would not support a strategy based on graduated pressure. In fact, the officers who played the role of the North Vietnamese leaders in the game "banked on [a lack of] American resolve" to see their effort to fruition. The vast majority of the participants voiced grave doubts that air power would end North Vietnamese support for the Viet Cong.[17] The game exposed fundamental flaws in the assumptions that underlay graduated pressure. First, it showed that North Vietnam was capable of responding to U.S. escalation by intensifying the war on the ground. Second, it suggested that the United States was underestimating Hanoi's resolve.

The participants thought there were two solutions to these perplexing problems: withdrawing from Vietnam or doing "enough the first time to convince [North Vietnam] that we really mean business." The test found that graduated pressure would lead to a protracted military commitment with little hope of success, as LeMay had originally predicted. One of the participants' remarks captured the frustration of those trying to draw conclusions from the outcome of the game: "If we back off like [sic] this looks like we should, we've lost Vietnam. We've got to use some other type of tactics, and my suggestion is that we've got to make it expensive for somebody to take on these excursions."[18] The SIGMA I test revealed the military and political difficulties associated with the application of graduated pressure to the war in Vietnam. Johnson, who had blocked the avenues by which he might obtain the Chiefs' advice, never received the results of the Pentagon war game.

McNamara was moving to sever all channels of communication between the JCS and the president. He shut off the back-channel communication between the JCS and Brigadier General Clifton. The defense secretary's position with the president depended on his control of information and advice on military matters, and he was determined to prevent the JCS from undermining his influence. All communications between the JCS and the White House went through his office. When, in early May, Clifton gave the president the Chiefs' views on matters unrelated to Vietnam, such as cost cutting initiatives in the services and employing women in uniform, McNamara became "very disturbed about the route which General Clifton used in going to the several services" directly. President Johnson supported McNamara and notified his staff that he wanted "all military requests for appointments or decisions" to come "through the McNamara channel."[19] McNamara sent to the president, however, only those assessments that supported his conception of prosecuting the conflict in Vietnam.

Robert McNamara was not interested in the outcome of SIGMA I. He had seen his strategy for Vietnam approved without effective opposition and had available other methods for gathering and analyzing information. Political scientist Alexander George has observed that people tend to "place more reliance on concrete information than abstract information in making predictions."[20] Indeed, the SIGMA test, largely a subjective evaluation based on military experience and diplomatic expertise, did not appeal to McNamara's penchant for systematic and quantitative analysis. McNamara used line charts to depict change over time in the counterinsurgency effort in Vietnam. He tracked the numbers of people killed on both sides, the rate of Viet Cong activity, weapons captured, number of aircraft sorties, North Vietnamese naval activity, the percent of South Vietnamese river boats on patrol, and the number of patrol days for South Vietnamese units.[21] He used his team of systems analysts to help him determine the meaning of this data. Alain Enthoven, chief of the systems analysis division, had broad responsibilities in the Department of Defense and believed that he could apply his analytical approach successfully to military operations. Enthoven argued that it would be "suicidal" for the secretary of defense to forgo quantitative analysis when considering the feasibility of his program for Vietnam.[22] McNamara did use such techniques and thought that his quantitative indices indicated progress.

Because his principal sources of information lay with Enthoven and other civilians in OSD, McNamara spent less time consulting with the JCS. Lieutenant General Buse, General Greene's operations deputy, recalled that, although McNamara met with the Chiefs every Monday in 1963, he met with them less frequently in 1964. Roswell Gilpatric, McNamara's deputy, often attended JCS meetings in McNamara's stead.

Eventually neither McNamara nor his deputy attended. Buse assumed that McNamara did all his business with Taylor.[23] To Admiral McDonald it seemed that when the secretary did attend he really "didn't expect to accomplish anything" and came down "just to show his face."[24] Lt. Gen. Harold K. Johnson, who attended the meetings as operations deputy to General Wheeler, regarded the infrequent encounters with McNamara as a "cosmetic" designed to guard against "criticism that there was not a relationship between the civilian bosses and military leaders." General Johnson likened conferring with McNamara to a "mating dance of the turkeys," in which participants "went through certain set procedures" but "solved no problems."[25]

In the beginning of April, the Joint Chiefs of Staff complained that they did not have political guidance sufficient to develop plans in support of graduated pressure.[26] White House special assistant Michael Forrestal wanted to pacify the JCS, so he forwarded a list of planned diplomatic maneuvers and domestic political initiatives to the Chiefs. Although McNamara was fixed on sharply limited strikes against North Vietnam, the scenario promised to consider "making the initial U.S. action strong." Included among the military options were the mining and naval bombardment of North Vietnamese ports and sustained air strikes against North Vietnamese supply depots, training sites, and petroleum reserves.[27] Yet Forrestal, who knew that the "President would never authorize anything like the actions proposed in the political scenario," deliberately misled the JCS because he knew that the promise of future actions and the impression that the administration would consider using a "hard knock" against North Vietnam would keep the Chiefs content for a while. Forrestal and McNaughton, who had recently taken over for William Bundy as assistant secretary of defense for international security affairs—cautioning that "more perceptive" people at the Pentagon might suspect the White House staff of "putting up a straw man"—persuaded McNamara to "put it to the Chiefs officially" to "stop the growing criticism that no formal political proposal has been made to them."[28] The political scenario on which the Chiefs based their first in-depth planning for escalation of the military effort in Vietnam assumed that the United States might take actions that the Johnson administration would resist taking during its entire tenure in office. By deceiving the Chiefs, civilians in the White House and Defense Department forestalled debate on the nature of the U.S. commitment in Vietnam and perpetuated misconceptions concerning the level of force that the commitment was likely to require.[29]

In April the JCS used Forrestal's political scenario to develop a list of military actions for McNaughton. The latter, in coordination with Forrestal and William Sullivan, the secretary of state's special assistant for Vietnamese affairs, then developed political and military scenarios for the gradual escalation of U.S. intervention in Vietnam, assuming that the situation in the South would deteriorate further and that the North would take certain actions. The scenarios listed political and military actions that the American government might take to bolster the counterinsurgency effort in the South or to respond to aggression from the North.[30] Despite their doubts about McNamara's strategic concept, the Chiefs were thus obliged to plan military actions in support of graduated pressure.

On April 17 the JCS forwarded to McNamara OPLAN 37–64, which identified military targets for a campaign of "graduated overt pressures" against North Vietnam. It was a three-phase plan "covering operations against VC infiltration routes in Laos and Cambodia and against targets in North Vietnam." Phase I provided for air and ground strikes within South Vietnam and permitted hot pursuit of enemy forces into the border regions of Laos and Cambodia. Phase II detailed "tit for tat" air strikes, airborne and amphibious raids, and aerial mining operations against North Vietnamese targets. Phase III laid out a program for "graduated overt pressure" against North Vietnam in the form of increasingly severe air strikes and other actions that went far beyond the "tit for tat" concept. The plan did not specify the degree of intensity with which American or South Vietnamese air forces would carry out the attacks. An annex attached to the OPLAN included a list of ninety-one targets in North Vietnam. In the next year McNamara and the president would select targets from a revised version in order to retaliate against the North for attacks on U.S. forces and thus begin applying graduated pressure to North Vietnam. Although the Chiefs suggested that "from a military viewpoint, it is considered that the most effective application of military force will result from a sudden sharp blow," they had mainly developed a plan for gradually intensifying military actions. McNamara, ignoring that qualification, used the Chiefs' document to plan his own program of graduated pressure against North Vietnam.[31]

■

Graduated pressure depended on the assumption that the limited application of force would compel the North Vietnamese to the negotiating table and exact from them a favorable diplomatic settlement. There was no need to pursue military victory because negotiations would achieve the same political objectives with only the threat of more severe military action. The only question was when, not if, the enemy would be induced to negotiate. On April 19 and 20, Rusk, General Wheeler, and Assistant Secretary of State for Far Eastern Affairs William Bundy traveled to Saigon to discuss OPLAN 37–64 with Lodge. During that visit Rusk supported Ambassador Lodge's suggestion that the United States make a diplomatic overture toward North Vietnam. On returning to the United States, he arranged for a Canadian official, J. Blair Seaborn, to deliver a warning to Hanoi that continued support for the insurgency in the South would result in great devastation to North Vietnam. The mission—the first of many attempts to couple the threat or use of force with diplomatic overtures to North Vietnam—failed.[32]

When he returned, Wheeler met with Taylor and the other Chiefs, as well as the outgoing CINCPAC, Admiral Felt. LeMay asked Felt what would be needed to "win" the war and whether action against the North would be necessary. Felt responded that, to achieve victory, the United States would need a reasonably secure base in the South and would "have to go North sometime."

To prevent dissension among his advisers and the military, Johnson led the Chiefs to believe that he was seriously considering expanding the military effort. The urgency with which the administration had encouraged JCS planning for military action in Vietnam, however, was inconsistent with its determination to constrain the level of commitment. Westmoreland recalled that officials in Saigon regarded OPLAN 37 as a "post-election plan."[33] When Wheeler asked the new deputy secretary of defense, Cyrus Vance, whether there was a ceiling on forces in Vietnam, Vance replied that the military is "fat out there" and told Wheeler that he would only accept a "validated requirement" (one that could be justified quantitatively) for additional forces.[34] William Bundy later viewed the planning effort in the spring of 1964 as "an emotional safety valve" for those who might otherwise pressure the president into taking actions that he was determined to avoid.[35] The planning efforts actually served the purpose of delaying genuine consideration of the situation in Vietnam until after the election,[36] keeping the JCS busy and, at the same time, permitting LBJ to keep the war low-key.[37]

Despite the president's efforts, however, calls to undertake additional action mounted. In early May, Ambassador Lodge became convinced that action against the North was not only desirable but necessary. He indicated that General Khanh was also dissatisfied with the course of the war. Khanh was prepared to declare a state of war between South and North Vietnam, impose martial law in the South, and issue an ultimatum to North Vietnam. He told Lodge that it was "illogical, wasteful, [and] wrong to go on incurring casualties just in order to make the agony endure." The general urged moving ahead to get a "real victory." Lodge, sympathizing, concluded: "This man obviously wants to get on with the job and not sit here indefinitely taking casualties. Who can blame him . . . ? He is clearly facing up to all the hard questions and wants us to do it too."[38] As assessments of the situation in Vietnam were generally growing more pessimistic,[39] the president again sent McNamara and Taylor to Saigon to defuse this latest challenge to the president's policy.

◼

Taylor found himself in the familiar role of defending the administration's policy against those who were anxious to fight the war in a less constrained fashion. He met with Harkins and the MACV staff on the morning of May 11.[40] Westmoreland, who would soon assume command of the American war effort in Vietnam, told Taylor that not only Khanh, but many Vietnamese generals were pressing for attacks against North Vietnam.[41] The staff officers at MACV pressed Taylor to lift restrictions on some of the South Vietnamese covert operations against North Vietnam that the United States had been supporting since the beginning of 1962. Operation Farmgate, for example, required that a South Vietnamese pilot accompany American pilots on their operations in order to preserve the pretense that the flights were training exercises. In practice Farmgate pilots took along South Vietnamese "observers" to whom they referred as "sandbags."[42] When the Air Force commander in Vietnam, Maj. Gen. Joseph H. Moore, spoke of the awkward arrangement, Taylor replied that the presence of South Vietnamese pilots would continue to be required. And when Moore, who had been Westmoreland's high school classmate, broached the possibility of introducing B-57s or another squadron of A-1E aircraft into Vietnam, Taylor again rebuffed him. Taylor, also voicing dissatisfaction with the targeting of fuel storage facilities under OPLAN 34-A, remarked that these missions might not be subtle enough to maintain "plausible deniability."[43]

The secretary of defense joined the conference on May 12 and further emphasized the restrictions on American involvement in direct combat actions. He also stated that U. S. Air Force pilots were never supposed to participate in combat.[44] When General Westmoreland asked for additional Special Forces units, McNamara replied that, when MACV put the requirement in writing, he would approve the request if he deemed it valid.[45] He ordered the MACV officers to base their requests on quantitative data so his staff could test their validity.[46]

Indeed, McNamara was confident that he could calculate precisely the amount of force necessary to secure the administration's objectives in Vietnam. To do so, however, he would have to exert tight control over his military officers—something he believed had been facilitated by his reforms in the Pentagon:

> We have been able to create and control the balanced, flexible forces now at our disposal. . . . To harness this wide array of human and material resources, and to form them into usable power requires an exceedingly precise degree of control. The engine of defense must be so harnessed that its vast power may be unleashed to the precise degree required by whatever threat we face.[47]

McNamara's faith in graduated pressure rested on the principle of precise control of the application of force. As a corollary he had to control the military precisely.

McNamara also had to exercise close control over U.S. "advisory" forces already engaged in combat alongside the South Vietnamese Army lest they compromise the president's election bid. Lieutenant General Krulak recalled that McNamara was "under tremendous pressure" from the president to cloak the military effort in South Vietnam until the November election.[48] McNamara had learned from the Cuban missile crisis that "political objectives do not disappear when we begin to exercise military power; indeed they are all the more seriously to be considered, for with the initiation of force we move into the zone in which errors may be irrevocable."[49] Accordingly, he thought that control over military forces must "be held firmly in the hands of the man preeminently responsible for national security; that is, in the hands of the president." McNamara was trying to preserve that control by emphasizing, rather than removing, restrictions on military actions.

The May meeting in Saigon was characteristic of the relationship between McNamara and the military. Neither side was forthright. The military tried gradually to erode barriers to further action,[50] while McNamara, suspicious of the military's behavior and eager to avoid increasing the troop strength in Vietnam, was determined to make the generals justify every request quantitatively, in writing. The secretary of defense was careful, however, not to alienate the military officers completely; requests that had the potential of becoming politically volatile if not accepted gained easy approval. Accordingly, McNamara told the senior MACV officers to ask for anything they needed and promised that "winning" the war in South Vietnam was his top priority.[51] He continued to conceal from the military the limitations on the level of effort the president was willing to approve.

The secretary of defense and General Taylor returned to Washington amid rising criticism of U.S. policy in the press. A May 13 editorial in the *Wall Street Journal* titled "Error Upon Error" observed that "it is almost impossible to figure out what is the U.S. strategy," and declared that "the evidence indicates the lack of any plan."[52] On May 15, perhaps to forestall further criticism, President Johnson cancelled the scheduled agenda for the noontime NSC meeting. Instead he invited congressional leaders of both parties to hear briefings from Rusk and McNamara. Taylor represented the Joint Chiefs of Staff. The discussion turned quickly to Vietnam, and the president asked the general for his assessment. Although the Chiefs had been pressing for action against the North, Taylor told the legislators: "If we attack North Vietnam, there would be a strong reaction by the Viet Cong in the South. . . . The larger the U.S. attack, the greater chance of Communist reaction." Taylor lent his support to McNamara's gradual approach to bombing, should it be undertaken. He argued that restraint would be necessary because "the level of the attack would be the determining factor in the Communist reaction." Although he had just received a briefing to the contrary, Secretary McNamara helped the president's cause further by claiming that "U.S. soldiers are not engaged in combat except in the course of their training the Vietnamese. . . . The bulk of the air effort is by South Vietnamese forces and does not involve exposing our men."[53]

■

On May 19 journalist Douglas Cater arrived at the White House for his first day on the job as an assistant to the president. McGeorge Bundy had not yet decided what duties to assign Cater, and the former national affairs editor for the *Reporter* magazine spent a boring time in the White House Situation Room. Later former Secretary of State Dean Acheson telephoned Cater to invite him to his Georgetown home for cocktails. Cater, who had accomplished nothing that day, thought "perhaps this is the way it works." That evening Acheson gave the White House aide a message that was obviously meant for President Johnson. He told Cater: "Things are going to hell in a hack in Vietnam and if the president does not do something that relates to getting the support of Congress in a Formosa-type resolution, it's going to be too late, and we'll go into this orgasm of a campaign period in which things will just have to stall." Cater hurried back to the White House, composed his first White House memo, and slipped it into the president's night reading.[54]

The next day, in response to Cater's memo and intensified attacks by the Pathet Lao guerrillas in Laos, President Johnson ordered McGeorge Bundy to look into the Vietnam problem with renewed vigor. On May 22, Bundy reported that four working groups were pulling together military and political plans to address the situation. The first group, under John McNaughton, developed a military plan based on the premise that actions would be designed to "hurt" but not to "destroy." He hoped that such limited action would convince the North Vietnamese to desist from their support of the Viet Cong. The second group, under William Sullivan, recommended a vast expansion of the American military and civilian advisory effort to put a "tall American at every point of the stress and strain." The third group, under NSC staff member Chester Cooper, analyzed possible enemy reactions to U.S. moves. The fourth, led by Under Secretary of State George Ball, drafted several congressional resolutions to give the president a "full range of choice" in seeking congressional "validation" of military action.[55]

Even though the subjects of three of the four groups clearly had military implications, the Joint Chiefs found themselves reacting to ideas from these groups and other agencies instead of contributing directly to the policy-planning process. The JCS received recommendations from these committees at the same time that they were sent to the president. The Chiefs gave their responses to the papers not directly to the president, but through the secretary of defense.

McNamara was anxious to dominate not only the JCS, but also civilian officials, during the planning for Vietnam. While the Chiefs were denied direct access to the White House, the *ad hoc* committees solidified inter-departmental relationships between second-level officials and gave them access to the White House staff. John McNaughton enjoyed a particularly close relationship with the NSC's assistant to the president for Far Eastern affairs, Michael Forrestal. Both McNaughton and Forrestal had confidence in the power of their own intellects and felt well qualified to give military advice.[56] McNamara often sat in on the working sessions of second-level officials such as Forrestal and McNaughton to ensure that the results were consistent with graduated pressure.[57] The recommendations of McNaughton's interdepartmental study group were based, therefore, on the same assumptions and premises that underpinned McNamara's blueprint for the war contained in the March memo, which became NSAM 288.[58]

On May 25 the Executive Committee of the NSC prepared a memo entitled *Basic Recommendations and Projected Course of Action on Southeast Asia*, which refined McNamara's earlier memo on graduated pressure. Rusk, McNamara, and Bundy discussed this document with the president during their luncheon on the following day.[59] They recommended that Johnson "make a presidential decision that the U.S. will use selected and carefully graduated military force against North Vietnam" if there was not "sufficient improvement of non-Communist prospects in South Vietnam and in Laos." Prior to applying military pressures, the United States would communicate the limited scope of its objectives to Hanoi, China, the Soviet Union, and France. Action against the North would "have more deterrent than destructive impact as far as possible" and would be accompanied by "active diplomatic offensives." The actions would be controlled to prevent the "unroll[ing of] a scenario aimed at the use of force as an end in itself." Sensitive to domestic political priorities, the advisers suggested that the president seek a congressional resolution only after crucial civil rights legislation was off the Senate calendar. The president agreed to call a meeting of government officials from Saigon and Washington in Honolulu from June 1 to 3.[60]

Taylor, McNamara, and Rusk joined Lodge and Westmoreland (who had recently replaced Harkins) at the Honolulu conference. Westmoreland and Lodge were generally optimistic and believed that the deterioration of the South's stability had leveled off. Westmoreland asserted that, with additional resources, he could turn the situation around. He unveiled a plan for a crash pacification program directed at eight critical provinces.[61] Three weeks later Westmoreland asked for an additional 900 U.S. advisers. By mid-July he had requested a total of 4,200 additional military personnel.[62]

Much of the discussion in Honolulu focused on the desirability of a congressional resolution to validate the administration's policy and on how to influence public opinion about it.[63] Taylor and Westmoreland were already involved in trying to put the best face possible on the American effort. Taylor had met with Hanson Baldwin of the *New York Times* on May 7 and told him, in contrast to the Chiefs' assessment, that he foresaw no difficulty in "holding on" in Vietnam until after the election.[64] On May 28 Ambassador Lodge gave MACV the task of composing a "definitive essay with detailed examples, facts and figures to support our claim that the Vietnamese are brave, effective fighters willing to sacrifice their lives in defense of their country," which he planned to bring with him to Honolulu.[65]

The conference attendees affirmed the basic concept of graduated pressure and agreed to refine plans to support it. There was a persistent lack of consensus, however, over the character of the attacks. The military and civilian planners had not reached a clear understanding "of just what should be hit and how thoroughly, and above all for what objective."[66] The ambiguity was deliberate, and Taylor played a critical role in preserving it.

■

On May 30, just prior to the Honolulu conference, the JCS met without Taylor present and prepared a memorandum expressing concern over the "lack of definition, even a confusion in respect to objectives and courses of action related to each objective," for Vietnam. The Joint Chiefs, citing their responsibilities as military advisers, argued that the military objective should be to "accomplish the destruction of the North Vietnamese will and capabilities . . . to compel [North Vietnam] to cease providing support to the insurgencies in South Vietnam and Laos." They argued that only courses of action consistent with destroying the will and capability of the enemy would end North Vietnamese support for the insurgency in the South. The memorandum criticized the gradual options under consideration because they were based on a "lesser objective" of persuading rather than compelling the North Vietnamese to change their policy and terminate their "subversive support." The Chiefs warned that there was "no basis to be hopeful about the situation . . . until and unless

North Vietnam is forced to stop supporting" the guerrillas in the South. They questioned the idea of using military actions to send "messages," which would waste both time and resources. If, however, the United States decided to pursue the "lesser" objective, the initial action against the North should be designed to "convey directly, sharply, even abruptly that the situation has indeed changed." Sharp initial action was necessary to convey to North Vietnam that the United States was "determined."[67] The Chiefs rushed to complete the memo before McNamara's departure for Honolulu, and urged that their concerns about the planning of the war be considered at the conference.[68] Taylor, however, obstructed their efforts.

On June 1 the director of the Joint Staff, Air Force lieutenant general David Burchinal, reported to the JCS that, just prior to Taylor's departure, the chairman had directed him to withdraw the memo from the defense secretary's office. Taylor had told Burchinal that he was unsure that the wording accurately reflected what the Chiefs had discussed in their May 30 meeting. LeMay, who had acted as chairman in Taylor's absence, was incensed. Greene believed that Taylor's refusal to present the memo to the secretary of defense prior to the conference was "a deliberate move to put the Joint Chiefs on ice until after the Honolulu meeting." Greene thought that Taylor wanted to "avoid presenting the views of the Joint Chiefs of Staff at this very important conference."[69]

Taylor underestimated JCS resolve. The Chiefs met briefly, made several changes in the language of the original document, cabled a revised copy to Honolulu, and requested that Taylor forward it to McNamara. Greene demanded that Taylor be notified by phone that "these views were of critical importance" to the subject of Vietnam and that the Chiefs wanted their assessment expressed to the conferees. Separately, Greene telephoned the commander of Marine forces in the Pacific, Lieutenant General Victor Krulak, whom he urged to attend the conference and report back to him so he could check what Taylor actually said during the conference against what the Chairman "professed his positions to be during JCS meetings."[70] Greene's suspicions were well founded. Despite the Chiefs' urging, Taylor refused to submit their paper to the conferees, and, after suppressing the memo, directly opposed the JCS position at the conference.

After Honolulu, Taylor finally forwarded the JCS memo to McNamara. He indicated his disagreement with it and promised to respond to it in a separate memo, which he wrote on June 5.[71] Taylor criticized his colleagues' paper for presenting neither an accurate nor a comprehensive expression of the military options available. He argued that, rather than choose between affecting the enemy's will and destroying his capabilities, the president might select one of three "patterns" of attack on North Vietnam. The first would entail a "massive air attack on all significant military targets in North Vietnam" to render the enemy "incapable of continuing to assist the Viet Cong and Pathet Lao." The second would involve a "lesser attack on some significant part of the military target system in North Vietnam," to convince the "enemy that it is to his interest to desist from aiding the insurgents" and obtain "his cooperation in calling off" the insurgency in South Vietnam and Laos. The third pattern of attack would have the same purpose as the second but include only "demonstrative strikes against limited military targets to show U.S. readiness and intent" to escalate the intensity of the attacks to either the second or first options. Taylor rejected the first because it risked escalation and was "unnecessarily destructive." Although he recommended the second option, Taylor observed that the JCS should focus planning efforts on the third because "political considerations" were likely to incline our "responsible civilian officials" in that direction.[72] McNamara agreed with Taylor that the JCS options were neither "accurate nor complete" and preferred the "least dangerous" third option to demonstrate U.S. willingness to move "up the scale if North Vietnam did not reduce insurgent support."[73]

Although Taylor attempted to minimize the importance of the Honolulu conference to the Chiefs, he had foiled another attempt to question the validity of the assumptions on which the concept of graduated pressure was based. He told the JCS on June 3 that Honolulu was the "most overbilled conference he [had] ever attended" and that it was "a disappointment to him." Indeed, Taylor said, military options were "never really fully discussed."[74] In fact, McNamara's memo on the conference's deliberations, based on the graduated pressure strategy, included a list of "illustrative military moves designed to demonstrate the U.S. intention to prevent further communist advances in Laos and South Vietnam."[75] The actions ranged from reconnaissance flights over Laos to military exercises in South Vietnam. While undercutting the JCS ability to influence Vietnam planning, Taylor fostered the false impression that policy deliberations to date had been inconsequential. He thereby bolstered McNamara's and Johnson's effort to keep the Chiefs divorced from the policy process while preventing them from openly dissenting.

■

Two days after his return from Honolulu, Taylor flew to Paris to attend a NATO conference. While he was in Europe, the situation in Laos became potentially explosive. The United States had begun photo and reconnaissance flights over Laos on May 19 to track the fighting between government forces and Pathet Lao guerrillas on the Plain of Jars. On June 6 the Pathet Lao shot down a photo reconnaissance jet. The pilot ejected from the aircraft and was quickly captured by Pathet Lao forces. Although the JCS had previously permitted forces in the region to undertake search-and-rescue operations, Deputy Secretary of Defense Cyrus Vance forbade using "U.S. resources" to do so. The pilot later escaped and made his way to friendly Lao forces.[76]

McNamara met with the Chiefs at 9:00 A.M. on June 6 to discuss the implications of the incident for further reconnaissance missions.[77] The Chiefs' failure to make a useful recommendation on what action to take next undercut their ability to influence the decision. LeMay argued for bombing antiaircraft positions before sending in additional aircraft. McNamara asked him, "How many [aircraft] would you send?" LeMay answered, "As many as we have." McNamara continued, "How many escorts will be required?" LeMay answered, "Just as many as we have." McNamara could easily dismiss LeMay's curt responses as the ravings of an unsophisticated airpower enthusiast. Greene, who supported LeMay, observed that he "did not impress the SECDEF [secretary of defense] with his belligerent and somewhat fumbling way of making recommendations concerning the problem at hand."[78] Wheeler, sensitive to the potential for escalation, agreed with McNamara that the reconnaissance missions should continue and fire only if fired on. McDonald waffled.[79] The divisions made it difficult for the Chiefs to challenge McNamara's position.

In Taylor's absence all the Chiefs, along with Goodpaster, attended a morning NSC meeting at the White House. Secretary McNamara began by recommending that aerial reconnaissance be conducted again the next day with two reconnaissance aircraft and six to eight escort jets. Their orders would be to fire only if fired on. LeMay and Greene indicated that they personally had recommended an attack on the antiaircraft position but concurred in the recommendation of the Joint Chiefs and the secretary of defense even though they were certain that future flights would be in jeopardy. Wheeler gave unqualified support to McNamara's position. The recorder noted that "all agreed," and Johnson decided to adopt the "unanimous" recommendations of his advisers.[80] The next day, June 7, another escort aircraft was shot down over Laos.

The president met with McNamara, McNaughton, Vance, and other civilian officials on June 10 to discuss the second incident and decided to delay further reconnaissance operations in order to avoid escalation.[81] Later in the day, the president's advisers reconvened without him to discuss what public position to take on the downed aircraft. McNamara suggested misleading the press by stating simply that the aircraft had been fired on and returned fire. McGeorge Bundy, contending that it would be imprudent to make an untrue statement, recommended that the administration continue to parry questions with "No comment." They agreed that the press furor would be short-lived. Rusk reported happily that there was "little Congressional interest" in the incident. The advisers decided to adopt Bundy's suggestion.[82]

■

At the same time, the president was presented with the opportunity to replace Lodge, who had entered the Republican presidential primary and had just won in New Hampshire. The ambassador was anxious to hit the campaign trail, so the president had to decide very quickly whom to appoint. On June 6 McGeorge Bundy prepared a list of six possible replacements including himself, Sargent Shriver, McNamara, and Robert Kennedy.[83] Lyndon Johnson, however, would accept none of these recommendations. He selected Taylor.

Before leaving, the general told McNamara that, during his service as chairman of the Joint Chiefs of Staff, he had worked hard to

> attenuate or if possible to eliminate the differences—sometimes real, sometimes imaginary—between the civilian and military authorities within the Department of Defense. I hope that our personal relationship of which I have been very proud has set an example for those around us and has contributed to proper team play. . . . In closing let me say what a pleasure it has been to have been associated with you in the last year and nine months. In my former unhappy days as Chief

of Staff of the Army, I cried out for a decisive Secretary of Defense to end the unending conflicts. I got one and am now content.[84]

Taylor met for the last time with the Joint Staff on July 2. He read an excerpt of NSAM 55 that he had composed for President Kennedy to deliver to the Joint Chiefs of Staff on June 28, 1961. The memorandum had directed the Chiefs to provide military advice in the broadest context. He told the officers assembled to maintain this breadth of view and look at all the factors—not just the military. He counseled them to view the problems of national security through the "eyes of the President." The general offered similar advice to his colleagues on the Joint Chiefs of Staff, enjoining them to be "more than military men."[85]

After meeting with Johnson on the same day, Taylor left for Cape Cod to bid farewell to former first lady Jacqueline Kennedy. He had remained close to the former president's family. Soon after his arrival in Saigon on July 7, he received a letter in which Mrs. Kennedy thanked him for demonstrating once again the "devotion you always showed to Jack." She credited Taylor with making "greatness" possible for her husband by helping him overcome the Bay of Pigs debacle and making the "second Cuba a triumph."[86]

Jacqueline Kennedy's letter evoked the memory of the crisis in civil-military relations that grew out of the Bay of Pigs incident, bringing the general to Washington and ending his three-year retirement from military service. Taylor had a profound impact on the Kennedy administration. He had helped the president replace recalcitrant members of the Joint Chiefs with men who would prove more sensitive to domestic political concerns. He had been instrumental in appointing Generals Harkins and Westmoreland and had helped to shape the American effort in Vietnam. He had developed and overseen the implementation of the advisory effort and, until November 1963, had joined McNamara in praising the "headway" that U.S. advisers and their South Vietnamese allies had made.

Perhaps Taylor's most significant legacy, however, was his shaping of the relationship between the JCS and the president that affected the decision making on Vietnam in 1963 and 1964. Long an advocate of the centralization of responsibility in the chairmanship of the JCS, Taylor possessed the dominant military voice in connection with U.S. policy toward Vietnam. Although he had lamented divisions among the Chiefs during the Eisenhower administration, he used those divisions to his advantage under President Johnson. When he found it expedient to do so, he misled the JCS, the press, and the NSC. He deliberately relegated his fellow military officers to a position of little influence and assisted McNamara in suppressing JCS objections to the concept of graduated pressure, reinforcing the secretary's confidence in his ability to develop strategic options for Vietnam independent of JCS advice. Ever loyal to the president, and sensing Johnson's election-year desire for unity and consensus, Taylor shielded him from the views of his less politically sensitive colleagues while telling the Chiefs that their recommendations had been given full consideration. To keep the Chiefs from expressing dissenting views, he helped to craft a relationship based on distrust and deceit in which the president obscured the finality of decisions and made false promises that the JCS conception of the war might one day be realized.

Neither the insidious relationship between the leading civilian and military officials in the Johnson administration nor the planning efforts in the spring of 1964 predestined the Johnson administration to escalate American military involvement in Vietnam. Nonetheless, they firmly established in the minds of key decision makers a flawed strategy for fighting what seemed to them a war without precedent.

6
Across the Threshold
July–August 1964

With the opportunity to observe the problems of a
President at closer range, I have come to understand the
importance of an intimate, easy relationship, born of
friendship and mutual regard, between the president and
the Chief's. It is particularly important in the case of the
Chairman.... The Chairman should be a true believer in the
foreign policy and military strategy of the administration
which he serves.

MAXWELL TAYLOR, 1972[1]

Like the Diem coup in November 1963, the American response to
reported attacks on U.S. Navy destroyers in the Gulf of Tonkin in
early August 1964 marked a turning point in the Vietnam War. After a
first attack on American destroyers, to which the "peace candidate,"
Lyndon Johnson, chose not to retaliate, the president ordered air strikes
on North Vietnam in response to confused reports surrounding an alleged
attack that probably did not occur. Johnson retaliated with sharply limited air strikes against North Vietnam based on McNamara's strategy of
graduated pressure. The American response to the Gulf of Tonkin incident solidified in practice McNamara's strategic concept. It became clear,
as well, that graduated pressure was ideally suited to the president's determination to base his Vietnam policy on domestic political needs.
Although the direct, overt action against North Vietnam represented an
important change in American military involvement in the war, the

most profound result was a congressional resolution that, in effect, gave the president carte blanche for the escalation of the war. Johnson wanted such a resolution to protect himself from future congressional attacks on his Vietnam policy.

Preoccupied with the campaign, Lyndon Johnson was determined to make only those decisions that would redound to his short-term political benefit. To enhance his chances for election, he and McNamara deceived the American people and the Congress about events and the nature of the American commitment in Vietnam. They used a questionable report of a North Vietnamese attack on American naval vessels to justify the president's policy to the electorate and to defuse Republican senator and presidential candidate Barry Goldwater's charges that Lyndon Johnson was irresolute and "soft" in the foreign policy arena.

In many respects the American response to the Gulf of Tonkin "incident" seems, in retrospect, a rehearsal for Lyndon Johnson's escalation of the war after he defeated Goldwater in the presidential election. When it turned out to his benefit, the president appeared restrained and measured in his approach. When pressure to take military action grew, he responded with apparent determination and resolve. All his decisions, however, betrayed his penchant for taking actions disconnected from military realities and without full appreciation of their consequences. The experience underlined what Lyndon Johnson wanted and expected from his "principal military advisers": the credibility lent his policy by their uniforms rather than their opinions.

■

How the Chiefs would respond to Johnson's expectations would depend largely on the character of the man who replaced Maxwell Taylor. Based on Taylor's recommendation, Johnson appointed the Army chief of staff, Gen. Earle Wheeler. Wheeler's selection continued a shift away from appointing combat commanders toward choosing officers more experienced in staff work and managing information. Wheeler lacked combat experience and was little known to the American public. The chairmen of the JCS who preceded him had distinguished themselves in battle during World War II and the Korean War.[2] Wheeler had spent most of World War II engaged in the important but unglamorous task of training National Guard units. He served in Europe during the last five months of the war as a division chief of staff.

Accordingly Wheeler's most notable qualities were those of a skilled staff officer. He was a master administrator who gave lucid, well-organized briefings. Because of his aptitude for staff work, Wheeler spent the preponderance of his career in Washington, D.C. In the late 1950s Army Chief of Staff Taylor entrusted him with the Army's strategic planning. Taylor soon promoted Wheeler to be his operations deputy, and the two worked together to change Eisenhower's defense policies. In 1958 Wheeler headed a joint committee charged with improving interservice planning and decision making. After serving two years as deputy commander in chief of the European Command, he returned to Washington as the director of the Joint Staff.[3]

The outcome of the 1960 presidential election gave Wheeler's career a boost. He gave weekly briefings on world military developments to presidential candidate John F. Kennedy. Kennedy shared the Army's dissatisfaction with Eisenhower's "new look" defense policies and was impressed with Wheeler's bearing and eloquence. Although he had never been an athlete, the handsome Wheeler was tall and fit. His manner was gentlemanly and affable. Kennedy was drawn instinctively to men who, like himself, were sharp witted and prepossessing in appearance. When Kennedy announced Taylor's appointment to the chairmanship of the JCS in August 1962, Taylor recommended his old operations deputy as the Army chief of staff. The *Washington Post* commented that Wheeler "might be called the beau ideal of a modern U.S. military commander. He fits like a glove the exacting specifications laid down by President Kennedy and Defense Secretary Robert S. McNamara."[4]

Wheeler, a former math instructor at West Point, established a good relationship with the analytical-minded secretary of defense. McNamara, furthermore, wanted "team players," not opinionated, irascible military heroes, and as a "new man," Wheeler fit the bill. As Army chief of staff, he worked amicably with the Whiz Kids and implemented McNamara's reforms without complaint. He supported the defense secretary when he needed it most, during congressional hearings on the Nuclear Test Ban Treaty and Pentagon budget reforms. Wheeler rebutted, point by point before the Congress, LeMay's concerns about proposed limitations on nuclear testing and told the Senate Appropriations Committee that McNamara's budgetary methods represented a "great step forward."[5]

Unlike a high-ranking officer coming to Washington for the first time, Chairman Wheeler was sensitive to and familiar with the political machinations of the Pentagon, the White House, and Capitol Hill.[6] For example, before General Westmoreland departed for his assignment to Vietnam, Wheeler told the MACV commander-designate to coordinate his actions very closely with the embassy in Saigon and to avoid statements or actions potentially embarrassing to the Johnson administration. Wheeler warned Westmoreland that the war could "be lost in Washington if Congress loses faith." Wheeler's sensitivity to the politics of executive-legislative relations made him an attractive choice for Lyndon Johnson.[7]

In time Wheeler developed a close association with the president. Johnson would count "Buz" (his actual nickname was "Bus," but Wheeler chose not to correct the president) as one of his ten best friends in Washington.[8] When asked about Wheeler's relationship with the president, Lt. Gen. Andrew Goodpaster recalled that Johnson had a way of "befriending" people and then using that friendship to exact acquiescence on controversial issues.[9] Wheeler did not like direct confrontation, and he was susceptible to the president's patronage. Loyalty was the criterion Johnson and McNamara thought essential for their appointees, and they thought that they could count on Wheeler to be a "team player."

Wheeler's appointment was immensely unpopular with many Pentagon officers, particularly those outside the Army. Navy and Air Force officers considered his appointment a blow to their services because it again undermined the precedent of rotating the chairmanship between the services. When Taylor replaced Army general Lemnitzer, it had been the Navy's "turn" to hold the chairmanship. Wheeler became the third Army officer in a row to hold the position. Many officers viewed Wheeler's appointment as a continuation of Taylor's and the Army's influence over defense policy.[10] LeMay was particularly suspicious of Wheeler and, referring to the new chairman's relationship with Taylor, called him "Polly Parrot." In an obvious allusion to Wheeler's lack of combat experience, LeMay said facetiously that Wheeler had earned one of his ribbons for "fighting the battle of Fort Benning [an Army post in Georgia where Wheeler trained National Guard units] during World War II."[11] Marine colonel William Corson of General Greene's staff bluntly criticized Wheeler as "the Army's highest-ranking sycophant."[12] Wheeler's lack of credibility with some officers in the Pentagon contrasted with the impressive military credentials of his predecessor, Maxwell Taylor.

Wheeler also lacked the drive and energy to discharge his responsibilities to the fullest[13]—something Taylor probably did not consider a draw-back. Taylor liked to weaken any post he left to guarantee that he had no rival to undermine his influence in his new position. In October 1962 when he departed the White House as President Kennedy's military adviser, he recommended abolishing that office.[14] Although Taylor could not modify the Chiefs' legal responsibilities, before leaving for Vietnam he drafted and had the president sign a letter that, in addition to his duties as the president's diplomatic representative, gave him complete control over the American military effort in South Vietnam:

> As you take charge of the American effort in South Vietnam, I want you to have this formal expression not only of my confidence, but my desire that you have and exercise full responsibility. . . . Specifically I want it clearly understood that this overall responsibility includes the whole military effort in South Vietnam and authorizes the degree of command and control that you consider appropriate. . . . At your convenience, I should be glad to know of the arrangements which you propose for meeting the terms of this instruction, so that appropriate supporting action can be taken in the Defense Department and elsewhere as necessary.[15]

Taylor's "mandate" eroded traditional military prerogatives and expanded civilian responsibilities in military affairs. McGeorge Bundy highlighted the fact that the letter gave Taylor "full control over everything in South Vietnam . . . something the military never let the Ambassador have before, and now that we have a man whom the military cannot refuse, it is time to establish the principle."[16] Taylor would work closely with General Westmoreland, whom, over the objections of his colleagues, he had installed in Vietnam three months earlier.[17] Indeed, Johnson's grant of plenipotentiary powers to Taylor as ambassador, combined with the appointment of Wheeler as his replacement at the JCS, further weakened the Joint Chiefs' ability to influence military policy and planning for Vietnam.

Other governmental departments and agencies quickly acknowledged Taylor's wide-ranging authority. The deputy director of the CIA, Lt. Gen. Marshall S. Carter, wrote to Taylor lauding him as "the coach, the captain, and the quarterback of the team" in Vietnam, and assuring him that the "assets of the Agency" were at his disposal.[18] Rusk vowed that "as the principal officer in the field," Taylor's views would be "of critical importance." He charged Taylor with developing a "concise military evaluation" for the White House as an alternative to the "reporting through military channels" that had presented a "fragmented picture."[19] Although Taylor enjoyed a broad mandate, the president's principal motivation in appointing him ambassador was to use Taylor's military reputation to protect his administration from charges that his Vietnam policy was soft.[20]

The president's letter had given the ambassador "great confidence," and Taylor wasted no time exercising his broad license. He promised to undertake a vigorous review of all mission activities. On July 7, the day he arrived in Saigon, he cabled that he was reorganizing operations in Saigon "under direction of a U.S. Mission Council over which I will preside."[21]

As soon as he began working in Saigon, Taylor realized that the situation in the South was worse than he had thought when he was in Washington. On July 15, he revised upward the estimate of Viet Cong strength in South Vietnam to between twenty-eight and thirty-four thousand and reported increased Viet Cong activity in the northern provinces. He argued that although this was "not an occasion for overconcern," the "growing magnitude of our problems" required the intensification of the South Vietnamese and American counterinsurgency efforts. Taylor required additional American military advisers to expand the pacification effort in the countryside surrounding Saigon (known as HOP TAC) and promised that a request for supplementary military personnel would be forthcoming.[22] His thorough reporting pleased McGeorge Bundy, who wrote to the president that there was "just no comparison with what we used to get from Ambassador Lodge."[23]

Two days later Taylor sent a message to Rusk detailing Westmoreland's request for about two thousand additional people. When added to previous requests, the proposal called for an increase of 4,200 in the advisory and support force. American military personnel in Vietnam would grow from sixteen to twenty-two thousand in the next six to twelve months. Taylor and Westmoreland envisioned doubling the advisory effort in South Vietnamese combat units, as well as a twofold increase in the number of places where U.S. advisers served. The plan also provided more Navy advisers on South Vietnamese vessels, expanded the MACV staff and logistic support activities, and introduced into South Vietnam an Air Force cargo squadron (sixteen aircraft), one Army airplane company (sixteen aircraft), and two Army helicopter companies (fifty aircraft). Taylor supported the proposal without qualification, estimating that the increases would satisfy pacification requirements for the next year.[24]

■

The Joint Chiefs were unable to influence President Johnson's consideration of the Taylor-Westmoreland request in part because Taylor had a direct line to the White House and in part because interservice rivalry prevented them from reaching agreement on the issue in time to affect the decision. According to established procedure, General Westmoreland should have sent the request to the JCS through CINCPAC. Although Ambassador Taylor sent a copy of the proposal to the JCS, he addressed his July 17 telegram to Rusk and McGeorge Bundy.[25] Yet it was the Chiefs' infighting that undercut their influence most. On July 20 McNamara discussed with them the introduction of additional troops into South Vietnam. The Chiefs could not agree on the issue and told McNamara that they wanted time to solicit from Westmoreland a detailed justification for the increase.[26] The next day, however, McNamara met with the president, Rusk, and Bundy for their Tuesday lunch. The proposed increase in the advisory and support effort was the first item on the agenda.[27] The president and his luncheon companions did not wait for the Chiefs' recommendation. After lunch Rusk informed Taylor that "highest authority has approved in principle . . . the requested increase in authorized military strength to approximately 22,000." He told Taylor to ensure that there was "no intentional or accidental release of information on this subject" because the president wanted to withhold public disclosure of the decision.[28] Thus the Joint Chiefs did not produce an assessment of the troop increase until three days after the president had approved it.[29]

In fact, because the Chiefs could not agree on the introduction of the Army airplane and helicopter companies, they did not respond fully to Westmoreland's request for additional Army aircraft until August 4—two days after North Vietnamese patrol boats revolutionized the situation in Vietnam by firing on two American destroyers in the Tonkin Gulf. Wheeler, the newly promoted Gen. Harold K. Johnson, who had replaced Wheeler as Army chief of staff, and McDonald supported the request without qualification. LeMay and Greene, however, did not believe that

Westmoreland's request represented a "potential contribution to the war." They argued that Westmoreland had not identified the need for these units in "specific operational" terms.[30]

The controversy over Army aviation was the principal reason why, for two weeks, the Chiefs were unable to render an opinion on Westmoreland's request for additional air assets. Gen. Bruce Palmer, operations deputy to Army Chief Johnson, recalled that the debate reached "bitter proportions" in the summer of 1964 and often affected discussions on Vietnam. LeMay and Greene questioned the need for more Army aircraft in South Vietnam because they believed that Westmoreland's request represented a surreptitious attempt to expand the Army's air arm.[31]

During one JCS session, as the Chiefs were discussing their response to the proposed increase in Army aviation assets, LeMay suddenly removed his cigar from his mouth, turned toward Johnson, and challenged the Army chief of staff to an aerial duel, shouting, "You fly one of these damned Huey's and I'll fly an F-105 and we'll see who survives. I'll shoot you down and scatter your peashooter all over the goddam [sic] ground." Johnson replied that he would be happy to learn how to fly and "take you on," suggesting that they could decide on a time and place later. He then calmly enjoined his colleague to discuss other matters at hand. The Air Force operations deputy left his seat to attempt to pacify his boss. Wheeler sought peace among his colleagues by recommending that the Chiefs postpone discussion of this controversial matter, without confronting a major operational issue that required speedy resolution.[32]

In fact, the Chiefs never reached a consensus on Westmoreland's request, so Wheeler finally sent a split recommendation to McNamara on August 4, two weeks after the president had decided the issue.[33] The Chiefs' chronic inability to transcend interservice rivalry had, once again, rendered them irrelevant to the policy-making process.

While the Chiefs fought over the services' roles and missions, Taylor was establishing his primacy as a military adviser on Vietnam policy. The OSD bypassed the JCS to solicit Taylor's advice. On July 23, for example, an OSD cable went directly to Saigon to request the ambassador's views on how to bolster the South Vietnamese counterinfiltration effort along the Mekong River.[34] Three days later McNaughton circumvented the Chiefs by sending a tentative list of military options through Forrestal to Taylor and Leonard Unger, ambassador to Laos. Under Rusk's signature, McNaughton and Forrestal recommended air attacks into the Laotian panhandle to "interdict and destroy facilities supporting infiltration into South Vietnam." The strikes, however, would mainly aim to boost morale in South Vietnam and quiet recent South Vietnamese calls for direct action against the North. McNaughton's plan specified the type of aircraft that would conduct the mission, the kind of armaments they would use, and the number of sorties they would fly per day. Although he predicted that some planes "would probably be downed in Laos during attacks on initial targets," losses would be "less than two percent."[35]

It was clear from Taylor's response that he intended to direct military planning from his post in Saigon. He argued that action against targets in the Laotian panhandle was not urgent, and expressed confidence that joint contingency planning with the South Vietnamese military for cross-border operations would mollify General Khanh and discourage future calls for action against the North. Sensitive to President Johnson's election-year concerns, he proposed an alternative to McNaughton's plan that would be more difficult to discern as an escalation of the war. The United States might avoid adverse international opinion if the Air Force conducted attacks under the pretense of "armed reconnaissance," for they had been flying low-level reconnaissance missions over Communist-occupied areas in Laos since May 21. Taylor observed: "In the course of flying reconnaissance missions . . . there would be ample opportunity and excuse to destroy targets such as those" in McNaughton's plan. He asserted that the Saigon embassy was the logical venue for planning such covert raids.[36]

On the same day that Taylor cabled the State Department, the Joint Chiefs of Staff responded to a specific request from President Johnson to develop contingencies for military action in Vietnam. Through Secretary McNamara, Johnson ordered the JCS to consider only those military actions that would:

A.   Contribute militarily to the success of the counterinsurgency effort in the Republic of Vietnam (RVN);

B.   Reduce the frustration and defeatism of the RVN leaders by undertaking punitive measures against the enemy outside the borders of the RVN;

C.   Entail minimum risk of escalatory measures by the enemy; and

D.   Require minimum US participation in a combat role.[37]

The Chiefs replied that "of the many courses of actions [sic] examined, only three fall within the established parameters." These included air strikes against infiltration routes through Laos into South Vietnam, ground operations into Laos against the Communist infiltration effort, and selected air strikes using non-U.S., unmarked aircraft against military targets in North Vietnam. Although these "limited actions . . . could prove militarily and psychologically beneficial to the war effort" in South Vietnam, they "would not significantly affect communist support of Viet Cong operations in South Vietnam and might have counterproductive results in Laos."[38]

McNamara and Johnson had solicited the Joint Chiefs' opinion in such a way as to force them to provide the advice that the president and his advisers wanted to hear. Two of the four objectives enumerated to guide the Chiefs' development of military options (C. and D., above) were "negative" ones. The Chiefs could minimize the risk of escalation and limit the involvement of U.S. forces *only* by *restricting* the application of military power.[39] By stipulating these negative aims, Johnson was able to interpret the JCS memorandum as an endorsement of the sharply limited military actions that the Joint Chiefs had hitherto resisted. Michael Forrestal, now the secretary of state's special assistant for Vietnam, reported that the JCS memo represented "a very significant step forward, since it gives [the Chiefs'] tentative approval to the very kinds of limited actions which we may want to use in the event Hanoi steps things up."[40]

Wheeler's weakness, Taylor's circumvention of the JCS, the Chiefs' infighting, McNamara's restrictions on the military options that the JCS could consider, and the exclusiveness of the Tuesday lunches removed the Chiefs entirely from policy deliberations on Vietnam. Still, Johnson's exclusion of the Chiefs had not gone unnoticed. Senator Goldwater charged Johnson with ignoring his military advisers. Much of the discussion during the July 14 luncheon, at which the president approved Taylor's and Westmoreland's requests, centered on answering Republican charges that the Johnson administration had "weakened the bonds of confidence between civilian leaders and the nation's top military professionals" and "bypassed seasoned military judgment in vital national security issues." McNamara responded that "the bonds of confidence and understanding between this administration's top civilian leaders and the nation's top military leaders has never been stronger." He trumpeted the achievements of EXCOM during the Cuban missile crisis and used quotations from former JCS Chairmen Lemnitzer and Taylor to support his characterization of civil-military relations as harmonious.[41]

They were anything but harmonious. Because Johnson was combining discussions of campaign strategy with Vietnam policy deliberations, he felt he should not include the Chiefs, whose interests and priorities focused on national security issues, in the policy discussions.[42] Johnson, however, did not conceive of Vietnam as primarily a national security issue. Rather, he saw it mainly as the issue that could cost him the election. His principal objective remained keeping Vietnam out of the campaign. Obviously the Chiefs did not conceive of Vietnam in that way, and they were, therefore, useless, and perhaps even threatening, to Johnson's Vietnam policy deliberations.

■

Although the president was preoccupied with the domestic political aspects of Vietnam, the American people persisted in regarding it as a foreign policy issue. Johnson's advisers, therefore, had to justify Vietnam policy decisions made solely on the basis of electoral concerns as having been made in response to the situation and actual American national security interests in Vietnam. Johnson's short-term political interests contradicted long-term planning for an escalation of the war. The president's advisers worried that their election-year rhetoric might make bombing North Vietnam "so unattractive" to the American people that, after the election, they would be unable to implement those plans. William Bundy and Forrestal, who recognized the inconsistency between the administration's stated and actual intentions, suggested how Democratic speakers might talk around the conflicting priorities of getting their president elected and preserving their freedom of action in Vietnam. Speeches were to emphasize that the primary problem existed within the borders of South Vietnam, but state that the administration would "spare no effort" in assisting its Southeast Asian allies. Speakers might downplay the seriousness of the situation in Vietnam by highlighting "the strengths of the South Vietnamese Army," which possessed "superior firepower and mobility." They should emphasize the unique qualities of Ambassador Taylor to create the impression that there existed "a strong possibility" that the situation in South Vietnam would "improve substantially."[43] Speeches, in other words, misrepresented the actual situation in Vietnam to justify the president's reluctance to take military action before the election, while preserving his options to escalate the war after November.

Bundy and Forrestal suggested that speakers couple reassurances that the admnistration was for "peace," with the qualification that future options had not been ruled out. The memo suggested raising the specter of higher American casualties to defend the president's prudent course, but advised that speakers temper their policy defense with a pledge that "preventing Communist domination of South Vietnam is of the highest importance to U.S. national security." Democratic candidates and supporters were to remind the electorate that, if South Vietnam fell, so too would "Burma and India to the west and the Philippines to the east." Speakers were to baffle the electorate with ambiguity and subtle qualification. Bundy and Forrestal concluded with a tribute to Lyndon Johnson's wisdom and patience. They recommended touting the administration's current policy as the most effective way to resolve the conflict "without resort to wider action" and "with the least possible loss of life either by Americans or Vietnamese."

■

Whereas Johnson's closest civilian advisers tried to protect his campaign image as peacemaker, his military advisers were not privy to the election strategy. Wheeler had been chairman of the Joint Chiefs for approximately two weeks when, during a background briefing to Pentagon reporters, someone asked him whether additional American soldiers would be going to Vietnam. He responded that additional advisers would soon embark for Southeast Asia. The July 15 editions of major newspapers gave the story front-page coverage. Although the press remained unaware of the extent of the advisory increase, the *New York Times* announced that "the withdrawals that were set in motion last Christmas when 1,000 of 16,500 men were withdrawn have been reversed."[44]

The general's forthrightness caused considerable consternation among McNamara, McGeorge Bundy, and President Johnson. McNamara offered the excuse that Wheeler was caught off-guard and was unable to "side-step" the question. Bundy was less sympathetic and expressed disbelief that Wheeler did not "hedge long enough" to give the White House staff a "crack at it."[45] Wheeler was expected not only to support the administration's policy, but to keep aspects of it concealed from the American public to bolster Johnson's election bid.

Wheeler's inadvertent revelation of the advisory increase in South Vietnam did not convince the administration to announce the full extent of the reinforcement. McGeorge Bundy reassured the president that the increase was "consistent with our policy of pacification in the South" and was "not the sort of thing that we would gain much from by announcing at the White House." He lamented the missed opportunity to make an earlier statement that would have misled the press and perhaps preempted the Wheeler disclosure. He would have told reporters that "these small numbers of people are connected with the critical provinces and other elements of our May and June decisions."[46] The assistant secretary of state for public affairs set out to control the potentially damaging effects of Wheeler's statement. He cabled Barry Zorthian, Taylor's counselor for public affairs, to suggest that he deceive the press by announcing that the sixteen thousand advisers in Saigon already included the increase that Wheeler had divulged. On July 27 Zorthian, who would later head the Saigon embassy's effort to convince correspondents that the war was being won, responded that the scheme was impractical because the announcement of additional advisers was so recent that the "new personnel could not have arrived by now." Zorthian recommended that the embassy stick to the "actual facts" to "save confusion and embarrassment in the numbers game in the future."[47]

On July 22 press reports from Saigon divulged further the degree to which Johnson was silently deepening American involvement in the Vietnam War. South Vietnamese air commodore Nguyen Cao Ky, perhaps hoping to pressure the American government into further actions against North Vietnam, announced to reporters that his planes had been dropping sabotage teams over the North. His remarks were the first official statement that South Vietnam was conducting military operations directly against North Vietnam.[48] In response to news stories covering Ky's revelation, the president asked McGeorge Bundy for an update on the air drops. On July 24 Bundy informed Johnson that there had been "a total of 8 drops since April 1964 as part of our overall covert plan 34A." He reported that the operations had been only "moderately successful" and the casualty rates "high."[49] The air drops had in fact been an abysmal failure. South Vietnamese soldiers regarded the covert operations as suicide missions. Fearful paratroopers failed to report for duty, and their officers often arrived in drunken stupors so they would be declared unfit for the operation. Those who did parachute into North

Vietnam were often detected by the enemy and never heard from again.[50]

■

Despite the failure of early 34A operations, McNamara remained an enthusiastic advocate of the program. The incursions provided him with an opportunity to test his statistical analysis techniques for tracking and controlling military operations. McNamara believed that covert operations were an ideal method for applying pressure on North Vietnam while minimizing the risk of escalating the war. The object of the covert operations, "maximum pressure with minimum risk," was a military translation of the economist's cost-benefits ratio.[51] Above all, covert operations appealed to McNamara because they allowed him to apply carefully measured pressure against North Vietnam without jeopardizing the president's campaign.

Eager to get on with the operations, McNamara had grown impatient with delays in the Navy's portion of the 34A program—seaborne strikes and raids against North Vietnamese naval and port facilities along the coast. Maritime operations (MAROPS) involved teams of South Vietnamese sailors and saboteurs using small, high-speed motor boats commanded and crewed by U.S. Navy SEALs. Equipped with 40-mm cannons or 81-mm mortars, the boats either shelled their objectives or landed frogmen to plant explosives. After hitting their targets, the teams withdrew to their base in Danang, South Vietnam.[52]

Senior naval officers had raised doubts about the operations. In May, Admiral Sharp noted that he had been "watching this program closely" and had seen some of his "early reservations . . . become a reality." He warned that North Vietnamese defenses against maritime attacks "may be more extensive and effective than originally assessed." McNamara remained undaunted, however, and Taylor and Wheeler supported him. After forcing American-built patrol boats on the advisory team (who believed that the craft were ill suited for these kinds of coastal strikes), McNamara pressed CINCPAC to begin the operations.[53] By the end of May, Americans had trained the South Vietnamese boat crews and sabotage teams and overcome various equipment and mechanical difficulties. Operations in May and June were generally successful. The maritime force captured several North Vietnamese junks and destroyed a storage facility and a bridge near the North Vietnamese port of Hao Mon Dong.[54]

Covert maritime operations became associated with another form of pressuring the Hanoi government, destroyer patrols along the North Vietnamese coast. The Navy had been conducting these DESOTO patrols sporadically since December 1962. MAROPS had increased MACV's requirements for current intelligence on the North Vietnamese coast and, after February 1964, the Navy assisted MACV in gathering photographic and electronic information for use in planning these covert operations.[55]

Probably in response to raids on their coastline, the North Vietnamese had reinforced their motor gunboat forces in the Gulf of Tonkin. On July 22 the Joint Chiefs authorized a July 31 DESOTO patrol to assess North Vietnamese naval capability. Separately, on the night of July 30–31, under orders from General Westmoreland, four of the MAROPS patrol boats departed Danang for targets on the islands of Hon Me and Hon Nieu in the Gulf of Tonkin. After shelling their targets from offshore, the boats returned with four wounded South Vietnamese sailors.[56]

At 3:40 P.M. Saigon time on August 2, the CINCPAC, Admiral Sharp, sent a flash message to Admiral McDonald and the Joint Chiefs. He reported that three torpedo boats had attacked the Navy destroyer *Maddox* in the Gulf of Tonkin. The *Maddox* returned fire. The torpedo boats, "after receiving numerous hits and near misses," closed on the destroyer and "because of [the] volume of fire made an ineffective launch of two torpedoes." Soon aircraft from the USS *Ticonderoga* joined in the engagement. The fire from the American planes and the *Maddox* damaged two of the vessels and left the third dead in the water. CINCPAC ordered the destroyer *Turner Joy* to join the *Maddox*, and the two ships continued patrolling sixteen miles from the North Vietnamese coastline.[57]

■

The president, convinced that the attack was a response to OPLAN 34A operations, decided to downplay the incident.[58] Accordingly the Pentagon issued a statement that did not mention North Vietnam. Later that evening Rusk, in New York for a speaking engagement, trumpeted a familiar election-year theme. When asked about the president's decision to forgo retaliation, he observed that many incidents since 1945 could have led to another world war "if sobriety had not exercised a restraining influence."[59]

Despite the president's desire to demonstrate restraint to the American people, he ordered the resumption of DESOTO patrols and the continuation of covert maritime operations to "show the flag" and convey to Hanoi that the United States did not "intend to back down."[60] After meeting with the president, General Wheeler cabled Admiral Sharp that the destroyers were authorized to continue DESOTO patrols no less than eleven miles from the coast. Wheeler ordered Sharp to take precautionary measures such as providing air protection for the patrols in daylight hours and avoiding "close approaches" to the coast "when maritime activities related to OPLAN 34A" were under way.[61]

Taylor felt that the president's statement that the U.S. intended to continue patrolling the Gulf of Tonkin was insufficiently forceful. In a cable to Secretary Rusk, the ambassador argued that the absence of retaliatory measures would encourage future North Vietnamese attacks and give the South Vietnamese the impression that America "flinches from direct confrontation." He recommended that the president consider the following actions: announce that American forces would attack North Vietnamese patrol boats whenever they were found in international waters; overfly North Vietnamese territory to accomplish regular air surveillance of North Vietnamese naval vessels; mine approaches to the patrol boats' harbors, and enhance the capability of the South Vietnamese Navy to hit targets in the North. In closing, Taylor pressured Rusk for immediate consideration of his recommendations so that he might inform the South Vietnamese government of U.S. intentions.[62]

Taylor's cable was not warmly received. On August 3 George Ball called McNamara to discuss it. Ball thought that Taylor's recommendations were extreme and amounted to a declaration of war. As an alternative Ball recommended that Forrestal work with McNamara's staff in the ISA division to develop some "announceable rules for engagement that would appear fierce." McNamara agreed that Taylor was "over-reacting" and recommended that they simply "ignore" his cable, rather than establish rules of engagement, which "would be a little difficult to announce." He recommended instead that the president make a succinct statement indicating American willingness to "attack and destroy any force that attacks us in international waters."[63]

After his conversation with Ball, McNamara telephoned the president, who took the advice of his most trusted adviser and called an impromptu press conference at the White House.[64] Johnson told reporters that he had instructed the Navy "to issue orders to the commanders of the combat aircraft and the two destroyers, (a) to attack any force which attacks them in international waters, and (b) to attack with the objective not only of driving off the force but of destroying it."[65]

No matter how much presidential authority Taylor carried with him to Saigon, he could not overcome his absence from the center of decision making. In Taylor's absence McNamara gained influence with the president, in part by keeping the ambassador's recommendations away from Johnson's eyes. In place of Taylor's suggested statement, McNamara had Lyndon Johnson make a public declaration that would, in Ball's words, "appear fierce." The president's statement was designed to placate Ambassador Taylor and members of Congress who favored direct retaliation for the Tonkin Gulf incident. McNamara thought it best that the president "lie low." If pressure to take retaliatory action continued to mount, Johnson might consider revealing to the public some of the covert activities already under way against North Vietnam.[66] Taylor, no longer under McNamara's direct influence, might have succumbed to "local" pressures in Vietnam and lost some of his sensitivity to political considerations in Washington.

The change in Taylor's relationship with McNamara and Johnson was significant. In Washington it had been easy for him to share their view of the situation in Vietnam and support their policy. When confronted with the reality of the situation in Vietnam, he revised his assessment of it. He then began to recommend actions that were not in accord with the president's electoral concerns. Rather than reexamine their view of conditions in Vietnam in light of the observations of a trusted member of their circle, McNamara and Johnson were so focused on the election and domestic priorities that they discarded Taylor's opinions and began to see him as a potential adversary rather than an ally.

Rusk cabled Taylor that he, the president, McNamara, and McGeorge Bundy had been "very sensitive" to his recommendations and hoped that Johnson's statement had addressed some of his concerns. Perhaps to keep the ambassador from becoming discouraged, Rusk told Taylor that the "ongoing 34A operations had begun to rattle Hanoi and the Maddox incident is directly related to their effort to resist these activities." He vowed that "we have no intention of yielding to pressure." He then made it clear that Taylor's prior recommendations were no longer open to discussion. At the end of the telegram, he stated plainly that he welcomed

Taylor's comments only on the "Saigon reaction to today's announcement" and on "the political temperature there."[67]

Although a letter he sent to Hanoi referred to the Gulf of Tonkin incident as an "unprovoked attack," President Johnson knew that the
American-planned and -supported raids on North Vietnamese territory
had provoked the naval engagement. To minimize the likelihood of further incidents, Bundy recommended that future DESOTO patrols appear
less directly connected with covert operations.[68] General Wheeler briefed
the president on plans for maritime operations against North Vietnam
scheduled for that night. His briefing must have reassured the president
and his advisers, for the meeting soon ended. Although the president
opposed retaliation, he affirmed his commitment to continuing covert
operations against North Vietnam. His decision was consistent with the
central tenet of the evolving strategic concept for Vietnam: demonstrate
restraint, yet appear steadfast and determined.

Meanwhile the MAROPS unit was preparing for another raid on the
coast of North Vietnam. After midnight on August 3, two PT boats, in
one of the many actions that Assistant Secretary of State William Bundy
described as "inherently small and unimportant," poured 770 rounds of
high-explosive munitions into the North Vietnamese radar facility near
Vinh Son. Another boat illuminated and shelled a security post near the
mouth of the Ron River, leaving it in flames.[69]

■

The president's decision to keep a low profile after the August 2 incident
proved short-lived. At 9:00 A.M. on August 4, Robert McNamara
received an urgent intelligence report based on North Vietnamese radio
transmissions. The report warned that the *Turner Joy* and the *Maddox*,
still on patrol off the coast of North Vietnam, might soon be subjected to
another North Vietnamese attack. The possibility of a second incident
aroused McNamara into a flurry of activity. After reading the message, he
telephoned the president with the news that the *Maddox* was "on the
alert again with the presence of hostile ships reported." Johnson asked
McNamara how long it would take to conduct a bombing raid on North
Vietnam. He then returned to the East Wing dining room to resume his
weekly breakfast meeting with Democratic congressional leaders.[70] No
attack had yet been confirmed.

The president recognized immediately the political desirability of retaliation should a second attack occur. After recounting his conversation with McNamara, he told the legislators that if there was another attack, the United States would have to retaliate. Johnson also communicated his hope that Congress would pass a resolution following retaliatory action to demonstrate the government's solidarity behind both the reprisal and his Vietnam policy in general. The legislators agreed that another incident would virtually require American military action against North Vietnam and they supported the president's idea of a congressional resolution.[71]

Although Johnson's prompt consideration of the possibility of military reprisals may seem inconsistent with his "holding strategy," he was willing to do so in order to win in November. His holding strategy was consistent with poll results showing that two-thirds of the American public paid little attention to the situation in Southeast Asia. A July 1964 poll conducted in Maryland indicated that voters cared little about foreign policy issues in general.[72] As a front-runner in the election, Johnson sought to "stress consensus issues, stay vague on controversial issues, and contrast the opponent's extremism with [his] centrism." Virtually all Americans supported "peace," and Johnson wanted to appear reluctant to order military action without first exhausting all other alternatives. His prudent image contrasted with Goldwater's hawkish stance on national security and military policy.[73]

The possibility of another attack in the Gulf of Tonkin, however, gave Johnson an opportunity for a political master stroke against his chief political adversary. Political analyst John Bartlow Martin observed that Lyndon Johnson not only wanted to win the election, he wanted to win "bigger than anybody had won ever."[74] A one-time strike on North Vietnam would allow Johnson to continue as the candidate for peace while demonstrating that he was neither indecisive nor timid.

After meeting with Democratic legislators, Johnson continued to discuss the possibility of retaliation with Kenneth O'Donnell, a White House assistant who had once been Kennedy's confidant. O'Donnell later recalled that he and Johnson "agreed as politicians that his leadership was being tested and that he must respond decisively." He told Johnson that the president must not allow Goldwater "to accuse him of vacillating or being an indecisive leader."[75] O'Donnell's advice resonated with counsel Johnson had received five months earlier from his trusted friend and mentor, Sen. Richard Russell. In February, Johnson had telephoned the senator to seek advice on Castro's decision to cut off water supplies to the American naval base at Guantanamo Bay. Russell warned Johnson that there was "a slowly increasing feeling in the country that we're not being as harsh and firm in our foreign relations as we should be—that is, we're worried more about our image than our substance." Although Russell believed that people did not "trust Goldwater's judgment," he warned the president that "any demagogue with any strength" could threaten the president's chances for reelection.[76] On the morning of August 4, Johnson was presented with an opportunity to preempt that possibility.

Aware that Johnson wished to retaliate should the North attack the patrolling vessels, McNamara took charge of formulating policy options. While Wheeler hurried back to Washington from New York, McNamara hastily convened an ad hoc planning group including Vance, Lieutenant General Burchinal, and other members of the Joint Staff. McNamara instructed Burchinal to act as liaison between the secretary of defense and Admiral Sharp, CINCPAC. He wanted to know how quickly Sharp could mount a retaliatory strike on North Vietnam. Burchinal told McNamara that the aircraft carrier *Ticonderoga*, which was operating near the North Vietnamese coast, could hit any target north of the demilitarized zone (DMZ) by 6:00 P.M. Washington time (6:00 A.M. Saigon time).[77]

■

After conferring for less than thirty minutes, McNamara received "flash" reports that the North Vietnamese torpedo boats had again attacked the American destroyers. He immediately told Johnson, who replied, "They have? Now, I'll tell you what I want. I not only want those patrol boats that attacked the *Maddox* destroyed, I want everything at that harbor destroyed; I want the whole works destroyed. I want to give them a real dose."[78] McNamara told Johnson that a retaliatory strike could be ready before 6:00 P.M. Shortly thereafter, the White House press office informed the major networks that, in time for the seven o'clock news, the president would appear before the American people to issue a statement of major importance about Vietnam. At the Pentagon naval officers familiar with carrier operations shook their heads in disbelief. Aircraft on the *Ticonderoga* were outfitted with weaponry for air-to-air or air-to-ship combat. It would take hours to reconfigure the aircraft for bombing and longer to brief pilots on their assigned targets. Although no officer challenged Burchinal's assessment directly, one told a McNamara aide: "We'll be lucky to get the order to the fleet in time for the evening news."[79]

McNamara continued to develop options for a retaliatory strike. He described the first four as both "sharp" and "limited." The fifth was designed to place "continuing pressure" on North Vietnam. The five options were:

1. Air strikes against PT boats and their bases.
2. Air strikes against petroleum installations.
3. Air strikes on bridges.
4. Air strikes on prestige targets, such as a steel plant.
[5.] The option for continuing pressure against the North Vietnamese is to mine important ports along their coastline.[80]

The president and his advisers had already planned to meet for their regular Tuesday luncheon, and McNamara wanted to have the options ready for the president before then. McNamara met with Rusk, McGeorge Bundy, Vance, and the Joint Chiefs of Staff (without General Wheeler) in the defense secretary's dining room.[81]

McNamara queried the Chiefs for specific information with which he could develop his own options for retaliation. Bundy and McNamara weighed the relative advantages and disadvantages of either retaliating with a "sharp limited blow" or mining the North Vietnamese coast to place "continuing pressure" on the Hanoi government. At the close of the meeting, McNamara charged the JCS with nominating targets for an immediate reprisal and recommending additional actions for twenty-four, forty-eight, and sixty hours ahead.[82] Leaving the JCS to complete these tasks, McNamara retired to his office with Vance, Bundy, Rusk, and Marshall Green, assistant to William Bundy. In the absence of the Joint Chiefs of Staff, they quickly narrowed the retaliatory options to three:

1. Sharp limited strikes against such target [sic] as PT boats, PT bases, oil depots, etc.
2. Continued pressure, i.e., mining the Vietnam coast.
3. A combination of both.[83]

The five men then left the Pentagon for the White House.

When they arrived, the president was at an NSC meeting. Johnson did not want the Gulf of Tonkin incident discussed in any detail outside the small circle of his closest advisers. He spoke of the incident only briefly at the NSC meeting, explaining that "Secretary McNamara and I are preparing recommendations but these are not yet ready." He warned that he wanted "nothing made public for the time being."[84]

Soon after McNamara arrived at the White House, the JCS, concerned that McNamara know which option they preferred before he met with the president, told General Burchinal to inform him of their recommendation. Although the Chiefs endorsed the general idea of a "sharp limited response option," they recommended a "heavy effort" to establish an "outer parameter" of how far the United States was willing to go should North Vietnam continue to undertake actions hostile to the United States.[85]

After the NSC meeting adjourned, McNamara, Rusk, Bundy, Vance, and Director of Central Intelligence John McCone joined the president for lunch. They determined that the American planned and supported raids on North Vietnamese territory provided the only "rational" explanation for the second attack. They concluded, however, that the covert forays above the seventeenth parallel did not justify attacks on American destroyers in international waters. McNamara laid out maps with possible targets highlighted. Much of the discussion, which lasted for nearly two hours, focused on the political ramifications of retaliation. The president and his advisers pondered retaliatory options in light of likely reactions from Barry Goldwater, Congress, the press, and foreign governments.[86]

Johnson agreed with McNamara's recommendation that the reprisal be both "sharp" and "limited," and rejected the Joint Chiefs' advice that the air strikes establish an "outer parameter" of how far the United States was willing to go. Rusk argued forcefully that the president limit the strikes to patrol boat bases and the Vinh oil refinery and not attack Hanoi, Haiphong, or more general targets. He convinced Johnson that the United States must "leave to the other side responsibility for escalation."[87] The president ordered retaliatory strikes against PT boats located at five North Vietnamese ports and the oil depot at Vinh. McNamara told Johnson that he would "work [the strikes] out carefully with the JCS upon his return to the Pentagon."[88] The president remained anxious for the American planes to strike their targets within the next four hours, in time for the seven o'clock news.

■

McNamara then met with the Chiefs to inform them of the president's decision. The JCS began to draft the order to initiate the strike. As the Chiefs went to work on the order, however, a reevaluation of the events in the Gulf of Tonkin reached the Pentagon. Capt. John Herrick, commander of the destroyer task force, reported that "review of action makes many reported contacts and torpedoes fired appear doubtful. Freak weather effects on radar and overeager sonarmen may have accounted for many reports. No actual visual sightings by *Maddox*. Suggest complete evaluation before any further action taken."[89] McNamara, well on the way to launching the operation against North Vietnam, called Admiral Sharp and asked, "There isn't any possibility that there was no attack, is there?" Sharp replied, "Yes, I would say there is a slight possibility." McNamara asked, "How do we reconcile all this?" Sharp said that he was trying to get further information and recommended that he hold the attack order until "we have a definite indication that this happened." McNamara told Sharp to leave the order in effect and instructed the admiral to call him with an update before six o'clock.[90]

At 4:47 McNamara again met with the JCS to "marshal the evidence to overcome the lack of a clear and convincing showing that an attack on the destroyer had in fact occurred."[91] In response to Sharp's requests for confirmation, Captain Herrick cabled that he was "certain that [the] original ambush was bonafide." He stated that sailors had made sightings of cockpit lights, and that the *Turner Joy* had reported that two torpedoes passed nearby. The JCS and McNamara considered Herrick's report, communications intelligence radio intercepts that the North Vietnamese had shot at two American aircraft and "sacrificed" two of their boats, and Admiral Sharp's personal determination that an attack had indeed occurred as conclusive evidence. Sharp, however, recalled having indicated to McNamara only that the "weight of evidence supported" the conclusion that an attack had occurred. The JCS retransmitted the strike order to CINCPAC at 5:19.[92]

General Wheeler, who had returned to Washington in time for the meeting, accompanied Secretary McNamara to the White House for pro forma consultations with the NSC and congressional leaders.[93] The NSC meeting convened at 6:15 and lasted less than half an hour. McNamara began by stating that "the North Vietnamese PT boats have continued their attacks on the two U.S. destroyers in international waters in the

Gulf of Tonkin." He mentioned that "our efforts to learn the exact situation and protect the patrol have been complicated by a very low ceiling." McCone predicted that the "proposed U.S. reprisals will result in a sharp North Vietnamese reaction, but such action would not represent a deliberate decision to provoke or accept a major escalation in the Vietnamese war." He told Johnson and the NSC that the North Vietnamese were "reacting defensively to our attacks on their off-shore islands" and had responded "out of pride and on the basis of defense considerations."[94] The meeting was aimed at ensuring that everyone was "on board" with the president's decision to retaliate, for the Joint Chiefs of Staff had already issued the strike order. Johnson asked a rhetorical question: "Are we going to react to their shooting at our ships over 40 miles from their shores?" He told his staff and cabinet officials that, as far as he was concerned, the only issue was "the numbers of North Vietnamese targets to be attacked."[95]

The meeting with congressional leaders began moments after the NSC meeting ended. The departure of cabinet officials and White House staffers no doubt gave the congressmen the impression that the president had just completed wide-ranging deliberations. Johnson began by warning that "some of our boys are floating around in the water" and asked that they keep the information about to be revealed in "closest confidence."[96] The congressmen learned of the alleged incident and of the president's plan to retaliate. Rusk articulated the reasoning behind the limited nature of the reprisal. He argued that while the United States must "make it clear that we are not going to run out on Southeast Asia," it also must convey to North Vietnam that its objectives were narrowly defined. Rusk hoped further that the reprisal would not only put an end to attacks on American vessels but also help coerce North Vietnam into desisting from its support for the insurgency in the South. He told Sen. Bourke B. Hickenlooper, the ranking Republican on the Foreign Relations Committee, that "we are trying to get across two points: (1) leave your neighbors alone and (2) if you don't we will have to get busy." Neither McNamara nor anyone else mentioned the uncertainty surrounding the actuality of the attack or the provocative role that 34A operations played in precipitating the reported North Vietnamese action.

Although General Wheeler and the Joint Chiefs of Staff had been on the fringes of the president's deliberations about the reprisal against North Vietnam, and their proposal for a "heavy effort" had been rejected,

Johnson used the chairman of the Joint Chiefs of Staff to lend uniformed credibility to his decisions. He announced that "the Joint Chiefs have gone over it all. General Wheeler is here. I would like him to report on the recommendations of General Taylor in Vietnam." Although Taylor had pressed for action after the first Gulf of Tonkin incident, he played no significant role in the development of plans for the second reported attack. The president had selected an option developed and presented by McNamara based primarily on how retaliatory action would affect his popularity with American voters.

Wheeler was to cast the president's "recommendations" in the light of military expertise and thereby increase their appeal to legislators generally sympathetic to the "military" point of view. Wheeler did not mention that he had already sent the "recommended" course of action to the Pacific Fleet in the form of an order, and he presented McNamara's plan for reprisal as a JCS proposal. After Wheeler summarized the plan, Johnson told the legislators that he "wanted the advice of each of you and wanted to consult with you. We felt we should move with action recommended by the Joint Chiefs, but I wanted to get the Congressional concurrence."

When the ambassador's views were more consistent with the president's than the Joint Chiefs', Johnson used them as a professional military endorsement of his decisions. Indeed, it is significant that Johnson asked the chairman of the Joint Chiefs of Staff, rather than the secretary of state, to report on the recommendations of an ambassador. The president also called his "diplomatic representative" in Saigon "General" Taylor, underlining the degree to which he considered the ambassador a military adviser. Taylor was more willing than the Joint Chiefs to accept substantial restrictions on the application of military power. Although Wheeler did not deliberately distort the Chiefs' views, as Taylor had done previously, he remained silent when the president misrepresented military advice.

After the president read the statement he intended to make to the American people, several of the legislators asked Johnson why he was describing the retaliation as "limited." Republican senator Leverett Saltonstall of Massachusetts commented that "three times in that little statement you use the word 'limited.' Why not use the word 'determined' and let the limitations speak for themselves?" Senate Republican leader Everett M. Dirksen suggested that the president put the "word 'limited' in deep freeze." The president replied that he wanted to communicate to North Vietnam that "we are not going to take it lying down, but we are not going to destroy their cities." Johnson stated clearly that this retaliation would be precedent-setting and provide a model for future action. The president hoped that the air strikes against North Vietnam, which would begin in the next several hours, would "prepare them for the course we will follow."

At the conclusion of the meeting, Johnson told the congressmen that he would soon ask them for a resolution to validate the use of force in Vietnam. The president concluded, "I have told you what I want from you." He then went around the table, asking for the views—and receiving the support— of each member of Congress. House Republican leader Charles A. Halleck assured the president that his resolution would "pass overwhelmingly." Johnson returned to the oval office to prepare for his appearance on national television.

■

When General Wheeler and McNamara returned to the Pentagon, they found that the attack had been delayed. Air crews were working vigorously to reconfigure armaments on the Navy jets, and the aircraft carrier *Constellation* was making its way toward the Gulf of Tonkin at "best speed" to join in the attack. It began to look as if the president's announcement, which had already missed the seven o'clock news, might be delayed until after the eleven o'clock program, which would also mean missing the final deadline for the major East Coast papers. The president grew more impatient with each passing minute. He telephoned McNamara at frequent intervals demanding to know precisely when he could go on the air. By eleven o'clock the president could no longer suppress his anger. He shouted into the phone, "Bob, I'm exposed here! I've got to make my speech right now."[97]

At 11:36 P.M. President Johnson, appearing somber and determined, sat behind his desk in the Oval Office and looked into the television camera. His statement placed the Tonkin Gulf incident in larger context of "the struggle for peace and security in Southeast Asia." He told Americans that "aggression by terror against the peaceful villagers of South Viet-Nam has now been joined by open aggression on the high seas against the United States of America." Johnson described the retaliatory strikes as "limited and fitting" and assured his audience that "we still seek no wider war." The president told Americans that his decision to order military action had been "solemn," but observed that "firmness in the right is indispensable today for peace." In closing, the president promised the people that, under his stewardship, "firmness will always be measured."[98]

One hour and thirty minutes after the president announced the attack, the first planes reached their targets. Naval pilots flew sixty-four sorties against North Vietnamese naval vessels and the oil storage facility at Vinh. They reported hitting thirty-three of thirty-four boats and the near-complete destruction of the oil depot. Two American planes were shot down. Lt. Richard C. Sather was the first naval aviator killed in action over Southeast Asia. Lt. Everett Alvarez Jr. ejected from his shattered aircraft and was captured near the North Vietnamese port of Hon Gay. In extreme pain from a fractured back, Alvarez was moved by his captors to a prison camp in Hanoi, where he was subjected to severe physical and mental abuse for eight and one-half years.[99]

■

After all was quiet in the Gulf of Tonkin, officials in the Johnson administration scrambled to push the president's resolution through Congress. George Ball had been hard at work finalizing the already drafted congressional resolution. The final version stated that "Congress approves and supports the determination of the president, as Commander in Chief, to take all necessary measures to repel any armed attack against the forces of the United States and to prevent further aggression." The resolution went on to describe American interests in Vietnam as "vital," and pledged that the United States was prepared "to take all necessary steps, including the use of armed force," to defend the "freedom" of its allies in Southeast Asia.[100] Rusk coordinated the text with congressional leaders. Ball then began to meet privately with key members of Congress to solicit their support for the resolution.[101]

On August 6 General Wheeler accompanied McNamara and Rusk to a joint session of the Senate Foreign Relations and Armed Services Committees.[102] The three men sat shoulder to shoulder in front of a massive oval table. Rusk and McNamara read prepared statements, and then the senators began to ask questions. The session was amicable until Oregon's Democratic senator Wayne Morse interviewed the three men. He had received a tip from a Pentagon official that the *Maddox* had not been on "routine patrol" but had been gathering intelligence for 34A operations when the incident occurred. The official had also intimated that "there was a hell of a lot of confusion" surrounding the August 4 attack on the *Maddox* and *Turner Joy*.[103] As a result Morse was the only senator to ask tough questions. Addressing Morse's concerns that 34A operations might have provoked the North Vietnamese response, McNamara assured the senators that the U.S. Navy "played absolutely no part in, was not associated with, was not aware of any South Vietnamese actions, if there were any. I want to make that very clear." McNamara went on to state that the *Maddox* "was not informed of, was not aware, had no evidence of and, so far as I know today, has no knowledge of, any possible South Vietnamese actions." Later in the hearing McNamara acknowledged that some shelling of North Vietnamese islands had occurred, but again denied U.S. knowledge of the actions. He also misrepresented the 34A raids as an effort to "patrol" the Vietnamese coast to interdict infiltration into South Vietnam. He described the boat operations as "in a sense pickets or patrols stationed in particular areas carrying out routine surveillance. . . ." After an hour and forty minutes, McNamara, Wheeler, and Rusk completed the Senate hearing and walked to the opposite side of the Capitol to testify before the House Armed Services and Foreign Affairs committees. The second hearing lasted considerably less than an hour.[104] The resolution passed the Senate and House committees without difficulty.

McNamara had done well for the president. Morse's questions about the role of 34A operations and the verity of the second attack attracted little attention. The defense secretary successfully misled the senators and representatives by misrepresenting America's role in the 34A attacks and by glossing over the confusion surrounding the August 4 incident.[105] At five o'clock in the afternoon, McNamara held a press conference in the Pentagon. When asked whether he knew of any incidents involving South Vietnamese vessels and North Vietnam, he replied, "No, none that I know of. . . . They operate on their own. They are part of the South Vietnamese Navy . . . operating in the coastal waters, inspecting suspicious incoming junks, seeking to deter and prevent the infiltration of both men and material." A reporter pressed him, "Do these junks go North, into North Vietnamese waters?" McNamara responded, "They have advanced closer and closer to the 17th parallel, and in some cases I think have moved beyond that in an effort to stop the infiltration closer to the point of origin."[106] It was a fitting end to a day of cunning responses to questions from reporters and legislators. [107]

■

McNamara dominated the responses to congressional questions during the August 6 hearings. Wheeler answered several technical questions, but McNamara responded quickly to those questions that were not directed toward a specific person.[108] Although Wheeler did not make any false statements to the senators or congressmen, by not revealing the truth he showed the president that he would go along with his and McNamara's attempts to mislead Congress and the American people. Military officers were not in the habit of challenging publicly and directly statements from their civilian bosses. Wheeler may have felt that expediency as well as loyalty justified his silence, while the defense secretary avoided or misrepresented the truth. The general, who had warned Westmoreland that the war in Vietnam could be lost in Congress, was reluctant to give the legislators information that could undermine the administration's commitment to South Vietnam.

Sitting silently next to McNamara, Wheeler, dressed in his uniform, the light from the Capitol's crystal chandeliers reflecting off his brass insignia, lent indispensable credibility to his defense secretary's remarks. Congressional faith in the integrity of the military was based, in part, on the expectation that JCS views and recommendations were independent of partisan political concerns and based solely on officers' experience and evaluation of the military aspects of the situation. Johnson and his advisers predicated the Gulf of Tonkin reprisal, however, on domestic political concerns and their election-year campaign strategy, hiding the true basis of their decisions behind the impression that they were simply supporting recommendations made by the Joint Chiefs of Staff. Wheeler's attendance at McNamara's side and his tacit support of the defense secretary's effort to obscure the nature of American military policy in Vietnam served as Wheeler's trial by fire. Although his influence as a military adviser was low, Wheeler had become a valuable "shield" to protect the administration from attacks on its decisions regarding Vietnam.

Although the second attack was not deliberately faked, domestic political considerations connected with the election impelled Johnson and McNamara to seize on uncertain circumstances as sufficient provocation for a retaliatory strike. Indeed, it soon became apparent that the retaliation against North Vietnam after the Gulf of Tonkin incidents was a political coup for the president. He received a surge of support in the polls. The decision to strike North Vietnam and the overwhelming passage of the Gulf of Tonkin resolution defused Goldwater's charges that LBJ had not been firm enough in matters of foreign policy.[109] William Bundy recalled that, after the air strikes on North Vietnam, a "feeling of satisfaction" pervaded the administration.[110] On August 10 Johnson met in the Cabinet Room with Wheeler, McNamara, Rusk, Vance, Ball, McCone, and McGeorge Bundy. He recognized the "instrumental" role of the secretaries of state and defense in securing such favorable responses from Congress and, "judging from the polls," from the American people.[111] Although Johnson did not mention him, General Wheeler deserved much of the credit for gathering support for the resolution by adding credibility to McNamara's and Rusk's testimony.

7
Contriving Consensus
August–September 1964

There have been no divisions in this government. We may
have been wrong but we have not been divided.

—LYNDON B. JOHNSON, 1967[1]

The period of self-congratulation after the air strikes was short-lived.
The taking of direct American action against North Vietnam forced
the president and his advisers to ponder their next moves. In Saigon the
Gulf of Tonkin reprisals raised hopes among some of the people that the
retaliatory raids were the beginning of a sustained campaign against their
adversaries north of the seventeenth parallel, and that direct U.S.
involvement would resolve their ten-year struggle with Hanoi and the
Viet Cong. In less than one week, however, it was apparent to all that the
United States would not undertake a sustained military campaign. Rising
expectations among the South Vietnamese gave way to dashed hopes and
heightened discontent.[2]

Although President Johnson took care to characterize the attack on
North Vietnam as "limited and fitting" and had assured the American
electorate that his administration sought "no wider war," others within

the administration, most notably the Joint Chiefs of Staff and Ambassador Taylor, wanted to keep the pressure on the Hanoi government. The JCS and Taylor regarded August 4 as a turning point in U.S. policy on direct action against North Vietnam, although they disagreed about both the form and the intensity of the operations following the reprisals.[3]

The American response to the Gulf of Tonkin incident had used up many of McNamara's plans for Vietnam, leading Lyndon Johnson and his advisers to consider future actions. In May, McNamara, McGeorge Bundy, and Rusk recommended that the president agree in principle to "use selected and carefully graduated military force against North Vietnam." The May memo called for a congressional resolution approving that plan and an "initial strike" against the North, "to have more deterrent than destructive impact." Based on the belief that "a pound of threat is worth an ounce of action," they asked the president to approve the deployment of American forces toward Southeast Asia to "maximize their deterrent impact and their menace." By mid-August he had acted on most of their recommendations. The initial strike occurred on August 4, the president got his congressional resolution on August 10, and on August 5 Secretary McNamara announced that the following military deployments were under way:

- transfer of an attack carrier group from the Pacific coast to the Western Pacific;
- movement of interceptor and fighter-bomber aircraft into South Vietnam [36 B-57's and 12 F-102's];
- movement of fighter-bomber aircraft into Thailand;
- transfer of interceptor and fighter-bomber squadrons from the United States to advance bases in the Pacific;
- movement of an antisubmarine force into the South China Sea;
- the alerting and readying for movement of selected Army and Marine forces.[4]

It was unclear when Johnson would approve additional actions in support of the central recommendation of the May memorandum: the gradual application of additional military pressures on North Vietnam.

Deliberations about Vietnam, conducted in the middle of a presidential campaign, solidified two critical assumptions: first, that the principal difficulty in South Vietnam stemmed from North Vietnam's support for the Viet Cong; and second, that the gradual application of military and diplomatic pressures on the Hanoi government would persuade North Vietnam's leaders to terminate that support. The period surrounding the 1964 presidential election also marked a subtle but significant shift in the nature of the advisory relationship between the Joint Chiefs of Staff and top policy makers in the Johnson administration. The Chiefs, still unable to reconcile their own differences, dropped their fundamental objections to McNamara's conception of the war, focusing instead on removing limits to the level of force and restrictions on its use. Taylor joined his former colleagues in urging direct American military action against North Vietnam.

■

Taylor's perspective on Vietnam had changed with his assignment as ambassador. Now exposed daily to the frustrations of organizing a counterinsurgency effort against an elusive and determined enemy, he began to view with sympathy the South Vietnamese government's calls for action against the North. General Khanh, who had come to believe that Communists in South Vietnam were no less than the "arms of the enemy monster"—and that the monster's "head was in Hanoi"—argued for the decapitation of his enemy. He wanted the United States and South Vietnam to "open the war up" with a decisive campaign to secure the objective of "total victory in order to liberate all the national territory."[5] Washington, however, was not going to let Saigon dictate the scope and tempo of the war.

Taylor's sympathy with Khanh's frustration put the ambassador at odds with Rusk and others in Washington. Although Taylor did not share Khanh's enthusiasm for immediate air strikes against the North, he advocated other military measures, such as the continuation of covert maritime strikes against North Vietnam and naval and air patrols in the Gulf of Tonkin to keep "pressure on North Vietnam" and "signal" American resolve. He suggested more permissive rules of engagement, allowing air and sea patrols to fire on enemy boats and aircraft. He warned that if the United States resisted "mounting pressures from the [South Vietnamese government] to win the war by direct attack on Hanoi," the South Vietnamese might pursue a negotiated settlement or an independent "military adventure" against North Vietnam. To placate the Saigon government, Taylor recommended that the United States apply limited pressure on the North immediately and prepare to implement a bombing campaign after January 1, 1965.[6]

Johnson, however, remained reluctant to take any action that might bring Vietnam once again to the forefront of public attention. The Democratic National Convention would begin on August 24, and the election campaign, combined with his domestic legislative agenda, dominated the president's attention. On August 10, less than an hour after he signed into law the Gulf of Tonkin resolution, the president charged his advisers with developing a plan of action for Vietnam that would allow the United States to retain the initiative gained during the Gulf of Tonkin reprisals "with maximum results and minimum danger." McGeorge Bundy whispered to Ray Cline, deputy director for intelligence at the CIA, "We know we're not going to do a goddamn thing while this goddamn election is going on." Rusk instructed Taylor to keep "General Khanh as far as possible on the same track as ourselves regarding possible action against [the] North."[7] The task of developing a Vietnam policy that would minimize dangers to the president's prospects for election fell to the man Johnson called "that other Bundy."

■

William Putnam Bundy had impeccable academic, professional, and social credentials. After receiving his law degree from Harvard in 1947, he entered the prestigious Washington law firm of Covington & Burling. Three years later, he joined the CIA as an intelligence analyst. Bundy was Dean Acheson's son-in-law, and, like his brother, was well connected within the Democratic establishment. Many thought that he would eventually rise to be director of central intelligence. In 1961, however, Bundy moved to the Defense Department as deputy assistant secretary of defense for international security affairs (ISA). When the head of ISA, Paul Nitze, became secretary of the Navy, Bundy succeeded him. Bundy liked working with McNamara and, in 1964, when he was named to replace Roger Hilsman as assistant secretary of state for Far Eastern affairs, he reluctantly left the Defense Department.[8]

It was from his desk in the State Department, however, that Bundy left his imprint on the American experience in Vietnam. He undertook to reconcile calls for further action against North Vietnam with the president's mandate that these actions present "minimum danger." McNamara recalled that the memorandum Bundy completed in mid-August 1964 set the agenda for policy deliberation and "became the focus of our attention" until January 1965.[9]

Despite his limited experience in the planning and application of military force, Bundy had confidence in his analytical ability. He found it unnecessary to consult the Joint Chiefs of Staff but coordinated his effort closely with McNamara and Rusk. Bundy's charge was to get the administration through the election with a "possible set of actions" that would "help morale in South Vietnam, put some pressure on North Vietnam, and yet present minimum risks of the war becoming more serious."[10]

The JCS, meanwhile, tried to answer the questions that Johnson posed to General Wheeler during the August 10 meeting. Wheeler and his colleagues focused on the following items:

1. What, if any, actions should be undertaken in the Laos Panhandle?
2. Should the tempo of Operations Plan 34A operations be increased?
3. Should we initiate a tit for tat program of retaliation, or should we do something more, against North Vietnam? If so, what and when?

Still encumbered by the need to forge consensus, the Chiefs, before submitting a response, were unable to complete this "major exercise" by the time Bundy circulated his draft policy paper. The senior military advisers, rather than examining the issue on their own terms, found themselves in the familiar position of responding to a paper that carried the weight of an agreed position between the secretaries of defense and state.[11]

Bundy called for a "short holding phase" of ten days to two weeks, during which the United States would avoid any actions that might divert international attention from North Vietnam's provocation in the Gulf of Tonkin. After this period of "military silence," American and South Vietnamese forces would undertake a program of "limited pressures" against the North Vietnamese government from September through December 1964. These pressures might include an intensification and overt acknowledgment of 34A operations, leaked information revealing joint U.S.–South Vietnamese planning for cross-border operations against North Vietnam and into Cambodia and Laos, intensified training of South Vietnamese pilots on jet aircraft, limited cross-border operations into Laos, the resumption of naval patrols in the Gulf of Tonkin, "tit for tat" retaliations for Viet Cong "dirty tricks," and the withdrawal of American dependents. Bundy recommended that the sequence be "played somewhat by ear, with the aim of producing a slightly increased tempo but one that does not commit us prematurely to even stronger actions." Although Bundy acknowledged that his scheme did not comprise a "truly coherent program of strong enough pressure," he expressed hope that the "pretty high noise level" might threaten North Vietnam with the possibility of "systematic military action" in the future. He recommended that the administration adopt General Taylor's contingency date of January 1, 1965, for direct American military action against North Vietnam.[12]

■

Although reluctant to accept the implicit objective behind Bundy's "limited pressures" against the North, the JCS offered no alternative plan. Bundy's program aimed to send a "signal" of resolve to the "Communists" and boost the morale of the South Vietnamese while minimizing the possibility of escalation before the November election. The Chiefs restated the position they had espoused consistently since January 22, 1964: Military action against North Vietnam should instead aim to destroy the Hanoi government's "will and capability" to continue support for the insurgency in South Vietnam. Caught without their own program for military action against North Vietnam, however, the Chiefs chose neither to challenge Bundy's concept of "limited actions" nor to question the wisdom of pursuing the short-term objective of "holding on" in South Vietnam until the New Year. They argued against the "holding strategy," only with the ambiguous observation that the "sudden advantage" gained in the wake of the Gulf of Tonkin incident "must be retained" through the application of "more serious pressures" against North Vietnam "as necessary." On August 14 the Chiefs informed McNamara that they would develop more detailed recommendations on military action as rapidly as possible.[13]

Sharp disagreements among the Chiefs over the nature of the problem in Vietnam and the type of military action necessary to improve the situation delayed the drafting of any response until August 26. Army Chief of Staff Johnson recalled that although there was general agreement among the Chiefs that the situation in Vietnam required some action, the services possessed a "wide variety of views" on what those actions should entail.[14] Differences of opinion among the Chiefs stemmed, in part, from their institutional perspectives as heads of their services. It seemed that each of the services, rather than attempt to determine the true nature of the war and source of the insurgency in South Vietnam, assumed that it alone had the capacity to win the war. The Air Force believed that bombing North Vietnam and interdicting infiltration routes could solve the problem of the insurgency in the South. Trained in the fluid application of destructive force, Air Force planners gave little thought to the more complex difficulties of pacifying the countryside and establishing South Vietnamese governmental control and security on the ground. The Army, whose mission would entail the introduction of ground troops, thought that the problem in South Vietnam was only partially connected with North Vietnam's support for the insurgency; it planned to pacify the countryside by means of political action and military security. The Army viewed increased American involvement in Vietnam in the context of a protracted commitment of ground forces, and believed that bombing the North might intensify the war in the South.

Since February General LeMay had pressed for the use of American air power against North Vietnam,[15] arguing that the Gulf of Tonkin retaliation should serve as a starting point for sustained air strikes which would destroy all ninety-four targets on the JCS list. On August 17 LeMay sent General Wheeler a study conducted by the RAND Corporation, whose thesis was that "the total commitment of Hanoi to the success of the insurgency is the key to the strength of the Viet Cong." The study argued that Hanoi provided the Viet Cong with leadership, a sophisticated political-military apparatus, a compelling ideological theme, and a secure military base. LeMay tried to use the study to persuade his colleagues on the Joint Chiefs that action against the North was necessary to defeat the insurgency in the South. Air power, he contended, offered the "best chance of success,"[16] and could win the war without the introduction of Army troops or Marines into South Vietnam.[17]

LeMay persuaded General Greene, commandant of the Marine Corps, to join him in urging action against the North. Greene, however, continued to advocate bombing as only the first step in a larger program that included the introduction of large numbers of Marines into South Vietnam to establish secure "enclaves" along the coast. The Marine Corps had been planning such a deployment of ground forces to the South Vietnamese coastal city of Danang since the Gulf of Tonkin incident. In August a Marine brigade commander conducted a reconnaissance of the port facility and the terrain surrounding the city.[18] Marine units established communications and combat outposts some thirty miles inland from the coast, just south of the DMZ.[19]

While Greene was aggressively seeking a wider role in the war for the Marine Corps, the Army chief of staff disapproved of a wider American role in the war. Harold Johnson viewed his JCS colleagues with suspicion. He harbored deep reservations concerning Air Force and Marine Corps views on how to wage war. He felt that the Marine Corps "head down and charge" mentality often led to ill-considered actions and excessive casualties. He thought that the Marine Corps should be kept "lean and mean and fairly small," and its mission limited to seizing advanced naval bases. Johnson's experience during the Korean War and his work on a committee charged with delineating the roles and missions of each service made him resentful of claims concerning the capabilities of air power.[20]

Although he was predisposed to conflict with his colleagues, Johnson proved more acquiescent with his civilian bosses. A survivor of the Bataan Death March in World War II, Johnson had endured three and a half years in a Japanese prison camp and when rescued at war's end weighed just ninety pounds. That harrowing experience had rekindled in him the deep religious faith of his rural South Dakota boyhood. Spiritual fortitude and a profound sense of loyalty led him to accept conditions outside his direct personal control and to work as best he could within the constraints of a difficult situation rather than confront directly the source of adversity. He therefore did not object to but reluctantly accepted wider American involvement in South Vietnam. Indeed, none of the Chiefs individually objected to William Bundy's policy of holding South Vietnam by applying limited pressure on the North.

■

The JCS still had not agreed on its position by August 18, when Ambassador Taylor sent his assessment of the Bundy memo to Rusk at the State Department. Taylor argued that American short-term objectives should be to "buy time" for the South Vietnamese government and "increase the morale" of the people while holding North Vietnam "in check." Long-term planning should continue to focus on "a deliberate escalation of pressure against North Viet Nam" to begin after January 1. He recommended a program consistent with Bundy's "limited pressures," which he termed "Course of Action A." The program would include the resumption of 34A operations and DESOTO patrols, U-2 surveillance flights over all of North Vietnam, and the initiation of air strikes and South Vietnamese ground raids in Laos to counter North Vietnamese infiltration. Taylor argued that, before progressing beyond these small pressures, the United States should "raise the level of precautionary military readiness" and introduce American air defense and Marine infantry units into South Vietnam to protect against possible North Vietnamese retaliation. After these deployments, the United States would initiate a "carefully orchestrated bombing attack" on military targets in North Vietnam. In case the situation in South Vietnam became far more urgent than anticipated, Taylor developed an accelerated program of "punitive action," Course of Action B, that would boost morale in South Vietnam and help hold the Saigon government together.[21]

Taylor's memorandum revealed the beginning of a significant shift in the administration's thinking about military action against the North. Previously Lyndon Johnson's principal advisers viewed instability in the Saigon government as a reason to delay or forgo action against North Vietnam. In the late summer of 1964, they began to consider air strikes as a method for enhancing the stability of that government. When he first departed for Saigon, Taylor had promised President Johnson that he would return periodically to Washington for deliberations on Vietnam. Now Taylor's impending visit, combined with a grim assessment of the situation from General Westmoreland, spurred the Chiefs into replying in detail to William Bundy's "holding strategy."

The Chiefs' deliberations between August 26 and September 8 reflected deep divisions about what course of action to recommend for Vietnam. How they chose to reconcile those differences established a pattern of advice that would continue through July 1965.

■

On August 26, while General Wheeler was on leave, General LeMay—the senior chief present—chaired the JCS meeting. Although LeMay and his colleagues remained unable to agree, the Air Force chief of staff was determined to produce a paper that was generally consistent with his view of the military action needed in Vietnam. Using General Westmoreland's recent assessment of a "distinct possibility of progressive deterioration in South Vietnam," LeMay urged the immediate adoption of Taylor's Course of Action B.[22]

LeMay emphasized the Chiefs' common belief that the expansion of Communism in Asia represented a serious threat to America's global political interests. In the aftermath of the Bay of Pigs, President Kennedy and Taylor had urged the Chiefs to consider national political interests when deliberating on the use of force. As chairman of the Joint Chiefs, Taylor exhorted his staff to consider matters in broad political context "through the eyes of the President." At the end of August 1964, the Chiefs began to take that advice to heart. LeMay warned his colleagues that there was simply "too much at stake" to let their differences prevent military action against North Vietnam. Vietnam was a test case for defeating Communist insurgencies. The United States could lose its position in Asia and, as it suffered a blow to its prestige and credibility with other nations, the Communist movement would gain momentum worldwide. Communism, like Hitler after the Munich Agreement in 1938, would become emboldened and continue to expand until the United States and its closest allies in Europe became the last bastions of freedom in the world.[23] Munich taught that the United States had to demonstrate an unyielding determination to protect non-communist governments from communist aggression.

The Chiefs did not question, as they had in the period from March to July 1964, the assumption that sharply limited military action against North Vietnam would reverse the deteriorating situation. Instead they expressed a willingness to go along with Taylor's Course of Action B and hope for permission to pursue more resolute military measures in the future. Because they favored more immediate military action than the postelection application of pressure called for in Course of Action A, they stated that Course of Action B was "more in accord" with their thinking and ought to be approved immediately "to prevent a complete collapse of the US position in Southeast Asia."[24]

While accepting for the moment Taylor's recommendation that initial strikes against the North be sharply limited, the Chiefs intimated that in the future, they would recommend removing limitations on the use of force. They thought that Course of Action B would not be "decisive" and suggested that the United States might have to take "more direct and forceful action," such as aerial mining of Haiphong Harbor, cross-border operations into Laos, "hot pursuit" into Cambodia, and U.S. aerial "reconnaissance" to attack Viet Cong bases outside South Vietnam. The Chiefs observed that these actions would "probably not in themselves accomplish our objective of compelling [North Vietnam] to respond favorably," but advocated their "adoption and implementation at once."[25] Although they voiced skepticism about the effectiveness of limited military actions, the Chiefs neglected to provide an estimate of what level of force would ultimately be required. Instead they sought an open-ended commitment from the secretary of defense and the president to increase the level of military effort when, as they clearly predicted, the limited measures failed.

The Chiefs' inability to formulate a specific proposal or estimate of the situation left the initiative for planning with the proponents of graduated pressure. Far from registering dissatisfaction with the ambiguity of the Chiefs' memo, however, McNamara seemed delighted with it. The JCS had given John McNaughton, McNamara's principal planner for Vietnam, the data he needed to continue developing courses of action. McNaughton was particularly pleased with an appendix to the memo that contained a revised list of ninety-four targets, along with ordnance and fuel requirements for hitting each target, aircraft availability and capability, and the number of sorties required. McNaughton lauded the hard work that had gone into the development of the target list and recommended that McNamara congratulate the Chiefs on what seemed to McNaughton to be "first rate studies of the 94 targets."[26]

Thus in August 1964 the JCS served more as technicians for planners in the OSD than as strategic thinkers and advisers in their own right. When McNaughton and William Bundy needed more information to develop their courses of action, they sent requests for data to the Chiefs through the secretary of defense. McNaughton asked if sufficient stocks of ordnance and fuel existed to carry out air strikes, and what effect bombing was likely to have on the capabilities of North Vietnam to sustain the insurgencies in Laos and South Vietnam. He also asked the Chiefs whether North Vietnam might respond to bombing by escalating the war on the ground using North Vietnamese regular forces.[27] While the Joint Staff categorized targets and determined the numbers of bombs and gallons of fuel required to hit them, the JCS left the development of strategic options to attorneys McNaughton and Bundy.

The JCS proved adept at providing technical information, but remained unable to respond to questions that had broad policy implications, the principal obstacle remaining the debate over the effectiveness of air power as a solution to the problem in Vietnam. On September 4 the Chiefs met to draft answers to McNaughton's questions. General Johnson demanded that the Chiefs remove a sentence in the memo asserting that air power offered the "best chance of success" in Vietnam and replace it with a sentence that described the proposed bombing of North Vietnam as merely one of the "essential elements" of a more comprehensive strategy. Johnson believed that Greene and LeMay had misdiagnosed the nature of the war itself; they thought that North Vietnam caused the war, whereas Johnson asserted that the insurgency in the South was essentially indigenous. Johnson predicted that the war "would continue at its present or increased intensity even if North Vietnam were completely destroyed." LeMay urged the Chiefs to press immediately for the destruction of the ninety-four North Vietnamese targets on their list, while Johnson insisted that any JCS recommendation state prominently that the war would ultimately be won or lost "in South Vietnam and along its frontiers." The JCS agreed to take offensive action to destroy all Viet Cong and Pathet Lao supply depots, staging areas, and way stations on the Ho Chi Minh Trail complex to stop the infiltration of men and materiél into Laos and South Vietnam. However, Johnson believed that a series of ground offensives into Laos would interdict supplies most effectively, whereas LeMay believed that air attack would work best. General Greene supported LeMay. Admiral McDonald—although sharing a degree of Johnson's skepticism about the effectiveness of aerial interdiction, and concerned that military action alone would do little to enhance political stability in South Vietnam—remained equivocal.[28]

Johnson also feared that bombing North Vietnam would lead to an escalation of the war. He was consequently more willing than his Marine Corps and Air Force colleagues to accept limitations on a bombing campaign. He disputed LeMay's and Greene's assessment that the "hard knock" would not provoke a response on the ground from North Vietnam and China, arguing that, if more moderate pressures did not dissuade the Hanoi government from supporting the Viet Cong, it was "illogical to conclude that . . . more severe pressures would have any other effect than to increase and intensify the insurgency in the South."[29]

Escalation did not worry LeMay, who firmly believed that air strikes against North Vietnam "had every prospect for success" and "entailed far less risk" than continuing on the present course. He thought that an air campaign against North Vietnam would actually lessen or remove altogether the possibility that U.S. ground forces would be needed in South Vietnam. If it showed a willingness to apply overwhelming destructive force, the United States could prevent Chinese Communist intervention. According to LeMay, only the introduction of American ground combat units into South Vietnam could provoke a Chinese response. Thus the Chiefs were at an impasse. They decided to adopt the draft JCS paper, which did not address strategy, as an informal "talking paper" for discussion with the secretary of defense and Ambassador Taylor on September 8.[30] They also decided to smooth over their differences: The talking paper incorporated elements of LeMay's and Johnson's positions without reconciling them. Instead of a coherent strategy for the war, the Chiefs recommended unconnected proposals for air operations against North Vietnam, air and ground operations into Cambodia and Laos, and intensified ground operations within South Vietnam—and attached them as appendixes to the talking paper. Because they chose not to air their differences in front of McNamara, General Johnson's reservations about the limited effects and dangers of using air power against North Vietnam never reached the secretary of defense.[31]

Johnson's failure to speak up may have stemmed from the tentativeness of his position as a new Chief appointed over thirty-two of his seniors, and from his strong belief that the United States had to confront the expansion of Communism. Later he recalled being "overwhelmed" early in his tenure as Army chief of staff, fearing that he did not have the stature, background, breadth of experience, web of contacts, or ease of relations with prominent individuals to succeed in that position.[32] The assertive LeMay, who had achieved great celebrity in World War II, did not lack self-confidence. Although Johnson ensured that the August 26 memo and the appendixes to the September 7 talking paper included plans for bolstering the pacification program, he did not include his warnings that an air campaign was likely to be ineffective and lead to an intensified war on the ground. In contrast to the bold LeMay, Johnson's strength was perseverance and his inclination was to compromise.

Despite his objection to the emphasis on air power, Johnson felt that something had to be done to stop Communist expansion in Southeast Asia. In Saigon, Ambassador Taylor was coming to the same conclusion.

■

Before he arrived in Washington, Taylor sent a cable recommending that the United States "accept the fact" that a stable government in South Vietnam was "unattainable" and recognize that there was "no George Washington in sight" to assume the leadership of the South Vietnamese people. Taylor thought that the United States should accept greater responsibility for the fight against the Viet Cong because the South Vietnamese government was so weak. He suggested that strikes against North Vietnam would help "hold South Vietnam together" and "create conditions required for a [negotiated] settlement on favorable terms." To attain domestic and international approval, the United States would, ideally, initiate attacks in response to a North Vietnamese act similar to the Gulf of Tonkin incident. According to Taylor, air strikes "would be orchestrated . . . to produce mounting pressure on the will of Hanoi" that would result in North Vietnam "calling off the insurgencies in South Vietnam and Laos." In closing Taylor recommended that the United States "take the offensive and play for the international breaks."[33]

Although the ambassador's observations in Saigon had led him to believe that military action against the North could no longer await a stable government in the South, his reacquaintance with Washington election-year priorities led him to reconsider. His recent recommendations that the United States undertake military action against North Vietnam without a stable political "base" in South Vietnam caused concern in Washington. With the election looming, the president was anxious to forge a consensus behind William Bundy's holding strategy. Action consistent with Taylor's recommendation might deepen American involvement in Vietnam before November. On September 7 and 8 Taylor met with Rusk, McNamara, Wheeler, the Bundy brothers, and Assistant Secretary of State for Public Affairs Robert Manning, and they sharply debated the timing of a bombing campaign against North Vietnam. After a meeting with the president on September 8, however, Taylor agreed to support William Bundy's program of "limited pressures." On September 8 McGeorge Bundy reported to President Johnson that the advisers in Washington had worked out a "consensus" with Taylor.[34] They secured the ambassador's support until the November election for the holding policy that William Bundy and McNaughton had already developed, however, without actually reconciling Taylor's opinions with their own.

To help the president justify the delay in action against North Vietnam, Taylor had to contrive an assessment of the South Vietnamese government that was more optimistic than the one contained in his report two days earlier. The delay ostensibly permitted "thickening the fabric of the Khanh government in the next two months," a task that Taylor had described as virtually impossible. William Bundy wrote a sanguine memo stating that the Khanh government "will probably stay in control and may make some head-way in the next 2–3 months." He went on to recommend that the military undertake some limited activities to guard against the perception that the United States and South Vietnam were "simply sitting back" in the months prior to the election. Naval patrols in the Gulf of Tonkin and covert 34A operations against North Vietnam should continue. In addition, the U.S. would plan and support initial South Vietnamese air and ground operations into the corridor areas of Laos, and prepare to respond on a "tit for tat" basis against North Vietnam in case of an attack on U.S. units.[35]

The president met with his advisers on September 9, not to examine options but to receive the consensus position. Despite McNaughton's assurance that the Chiefs' August 26 memorandum would get careful attention, their assessment of the situation in Vietnam had been "rejected outright" at the beginning of the September 7 meeting between McNamara, Taylor, Rusk, Wheeler, and others.[36] McNamara used the ambiguity in the language of the Chiefs' recommendations to obscure their opposition to the limitations contained in Bundy's memorandum. The defense secretary told the president that the objective and actions in Bundy's memo "with minor adjustments, had the approval of the Joint Chiefs." McNamara and Wheeler did inform the president that Generals Greene and LeMay "believed that it was now necessary . . . to execute extensive U.S. air strikes against North Vietnam"; Wheeler went on to say, however, that he, General Johnson, and Admiral McDonald agreed with Ambassador Taylor, "the man on the spot," that it was unwise to strain the weak South Vietnamese government by taking direct action against the North.[37] This was not Taylor's original assessment based on his observations in Vietnam, but the new position he had adopted to placate the president.

■

The meeting on September 9 revealed the degree to which Taylor's appointment as ambassador had weakened the influence of the Joint Chiefs of Staff in the formulation of military policy toward Vietnam. In Taylor the president had someone who could combine the credibility of distinguished, publicly recognized military experience with support for the president's domestic political concerns. LBJ could count on Taylor's recommendations to take advantage of the Joint Chiefs' split position on Vietnam because JCS Chairman Earle Wheeler, Taylor's protégé, was willing to defer to Taylor's judgment. Years afterward McNamara included Taylor among the president's "military advisors" who were "deeply divided."[38] Johnson and McNamara did not explore the reasons behind the disagreements among the Chiefs but noted the lack of a united opinion.

Johnson conveyed the impression to his advisers that he had made a decision consistent with Taylor's counsel. He asked Taylor to explain further his "unreadiness to recommend larger action." Taylor spoke the opposite of what he had written from Saigon, saying that "there was a real possibility, at the optimistic end of the spectrum" that General Khanh would gain "more true support in the country as a whole." After Taylor warned that "on balance . . . the government was in a more uncertain condition than before," LBJ pressed him for some final words of optimism. The president told Taylor that "what disheartens me is that we had our best team out there for sixty days and have lost ground." Taylor objected that the president might have the wrong impression. He argued that "in the field" he and General Westmoreland were "doing better," there was "real strengthening of the pacification effort," and the "tactics and performance" of the South Vietnamese Armed Forces were improving. He stated that the overall program in half the provinces was "going well" and that "progress was being made at the grass roots." Johnson asked if anyone in the room objected to the consensus position contained in William Bundy's memo of September 8. All reassured him of their support.[39]

Taylor then testified before Congress. When Senator Morse questioned the events surrounding the Gulf of Tonkin incident, Taylor gave misleading answers. When asked about the role of 34A operations in provoking the North Vietnamese attack on the destroyers, the ambassador feigned ignorance and led the Senators to believe, as McNamara had before, that covert maritime raids against North Vietnam were little more than patrols trying "to block naval infiltration." Although, as chairman of the Joint

Chiefs, he had presided over their implementation, Taylor claimed that he did not know how long 34A operations had been in effect. Perhaps forgetting the broad authority given him by President Johnson, Taylor begged off their most trenchant questions by reminding the legislators that "I am the Ambassador, not the commanding General." In his memoir he recalled that his opportunity to brief congressional leaders had been one of the "advantages" of his trip.[40]

Thus presidential candidate Lyndon Johnson got from his advisers what he wanted. On September 10, 1964, the president signed NSAM 314 approving the resumption of U.S. naval patrols in the Gulf of Tonkin, 34A operations (including maritime raids, air drops, and leaflet operations), and planning for South Vietnamese cross-border air and ground operations into Laos.[41] William Bundy's "holding strategy" was policy until after the election.

Yet Johnson remained sensitive to preventing dissent from his "principal military advisors." The president asked Wheeler to tell LeMay and Greene that, although he had been reluctant to enter the fighter (South Vietnam) "in a ten-round bout when he was in no shape to last through the first round," he "would be ready to do more" at a later time. He vowed that when "larger decisions are required at any time by a change in the situation, they will be taken." To appease LeMay and Greene, NSAM 314 promised reprisals in case of North Vietnamese or Viet Cong attacks on U.S. units or severe attacks against the South Vietnamese. The memo indicated that the decision to forgo bombing North Vietnam was not final and would be under "constant review."[42] Speaking more openly with Wheeler in private, President Johnson promised him that although he didn't want "problems to arise with respect to Vietnam that would have an effect on the election," he was "going to do something" after November. In the meantime the president was gambling that he could avert disaster in Vietnam. He told Wheeler, "If the roof caves in I will have been proved wrong, but I am going to take the chance that it won't."[43] Despite these assurances, however, LBJ would later delay or disapprove many of the actions that NSAM 314 ostensibly cleared for implementation.

■

As a result of the shift in the JCS approach to offering military advice, and the president's efforts to suppress objections to his policy, the assumptions that underlay the maturing policy of graduated pressure went unchallenged. Nineteenth-century military philosopher Carl von Clausewitz observed that "the first duty and the right of the art of war is to keep policy from demanding things that go against the nature of war, to prevent the possibility that out of ignorance of the way the instrument works, policy might misuse it."[44] Even though the Joint Chiefs of Staff believed that the concept of graduated pressure was inconsistent with the "nature of war," they planned for the war within the parameters of that concept.

In the ensuing months the Chiefs' suppression of their differences to gain approval for stronger military action and the contrived consensus between the president and his civilian and military advisers would permit planning for the Americanization of the war without full consideration of the potential costs and consequences. Momentum continued to build behind McNamara's concept of graduated pressure, and other options, such as a negotiated withdrawal, were discounted without due consideration. Despite LBJ's retrospective assertion that his government may have been wrong but was not divided, his government was, as historian George Herring has observed, "both wrong *and* divided."[45]

8
Prophecies Rejected and the
Path of Least Resistance

September–November 1964

Eager to get moving, we never stopped to explore fully
whether there were other routes to our destination.

—Robert S. McNamara, 1995[1]

As the president signed NSAM 314 and Ambassador Taylor prepared
to return to Saigon, the Defense Department began a simulation
designed to predict the likely consequences of bombing North Vietnam.
The reprisals and deployments after the Gulf of Tonkin incident had
served as a rehearsal for the application of the new concept of graduated
pressure. A policy of coupling military pressure with diplomacy to coerce
North Vietnam into desisting from its support of the Viet Cong had been
in effect since February, when covert 34A operations against the North
began. The policy authorized only covert actions; direct attacks against
North Vietnam or "continuous overt pressures," such as a progressively
intensifying bombing campaign or the mining of North Vietnamese
ports, remained "possible later actions."[2]

After the April 1964 SIGMA I test had concluded that air power
would not destroy North Vietnam's capability to support the insurgency

in the South, Walt Rostow argued that air power only had to coerce Hanoi's leaders to stop supporting the insurgency rather than destroying their ability to do so. In September, a new war game, SIGMA II–64, would test the "Rostow thesis":

> By applying limited, graduated military actions, reinforced by political and economic pressures, against a nation providing external support for an insurgency, we could cause that nation to decide to reduce greatly, or eliminate altogether, its support for the insurgency. The objective of the attacks and pressures is not to destroy the nation's ability to provide support but rather to affect its calculation of interests.[3]

Rostow also predicted that there would be "bonus effects" of boosting the "morale of the country under insurgent attack and improving U.S. bargaining leverage in any international conference on the conflict."[4] Organized by the War Games Division of the Joint Chiefs of Staff, SIGMA II would evaluate, among other issues, how a bombing campaign against North Vietnam might affect Hanoi's behavior.

SIGMA II's broad purpose was to "consider the major political and military questions that should be answered prior to making a decision to commit . . . U.S. Armed Forces to combat in Southeast Asia." From September 8 to 17 military officers and civilians from both inside and outside the government attempted to replicate as closely as possible the outcome of an air campaign against North Vietnam. The game director was the head of the Department of Social Sciences at West Point, Col. George Lincoln. Lincoln, who had an impeccable reputation in government and academia, was best known for his contributions to victory in World War II as Army Chief of Staff Marshall's war planner. "Senior participants" included McGeorge and William Bundy, McCone, McNaughton, Vance, and the JCS. Others—including McNamara, Rusk, Ball, and Rostow—observed the game and received briefings on SIGMA's conclusions.[5]

The game's result raised troubling questions about the viability of the Rostow thesis. After initiating a bombing campaign, the United States confronted "the question of what to do since escalation of the war into NVN had failed to achieve desired results in SVN, and the enemy appeared to be raising the ante toward major ground warfare." The

American "team," however, remained "anxious to continue trying to force the DRV out of the war through air attack." Lincoln noted that once open hostilities began, consideration of "possible alternative strategies such as to negotiate" was minimal and the United States "followed through with escalation of pressures against North Vietnam to include wiping out *all* DRV industrial targets" and the mining of North Vietnamese ports. The bombing, however, had minimal effect and actually stiffened North Vietnamese determination, as the Viet Cong used existing stockpiles and civilian support to sustain the insurgency in the South. General Wheeler seemed particularly impressed by the game's findings that the Viet Cong's low demand for supplies, coupled with the agrarian nature of North Vietnam's society, made the enemy resistant to the use of air power.[6]

Although "both sides felt that they were making themselves clear to the opposition in a way that [made evident] the futility of the opponent's action," neither side "seemed to 'read' this message," and the war continued to escalate gradually. Frustration in the air campaign compelled the introduction of U.S. ground combat units into South Vietnam. The "Red" or Communist team observed that once American troops arrived in South Vietnam and began to take casualties, "You're there, you're committed. Your honor is at stake, now you've got to do something." At the game's conclusion the United States had deployed more than ten ground combat divisions to Southeast Asia and was contemplating an amphibious invasion of North Vietnam.[7]

Ultimately SIGMA II predicted that the escalation of American military involvement would erode public support for the war in the United States. Continued political instability in Saigon drew into question the worthiness and dependability of America's ally, and the subtlety of the Communist strategy made it difficult for the U.S. government to sustain its case for military intervention. The Red team concluded that the American public would rather pull out of South Vietnam than commit to a protracted war.[8]

SIGMA II questioned the fundamental assumption on which graduated pressure depended: that, "like the commitment to get the missiles out of Cuba in 1962," the enemy would be convinced that the United States was "prepared to meet any level of escalation they might mount"; that it had "established a consensus to see through this course of action both at home and on the world scene"; and that it would "not buckle politically" if North Vietnam failed to "comply."[9] Deputy Secretary of

State Ball found particularly striking the outcome that "exhausting the 1964 target list presently proposed for air strikes would not cripple Hanoi's capability for increasing its support of the Viet Cong, much less force suspension of present support levels." William Bundy recalled that, when the game ended, the North Vietnamese "stood in a strong position within South Vietnam and the United States was faced with the decision whether to send in major ground forces in support of a weak South Vietnamese government and a shaken population."[10] The results of SIGMA II suggested that graduated pressure could lead to disaster in Vietnam. The president, it seemed, would have to confront a difficult decision between a large-scale protracted war or disengagement under the auspices of a negotiated agreement.

The conclusions of SIGMA II, however, were never seriously studied and had no discernible impact on American policy. According to William Bundy, the effect of the game on him and others charged with responsibility for Vietnam planning "was not great."[11] The growing consensus behind the strategic concept of graduated pressure overpowered SIGMA II's unpromising conclusions because the president and his advisers were unwilling to risk either disengagement or escalation. In their minds the rash application of force could be disastrous and lead, in the worst-case scenario, to nuclear war with the Soviet Union.[12] Doing nothing would lead to defeat in South Vietnam and an associated loss of credibility that could undermine the West's alliance structure and result in defeat in the Cold War.

Although SIGMA II highlighted the possible negative consequences of following graduated pressure, the strategy's proponents could claim that their approach had a historical precedent. The crisis atmosphere of the Gulf of Tonkin incident had reminded those who had served in the Kennedy administration of their "triumph" over the Soviet Union during the Cuban missile crisis. Now the direct confrontation with Hanoi seemed to reveal similarities between Ho Chi Minh's ongoing support for the Viet Cong and Khrushchev's decision to introduce missiles into Cuba. The Tonkin Gulf incident focused the administration on what many believed to be North Vietnam's central role in directing and providing support for the insurgency in the South.

■

The parallel between the situation in Vietnam and that in Cuba was comforting to American policy makers. Counterinsurgency warfare by proxy in South Vietnam had proved immensely frustrating. The principal elements of American military strength were of little use in fighting guerrillas who would engage the South Vietnamese Army only at times and in places of their own choosing. Unlike the guerrillas, however, the Hanoi government was vulnerable to the projection of American firepower. If North Vietnamese support for the insurgency was the root of the conflict, bombing North Vietnam accomplished American goals without the vexing problems of counterguerrilla warfare and building a legitimate government around leaders who seemed more concerned with self-aggrandizement than with the challenges of governing a fractious society. The Gulf of Tonkin incident helped focus war planning on a solution for which American power was well suited. Just as Khrushchev broke under the pressure of a naval quarantine, aerial overflights of Cuba, menacing troop deployments and mobilization, and the threat of something far more destructive, Ho might fold under the specter of American military power.

Under graduated pressure, the threat of using force was more important than its use. The Johnson administration continued to use Canadian emissary J. Blair Seaborn, in conjunction with the air strikes and deployments of forces. In keeping with graduated pressure, Seaborn sought to "make very clear [to the Hanoi leadership] both the seriousness of the U.S. will and the limited character of U.S. objectives" while emphasizing that U.S. policy goals were limited to preserving the "integrity of South Vietnam's territory against guerrilla aggression." Seaborn highlighted the overwhelming approval of the congressional resolution, which permitted the deployment of "additional air power" to South Vietnam and Thailand. Lest the North Vietnamese government overlook the depth of American resolve, he warned that U.S. "patience with North Vietnamese aggression is growing extremely thin," and that if North Vietnam "persists in its present course, it can expect to suffer the consequences."[13] The use of force in Vietnam was aimed not at "destroying the enemy's will and capabilities" but at achieving a psychological victory over the minds of enemy leaders.

The fear of escalation reinforced the perception that JCS advice about Vietnam, based on the belief that the proper military objective in war is the "destruction of the enemy's will and capability to fight," was not only irrelevant but dangerous. Khrushchev had put President Johnson on notice that following aggressive policies, such as those recommended by

Generals Greene and LeMay, could lead, in the worst-case scenario, to nuclear war.[14] McGeorge Bundy remarked that General LeMay assumed away the possibility of an escalation of the war. McNamara agreed that the Chiefs "downplayed" risks of escalation and that he had to keep the Chiefs in check to "avoid the risk of nuclear war."[15]

Considering military action as an extension of diplomacy discouraged analysis based on military considerations such as the SIGMA II findings. McNaughton shared McNamara's and Bundy's views that the use of force should aim to communicate with the enemy rather than to inflict destruction. Even Taylor had come to believe that military force should "signal intention." Referring to the Cuban missile crisis to support his view, he warned that "too much in this matter of coercing Hanoi may be as bad as too little." Taylor hoped that Rostow's thesis was true, so that severely limited force would induce the leadership in Hanoi to become "cooperative" and "wind up the VC insurgency on terms satisfactory to us and our South Vietnamese allies."[16] To satisfy the conflicting objectives of avoiding escalation and demonstrating resolve to the enemy, civilian leaders felt not only justified but compelled to discount the advice of the Joint Chiefs.

The blurring of the distinction between diplomatic communication and military action helped to draw military planning for Vietnam further away from the JCS and toward the State Department and interdepartmental committees. William Bundy of the State Department and McNaughton of the Defense Department became the principal planners for Vietnam. Both men believed that coordinating the use of force with diplomacy called for a high degree of precision and control, a lesson they drew from the Cuban missile crisis. These two civilian advisers, along with McNamara, would determine the right "mix" of military and diplomatic measures necessary to attain a settlement in Vietnam. They would then supervise military operations to "tighten the screw" on North Vietnam's leaders.[17]

■

The control of covert 34A operations approved in NSAM 314 typified this close supervision of military action. Each month the Joint Chiefs submitted a detailed schedule of raids for review to McNaughton, Deputy Secretary of Defense Vance, McGeorge Bundy, and Llewellyn Thompson of the State Department. Before the JCS could draft any orders, each action was subject to another review, usually involving the president. After the Joint Staff drafted the order, the JCS could dispatch instructions only after McNaughton, McGeorge Bundy, and Thompson initialed the cable.[18]

Yet it was difficult to control events halfway around the world. On September 12 destroyer patrols in the Gulf of Tonkin resumed in accordance with NSAM 314. Five days later destroyers reported firing at and hitting several North Vietnamese patrol boats. Like the alleged second Gulf of Tonkin incident, however, the reality of the North Vietnamese attack was in doubt. The president was reluctant to act without conclusive evidence. He already had his congressional resolution, and his authorization of military actions had defused Senator Goldwater's criticisms of his Vietnam policy. "Hell," Johnson said, "those dumb, stupid sailors were probably just shooting at flying fish." The president rejected the Joint Chiefs' and secretary of state's recommendations for reprisal strikes because Johnson and his advisers were afraid of losing control. A press report on the latest "incident" in the Gulf of Tonkin had nearly forced his hand. Ball urged LBJ to discontinue the operations. Ball thought that Congress would react badly should one of the destroyers be sunk, and might accuse the president of using "American boys as decoy ducks" and "throw[ing] away lives just so you'd have an excuse to bomb." After hearing Ball's assessment, the president told Robert McNamara, "We won't go ahead with it, Bob. Let's put it on the shelf."[19]

The ability to control events precisely—rather than what effect those operations might have on the enemy—became a principal criterion for approving operations. As an alternative to the DESOTO patrols, Forrestal recommended to McNaughton that the United States initiate cross-border air operations into Laos. The principal virtue of these undertakings was that they were "controllable." Sharp limitations on the severity of the air strikes would allow the United States to "give a strong impression to Hanoi that we are slowly walking up the ladder" without destroying "a large number of the targets in massive attacks." Those charged with launching the air strikes would be ordered "to proceed with caution and would not be pressured to produce immediate visible results."[20]

The belief that they could maintain close control from Washington of the actions of American forces engaged in combat in Vietnam carried over to an assumption that they could anticipate, even script, the enemy's response to military operations. On September 3 McNaughton proposed a scheme for controlling events in Vietnam in accordance with the president's election concerns, reassuring South Vietnamese allies, and signaling determination to North Vietnam. He wrote:

> during the next two months, because of the lack of "rebuttal time" before the election to justify particular actions which may be distorted to the U.S. Public, we must act with special care—signaling to [North Vietnam] that initiatives are being taken, to [South Vietnam] that we are behaving energetically despite the restraints of our political season, and to the U.S. people that we are behaving with good purpose and restraint.

McNaughton felt that he could enlist the assistance of Hanoi to solve his planning dilemma. "By doing legitimate things," the United States could provoke a North Vietnamese attack which would "commence a crescendo" of military actions against North Vietnam. In retrospect, McNaughton's colleague William Bundy admitted that the paper seemed to combine realpolitik with the hypernationalist belief in control of the most refined American think tank. It was, in essence, "an attempt to devise more Tonkin Gulfs to order."[21]

■

Despite SIGMA II's findings, unrealistically sanguine assumptions about how Hanoi's leadership would respond to coercive military pressures continued to shape the evolving strategy for the war. The principal elements of the policy of graduated pressure—maximum results with minimal investment, and the belief that the enemy would respond "rationally" to precisely controlled military stimuli—were consistent with the educational backgrounds and professional experiences of those who became the architects of American intervention in Vietnam. The economists, managers, and systems analysts, such as Rostow and McNamara, tried to achieve maximum political payoff with minimal investment of military force, which they planned to use to affect Hanoi's calculations of future costs and benefits. When faced with the "cost" of continuing his support for the Viet Cong, Ho Chi Minh and his government would recognize the benefit of abandoning the attempt to unify Vietnam under Hanoi's leadership.[22]

Those who believed in the application of systems analysis to military strategy thought it incorrect to argue that the enemy "will do his worst." Instead planners should assume that the enemy "is in much the same position as we" and will "adapt his behavior." Controlled, rational application of military force would result in the United States and its adversary reaching "simultaneously a judgment about what is the most reasonable choice for us to make and what is a reasonable choice for him to be making."[23] The traditional military precept of using overwhelming force seemed unnecessary, wasteful, and inefficient to these analysts. Undaunted by the outcome of SIGMA II, Rostow wrote that the essence of applying military force would not be "the damage we do but the character of our military dispositions and our diplomatic communications."[24]

William Bundy's, Forrestal's, and McNaughton's education and experience in the law reinforced the analysts' assumptions. In English common law, lawyers and judges must view human behavior through the lens of the "average reasonable man." That theory underlay predictions of how Hanoi would respond to limited air strikes. Bundy found "too harsh" SIGMA II's conclusion that bombing would reinforce Hanoi's determination to win in the South. That conclusion succumbed to the attorneys' belief that as the "average reasonable man" would alter his behavior to remove the threat of great personal damage, so, too, would North Vietnamese leaders respond to the threat of military force. Otherwise Ho Chi Minh and his colleagues would be negligent. In a Vietnam planning paper, McNaughton and William Bundy wrote that U.S. policy would be to establish a "common law" justification for bombing. In a separate memo Bundy planned for negotiations to begin soon after the United States had established a clear "common law pattern of attacks" against North Vietnam.[25]

The attorneys, managers, and analysts failed to consider that Hanoi's commitment to revolutionary war made losses that seemed unconscionable to American white-collar professionals of little consequence to Ho's government. They discounted instinctively advice that questioned their assumption that Ho, when confronted with military action designed to affect his "calculation of interests," would respond as they anticipated. Lieutenant General Goodpaster protested to Secretary McNamara in the fall of 1964, "Sir, you are trying to program the enemy and that is one thing we must never try to do. We can't do his thinking for him."[26] Goodpaster's words fell on deaf ears.

Graduated pressure had practical as well as intellectual appeal. The concept permitted the president to postpone difficult policy decisions. Since August 1963, French president Charles de Gaulle had called for the neutralization of Indochina and the withdrawal of all foreign forces. In April 1964 he warned the U.S. ambassador to France, Charles Bohlen, that the United States was repeating "the experience that the French had earlier." De Gaulle argued that, in contrast to Hanoi's determination, the South Vietnamese "had no stomach for the war." He recommended strongly that the United States pursue immediate neutralization, telling Bohlen that America had either to choose "this neutralization as an announced policy" or demonstrate the "willingness of the US to really carry the war to the North and if necessary against China."[27] In June, DeGaulle pressed his views with Ball,[28] who recalled that LBJ was "unimpressed, or at least unwilling to listen, as he was then preoccupied with strengthening his domestic flanks."[29]

Thus, by the end of the fall of 1964, graduated pressure had become the policy of the Johnson administration, at least temporarily; adherents squelched isolated calls to examine alternative approaches. Initiatives from de Gaulle and UN Secretary-General U Thant fell prey to the momentum behind the policy. In response to diplomatic initiatives, Taylor warned Secretary of State Rusk that negotiations held "little hope for a settlement consistent with U.S. interests." He continued to believe that the coercive application of military force was a necessary precursor to a negotiated settlement. The president observed that an international conference in the fall of 1964 would only "tie our hands" and preclude the U.S. military action against North Vietnam planned for after the November election.[30]

■

Meanwhile, events in South Vietnam during September and October led some to question the value of the American commitment to Saigon. General Khanh's proclamation of a new constitution in mid-August sparked renewed protests from the Buddhists. After opponents forced him to withdraw the constitution, Khanh suffered a mild nervous breakdown, but he returned to government on September 3. During Taylor's absence from Saigon in mid-September, Brig. Gen. Lam Van Phant attempted a coup, but Khanh retained a tenuous hold on power. On his return to Saigon, Taylor promised to put his embassy's full effort behind creating an effective South Vietnamese government.[31]

At the end of October, despite the efforts of Taylor and his staff, the political situation in Saigon was at its most chaotic since the Diem coup a year earlier. Taylor blamed Khanh for the lack of stability in the government; the ambassador's attitude toward the South Vietnamese leader was fast becoming one of deep contempt. Complicating the political scene in Saigon was the emergence of several civilian politicians who, in the words of William Colby, chief of the CIA's Far Eastern Division, "divided and sub-divided into a tangle of contesting ambitions and claims to power and participation" in the government.[32]

Khanh, who had presided over the High National Council (HNC) since September 26, presented another new constitution on October 20. Taylor reviewed and edited the document, which called for a change in government from military to civilian rule. Although he supported Khanh's effort at reform, Taylor warned the South Vietnamese politicians and generals that he "did not wish to be presented with the *fait accompli* of a governmental slate containing individuals with whom we could not work." Without consulting the ambassador, the HNC elected Phan Khac Suu as chief of state and, several days later, designated Tran Van Huong as the next prime minister. Taylor scolded the Vietnamese for not consulting him. He thought that Suu was incompetent and Huong "handicapped by poor health and by a highly developed bump of stubbornness." Taylor, however, resolved to do the best that he could with the government at hand and began reviewing all nominees for cabinet positions. To enhance the government's chances of survival, Taylor coaxed likely competitors for power either to leave the country or to participate nominally in the new administration.[33] It was clear to any informed observer that the Saigon government existed only because of constant U.S. intervention.

Persistent governmental instability gave rise to renewed calls for negotiations and withdrawal. At the end of October, Senator Russell suggested separately to Johnson and DCI McCone that to "save face" the United States "bring a man to the top of the government in South Vietnam who would demand that the U.S. withdraw its forces from that country." A week earlier General Westmoreland had sent a cable to General Wheeler indicating his concern about the South's political problems. Westmoreland argued that unless a "fairly effective government" existed in South Vietnam, "no amount of offensive action by the United States either in or outside South Vietnam has any chance by itself of reversing the deterioration underway," although, he added, "the situation is not yet desperate." He stated that political stability was a "prerequisite for major overt military action against [North Vietnam] except in retaliation for attack[s] on U.S. forces." As early as September 25, Admiral Sharp warned that the unstable political situation in South Vietnam might render Saigon itself "untenable." He thought that "conceivably the decision could be one of disengagement." In closing, Sharp urged Wheeler to "consider as a matter of urgency" America's future in South Vietnam "in the light of all possible contingencies."[34]

Separately, George Ball developed a strictly confidential memorandum in which he argued strongly for disengagement from Vietnam. After Ball persuaded the president to forgo future DESOTO patrols in the Gulf of Tonkin, Johnson asked him to critique General Wheeler's proposal to continue them.[35] On October 3 Johnson asked Ball also to play devil's advocate against Vietnam policy in general and the strategic concept of the war. The president told McNamara to continue developing the plan for Vietnam and instructed Ball to "shoot holes in it."[36] On October 5 Ball completed a sixty-four-page memorandum, which he described as a "challenge to our assumptions of our current Viet-Nam policy."

Partially echoing LeMay's and Greene's argument for a "hard knock," Ball's paper raised criticisms consistent with those of senior military officers, arguing that military action against North Vietnam would "have to be substantial and sustained." Like Harold Johnson, however, Ball doubted the ability of even the most severe air campaign to persuade Hanoi that it should "permanently abandon its aggressive tendencies against South Vietnam," and warned that air strikes could precipitate a more serious challenge from the North. He echoed Westmoreland's concerns that without political stability in Saigon, military pressure would be dangerous. He argued that air strikes would force Hanoi to "retaliate using ground forces" to "increase the intensity of the insurgency in South Vietnam" and launch "terror attacks on American personnel." Unable to "counter ground forces by air power alone," the United States would be compelled to deploy "American ground units to defend our bases from attacks by the North." After U.S. forces were engaged on the ground, it would be difficult to resist pressures to take over primary responsibility for the war. In closing, Ball urged the president to assess the potential cost of the war "before we commit military forces to a line of action that could put events in the saddle and destroy our freedom to choose the policies that are at once the most effective and the most prudent." Ball warned that "once on the tiger's back, we cannot be sure of picking the place to dismount."[17] As McNamara recalled years afterward, however, "no one was willing to discuss getting out."[38]

In the fall of 1964, with the president's advisory system rigged for consensus, Ball stood little chance of triggering a serious examination of Vietnam policy. Afraid of leaks, he limited distribution of his memo to Rusk, McNamara, and the Bundy brothers. These men sought to spare the president from making tough decisions on Vietnam policy during an election campaign. Accordingly William Bundy annexed to Ball's paper one of his own that countered all of Ball's "heresies" against graduated pressure.[39]

Ball's opposition to graduated pressure was as fainthearted as Bundy's defense was spirited. Because the president had given Ball the task of "shooting holes" in McNamara's planning effort for the war, he and his closest advisers viewed Ball's opinion skeptically, as if he were a devil's advocate who was only fulfilling his task as the lone dissenter. Ball was simply acting as a good lawyer for the president by developing dispassionately an argument diametrically opposed to McNamara's.[40]

Although the JCS held views consistent with those of Ball, they, too, failed to press their case for a reexamination. Their silence helped to impel the very strategic concept they opposed. One week after Ball sent his memo to the members of Lyndon Johnson's inner circle, the Chiefs met to consider recent developments in Vietnam.

■

LeMay brought to the meeting two Special National Intelligence Estimates (SNIEs) prepared during the first ten days of October 1964. Both, he pointed out, predicted continuing deterioration of the situation in Vietnam. The reports were as "clear a forecast of impending disaster as we can expect to receive from the intelligence community." He predicted that "unless we can, without delay, define and initiate some positive course of action to counter the present trend, we must accept what looms before us as an inevitable consequence."[41] Lamenting that previous JCS recommendations for action against North Vietnam had gone unheeded, LeMay warned that "time is not on our side" and any delay would be disastrous. He urged his colleagues to renew within seventy-two hours their previous recommendations and urge the president to take immediate action.[42]

The Joint Staff, still unable to reconcile competing service positions, could not move quickly enough for LeMay. Four days later, on October 16, LeMay again attempted to gain JCS endorsement for the Air Force position. He invoked the recent assessments of Taylor, who, removed from the maelstrom of Washington election-year politics, had returned to his earlier position of urging "new and drastic methods to reduce and eventually end" infiltration from North Vietnam regardless of the political stability of the Saigon government. LeMay used Taylor's argument that infiltration from North Vietnam constituted "an invasion of hostile forces into the territory of an ally of the U.S." He pressed his colleagues to recommend what he had advocated continuously since September 14: a large-scale bombing campaign against North Vietnam.[43]

On October 21 LeMay finally persuaded his colleagues to incorporate some of his concerns in a memorandum to the secretary of defense. Although the memo made no specific recommendations for American action, it communicated clearly LeMay's assessment that the United States was "fast running out of time in Southeast Asia." Noting that the administration had ignored their previous calls for an expansion of the war, the Chiefs promised once again to provide the defense secretary with a new set of recommendations.[44]

Harold Johnson, Wheeler, and McDonald insisted on muting General LeMay's advocacy for bombing North Vietnam. Johnson opposed LeMay the most, because he continued to believe that the principal problem in Vietnam involved "a struggle for the loyalty and support of the population" rather than North Vietnam's support for the insurgency. He held, therefore, that without a stable political base in the South, bombing North Vietnam would not help and could hurt the situation. LeMay, unrelenting, argued that the solution to the problem in Vietnam would not be found through "political, economic, psychological, and military actions proposed by the Army," but rather in the unconstrained application of firepower against North Vietnam. LeMay chastised Johnson for diluting the "firm stand" that the JCS had taken in the past. Without "positive military action," he continued, the pursuit of a stable political base in the South was a "lost cause."[45]

With help from General Wheeler, LeMay finally broke through his colleagues' resistance. On October 23 the JCS issued a memo recommending action against the North to destroy its "will and capability" to support the insurgencies in South Vietnam and Laos.[46] The Joint Chiefs decided to advance ambiguous versions of both LeMay's and Johnson's recommendations. "Accelerated and forceful actions both inside and outside of the Republic of Vietnam" would support a fourfold strategy of cutting off the Viet Cong from assistance from the North, separating the Viet Cong from the population in the South, continuing to seek a viable and legitimate South Vietnamese government, and maintaining a threatening "readiness posture" in Southeast Asia for the purposes of coercion and deterrence. Appendix A to the memo comprised actions within South Vietnam and Appendix B actions outside South Vietnam. Because of the South's precarious political stability, the memo described the struggle in Vietnam as needing "a combination of political and military action" and argued that "there is an interaction between the two that permits a political success to be exploited militarily and vice versa."[47] Wheeler's compromise softened the Chiefs' opposition to graduated pressure and signaled that they would go along with the concept.

Consistent with their willingness to accept restrictions on the use of force at the outset and then lobby for their future relaxation, the Chiefs organized military actions in "ascending order of severity." They recommended immediate implementation of the first six actions designed to influence the situation within South Vietnam and the first eight actions aimed at isolating the insurgents in the South from their base in the North, but they seemed content to postpone additional measures until they could convince the defense secretary and the president that they had become necessary, as they knew would be the case.

Actions to be taken immediately in South Vietnam included an intensification of the pacification and civil affairs efforts and air strikes against the Viet Cong by U.S. fixed-wing aircraft. Immediate actions outside South Vietnam included a resumption of destroyer patrols in the Gulf of Tonkin, intensified 34A operations, forward deployments of U.S. combat units in Southeast Asia, cross-border operations into Cambodia and Laos, retaliatory actions against North Vietnam, low-level aerial reconnaissance of North Vietnam, and cross-border air strikes against Viet Cong supply lines in North Vietnam and Laos at points near the border with South Vietnam.[48]

The memorandum stated that the Joint Chiefs of Staff disagreed only in the matter of timing. Foreseeing a "great likelihood of a VC victory" in the near future, Generals Greene and LeMay recommended the deployment of U.S. ground troops and fighter aircraft to Vietnam and adjacent areas and air strikes against infiltration targets in North Vietnam by American and South Vietnamese aircraft. Johnson, Wheeler, and McDonald supported deploying additional aircraft and the first ground combat troops to Southeast Asia (an Army brigade to Thailand and a Marine brigade to Danang for air base defense), but thought that these deployments should occur only after the "appropriate implementation" of the first eight measures on the list.[49] In addition to diluting the Chiefs' opposition to graduated pressure, the memo obscured the ultimate cost of pursuing a military solution to the problem in Vietnam.

The JCS memorandum aimed to gain approval for particular actions rather than for a comprehensive strategy to guarantee the freedom and independence of South Vietnam. Although the Chiefs warned that "the entire program of courses of action may be required," they observed that the list of actions was "arranged so that any of the actions may be selected, implemented, and controlled, as required to produce the desired effect while analyzing and estimating the communist reaction." At the extreme end of the scale, the JCS program of actions included mining and blockading North Vietnamese ports, an all-out air campaign against North Vietnam, amphibious and airborne ground offensives into the coastal areas of North Vietnam, and the commitment of increasingly large numbers of ground forces into Southeast Asia. The JCS recommendation nourished hopes that the United States could wage the war at a minimal and carefully controlled cost. The JCS noted that the program could be "curtailed or terminated" as soon as the United States achieved its objectives.[50] No one considered whether any particular action might force an end to the war on American terms, because the government could always take the next step on the list.

The specific consequences of further military action also went unexplored. Military actions would show force, "demonstrate resolve," display American destructive power, "increase pressure," and cause North Vietnam "to make a political decision to cease support of the insurgencies." Even an amphibious and airborne invasion of North Vietnam would aim only to "pose a plausible threat" to North Vietnam.[51] The JCS recommended actions in "ascending order of severity" without warning that once the United States entered the war directly, the level of military effort could quickly escalate in response to enemy initiatives. There was no mention of General Johnson's belief, consistent with the SIGMA II findings, that air action against the North would provoke an intensified ground war in the South, which in turn would require the introduction of large numbers of American ground troops. The Chiefs wrote that there was "not a high risk" of Chinese intervention on the ground unless the United States and South Vietnam occupied areas of North Vietnam or Northern Laos, or the United States attacked Chinese air bases. They observed that, if the Chinese did intervene, it was "within the capability of US force to deal with large-scale aggression." Missing was any analysis that explored Clausewitz's observation that in war, because "each side is driven to outdo the other," states tend to escalate their efforts. In the beginning of October, Ball echoed Clausewitz, writing, "It is in the nature of escalation . . . that each move passes the option to the other side, while, at the same time, the party which seems to be losing will be tempted to keep raising the ante." Ball had warned that "to the extent that the response to a move can be controlled, that move is probably ineffective. If the move is effective, it may not be possible to control—or accurately anticipate—the response."[52] The Chiefs, however, failed to make these points.

After taking six weeks to develop the memo, the JCS wanted the president to consider their recommendations immediately. Instead of forwarding the memo to the president as the Chiefs requested, however, McNamara sent it to Ambassador Taylor in Saigon for comment.[53] He wanted Taylor to act again as a foil to the professional military. Taylor, meanwhile, had another agenda, which he pursued first.

■

On October 3 Taylor recommended the establishment in Saigon of a committee that would, under his supervision, coordinate "policy recommendations and military operational matters." Rusk was "completely sympathetic" with Taylor's request, but instructed him to "avoid giving the impression at this time" that he was presiding over a "political and military command structure." Taylor received Rusk's official permission to form the committee on October 7 and held the organizing session the next day. Military subjects dominated the agenda, and topics discussed included a recommendation that U.S. aircraft participate in air operations in the Laotian corridor. On October 10 Taylor informed Rusk that his committee would be known as "Coordinating Committee for US Mission Southeast Asia (SEACOORD)." Taylor's protégé, General Westmoreland, would chair an element of SEACOORD named the "Standing Military Committee."[54]

The formation of SEACOORD further diffused responsibility for military planning. CINCPAC, Admiral Sharp, complained to the Joint Chiefs that SEACOORD might confuse military command channels and result in "reduced effectiveness." He argued that the "coordination and direction of U.S. military operational matters is a function of the existing national military command structure and is included in the statutory responsibilities of the secretary of defense, the JCS, and the Unified Commanders." Lieutenant General Krulak, commander of Marine forces in the Pacific, thought that SEACOORD formalized many of the military responsibilities that Ambassador Taylor had already assumed. The ambassador routinely submitted military recommendations through Secretary Rusk and the State Department which bypassed completely CINCPAC, the JCS, and the secretary of defense. Taylor's broad charter in Vietnam had already confused the military chain of command.[55]

■

Before Taylor could intervene in military affairs in Washington by responding to McNamara's request for advice on the JCS memo, however, an event in a suburb of Saigon changed the policy perspective. Just after midnight on November 1, 1964, the Viet Cong launched a raid on Bien Hoa airfield that left four Americans dead and seventy-two wounded. Americans at Bien Hoa were part of a B-57 bomber unit that McNamara had sent to Vietnam to signal U.S. resolve in the wake of the Gulf of Tonkin incident. Soon after the aircraft arrived in South Vietnam, Admiral Sharp warned Westmoreland that "heavy concentrations of recently deployed U.S. aircraft on airfields such as Bien Hoa" were vulnerable to Viet Cong attack. The Viet Cong, Sharp observed, would "derive tremendous psychological advantage" from such a strike. General Westmoreland replied two days later that he had given the matter his "personal attention" and that he and his staff had organized their resources to meet the threat.[56] Sharp's assessment proved prophetic.

November 1 was set aside as a day of celebration in South Vietnam in honor of the new civilian government under Tran Van Huong. The presidential election in the United States was only two days away. If the Viet Cong intended to disrupt both the South Vietnamese holiday and Lyndon Johnson's last campaign push, the attack on Bien Hoa was ideally timed. Fourteen miles northeast of Saigon, Viet Cong guerrillas crept through the rice paddies, palm groves, and villages outside the airfield and set up their mortars. As the new day began, they initiated a thirty-nine-minute barrage. Four U.S. servicemen were killed and seventy-two wounded or injured. In addition to the human loss, the attack damaged or destroyed seventeen of the thirty-six B-57 aircraft in South Vietnam. The Viet Cong escaped.[57]

Taylor was outraged. In a cable to Washington, he described the attack as "a deliberate escalation and a change of the ground rules" and recommended that the attack "be met promptly by an appropriate act of reprisal." Westmoreland and Sharp agreed with Taylor that Bien Hoa was precisely the kind of attack for which the president, just over a month earlier, had approved "tit for tat" reprisals. On the principle that "tit be as close to tat" as possible, Taylor recommended that U.S. aircraft strike Phuc Yen airfield to eliminate recently arrived MIG fighter aircraft. Simultaneously South Vietnamese aircraft would join American jets in striking three barracks in the southern portion of North Vietnam. Taylor sent very detailed military recommendations to the secretary of state. He identified specific target numbers on the Pentagon's ninety-four-target list, calculated the number of sorties per target and time of attack, and named the units that would carry out each strike. Taylor recommended that the United States and South Vietnam announce jointly after the reprisal that "retaliation will henceforth be the rule."[58]

It was Sunday morning in Washington. General Wheeler met first with General LeMay to discuss JCS reprisal plans and Taylor's cables. LeMay and Greene were upset that Wheeler planned to attend a noon White House meeting before consulting the other Chiefs. LeMay demanded that the JCS meet and Wheeler agreed.[59] When the meeting began at 10:00 A.M., the Chiefs did not think that Taylor's cable and Westmoreland's concurrence with it went far enough. They viewed the raid as an opportunity to begin "systematic bombing" of North Vietnam and recommended progressive attacks against all the targets on the ninety-four-target list. In conjunction with the initial strikes, the Chiefs planned to dispatch Marine and Army units to secure the Danang and Saigon areas. After flying American troops and supplies into Saigon, the aircraft would evacuate American dependents. Although the bombings might initially appear to be reprisals, they would mark the beginning of a sustained air campaign to "punish" North Vietnam and interdict infiltration routes to the South. The Chiefs did not have time to prepare a memo and charged General Wheeler with communicating their views to the president and the secretary of defense. Wheeler left his colleagues at 11:00 to brief McNamara. The two then attended a preliminary meeting to prepare for discussions with the president at 12:30 the following day.[60] Immediate retaliation, however, was out of the question. The president asked William Bundy to explain to Taylor his decision to forgo reprisal.

Bundy reassured Taylor that the president and his closest advisers had "weighed carefully" his recommendations but did not consider the attack on Bien Hoa as "a major escalation in itself." Comparing the attack to "recurrent attacks on US personnel and equipment playing military roles" in order to decrease its significance, Bundy argued that it had to be considered in the "wider context" of the Chiefs' advocacy of a bombing campaign. He observed that the Bien Hoa attack had "brought measurably nearer" a "decision on systematic wider actions against [the] North."[61] Although Bundy's memorandum contained the official rationale for disapproving a reprisal, Rusk transmitted an "eyes only" cable to the ambassador one minute later that gave the president's real reasons for rejecting retaliation.

Rusk admitted to Taylor that the decision was "inevitably affected by election timing." To assuage the ambassador, the secretary of state coupled promises of future action with reassurances that the ambassador's views were valued and welcome. He affirmed William Bundy's judgment that "we are reaching [the] point where policy hardening must be acutely considered." Rusk acknowledged, however, that any decision must be postponed until after the election. Taylor might return again to Washington in mid-November to "look at the whole problem and possible decisions."[62]

As Rusk had indicated, the election dominated Johnson's decision to reject retaliation. Earlier Johnson had directed Special Assistant Bill Moyers to telephone pollster Lou Harris. Moyers asked Harris "if a failure to respond to this attack immediately will be taken by the voters as a sign of weakness by the administration." Harris responded that bombing was "the sort of thing people would expect from Barry Goldwater and probably the main reason they are voting for [LBJ]." In light of Harris's assessment, Johnson would hardly entertain seriously Taylor's and the Chiefs' recommendations. General Greene first heard of the president's decision while listening to a radio news broadcast. Reflecting on the president's assurance in September that the United States would respond against North Vietnam for attacks on American units, Greene thought that the administration had released the story as a cover for a later attack.[63]

In retrospect the Bien Hoa attack and the Johnson administration's reaction might have highlighted the difficulties associated with gradually increasing American military involvement in Vietnam. After the Gulf of Tonkin incident, the United States deployed B-57s to Bien Hoa airfield to demonstrate its determination. That step, however, which appeared innocuous at the time, had subjected American forces to a Viet Cong response. The Viet Cong attack, in turn, left the United States with a choice of either backing down or escalating the conflict. What had been meant as a "signal" of U.S. determination increased America's vulnerability and forced the administration to consider further military action.

The response to Bien Hoa typified what would become a pattern in the relationship between the JCS and Lyndon Johnson's administration. The Chiefs tried to use the attack to gain approval for additional actions on the list they had developed less than a week earlier. To keep the Chiefs "on board," President Johnson and his closest advisers appeared sympathetic to the JCS recommendation and held out the promise of future action. In September, to sign the JCS up for his "holding strategy," Johnson had promised to approve retaliation against the next Viet Cong or North Vietnamese attack. When his domestic political priorities conflicted with retaliation, however, the president reneged. After Bien Hoa, Johnson promised action later, stating ambiguously that retaliation was "in order, but such a response need not be immediate." In November, Wheeler received assurances from the president that another Viet Cong attack similar to the one launched on Bien Hoa would result in the systematic bombing of North Vietnam.[64]

■

Despite the president's sensitivity to the Chiefs' loyalties, the decision to forgo retaliation strained the civil-military relationship. On November 1 Wheeler reported to McNamara that the Chiefs were frustrated and believed that, if the United States did not take action against North Vietnam immediately, it should withdraw all forces from South Vietnam. They wanted a memo to that effect to go to the president.[65] McNamara responded on the president's behalf by promising that LBJ would soon decide to use American military force in Vietnam. He reassured them that their recommendations were vital to the decision-making process. In a meeting with the Chiefs on the morning of November 2, McNamara appeared sympathetic to their view that "disaster" would ensue if the United States followed the current policy in Vietnam. He told the JCS to "reexamine the forces which should be required to support a major effort in South Vietnam and the logistics to back up these forces." LeMay took solace in McNamara's tough talk about a systematic bombing program. The defense secretary spoke expansively about air strikes against China, suggesting that once the United States completed the destruction of the ninety-four targets on the JCS list, air strikes might be launched against Mao Tse-tung's nascent nuclear facilities. McNamara reassured Harold Johnson by stating that ground troops should deploy at the outset of an air campaign because bombing alone would "not bring any major changes in the attitude of the dissident 'Viet Cong' in the South." McNamara even spoke unreservedly about a land war in Southeast Asia that would pit U.S. armed forces against the combined armies of China and North Vietnam.[66] Years afterward, however, McNamara recalled that he had a constant personal dread of escalation. McNamara's empty promises of future action, combined with his requests that the JCS reexamine plans for a large-scale war in Asia, overcame the Chiefs' initial discontent with the president's reluctance to retaliate.

Similar encouragement went to Ambassador Taylor in Saigon after Bundy informed him that there would be no reprisals for Bien Hoa. Bundy asked Taylor what actions would give the "right signal level to [the] North and keep up morale in the South." In addition, he solicited Taylor's opinion about U.S. air strikes against the Viet Cong in the South and the deployment of ground units. According to Bundy, ground forces might give the "desirable appearance [of] securing decks for action." Although Bundy thought that the introduction of ground forces might "add to our casualties and general exposure," he thought that these deployments might deter the North Vietnamese from launching a ground offensive in response to the promised American air strikes. In short, William Bundy communicated the administration's firm commitment to South Vietnam, requested advice, and promised future action—just as McNamara had done with the JCS.[67]

■

After the dust from the Bien Hoa raid settled, Taylor had time to respond to the October 27 JCS memorandum; he forwarded his assessment to McNamara on Tuesday, November 3, election day. Taylor commented on the memo item by item, but he did not point out that the recommended actions lacked coherence because no strategic concept guided them. Taylor did not, therefore, discuss the differences between the Chiefs' vision of the war and his own. Instead he focused on the JCS position, with which he agreed, that "the deteriorating situation in South Vietnam requires the application of measured military pressures on [North Vietnam] to induce their government to cease to provide support to VC and to use its authority to cause VC to cease or at least to moderate their depredations." Like McNamara, however, Taylor ignored the most severe military actions on the Chiefs' ascending list; he wished to use limited force to achieve his policy objective.[68] Instead of fostering debate over different concepts of the war, then, the JCS memo and Taylor's evaluation of it created the veneer of agreement.

It was clear well before midnight that Lyndon Johnson was on his way to an overwhelming victory. Johnson gained the highest proportion of the popular vote in American history and swept many Democrats to victory along with him. Members of his party would enjoy wide majorities in both houses during the next Congress.

Although it was not immediately apparent in Washington, the growing momentum behind the evolving strategy of graduated pressure would have profound consequences. Because the president and his key policy makers were preoccupied with the election and continued to regard the strategy of graduated pressure as a sensible way to prevent a wider war, they never considered alternatives to that ostensibly inexpensive policy, such as neutralization or diplomacy. Despite predictions that graduated pressure would fail and isolated calls for consideration of a negotiated settlement to extricate the United States from a commitment with little prospect for success, U.S. involvement in Vietnam continued, in the face of increasing governmental instability in Saigon. Instead of considering what deepening American involvement in Vietnam might ultimately cost or voicing individual doubts, the Joint Chiefs compromised, listed actions that would contribute to the war effort, and contented themselves with gaining incremental approval for them. Everyone—the president, his closest civilian advisers, *and* the Joint Chiefs of Staff—had taken the path of least resistance. As a result the most difficult questions about the nature of American involvement in Vietnam remained unanswered, and the assumptions that underlay the president's policy went unchallenged by the one formal body charged by law and tradition with advising the president of the United States about strategy and warfare.

9
Planning for Failure
November–December 1964

The first point I want to make—and I want to make it with emphasis—is that no matter what rumors or assertions you may have heard to the contrary, there is no boiling dissention between the military and civilian leaders within the Department of Defense. It appears to me that the current relationship between the soldier and the state is possibly the best we have had in many years.

—GEN. EARLE WHEELER, JANUARY 14, 1965[1]

On November 2, the day after the Bien Hoa attack and the day before Lyndon Johnson's crushing defeat of Barry Goldwater, McGeorge Bundy recommended that "a period of quiet and a period of preparation" with regard to Vietnam follow the election. Accordingly, with the exception of two short visits to Washington, Johnson remained at his Texas ranch until the end of the month. The president's first priority was to pull together the Great Society program that he had promised during his campaign. His grand ambition, the Great Society would provide medical care for the old, educational assistance for the young, lower taxes for big business, a higher minimum wage for workers, subsidies for farmers, job training for the unskilled, food for the hungry, housing for the homeless, income redistribution for the poor, legal protection for African-Americans, and reduced quotas for immigrants.[2] Johnson was determined to pass this social legislation, which he believed would secure his place in history.

179

Because the Great Society constrained the exploration of policy options in Vietnam, the probable consequences of the favored course—the gradual application of military pressure against North Vietnam—received relatively little attention. Indeed, those who developed plans for that strategy recognized that their proposals were unlikely to achieve the administration's stated foreign policy objective of guaranteeing the freedom and independence of South Vietnam. Rather than explore alternative courses of action, however, planners such as McNaughton and William Bundy rationalized that committing the U.S. military to a war in Vietnam and losing would be preferable to withdrawing from what they believed was an impossible situation. They believed that if the United States demonstrated that it would use military force to support its foreign policy, its international stature would be enhanced, regardless of the outcome. Because the civilian advisers conceived of the gradual application of force as a political, rather than a military, operation, they did not seriously evaluate its practical military consequences. The men charged with a comprehensive examination of U.S. policy toward Vietnam were planning for failure.

■

After the election McGeorge Bundy recommended and Johnson approved the formation of yet another interdepartmental committee to examine U.S. interests and objectives in Vietnam, assess the situation there and its global and regional implications, define the major courses of action, and argue the pros and cons of each. William Bundy headed the committee. As President Johnson celebrated the election returns in Austin, Texas, William Bundy met with McNaughton in Washington. The attorneys-turned-strategists were glad that the election and its attendant influence on Vietnam planning was over.³ Within two weeks the committee completed a draft paper entitled "Courses of Action in Southeast Asia."

According to William Bundy, the working group represented a "full-scale mobilization of the relevant men in Washington." Joining Bundy were McNaughton; McNaughton's assistant Daniel Ellsberg (who would later gain notoriety by expropriating and releasing the top-secret *Pentagon Papers*); Harold Ford of the CIA; and Michael Forrestal, Marshall Green, and Robert H. Johnson of the State Department. Vice Adm. Lloyd Mustin, senior operations officer (J-3) of the Joint Staff, represented the JCS. McNamara, Rusk, and McGeorge Bundy generally supervised and occasionally participated in meetings. William Bundy and McNaughton, however, steered the committee's deliberations so that its final recommendation agreed with their own ideas and with those of McNamara, who monitored the committee's progress closely through McNaughton.[4]

During the first two sessions of the working group, on November 3 and 5, Bundy and McNaughton developed three possible courses of action. Option A would "continue on present lines." Option B included "present policies plus a systematic program of military pressures against the North, meshing at some point with negotiation but with pressure actions *to be continued until* we achieve our central present objectives." Option C called for a continuation of "present policies plus additional forceful measures and military moves, followed by negotiations in which we would seek to maintain a believable threat of still further military pressures but would not actually carry out such pressure to any marked degree during the negotiations."[5]

■

The Joint Chiefs were unable to inject their views into the committee's vital early deliberations. Although Admiral Mustin served as the Chiefs' representative, the committee moved too fast for him to provide advice from the JCS. Bundy recalled that because the admiral was unable "to speak authoritatively in the absence of a written paper endorsed by the Chiefs as a whole, Mustin was from the first in a somewhat difficult position." The Joint Staff did provide Bundy's committee with "specific military facts," but neither the JCS nor the Joint Staff exerted any real influence over the working group's effort. The committee established the limits of its examination in the first two meetings, and all of Bundy's options called for the gradual application of limited military force against North Vietnam.[6] By the time General Wheeler first received a coordinating draft of the committee's analysis, Rusk, McNamara, and McGeorge Bundy had already briefed the president on the scope of the study.[7] The JCS was forced once again to dissent from a consensus position devised through interdepartmental coordination.

Because Mustin could not obtain approval of his positions from the Chiefs, he and the Joint Staff commented only when they felt sure that each of the Chiefs agreed with their position. Consistent with General

Taylor's prior directive that the Joint Staff provide advice "through the eyes of the President," their early submissions to the committee focused almost exclusively on the strategic importance of South Vietnam and the dire consequences should that country fall to Communism.[8]

The Chiefs devised alternative courses of action to the gradual application of force recommended by the committee. On November 11, before the committee's report was released, General Wheeler conferred with Director of the Joint Staff Lieutenant General Burchinal, Lieutenant General Goodpaster, Vice Admiral Mustin, and Lieutenant Colonel Rogers. Wheeler was agitated because of the weakness of the committee's recommendations. McNaughton had admitted that Option B, like Option C, consisted of the "progressive application of increasing military pressures." The two differed only in phraseology, such as air strikes on "major military or prestige targets" or military "displays of real muscle in action." McNaughton described the first military actions under B as a "gradual, even though somewhat rapid squeeze" that "would be preferable to dramatic actions." For fear of antagonizing either the Chinese or the Soviets, vital military targets, such as the North Vietnamese MIG fighter base at Phuc Yen, would be off limits under any of the working group's options.[9]

Wheeler took out a legal pad and outlined in pencil a course of action that would begin with a "hard knock" against North Vietnam in order to maximize the psychological and military impact on the enemy from the outset.[10] The Joint Staff went to work on the chairman's outline. Six days later, on November 17, William Bundy forwarded to General Wheeler the first full draft of the working group's study. On November 23 the Joint Staff finally completed a memorandum that defined five courses of action in the Joint Chiefs' own terms. Their preferred course, the "hard knock," appeared there as a rewritten Course of Action B.[11] It was too late. The issue had already been decided.

■

Momentum formed behind Option C. George Ball observed that the committee had developed options on the "Goldilocks principle." Option A was "too soft," B was "too hard," and C was "just right."[12] A was dismissed almost immediately. C, termed the "progressive squeeze and talk," was most consistent with the concept of graduated pressure. According to McNaughton, Option C was just right because it was "more hopeful" than continuing the current policy, and "more controllable and less risky than Option B."[13]

McNaughton began to develop in earnest an "evaluation" of the favored option. He and Daniel Ellsberg completed a twenty-page draft analysis of Option C in less than five days. On the same day William Bundy distributed a five-page analysis of Option B, dubbed the "fast full squeeze." Although the "cons" of B listed "major U.S. casualties" and "substantial deployments," McNaughton and Ellsberg included no such consideration of casualties or military deployments in their analysis of Option C. On November 23 McNaughton recommended that option.[14]

Despite his advocacy of Option C, McNaughton began to doubt that the acutely limited military action he favored could persuade North Vietnam to stop supporting the Viet Cong. He feared that, no matter what action the United States took against North Vietnam, governmental instability and popular discontent would exhaust South Vietnam's ability to resist the Viet Cong. In a November 7 draft memo, he wrote that Option C stood "some chance of coming out very badly." He shared his doubts only with William Bundy and Forrestal. McNaughton went to Forrestal's office almost every evening to sit with his friend and worry about the deepening American involvement in a war that was unlikely to succeed. Bundy, sharing McNaughton's doubts, recognized that Option C was based on a "thin wedge of hope."[15]

Despite their misgivings they continued to support Option C because, in part, they believed that it offered them the best opportunity to control precisely the application of military force. McNaughton and other officials in the Defense and State Departments believed that if the North Vietnamese did not respond to the gradual application of military pressure, the United States could simply stop using force. Forrestal recalled years later:

> It was sort of a creeping thing. The theory was that you could always stop it if it didn't work. Or if you got any kind of signal, because we kept listening for signals all the time from the North Vietnamese, we would stop it. . . . You always kept telling yourself, "Well, if it doesn't work, we stop."[16]

McNaughton wrote that Option C was designed to allow "maximum control at all stages and to permit interruption at some appropriate point or points for negotiations, while seeking to maintain throughout a credible threat of further military pressures should such be required."[17]

■

McNaughton, Forrestal, and William Bundy concluded that it would be preferable to fail in Vietnam after trying some level of military action than to withdraw without first committing the United States military to direct action against North Vietnam. They thought that the principal objective of military activities was to protect U.S. credibility. Because they believed that graduated military pressure could be stopped at any time and would not commit them to any further military measures, they saw less risk in using force than in not doing so. Failure to uphold the administration's commitment to preserve the independence of South Vietnam would be acceptable as long as the world recognized that the United States had done all that it could under the circumstances. McNaughton believed that the United States would be in "no worse position" in Southeast Asia if graduated pressure failed to secure American policy objectives there than it was already. Indeed, the loss of South Vietnam after the direct intervention of U.S. armed forces "would leave behind a better odor" than an immediate withdrawal and would demonstrate that the United States was a "good doctor willing to keep promises, be tough, take risks, get bloodied, and hurt the enemy badly."[18]

This shift in thinking about the U.S. objective in Vietnam became apparent during the working group's deliberations. On October 13 McNaughton had placed helping South Vietnam and Laos "develop as independent countries" at the top of his list of goals in Southeast Asia. Three weeks later McNaughton listed the following "aims" of U.S. military action in Vietnam for the use of the Bundy committee:

A. To protect US reputation as a counter-subversion guarantor.

B. To avoid domino effect especially in Southeast Asia.

C. To keep South Vietnamese territory from Red hands.

D. To emerge from crisis without considerable taint from methods.[19]

For McNaughton and others the goal of American military intervention in South Vietnam had less to do with that country than with containing Communism and maintaining America's "international prestige."

McNaughton wrote that "it might become desirable to settle for less than complete assurances on our key objectives," namely the U.S. pledge to guarantee South Vietnam's freedom and independence.[20]

The final report Bundy and McNaughton completed on November 26 ostensibly reaffirmed the American commitment to a free and independent South Vietnam and Laos, but it contained "fall-back objectives" consistent with McNaughton's "good doctor" metaphor:

1. To hold the situation together as long as possible, so that we have time to strengthen other areas of Asia.

2. To take forceful enough measures in the situation so that we emerge from it, even in the worst case, with our standing as the principal helper against Communist expansion as little impaired as possible.

3. To make clear to the world, and to nations in Asia particularly, that failure in South Vietnam, if it comes, was due to special local factors—such as bad colonial heritage and a lack of will to defend itself—that do not apply to other nations.[21]

While the Bundy committee completed its work, Secretary of Defense Robert McNamara tried to obtain from the Joint Chiefs a specific plan for applying graduated military pressure. On November 10 McNamara asked Wheeler to have the JCS develop courses of action to apply "controlled and increasingly severe military pressure on North Vietnam." Although the Chiefs did not support Option C, McNamara's instructions forced them to develop a military plan to implement it. The Chiefs argued that the limited intervention would not secure the freedom and independence of South Vietnam and Laos; rather, it would only "signal" determination, "reduce progressively" North Vietnam's support of the insurgencies in South Vietnam and Laos, and "punish" North Vietnam for actions against the Laotian and South Vietnamese governments.[22]

Because the Chiefs did not believe that Option C would secure American objectives in Southeast Asia, they urged McNamara to develop a "clear set of military objectives before further military involvement in Southeast Asia is undertaken." They were reluctant to accept the "fall-back" objectives then under development. They argued that the

United States, once it had begun using force in Vietnam, could not terminate military activities until it had attained freedom and independence for South Vietnam. The Chiefs therefore rejected the very idea that underlay the widespread support of Option C, namely, that gradual military pressure would enable the United States to pull out of Vietnam whenever it wished. The senior military officers did not believe that the United States should commit military force and expend the lives of Americans without fully committing to the policy objective that the intervention was supposed to achieve. They did not support using military force to leave "behind a better odor" should the United States lose.

The Chiefs also reminded McNamara that their preferred course of action was an intensive air campaign against North Vietnam to destroy the ninety-four targets on their list. The Chiefs asked that their recommendation for a "hard knock" be forwarded to the president for his consideration. On November 18 the JCS submitted their plan to McNamara, who refused to forward the memo to the president on the grounds that he would receive the JCS position when the working group completed its study.[23] He also ignored the Chiefs' call for a clear articulation of military objectives and forwarded their plan for gradually intensifying military action to William Bundy and McNaughton for use in the development of Option C.[24]

Even as McNamara excluded the Chiefs from the policy process, he attempted to preserve the impression that the working group's study represented a wide range of opinions. On November 19 he attended a meeting at the White House with the president, Rusk, McGeorge and William Bundy, Deputy Secretary of Defense Cyrus Vance, and CIA Director McCone. After Rusk and William Bundy explained the three options the committee had generated, McGeorge Bundy told the president that "the focus of attention was increasingly on Option C" and that Ball's "devil's advocate exercise" of proposing a negotiated withdrawal had made little progress. McNamara, however, tempered Bundy's statement and explained that work was "well advanced" on Option B. Rusk and William Bundy assisted McNamara, agreeing that Ball had made "some progress" on the "devil's advocate exercise." Rusk assured the president that the working group would not permit irresistible momentum to develop in favor of any one option to the exclusion of others. McNamara did not mention the Chiefs' call for a clarification of objectives or their advocacy of a "hard knock" military option that went beyond those being considered by the working group.[25]

When the president expressed his desire that no "firm decisions" be made without military advice, McNamara assured him that the "military were already deeply involved in the planning" and that the JCS had been "working for weeks on this problem." The defense secretary, however, failed to disclose how closely he had curtailed the scope of JCS planning to conform with his own preconceptions of how the war ought to be fought. He also assured the president that General Wheeler would be present at the meetings scheduled for Ambassador Taylor, who planned to visit Washington during the following week.[26] The president warned McNamara and the others that he "could not face the congressional leadership on this kind of subject unless he had fully consulted with the relevant military people." Shortly after the meeting, the president returned to his Texas ranch, taking with him William Bundy's and McNaughton's latest drafts of the so-called "hard/fast squeeze" and the favored "slow, controlled squeeze."[27]

■

Meanwhile the JCS tried to design their version of Option B so that it would appeal to the president's top advisers. They described their bombing program as "controlled" and "swiftly yet deliberately applied." Despite their efforts the "hard knock" faced insurmountable opposition. On November 24 William Bundy prepared a memo that revealed unambiguously his, McNamara's, and McNaughton's advocacy of Option C. Bundy argued against the "hard knock" noting that "many of us feel the actions should be progressive, with the prospect of more to come at least as important psychologically as present damage." He highlighted the virtues of "focusing at length on low-key targets not so much for the sake of damage as to show how hopeless the DRV [North Vietnam] is." Bundy contended that his "undramatic 'water drip' technique" would actually have a more disquieting psychological effect on North Vietnam than the "more dramatic attacks" that the JCS advocated.[28]

The military was far from united behind the "hard knock." Admiral Sharp and General Westmoreland had dissented from the JCS position. CINCPAC seemed to favor Option C, or as he described it, "a campaign of systematically and gradually increased measured military pressures . . . to convince the Communists that destruction will continue to occur until they cease supporting the insurgency."[29] The MACV commander recommended Option A or a continuation of the current policy for the next several months. Westmoreland—deeply involved in what he considered a "laboratory experiment in pacification" to clear and hold the area around Saigon—feared that early strikes against the North would divert the South Vietnamese government from the fight against the Viet Cong.[30]

Faced with overwhelming opposition and a lack of consensus within the military, the JCS devised a "fall-back" option, C-prime (C').[31] Option C' differed from Option C only in its commitment to "continue military pressures, if necessary, to the full limitations of what military actions can contribute toward US national objectives." The JCS provided no estimate of what level of force would ultimately be required to achieve a free and independent South Vietnam. Instead they wanted a blank check that would permit the war to escalate after the gradual approach failed. The Chiefs wrote that Option C' was "not recommended" but indicated that they would support that option "should a controlled program of systematically increased pressures be directed." Wheeler presented the fall-back option at a November 24 meeting with Rusk, McNamara, McCone, Ball, and the Bundy brothers. The purpose of the meeting was to arrange a "consensus" position before Taylor's visit.[32] Wheeler agreed to support Option C in exchange for an open-ended commitment to escalate the war to whatever level of force became necessary.

The JCS intended to try to intensify the bombing to a level more consistent with their concept of a "hard knock" after the president approved the gradual option. The Chiefs recognized that the sharp limitations on U.S. force imposed by Option C "would encourage the enemy to match each progressive step with a new level of effort" until the "scale of hostilities would eventually reach those in Course of Action B." After the November 24 meeting, William Bundy composed a memorandum that recorded the "consensus or majority view of key issues discussed." General Wheeler had not dissented from the position that "maintaining military pressure and a credible threat of major action while at the same time being prepared to negotiate could in practice be carried out."[33]

■

The president's desire for consensus and Wheeler's sensitivity to that desire helped preclude a full examination of differences between the opinions of the JCS and of William Bundy's working group. These areas of disagreement included points as fundamental as the appropriate objective for military action and, as William Bundy put it, "the degree of firm-ness" with which the United States should pursue those objectives. The Chiefs remained committed to the application of the "full limits" of American military power to secure the freedom and independence of South Vietnam.[34] McNamara, McNaughton, and Bundy, however, sought only a "limited objective" in South Vietnam itself and were interested primarily in preserving America's "credibility" worldwide. Indeed, the initial outline of Option C indicated that the United States would accept "the possibility that we might not achieve our full objectives."[35] Because Wheeler failed to confront civilian officials with these disagree-ments, planning for the war continued without agreement on either the objective or the level of commitment the United States was willing to make.

The Joint Chiefs, and Wheeler in particular, were working within the constraints of graduated pressure rather than questioning its assumptions. Since the Gulf of Tonkin incident, the Chiefs had focused much of their time and energy on removing obstacles to more resolute military action. While the working group was in session, the JCS continued to submit memos aimed at the intensification or activation of military operations already approved. These included expanded covert raids against North Vietnam and the resumption of DESOTO patrols.[36] The Chiefs' advo-cacy of minor military actions occurred even while the Joint Staff worked on a memorandum aimed at persuading U.S. policy makers that a "hard knock" was preferable to the incremental application of military pres-sure. The JCS adopted the language of graduated pressure to strengthen their argument that restrictions on military actions should be relaxed. On November 14 the Joint Chiefs recommended that the president approve air strikes against North Vietnam by unmarked aircraft of the South Vietnamese Air Force. The Chiefs argued that these "additional harassment actions" would apply "pressure" against North Vietnam and "provide a stimulus" to the Saigon government.[37] The Chiefs' preoccupa-tion with minor intensifications of the war diverted them from strategic planning and thereby excluded them even more from the policy process. It also reinforced in practice the concept of graduated pressure.

■

Maxwell Taylor arrived in Washington on Thanksgiving, November 26, 1964. He brought with him an assessment of the situation in Vietnam and a recommended plan of action. Over the next four days the president's advisers worked to combine the Bundy group's papers with Taylor's latest recommendations. Michael Forrestal had met Taylor in Saigon to brief him on the working group's early drafts. Taylor's proposed plan of action strikingly resembled McNaughton's and Bundy's Option C.[38]

The purpose of Taylor's visit was to preserve consensus. He joined an Executive Committee (EXCOM) meeting, similar to the forum that President John Kennedy's advisers used during the Cuban missile crisis. In addition to Taylor, the Vietnam EXCOM included Rusk, McNamara, McCone, Wheeler, Ball, the Bundys, McNaughton, and Forrestal. The EXCOM planned to present its proposal to the president on Johnson's return from Texas to Washington on December 1.[39]

Taylor's assessment of the situation was dismal. He argued that Westmoreland's hope for progress in the pacification program was unrealistic. He lamented the malaise that seemed to have gripped the South Vietnamese populace and expressed surprise over the strength and resiliency of the Viet Cong, who demonstrated the "recuperative powers of the phoenix" and an "amazing ability to maintain morale." He blamed this situation largely on the ineffectiveness of the Saigon government, but he admitted that prospects for improvement in that area were dim. He argued that only direct military action against North Vietnam would provide a "glimmer of light" that might boost morale among the South Vietnamese people and strengthen the government. He believed that gradually intensified bombing of North Vietnam might provide a "pulmotor treatment" to keep a dying South Vietnamese government alive. McNamara agreed that air action against the North might "buy time even measured in years" before the Saigon government "crumbled."[40]

Taylor proposed a two-phase "Scenario for Controlled Escalation" to begin the application of military pressure on North Vietnam. Phase I of the scenario, approximately thirty days long, would aim to "bolster the local morale and restrain the Viet Cong" by conducting covert operations, air strikes against infiltration targets in Laos, and reprisal bombing. If, as hoped, the Saigon government survived, the United States would initiate Phase II, which Taylor described as a "methodical program of mounting air attacks" against North Vietnam. Taylor continued to believe that the gradually applied pressure of air strikes on the North might force Hanoi to "use its directive powers to make the Viet Cong desist from their efforts." McNamara asked Taylor if this second phase of actions against the North would be justified if the Saigon government were unstable, and quickly answered "yes" to his own question; Taylor agreed with the defense secretary.[41] The EXCOM ordered William Bundy to draft a specific plan based on Taylor's two-phase course of action.[42]

General Wheeler convened a meeting of the Joint Chiefs of Staff upon his return from the EXCOM meeting on November 27. Perhaps in deference to Taylor, his old boss and mentor, Wheeler had not pressed the JCS view during the EXCOM meeting. He may also have recognized the futility of doing so. The chairman reported to his colleagues that they alone advocated Option B. Although the Chiefs decided to continue recommending a "hard knock," they again made it clear that they would agree to the gradual application of force in exchange for a commitment to use whatever force became necessary to assure South Vietnam's freedom and independence.[43]

Planning responsibility remained with William Bundy's working group after Taylor's arrival. Bundy and his colleagues were too preoccupied with conflicting political priorities to consider adequately military issues such as the level of force necessary to affect the enemy's will and ability to continue the war. They had to "weigh at every point" possible reactions of the U.S. Congress, the Saigon, Hanoi, and Beijing governments, and American and international opinion. After the November 28 meeting, William Bundy drafted an NSAM that detailed thirty days of Phase I "immediate actions," followed by a second phase consisting of "graduated military pressures directed systematically" against North Vietnam. Taylor, McNaughton, Rusk, and Forrestal reviewed Bundy's memo; the draft NSAM was ready to go to the president on November 29. McNaughton developed and McNamara approved an appendix to the NSAM, entitled "Graduated Military Pressure and Related Actions," which included time-phased military actions such as air deployments, bombing targets, and the numbers of sorties required per target. The JCS did not contribute to this document. William Bundy thought McNaughton's "impressive array of facts on available forces" represented "the best thinking available."[44]

The Joint Chiefs did not recommend changes to the substance of Bundy's memo. In fact General Wheeler asked only that, in the discussion of U.S. operations in Laos, the phrase "armed reconnaissance" be changed to "air strikes" so as not to preclude attacks on bridges. The Chiefs approved the document because it held out the promise of future action and indicated that the president would escalate the level of military activities. In fact, on November 30, Taylor told the JCS that the rate of escalation under Option C was ambiguous and speculated that it might shift quickly to the "hard knock."[45] The memo stated that America's policy objective in Vietnam, to secure an independent, non-Communist South Vietnam, was "unchanged." The document did not list "fall-back" objectives. It permitted air strikes on all ninety-four targets recommended by the JCS, as well as aerial mining of North Vietnamese ports and a naval blockade of North Vietnam.

The Chiefs supported the memo, furthermore, because the draft that they reviewed included a paragraph describing the "hard knock." They were naturally under the impression that the Bundy memo that the president received contained this information. They were misled:[46] Prior to submitting the memo to the president, McNamara removed the description of the "hard knock." William Bundy later explained that this excision was natural because the president's other advisers had reached a "crucial consensus" and the JCS position was "without institutional support." According to Bundy the JCS were lucky that their proposal survived as long as it did because it had already been "completely accepted that the military elements of any bombing program would be gradual in character." Bundy said that the consensus that had "formed slowly over a long time" had finally moved "out in the open."[47]

General Wheeler had his only opportunity to propose the "hard knock" during a December 1 meeting with the president, Vice President Hubert H. Humphrey, and the EXCOM members.[48] When his turn came to speak, Wheeler told Johnson that the Joint Chiefs of Staff recommended "sharp military actions" including the destruction of the Phuc Yen MIG fighter base, other airfields, and major petroleum facilities in three days. These initial attacks would "establish the fact the US intends to use military force, if necessary, to the full limits of what military force can contribute to achieving US objectives in Southeast Asia." Air strikes would then continue on infiltration targets in North Vietnam and expand eventually to areas throughout the country. Wheeler stated that the program "could be suspended short of full destruction of [North Vietnam] if our objectives were earlier achieved."[49]

Wheeler reported the Chiefs' judgment that solving the conflict in Vietnam would ultimately require a greater level of force than that proposed in the Bundy committee's Option C. He read the following passage verbatim from a sheet of paper:

The JCS recognize that any course of action we adopt, except early withdrawal from SVN, could develop eventually into the course they advocate. This fact reinforces our belief that we should profit by the several advantages of forthright military action initiated upon our decision. In other words, if we must fight a war in Southeast Asia, let us do so under conditions favorable to us from the outset and with maximum volition resting with the United States.[50]

By all accounts Wheeler did not present the Chiefs' position forcefully. He did not dissent from the Bundy memo. He did not highlight the Chiefs' disagreement with the consensus policy. He did not confront President Johnson with the things he feared: division among his advisers and the possibility that the country would learn that the Chiefs dissented from the policy choices he favored.

Wheeler's presentation of the Chiefs' position preserved a facade of consultation between the president and the JCS. Before Wheeler first spoke, the president had already approved the consensus position of his civilian advisers. After Wheeler gave the JCS position, however, Johnson expressed agreement with several points and appeared amenable to tougher military action. He seemed to leave open the degree to which he was willing to commit military force, and concurred with Wheeler's statement that military actions should aim to preserve "maximum volition." The president indicated that he was reluctant to take immediate military action due to the instability of the South Vietnamese government and the precarious position of American civilian dependents living in South Vietnam, but he pledged a willingness to reconsider Wheeler's proposal at a later time. Just prior to the end of the meeting, LBJ reassured Wheeler that if the situation did not improve, "I'll be talking to you, General."[51]

On his return to the Pentagon, Wheeler reported to LeMay and the other Chiefs that the president had essentially opted for the Chiefs' Option C' or "fall-back" proposal. Although the president and his advisers had rejected the "hard knock" for the present, it seemed likely that the JCS would eventually secure approval for the level of military force they advocated. Wheeler noted that no one at the meeting questioned the importance of Southeast Asia or the validity of U.S. objectives there as the JCS had defined them.[52] Yet the JCS and the civilian presidential advisers had not resolved their fundamental disagreement over the objectives that the United States was pursuing in Vietnam or over the level of military force that the president was willing to commit to the war. On December 3 Johnson again met with his advisers to approve the EXCOM's two-phase plan for slowly deepening America's involvement in the war.

On the same day the president gave Taylor final instructions before the ambassador departed for Saigon. He put tremendous pressure on the ambassador to make improvements in the South Vietnamese government—a task that Taylor had described as virtually impossible. LBJ emphasized that the South Vietnamese government would have to meet "minimum criteria of performance" before the United States attacked North Vietnam. In short, the Saigon government had to maintain control of the population while the military remained subordinate and responsive to civil authority. Specifically Taylor should instruct the South Vietnamese government to increase the size and effectiveness of its armed forces and police, replace incompetent commanders and civilian officials, broaden the civic action program, demonstrate progress in pacification, and, finally, carry out a sanitary cleanup of Saigon. The president authorized Taylor to begin joint planning for air strikes against the North to show the South Vietnamese leaders that the United States was willing to reward them with bombing runs on North Vietnam if they satisfied the American criteria for an effective government. It was time to "quit talking and go to work," the president announced.[53]

■

Johnson's reluctance to approve a bombing program ran deeper than his concern over the stability of the South Vietnamese government. Vietnam was demanding his attention when he could least afford to give it. Preoccupied with putting the finishing touches on his Great Society program for the next Congress, Johnson planned to push 150 bills in as many days. From his long experience in the House and Senate, he knew that he had to win congressional support for this program in the first year of his presidency, when his influence was greatest. Vietnam must not divert congressional or public attention from the Great Society.[54] He moved to obscure the depth of the difficulties in Vietnam and to minimize the significance of Taylor's visit.

Although Johnson had already authorized air raids against Laos, an intensification of reconnaissance flights over North Vietnam, and

U.S.–South Vietnamese joint planning for air strikes into North
Vietnam, he was anxious to keep these decisions from the American people. He ordered that the National Security Action Memorandum be
issued as a less conspicuous "policy paper" and decreed that the word
"EXCOM" no longer be used to describe the group of Vietnam advisers.
The State Department press release about Taylor's visit quoted his reporting an increase in the strength of the South Vietnamese armed forces,
rather than publicizing his pessimistic assessment of affairs in Saigon.
The president attempted to conceal from the American public the difficulties in the South Vietnamese armed forces and the gains in Viet Cong
strength. On McNamara's recommendation, he removed from a draft of
an official White House statement an announcement that the State
Department would soon release a study of increased infiltration from
North Vietnam. Johnson told his advisers on December 1 that he would
"shoot at sunrise" anyone who leaked information on infiltration to the
public.[55]

Lyndon Johnson knew how dramatically any action against North
Vietnam would contrast with his position during the election. Only two
months prior to the December meetings, he had told a crowd in
Manchester, New Hampshire, that his administration would "start dropping bombs" only as a "last resort" and that he planned to "get them [the
South Vietnamese] to save their own freedom with their own men." A
November 25 New York Times editorial reminded readers of the president's campaign remarks and suggested: "If there is to be a new policy
now, if an Asian war is to be converted into an American war, the country has a right to insist that it be told what has changed so profoundly in
the past two months to justify it."[56] Johnson was caught in a web of his
own spinning. Even if he did not prefer subterfuge to frank communication, he now had no choice.

Consistent with Johnson's effort to keep Vietnam out of the press, the
president's top civilian advisers were determined to keep the Phase I
pressures sharply limited. The Joint Chiefs continued to press for a relaxation of restrictions on military action. Their requests, however, received
only partial approval from the secretary of defense and the president.
During the month following the president's decision to begin Phase I,
U.S. aircraft flew only six armed reconnaissance missions, spotting no
enemy soldiers or military traffic. While the JCS complained that the
program had fallen far short of what the president had approved,

McNamara and McNaughton continued to block the Chiefs' calls for further action. McNaughton argued that "the purpose of the missions was to send a signal of deeper US involvement, the signal to be more psychological in nature than pure military effectiveness." Although the Chiefs scoffed at the idea of using military force to "send signals," they remained unwilling to confront the rationale that lay behind the concept of graduated pressure or make a forceful issue of their disagreement with the secretary of defense or the president.[57]

10
A Fork in the Road
December 1964–February 1965

In retrospect, I'm absolutely convinced that we lost the war wrong. We should have fought that war in an advisory mode and remained in that mode. When the South Vietnamese failed to come up and meet the mark at the advisory level, then we never should have committed US forces. We should have failed at the advisory effort and withdrawn.

—GEN. VOLNEY F. WARNER, 1983[1]

From December 1964 to February 1965, after the president had approved the report of William Bundy and his "working group," a deteriorating political and military situation in South Vietnam combined with pressure from LBJ's advisers to move LBJ toward deepening American military intervention. The planning efforts of 1964 and the president's promises of future action, which fabricated a consensus behind graduated pressure and postponed difficult decisions, had laid the foundation for the Americanization of the war. As George Ball had warned, "events" were now "in the saddle."[2]

■

On December 12 Army Chief of Staff Harold Johnson returned from a four-day trip to South Vietnam, where he visited fifteen locations. At best the general received only a superficial impression of the situation.

The main purpose of his visit was "to convey to a maximum number of U.S. Army personnel . . . an appreciation of the Army chief's keen interest in the welfare of his people and the *success* of the US advisory and support mission in the Republic of Vietnam."[3]

In purpose and itinerary General Johnson's trip prepared him to see only the positive aspects of the U.S. effort in Vietnam. Army advisers and staff officers who briefed the Army chief of staff were reluctant to bring bad news. Johnson, a compassionate leader whose principal concern was the morale of his soldiers, did not probe deeply into the reports of progress. On his return, the general rendered an unrealistically sanguine report to McNamara. He described various improvements in the South Vietnamese armed forces and government, lauded the accomplishments of the American military's advisory and support effort, and reported that, "given political stability and popular support of the government, the positive factors, on balance, appear to outweigh the negative ones. They encourage some optimism about the results of programs already underway and prospects for the future."[4] He could not have been more mistaken.

■

When Taylor returned to Saigon, he undertook LBJ's charge to straighten out the South Vietnamese government seriously and with all the subtlety of a colonial governor. Taylor invited a score of senior South Vietnamese commanders, including a group of influential officers whom Washington officials called the "Young Turks," to General Westmoreland's residence for a steak dinner, at which he told them that the United States could no longer support South Vietnam if the military continued to engage in political intrigue. He exacted from the generals a pledge to support the fledgling civilian government of Prime Minister Tran Van Huong and his interim legislative body, the High National Council. Separately Taylor notified Huong that if the South Vietnamese government demonstrated "minimum" effectiveness, the United States would consider commencing a program of "direct military pressure" on North Vietnam. In the meantime the United States would monitor the government's progress and take military actions directed toward "reducing infiltration and warning the government of North Vietnam of the risks it is running."[5]

General Westmoreland's steak dinner probably gave the South Vietnamese generals a bad case of indigestion. Although they depended on U.S. support, the Young Turks and their commander in chief, Nguyen Khanh, were painfully aware of their country's historical struggle against colonial domination. These proud men resented any implication that they had become "puppets" of the American government, something that, in addition to a personal affront, would be a boon to Communist propagandists and an obstacle to gaining popular support. Taylor incorrectly believed that his guidance had been "well received." On December 20 the Young Turks, with Khanh's approval, dissolved the High National Council and arrested twenty-two of its members. Taylor was furious. He considered their action treachery and, coming so soon after his appeal for good behavior, a personal insult.[6]

Taylor called the Young Turks to his office and scolded the generals: "We cannot carry you forever if you do things like this." Addressing them in a condescending manner, he asked, "Do all of you understand English? I told you clearly at General Westmorland's dinner we Americans were tired of coups." The South Vietnamese generals, unaccustomed to reprimands, responded with equal vigor. Air Vice Marshal Nguyen Cao Ky told Taylor that not only did he and his colleagues understand English, but they also understood their responsibilities: "We did what we thought was good for this country." Taylor did not waver. The generals had "broken a lot of dishes and now we have to see how we can straighten out this mess." Ky later recalled that he had felt like a West Point cadet being raked over the coals by the superintendent.[7]

The next day Taylor provoked a feud with Khanh that would continue until Khanh's departure from the government in February 1965. Nine months had passed since Taylor, then chairman of the JCS, had traveled with McNamara to Saigon to demonstrate American support for Khanh as prime minister. Now Taylor told Khanh that the South Vietnamese general had "outlived his usefulness." When Khanh, frustrated, offered to quit as commander of the South Vietnamese armed forces, Taylor suggested that he not only resign but leave the country. Just before Christmas the rift between the ambassador and the South Vietnamese military became public. Accusing Taylor of "activities beyond imagination," Khanh stated publicly that the ambassador was "not serving his country well" and suggested privately to Premier Huong that the South Vietnamese government declare Taylor persona non grata.[8]

On December 23 Taylor told Washington: "We are in the midst of a first-class governmental crisis in Saigon." He described the problem as "infighting on three fronts: the govt versus the Generals, the Generals versus the US Ambassador, and the Buddhists versus the govt."[9] Gone was any hope for an improvement in the South Vietnamese government during Phase I of the plan Lyndon Johnson had approved three weeks earlier. In the midst of the turmoil in Saigon, the Viet Cong struck.

On Christmas Eve a powerful explosion destroyed the Brinks Hotel, an American bachelor officer quarters (BOQ) in Saigon. Viet Cong terrorists had planted a car bomb in the parking garage. The blast killed two Americans and left sixty-three others injured.[10] Taylor was anxious to launch a reprisal, but he acknowledged that several factors militated against an early decision to retaliate. Amid the turmoil in Saigon, some American officials actually suspected that South Vietnamese government agents planted the bomb. Relations were so poor with Air Vice Marshal Ky and the South Vietnamese Air Force, moreover, that any air strike would most likely be an exclusively American operation. Taylor withheld his recommendation until he had first conducted an investigation into responsibility for the bombing. Finally, on December 28, he recommended a retaliatory strike against North Vietnam.[11]

■

The Joint Chiefs quickly supported Taylor's suggestion. Wheeler asked McNamara for permission to order a reprisal raid against Taylor's preferred target, a military barracks in the southern portion of North Vietnam. Because the president was away at the Texas ranch for the holidays, Rusk presided over a meeting with Wheeler, Deputy Secretary of Defense Vance, and Forrestal.[12] McGeorge Bundy and Rusk opposed a retaliatory strike. Bundy thought that the "signal" to the North Vietnamese would be blurred as long as there was such political confusion in Saigon, and that the four-day interval since the Brinks bombing had already compromised Washington's ability to send its message. Bundy also asserted that it would be "unwise" to strike North Vietnam "merely because security control in a U.S. BOQ is bad." Bundy's and Rusk's opinion prevailed, although the former included Taylor's and the Chiefs' arguments in favor of a reprisal in a memo to the president. The two men traveled to Johnson's ranch on December 29. The president seized on Bundy's rationale for denying a reprisal strike and sent the ambassador a cable in which he emphasized the uncertainty surrounding responsibility for the attack and the "general confusion in South Vietnam."[13]

■

The "holiday" deliberations revealed that Taylor was falling out of favor with the president and his closest advisers. McGeorge Bundy and Dean Rusk openly criticized the ambassador and seemed to blame him, in part, for both the political crisis in Saigon and the BOQ bombing. Rusk wondered if Taylor had become "used up" politically as a result of his clash with General Khanh and the Young Turks. McGeorge Bundy questioned the objectivity of Taylor's advice. He invoked the authority of Winston Churchill to suggest that the president should "never trust the man on the spot." He suggested that it was easy for Taylor to be "brave," but it would be Johnson who would have to "live with the decision."[14] The Brinks bombing and the confused political situation in Saigon presented Rusk and Bundy with an opportunity to challenge Taylor's influence over Vietnam policy.

Johnson sent Taylor a cable that combined an explanation of the decision to forgo retaliation with a stinging critique of the ambassador's performance. The president seemed to blame Taylor and his country team for the bombing and the conditions that precluded an American reprisal. Repeating Bundy's criticism of American security arrangements, the president vowed that he would not "be drawn into a large-scale military action against North Vietnam simply because our own people are careless or imprudent." Johnson told Taylor that he did not understand "why aircraft cannot be protected from mortar attacks and officers quarters from large bombs." He insinuated that Taylor had been insensitive and inept in his dealings with "the various groups in South Vietnam" and expressed disappointment that Taylor had not accomplished all that he could have in the area of "political persuasion" with the South Vietnamese politicians and generals. The president suggested that the ambassador seek counsel from Vietnam experts who might help him deal with his present difficulties.[15]

After he admonished Taylor, Johnson enumerated conditions that would have to be met before he would "look with favor" on reprisal actions. These included:

1. The removal of dependents.
2. The stiffening of our own security arrangements to protect our own people and forces.
3. A much wider and more varied attempt to get good political relations with all Vietnamese groups.

4. An intensified US stiffening on-the-ground by Rangers and
    Special Forces or other appropriate elements.

While rejecting Taylor's request for a bombing reprisal, Johnson suggested that American ground troops would be "more effective" in reversing the deteriorating situation. The suggestion had come from Bundy,
who, as early as March 1964, had pressed Johnson to consider deploying
ground troops to South Vietnam as "a stiffener . . . not because they're
needed to win the war but only to show them that this damn thing can
be done." Johnson told Taylor that he was "ready to look with great favor
on that kind of increased American effort, directed at the guerrillas and
aimed to stiffen the aggressiveness of Vietnamese military units up and
down the line."[16]

Taylor could not understand how the president could balk at what the
ambassador considered a low-cost, low-risk bombing reprisal and simultaneously propose the introduction of U.S. ground forces to Vietnam.[17] At
the end of 1964, there were more than 23,000 American military advisers
in South Vietnam, fighting side by side with their South Vietnamese
counterparts. During 1964, 149 Americans had been killed in action and
19 were either missing or had been captured by the enemy.[18] The introduction of American ground combat units, however, would change the
nature of U.S. involvement in the war. Vietnam would become an
American war rather than a U.S. effort to help the South Vietnamese
fight their own conflict.

Although McNamara would write in 1995 that the president's suggestion for ground troops came "out of the blue," the secretary of defense
and the EXCOM had considered the introduction of ground troops as
part of Option C during their deliberations in November 1964. On
November 24 Rusk and McGeorge Bundy expressed an interest in the
deployment of ground combat forces as a "signal of determination" on
the part of the United States. McNamara disagreed and argued that
ground troops were not needed under his proposal for graduated pressure
against the North. McNamara carried the argument, and the working
group's final draft reflected his assessment. In his November 26 memo
William Bundy observed that by deploying ground troops early in the
game of graduated pressure, the United States "would play a card that we
might wish to hold in reserve for a later stage." After Taylor arrived in
Washington, the ground troop issue was suppressed completely. Like

McNamara the ambassador remained opposed to American ground combat units in Vietnam. William Bundy's NSAM on Vietnam did not mention the deployment of ground troops. As William Bundy subsequently stated, McNamara and Taylor guaranteed that the issue "simply died away."[19] Although Rusk and McGeorge Bundy had deferred to McNamara and Taylor in early December, they had the opportunity to suggest ground troops directly to the president during a trip to Texas in the wake of the Brinks bombing, when Taylor's opinions were most vulnerable to rejection.

The president's casual proposal to deploy ground troops reflected thinking that ground forces could be used in much the same way as air power. During the November 1964 deliberations, Robert H. Johnson of the State Department's Policy Planning Council and Paul Kattenberg, also of the State Department, advocated the introduction of ground combat units into South Vietnam as an alternative to bombing North Vietnam. Ground forces would be deployed not with the mission to defeat the enemy on the battlefield but to coerce Hanoi into negotiations designed to "extricate" the United States from its commitment to South Vietnam. Johnson and Kattenberg predicted that the presence of ground forces would "forecast" to the North Vietnamese "the likelihood of a much longer and more costly war." They thought that they could maintain tight control over ground forces, just as they planned to do over air strikes. Robert Johnson suggested that ground forces could undertake limited military action to "turn military pressure off and on" during negotiations.[20]

Like the threat of continued bombing, ground forces such as the First Marine Division and advance elements of the Army's Eighty-second Airborne Division would serve as a "bargaining lever" in these hypothetical negotiations. Johnson and Kattenberg suggested that ground combat units would convince North Vietnam to desist from its support of the insurgency in the South because, unlike air strikes, which would have to stop once negotiations had begun, ground forces "could not readily be removed by international pressures in negotiations." The chairman of the Policy Planning Council, Walt Rostow, agreed with their assessment. In a letter to McNamara on November 13, Rostow had argued that "ground troops can sit during a conference more easily than we can maintain a series of mounting air and naval pressures." During negotiations, the United States could take the "reasonable position" that it would remove ground forces when North Vietnam had pledged to end its support for the insurgency in the South.[21]

■

As he composed a six-part telegram responding to the president's cable, Taylor was besieged on all fronts. He received information that suggested an impending collapse of the American position in South Vietnam. While South Vietnamese generals occupied themselves principally with political intrigue, the Viet Cong were growing stronger, to a point where they controlled half of the countryside and one-quarter of the rural population. They had infiltrated the once-safe major cities and seemed poised to cut off the northern portion of South Vietnam by driving from their highland bases to the coastal provinces on the South China Sea. The pacification program that Westmoreland had hoped would secure the area around Saigon and serve as a model for the entire country had come to a standstill. The South Vietnamese armed forces were exclusively on the defensive and had suffered major defeats in spite of their superiority in numbers and equipment. Morale was sagging. In January alone more than seven thousand South Vietnamese deserted from the ranks.[22] Taylor, however, never considered reexamining the U.S. commitment to South Vietnam. He later recalled that "there were many untried military and other possibilities for improving the situation." With the South Vietnamese government in disarray and its armed forces on the ropes, it was time for the "pulmotor treatment" that Taylor had predicted might become necessary to revive an expiring South Vietnam.

After reaffirming his advocacy of bombing, Taylor explained in great detail why deploying ground combat units to Vietnam would be a grave mistake.[23] First, the United States had "gone about as far down the advisory route as it is practical to go without passing the point of clearly diminishing returns." "After much soul searching," Taylor and Westmoreland concluded that any military advantages gained as a result of the introduction of ground forces would be more than offset by the political liabilities. Taylor argued that the South Vietnamese had the physical and logistical capability to win the war but lacked the motivation to fight effectively. In light of the massive advisory effort that the United States had undertaken over the past ten years, it seemed unlikely that the introduction of U.S. combat forces would inspire the South Vietnamese to press the war more vigorously. On the contrary, he argued, U.S. combat forces would simply encourage the South Vietnamese armed forces to let the United States carry the full burden of the war effort. He feared that large numbers of U.S. ground troops would raise the specter of French colonialism and encourage a majority of the population to turn against the United States. Ultimately, Taylor predicted, U.S. soldiers and Marines would find themselves occupying a hostile foreign country.[24]

Taylor also considered the introduction of ground forces too expensive in money, manpower, and public opinion. General Westmoreland estimated that it would take thirty-four battalions or 75,000 troops to provide security to U.S. personnel and facilities. The ambassador observed that it would be difficult to confine Americans to their secure enclaves "in the face of guerrilla attacks" and predicted that ground units would inevitably have to expand operations beyond defensive perimeters. Due to the expanding mission, Taylor argued that the ultimate "cost in U.S. forces" would be "unpredictable" and warned that U.S. casualties would be "high." Offensive operations outside the enclaves would inevitably kill South Vietnamese civilians—casualties that would increase anti-American sentiment and give "appearances of a white man's war against the brown." The tactical operations conducted over the previous two years revealed that, due to the guerrilla nature of the fighting, it would rarely be feasible to use large U.S. combat formations in battle.[25]

Although Taylor objected to the introduction of ground combat units, he observed that the current situation in Vietnam demanded some sort of action: "We are presently on a losing track" and "must risk a change." He rejected the president's hint that old Vietnam hands like Gen. Edward Lansdale and CIA station chief Lucien Conein might assist him. No one would be able to "change national characteristics, create leadership where it does not exist, raise large additional combat forces or seal porous frontiers to infiltration." Improvements in these areas would take time; South Vietnam might collapse in the very near term. The president and other senior officials in Washington should be satisfied with a "marginal government" and add a "new element" to American policy to compensate for those factors that were beyond American control.

Taylor urged the United States to "look for an occasion" to conduct a reprisal air strike and "set the stage" for Phase II continuing actions against the North. The U.S. government could "justify" systematic bombing to the American public by publicizing reports of North Vietnamese infiltration into the South and by provoking a North

206 I DERELICTION OF DUTY

Vietnamese attack on U.S. destroyers in the Gulf of Tonkin.[26] As for the president's concerns that air power could not win the war in the South, graduated pressure would influence the North Vietnamese leaders, who were "practical men"; faced with the prospect of damage from the air, they would try "to find some accommodations which will excise the threat."[27]

On January 6 the president met with Rusk, Ball, and McNamara to discuss Taylor's cable and the situation in Vietnam. No military leader was present. Rusk argued that the United States had to make the current policy of supporting South Vietnam work because "the alternatives are so grim." Ball appeared almost resigned to defeat, but he agreed with Rusk that "we should make a heroic effort, but not delude ourselves" about a regime that had the "smell of death." Lyndon Johnson committed himself to a reprisal against North Vietnam after the next raid on American forces or facilities.[28]

Perhaps to assuage Taylor's feelings after the highly critical cable sent earlier, Lyndon Johnson thanked Taylor for his "exceedingly helpful and thoughtful analysis of the situation." Johnson told Taylor that the United States would reply by air to the next act of aggression against U.S. personnel and equipment, although he doubted that bombing would raise South Vietnam's morale. He was not yet willing, however, to commit to "the timing and scale" of Phase II graduated pressures on North Vietnam.[29] William Bundy and McNaughton, meanwhile, shared Ball's feeling that although the United States should deepen its military involvement in Vietnam, it should be prepared to accept defeat.

■

Despite their doubts that military force would secure American objectives in Vietnam, McNaughton and Bundy found the commitment of U.S. ground combat units to be an attractive option. On January 4 McNaughton restated his belief that the important "stakes" in Vietnam were the "buffer real estate near Thailand and Malaysia" and "our reputation." He felt that America's "reputation" would suffer least if it continued to support South Vietnam. Even if the United States did not "reverse the tide," a failure after deeper American involvement would permit "a departure of the kind which would put everyone on our side, wondering how we stuck it out and took it so long." Besides, if things "slipped," McNaughton had plans to "shore up Thailand and Malaysia." The secretary of defense concluded that a loss at the current level of commitment would be worse than failure after the commitment of hundreds of thousands of American soldiers, airmen, and Marines. On January 6, just before Rusk met with the president, William Bundy handed him a memo in which he and Forrestal concluded, like McNaughton, that "stronger action" would put the United States in a better position to "hold the next line of defense." The application of bombing pressure on North Vietnam would "have appeared to Asians" to have been the Americans' best shot. As Bundy later recalled his thinking:

> If, as appeared quite possible, South Vietnam was too far gone to save, nonetheless a final additional American effort would greatly increase the chances of holding the line at Thailand, the fallback geographical bastion and, as it increasingly appeared, the psychological key to the rest of mainland Southeast Asia at least.

Like McNaughton, Bundy was not opposed to the deployment of ground troops to keep up appearances. As his brother had suggested earlier, Bundy thought that ground combat units introduced at the outset of bombing the North might have "a real stiffening effect in Saigon, and a strong signal effect to Hanoi."[90]

The Joint Chiefs had accepted the strategy of gradual application of force in Vietnam on the condition that once U.S. forces became directly involved in the war, the U.S. government would pursue its stated policy goals and objectives without qualification. The president and his civilian advisers did not intend to fulfill this condition. The advisers also had developed among themselves, they thought, a Southeast Asia policy that allowed them to work within Johnson's domestic political constraints and achieve their political international goals. They consequently circumvented the Chiefs rather than allowing them to plan for the deployment of American ground troops.

Although Taylor persuaded Lyndon Johnson not to use ground troops in the near term, he was unable to hold the president to this position in the long run. Johnson's closest advisers, who had already voiced doubts about Taylor's effectiveness, continued to undercut the ambassador's influence. McGeorge Bundy, pointing to his own three-year experience as an Army staff officer, suggested that Taylor and Westmoreland, as "regulation officers," were running operations in Vietnam "in a regulation way" with "too much staff, too much administration, too much clerical work, too much reporting, too much rotation, and not enough action." Rusk shared Bundy's doubts about Taylor. He and others suggested that only Taylor's assistant, U. Alexis Johnson, kept the Saigon embassy functioning effectively. By the end of January, rumors of the attacks on Taylor had reached Attorney General Robert F. Kennedy. Kennedy warned him of "an effort on behalf of at least some important segments of the administration to place the blame on you" for the difficulties in Vietnam.[31]

Policy differences, particularly over the use of ground troops in Vietnam, in part underlay the opposition to Taylor. McGeorge Bundy, consistent with the views of his brother, rejected Taylor's argument that ground combat units should not be introduced into Vietnam at an early date. He suggested to the president that McNamara opposed sending more American soldiers to Vietnam only because he believed that a larger number of troops would mean more "overhead and administration and general heaviness." On January 7 Bundy drafted for Johnson a memo to McNamara suggesting that he develop a "new plan for volunteer fighting forces that would proceed with a minimum of overhead and a maximum of energy in direct contact with the Vietnamese at all levels." The memo directed McNamara to "develop some alternatives" for the employment of U.S. ground forces in Vietnam. Bundy had LBJ attach to the memorandum a copy of a *U.S. News & World Report* article critical of Taylor's and Westmoreland's operation in Saigon.[32]

■

As McGeorge Bundy and Rusk chipped away at Taylor's and McNamara's influence with the president, the JCS remained excluded from the president's review of Vietnam policy. The president and his closest advisers did not solicit military advice on either the introduction of ground forces or Taylor's recommendation to begin a regular bombing campaign. Someone aware of their frustration leaked a story that was published in the *London Times* on January 18: The "uniformed military had been excluded from the inner counsels in Washington." One of Bundy's staff received a copy of the article and warned him that:

> there is considerable concern in the JCS about their exclusion from
> these [Vietnam] meetings. Since the Joint Staff is frequently asked for
> briefing materials, General Wheeler is well aware that the meetings

are taking place. There may be a good reason for excluding Wheeler, but I wonder whether it outweighs the disadvantages that might arise from his absence. . . . I know that this is McNamara's problem, not yours, but you might want to raise the issue with him.[33]

In his memoir McNamara wrote that Johnson was frustrated by the shallowness of advice that the JCS sent him.[34] McNamara himself, however, was largely responsible for the inadequacy of the JCS's counsel, and therefore, for the president's frustration.

Excluded from substantive deliberations on Vietnam, the JCS continued to try to erode the barriers to more resolute military action and to prepare for a larger American military commitment. General Wheeler, disappointed in the decision to forgo retaliation for the Brinks bombing, moved to guarantee that future incidents would precipitate a retaliatory air strike. He sent a cable to General Westmoreland and Admiral Sharp expressing astonishment at the argument that "lax security not only invites but in some curious way justifies a VC attack and thereby inhibits us from retaliatory action." Sharp and Westmoreland must "somehow convince the Washington policy-makers that our security arrangements are as good as the type of war we are fighting will permit." "Hurdles" to direct American action against North Vietnam could be reduced, and the commanders should be ready to conduct reprisals. U.S. dependents should be evacuated to preclude them from hindering action against the North. Finally Wheeler asked Westmoreland to "press the military and civilians in Saigon to submerge their differences and fabricate a reasonably sound governmental structure."[35]

Wheeler and the JCS now sought an increased level of military activity as a goal in itself. On January 15 the Chiefs reminded McNamara that the period allocated for Phase I pressures had elapsed, and at their suggestion he permitted the use of U.S. jet aircraft within South Vietnam, subject to Ambassador Taylor's approval. They urged a resumption of destroyer patrols in the Gulf of Tonkin and prepared a series of reprisal options aimed at "low-value" military targets. Their reprisal "packages" were designed to appeal to Washington officials' penchant for control and for limiting the scale of air strikes. Through an Air Force colonel on the NSC staff, the Chiefs requested the relaxation of geographic restrictions on Operation Barrel Roll, the air strikes in Laos.[36]

The JCS responded to civil unrest in South Vietnam by preparing to intervene directly on the ground. From January 23 to 25 Buddhist uprisings in major South Vietnamese cities unmasked strong anti-American sentiments. The Buddhists directed assaults against symbols of the American presence in South Vietnam. In Hue, the center of the unrest, students sacked the United States Information Service library. Demonstrators shouted "Taylor go home!" and Buddhist leaders denounced Premier Huong as the ambassador's "lackey." On January 25 the JCS ordered an amphibious readiness group to move within twenty-four-hours' striking distance of Danang, and two naval task groups to move to a location six hours away from Saigon.[37] Although the crisis passed, it showed that concerns over the security of American citizens and property might easily overwhelm Taylor's objections to the introduction of ground combat forces.

McNamara resisted the Chiefs' requests for further action, although he was willing to make minor concessions. On January 13 the Chiefs asked McNamara to approve the deployment of a 6,200-man Army logistical command in Vietnam to prepare for the possibility of large-scale troop deployments. McNamara, who had ordered McNaughton to "hold the line" on the numbers of U.S. troops in Vietnam, sent a Defense Department team to Saigon to study the request, which Westmoreland had initiated. The team notified Westmoreland's staff that they would approve 125 logistical troops and, if MACV used them properly, 250 more. The team's odd decision reflected McNamara's attempt to accede to the military's request on the one hand, and his belief that introducing more U.S. troops in Vietnam was "as likely to be counterproductive as productive" on the other.[38] The defense secretary, who in November had helped suppress discussion on the introduction of ground troops, thought that applying pressure to North Vietnam would solve the problems in South Vietnam. He only had to pull the president away from his preoccupation with the Great Society and force him to decide to implement Phase II.

■

Johnson's preoccupation with his domestic legislative program led him to obscure from the public and the Congress the extent of the difficulties in Vietnam. Despite his efforts to suppress the stories, however, newspapers had carried front-page articles on the U.S. ambassador's row with the South Vietnamese generals and on the military defeats suffered by the

South Vietnamese Army at the hands of the Viet Cong. On January 21 Johnson arranged a meeting with key Democratic and Republican members of the House and Senate. The meeting convened as General Khanh was charging the adminstration with grossly understating the degree of Communist infiltration from North Vietnam. Coincidentally, the purpose of the meeting with the legislators was to propagate the adminstration's spuriously optimistic assessment.[39]

On the first day of his four-year term, Johnson hid the truth about Vietnam for the sake of a domestic political agenda. McNamara assisted his dissembling.[40] For those who might urge the adminstration to take additional action against North Vietnam, McNamara indicated that tough measures were already under way. He divulged the nature of covert operations against North Vietnam under OPLAN 34A and revealed that U.S. aircraft were bombing infiltration routes in Laos under Operation Barrel Roll. Contrary to reality, he depicted both operations as highly successful. For those wary of deepening U.S. involvement, McNamara struck a note of reassurance. He suggested, contrary to recent reports from the field, that the South Vietnamese Army had increased its effectiveness in response to increases in the size and strength of the Viet Cong. He misrepresented the Chiefs' assessment of the situation, stating that they believed that the South Vietnamese armed forces were stronger than a year before. For those who feared that the American commitment to Vietnam had grown too costly, he minimized the price of American involvement. McNamara stated that only 254 Americans had been killed in action there in the past decade, without mentioning that more than half of the American combat deaths in Vietnam had occurred within the last year. He did not disclose plans to begin reprisal bombing of North Vietnam, and stated that there would be "no need" for U.S. troops.[41]

The president reinforced McNamara's effort. At the end of the meeting he interjected that he and his advisers had "decided that more U.S. forces are not needed in South Vietnam short of a decision to go to full-scale war." Johnson emphasized that the "war must be fought by the South Vietnamese. We cannot control everything that they do and we have to count on their fighting their war." The day following the meeting, the *New York Times* reported that the president and top administration officials had engaged the representatives and senators in a "very frank and thorough discussion of the international situation."[42]

The disparity between the adminstration's declarations and the truth necessitated tight control over the military's access to the press. Two days after the meeting with congressional leaders, an Associated Press story recounted senior naval officers' views on the president's Vietnam policy. The report that "some top officers in the 7th Fleet believe the United States has lost face in Vietnam for stopping destroyer patrols in the Tonkin Gulf" undermined official government pronouncements that the United States had continued its patrols since the incidents in August and September 1964. In response McNamara ordered CINCPAC to deny that the official policy had changed and to ban media representatives from naval operational units and sensitive installations without prior approval from the Defense Department. Rather than announce the information control policy, CINCPAC would simply respond to reporters' requests by placing them under review.[43]

■

To support the president's desire to keep Vietnam from encroaching on his domestic political agenda, McNamara had disconnected what he said from what he knew. By the end of January—in contrast to the optimistic assessment that he had given to the representatives and senators—he concluded that he had to force LBJ to make a decision because he thought that South Vietnam was "on the brink of total collapse." McGeorge Bundy agreed. Both had supported the president's holding strategy, but they now believed that unless they focused his attention on Vietnam, his indecision would lead to "disastrous defeat." They asked to see Johnson on January 27, and with McNamara's approval, Bundy wrote a memo to prepare the president.[44]

Bundy and McNamara argued that the persistent instability in the Saigon government stemmed from a lack of hope in the future among South Vietnamese officials and the public at large. In part they blamed American inactivity in recent weeks for a feeling of "uncertainty and lack of direction" among both Vietnamese authorities and U.S. government officials in Saigon and Washington. They argued that the president's policy of waiting for a stable South Vietnamese government limited the United States to a "policy of first aid to squabbling politicos and passive reaction to events we do not try to control." Bundy and McNamara told the president that the current policy was the "worst course of action" and condemned the United States to an "essentially passive role which can only lead to eventual defeat and an invitation to get out in humiliating circumstances."[45] They then pressed him to choose between two alternatives: Use American military power to "force a change of Communist policy" or negotiate a withdrawal aimed at "salvaging what little can be preserved with no major addition to our present military risks." They recommended the first option.

> Both of us have fully supported your unwillingness, in earlier months, to move out of the middle course. We both agree that every effort should still be made to improve our operations on the ground and to prop up the authorities in South Vietnam as best we can. But we are both convinced that none of this is enough, and that the time has come for harder choices.

Bundy alerted the president that Rusk did not agree with their assessment, but closed by emphasizing that he and McNamara had "reached the point where our obligations to you simply do not permit us to administer our present directives in silence and let you think we see real hope in them." William Bundy recalled later that his brother's memo "summed up the feelings of all of us at the time."[46] Johnson's closest advisers had put the president at a "fork in the road."

The memo and the meeting galvanized LBJ to action. He had avoided decisions on Vietnam earlier, first because of the election, then because the Great Society had preoccupied him. Now, faced with a strong argument for action from the men who had helped him navigate a middle course, and confronted with the danger of division within his own adminstration, he vowed that "stable government or no stable government, we'll do what we ought to do. . . . *We will move strongly.*"[47] The president, however, needed an incident to which the United States could respond with military force.

In hopes of provoking a North Vietnamese attack, he authorized the resumption of destroyer patrols in the Gulf of Tonkin. The Joint Chiefs of Staff responded immediately. On January 28, General Wheeler ordered Admiral Sharp to resume DESOTO patrols on February 3; they would be the first since September of 1964. The patrols' principal mission was to provoke a North Vietnamese attack that would, in turn, trigger an American reprisal. Wheeler ordered retaliatory forces into position before the destroyer patrols commenced and told Sharp to anticipate hitting five reprisal targets in the southern portion of North Vietnam. A few days later Wheeler modified his instructions to allow more flexibility and to include targets "more suitable in terms of Washington objectives." It was, McGeorge Bundy recalled, "like waiting for a streetcar." The president wanted an unassailable justification for retaliation. Accordingly, the patrols were designed to avoid the criticisms of Oregon Senator Wayne Morse and others that attended the August 1964 incident. Unlike previous patrols that had passed within three miles of the North Vietnamese coast and had been conducted in close proximity to Operation 34A raids, the February 1965 patrol would stay thirty nautical miles from the coast, and the Navy would launch no 34A raids forty-eight hours before and after the patrol.[48]

Although he supported the DESOTO patrols and preparations for reprisal, Gen. Harold Johnson still harbored doubts about the effects of bombing North Vietnam. On February 1 Johnson warned the Chiefs that *any* direct military pressure against North Vietnam could cause Chinese intervention. To avoid the errors of hasty deployment, which he had experienced at the outset of the Korean War, Johnson urged the Chiefs to prepare for an escalation of the war on the ground. He wanted his colleagues to consider the consequences of their actions, but they never acted on his memo.[49] The planning for air action against the North continued without consideration of its possible costs and consequences.

■

The same day that General Johnson signed his memo, Lieutenant General Goodpaster, McGeorge Bundy, Bundy's assistant Chester Cooper, McNaughton, and William Bundy's deputy, Leonard Unger, left for Vietnam. President Johnson decided to send Bundy on the mission during his meeting with him and McNamara on January 27. Although the president had already agreed to reprisals against North Vietnam, and action was planned to provoke a North Vietnamese "act of aggression," he kept his decisions from all but his closest advisers. Cooper recalled that the president "damn well had decided already what he was going to do" and that Bundy's trip was "part of Johnson's effort to demonstrate he was considering all the options." The trip was designed to build consensus behind the decision to bomb North Vietnam.[50]

On February 6 in Saigon, Bundy and his team began to draft their report to the president, while the American Embassy continued its attempt to remove General Khanh from power. Despite disturbing evidence of political instability in South Vietnam, Bundy's group recommended that the United States take advantage of the first opportunity to strike North Vietnam. Galvanizing American public opinion behind the change of policy remained the only obstacle to its success. They agreed that the Communists would have to do something dramatic in order to justify an air strike against North Vietnam. According to Cooper, "The thought was we would take our lumps until something very dramatic came along."

Bundy planned to spend his last day in Vietnam, Sunday, February 7, making a leisurely inspection of economic and military assistance programs in the countryside. However, the Viet Cong disrupted his plans even before breakfast.[51] Early that morning Viet Cong demolition teams infiltrated the adviser's compound and airfield at Pleiku in the Central Highlands of South Vietnam. A barrage of mortar rounds caused explosions that killed eight American servicemen, wounded more than one hundred others, and set fire to twenty aircraft on the airstrip. Goodpaster and Bundy accompanied General Westmoreland to the site of the attack. The airfield was in shambles. The sight of gravely wounded American servicemen evoked in Bundy uncharacteristically strong and visible emotion. In the White House he and his staff had compared casualties in Vietnam to traffic-related injuries in the Washington, D.C., area and concluded that the numbers of American dead and wounded in the war were insignificant.[52] The scene at Pleiku, however, brought home the reality of the war. Thrust suddenly into a chaotic environment that contrasted sharply with the relatively orderly, controlled surroundings of the White House, he began to mutter, "We cannot stand by . . . just can't do this to our country." Westmoreland recalled that Bundy became "intense, abrupt, and arrogant," as if under a "sort of field marshal psychosis."[53] The opportunity to urge the bombing of North Vietnam was cathartic for the emotional Bundy. The "streetcar" for which he had been waiting had arrived.

Taylor and the Joint Chiefs supported Bundy's call for a reprisal. In Washington, Deputy Secretary of Defense Cyrus Vance briefed Lyndon Johnson on the attacks and the plan for retaliation against military targets in the southern portion of North Vietnam. Taylor made his own recommendation separately. The president deferred to the "man on the spot" in Saigon. General Wheeler issued the order to CINCPAC the following day: U.S. forces would strike three North Vietnamese barracks while the Vietnamese Air Force and Farmgate struck a fourth. As Bundy's plane was making its way eastward across the Pacific, he and the members of his group heard the White House statement on the radio:

> On February 7, U.S. and South Vietnamese air elements were directed to launch retaliatory strikes against barracks and staging areas in the southern area of North Viet-Nam which intelligence has shown to be actively used by Hanoi for training and infiltration of Viet Cong personnel into South Viet-Nam. . . . Today's action by the U.S. and South Vietnamese governments was in response to provocations ordered and directed by the Hanoi regime. . . . As in the case of the North Vietnamese attacks in the Gulf of Tonkin last August, the response is appropriate and fitting. As the U.S. government has frequently stated, we seek no wider war. . . . The key to the situation remains the cessation of infiltration from North Viet-Nam and the clear indication by the Hanoi regime that it is prepared to cease aggression against its neighbors.[54]

After months of dutifully adhering to their president's instruction that Vietnam not interfere with the Great Society, Johnson's advisers, assisted by the Viet Cong, had finally pushed him into acting.

11
The Foot in the Door
February–March 1965

I believe that effective interdepartmental coordination is
leading the United States Government down the path to a
major contribution to the solution of what may be the
greatest problem facing the Free World today, subversive
counterinsurgency.

—GEN. EARLE WHEELER, MARCH 23, 1965[1]

In February 1965 President Johnson made decisions that transformed
the conflict in Vietnam into an American war. The February 7 Viet
Cong attack on Pleiku triggered the next step up the ladder of Secretary
of Defense Robert McNamara's campaign of graduated pressure: carefully
limited bombing of selected targets in North Vietnam. Although overt
aerial attacks on the North escalated American involvement to a new
level, the president's decision, at the end of February, to introduce U.S.
ground combat units into South Vietnam represented an irrevocable
commitment to the war. The president, however, would refuse to consider or even to acknowledge the consequences of his decisions, and thus
still imagined that he could pursue a policy of gradual escalation without
involving the United States in a major war.

Although the JCS thought that the president's policy was fundamentally flawed, their actions supported and reinforced it. Unable to resolve

interservice differences or to agree on the primary source of the problem in Vietnam, the Chiefs submitted consensus recommendations that focused on individual military actions and avoided strategic issues. As a result they did not force the president to face the fact that the commitment of ground forces would make it harder than ever to withdraw, and that additional forces would certainly be necessary. Instead they resolved to push the president gradually along the course toward Americanization of the war. A member of the Army operations staff, then Maj. Gen. Arthur Collins, recalled that "all the services were anxious to get their foot in the door, and it reminded me of the story of not letting the camel get its nose in the tent."* It was apparent to Collins that "the US would get far more committed than it intended, and it was obvious from the civilian influence on the tactics and strategy that we were just going to nibble away at this Vietnamese problem."[2]

∎

On February 7, 1965, U.S. Navy aircraft carriers *Ranger*, *Coral Sea*, and *Hancock* were afloat in the South China Sea, waiting for orders to bomb North Vietnam. The Viet Cong attack on Pleiku provided the occasion to launch Flaming Dart I, the name for the reprisal strikes against military barracks in the southern portion of North Vietnam. *Ranger* would strike military barracks at Vit Thu Lu, while *Coral Sea* and *Hancock* would target a barracks facility at Dong Hoi. The South Vietnamese Air Force would bomb a third facility. The air strikes would comprise the first overt attack on North Vietnam since the Gulf of Tonkin reprisal in August 1964.

All did not go as planned, however. Low cloud cover obscured *Ranger's* target, so the aviators aborted the mission. Pilots from the other two carriers also encountered poor weather conditions but decided to press the attack at low altitude, underneath the clouds. Streaking in at high speed, twenty-nine aircraft from the *Coral Sea* began their run at the Dong Hoi barracks. Intense antiaircraft and small-arms fire reached up at the low-flying aircraft, shooting down one plane and killing its pilot. Fire from the ground and poor weather conditions limited the damage inflicted on the barracks. When the raid was complete, Vit Thu Lu had escaped

---

*Collins's metaphor implied that once the camel's nose was in the tent, the occupant would be unable to prevent the unwelcome animal from entering.

attack, and the strike on Dong Hoi had destroyed only 16 of its 275 buildings.[3]

McGeorge Bundy and his party returned from South Vietnam late on Sunday, February 7. Bundy went immediately to the White House to deliver the memo that he and his group had finished on the trip. He assured the president that the memo represented the consensus between his party and Taylor's embassy. Like his brother and McNaughton, McGeorge Bundy believed that protecting American credibility was the principal objective of U.S. policy. He argued that, in the eyes of the world, the United States was responsible for the outcome in Vietnam. American "international prestige" and influence were "directly at risk." He told the president that "without new U.S. action defeat appears inevitable—probably not in a matter of weeks or perhaps even months, but within the next year or so." He suggested that the Pleiku raid gave the United States "a practicable point of departure" for a new policy centered on the bombing of North Vietnam. According to Bundy the United States was at a "turning point" in the war.[4]

Bundy shared not only McNaughton's doubts about the chances of success but also his belief that it was better to commit American military force and lose than to forgo acting. Although Bundy put the odds of a favorable outcome of the war at as low as twenty-five percent, he was one hundred percent certain that "even if it fails, the policy will be worth it." To preserve American credibility, Bundy told the president, "the policy of graduated and continuing reprisal" was "the most promising course available."[5] Domestic and foreign political concerns reinforced Bundy's conviction that the president should deepen American involvement in Vietnam. Bundy's report argued that defeat after a substantial U.S. military effort would "damp down the charge that we did not do all that we could have done, and this charge will be important in many countries, including our own."[6]

Although Bundy was impressed with the cost of "losing" South Vietnam without first committing U.S. armed forces, his examination of the possible consequences of deepening American military involvement in the war was cursory. He admitted that "U.S. casualties would be higher—and more visible to American feelings," but he dismissed that expense as "cheap" relative to the costs of withdrawal. He and his group concluded ambiguously that "the value of the effort seems to us to exceed its cost."[7]

The president, preoccupied with his domestic legislative program, did not examine Bundy's program in any depth. When Bundy finished briefing the president, he was surprised when Johnson asked if there was anything new in his report. He replied, "Well, we thought we made a sketch of a program that didn't exist." Anxious to keep his decision to begin the systematic bombing of North Vietnam secret, Johnson disagreed. "No, that's where we are already. Let's just not talk about it anymore." As Bundy was about to depart, Johnson asked, "How many copies of this are there?" When Bundy told him that several memos had been distributed, Johnson erupted: "Get them back!"[8]

■

On February 8 Johnson cabled Ambassador Taylor that he was "now prepared to go forward with the best [South Vietnamese] government we can get, and accordingly I wish you to know that I have today decided that we will carry out our December plan for continuing action against North Vietnam." Johnson warned Taylor, however, that it was "most important that this decision not be publicized."[9]

Taylor and McGeorge Bundy supported the president's desire to slip the country into war without public or congressional debate. Taylor agreed that the United States should explain the bombing of North Vietnam "on the basis of retaliation" to manage "domestic and international opinion."[10] Until the president deemed it appropriate to make public the decision to bomb North Vietnam on a continuing basis, Bundy would have Cooper of the NSC staff compile "weekly lists of outrages" by the Viet Cong and North Vietnam to justify the continuing air strikes on the North. Over time, as the American public became accustomed to the bombing of North Vietnam, air strikes could become less associated with specific Viet Cong actions.[11]

To preserve consensus and prevent a divisive debate over Vietnam, Johnson kept his policy deliberately ambiguous. The morning after the Pleiku reprisal strikes, he invited key senators and congressmen to an NSC meeting. McNamara and Wheeler helped Johnson maintain a facade of consultation with Congress even as the president obscured the changing role of the United States in the war. To appease both Senate Majority Leader Mike Mansfield, a Democrat, who favored a negotiated settlement, and Republican Representative Gerald Ford, the House minority leader, who advocated additional air strikes against the three targets that had been "weathered in" the day before, the president's advisers described the air strikes against North Vietnam as mere reprisals. McNamara explained that he did not want the Communists to get the "wrong signal and think we are launching an offensive." Wheeler supported McNamara's distortion as he had done during the Gulf of Tonkin affair, although he personally favored another reprisal strike and had just been ordered to develop plans for an eight-week air campaign against North Vietnam. Wheeler told the legislators that, because the bombing was merely a reprisal, subsequent "air strikes on the three targets are not necessary from a military point of view," even though he was planning an extended campaign.[12]

After hearing the arguments for and against additional strikes on North Vietnam, the president approved a South Vietnamese attack against one target but denied permission for additional strikes by American aircraft.[13] Three days later another Viet Cong attack permitted Johnson to maintain the facade of reprisal bombing while embarking on the long-anticipated program of graduated pressure against North Vietnam. On February 10 Viet Cong terrorists bombed an American enlisted soldiers' barracks in the coastal city of Qui Nhon. The blast left twenty-three dead and twenty-two others wounded. In an NSC meeting on the same day, the president approved a "reprisal" strike on two military targets in the southern portion of North Vietnam. Johnson and his advisers again agreed that they "should not spell out in detail what we had undertaken to do."[14]

The results of the strike after the Qui Nhon attack were as disappointing as those of the attack after Pleiku. The Joint Chiefs had proposed a massive raid against seven targets. McNamara recommended only three, and Ball urged the president to limit the strikes further to the two southernmost targets. Johnson accepted Ball's position.[15] American naval aircraft were to strike Chanh Hoa barracks while South Vietnamese Air Force and Farmgate aircraft hit Vu Con barracks. Cloud cover once again forced naval aircraft to fly below optimal altitude, and North Vietnamese antiaircraft gunners barraged them. One hundred bomb- and rocket-laden aircraft hit only 23 of the 76 buildings in the target areas, and three aircraft fell to enemy fire. On February 7, 8, and 11, the United States had launched 267 aircraft sorties against 491 buildings and had destroyed only 47 of them. Operations at the North Vietnamese barracks continued unimpaired.[16]

McNamara, disappointed by the results, addressed a memo to Wheeler that reflected the general confusion surrounding the gradual application of force against North Vietnam. He was torn between his expectation that the raids would have inflicted greater damage and his belief that the objective of the air strikes was "communication." He told Wheeler, "Surely we cannot continue for months accomplishing no more with 267 sorties than we did on these missions." Simultaneously, however, the secretary of defense seemed to reassure himself with the observation that "our primary objective, of course, was to communicate our political resolve. This I believe we did." Still, he urged Wheeler to take corrective measures. He told the chairman that "future communications of resolve" would carry a "hollow ring" unless American aircraft could inflict more damage. The former Air Force statistician suggested that Wheeler and the Joint Chiefs choose different targets, change the weights of effort against them, or change the composition of the attacking force.[17]

Limitations on the use of force and the centralization of decision making in the White House compounded the difficulties of bad weather, enemy air defenses, and the general imprecision of bombing. Prior to the Qui Nhon strikes, separate proposals for reprisal targets came from the JCS, McNamara, and Taylor. The Joint Chiefs sent General Westmoreland and Admiral Sharp a series of orders and counterorders that confused the planning process. Air crews could not make final preparations until the president decided to strike yet another combination of targets. Westmoreland reported that conflicting orders had exhausted and confused his staff and "whiplashed" the South Vietnamese Air Force.[18]

Despite the poor results of the initial air strikes, McNamara's guidance to the Chiefs sharply limited the scope and intensity of the bombing. On February 8, when the defense secretary asked Wheeler to develop an eight-week program of preplanned air strikes against North Vietnam that would appear as reprisals for North Vietnamese and Viet Cong "provocations," he told the Chiefs to plan for no more than two to three attacks per week. All targets were to be south of the nineteenth parallel, and the MIG fighter base at Phuc Yen airfield remained off limits.[19] McNamara had once again structured his request to constrain the Chiefs from providing broad-based advice.

■

One might have expected General LeMay to contest McNamara's limitations and controls over the air campaign. One week prior to McNamara's request, however, LeMay had brought to a close his thirty-four-year career as a military officer. His replacement was Gen. John P. McConnell. The president and his top advisers, long anticipating LeMay's retirement, had selected McConnell ten months earlier and installed him, meanwhile, as Air Force vice chief of staff. The contrast between McConnell and LeMay seemed stark. *Newsweek* ran side-by-side photos of the two officers and opined that McConnell's "brains and thrust" had replaced LeMay's "dedication and crust." Unlike LeMay's gruff manner and appearance, McConnell's countenance was kind and thoughtful. *Time* announced that McConnell's appointment "marked the end of an era in military leadership." Pentagon analysts predicted that, under the management of this "new breed" of officer, interservice rivalry would diminish and relations between civilian and military officials would "flourish." Indeed, McConnell had a friendlier relationship with McNamara and other civilian officials in the Pentagon than did LeMay. As deputy NATO commander in Europe, he had impressed the secretary of defense with incisive, well-organized briefings. By appointing McConnell, Johnson appeared to have completed the shift of the JCS away from "heroes" to military men who were McNamara-style "planners and thinkers."[20]

Taylor had recommended McConnell as LeMay's successor as early as January 1964. In addition to his reputation as a "McNamara man" who supported the defense secretary's Pentagon reforms, the general had established a close personal rapport with the president, becoming acquainted with Johnson in 1957, when he traveled to his Texas ranch to brief him on issues concerning the Strategic Air Command (SAC). McConnell recalled that Johnson "was a great host" and "very keen." The Air Force officer shared a "very enjoyable association" with Johnson as they rode all over the ranch, swam in the pool, shot pistols, and visited neighbors. The future president had even personally served McConnell breakfast in bed.[21] LBJ again wanted to appoint a Chief on whose support he could count, because he continued to fear resistance to his Vietnam policy from the military. McConnell was a wise choice.

Despite their previous association, the president wanted to confirm McConnell's dependability. In early 1964, when he was considering McConnell for the chief of staff position, Johnson arranged for the general to return from Europe for an interview in the White House. Getting right to the point, Johnson asked if McConnell would support policies inconsistent with his professional military opinion. The general assured the president that, even if he did not have faith in the administration's policies, he "would still go ahead and carry out his decisions to the best of my ability, and I would see, also, to it that the entire Air Force did the same." The new Air Force chief of staff saw his role as providing McNamara and Johnson "suitable alternatives for the application of military power" so they might "choose the one which best solved the problem *as they saw it*."[22] McConnell had given Johnson the right answer. McConnell's "can-do" attitude and personal loyalty predisposed him to serve more as a technician than as an adviser. He would support the strategy of the president and the secretary of defense with as many or as few bombing runs on North Vietnam as the civilian leaders required. McConnell later recalled that he, like Wheeler, went on to develop a "close personal friendship" with the president.[23]

■

McConnell's relationship with Army Chief of Staff Johnson, however, was less than tranquil. Not only did the two men differ in their institutional perspectives concerning the use of military force, but the two future heads of their respective services had experienced a difficult relationship as cadets at West Point. McConnell, an Arkansan, arrived at West Point with Earle Wheeler in 1929 after graduating magna cum laude from his home state's Henderson-Brown College. In contrast to Harold Johnson's mediocre record as a cadet, McConnell rose to the highest cadet rank of first captain. During his last year at West Point, McConnell was manager of the football team and Johnson, a year behind McConnell, was assistant manager. Johnson remembered that McConnell had delegated the hard work to Johnson but kept all the credit for himself.[24] Johnson may also have been uncomfortable with McConnell's heavy drinking, which, as the Vietnam War escalated, developed into alcoholism. It would be up to Earle Wheeler, a West Point classmate of McConnell's, to mediate between the two.

Johnson's and McConnell's institutional perspectives, however, were irreconcilable. Like LeMay, McConnell advocated a massive air campaign that would bring North Vietnam to its knees and obviate the use of American ground forces. To prepare for the campaign, he proposed deploying fifteen additional squadrons of aircraft to the Pacific. Harold Johnson, who recalled the bitter experience of land warfare in Korea and believed that bombing North Vietnam would actually cause the deployment of U.S. ground combat troops to Southeast Asia, remained more concerned than his colleagues about the possibility of Chinese intervention in Vietnam. Worried that the war might escalate, Johnson favored sharp limitations on the air campaign. He argued that the deployment of fifteen squadrons was overkill and, noting that there were already 865 U.S. aircraft in the Pacific, suggested that the Air Force defer deploying additional aircraft until there was a demonstrable need for them. He recommended that to deter a Communist ground offensive, two Army divisions deploy to Thailand before air strikes against the North began.[25]

Rather than express their differences of opinion to the secretary of defense and the president, General Wheeler talked Johnson and the other Chiefs into submitting a consensus position. Wheeler's motivation was practical, consistent with his desire to create a compromise and avoid confrontation. He sought to protect the limited influence of the Joint Chiefs, and he believed that McNamara and the president would use the Chiefs' differences to weaken JCS influence over Vietnam policy decisions.[26] McNamara, who believed that "one raid each week" would make the air campaign sufficiently intense, further encouraged Wheeler to broker a compromise between his colleagues on the JCS.[27] He suggested to the general that the JCS go along with the limitations on the use of force in the near term and promised that, if the early actions failed, the president would increase the military effort against North Vietnam. What was needed immediately, McNamara argued, was a bombing campaign that could gain LBJ's approval. Besides, McNamara observed, the Chiefs could not prove that the sharply limited actions against North Vietnam would not work.[28]

To form a consensus, Wheeler suppressed JCS misgivings about McNamara's strategy for deepening American involvement in the war and advocated force deployments that he knew would prove inadequate in the long term. Despite the Army staff's assessment that air strikes would be ineffective and instigate the deployment of U.S. ground combat units to Southeast Asia, the Army deputy chief of staff for plans and operations, Lt. Gen. Bruce Palmer, recalled that he and General Johnson were persuaded to "pursue the air war solution on the grounds that all could agree at least that it was worth the effort and there was no harm in trying it." Wheeler suggested that the Chiefs focus first on gaining approval for the deployment of smaller numbers of aircraft and ground troops. Once those forces had been approved and reached their stations, the JCS would "study" further deployments as a matter of priority. In retrospect, Palmer concluded that concealing the Chiefs' reservations about the incremental escalation of the war was a "disservice."[29]

Wheeler appealed to the Chiefs' common belief that Communism had to be stopped in Vietnam, and he structured his compromise to appeal to each of the services. For the Army, Wheeler reduced the number of air squadrons from fifteen to nine, writing that air strikes "almost certainly would not lead Hanoi to restrain the Viet Cong." In further deference to Harold Johnson's view that the war would be won or lost on the ground, the Chiefs pressed for invasions into Laos by South Vietnamese forces. Under Wheeler's proposal, the Army would send a brigade (one-third of a division) to Thailand and the Marine Corps would deploy a brigade to the South Vietnamese port city of Danang. The Air Force would have to settle for six fewer squadrons of aircraft and a limited air campaign in the short term, but could look forward to larger deployments and less constrained action in the future. The Navy would participate in the air strikes and augment bombing with naval bombardment.[30]

On February 11 the JCS gave McNamara its plan for an eight-week program for the air campaign consistent with the restrictions he had imposed. The plan called for U.S. and South Vietnamese aircraft attacks on four fixed targets and air interdiction missions over two road segments per week. If "the insurgency continues with DRV [North Vietnamese] support, strikes against the DRV will be extended with intensified efforts against targets north of the 19th parallel," the plan continued. In case the president was willing to approve more intensive air strikes immediately, the Chiefs presented options to strike either seven or ten targets per week. All targets were "military": barracks, storage depots, and bridges. The JCS estimated for each option the number of sorties per target and the type of aircraft that should conduct each mission. The code name for the air campaign was Rolling Thunder.[31]

■

The president approved continuing air strikes against North Vietnam without considering the possibility that his decision might accelerate the deployment of U.S. ground combat units to South Vietnam. Years afterward McNamara claimed that the beginning of the air war "unexpectedly triggered the introduction of U.S. troops into ground combat."[32] Harold Johnson, however, had warned that this might happen. But McNamara, along with Taylor, had suppressed any discussion of the use of ground forces during the policy deliberations in November and December 1964. In February 1965, the secretary of defense, while pursuing relentlessly the implementation of graduated pressure on North Vietnam, continued to ignore JCS recommendations that U.S. Marines and Army troops deploy to Southeast Asia concurrent with the initiation of Rolling Thunder. Wheeler's compromise clouded the recommendation for ground troops, and McNamara's control over and selective use of the advice he received overshadowed the issue completely.[33]

After gaining presidential approval for "continuing action" against North Vietnam, it proved difficult to get Rolling Thunder under way. On February 18, one week after they submitted their compromise memo to McNamara, the JCS issued the execute order for Rolling Thunder I. United States and South Vietnamese aircraft were to strike a North Vietnamese naval base on February 20. The first six attempts to begin the bombing, however, failed due to an attempted coup in Saigon, poor weather, and concern over initiating the air strikes concurrent with a Communist conclave in Moscow. The first Rolling Thunder mission was not conducted until March 2.[34]

■

Although bolstering the morale of the South Vietnamese people and enhancing the stability of the Saigon government had become one of the objectives of the air campaign, the chronic political turbulence in the South remained the principal obstacle to extending the war to the North. In mid-February 1965, even though there was virtually "no government" in Saigon, Taylor remained sanguine about Rolling Thunder's prospects.[35] Although President Johnson had concluded that General Khanh was the de facto leader in South Vietnam, Taylor, like Lodge before him, had decided to take an active role in forcing a change in the political power structure. On January 26 General Khanh had installed Nguyen Xuan Oanh as premier. Oanh, a Harvard-trained economist who had worked for the United States government and was considered very pro-American, came to power in the midst of newly intensified Buddhist protests and riots. Students burned the United States Information Service (USIS) center in Hue and sacked the center in Saigon as well. A CIA report attributed the unrest to a nationalistic "social and political revolution." Taylor, however, blamed General Khanh for the latest outburst of anti-

Americanism, labeling him a Communist sympathizer and hoping thereby to undermine his credibility with the South Vietnamese military.[36]

The weakening of Khanh's authority without an heir apparent to the leadership of the military threw Saigon into another round of turmoil as senior South Vietnamese military officers scrambled to fill the power vacuum. Between February 19 and 27, U. Alexis Johnson felt as if he were "living through a movie shown several times normal speed; I had to strain just to follow what the actors were saying and doing, let alone make sense of it all."[37] General Phat and Col. Pham Ngoc Thao, a secret agent of Hanoi, attempted to kidnap Khanh and wrest power from the Armed Forces Council. Khanh and Air Vice Marshal Ky narrowly escaped capture. Ky found sanctuary at the Bien Hoa air base, from which he issued orders to bomb the coup headquarters in Saigon. Johnson, Taylor, and the embassy staff worked around the clock to prevent chaos. While bombers flew low over the embassy, General Westmoreland frantically attempted to dissuade Ky from attacking units of his own armed forces. At the last moment Westmoreland and U. Alexis Johnson arranged a temporary cease-fire. As tensions eased, General Khanh and the officers of the Armed Forces Council used the respite to gather troops loyal to their cause.[38]

The strain of the coup attempt and Taylor's effort to undermine Khanh widened the rift between Khanh and the Armed Forces Council. The council resented Khanh's attempts to bypass them and to solicit support from lower-ranking officers. The generals demanded Khanh's resignation. Recognizing that he had lost his base of support, Khanh reluctantly acquiesced. On February 25, after receiving full military honors, Khanh and his family boarded a Paris-bound Pan Am clipper. It seemed a victory for Taylor. Alexis Johnson recalled that "there was not a wet eye in the crowd."[39]

Taylor regarded Khanh's departure as a personal triumph and urged the bombing of North Vietnam with renewed enthusiasm. After Khanh's plane lifted off, Taylor sent a terse cable to Washington: KHANH AIRBORNE. QUAT HAS GIVEN POLITICAL CLEARANCES FOR FEBRUARY 26 STRIKE. The day after Khanh's departure, Taylor told Premier Phan Huy Quat and other top officials of the South Vietnamese government that direct American action against North Vietnam may be the "turning point" that could "reverse the trend of the war." He informed the South Vietnamese generals and reported separately to Washington that the initial bombing of the North had resulted in an "upsurge of hope" among the people of South Vietnam. Taylor urged the South Vietnamese generals to unite, "set [their] sights on victory and vigorously pursue" it. He told them that they could make theirs the "victory government."[40]

Taylor's "victory" over Khanh proved ephemeral, for the military situation in South Vietnam had become desperate. The Viet Cong controlled over half of the country and the fighting reached a new level of intensity. In January, Hanoi's leaders had decided to risk an attempt to destroy the South Vietnamese Army (ARVN) before the United States could intervene directly in the war. The Viet Cong launched concentrated attacks on isolated ARVN outposts and lines of communication. American and South Vietnamese casualties rose sharply. In the week prior to Khanh's departure, 36 Americans were killed in action, 196 wounded, and 1 was missing. Even more ominous, ARVN forces lost 1,555 men during the same period. Due to battle losses and the inattention of commanders preoccupied with political intrigue in Saigon, morale in the South Vietnamese armed forces fell dramatically. As Taylor sent his message of hope for what bombing North Vietnam might accomplish, ARVN soldiers were deserting at a rate exceeding 350 per day.[41]

■

In contrast to Taylor's belief that air strikes against the North could reverse the deteriorating situation, the U.S. Intelligence Board concluded that bombing North Vietnam would probably not cause the Hanoi government to cease supporting the insurgency in the South and might even result in an intensification of Viet Cong efforts "in the expectation of early victory."[42] Despite the ambassador's hope that bombing would enhance governmental stability in the South, the CIA predicted "further power struggles within the South Vietnamese government" and noted that "Khanh's departure with no specific heir to the leadership of the military, merely opens up new opportunities for numerous aspirants to the role of military strongman." In short, the prospects for achieving a stable and effective government in the near future remained "exceedingly slim."[43]

Taylor, however, staunchly advocated Rolling Thunder. Westmoreland recalled that Taylor was "really convinced that graduated response was going to work" and continued to believe that Hanoi would "collaborate in obtaining cessation of the insurgency, not just stop its support." The ambassador predicted that bombing North Vietnam would "affect the minds of the Hanoi leadership, to convince them that they must stop their aggression and dissuade the VC from continuing their sabotage, or else pay a prohibitively high price." According to Taylor the bombing would "raise GVN morale and depress that of the VC, who would see they no longer had a safe haven." Although he did not agree with what he regarded as Taylor's "pie in the sky" hopes for Rolling Thunder, Westmoreland "saw no harm coming from it." He was skeptical, but like the JCS, he concluded that the limited strikes against North Vietnam were worth trying. If the bombing failed, the United States would simply expand its effort to save South Vietnam.[44]

It might seem inconsistent that Taylor, once an avowed critic of air power, would have become such an energetic advocate for bombing North Vietnam. Although Taylor had recommended introducing ground troops into South Vietnam as early as November 1961, he thought that U.S. combat units should join the fight against the Viet Cong only as a last resort.[45] To Taylor, Vietnam was an "experiment" in stopping Communist insurgencies. Since the end of 1961, Taylor had tried to ensure that the experiment succeeded.[46] The large-scale deployment of American ground combat units, however, eventually revealed that it had failed. U. Alexis Johnson recalled that Taylor's persistent advocacy of bombing the North was based, in part, in the ambassador's desire to "quiet the growing push for the commitment of American ground forces."[47] Bombing North Vietnam seemed to be the only remaining option for a man whose personal reputation and legacy had become inextricably linked to the counterinsurgency effort in Vietnam. Westmoreland recalled that Taylor considered Rolling Thunder a "cheap way of casting our lot toward some course of action that might have some prospect of success."[48] So desperately did Taylor want the experiment in counterinsurgency to succeed that he deleted paragraphs of CIA reports that expressed doubts about the air campaign before forwarding them to keep the president from losing faith in the bombing.[49]

■

General Westmoreland did not share Taylor's reluctance to introduce American ground combat units. Like Harold Johnson, Westmoreland believed that ground forces should deploy to South Vietnam *before* the initiation of Rolling Thunder. On February 9, in the wake of the Pleiku attack, Westmoreland sent a cable to Wheeler alerting the chairman that the situation in South Vietnam might require U.S. combat forces "in division strength" to protect U.S. personnel and installations. In reply Wheeler asked him for the numbers and types of units he needed. On February 17 Westmoreland prioritized three places that required Americans for security: Danang, the greater Saigon area, and Nha Trang. Admiral Sharp agreed with Westmoreland's assessment and recommended the deployment of a Marine Expeditionary Brigade (MEB) to Danang. The Chiefs had recommended deploying an MEB in their "compromise" memorandum of February 11 and, on February 18, the JCS once again forwarded the recommendation to McNamara. It would be up to Westmoreland to persuade Taylor to go along with the deployment.[50]

Taylor resisted. On February 22 the ambassador objected strenuously to any deployment of American combat troops to South Vietnam. Taylor argued that "white-faced" American soldiers were "not suitable guerrilla fighters for Asian forests and jungles" and warned that U.S. troops would do no better than had the French ten years earlier. He predicted that the introduction of U.S. ground combat forces would sap ARVN's determination to fight and lead to tensions between American soldiers and Vietnamese civilians. Taylor considered the JCS plan to introduce an entire MEB a "grandiose scheme" that far exceeded any military requirement for security.[51]

Despite these objections, Westmoreland got Taylor to compromise. Taylor hoped that the deployment of a small force would quell calls for the Marine brigade and other units. Instead of an entire brigade, Westmoreland and Taylor asked for one-third of that force, a Marine Battalion Landing Team (BLT) of 1,200 men, to deploy to Danang. Taylor suggested that a small force would "be more manageable . . . from the point of view of accommodating it on base and absorbing it into the Danang community." He recognized, however, that once American ground forces arrived in any number, "it will be very difficult to hold the line" on further deployments. He conceded the need for one battalion, but urged that the United States "adhere to our past policy of keeping our ground forces out of [a] direct counterinsurgency role."[52]

On February 26, during a meeting with Rusk, McNamara, Ball, and McGeorge Bundy, LBJ approved deploying a helicopter squadron and two Marine battalions to Danang, a force more than twice as large as

Taylor thought necessary. The decision was casual and made without consideration of the radically changed nature of the American commitment once U.S. ground combat units entered South Vietnam.[53] It seemed an easy decision to the president because it represented a consensus among his civilian advisers and the action could be justified under the compelling argument that U.S. installations and people had to be protected. His civilian advisers viewed the deployments as a reversible show of force or a benign defensive action. His military advisers, anxious to gain approval for further deployments, viewed the initial Marine deployments as the first step in transforming the war in the South to an American war.

As Taylor had feared, his compromise on the principle of troop deployments opened the door for much larger deployments and moved America one step closer to direct intervention on the ground in South Vietnam. Westmoreland had agreed to a small force, but resolved to keep his "options open for reinforcement." Although his compromise with Taylor forced him to request only one Marine battalion "initially," Westmoreland urged that the entire Brigade deploy "on a phased basis." Westmoreland must have been encouraged by the president's approval of two battalions and a squadron of helicopters.[54]

Like Westmoreland, Earle Wheeler considered the introduction of the ground troops as the first installment on a much larger deployment. It meant an Americanization of the war. Although the JCS memorandum to McNamara of February 11 recommended deploying only one Army brigade to Thailand and additional aircraft to the western Pacific region, Wheeler had begun planning for the deployment of two Army divisions and six additional air squadrons to Southeast Asia. He had also begun to consider moving a third U.S. division into a position along the demilitarized zone between North and South Vietnam.[55] The first deployments would provide security for U.S. bases and personnel, and the third would act in offensive operations against the Viet Cong. Admiral Sharp shared Wheeler's determination to expand the size and mission of U.S. ground forces. Wheeler told Sharp that one of the purposes of deploying an Army division to South Vietnam would be to position "forces of substantial size into forward areas in advance of expanded conflict."[56] Sharp, receptive to Wheeler's suggestion, challenged Taylor's arguments against using Americans as counterinsurgents, saying that Taylor's remark that the American soldier, "armed, equipped and trained as he is, is not [a] suitable guerrilla fighter for Asian forests and jungles" ignored the Marine Corps' "distinguished record in counter-guerrilla warfare."[57] Wheeler assured Sharp that the president would soon approve the deployment of additional Marine units. He told the admiral that the "deployment of the third battalion and the remainder of the Brigade's command and support units" had merely been "deferred for later action." Wheeler assured Sharp that the president wanted to "do everything possible to maximize our military efforts to reverse [the] present unfavorable situation."[58] As Maxwell Taylor was arranging for a South Vietnamese "request" for U.S. Marines, the JCS were still trying to launch the first Rolling Thunder strike.[59]

∎

Three weeks had passed since the president's decision to begin "continuous action" against North Vietnam, but the unsettled political situation in Saigon and tight control from Washington had impeded the effort to begin the bombing. Washington retained the authority to cancel missions due to poor weather, and the JCS called off several planned strikes between February 22 and March 2. Westmoreland told Wheeler that this form of control from Washington was absurd, considering that the weather changed faster than people in Vietnam could inform Washington of those changes. Last-minute orders and counterorders from Washington continued to confound planning staffs and exhaust pilots, who had to remain on almost constant alert. Westmoreland asked for greater authority in "orchestrating" the air strikes with other operations over which he enjoyed more control, such as the Barrel Roll armed reconnaissance into Laos and the OPLAN 34A covert raids into North Vietnam. In a prophetic closing, Westmoreland warned Wheeler that "experience indicated that the more remote the authority which directs how a mission is to be accomplished, the more we are vulnerable to mishaps resulting from such things as incomplete briefings and preparation, loss of tactical flexibility and lack of tactical coordination."[60]

Wheeler recognized "the policy and procedural difficulties" flowing from the "close control of Rolling Thunder exercised by Washington," but he sensed that the time was not propitious for raising those issues with the president. What Wheeler regarded as "most important" was to "get off this next ROLLING THUNDER to break what seems to be a

234 | DERELICTION OF DUTY

psychological/political logjam." Wheeler urged Westmoreland to be patient and to let him handle the "political" problem of control over Rolling Thunder. He assured Westmoreland that he and McNamara would do their best to clear away restrictions and relax Washington's tight control. He asked the MACV commander to be sensitive to the "sizable and vexing" domestic and international political considerations that impinged on operations against North Vietnam. Once Rolling Thunder was under way, Wheeler believed he would have greater success in removing the restrictions on the operation. He reminded Westmoreland of their successful effort to loosen control over Barrel Roll and Yankee Team air operations in Laos.[61] Like the decision to deploy the first U.S. ground combat units to South Vietnam, the systematic bombing of North Vietnam would begin without a comprehensive estimate of how much force would ultimately be required. Wheeler focused only on gaining permission to take the first step.

On March 2 the initial mission of a bombing campaign that would last more than three years and drop 643,000 tons of bombs on North Vietnam was finally undertaken. U.S. Air Force and South Vietnamese aircraft struck North Vietnamese military facilities at Xom Bang and Quang Khe. The North Vietnamese, however, had used the eight months since the Gulf of Tonkin reprisals to improve their air defense capabilities. Five American and one South Vietnamese aircraft went down in flames.[62]

■

The beginning of Rolling Thunder revealed a wide disparity in expectations. Graduated pressure, an intentionally ambiguous strategy, permitted different interpretations of how the air campaign ought to be conducted and what it should achieve. Various senior members of the Johnson administration and the military had differing objectives for the air campaign, including forcing Hanoi to negotiate, coercing Hanoi either to reduce its support for or "call off the insurgency," interdicting supplies and infiltration into South Vietnam, "punishing" Hanoi, boosting morale in South Vietnam, destroying North Vietnamese military capabilities, and protecting U.S. credibility by posing as the "good doctor" trying his best to keep South Vietnam from succumbing to the disease of the Viet Cong insurgency.[63]

Deputy Secretary of State Ball had recognized the wide disparity in expectations for Rolling Thunder and sought clarification from the president. Three weeks before the sustained bombing began, Ball urged LBJ to "smoke out" the differences among his colleagues. Although Ball and Llewellyn Thompson, also of the State Department, supported the bombing of North Vietnam, Ball emphasized what he considered important differences among the president's principal advisers. McNamara, McGeorge Bundy, and Taylor agreed that bombing North Vietnam would not only decrease infiltration from the North but actually coerce Hanoi to "call off the insurgency in the South and withdraw those elements infiltrated in the past." Ball thought that objective tantamount to demanding "unconditional surrender," observing that "short of a crushing military defeat Hanoi would never abandon the aggressive course it has pursued at great cost for ten years and give up all the progress it has made in the Communization of South Vietnam."[64] Ball, a member of the American Strategic Bombing Survey team of 1944–45, which concluded that bombing had actually increased, rather than decreased, the resolve of the German people, was familiar with the inflated claims and expectations of air power enthusiasts.

Instead of aiming to coerce Hanoi into forgoing its support for the Viet Cong, Ball suggested that the air campaign focus on interdiction. According to Ball, Bundy's and McNamara's expectations for the bombing would require escalation in pursuit of an elusive objective. Escalation, Ball warned, might lead to a ground war and nuclear confrontation with China. Although the bombing would not be decisive in itself, it would reduce the flow of supplies to the Vietnamese communist forces and "boost morale" in the South, enabling the South Vietnamese armed forces to cope better with the insurgency. Ball hoped to accomplish through negotiations what he thought unattainable through military action. After an unspecified period, an international agreement would permit the United States to reduce its involvement in the war. That agreement would, Ball hoped, "stop the insurgency in South Vietnam and deliver the entire country south of the seventeenth parallel to the government in Saigon free and clear of insurgency."[65] Ball's expectations for diplomacy seemed as unrealistic as McNamara's, Taylor's and McGeorge Bundy's expectations for air power.

Although bombing advocates could see the weakness in Ball's hopes for a negotiated settlement, and although Ball viewed the expectations for the air campaign as unrealistic, all assumed that some combination of bombing and diplomacy would achieve a settlement in Vietnam more favorable than a U.S. withdrawal. Each sought to convince the president that his "mix" of diplomatic and military activity was most appropriate to the situation. Disagreements centered on the timing of negotiations. Ball urged that the United States go to the UN Security Council "as soon as possible" to call for a cease-fire and the end of support for the Viet Cong from the North. Taylor, McNamara, and Rusk thought that negotiations ought to be postponed until the United States had evidence that North Vietnam was "hurting" and was prepared to "stop doing what it is doing against its neighbors."[66]

Ball's memo failed to inspire a reexamination of expectations for air strikes against North Vietnam, and Rolling Thunder continued without a clear definition of what it was to accomplish. Ball found McGeorge Bundy and McNamara defensive about the air campaign. McNamara dismissed Ball's caveats concerning Rolling Thunder without discussion. McGeorge Bundy supported McNamara and argued that the absence of a clearly defined policy objective was a positive feature of the bombing campaign. Bundy told Ball that there was no need for the United States to "follow a particular course down the road to a particular result." Bundy's belief had led him to support his brother's "fall-back objectives," discussed briefly in November 1964. Ball recalled that Bundy was "qualifying" the U.S. war aim (declared in NSAM 288 on March 17, 1964) to maintain "an independent non-Communist South Vietnam." He concluded that Bundy was leaving "our objective unformulated and therefore flexible." Without a clearly defined objective, Ball said later, he and his colleagues were "charging more deeply into the mire without clearly acknowledging where we were going and on what basis we would call a halt."[67]

■

Like Ball, McNaughton sensed the ambiguity of U.S. policy and attempted to clarify his own thinking about what the United States hoped to achieve in Vietnam, weighting each objective by percentage:

70%—To avoid a humiliating US defeat (to our reputation as guarantor).

20%—To keep SVN (and then adjacent) territory from Chinese hands.

10%—To permit the people of SVN to enjoy a better, freer way of life.

ALSO—To emerge from crisis without unacceptable taint from methods used.

NOT—To "help a friend," although it would be hard to stay if asked out.[68]

McNaughton, the principal civilian war planner in the Department of Defense, had abandoned the stated objective of maintaining a "free and independent" South Vietnam.

For McNaughton the objective of protecting American credibility had displaced the more concrete aim of preserving a free and independent South Vietnam. Even as Rolling Thunder began and Marines landed at Danang, McNaughton continued to plan for failure. He concluded that to avoid humiliation the United States must be prepared to undertake a "massive" effort on the ground in Southeast Asia involving the deployment of 175,000 ground troops. Even if the Communists won, McNaughton believed that the United States would have protected its international image. On the occasion of an American defeat, the United States might use the following excuses: the chronic instability of the South Vietnamese government and the "uniqueness and congenital impossibility" of the situation. To cover its retreat from Vietnam, America might launch "diversionary 'offensives' elsewhere in the world" or begin "multi-nation negotiations for propaganda purposes." Although McNaughton repeated his belief that the likelihood of winning the war was small, but all the United States had to do was "get bloodied" and "hurt" the North Vietnamese and Viet Cong to demonstrate to the "world [the] lengths to which [the] United States will go to fulfill its commitments."[69] McNaughton did not attempt to calculate how much "blood" it would take to protect American credibility.

Although General Wheeler recognized that the lack of a clearly defined objective had created "confusion among the command echelons between Washington and Saigon," he did not seek clarification from the secretary of defense or the president. Wheeler continued to plan for deepening involvement in Vietnam under the assumption that the president and his advisers were pursuing the objective articulated in March 1964 to maintain "an independent non-communist South Vietnam."[70] With that unqualified objective in mind, Wheeler believed that the

United States would have to destroy North Vietnam's capability to support the insurgency in the South. Wheeler and the Chiefs had resolved to do what they could within the constraints of graduated pressure, postponing aerial interdiction missions and attacks against radar and communications facilities until they could bomb targets north of the nineteenth parallel. Reluctant to use one of their bombing allocations on a low payoff target, they postponed the Rolling Thunder strike scheduled for March 11 because the most lucrative target was weathered in. American and South Vietnamese aircraft did not conduct the mission until four days later.[71]

Taylor, anxious to get Rolling Thunder under way, railed at the delay. Even as the Chiefs focused on destroying North Vietnam's military capabilities, Taylor, like McNaughton, thought that the bombing should be aimed at strategic persuasion. Whereas McNaughton focused on demonstrating to Asia and the world that the United States was prepared to back up its commitments to the best of its ability, Taylor continued to believe that air strikes would induce in the North Vietnamese leadership "an attitude favorable to U.S. objectives." He believed that the JCS had placed "too much importance" on striking targets because of their "intrinsic military value." He contended that the "really important target is the will of the leaders in Hanoi" and that "virtually any target north of the 19th parallel" would "convey the necessary message." Taylor lamented that "repeated delays" had failed to "give the mounting crescendo to Rolling Thunder which is necessary to get the desired results."[72]

Confusion over the objectives and nature of the air campaign, however, did not concern the president. President Johnson helped to preserve the confusion and lack of clear direction that attended deepening American military involvement in the war. To achieve his primary goal—the preservation of the fragile consensus behind his Vietnam and domestic policies—his tactics included deliberate ambivalence, obfuscation, and subterfuge. Moreover, the ambiguous nature of his Vietnam policy bestowed certain advantages in the domestic political realm, permitting disparate constituencies to read into the president's policy what they wanted to. For those opposed to deepening the American commitment to Vietnam, Johnson would remain devoted to the pursuit of "peace" and would emphasize careful controls and tight restrictions on the use of military force. For the Joint Chiefs and others who pressed for more resolute military action, Johnson would appear tough and privately characterize initial military actions as first steps toward a much larger war effort. To both doves and hawks, he stressed continuity with the policies of previous administrations. For the doves he described the intensified American military role as essentially no different from the policies of Kennedy, Eisenhower, or even Truman. For the hawks he affirmed his commitment to "save South Vietnam and to help the South Vietnamese to preserve their freedom."[73]

■

Johnson moved to suppress any news of the shift in U.S. policy toward direct action against North Vietnam. On February 15, *New York Times* reporter Tad Szulc published a front-page article predicting that the Johnson administration would soon release a "broad" definition of its Vietnam policy and reveal a willingness to begin early negotiations with Hanoi. The president detected similarities between the article and George Ball's February 13 memo and was incensed. He telephoned Ball, described the publication of the article as a "crisis," and demanded that the State Department determine the source of the leak. Johnson feared that a definitive policy statement would invite criticism from hawks and doves alike. He believed that such Republicans as Senate Minority Leader Dirksen would demand more resolute military action while "peacemakers" such as Democratic Senators Frank Church and George McGovern would criticize any level of military force as dangerous and excessive.[74]

Faced with the danger of leaks revealing America's deepening involvement in the war to the Congress and the public, Johnson drew his advisory group even tighter. He warned Ball that he was going to "put watches on the top people" in the State Department and even suggested that Sen. Joseph McCarthy had been "right" in the 1950s, when the Wisconsin Republican made sensational, unsubstantiated claims that the State Department was full of Communist subversives. LBJ instructed Ball to obscure the changed nature of the war, demanding that

> whenever possible, Rusk, Ball, [and] McNamara feed out enough repetition of what our position is so the "folks" won't say we don't tell them anything. Take the position we have the same policy, we don't believe in moving out and we are not; we do believe in helping other people defend themselves; we did this in the Gulf of Tonkin and

when our soldiers were caught sleeping in their barracks. It does not change our policy or go north attitude.

The president told Ball that if necessary he would make all decisions by himself and "get one man alone with him in the room and bar all others."[75]

The president's reluctance to discuss Vietnam in a forthright manner confused even his closest advisers. On February 16 McGeorge Bundy told Johnson that he was unclear as to "the firmness of your own decision to order continuing action" and urged him to "at least make the decision known to enough people to permit its orderly execution." Bundy explained that McNamara, too, was confused and needed to know where the president stood so that he could "make his military plans and give his military orders." Bundy reminded Johnson that his policy was "very different indeed" from that of previous operations and recommended that the president reveal the bombing of North Vietnam to the public as a "major watershed decision."[76]

Instead of taking Bundy's advice, Johnson intensified his effort to portray his policy as one of continuity with those of previous administrations. He met with Dwight D. Eisenhower. He briefly mentioned this meeting to the National Industrial Conference Board in a speech that, although it focused primarily on aspects of the Great Society, did mention Vietnam:

> As I have said so many, many times, and other presidents ahead of me have said, our purpose, our objective there is clear. That purpose and that objective is to join in the defense and protection of freedom of a brave people who are under an attack that is controlled and that is directed from outside their country.[77]

On the same day Harry S. Truman issued a statement in support of Johnson's Vietnam policy.[78]

Johnson's effort had the desired effect. The New York Times published photos of Johnson with Eisenhower on the front page, and an accompanying article reported broad Republican support for Johnson on Vietnam. Republican senators had remained the president's principal concern because, if dissatisfied over Vietnam, they might join with conservative Democrats to derail the Great Society. During his meeting with Johnson,

Eisenhower told the president that "the U.S. Government must tell our people just what we are doing, . . . what our policy is, and what course of action we are following." Even with Eisenhower's support in hand, however, Johnson remained determined to avoid clearly defining his policy in Vietnam. Doves heard restraint in his promise to take only "measured and fitting" actions that are "justified" and "made necessary by the continuing aggression of others." Hawks were reassured by his pledge to "persist in the defense of freedom."[79]

Those who questioned the direction of LBJ's policy were excluded from future deliberations on Vietnam. Vice President Humphrey, impressed by recent intelligence estimates that questioned whether bombing North Vietnam would persuade Hanoi to end the insurgency, asked his former senatorial assistant, Thomas Hughes, to brief him on the current situation in Vietnam. On February 1, Hughes, then director of the State Department's Bureau of Intelligence and Research, carried the latest CIA and Special National Intelligence estimates with him to meet Humphrey, who was vacationing in Georgia. When the vice president returned to Washington he forwarded a memo to LBJ saying that he would support any presidential decision on Vietnam but felt obligated to apprise the president of his growing concern about the deepening U.S. involvement in the war. He observed that the Truman and Eisenhower administrations had not been able to sustain public support during the Korean War and argued that the situation in Vietnam was fraught with even greater difficulties. He told Johnson that there was little hope for success and warned, as Ball had earlier, that the United States would become the "prisoner of events" in Vietnam. He suggested, as Senator Russell had in November, that the president's landslide victory had put the administration in a stronger position to distance the United States from the war "than any administration in this century." Humphrey added that pulling out of Vietnam would present "minimal political risk" to the administration and warned that, on the contrary, a slow escalation of American involvement would lead to considerable political opposition. Johnson responded by excluding Humphrey from future deliberations on Vietnam.[80]

Johnson's other advisers considered Humphrey's treatment an object lesson. Ball later recalled that "faced with a unanimous view" among the president's top advisers, he "saw no option but to go along." Although Ball would attempt to postpone and minimize the scope and intensity of the bombing, he would no longer question the general direction of the policy or the assumptions that underlay it.[81] He and others had come to the paradoxical conclusion that to protect their influence with the president, they had to spare him their most deeply held doubts. If they voiced their reservations, they would join Humphrey in exile.

12
A Quicksand of Lies

March–April 1965

The Constitution assigns to Congress the right to declare war. How can Congress discharge this function if its members and the citizens who have elected them are precluded from discussing the merits of the issues that might lead to war? The Constitution implies that Congress has a choice in the matter of war. How can it make that choice if neither it nor the people it represents have the right to debate the issues? To say that the most momentous issues a nation must face cannot be openly and critically discussed is really tantamount to saying that democratic debate and decision do not apply to the questions of life and death and that, as far as they are concerned, the people have given carte blanche to one man. Not only is this position at odds with the principles of democracy, but it also removes a very important corrective for governmental misjudgment.

—HANS MORGENTHAU, APRIL 3, 1965[1]

The movement toward war seems in retrospect to have been inexorable largely because LBJ succeeded in minimizing the participation of Congress in his decisions that escalated American military involvement in Vietnam. McNamara, reflecting on the decisions of the spring and early summer of 1965, recalled that "we were sinking into the quicksand."[2] It was, however, a quicksand of his and the president's making—a quicksand of lies. The support of the Joint Chiefs of Staff would prove crucial to LBJ's and McNamara's efforts to conceal the changed nature of American involvement in Vietnam.

On March 1 the *New York Times* reported that Johnson had begun a "continuing but limited air war against North Vietnam to force a negoti-ated settlement on honorable terms." On March 2, the day after Taylor received permission from the Saigon government to land Marines at Danang, reporter Szulc quoted "administration officials" revealing the president's decision to deploy a twelve-hundred-man Marine battalion landing team. The article reported that the Marines would "be assigned to guard air bases and other installations in areas where Vietcong guerril-las are particularly active . . . but would not be sent into combat."[3]

The stories incensed Johnson. He issued a strong rebuke to the mili-tary through McNamara, who sent a message directly to General Westmoreland describing the leaks to the press as "irresponsible if not insubordinate." McNamara was "taking action to prevent similar occur-rences in the future . . . including the application of severe disciplinary penalties," and he asked Westmoreland to "do the same in Saigon."[4] The president called the Army chief of staff to the White House to express his dissatisfaction with the leaks and to charge General Johnson with reassessing the situation in Vietnam. Joining the general and the presi-dent were Rusk, McNamara, and McNaughton. LBJ indicated that he was willing to look with favor on a recommendation for the deployment of more U.S. ground combat units to Vietnam.[5] Like McGeorge Bundy's trip in February, Harold Johnson's visit to South Vietnam would legit-imize a military action for which strong sentiment already existed among the president and his closest advisers.[6] His trip would give the JCS a sense of participation in the policy process.

Over breakfast at the White House, the president told General Johnson to return with recommendations that would boost the coun-terinsurgency effort in South Vietnam without drawing public attention to the escalation of the war. LBJ made it clear to the general that his domestic political concerns would not permit a large-scale troop deploy-ment. The president suggested that, after the first Marine battalion landed, the next increment of troops consist of two Army rather than Marine Corps battalions, thinking that the deployment of Army units would blur the distinction between combat formations and advisers already in Vietnam and produce a "lower noise level."[7] After breakfast the general joined LBJ on the elevator. As Harold Johnson was about to part company with his commander in chief, the president leaned down,

pushed his forefinger into the general's chest, and said: "Get things bub-
bling!"[8] Johnson's instructions included twenty-eight "possible actions"
to discuss with Westmoreland, Taylor, and their staffs on arrival in
Saigon. Although the president had initially directed the general to consider the possibility of deploying ground forces, LBJ ordered that passage
deleted from the general's written instructions.[9] General Johnson's team
consisted of eleven men, including McNaughton and Lieutenant
General Goodpaster.

■

Because Johnson's visit was so short and its focus so broad, he did not
have time actually to reassess the situation there, but only to compile
more actions to take inside and outside South Vietnam. Johnson was
inundated with information from various agencies that briefed him on
more than sixty topics. After only four days in Saigon, he was already
"saturated" with information. He committed only one full day to visits
with U.S. advisers and South Vietnamese officials in the field. He
stopped at eight locations in that short period and had only thirty minutes per stop, which left little time for more than introductions and brief
chats.[10]

Johnson found Taylor and Westmoreland pessimistic about the
prospects for improvement in the situation, but fully committed to additional U.S. action. Although Taylor acknowledged the extreme dedication of the Viet Cong to their cause and the "apathy" among the South
Vietnamese, he focused on the "infiltration problem" and urged an
intensification of Barrel Roll and Rolling Thunder air operations in Laos
and against North Vietnam. He continued to resist further troop deployments but conceded that U.S. combat units might be needed eventually
to offset shortages in the South Vietnamese Army.[11] Johnson found
Westmoreland more receptive than Taylor to the introduction of more
troops into South Vietnam.

At the end of a long day of briefings, Johnson asked that everyone
leave the room except the generals. He then told them that President
Johnson was not convinced that air power alone could reverse the downward trend in South Vietnam. "I am here as a representative of the president of the United States," who was making the "momentous decision"
to commit American ground combat units on a large scale to South
Vietnam. Westmoreland believed that defeat in Vietnam was imminent

and recommended to General Johnson that the U.S. "take whatever actions are necessary," including the deployment of additional ground combat units, to "postpone indefinitely the day of collapse."[12]

The Army staff had already accomplished some planning of its own. Harold Johnson had long believed that the deployment of ground troops to Southeast Asia should precede any air strikes against the North. He wanted well-equipped and well-trained Army units ready to fight if the situation continued to deteriorate in South Vietnam. In February, Johnson had sent his operations deputy, Lieutenant General Palmer, to South Vietnam. Palmer had found the South Vietnamese Army inept, poorly led, and incapable of fighting effectively against the Viet Cong, and told Johnson that the United States had two choices: withdrawal or direct intervention on the ground. The Army staff had concluded then that a five-division force would be necessary. One division would occupy the Central Highlands and also establish secure "enclaves" on the coast, while the other four (three U.S. and one South Korean) would interdict the main infiltration route—the Ho Chi Minh Trail—from positions in Laos and along the DMZ in South Vietnam.[13]

Johnson's trip to Vietnam confirmed Palmer's findings. In the northern half of South Vietnam, the Viet Cong had cut almost all of the transportation routes, limiting government control to the major cities. In Kontum Province government forces had abandoned several districts completely. The only means of supply into the high plateau was by air. In short, the South Vietnamese government controlled only a small part of the population, concentrated in the coastal urban centers. In addition to almost routine accounts of ARVN defeats at the hands of the Viet Cong, Westmoreland reported that North Vietnamese Regular Army regiments had infiltrated into the Central Highlands and were preparing for a large-scale offensive. On his return to Washington, General Johnson reported that U.S. ground forces would have to intervene directly in the counterinsurgency.[14]

Although the general remained a private critic of the air campaign, he argued that the slow tempo and "self-imposed restrictions" on the bombing of North Vietnam had "severely reduced" its effectiveness and made the successful execution of four Rolling Thunder missions per week virtually impossible. He submitted a list of twenty-one recommendations that included requests for an elimination of Washington's control over targeting and munitions, the deployment of additional helicopter companies, the construction of airfields, and an intensification of covert operations against North Vietnam. Johnson based his list of actions on McNaughton's memo and on discussions with General Westmoreland and Ambassador Taylor. Johnson provided no strategic concept, however, to lend coherence to his list of actions, and his report did not demonstrate how those actions would resolve what Taylor identified as the central difficulty in Vietnam: "popular apathy" and "no popular commitment" to the South Vietnamese government. The general warned LBJ that "temporizing or expedient measures will not suffice," but all the suggestions that he offered the president were expedients aimed at averting immediate disaster in Vietnam.[15]

Although Johnson had predicted in December that it would take five years and five hundred thousand troops to win in Vietnam, he also agreed with Westmoreland's appraisal that the United States should "take whatever actions are necessary" to "buy time." Once the impending disaster in Vietnam was averted, the general and his colleagues could press for further deployments. Westmoreland had shared with Johnson his observation that the president's policy had evolved into one of gradually and incrementally intensifying the war. He suggested that the military support LBJ's policy as long as the president remained committed to "do whatever is necessary militarily to prevent defeat." General Johnson agreed. Instead of recommending that the president deploy five divisions, the level of force he and Army planners felt was necessary to achieve a free and independent South Vietnam, he made the "politically feasible" recommendation for one division, as long as the others were added later.[16] Years afterward he regretted that he did not "push" for the deployment of the four-division anti-infiltration force.[17]

Johnson's colleagues on the JCS were anxious to take full advantage of any opportunity to intensify the military effort. While General Johnson was in Vietnam, the JCS submitted separate memoranda urging approval for "hot pursuit" of the Viet Cong across the Cambodian border and a relaxation of restrictions on Farmgate, OPLAN 34A activities, and U.S. air strikes within South Vietnam.[18] The Chiefs thus attempted to remove gradually the barriers to more resolute military action. They pursued that course without thinking about how, collectively, those actions fit together to accomplish their objective, for they had already accepted working within the flawed strategy of graduated pressure, which discouraged such considerations.

■

By the time Johnson and his team returned to Washington on March 12, the president had already discussed the introduction of additional ground forces with his civilian advisers. On March 5 McGeorge Bundy, McNamara, and Rusk met to consider contingencies in the event of a "sharp deterioration" in the situation in Vietnam. After the meeting, in a "personal and sensitive" memorandum, Bundy felt it necessary to assure the president that he and his colleagues had not generated any paperwork and that the discussions had been closed to everyone but "the three of us and one subordinate each." On March 9, as the Marines landed at Danang, McNaughton returned early from the trip to South Vietnam and reported to Bundy that the situation there was "troubled" and the prognosis "grim." He suggested that the president consider sending "lots" of troops to prevent the collapse of South Vietnam. Bundy invited McNaughton to join him, McNamara, Rusk, and the president for that day's Tuesday lunch, at which the former law professor gave the president the same assessment. On March 10, during a meeting at Camp David with McGeorge Bundy, McNamara, and Rusk, LBJ concluded that to withdraw from Vietnam would be the equivalent of British Prime Minister Neville Chamberlain's appeasement of Hitler at Munich in 1938, resolving that "come hell or high water, we're gonna stay there." McGeorge Bundy recalled that the president "had decided to do whatever he had to do, but he had not decided how much he had to do."[19]

Two days later General Johnson and his team returned from Vietnam. On March 15 the president called the JCS to the White House for consultation. Although he continued to delay approval for the deployment of additional ground forces, he talked tough and convinced the Joint Chiefs that he was committed to taking any action necessary to preserve South Vietnam. Even as he postponed his decision on ground troops, LBJ made concessions to the Chiefs in other areas and held out the promise of more decisive military action in the future. The president loosened controls on Rolling Thunder, approved most of the actions contained in Harold Johnson's report, and charged the Chiefs with finding ways to improve the military situation in the South. He ended the meeting with a pep talk. He told his military officers that he wanted them to employ any means necessary to "kill more Viet Cong." He expected a weekly report totaling the Viet Cong dead.[20] The meeting did nothing to clarify U.S. objectives in South Vietnam or determine what level of military force would ultimately be required to meet those objectives. The president's tough talk, however, galvanized the Chiefs and convinced Wheeler that his commander in chief was committed to "do everything possible to better our situation" in Vietnam.[21]

■

When the Chiefs endeavored to carry out the president's instructions, interservice differences over how to fight the war in Vietnam resurfaced. General Greene put forward a plan for the establishment of "six beach heads" similar to his proposal of February 1964. The commandant's plan would guarantee Marine participation in Vietnam in large numbers. Greene had suspected the Army of trying to minimize the Marines' role in Vietnam; his concept emphasized securing logistical bases adjacent to the sea from which U.S. forces could strike inland. Wheeler set the Joint Staff to work on a proposal that would deploy the remainder of the Marine Expeditionary Force to Danang and place one U.S. and one South Korean Army division in the Central Highlands to take an active role in counterinsurgency operations. Air Force Chief of Staff McConnell was opposed to both Wheeler's and Greene's proposals and continued to argue that air strikes against North Vietnam would be decisive only if the bombing restrictions were lifted. To carry out his unrestricted air campaign, McConnell proposed accelerating the deployment of four additional squadrons to Southeast Asia. Instead of recommending more troops, McConnell contended that the JCS should urge "immediate and more forceful application" of air power against the "source of DRV strength." He envisioned intensified bombing within the South to destroy Viet Cong concentrations, while more Air Force and Navy jets pounded vulnerable resources of the enemy in the North. Under McConnell's plan Marine Corps and Army units would guard air bases and logistical facilities and aid the South Vietnamese Army's counterinsurgency efforts.[22] Although the Joint Chiefs had concealed their differences from the secretary of defense and the president, they failed—as usual—to reconcile any of the disagreements because of their inability to overcome service parochialism.

While the Chiefs were divided, McNamara retained the initiative in planning the air war against North Vietnam. As a result of the Chiefs' delaying, and without their prior approval, the Joint Staff briefed McNamara on a twelve-week program of military activities. It called for a three-week interdiction campaign south of the twentieth parallel, followed by a more comprehensive bombing program against the transportation network and radar facilities throughout North Vietnam.[23] McNamara and the Air Force had begun Rolling Thunder as a campaign of strategic persuasion aimed at coercing North Vietnam to end its support for the insurgency in the South. The Joint Staff proposal marked a shift from that strategic objective to the tactical mission of interdicting the flow of supplies to the Vietnamese communist forces in South Vietnam.[24]

The Chiefs' confusion about the objectives and scope of the bombing persisted. On March 27 all that Wheeler could do was to tell McNamara that the JCS was continuing to study alternatives. In mid-April the JCS, still unable to reach agreement, referred the matter back to their staff.[25]

■

Meanwhile sharp restrictions on the air campaign continued. The president's exhortation to "kill more Viet Cong" was aimed more at appeasing the Chiefs than reflective of a genuine willingness to remove constraints on military activity. Although Rolling Thunder VII (the first strikes following General Johnson's report) lacked specific restrictions, such as Washington's approval to attack alternate fixed targets, the president imposed more general constraints that negated those changes. LBJ directed that the JCS avoid air operations in North Vietnam that might lead to clashes with North Vietnam's MIG fighters. That general restriction obliged General Wheeler to limit air operations to the area of North Vietnam south of the twentieth parallel. Reconnaissance aircraft and fighter escorts could operate between the nineteenth and twentieth parallels, but had to withdraw immediately upon detecting MIG fighters.[26]

The contradiction between the president's tough talk in the meeting with the JCS and the continuation of restrictions on the use of force confused General Greene. After their meeting with the president on March 15, Greene told his JCS colleagues that the Marine force at Danang was ready to "commence offensive killing operations" within twenty-four hours. On Friday, March 19, Greene noted that the president had wanted a report on what measures had been taken to "kill more Viet Cong" and could not understand why "no orders had gone out" to satisfy his desire.[27] The other chiefs shared Greene's confusion and, on the same day, decided to press Johnson to deploy additional ground forces and expand the mission of those forces to include offensive operations.

Under the JCS proposal the first additional units to deploy would be the remainder of the Third Marine Expeditionary Force (MEF) totaling 39,000 Marines. In addition the Chiefs urged the approval of Harold Johnson's "fall-back" proposal for the deployment of one U.S. Army division (26,000) to the central plateau area for offensive operations and the deployment of the South Korean (ROK) division (21,000). McConnell, who had opposed Army deployments, agreed to support the memorandum in exchange for a JCS recommendation that the president intensify the air war against North Vietnam and approve the deployment of nine more Air Force squadrons. Without ground forces along the DMZ and in Laos, the Air Force would thus retain primary responsibility for the interdiction effort. As they had in the past, the Chiefs sought an expansion of the war effort while suppressing doubts about the effectiveness of those intermediate steps. The justification was short term. Wheeler warned McNamara that this "direct military action" was essential "if defeat [was] to be avoided."[28]

■

Ambassador Taylor, however, continued to oppose Westmoreland's and the Chiefs' proposals for expanding the numbers and broadening the mission of ground combat units in Vietnam. Wheeler pressed Westmoreland to request additional troops without regard for preserving the "past policy" of advising the South Vietnamese, but the MACV commander had to move cautiously, for he and Taylor had clashed when the first Marines landed in Danang. At that time Taylor reminded Westmoreland that he was in charge of the military effort in Vietnam. Westmoreland therefore had to limit his recommendations for the time being to whatever forces Taylor would allow.[29] On March 18 Westmoreland persuaded Taylor to endorse a request for a third Marine battalion. Taylor gave in to Westmoreland's request in the hope that the battalion would comprise the final American troop deployment.[30]

As Westmoreland sent his request to the JCS, Taylor cabled Rusk, emphasizing the "numerous disadvantages" of sending additional forces to South Vietnam. He warned of "greater losses" and an increase in American "vulnerability to communist propaganda and third world criticism as we appear to assume the old French role of alien colonizer and conqueror." He conceded that the introduction of an Army division would make "some contribution" to the war effort, but warned that U.S.

forces would encourage the South Vietnamese to pass the "Viet Cong burden to the U.S." He argued that there were problems with each of the locations where ground troops might deploy. The introduction of an American division into the Central Highlands, an area controlled by the Viet Cong, "permits one to entertain the possibility of a kind of Dien Bien Phu." A coastal enclave mission would involve U.S. troops in an "inglorious static defensive mission unappealing to them and unimpressive in the eyes of the Vietnamese." U.S. troops operating in major population areas would "maximize the possible points of friction" with the people. Westmoreland, however, was more concerned about recent battlefield defeats inflicted on the South Vietnamese Army than impressed by Taylor's arguments against the deployment of U.S. troops.[31]

Wheeler and Westmoreland began to work together to overcome the ambassador's opposition to ground combat troops. As the Chiefs recommended to McNamara that the remainder of the Third Marine Expeditionary Force, one U.S. Army division, and one ROK division deploy to South Vietnam with the mission of conducting "counterinsurgency combat operations," Wheeler solicited from Westmoreland and Sharp their estimates of the logistical requirements and command arrangements necessary to implement the proposal. Wheeler requested that Westmoreland and Sharp keep the JCS proposal secret and limit planning actions "to the smallest possible U.S. military repeat military group" until he had an opportunity to press his recommendations with the president.[32]

■

Meanwhile, Johnson's closest civilian advisers had become convinced that the introduction of U.S. ground forces to Vietnam was necessary and sought to portray Taylor's views as emotional and illogical. As early as March 6, McGeorge Bundy, who advocated the introduction of ground forces to improve the U.S. "bargaining position" in Vietnam, recommended to the president that Taylor be replaced no later than June 1. Bundy noted that, although Taylor's prestige had been instrumental in "keeping American opinion from division and criticism," the ambassador had become "rigid, remote, and sometimes abrupt." Bundy thought that Taylor's deputy, Alexis Johnson, would be the best replacement and that a "younger man," such as McNaughton, would be an ideal choice for deputy ambassador. In a thinly veiled criticism of Taylor's performance,

McGeorge Bundy told the president that what the United States needed was an "ambassador who understood the essentially political nature of the problem and applied himself to decentralized action with U.S. advice, assistance and support at every level."[33]

Until Taylor's one-year tenure was up, however, the president felt he needed the ambassador's support to preserve the delicate consensus behind his Vietnam policy. Moreover, Taylor would have to gain South Vietnamese approval for U.S. ground troop deployments. As he contemplated candidates to succeed Taylor, Johnson asked the ambassador to return to Washington at the end of March for another round of interdepartmental consultations on Vietnam. On March 29 Taylor joined McNamara and the JCS for a meeting at the Pentagon. The ambassador and the Chiefs disagreed about how many U.S. troops should be deployed to Vietnam and how those troops ought to be used. In an "Estimate of the Situation," sent to Washington in advance of Taylor's arrival, Westmoreland supported Wheeler's proposals to change the mission of American forces from maintaining security in the South to conducting active counterinsurgency operations and to introduce a three-division force to secure coastal areas and fight communist forces in the Central Highlands region. Taylor, however, remained opposed to additional ground forces He thought that a three-division force was "too large" and argued that the South Vietnamese government did not think that U.S. troops were necessary. Taylor again warned that U.S. troops would trigger latent anti-American sentiments among many South Vietnamese. If additional forces did deploy to South Vietnam, Taylor argued that their mission ought to be carefully circumscribed. He recommended that U.S. troops occupy secure enclaves along the coast and in the highlands, leave the preponderance of the fighting to the South Vietnamese, and conduct offensive operations only as a mobile reserve force. Harold Johnson disagreed with Taylor, observing that poor intelligence would result in "quick reaction" strikes falling on air rather than on the Viet Cong. General Johnson, countering the ambassador's proposal, suggested that U.S. ground forces establish model pacification programs in the three plateau provinces northwest of Saigon to provide security, undertake political reforms, and enhance economic development.[34]

Taylor's meeting with the JCS resolved little. Although McNamara believed that some U.S. troops were needed, he agreed with Taylor's assessment that three divisions "seemed high." McNamara, who still wished to control carefully each incremental increase in the use of force in Vietnam, recommended that only two additional Marine battalions deploy to redress the "adverse force ratios" between the Viet Cong and the South Vietnamese Armed Forces. He suggested that, if the situation required more troops, an additional brigade or division could follow the Marines at a later date. McNamara thought that the primary contribution of ground forces would be to signal resolve to Hanoi, and gave his tentative endorsement to Taylor's "enclave" concept.[35]

Taylor and McNamara together overruled the Chiefs' calls for an intensification of Rolling Thunder. Taylor argued that the latest air strikes had established a "good tempo." To forestall opposition from the JCS, McNamara held out the promise of future action. The defense secretary suggested that in four to twelve weeks the mining of Haiphong Harbor and other actions that the Chiefs had previously recommended might become "politically feasible." McNamara assured the Chiefs that if they supported restrictions on the air campaign in the short term, they would eventually be permitted to place "very strong pressure" on North Vietnam.[36]

■

Despite LBJ's efforts to minimize his recent decisions to intensify and widen the U.S. effort in Vietnam, public and congressional opposition to his policy had increased in March. Discontent over the president's policy was growing principally on college campuses and among liberal intellectuals. A State Department white paper, designed to prove North Vietnamese complicity in the insurgency in the South, was weak in its argument and short on evidence, the bulk of which remained classified. A week prior to Taylor's arrival in Washington, the students and faculty at the University of Michigan held the first Vietnam War "teach-in" to voice opposition to the president's policy.[37] In response to the growing opposition, LBJ redoubled his effort to prevent leaks and to conceal deepening American involvement in the war.

The president denied that his policy had changed significantly since his election in November. On April 1, an hour before he met with his advisers on Vietnam, he held an impromptu press conference in the White House theater. Johnson emphasized progress in getting Great Society legislation through Congress. When asked specifically about his Vietnam policy, he highlighted continuity with previous administrations, claiming that he was simply honoring the commitment to the Southeast Asia Treaty Organization (SEATO) that Eisenhower and Congress had made.* Johnson cited the Gulf of Tonkin resolution as evidence of congressional support for his policy and stated that he knew of "no division in the American Government" over Vietnam. To dispel reports that he was discussing major military decisions during Taylor's visit, he denied knowledge of any "far-reaching strategy that is being suggested or promulgated." He said that those who publicly opposed his Vietnam policy and journalists who speculated about it disregarded "our soldiers who are dying" in Vietnam.[38] Immediately after the press conference, the president joined McCone, Rusk, McNamara, Wheeler, McNaughton, Taylor, and the Bundy brothers for consultation on Vietnam.

Johnson made it clear at the outset that the meeting was off the record and that "no great decisions" would be reached. Rusk and CIA Director McCone expressed doubts about the effectiveness of the air strikes against the North and suggested that North Vietnamese leaders, even if they were so inclined, would not be able to call off the insurgency in the South. The president seemed frustrated, wondering how he could get his "feet on their neck." In contrast to his tone at the press conference, he ended his opening remarks with the statement: "We got to find 'em and kill 'em."[39]

General Wheeler picked up on the president's exhortation with an argument for the expansion of the air campaign and the deployment of ground combat units to Vietnam. Although interservice disputes had prevented the JCS from generating its own proposal, Wheeler argued that the twelve-week bombing program developed under McNamara's guidance was inadequate. It did not make sense militarily to avoid hitting the MIG airfields in North Vietnam. Because the United States was "losing the war," the president should approve the JCS recommendation to deploy the remainder of a Marine division, a U.S. Army division, and a South Korean division. Wheeler argued that ground forces would have a major effect on the war, signal American determination and purpose to North Vietnam, serve as a deterrent to escalation, position U.S. military

*Conceived in 1954, SEATO was a collective security arrangement among the United States, Britain, France, Australia, New Zealand, Thailand, Pakistan, and the Philippines. Later, a protocol to the original agreement put South Vietnam, Cambodia, and Laos under its protection.

power forward if deterrence failed, and provide bargaining leverage for negotiations. Wheeler pressed the president for a decision, telling him that with three divisions and logistical improvements, "your problem [is] solved." Wheeler, minimizing the cost of his proposal, noted that reserve forces would not have to deploy and could be used to replenish the strategic reserve.[40]

Instead of producing a debate on the nature of the problem in Vietnam and examining possible U.S. responses, Wheeler's proposal ran into the president's preoccupation with consensus and his desire to keep American involvement in the war as quiet as possible. The president took a middle course designed to satisfy all parties. Johnson deferred making a decision on Wheeler's three-division recommendation. Instead he approved the deployment of two additional Marine battalions and expanded the Marine mission from defensive security to offensive counterinsurgency operations. In the long run the change of mission that committed American troops to offensive combat was more significant than the deployment of additional troops, but the former decision was easier to conceal from the American public in the short term. The president reassured Wheeler that he would consider sending additional forces to Vietnam in the near future and told him to prepare two American divisions for deployment.[41]

■

After the meeting DCI McCone realized that the president had made his decision without an informed comprehensive estimate of the situation and without considering fully the consequences of expanding the mission of U.S. ground forces in Vietnam. McCone attempted to relate the issue of additional ground forces to the ongoing Rolling Thunder campaign and challenged Taylor's assertion that the tempo of the air strikes was "about right." In a memo to Rusk, McGeorge Bundy, McNamara, and Taylor, McCone argued that the bombing had not been "sufficiently heavy and damaging really to hurt the North Vietnamese" and had only "hardened their attitude." Although Taylor had excised paragraphs of CIA reports that questioned the effectiveness of the air strikes, McCone's officers in Saigon had forwarded unedited versions of the reports through back-channel communications. McCone argued that the decisions to change the mission of U.S. ground forces in Vietnam to one of "active combat" was correct only if we "hit" North Vietnam "harder, more frequently, and inflict greater damage." He urged:

Secretary of Defense Robert McNamara reviews dispatches during a two-day trip to South Vietnam in May 1962. He told reporters that he had seen "nothing but progress and hopeful indications of further progress in the future." His notebook full of statistics, McNamara reassured one persistent reporter that "every quantitative measurement we have shows that we're winning this war." *(Courtesy U.S. Army)*

November 23, 1963. The day after John F. Kennedy's assassination, Lyndon Johnson (*at head of table*) holds his first Vietnam meeting as president in the vice-presidential quarters. Seated with Johnson are (*left to right*) Ambassador Henry Cabot Lodge, Secretary of State Dean Rusk, Secretary of Defense Robert McNamara, and Deputy Secretary of State George Ball. (*Photograph by Cecil Stoughton, courtesy LBJ Library Collection*)

January 10, 1964. McNamara advises Johnson on Vietnam. Days after this meeting, the president approved OPLAN 34A covert operations against North Vietnam. (*Photograph by Yoichi R. Okamoto, courtesy LBJ Library Collection*)

March 13, 1964. General Maxwell Taylor (*far left*), McNamara (*third from left*), and Director of Central Intelligence John McCone (*standing*) brief the president after spending five days in South Vietnam. Their report, written by McNamara, provided a blueprint for the escalation of American involvement in the war. Also present is Rusk (*second from left*). (*Photograph by Cecil Stoughton, courtesy LBJ Library Collection*)

March 22, 1964. With the Joint Chiefs of Staff relegated to a position of little influence, McNamara, whom Johnson called a "can-do fellow" and "the best thing I've found in government," became the president's "oracle" for Vietnam. *(Photograph by Yoichi R. Okamoto, courtesy LBJ Library Collection)*

In August 1964 crewmen aboard the USS *Midway* prepare an F–4 "Phantom II" for operations off the coast of North Vietnam. LBJ ordered strikes against North Vietnamese ports on August 4 in retaliation for an alleged attack on U.S. destroyers operating in the Gulf of Tonkin. *(Courtesy U.S. Navy)*

LBJ on the campaign trail in October 1964. Anxious to draw a contrast between himself and the Republican candidate for president, Sen. Barry Goldwater, Johnson cast himself as a "peace candidate" even as his advisers planned the Americanization of the Vietnam War. *(Courtesy LBJ Library Collection)*

December 1, 1964. Meeting in the cabinet room on the occasion of Ambassador Taylor's visit to Washington *(from left to right)*: William Bundy, Rusk, LBJ, McNamara, Taylor. The president's advisers had formed a consensus behind William Bundy's program for a gradual escalation of American military intervention in Vietnam. *(Photograph by Cecil Stoughton, courtesy LBJ Library Collection)*

December 1964 at Johnson's Texas ranch. Behind McNamara and LBJ are *(left to right)* Gen. Harold Johnson (Army Chief of Staff), Adm. David McDonald (Chief of Naval Operations), Gen. Curtis LeMay (Air Force Chief of Staff), Gen. Earle Wheeler (JCS Chairman), Deputy Secretary of Defense Cyrus Vance, and Gen. Wallace Greene (Marine Corps Commandant). *(Photograph by Yoichi R. Okamoto, courtesy LBJ Library Collection)*

February 7, 1965. National Security Advisor McGeorge Bundy, pictured with General William Westmoreland *(right)*, surveys the scene of the Viet Cong attack on Pleiku. Upon his return to Washington, Bundy recommended that the president authorize the "systematic" bombing of North Vietnam. *(Courtesy U.S. Army)*

March 2, 1965. McNamara briefs members of Congress on LBJ's "gimmick" to secure additional funding for Vietnam. The president connected the request to intervention in the Dominican Republic and equated a negative vote with abandoning American troops in the field. LBJ and Vice President Hubert Humphrey are seated in the front row. *(Photograph by Yoichi R. Okamoto, courtesy LBJ Library Collection)*

Marine Corps tanks and their crews prepare to land at Danang on March 8, 1965. While the Marines prepared for an offensive role in the war, the Johnson administration described their deployment as a defensive security measure. *(Courtesy U.S. Navy)*

April 8, 1965. McNamara meets with LBJ in the Oval Office just prior to the arrival of the Joint Chiefs of Staff. (*Photograph by Yoichi R. Okamoto, courtesy LBJ Library Collection*)

April 8, 1965. Air Force Chief of Staff John McConnell (*left*) and JCS Chairman Earle Wheeler use a map to brief LBJ concerning early Rolling Thunder air strikes against North Vietnam. Army Chief of Staff Harold K. Johnson is seated in the background. LBJ instructed the JCS to "kill more Viet Cong." (*Photograph by Yoichi R. Okamoto, courtesy LBJ Library Collection*)

April 8, 1965. The "Coach" and his "Team" pose on the White House lawn (*from left to right*): Air Force Chief of Staff John McConnell, Army Chief of Staff Harold K. Johnson, JCS Chairman Earle Wheeler, LBJ, Deputy Secretary of Defense Cyrus Vance, Chief of Naval Operations David McDonald, and Marine Corps Commandant Wallace Greene. (*Photograph by Frank Viola, courtesy LBJ Library Collection*)

April 1965. At the Pentagon, McNamara briefs members of the press on the progress of Rolling Thunder. He often impressed his audiences with what seemed to be a firm grasp of details and statistics. Although McNamara portrayed the initial bombing missions as successful, their results had been disappointing. (*Courtesy U.S. Army*)

July 26, 1965. With Rusk and Wheeler looking over his shoulders, McNamara briefs LBJ on his plan to deploy 125,000 additional troops to South Vietnam without mobilization and without asking Congress for an additional funding authorization. (*Photograph by Yoichi R. Okamoto, courtesy LBJ Library Collection*)

Instead of avoiding the MIG's, we must go in and take them out. A bridge here and there will not do the job. We must strike their air fields, their petroleum resources, power stations and their military compounds. This, in my opinion, must be done promptly and with minimal restraint. If we are unwilling to take this kind of decision now, we must not take the actions concerning the mission of our ground forces.

McCone warned that unless the president made a clear choice between a negotiated settlement and a decisive expansion of the war, the United States would incur an "ever-increasing commitment of U.S. personnel without materially improving the chance of victory."[42]

The president heard McCone's views in an NSC meeting on April 2, but he remained resolved to take only the minimal actions necessary to prevent defeat in South Vietnam. McCone had become increasingly frustrated with his limited access to the president as well as with the administration's apparent disinterest in intelligence. Unlike graduated pressure McCone's assessment provided no easy solutions to the problem in Vietnam and demanded, in effect, that the president make a difficult choice between commitment to a large-scale war and a negotiated withdrawal. Johnson, however, would not make a tough decision that would alienate constituencies on which his Great Society depended. Three weeks after he composed his memo, McCone resigned in frustration.[43]

Although he had come to the same conclusion as McCone about what the situation in Vietnam demanded, Wheeler did not consider resignation. He responded to the president's reluctance to commit fully to either negotiation or the use of military force by pressing for a gradual intensification of the war effort, as the president's domestic political concerns permitted. His approach allowed Johnson to avoid deciding whether to go to war in Vietnam even as the country sank deeper into that war. The president remained more interested in preserving consensus about his policy than in entertaining a wide-ranging discussion on the situation in Vietnam.

■

Taylor's final meeting in Washington revealed that the principal purpose of his visit had been to preserve the superficial harmony and consensus among the president's principal Vietnam advisers. In a meeting with

258 I DERELICTION OF DUTY

Taylor and the Bundy brothers, Rusk told Taylor that "the president felt that he must not force the pace too fast or the Congress and the public opinion, which had been held in line up to now through the president's strenuous efforts, would no longer support our actions in Vietnam." Rusk emphasized that Taylor must keep the few decisions that the president did make as quiet as possible. The secretary of state recognized that Taylor would have to get South Vietnamese permission to deploy the additional Marines, but "did not yet want to give up the ability to describe their mission as defensive." Rusk attempted to qualify the president's decision on the mission change by suggesting that the Marines already in country delay offensive operations until the additional battalions joined them, and by claiming that any offensive be described as "aggressive patrolling." Under no circumstances would Taylor indicate to the South Vietnamese government that the president was considering large-scale American troop deployments. At the end of the meeting, McGeorge Bundy, who had congratulated the president for his "personal achievement" in presenting his decisions to expand the war "within the framework of a continuing policy and a continuing purpose and not as major new departures," stressed to Taylor the need for "very tight public information controls on these matters." Taylor indicated that he now "understood the situation in the United States."[44]

Assured of harmony within his administration, the president moved to defuse opposition from those who favored an immediate move toward a negotiated settlement. Since first authorizing "continuing action" against North Vietnam in mid-February, he had ignored and discouraged calls for negotiation. He shared Taylor's view that an early willingness to negotiate would appear to the North Vietnamese as a sign of weakness. Johnson told Ball that early calls for negotiation had him feeling as if he were "getting crowded into a corner." Johnson instructed Ball to act as "his lawyer" and forestall calls for negotiations until North Vietnam had felt the effects of the bombing campaign. In response to peace initiatives from the British prime minister, the secretary general of the UN, and others, the president threatened "to get sick and leave town" to avoid having to receive their proposals.[45]

■

By the end of March, however, it had become apparent to the president that he would have to confront growing public and congressional opposition to his policy. Democratic Senators Mansfield and McGovern had warned him that his policy of expanding the American military effort in Vietnam would have dire consequences. Mansfield argued that U.S. interests on the Southeast Asian mainland did not justify the cost in lives and resources. He urged Johnson to pursue negotiations even if the United States had to accept a less than favorable settlement.[46]

Just as he had used tough language to convince the JCS of his determination to commit whatever force was necessary in Vietnam, the president turned to the language of peace to quell opposition to military action. On March 25, two days after receiving Mansfield's memo and the day after the University of Michigan teach-in, Johnson released a statement that stressed the limited nature of American military actions in Vietnam and cited his readiness to "go anywhere at anytime and meet with anyone whenever there is promise of progress toward an honorable peace." The president hoped that there would be a time when Southeast Asia would be "free from terror, subversion, and assassination" and would be able to reap the benefits of "economic and social cooperation with the United States."[47]

One week later, Averell Harriman sent a memo to McGeorge Bundy urging the president to develop more fully a proposal for economic development for both Vietnams. Harriman suggested that to regain the support of those who had begun to question the president's Vietnam policy, Johnson offer North Vietnam a "political and economic carrot" in the form of an exported Great Society. Bundy, who had come to believe that the president ought to give the American public "a more detailed exposition of our conditions for peace and our view of the future in Southeast Asia," began to draft a speech for the president. LBJ chose April 7 to deliver a nationally televised address on Vietnam at Johns Hopkins University in Baltimore.[48]

In that much-publicized speech, Johnson reemphasized his commitment to guarantee "the independence of South Viet-Nam and its freedom from attack" and stressed the continuity between his policy and that of President Eisenhower in the 1950s. He vowed "never [to] be second in the search for a peaceful settlement in Viet-Nam." While emphasizing his commitment to use military force, Johnson held out the promise of a comprehensive economic and public works development program for all of Southeast Asia. He evoked images of progress that, as a New Deal congressman and senator, he had helped bring to his native Texas hill country. He promised North Vietnam a Mekong River development program that would "provide food and water and power on a scale to dwarf even our own TVA" (Tennessee Valley Authority) and "revolutionary advances in medical care, agriculture, and education." Under Johnson's program, North Vietnam could feed its people with food from American warehouses and allow its people to trade in their "rags" for decent clothing. Johnson's words, as he and his advisers had described them at lunch the day before, were aimed at placating the "sob sisters and peace societies" in the United States.[49]

The president's stated objective of "an independent South Viet-Nam—securely guaranteed and able to shape its own relationships to all others—free from outside interference" was nonnegotiable to North Vietnamese leaders, who remained determined to unite Vietnam under Hanoi's domination.[50] The North Vietnamese Politburo had concluded that negotiations would only be useful "to pave the way for a U.S. withdrawal with a lesser loss of face." They planned to negotiate only after the insurrection in the South succeeded. The day after the Johns Hopkins speech, Hanoi responded with "four points" as preconditions for any negotiations. The United States was to withdraw unconditionally from Vietnam. A coalition government in the South (which Hanoi planned to dominate) would be formed to negotiate the unification of Vietnam. Until that government was formed, the Viet Cong's political arm, the National Liberation Front (NLF), would be the only legitimate representative of the Vietnamese people.[51]

Although it had taken less than twenty-four hours for Ho to reject LBJ's export version of the Great Society, the response in the United States was generally positive. Former ambassador to India, economist John Kenneth Galbraith, who had recently returned to the faculty of Harvard University and would become an outspoken critic of the Vietnam War, wrote an open letter to the New York Times. Galbraith praised the president's reversal of what had seemed a military approach to the problem in Vietnam and expressed relief that Johnson was not embarking upon an "infantry war in Asia."[52]

When Galbraith wrote his letter to the editor, however, U.S. Marines had already received orders to begin "offensive killing operations," and two additional Marine infantry battalions, one Marine air squadron, and twenty thousand logistical troops capable of supporting three more divisions of combat troops were preparing for deployment to South Vietnam.

In pursuit of consensus and not wanting to confront the implications of his decisions, the president had quietly committed the United States to war.[53]

■

The body charged with providing the president with military advice and responsible for strategic planning permitted the president to commit the United States to war without consideration of the likely costs and consequences. Comprehensive estimates of the number of troops necessary to win existed, but to conceal interservice divisions and to increase the likelihood that the president would approve the actions that they recommended, the Joint Chiefs suppressed them. In late January 1965, Vice Admiral Rufus Taylor, director of Naval Intelligence, had reported to Admiral McDonald that the United States "should be prepared at an early date to either commit U.S. forces in sufficient strength to ensure victory for our side or get out before it is too late." A JCS study conducted under the direction of the Marine Corps staff estimated that seven hundred thousand troops would be needed to win in Vietnam. Harold Johnson had concluded that it would probably take five years and five hundred thousand men to defeat the insurgency in the South. The failure of early Rolling Thunder strikes came as no surprise to Admiral McDonald and Harold K. Johnson, but neither had expressed his doubts about the bombing to his civilian superiors.[54] They accepted an open-ended commitment to fight in Vietnam rather than press for the deployment of the number of troops that they thought would be required to win the war or develop a strategic plan integrating the air, ground, and naval efforts into a coherent military program. Each member of the JCS continued to suppress his reservations about the strategy of graduated pressure and optimistically advanced his own service's solution to the problem.

The Chiefs, however, had given the president the military advice he wanted. While excluding the JCS from substantive deliberations, LBJ and McNamara bought the support of the military with a combination of pro forma consultation and promises of stronger action in the future. With Rolling Thunder under way and combat units arriving in South Vietnam, the JCS had begun to press McNamara and Johnson to deliver on their promises. It was time for LBJ to communicate to the JCS precisely what he expected from his military advisers.

13
The Coach and His Team
April–June 1965

Maybe we military men were all weak. Maybe we should have
stood up and pounded the table. ... I was part of it and I'm
sort of ashamed of myself too. At times I wonder, "why did I
go along with this kind of stuff?"

—ADM. DAVID LAMAR McDONALD, 1976[1]

In the spring and summer of 1965, LBJ was responding to political
pressures. Having placated the "sob sisters and peace societies" with
his April 7 Johns Hopkins speech, the president felt compelled to
respond to pressure from another quarter, the Joint Chiefs. Indeed, two
days prior to the president's speech, McNamara asked the JCS for a
detailed schedule for the introduction into Vietnam of a force of two to
three divisions "at the earliest practicable date." Assuming that the president would soon approve the deployment, the JCS ordered units to prepare for shipment to South Vietnam. Lieutenant General Burchinal, the
director of the Joint Staff, cabled CINCPAC expressing the JCS's desire
to "ram" logistical units into South Vietnam "as rapidly as MACV wants
them and we can send them" in order to prepare for the support of large
ground combat forces.[2] The first confirmed reports that North
Vietnamese Regular Army units had infiltrated into the South added

urgency to JCS recommendations for an intensification of the air campaign against the North and for deployment of three divisions to South Vietnam.[3]

Johnson, however, was unwilling even to entertain the Chiefs' recommendations. He was impressed by the vehemence and strength of the antibombing protests, and feared that the large-scale troop deployments the Chiefs were recommending would raise to a higher level the public and congressional attention directed toward the war. He was still concerned that greater congressional scrutiny on Vietnam meant less attention to the Great Society. He responded to competing pressures with decisions that he hoped would satisfy, or at least placate, critics and potential critics. He refused to consider an intensification of the Rolling Thunder air campaign because it would incite further protests and opposition. He would, however, approve small increases in the level of force in South Vietnam and change the mission of U.S. ground units from defensive to offensive operations—actions, in other words, that he could conceal from the American public and Congress. Units smaller than division size already stationed overseas could be relocated to South Vietnam with less fanfare than the deployment of entire divisions from the United States. Offensive operations could be portrayed as active patrolling in support of what the administration would continue to describe as a primarily defensive operation. The president hoped that his middle course, dependent on lies and obfuscation, would minimize criticism from those opposed to deepening American involvement in the war as well as those, like the JCS, who urged further action.

To continue to hold the "middle ground" on Vietnam, the president needed the cooperation of the Joint Chiefs. Because he was deceiving the American people and the Congress, keeping the Chiefs "on the team" would become more important to him than it had been previously. The JCS had recognized that graduated pressure was a strategy driven by domestic political objectives. Most of all, the introduction of ground troops to Vietnam was the first natural breakpoint in Johnson's Vietnam policy since graduated pressure had become the administration's strategy in March 1964. The arrival of ground troops in South Vietnam and their employment in offensive operations against the Viet Cong gave the Chiefs an opportunity to voice their opposition to Johnson's Vietnam policy.

Indeed, the Chiefs attempted to press the president to take more resolute action in Southeast Asia. They reached an agreement to tell the president that the immediate deployment of three divisions was necessary to win the war in Vietnam. Wheeler asked his colleagues to stand firmly behind this recommendation. The Chiefs failed, however, to take advantage of a clear opportunity to question Johnson's policy, and graduated pressure continued to guide the deployment of ground troops while the president's advisers focused on tactical details rather than on strategic issues. From April through June of 1965, the president failed to confront the likely consequences of military actions and the Joint Chiefs of Staff continued to recommend an escalation of the military effort without presenting a strategy aimed at forcing an outcome consistent with U.S. interests.

■

Johnson's determination to conceal the scale of America's deepening military involvement in Vietnam militated against approving the Chiefs' recommendations. Although he authorized the deployment of two additional Marine battalions and one air squadron, he was particularly concerned about changing, without the knowledge of Congress, the Marines' mission from defensive to offensive combat operations. In an NSAM issued on April 6, "the president approved a change of mission for all Marine battalions deployed to Vietnam to permit their more active use under conditions to be established and approved by the Secretary of Defense in consultation with the Secretary of State." The final paragraph of the NSAM made clear the president's desire to avoid "premature publicity" about his recent decisions. Although "the actions themselves should be taken as rapidly as practicable," the military should "minimize any appearance of sudden changes in policy." Only the secretaries of defense and state could issue official statements concerning troop deployments and mission changes. Finally the NSAM reemphasized that "these movements and changes should be understood as being gradual and wholly consistent with existing policy."[4]

Meanwhile, because of international and domestic political pressure to stop Rolling Thunder,[5] LBJ assured the American people that he would continue to exercise "restraint" in connection with the air campaign.[6] Concerned about this issue, Johnson arranged a meeting on April 8, 1965, the day after the Johns Hopkins speech, with the JCS, McNamara, and Deputy Secretary of Defense Vance.[7] The president was determined to avoid any discussion of the bombing of North Vietnam and made it clear to the Chiefs that he expected results in Vietnam even under the restrictions that he had placed on air and ground operations.

The Joint Chiefs, however, based on assessments that Rolling Thunder had not reduced the overall military capability of Vietnamese communist forces in "any major way," continued to recommend lifting the restrictions on the air campaign.[8] Using enlarged photographs Wheeler recounted recent Rolling Thunder strikes on two key bridges in North Vietnam. McConnell noted that U.S. aircraft had dropped 432 bombs on one bridge and, although it was damaged, no part of it had been knocked down. Two American fighters, furthermore, had been shot down by North Vietnamese MIGs. The president asked the Chiefs what had "gone wrong" with the attack. McConnell responded apologetically that neither mission had been well-planned or -executed. He promised that missions would improve in the future, and noted that he had sent to South Vietnam a team of four men to "get them straightened out." He made no mention, however, of the continued prohibition against targeting the enemy's fighter bases as a possible contributing factor to the fate of the two Air Force F-105s. The president said, "It looks to me as if the boys are inexperienced." Nodding in agreement, McConnell muttered that this was so.[9] The Chiefs allowed the president to blame the mission's failure on the "boys" who executed it rather than emphasize how both the restrictions on the amount of force and the rules of engagement compromised the Rolling Thunder attacks. They therefore put themselves on the defensive rather than force the president to face the consequences of his policies.

LBJ told the JCS: "Now, I'm like a coach I used to know, and you're my team; you're all Johnson men." Referring to the situation in Vietnam, the president continued with his metaphor: "We played the first half of the game and the score is now 21–0 against us; now I want you to tell me how to win." LBJ's eyes turned to Wheeler: "You're graduates of the Military Academy and you should be able to give me an answer. I want you to come back here next Tuesday and tell me how we are going to kill more Viet Cong." The president appeared committed to invest whatever level of force the JCS determined was necessary to "win" the war in the South. He observed that "at present we are limited as to what we can do in North Vietnam, but we have almost free rein in South Vietnam, and I want to kill more Viet Cong." Although he had essentially placed any discussion of intensifying the air campaign against North Vietnam off limits, Johnson pledged a willingness "to spend the money and, if necessary, to move the Joint Chiefs of Staff right out to Saigon" to improve the situation. He asked them to tell him "what we can do to win."

Despite his professed desire to "win," the president attempted to exact from the Chiefs a recommendation consistent with his desire to maintain domestic political consensus. He hoped to generate among them an understanding of his need to limit military action against the North. He told them that he was "having trouble" with Congress and the public. He leaned backward in his chair, pointing out a pile of telegrams on the desk behind him. He told the JCS that the telegrams were "all criticisms of the speech I made last night at Johns Hopkins. I thought I was doing pretty well—I got 14 applauses in 40 minutes, but those letters don't look that way." After making clear his insecurity and need for support, "Coach Johnson" told his team what he expected.

First the president wanted the JCS to prevent criticisms from the field from reaching the media and the American public. He referred to recent press reports that the war had been controlled too tightly from Washington, and told the JCS that "as long as I am Commander in Chief, I am going to control from Washington." He ordered Wheeler to identify and punish those who had complained to reporters. Wheeler promised that he would. Johnson then told the JCS to shift their strategic focus away from the controversial bombing of North Vietnam and toward additional action in South Vietnam. He asked Wheeler, "How many Viet Cong have we killed since you were here last time?" Wheeler had no figures, so Deputy Secretary of Defense Vance helped the chairman make an estimate. The president appeared disappointed. He wanted to "know how many Viet Cong have been killed since the first of January and how many Vietnamese have been killed by the Viet Cong and how many Americans." It appeared that the president, having discussed the war in terms of a football game, was intent on keeping score by tracking the numbers of dead on both sides.

Greene, who had grown frustrated with the disparity between the president's tough talk and limitations on the use of force, leaned forward and told Johnson:

> Mr. President, the last time I came over here was last month on the
> 15th of March. When I left the meeting that day, I had the clear idea

you wanted more VC killed. I thought that you really meant that, but here it is almost a month later—the 8th of April—and we are just getting permission to modify our security mission to permit us to go out and kill Viet Cong. Furthermore, we're just getting approval from the Vietnamese Government . . . for the introduction of more Marines into the Danang area and also I assume approval of a combat killing mission for the Danang Marine forces.[10]

Greene told the president that the Marine force currently in the South (two reinforced battalions of about sixteen hundred men each) was inadequate.

Greene used the president's demand to kill more Viet Cong to argue for a much larger U.S. Marine effort in South Vietnam. He observed that offensive operations against the enemy would require "additional troops" and suggested that the "Marine commander on the ground" be given the authority to bring in as many Marines from the Third Marine Expeditionary Force based in Okinawa as he deemed necessary to "expand his operations." Greene suggested that South Vietnamese Marine units supplement U.S. Marine forces to conduct combined "Viet Cong killing operations." Noting that the Marines were "trained to operate together as an air-ground team," he observed that a Marine air squadron was not yet positioned in Danang. Once the first squadron arrived, he would need a second to "operate in close teamwork with our ground Marines."

LBJ was not yet prepared to consider specific proposals. Having told the JCS why further action against the North was out of the question and having communicated his need for support, he deferred any consideration of Greene's recommendation until their next meeting. He told the JCS that Greene's proposal was "the kind of information I want you all to give me next Tuesday when you come back to talk again."

As the Chiefs rose to leave, the photographer continued to move about the room to record the president's "consultation" with his military advisers. LBJ motioned for the Chiefs to gather around his desk. Picking up a handful of the telegrams he had referred to earlier, the president told them, "This is the sort of thing I am up against—This is the sort of stuff I am getting from the public." Johnson then asked the officers to step outside into the garden for some additional photographs. During the second photo, Greene switched positions with McDonald and stood next to the president. Having read the Johns Hopkins speech in the morning paper, the Marine Corps commandant sought to reassure the president, telling him that the speech was "the best one given during the past administrations," and that he was "sure that there were a lot of people in the country who felt just as I did."

LBJ had performed well. Greene was impressed by the "clear worry" that dominated the president's demeanor. To prevent the Chiefs from questioning limitations on the use of force against the North, the president played for their sympathy, asking that they be team players. Lest the Chiefs underestimate the seriousness with which he regarded their support, LBJ made veiled threats to relieve his military advisers or supplant their role. He said that he had considered sending General Shoup, the retired Marine Corps commandant, to "take charge of the whole military situation" in South Vietnam, but had decided against it because there were already too many generals "out there." Unwilling to intensify the air campaign or deploy large numbers of U.S. troops to the South, he pressured the Chiefs to "kill more Viet Cong" with troops and matériel currently available to them.[11]

Although he registered no objections during the meeting, Greene recorded that the president "does not seem to grasp the details of what can and cannot be done in Vietnam!" Recognizing that temporizing measures would not produce tangible results, Greene believed that the United States faced the difficult decision of either withdrawing from Vietnam or staying to fight a "major campaign." In a memo that he passed out to his colleagues just prior to the meeting with the president, Greene had recommended the immediate deployment of one Marine expeditionary force, one Army division, and one South Korean division to South Vietnam. After a ten-day "grace period" following the Johns Hopkins speech, the United States would "commence a rapid, significant, sustained increase" in pressures against North Vietnam, including unrestricted air strikes on enemy military and industrial targets, the mining of Haiphong Harbor, shore bombardment of coastal and island targets, and seizure of the latter with South Vietnamese troops. Simultaneously the United States would prepare for a "total blockade" of North Vietnamese ports and put the American economy "on a wartime footing."[12] The president, however, did not wish to make such a firm commitment to war, lest he alienate any of his constituencies.

∎

Secretary of Defense McNamara remained Johnson's principal assistant in pursuing a "middle ground" in Vietnam[13] and in concealing from Congress and the public the fact that an expanded U.S. effort on the ground in South Vietnam was under way. The defense secretary told the Senate Foreign Relations Committee that "it will be the president's desire and purpose to consult with the Congress, the leadership of the Congress, members of this committee, before undertaking any combat moves of personnel that would potentially enlarge the war."[14] Taylor assisted McNamara in this deception. Before he returned to Saigon, the ambassador had assured the Senate Foreign Relations Committee that "no one is approaching a decision of this magnitude at this moment." He promised the senators that if a large-scale deployment was needed, "you are going to be consulted, I am perfectly sure." Separately Dean Rusk had assured Senator Church and his colleagues that large scale troop deployments were not "at all in contemplation and that we would naturally consult with appropriate Senate leaders before we seriously considered such a step."[15]

Based on consultation with Taylor, Westmoreland sensed that "the deployment of division-sized forces is not in the immediate offing."[16] Accordingly, he suggested that he and the JCS work within the president's approach to gain approval for sending to Vietnam the largest number of troops possible without attracting intense congressional scrutiny. On April 11 he suggested that the JCS recommend redeployment of the 173rd Airborne Brigade from Okinawa to the Central Highlands of South Vietnam.[17] He reasoned, as he had earlier, that the deployment of brigade-size forces from Okinawa would attract less public and congressional attention than that of division-size forces from the United States. Westmoreland suggested that the JCS work within the constraints of the president's domestic agenda by gradually, rather than suddenly, expanding the U.S. commitment in Vietnam.

On April 13 the JCS and McNamara returned to the White House for lunch with the president.[18] Johnson continued to play for sympathy from the Chiefs while criticizing their performance. He thought it unfair that he had borne the "blame for some eighteen months by himself." If the situation in Vietnam continued to deteriorate, he threatened, he would "share [the blame] with those who had been giving him advice."

Johnson also remained determined to preempt discussion of an intensification of military actions against the North. He again made clear his intention to retain tight control over military operations. He promised more determined action in the future, however, and vowed to increase the tempo of bombing targets below the twentieth parallel. Because the president limited the discussion to actions within South Vietnam and wished to maintain tight control over the air campaign against the North, McConnell restricted his recommendations to minor changes that he could carry out "in house" without presidential approval. Similarly, McDonald indicated that the Navy was taking measures to improve sea surveillance of the North Vietnamese coast.

Although he forestalled discussion of the air campaign against North Vietnam, Johnson professed enthusiasm for any JCS proposal to intensify the war in the South. He again emphasized that he would even move the JCS to Saigon "to handle the situation themselves." LBJ assured the Chiefs that he would invest whatever amount of money, matériel, or effort necessary "to win the game in South Vietnam" and "start killing more Viet Cong."

The president asked for Wheeler's recommendations. The chairman restated the JCS recommendation of March 20 that three divisions deploy to South Vietnam. As Wheeler spoke the president began to calculate the total number of troops that would then be deployed in South Vietnam, arriving at a total of 180,000. Despite his pledge to commit to South Vietnam the forces the JCS deemed necessary, the president said that he could never get Congress to go along with that large a number of troops. Besides, the president noted, a large troop deployment might incite a reaction from North Vietnam and China.

Unhappy with Wheeler's advice, the president indicated that he would be willing to approve the deployment of five thousand troops, instead of the ninety thousand that would attend the deployment of three divisions. He made his point with an analogy: "It is just as if you went to a bank owned by Mr. McNamara and asked him for a loan of $90,000, and he told you that no he couldn't let you have that amount, but that he would loan you $5,000. What would you do? Let your business go into bankruptcy, or would you take the $5,000 and try to do something with it?" Johnson wanted the JCS to tell him how to reverse the deteriorating situation in South Vietnam cheaply and quickly. He told his senior military officers that he was "willing to send a reasonable number of troops into South Vietnam," but was "never going to agree at this time to three divisions; something else on a smaller scale would have to be tried." After making his point, the president turned to Harold Johnson and asked for his assessment. When the Army chief of staff reiterated the JCS estimate that three divisions were the minimum force necessary, LBJ turned quickly to General Greene. The president was counting on the commandant of the Marine Corps (whom McNamara had earlier described to him as "immature")[19] to break with his colleagues and make a recommendation that would not precipitate a congressional debate. When the Chiefs first arrived at the White House, LBJ had shaken the general's hand warmly and said in a low voice, "I want some good recommendations from you today." After General Johnson reinforced Wheeler's three-division proposal, the president addressed the group: "The last time you were over here, Wally Greene had a proposal to make which we partially heard that had to do with combined operations with the South Vietnamese. Now let's hear what he has to say." The president's pandering had the desired effect.[20]

Greene gave Johnson the advice he wanted. The commandant described a proposal for combined operations as a program that "could be bought cheaply and might be successful." Johnson responded that he was willing to "throw another chip on the table amounting to 5,000 more U.S. Marines, if necessary, in order to carry this plan out." Although McNamara interjected that Greene's proposal would require some study, the president remained enthusiastic. LBJ thought that "this recommendation should be tried out and if it failed, we wouldn't have lost and could go on and try something else."[21] After his meeting with the Chiefs, Johnson approved Westmoreland's request for the 173rd Airborne Brigade.[22]

■

The two April meetings between the president and the JCS added greater confusion to an already muddled strategic picture of what the U.S. military was to accomplish in Vietnam. The president's curtailment of their discussion to only those initiatives that would "kill more Viet Cong" prevented the development of a comprehensive plan for the war. Instead of defining policy goals precisely and then determining how military force might contribute to those goals, the president's discussion with the Chiefs began with how much force he was willing to invest in the near term and assumed, with no thought for the nature of the war, that any action would constitute progress in the war effort. The Chiefs were to make their recommendations not according to agreed-on objectives but according to the means the president made available, based on domestic political priorities.

In the absence of clearly defined strategic objectives, "killing more Viet Cong," a tactical mission, became the basis for JCS plans and recommendations. After their meetings with the president, the JCS set the Joint and Service Staffs to work to "determine how we can increase the Viet Cong (VC) kill rate within the framework of our present posture in Southeast Asia." The JCS concluded that, with the current force levels, they might "kill more Viet Cong" through the massive application of air power in the South.[23] It remained unclear, however, how the tactic of using massive air strikes against an enemy who was intertwined with the noncombatant population would help to establish strategic conditions conducive to ending the war.

Because the bombing of North Vietnam had incited opposition, the piecemeal introduction of small numbers of ground troops seemed to the president the path of least resistance. Through this course of action, Johnson might assuage the Chiefs' desire for additional action, while continuing to obscure the nature of America's growing military commitment from those who were opposed to military intervention in Vietnam. Public, congressional, and international opposition to bombing North Vietnam had dimmed the luster of what had been the politically cheap course of action.[24] Although intensified action against the North might inflame emerging critics of the Vietnam policy, such as Senators Morse, Fulbright, and Church, a few more Marines or an Army brigade stationed in the Philippines might slip into South Vietnam without inciting a politically damaging debate.[25]

The president had used differences among the Chiefs to his advantage before, and service parochialism continued to be a debilitating influence on the JCS. Greene's desire to increase the Marine Corps' role in Vietnam led him to spare the president the "hard, cold facts" that he and the Marine Corps Staff had recorded in an estimate of the situation. Instead, he urged a "cheap" deployment of five thousand more Marines, one-hundredfold fewer than he thought would ultimately be required to fight a "major campaign."[26] LBJ had impressed Greene with his "very forceful and impressive manner" and had left the general with "no doubt in my mind that he meant business and that he expected the Joint Chiefs to produce and that he wanted more Viet Cong killed."[27]

Wheeler recognized how Lyndon Johnson had manipulated the JCS, but he remained unwilling to confront his commander in chief. When he returned to the Pentagon, he summoned his colleagues to his office. Greatly distressed, he told the Chiefs that they had been "led into a trap." When Greene asked Wheeler what he meant, the chairman responded heatedly that they had not "stuck by their original agreement to hold fast on the Chiefs' previous recommendation to introduce three divisions into South Vietnam."[28]

Greene protested. Although he affirmed his support for the introduction of three divisions, he argued that he "wasn't going to sit at the table and tell Mr. Johnson that I didn't have anything to say, or refer him to the Chairman indicating that the Chairman would speak for me." Greene contended, furthermore, that his "recommendations were perfectly sound . . . , that everyone present had the opportunity to examine them and discuss them if they didn't like them—and that no one had done this."[29]

Wheeler, who had already reconciled himself to working for a gradual intensification of the war, suppressed his anger and got on with the business of deploying more troops to South Vietnam. On April 14 he sent a message to CINCPAC, MACV, and the Saigon embassy, detailing the decisions that the president had made in his April 13 meeting with the JCS. He instructed the military commanders to accomplish the following actions as soon as Ambassador Taylor obtained approval from the South Vietnamese government:

DEPLOY 173D AIRBORNE BRIGADE AND NECESSARY SUPPORT ELEMENTS TO BIEN HOA–VUNG TAU AREA WITH THE INITIAL MISSION OF SECURITY OF US INSTALLATIONS AND FACILITIES.

EXPAND INITIAL MISSION TO INCLUDE ENGAGEMENT IN COUNTERINSURGENCY COMBAT OPERATIONS.

The final paragraph of the JCS cable instructed addressees to make "no public statements" and ordered that the deployment "be treated as low-key."[30] In a separate cable Wheeler informed Westmoreland that he would "personally control and carefully monitor" the initial Marine Corps offensive operations and directed that those operations begin with small patrols. Wheeler concluded that, barring an emergency, he did not "visualize" battalion-size operations occurring for several weeks.[31]

Thus, despite his feeling that Johnson had "trapped" the JCS, Wheeler supported the president's deception of Congress and the American public about the changed nature of the American involvement in the war. Westmoreland, in response to Wheeler's instruction to keep the president's decisions "low-key," suggested that the administration take the "public stance" that U.S. ground forces were merely providing support for South Vietnamese units rather than conducting independent offensive operations.[32]

14
War without Direction

April–June 1965

He [LBJ] played a role between the doves and the hawks, and
he did it much the way he used to conduct his majority
leadership. He did it on the notion that here was some middle ground, always, on which the majority of the votes
could be secured. That was true in the Senate where you
have to find that consensus in order to enact legislation.
But I think the role of the president is different from
that of a senator and that this was a matter of policy that
could not be cut down the middle. And his constant attempt
to do it led him always to temper the military on the one
hand and yet to generally move in the direction of larger
warfare, reluctantly reaching out left and right in the
hope that maybe something would give, some kind of peace
would become possible, but, nevertheless, moving with the
mainstream, and, on that, trying to base a consensus.

—Sen. Frank Church, 1969[1]

The United States was at war, but LBJ's preoccupation with pursuing a
"middle course" in Vietnam prevented a clear articulation of the
objective of military force. American soldiers, airmen, and Marines went
to war in Vietnam without strategy or direction. Because he continued to
deceive the Congress and the public, the president could ill afford dissention within his own administration that might reveal his actual policy
decisions. Having secured his political flanks against opposition from the
JCS, the president now faced a potential threat from his ambassador in
Saigon.

■

The decision to deploy the 173rd Airborne Brigade came as a "complete surprise" to Taylor.[2] He responded to the news by arguing that the presence of American ground combat units was not only unnecessary but counterproductive. He observed that the principal rationale for the introduction of more troops "could be adduced to justify almost unlimited additional deployments." He restated his earlier arguments against deploying American ground combat units, including his judgment that their presence would "sap the GVN initiative and turn a defense of the GVN homeland into what appears a foreign war." Although Taylor approved of logistical preparations for future contingencies, he recommended that American units remain "outside of SVN just as long as possible and until their need is uncontrovertible." He described the deployment of the 173rd Airborne and more Marine units as "wasteful."[3]

McGeorge Bundy reported to the president that Taylor had discovered the planned deployment of the 173rd Brigade due to a "premature JCS message" and had "already come in questioning it." Bundy suggested that, based on Taylor's assessment, "it is not clear that we now need all these additional forces." He indicated to the president that he was "*not* sure that you yourself currently wish to make a firm decision to put another 10,000–15,000 combat troops in Vietnam today." Bundy's resistance to the deployment stemmed primarily, however, from his desire to protect the president from a public or congressional flap that would attend any inkling of dissent from Taylor.[4]

Bundy recommended, in light of Taylor's opposition to the deployment of the 173rd Airborne, that the president delay "direct orders of this sort to Taylor" because they "would be very explosive right now." Taylor's opposition, Bundy explained, was based partially on the feeling that he had "not been consulted." Bundy reassured the president that "we can turn him around if we give him a little time to come aboard."[5]

To soften the tone of instructions to Taylor, Bundy described the troop deployments and other measures as "experimental steps" that the "highest authority" thought were needed to add "something new . . . in the South to achieve victory." Those experiments included Greene's proposal for American and South Vietnamese combined operations, the introduction of the 173rd Airborne to the Central Highlands region "both to act as a security force for our installations and also to participate in counterinsurgency combat operations," and the deployment of "multi-battalion forces into 2 or 3 additional locations along the coast . . . to experiment further with U.S. forces in a counter-insurgency role."[6] Despite Bundy's efforts to mislead Taylor, the ambassador was incredulous.

Taylor sensed that U.S. policy had devolved into a collection of disparate initiatives lacking any unifying strategic concept or clear objective. Accordingly he expressed confusion over the "rapidly changing picture of Washington desires and intentions with regard to the introduction of . . . combat forces." He stated that he needed "a clarification of our purposes and objectives" in "a new policy of . . . participation in ground combat."[7] Taylor was "greatly troubled" by Washington's proclivity to equate any new program or initiative with an improvement in the situation in Vietnam. He expressed frustration over trying to get a weak South Vietnamese government to implement a twenty-one-point military program, a sixteen-point propaganda program, and a twelve-point CIA program as well as organize and gain approval for the introduction of U.S. ground combat forces. It seemed to the ambassador that Washington was trying to win the war on a "point score," and he protested that he was getting "helped to death."[8]

■

When Taylor's response arrived, the president was at his ranch, relishing the progress that his domestic legislative program was making through Congress, but he remained concerned about international and domestic opposition to his Vietnam policy.[9] Although the Johns Hopkins speech had been a success, it had done nothing to appease those who were urging the president to stop the bombing of North Vietnam.[10] McGeorge Bundy, therefore, had suggested that the president make "a strong peaceloving statement" designed to defuse emotion behind planned anti-bombing demonstrations in Washington and at the gates of LBJ's ranch.[11]

Addressing reporters from the front porch on April 17, the president stressed the familiar themes of restraint and determination that remained the rhetorical foundation for maintaining consensus behind his Vietnam policy. He told reporters that he regretted that the "necessities of war have compelled us to bomb North Vietnam" and emphasized that his administration had "carefully limited those raids" and directed them toward "concrete and steel, and not human life."

To pacify those who might oppose his policy on the grounds that he was irresolute, Johnson publicly committed himself to win the war in

Vietnam. Although he understood and shared "the feelings of those who regret that we must undertake air attacks," he pledged that until the freedom and independence of South Vietnam were "guaranteed[,] there is no human power capable of forcing us from Viet-Nam." He promised that the United States would remain in South Vietnam "as long as is necessary, with the might that is required, whatever the risk and whatever the cost."

To placate those who opposed American military action against North Vietnam, the president at once reverted to the language of peace with a restatement of his desire to "help the poor and the weak" nations in Southeast Asia through economic development and technological progress on the American model. Although he made no mention of the change of mission for U.S. troops or the impending deployment of additional units, he told reporters that "yesterday, only yesterday, I sent a team of rural electrification experts to Saigon to help extend the healing miracles of electricity to the Vietnamese countryside."[12]

Taylor, meanwhile, warned that the arrival of the 173rd Brigade would signal a "new policy," and that any initiative that resembled military occupation would receive "wide publicity."[13] As Taylor pressured the president to halt the increase in U.S. forces, the JCS urged McNamara to dismiss Taylor's objections. The Chiefs' plans called for troops actively to seek out and engage the enemy in close combat and highlighted the need for more troops to secure U.S. bases. They used the circular argument that logistics bases, established to prepare for the possibility of larger troop deployments, required more combat troops to secure them. The Chiefs implied that Taylor was dragging his feet in gaining South Vietnamese approval for additional troops, and suggested that the president determine whether the ambassador was obstructing military deployments already approved by "highest US authority."[14] Rather than assess the validity of Taylor's reservations about the consequences of introducing progressively larger numbers of troops, the JCS remained fixated on gaining approval for additional deployments.

The president, unwilling to risk open dissent with either Taylor or the JCS, depended on McNamara to effect a compromise between them. Johnson suspended the deployment of the 173rd Airborne Brigade while McNamara met with Taylor, McNaughton, Westmoreland, Wheeler,

Sharp, and William Bundy in Honolulu. McNamara would have to persuade Taylor to accept the deployment of additional troops while parrying calls from the military for an intensification of the air campaign against North Vietnam.

McNamara did not disappoint the president. On his way back from Hawaii, he summarized the agreement arranged between civilian and military officials. He told the president that it would take about one or two years for U.S. ground troops to "demonstrate VC failure in the South." He reported that the conferees had agreed that the troops that he and the others were currently recommending "might not be enough" and "that it would be unwise to attempt to fix any time limit to the war." The strategic objective had shifted from coercing Hanoi with limited air strikes and other pressures to frustrating Communist designs for domination of the South by "denying them victory." McCone recorded that McNamara returned from Honolulu arguing to "change the purpose of the bombing attacks on North Vietnam" to one of "continual harassment" while U.S. and South Vietnamese ground forces in the South convinced North Vietnam that the Viet Cong effort was hopeless. McNamara had gained Taylor's support for increasing U.S. forces in Vietnam to 82,000, which would be followed by a possible deployment of 41,000 more U.S. troops.[15]

The outcome of the Honolulu conference was the sort of compromise that might result from a congressional committee meeting. McNamara had been the president's "committee chairman," charged with persuading others to support the president's approach to Vietnam. He allied himself with Taylor to oppose Wheeler's and Westmoreland's request for three divisions and then persuaded Taylor to support an increase in U.S. strength in Vietnam by promising that future troop deployments would be subject to strict scrutiny. For Westmoreland and Wheeler, McNamara suggested "possible later deployments, not recommended now," including over 56,000 more troops from the Army's airmobile division, a corps headquarters, and the remainder of the Marine Expeditionary Force.[16] Westmoreland recalled that, although the consensus position of the Honolulu conference did not contain a force to retake the "critical Central Highlands," he "took solace" in the larger forces included as "possible later deployments."[17] The JCS did not receive permission to deploy three divisions, but troop strength in Vietnam more than doubled from 33,000 to 82,000.

If disagreements persisted, McNamara suppressed them. The report to the president, Sharp observed years later, reflected McNamara's "own views, not necessarily a consensus."[18] Wheeler and Sharp had recommended intensifying the air campaign, but McNamara reported to LBJ that "with respect to strikes against the North, they all agree that the present tempo is about right." Sharp later described McNamara's memo as a "distortion."[19]

George Ball recognized that the president was failing to consider the likely consequences of his decisions to increase gradually the number of U.S. troops in Vietnam. He recalled years afterward that before McNamara returned from Honolulu, he warned the president not to take "such a hazardous leap into space without further exploring the possibilities of a settlement."[20] Ball echoed Humphrey's warning that the situation in Vietnam was "more ambiguous—and hence more dubious—than in the Korean War." The American public, Ball argued, would not tolerate U.S. casualties if the war continued without a resolution in sight. Ball stopped short, however, of objecting forcefully to the direction of U.S. policy. He described his resistance to the growing ground troop commitment as a "deliberate stalling tactic."[21] Like the JCS, Ball was unwilling to press the president to choose between large-scale intervention and withdrawal.

As the president's advisers would not confront directly the confusion and contradictions apparent in LBJ's "middle course," the United States continued to deepen its involvement in the war without a clear objective or strategy for the employment of American military force.[22] According to Admiral Sharp, at the outset of the Honolulu meeting, it was clear that McNamara had decided to "downgrade the air war against North Vietnam and to emphasize the air and ground war in South Vietnam."[23] McNamara recalled in his memoir that his and the Chiefs' focus on "day to day" events had prevented them from "developing a military strategy and a long-term plan for the force structure to carry it out."[24] More precisely McNamara's effort to satisfy the president's desire for consensus obscured the long-term implications of the administration's decisions.

Having secured a "consensus" in Honolulu behind the shift in objectives, the president sought to widen that consensus to include all of his Washington advisers. On April 21 he met with McNamara, Rusk, Ball, McGeorge Bundy, Director of Central Intelligence McCone, and Vice Adm. William Raborn, who would replace McCone in two days. The president, who had squelched JCS recommendations for the expansion of

Rolling Thunder, feigned confusion. He asked McNamara why the Honolulu group had not recommended more resolute military action against North Vietnam. "Are we pulling away from our theory that bombing will turn 'em off?" McNamara, the "father" of graduated pressure, responded, "That wasn't our theory. We wanted to lift morale; we wanted to push them toward negotiations—we've done that."[25]

McCone sounded the lone objection. As he had done before, he urged the president to consider possible enemy reactions to the introduction of U.S. ground forces. McCone again predicted that the North Vietnamese would respond in kind to the U.S. effort in South Vietnam so that troop deployments would produce "no definite result."[26] Wheeler and Ball, both of whom questioned the wisdom of the president's chosen course, nevertheless supported Johnson's decisions. Ball resolved to impede greater military involvement, whereas Wheeler sought to accelerate it.

The next day, as U.S. Marines saw their first combat in South Vietnam, the president approved the Honolulu recommendations. Although Johnson's advisers had recommended that he include Congress in his decision, there was no consultation. No memorandum promulgated the decision, and there was no public announcement. In his instructions to Ambassador Taylor, the president directed that it was "not our intention to announce the whole program now but rather to announce individual deployments at appropriate times."[27]

Meanwhile, the Communist buildup that McCone predicted was well under way. Encouraged by popular unrest in the South, the persistent instability in the Saigon government, and the growing antiwar sentiment in the United States, Hanoi's leaders sensed an opportunity to gain decisive victory. As American ground combat units arrived in the South, the chief of the North Vietnamese Politburo, Le Duan, advocated a combined Viet Cong/North Vietnamese Army offensive aimed at achieving victory before the United States could intervene in force. By mid-April, it was clear to U.S. intelligence officials that Hanoi was dispatching not just individual soldiers, but trained and ready North Vietnamese Army (NVA) units to South Vietnam. The offensive was set to begin in May, with the onset of the monsoon season.[28]

■

As Vietnamese communist forces prepared for the summer offensive, a crisis in the Caribbean temporarily diverted U.S. attention from

Southeast Asia. Beginning on April 24 supporters of the former civilian president of the Dominican Republic, Juan Bosch, tried to overthrow the military junta that had forced Bosch from office. On April 28 President Johnson ordered U.S. Marines into the capital, Santo Domingo, for the "protection of U.S. citizens." Whatever the initial justification, the operation grew rapidly in scale, involving more than twenty thousand troops, in order to prevent a Communist takeover that would result in another "Cuba" in the Caribbean. Although he was aware that the intervention would expose him to charges of gunboat diplomacy, Johnson thought that the public and congressional criticism would be "nothing compared to what I'd be called if the Dominican Republic went down the drain."[29] Faced with growing congressional criticism and the prospect of Vietnam protests and debates, the president sought to defuse opposition. William Bundy—recalling that the Dominican intervention "and its rationale came under heavy fire in the very quarters, both at home and abroad, that were already skeptical or hostile to the Vietnam actions"—wrote later that "the president responded to the congressional pressure by what can only be described as a gimmick."[30]

The Dominican "crisis" gave the president an opportunity to overcome opposition to his Vietnam policy. On May 4 Johnson sent to Congress a request for seven hundred million dollars to support additional efforts both in Vietnam and the Dominican Republic. The president told Congress:

> This is not a routine appropriation. For each member of Congress who supports this request is also voting to persist in our effort to halt communist aggression in South Vietnam. Each is saying that the Congress and the president stand united before the world in joint determination that the independence of South Viet-Nam shall be preserved and communist attack will not succeed.[31]

Reminding the legislators that "more than 400 Americans have given their lives in Vietnam," the president made it clear that a vote against the bill was a vote against "those brave men who are risking their lives for freedom in Viet-Nam."[32] William Bundy recalled that the president's tactic was to "make the appropriation of a relatively small sum—not in fact related to any specific program or its costs—into a small-scale new Tonkin Gulf Resolution. And all this in a week when the American people were confronting the idea of a 'second Cuba,' of a Communist threat at their doorstep."[33] Like the Tonkin Gulf resolution, the president's bill passed overwhelmingly (408–7 in the House and 88–3 in the Senate). As Rhode Island's Claiborne Pell, a Democrat, observed, voting against the appropriation would have been "like voting against motherhood."[34] The president had presented the legislators with a fait accompli. After U.S. ground combat troops arrived in Vietnam, the president could equate a vote against his policy with the abandonment of American soldiers and Marines at the front. Representative Dante Fascell, a Democrat from Florida, recalled that the patriotic impulse to support the troops had become the "linchpin for greater involvement in Vietnam."[35]

■

Despite the president's coup over the legislators, domestic and international pressures to stop the bombing of North Vietnam persisted. McNamara set McNaughton to work on a bombing pause designed to "marshal world opinion in support of GVN/US position for peace and for an independent South Vietnam."[36] In addition, the president had received a recommendation from the new CIA director, Vice Admiral Raborn, to halt the bombing temporarily to see if Hanoi was interested in "serious negotiations." A pause in Rolling Thunder, Raborn argued, would alleviate "extreme world pressures." Like his predecessor, however, Raborn believed that Rolling Thunder had to be intensified to "hurt North Vietnam badly enough to cause the Hanoi regime to seek a political way out through negotiation rather than expose their economy to increasingly serious levels of destruction." After the United States proffered the olive branch, it might reapply the sword with renewed vigor.[37]

On May 10 the president approved a five-to-seven-day bombing pause, code-named Mayflower. The administration informed Moscow and Hanoi that it was prepared to open negotiations. The president intended to keep the pause secret and, after it failed, to publicize the administration's effort to make peace with Hanoi.[38] Designed more to influence public opinion than to explore a diplomatic alternative, the bombing pause was destined to fail. Planning for the pause was rushed and the American message to Hanoi was imprecise in language and threatening in tone. Soviet Foreign Minister Andrei Gromyko referred to the American offer as an "ultimatum" and refused to serve as intermediary between Washington and Hanoi. When the U.S. ambassador to

Moscow, Foy Kohler, had the message delivered to his North Vietnamese counterpart, the Hanoi embassy returned it without comment in a sealed envelope. When the British made a follow-up delivery, the Hanoi government rejected the offer unequivocally.[39]

The president kept knowledge of the pause limited to Rusk, McNamara, Raborn, and the Bundy brothers. He did not inform the JCS until it was necessary for them to issue the orders to stop the bombing. Even then the plan was not to be discussed "by anyone at any time with anyone inside or outside the government."[40] On May 12, the day the pause began, LBJ sent Goodpaster to brief former president Eisenhower. Eisenhower supported the ultimatum that accompanied the bombing pause, recalling that, during the Korean War, he had passed word to the Chinese that if they failed to stop the war, the United States would use nuclear weapons. Eisenhower advised Johnson, however, that the real problem in Vietnam seemed to lie with the South Vietnamese people. Goodpaster recorded Eisenhower's assessment that "the important thing is that the people see real hope of progress." Eisenhower's final advice to Johnson was to "not be too surprised or disturbed at the 'chatter' from [the incipient antiwar movement] over the firm course the president is pursuing. . . . A certain amount of this has to be expected. . . . So long as the policies are right . . . too much attention need not be given to these people."[41]

The president and his advisers, however, remained preoccupied with public opinion. On May 16 a Gallup poll revealed that 59 percent of the respondents favored the bombing of North Vietnam while only 21 percent were against it.[42] At 6:45 P.M. on the same day, the president met with Rusk, McNamara, Acheson, Ball, Raborn, and presidential aide Jack Valenti to discuss when to end Mayflower. Once again the JCS were left out of the decision-making process. Having undertaken the bombing pause principally to quiet the opposition to Rolling Thunder, the president had begun to grow wary of potential charges from conservatives that the pause indicated a soft policy and a weak commitment to South Vietnam. McNamara seemed more concerned with the president's liberal constituency, however, and recommended letting the pause continue for seven full days to satisfy the expectations of the New York Times editorial page. The president stated unambiguously that it was "a pure question of what happens in this country. If we hold off the bombing any longer, people are going to say 'What in the world is happening?'" The president told McNamara, "My judgment is the public has never wanted us to stop the bombing. We have stopped in deference to Mansfield and Fulbright, but we don't want to do it too long else we lose our base of support." At the end of a laborious discussion concerning domestic reaction to bombing, the president and his advisers decided to resume Rolling Thunder on May 18.[43]

■

Despite Raborn's recommendation that the first air strikes after the pause apply force more dramatically, tight restrictions on the air campaign continued. At the May 16 meeting with the president, McNamara had argued against JCS recommendations to attack North Vietnamese surface-to-air-missile (SAM) sites. He spoke with the confidence of a seasoned air commander, explaining, "We have to go after the MIG airfields first. First, B-52's to plaster the airfields at night. There may be civilians involved since all bombs won't hit target. Then fighter-bombers go in. And then we take out the SAM's." McNamara observed that Hanoi would view the attack as "a major operation" and noted that, if the president delayed the attack on the missile sites until after they became operational, the "most you would lose would be 3 or 4 crews." (In August 1965, when the JCS received permission to strike the already-established SAM sites, the attempt failed with thirteen jets lost.) To keep the Chiefs from asserting that the administration had "gone soft," McNamara gained approval for an attack on a "military barracks 10 miles further [north] than we have ever gone." He promised Dean Rusk, however, that he would keep the barracks off of the first day's target list.[44]

As McNamara endeavored to keep the bombing restricted, the Joint Chiefs continued to press for its intensification. McNamara, however, retained tight control of the air campaign and coordinated all targets with Rusk. On May 22 the JCS forwarded to McNamara a CINCPAC proposal to shift the air effort against the North to a combination of around-the-clock small strikes and deliberately planned large strikes aimed at inflicting maximum damage in a single day. Initially CINCPAC would limit strikes to the area south of the twentieth parallel, but subsequent raids would hit major military targets further north. The proposal would give CINCPAC greater autonomy in planning missions and increase the weekly allocation of sorties. McNamara took a full month to respond. He told the JCS that he saw "no serious defects in the present method of planning Rolling Thunder operations." He stated that the air strikes were "militarily effective" and "managed in such a way as to permit political considerations to be taken into account on a timely basis." He doubted that "a change in our method of planning Rolling Thunder operations would be desirable."[45]

The development of a weekly Rolling Thunder program, however, remained cumbersome and fragmented. The JCS focused on the "positive" objectives of interdicting the flow of men and supplies from north to south and of destroying the will and capability of North Vietnam to continue its support for Communist forces in South Vietnam, whereas civilian officials in the Departments of State and Defense emphasized the "negative" objectives of preventing further international and domestic opposition to the war, minimizing civilian collateral damage, and preventing the conflict from escalating.[46]

The development of Rolling Thunder Program 20 (RT20), to be executed in June 1965, was typical of the planning process. The JCS recommended that RT20 include fourteen targets. McNamara removed six from the JCS proposal. Wheeler then sent a draft planning message to CINC-PAC. Simultaneously the State Department and McNaughton at ISA received a copy. The State Department objected to one of the targets because it was "too close" to the port city of Haiphong, a SAM site, and Phuc Yen airfield (the target was actually twenty-seven miles from the SAM site and fifty-one miles from the airfield). State Department officials also objected to the strike because it was too close to populated areas and could lead to "high" civilian casualties. McNaughton similarly informed McNamara that the target was the closest to Hanoi and Haiphong of those that Wheeler had recommended, and predicted that an air strike in that vicinity might result in thirty civilian casualties. McNaughton argued that the strike was worth the potential collateral damage, however, and urged McNamara to approve it.[47] McNamara, in deference to the State Department, deleted the target, while persuading Rusk to approve another "good solid target" to offer the Chiefs in compensation. On June 23 the president met with his advisers to approve the target package personally. Using a large map, McNamara briefed the president on the compromise he had worked out with Dean Rusk. Although McNamara brought Vance and McNaughton to the meeting, no military officer was present.[48] Six days after the JCS had made their initial proposal, Wheeler sent the final orders for RT20, consisting of seven targets, to CINCPAC.

The process focused civilian and military officials in the Department of Defense on choosing what specific targets would be hit in each Rolling Thunder program, rather than on developing a comprehensive strategic assessment of the air campaign. It is not surprising, then, that reports indicated that Rolling Thunder neither significantly impeded the flow of supplies to Communist forces nor discouraged North Vietnam from continuing its support for the war in the South. The JCS continued to press for a gradual relaxation of restrictions on the bombing, hoping to increase its effectiveness. Between May and July, McNamara permitted several extra armed reconnaissance missions against North Vietnamese supply lines, but only when such increases "appeared necessary." Meanwhile geographic limitations on interdiction missions and strikes against fixed targets gradually receded.[49]

■

Even as the president resisted JCS requests to intensify the air campaign, he emphasized the ground war in the South. Sending U.S. troops to fight in the South seemed the least expensive course of action in terms of domestic political reaction, even though McNamara and the president were aware of predictions that an expansion of the American effort on the ground would lead to a protracted, indecisive war that the United States would ultimately lose. On May 8 DCI Raborn wrote to Johnson predicting—based largely on the French experience—that "we will find ourselves pinned down, with little choice left among possible subsequent courses of action: i.e. disengagement at very high cost or broadening the conflict in quantum jumps." Raborn warned that the administration should not become "preoccupied with military action and lose sight of the basically political aspect of the war." He agreed with Eisenhower that the critical factor was the loyalty and morale of the South Vietnamese people: The war would be won or lost at the "hamlet level."[50] He had based his letter in part on a special assessment from the CIA mission in Saigon. Although Taylor had once again deleted the worst news from the embassy's intelligence report, CIA officials transmitted the omitted text directly from their Saigon station to CIA headquarters.[51]

Johnson was sufficiently concerned to send Raborn's assessment to his old friend and adviser Clark Clifford. The Washington attorney responded with a one-page letter in which he made "one major point." He advised the president to keep the number of U.S. ground troops in

South Vietnam "to a minimum consistent with the protection of our installations and property in that country." He warned the president that "this could be a quagmire. It could turn into an open end [sic] commitment on our part that would take more and more ground troops, without a realistic hope of ultimate victory." He recommended that the president pursue a negotiated settlement that the United States "could learn to live with."[52]

As Ball recalled, the president and McNamara remained "preoccupied with operational problems," however, because decisions based on political expediency had backed LBJ into a corner. More than fifty thousand American troops were in South Vietnam by the first of June and an additional thirty thousand were on the way. Marine units were actively seeking close combat with Vietnamese communist forces in the Danang area. When Ball and former secretary of state Dean Acheson designed a plan to avert the "gradual escalation of the conflict" that they feared was inevitable under the current policy, it was already too late.[53] Once Johnson committed ground combat troops, the actions of Vietnamese communist forces would determine the level of American effort necessary to prevent a collapse of the South Vietnamese regime.

The Communist summer offensive had begun on May 11. Viet Cong troops quickly overran Song Be, the capital of Phuoc Long province near Saigon. The attack inflicted high casualties on U.S. advisers and on South Vietnamese troops. Later in the month, the Viet Cong ambushed and destroyed a battalion of South Vietnamese troops in Quang Ngai province. In the ensuing battle another ARVN battalion was lost. In addition to disastrous ARVN defeats, intelligence reports confirmed that the North Vietnamese had infiltrated an entire division into South Vietnam. Another division was moving south along the Ho Chi Minh Trail.[54]

To make matters worse the South Vietnamese government was again in turmoil. A confrontation between Premier Quat and Chief of State Suu over the reorganization of the cabinet weakened the government. On June 11 Quat ceded the Saigon government to the military and the eight-month interlude of civilian rule in South Vietnam ended, never to return. Taylor reported that Quat, the quiet and unassuming physician who had tried to heal South Vietnam's destructive divisions, had fallen prey to "jugular-vein politics in Saigon."[55] Air Vice Marshal Ky took over as prime minister.

As the Saigon government faltered and the Viet Cong summer offensive gathered momentum, the president and his advisers remained ambivalent about how U.S. military force ought to be used in Vietnam and, indeed, for what purpose. On Saturday, June 5, McNamara, Rusk, Ball, Llewellyn Thompson, McNaughton, and the Bundy brothers met for "an across-the-board discussion" on Vietnam.[56] About two hours into the meeting, LBJ joined his advisers, unannounced and appearing confused. The questions that he posed revealed that he had not fully considered the dynamics or the consequences of his decisions to escalate the war effort to its current level.[57] He asked: "Who sees our purpose and means of achieving it, out there?" He wondered: "Will it be so costly? How do we expect to win?" Johnson remained equally concerned about the possibility of a protracted commitment complicating his bid for reelection in 1968. Referring to Eisenhower's 1952 presidential campaign vow to end the Korean War, Johnson asked, "How do you expect to wind things up? You'll get, 'I'll go to Korea.'"[58]

Although it may have seemed that McNamara had moderated his enthusiasm for graduated pressure to help the president fend off recommendations for an intensification of Rolling Thunder, the secretary of defense remained hopeful that U.S. military power could coerce North Vietnam into giving away at the negotiating table what policy constraints and the nature of the war would not permit U.S. forces to achieve on the battlefield. He concluded that the deterioration of the military situation in South Vietnam had made achieving a military "stalemate in the South" as important as "causing pain in the North." Rusk agreed, stating that U.S. military force would simply have to demonstrate to the "other side" that they could not win without a major escalation of the war. He said that although Hanoi's response might be only to stop infiltration and emphasize political rather than military means of unifying the country under its leadership, at least they would have abandoned their current strategy of pursuing victory in the short term. According to Rusk the objective of U.S. military force would be to force a return to the situation that had existed in 1958, when the South Vietnamese government battled an indigenous guerrilla force that did not have the benefit of extensive support from the North. Ball concurred, adding only that the United States had to present Hanoi with an opportunity to end the war through negotiation. The meeting ended with the president and his advisers hoping that they could "carry through" in Vietnam with the 82,000 U.S. troops that the president had already approved on April 22. Before LBJ left his advisers, he mused that "the great danger is that we'll pick up a very big problem any day."[59] That day arrived forty-eight hours later.

■

On June 7 General Westmoreland sent a cable to CINCPAC requesting more American troops and permission to use them to locate and destroy Vietnamese communist forces in the South.[60] He argued that, in light of recent Viet Cong successes and the ominous presence of NVA units in the South, the South Vietnamese armed forces were near collapse. To avert disaster he requested an immediate increase of 41,000 troops. Later he would need an additional 52,000, bringing the total to 175,000. The total would comprise thirty-four "maneuver" battalions (twenty-two Army and twelve Marine), along with combat support battalions and additional Navy and Air Force units. Westmoreland also requested the immediate deployment of ten additional battalions of South Korean and Australian troops. If those "third country" units were not forthcoming, he asked that the United States make up the shortfall, increasing the number of U.S. troops to approximately two hundred thouand, or forty-four battalions. The number of troops Westmoreland requested was more than two and one-half times larger than the limit the president had approved on April 22. Westmoreland planned to position the forces "both along the coast and inland" and to use them "both offensively and defensively." He recalled later that there would be "no more niceties about defensive posture and reaction." It was time to "forget about enclaves and take the war to the enemy."[61]

Even as he received Westmoreland's request, the president remained determined to conceal the depth of American intervention. Astute reporters had discerned the shift in the U.S. ground forces' mission from defensive security to offensive operations. Although the president had authorized the change on April 13, he had ordered that it be kept secret. Since that time, civilian and military officials had made misleading statements to obscure the change of mission.[62] On June 8 a reporter asked Robert McCloskey, assistant secretary of state for public affairs, about the mission of American ground troops in South Vietnam. McCloskey, who felt that his reputation and the credibility of the State Department were at risk, responded that U.S. forces would be used in offensive combat operations. An editorial in the next morning's *New York Times* expressed disbelief that "the American people were told by a minor State Department official yesterday, that, in effect, they were in a land war on the continent of Asia. . . . The nation is informed about it not by the president, not by a Cabinet member, not even by a sub-Cabinet official, but by a public relations officer."[63]

Despite McCloskey's indiscretion, the president was still resolved to conceal the change of mission. After the *New York Times* editorial appeared, White House Press Secretary George Reedy met reporters to issue a brief statement:

> There has been no change in the mission of U.S. ground combat units in Viet Nam in recent days or weeks. The president has issued no order of any kind in this regard to General Westmoreland recently or any other time. The primary mission of these troops is to secure and safeguard important military installations like the airfield at Danang. They have the associated mission of active patrolling and securing action in and near the areas thus safeguarded.

Reedy allowed only that General Westmoreland had authority to assist beleaguered South Vietnamese units if "the general military situation requires it." In response to a question, he told the reporters for "background" that the discrepancy between his statement and McCloskey's the day before was due to "certain speculative matters and certain contingencies, which are inherent in the situation" that "came out the other end as though these were decisions which had been taken and orders which had been issued."[64]

■

Westmoreland, although confused by the White House statement, remained more interested in obtaining permission to take wider military action than in questioning the president's effort to mask the nature of American involvement in the war. He reassured Honolulu (CINCPAC) and Washington that he saw "no difficulty in explaining" U.S. offensive operations as consistent with Reedy's statement that U.S. troops were in South Vietnam to guard military bases. He stated that American offensive operations were already under way and the South Vietnamese "now expect and anticipate this kind of participation." He observed that "we have reached a point in Vietnam where we cannot avoid the commitment to combat of US ground troops" because the South Vietnamese "can no longer cope alone" with Vietnamese communist forces.[65]

Sharp supported Westmoreland's approach. He told Westmoreland to proceed with the battalion-sized operations that Westmoreland was planning for the 173rd Airborne Brigade, but warned him to be cautious. "I'm sure you realize that there would be grave political implications involved if sizable U.S. forces are committed for the first time and suffer a defeat."[66]

On June 8 Ambassador Taylor arrived in Washington for another round of consultations with the president and his principal advisers. Westmoreland's troop request dominated the discussions. Taylor's resistance to additional troop deployments and to State Department negotiating proposals had further diminished his popularity among top administration officials. He was due to leave his position in the late summer or fall. Bundy, however, thought that the sooner Taylor left the better.[67]

Taylor opposed Westmoreland's troop request, but, consistent with his compromise with McNamara at the Honolulu conference, he merely proposed a smaller number of troops. He suggested that the situation in South Vietnam was not as bad as Westmoreland had reported. Instead of the 85,000 additional troops that Westmoreland had estimated would eventually become necessary, Taylor recommended that the president consider deploying 8,000 troops beyond the 82,000 already authorized. In response to Taylor's proposal, Wheeler told the president that the JCS supported Westmoreland's request in full. McNamara and McGeorge Bundy argued that 18,000 more troops (which would bring the total number of American troops in Vietnam to 100,000) was most appropriate.[68]

Ball pointed out that the number of troops was not as important as how they affected the nature of American involvement in Vietnam. He asked, "When does this become a white man's war?" Ball's question begged a discussion of military strategy. It was still unclear whether American forces would remain in enclaves to provide security and serve as "ready reaction" forces or whether they would engage in large-scale offensive operations aimed at finding and destroying the enemy. Taylor and Greene favored the enclave concept, whereas Westmoreland and the other Chiefs advocated aggressive, offensive operations against enemy troop concentrations.[69] A discussion of strategic options and analysis of their feasibility, however, did not occur. McNamara recommended that the president delay making a comprehensive assessment and deploy only enough troops to hold the situation together through the summer.[70]

■

Having decided to do only what was necessary to avert disaster, LBJ focused on how he would gain popular and congressional approval for his latest escalation of the war. The president met with his advisers once again on June 9. His longtime friend and mentor, Senator Russell of Georgia, joined Rusk, McNamara, Ball, Vance, Raborn, Reedy, and Moyers.[71] The presence of Reedy and Moyers as well as the absence of General Wheeler facilitated discussion of the public relations "war."

Describing his area of disagreement with Westmoreland's request as "limited," McNamara proposed that the president approve eighteen additional battalions for South Vietnam, sixteen short of the number Westmoreland had recommended. McNamara predicted that the smaller force would "cover us until the end of the year." Later in the meeting Johnson asked "What do they [the military] want now?" McNamara replied, "More explanation." Ball attempted to delay a decision and reinforced McNamara's focus on a short-term, limited response to Westmoreland's request. He advised the president to be "careful not to regard this decision as defining or pre-deciding what we can do after we see what happens."[72] The president asked if anyone disagreed with McNamara's proposal. Rusk and McNamara reported that the senior people in State and Defense agreed.[73]

After Johnson approved the deployment of fourteen more battalions as a short-term expedient, the meeting evolved into a rehearsal for justifying the president's policy to critics. Anticipating public and congressional arguments against a further increase in the U.S. military commitment to South Vietnam, the president asked whether this latest escalation of the war would mean a "land war in Asia." Taylor responded, "We have to explain that this is not that—not a Korean War." Johnson asked, "What is the answer to the argument that the bombing has had no results?" Rusk suggested: "We never thought that it would bring them running," and "it has had a good military effect." Taylor added that the president might point to increased morale among the South Vietnamese. According to McGeorge Bundy's notes, LBJ put his advisers on notice that his reason for going North was "to raise morale in the South." Johnson then summarized the arguments against his policy. He read from a memorandum that Senator Mansfield had sent him on June 5 listing reasons against transforming Vietnam into an American war. Rather than explore the validity of Mansfield's objections, however, the president asked his advisers to answer the objections to deeper involvement "line by line." The key, his advisers concluded, would be for the president to keep public relations "pressure on left and right to prove" that he was moving "carefully."[74] Responding to the president's need for support, senior officials in the Johnson administration had become more apologists than advisers.

The president remained determined to deepen American involvement in Vietnam without a congressional debate. With Senator Russell listening, he asked if the administration had adequately described the mission of U.S. ground forces in South Vietnam. Rusk responded that they had. LBJ ordered Leonard Meeker, the State Department's legal adviser, and Attorney General Nicholas Katzenbach to prepare legal justifications under the Gulf of Tonkin resolution for McNamara's proposed troop increase.[75] Even as he circumvented the Constitution, LBJ abdicated leadership in connection with Vietnam.

The focus on justifying the president's middle course preserved confusion in strategic planning. When the president asked his advisers "What is our objective?" some answered, "stalemate in the South." Others hoped that military action against the North would coerce Hanoi into negotiations. The meeting ended without a clear answer to Johnson's question. Ball concluded that the short range objective of "holding on" preempted further discussion. The president and his advisers hoped that, despite Westmoreland's estimate that at least 123,000 and probably 175,000 troops were needed, 95,000 would keep South Vietnam from disintegrating until September. Consideration of the consequences of deeper involvement was deferred. The president's advisers concluded that the additional troops "should not get the US into deep trouble; there was still room to pull back, or even out if the ARVN could not carry on."[76] When the president asked "what kind of losses" U.S. ground troops might suffer, McNamara responded with a short-term estimate of "another 400 between now and October." Although McNamara contrived to enjoy virtually unchallenged credibility as a brilliant analyst, it was unclear on what facts and interpretations he had based his estimate. Without a clear idea of the objective, the military strategy under which U.S. forces would operate remained unclear as well. When the president asked McNamara "what are we doing" with the 95,000 troops, he responded "not too much," and offered "general need" as justification. In opposition to Westmoreland's concept for expanding offensive operations, Taylor emphasized the "strike/reserve" proposal that he had advocated in March. He linked the air campaign to the troop increase with the vague observation that they were "complementary."[77]

■

McNamara faced the challenge of explaining to the JCS the decision to grant only a portion of Westmoreland's request. After he returned to his Pentagon office, the defense secretary telephoned the president. McNamara recognized the incompatibility between the president's desire to take the middle approach and pursue a "stalemate" in the near term and the Joint Chiefs' belief that, once committed, the United States should apply the level of force necessary to defeat Vietnamese communist forces. McNamara told the president that, "in the back of my mind, I have a very definite limitation on commitment in mind, and I don't think the chiefs do. In fact, I know they don't." LBJ asked "Do you think that [the Westmoreland request] is just the next step with them up the ladder?" "Yes," McNamara responded. "They hope they don't have to go any further. But Westmoreland outlines in his cable the step beyond it. And he doesn't say that's the last."[78]

McNamara, however, neither communicated to the Chiefs the "limitation on commitment" nor asked them what might be achieved with the additional troops or what strategy was appropriate to that level of force. Wheeler first became aware of the president's decision to commit only those troops necessary to hold on through the summer at a June 11 NSC meeting. The meeting, designed to build consensus behind the president's decision, included Wheeler, McNamara, McNaughton, Rusk, Ball, Raborn, Katzenbach, U.N. Ambassador Adlai Stevenson, Reedy, the Bundy brothers, and several other officials.[79]

Beginning the meeting with an explanation of the legal justification for his policy under the Gulf of Tonkin resolution, Johnson limited the scope of the discussion to "ways of holding the situation." Taylor, who had agreed to McNamara's force ceiling of 100,000 troops, minimized the difficulty of the situation in South Vietnam. He told the audience that "the present VC campaign will be terminated without serious losses."[80]

After preliminary remarks that put Westmoreland's request in the context of a difficult but far from desperate situation in Vietnam, McNamara misrepresented its scale. He ignored the second portion (a total of thirty-four battalions and 175,000 troops), stating instead that Westmoreland "recommends that the 13 battalions . . . authorized be increased to 23 battalions—123,000 men." McNamara highlighted divisions among the Chiefs to suggest that they did not fully support Westmoreland's request or his advocacy of an aggressive war against the Viet Cong. He claimed that the Chiefs opposed the deployment of U.S. forces in the Central Highlands of South Vietnam and wanted the new forces to be used as a mobile reserve near the coast.[81]

Wheeler quietly challenged both Taylor's depiction of the situation and McNamara's portrayal of the JCS position. He stated that the

> Chiefs are impressed by General Westmoreland's presentation of the need for more U.S. forces. . . . The Defense Department's proposal calls for deploying fewer troops now than either General Westmoreland or the Joint Chiefs recommend. The Chiefs favor taking a decision now on sending the number of troops recommended by General Westmoreland. The McNamara plan would send fewer forces now and keep our options open to send additional forces later.[82]

Wheeler's effort was futile. The decision had already been made. The president closed the meeting with the following statement:

> We must delay and deter the North Vietnamese and Viet Cong as much as we can, and as simply as we can, without going all out. When we grant General Westmoreland's request, it means that we get in deeper and it is harder to get out. They think they are winning and we think they are. We must determine which course gives us the maximum protection at the least cost.[83]

The president had used the "logic" of graduated pressure to rationalize his continued pursuit of a policy that would allow him to maintain a consensus. William Bundy recalled that Johnson had decided to "try to keep the middle ground; just what this meant in terms of U.S. forces was not spelled out or decided."[84]

As the president spoke of keeping his options open, two Viet Cong regiments were overrunning the U.S. Special Forces camp at Dong Xoai and inflicting another disastrous defeat on the South Vietnamese Army.[85] The "middle ground" that the president had occupied for so long was crumbling beneath him.

Despite his recognition that his advisers had "no plan for victory militarily or diplomatically," Lyndon Johnson remained resolved to do only what was necessary to avoid defeat in Vietnam. Fixated on short-term expedients and lacking a comprehensive estimate of what the war might cost the United States in the long term, the president focused on the more easily discernible price of withdrawal. Pulling out, Johnson confided to his most trusted advisers, made him "shudder to think what all of 'em would say."[86]

As Johnson approved additional troop deployments to prevent defeat in the South, he continued to defer a decision on the fundamental nature of his policy. LBJ told Ball that he wanted to "keep his options open" until after the monsoon season, when he planned to get an appreciation for congressional sentiments in connection with Vietnam.[87] After September, Johnson hoped to forge a "united front" in Congress behind his policy. Ball suggested that Johnson keep new troop deployments to a minimum so he could "keep the power of decision" and "keep control."[88] With each troop deployment, however, Johnson was sinking the United States deeper into what his old friend Clifford had described as a "quagmire."

∎

On June 18 the president formally approved a portion of Westmoreland's request. The air mobile First Cavalry Division (nine battalions, 23,000 troops) would be sent to South Vietnam. Depending on the situation, two brigades already approved for deployment might withdraw sometime in the future. Consistent with McNamara's recommendation of one week earlier, if those brigades were to remain, twenty-three battalions (123,000 troops) would be committed to South Vietnam.[89]

The JCS had found the twenty-three-battalion force level "acceptable" because McNamara promised to consider leaving in South Vietnam the battalions marked for possible withdrawal. Westmoreland, however, protested. He thought unrealistic McNamara's suggestion that 123,000 U.S. troops represented an "upper threshold of our ground commitment; and that thereafter a cut of 3–6 battalions might be enforced."[90] Westmoreland reminded Sharp and Wheeler of his belief that "extraordinary measures were necessary just to stabilize the situation; and that more combat strength would probably be required to carry the war to the enemy." Westmoreland disagreed with McNamara's argument that the piecemeal approval of his request had provided the MACV commander with "maximum flexibility."[91]

McNamara kept the military on the president's "team" while hiding from them his determination to keep the U.S. commitment sharply limited. To help the president steer the middle course, McNamara began to develop a program aimed at achieving a "stalemate in Vietnam."[92] By definition, McNamara's objective did not entail compelling the enemy to accept terms favorable to U.S. interests. American involvement in the war continued to escalate in a vacuum of strategic thought and without a clear plan of action aimed at achieving decisive results.

■

McNamara recalled that at the end of June 1965, Lyndon Johnson "felt tortured" and was "deeply torn over what to do" about Vietnam.[93] The president had finally begun to recognize the consequences of the decisions he had made during the previous five months. He had discovered that once Americans were committed to direct combat in the air against the North and on the ground in the South, he had no option but to continue to deepen American intervention and assume even greater responsibility for the war effort. The rationale of graduated pressure, that incremental intensifications of the war were reversible and therefore could be pursued at low cost, had committed the United States to war before Johnson had given himself and the country an opportunity to decide whether that commitment would be in the interest of the United States. Blinded by his desire to pass the Great Society legislative program, the president had found Vietnam a nuisance that he hoped would go away. Sensing LBJ's desire for an easy answer to what seemed an intractable problem, his most trusted civilian advisers gave Johnson what he wanted. The JCS, moreover, let the assumptions on which the president's policy was based go unchallenged and chose instead to work within his constraints in an effort to intensify the war effort by degrees. By the end of June, however, the path of least resistance had left Lyndon Johnson at a dead end. He had used rhetoric equating opposition to his policy with the abandonment of American soldiers on the front lines. If he rejected military requests for additional forces, those same charges could be leveled against him. In the next weeks, LBJ's series of "small decisions" on ground troops would push the number of troops approved for deployment to South Vietnam over 120,000. Decisions made from the beginning of OPLAN 34A operations in January 1964, through the first air strikes against North Vietnam in response to the real or imagined Gulf of Tonkin incidents, to the incremental decisions of February through June 1965 had already committed the United States to war. By July 1965 it was no longer a question of *whether* the United States would deepen its involvement in Vietnam, but *how* the president would reconcile the demands of war with those of the Great Society.

15
Five Silent Men
July 1965

What [the military officer] isn't taught is how to cope with the accommodation required in the political process. There must be clearer and more rigid standards for the man in uniform whose responsibility ends in human life in contrast to standards for the man in civilian clothes who does not face the specter of death in his mind as he deliberates on actions that might be taken.

—GEN. HAROLD K. JOHNSON, 1973[1]

As George Ball made one last futile attempt to prevent what had already become an American war in Vietnam, the president continued to rely on McNamara to maintain consensus behind his pursuit of the "middle ground." On June 23 Ball recommended that the United States cut its losses in Vietnam. When McNamara and Rusk opposed this proposal and argued for deepening American military involvement, the president directed that McNamara and Ball put their views in writing.[2] Before the memos were complete, however, McNamara persuaded Ball to abandon his radical proposal for withdrawal in favor of a proposal that the United States minimize its liabilities by limiting troop deployments to 72,000 and restricting their combat role.[3] Bombing would continue, but the area around Hanoi and Haiphong would remain off limits. McNamara, arguing that Ball's paper was unacceptable because it did not offer a "good way out," received assistance from Rusk, who predicted that

300

pulling out of Vietnam would damage U.S. credibility, which "is the pillar of peace throughout the world." Rusk argued that such a diminution of American reputation would "lead to our ruin and almost certainly to catastrophic war.[4] With Ball's "dangerous" paper suppressed, McNamara continued to build consensus behind the proposal that he was developing in the Pentagon.[5]

McNamara told McNaughton to outline a political and military "scenario" for American intervention in Vietnam. Following the president's instructions to include the smallest group possible in the planning effort in order to minimize the possibility of leaks,[6] the defense secretary asked the Joint Staff to develop a list of specific military actions that could be taken in Vietnam, but did not permit the JCS themselves to participate in higher-level discussions concerning policy or strategic options. Indeed, McNamara, with Wheeler's assistance, kept the other chiefs in the dark about the latest planning effort.[7] Although McNamara ostensibly included Wheeler in the process, he excluded the general from substantive deliberations by lying to him about the subject of meetings with Ball, Rusk, McGeorge Bundy, McNaughton, and others.[8] With the Joint Staff providing only technical advice and the JCS shut out of policy meetings, the list of military actions were consistent with the president's call to "kill more VC," and so the discussions emphasized tactics and means rather than strategy and the endstate desired in Vietnam. Overlooking the complexities of countering the political and military challenges of defeating an insurgency, military operations were aimed at killing large numbers of the enemy in conventional battles and at "hounding, harassing, and hurting the VC should they elect not to stand and fight." The report requested more troop deployments and emphasized the tactic of launching eight hundred B-52 strikes against "VC havens" and following up each air raid with a prompt "entry of ground forces into the struck area." The latest planning effort continued to equate any activity with progress rather than providing a vision for ending the war on terms favorable to the United States. These "expanded military and political moves," McNamara wrote to LBJ, would convince North Vietnam and the Viet Cong "that the odds are against their winning."[9] By default, attrition had become the military strategy and stalemate was its objective.

Even as he excluded the JCS from policy discussions, McNamara remained committed to keeping the Chiefs "on the team." He retained in his paper the full list of military actions developed by the Joint Staff, even though it included military measures that went far beyond the limitations he envisioned. In the first draft of his paper on the expansion of U.S. military pressure, McNamara recommended the deployment of forty battalions to raise the number of U.S. troops to two hundred thousand. Consistent with JCS plans for mobilization, the paper suggested a reserve call-up of one hundred thousand and the extension of tours of duty for those already in the service. The paper also proposed expanding the air campaign against North Vietnam, including bombing port facilities, mining harbors, destroying transportation and industrial targets closer to Hanoi, and intensifying aerial interdiction. Aircraft would attack North Vietnamese airfields and SAM sites "as necessary."[10] But McNamara never genuinely considered advocating the measures that the Joint Staff had recommended. McGeorge Bundy, who thought that the principal purpose of ground troops would be to preserve American credibility by covering "an eventual retreat," criticized the military actions contained in McNamara's paper as "rash to the point of folly."[11] McNamara responded that he would be more than willing to abandon controversial military recommendations, noting, however, that the Joint Chiefs of Staff "are strongly in favor of going even further."[12] McNamara appeased the JCS by keeping his memo unchanged while, by privately professing a willingness to drop military recommendations, he preserved the support of McGeorge Bundy and Rusk, who favored limited military actions.

Although William Bundy described the last week in June as the "time for pleadings," the president's advisers settled their differences out of court. Before the president met with his advisers on July 1, McGeorge Bundy sent him a memorandum to which he attached the Vietnam policy papers from McNamara and Ball, and from Rusk and William Bundy. Rusk's paper highlighted the damage to U.S. credibility that would attend a withdrawal from Vietnam, and William Bundy proposed that the administration limit additional troop deployments while waiting to "see what happens."[13] McGeorge Bundy advised Johnson to "listen hard to George Ball and then reject his proposal." Bundy suggested that Johnson then choose between McNamara's and William Bundy's options, and told the president that McNamara was willing to "tone down" the recommendations in his paper.[14] Two days before McGeorge Bundy forwarded the advisers' memos to the president, however, LBJ had rendered Ball's and William Bundy's recommendations irrelevant to the current situation by approving the immediate deployment to Vietnam of three additional Marine units comprising eleven thousand men in response to an urgent request from Westmoreland.[15]

■

With the pattern of slowly deepening American military involvement in Vietnam well established, the president attempted to build support within his administration, in Congress, and among the public. On July 2, as more U.S. Marines landed at Danang and Qui Nhon, Johnson met with his closest advisers.[16] To protect the consensus they had reached around McNamara's "toned-down" recommendation for further military action, McNamara and Rusk wanted the meeting kept small because, according to McGeorge Bundy, they felt

> strongly that the George Ball paper should not be argued with you in any audience larger than yourself, Rusk, McNamara, Ball and me. They feel that it is exceedingly dangerous to have this possibility reported in a wide circle. Moreover, both of them feel great reticence about expressing their innermost thoughts to you in front of any larger group.

Johnson, however, was already following the consensus that McNamara had worked to contrive. To build further support for his decision to gradually introduce more troops into South Vietnam while maintaining the sharp limitations on the use of force against the North, McNamara would travel to Saigon in mid-July for "further consideration" of Westmoreland's request.[17]

The JCS—with whom McNamara had last met on June 28—had no influence over the administration's response to Westmoreland's request. Even as the Joint Staff worked with McNaughton, Wheeler kept the service chiefs ignorant of the McNamara memo until it was completed. Wheeler was determined to give Westmoreland his unqualified support and present McNamara with a unified view from the Chiefs, and Greene, who preferred the enclave strategy to Westmoreland's concept of offensive action aimed at destroying concentrations of Vietnamese communist forces, might have complicated Wheeler's effort. When Greene discovered on June 28 that he and his colleagues had been kept uninformed about the McNamara memo for nearly a week, he concluded that JCS influence had reached a new low.[18]

Despite Greene's disappointment, however, service parochialism continued to undermine the Chiefs' ability to cooperate on urgent matters of national security. Admiral Sharp, who was in Washington for a brief visit, warned Greene that "General Westmoreland and Ambassador Taylor do not like Marines and will do everything they can to prevent the Marine Corps from getting credit for their accomplishments in South Vietnam." Greene's conversation with Sharp turned him toward improving press coverage of Marine Corps actions rather than evaluating the decision to deploy more troops.[19]

Believing that the war would require up to three times as many troops as the president was currently considering, the JCS, meanwhile, continued to advocate incremental troop deployments. Harold Johnson estimated that to guarantee a free and independent South Vietnam would take six to seven hundred thousand troops and five years of fighting. Wallace Greene's figure also went as high as seven hundred thousand. General Johnson recalled that, despite their personal estimates, the JCS never made a recommendation for the total force. In addition the Chiefs' disagreements on how to use U.S. military force went unheard and unresolved. As the president enlarged the American commitment in Vietnam, he had yet to hear from his military advisers concerning how the U.S. military would fight the war or how many troops it might take to force a settlement consistent with the stated policy goal of maintaining the freedom and independence of South Vietnam.[20]

In a July 10 meeting with the JCS, McNamara told the Chiefs that the president had decided to "move forward" in South Vietnam but had not yet decided on a specific course of action. He warned the JCS to keep what he was about to tell them "out of the news." He divulged that the president had, on July 8, approved the deployment to South Vietnam of the full thirty-four battalions that Westmoreland had requested. The total force of more than two hundred thousand would be in South Vietnam by November 1. After making the announcement, McNamara reviewed the details of the impending mobilization and deployment. The Marine Corps would mobilize a fourth Marine division and air wing and add three new brigades (three battalions each) to the force structure. The reserve and newly formed units would be combat ready within four to six months. The Army would call up twenty-seven reserve battalions and, to replace eventually the reserve units, would organize another twenty-seven Regular Army battalions from scratch. If the need existed, the reserves might remain on active duty. McNamara told the Chiefs that the first priority would be to get troops "into South Vietnam as fast as they can be absorbed." All that remained, he said, was the formal announcement of the decision. The Congress and the American public, however, would have to be "softened up." Public relations, McNamara told the Chiefs, was the principal reason for his impending trip to South Vietnam.[21]

Greene found McNamara's announcement "astonishing." He thought that the "requirement for additional forces and the deployment of both regulars and reserves had not been carefully thought through." Greene recorded at the time that McNamara conducted the JCS meeting in a "condescending and impatient" manner. He left Greene with the impression that the Chiefs had become technicians whose principal responsibility was to carry out decisions already made rather than fully participating in the planning and advisory process.[22]

While preparing deployment plans and a concept for how to use U.S. forces, McNamara and Wheeler bypassed the other members of the JCS. Greene would not discover until July 12 that, since July 2, an ad hoc committee under Goodpaster's direction had been charged by Wheeler with determining what "assurance the U.S. can have of winning if we do everything we can."[23]

As Goodpaster's committee scrambled to develop a military strategy for Vietnam, civilian officials in the Department of Defense made the effort frivolous. Although McNamara had told the president that he had a "very definite limitation on commitment in mind," he did not tell Goodpaster or the JCS that such a constraint existed, lest the Chiefs balk at explicit limitations.[24] After he arrived in Saigon, McNamara asked Westmoreland whether, based on the assumption that enemy efforts did not increase, thirty-four U.S. battalions would suffice "to prove to the VC/DRV that they cannot win in South Vietnam."[25] Although he had assumed away the possibility of an enemy response to an American buildup and limited the military objective to stalemate, McNamara did not get the answer he wanted. Implicitly rejecting stalemate as a military objective, Westmoreland argued that the enemy was "too deeply committed to be influenced by anything but [the] application of overpowering force." Even the full level of force that Westmoreland had requested would "not per se cause the enemy to back off." Westmoreland told McNamara that, "instinctively, we believe that there may be substantial additional U.S. force requirements." After the forces included in his request had stabilized the military situation, Westmoreland intended to use unspecified numbers of additional troops in 1966 "to gain and maintain the military initiative."[26] Even though McNamara had hoped to exact from Westmoreland an estimate of the number of troops needed to impose a stalemate, Westmoreland sought an open-ended commitment to the objective of "overwhelming" the enemy.

■

McNamara's guidance to Goodpaster's group clearly revealed that civilian and military officials were going to war with dramatically different objectives in mind. McNamara and McNaughton, who continued to define the policy goal as maintaining U.S. credibility and prestige, envisioned achieving that goal by pursuing the military objective of stalemate in South Vietnam. In a July 2 memo that he had cleared with McNamara, McNaughton suggested to Goodpaster that, to "win" in Vietnam, the United States would merely have to "succeed in demonstrating to the VC that they cannot win." A stalemate, McNaughton suggested, would be tantamount to "victory" if it served as a "way station along toward a favorable settlement."[27] Goodpaster did not take McNaughton seriously and continued to develop plans based on the *stated* policy goal of maintaining a stable and independent non-Communist government in South Vietnam. He established objectives that would require larger forces and fewer restrictions on military planning and operations than McNaughton and McNamara envisioned. Goodpaster urged the destruction of the "war-supporting power of North Vietnam" and the defeat of Viet Cong and North Vietnamese main force units in the South. Military action would not impose a stalemate as a "way station" to negotiations, but force the enemy to stop the war or render them incapable of continuing it. Goodpaster recalled that he had taken special care to "make clear that the proposal was based on avoiding a stalemate."[28] He did not, however, directly confront McNamara and McNaughton over what were apparent, if not explicit, disparities in the objectives pursued by military and civilian officials, which underlay recommendations of vastly different levels of force.

Although McNamara implied that Goodpaster's study group should limit the scope of military actions it recommended, he failed to make explicit the limits and restrictions on the use of force that he had in mind.   After a conversation with McNamara, McNaughton asked Goodpaster to "minimize the amount of the team's creative effort that must go into analyzing the ROLLING THUNDER program or such proposals as the mining of the DRV harbors." Despite the insinuation that he should not study the effectiveness of the most controversial military measures taken or recommended so far, the guidance that Goodpaster received from McNamara permitted military planning based on the assumption that the United States would do everything it could.[29]

Goodpaster's reply to the question of whether the United States could win in Vietnam was a qualified yes. To win, the study argued, the administration must lift restrictions and controls on the use of military force, with the exception of prohibitions on a land invasion of North Vietnam, the use of nuclear and chemical weapons, and mass bombings of population centers. Short of those few prohibitions, Goodpaster assumed, the military would have complete freedom of action, including ground operations in Laos to cut the Ho Chi Minh Trail, a "full-scale" air campaign against the North, and offensive operations in the South aimed at the "destruction" of enemy units. Once the president approved Goodpaster's strategy, military actions would "not be subject to restriction, delay, or planning uncertainties."[30] In essence Goodpaster told McNamara that the United States would have to remove virtually all restrictions on the application of conventional military power to win in Vietnam.

Because McNamara's military objectives were undefined and because he had not communicated frankly with Goodpaster concerning limits on the use of force, Goodpaster's study offered military advice in a vacuum of political guidance. McNamara even attempted to persuade Goodpaster to drop from his study all assumptions concerning the limits of the U.S. effort and replace them with an assumption that the large-scale introduction of U.S. troops would not provoke intensified enemy efforts. Goodpaster replied that, without making assumptions about what level of force the U.S. was willing to commit, he could not tell McNamara whether the U.S. could win. He also argued that the estimate should be based on the enemy's capabilities rather than on unrealistic assumptions concerning enemy intentions.[31]

The American military commitment in Vietnam grew without a reconciliation of Goodpaster's and McNamara's fundamentally different conceptions of how to prosecute the war. McNamara did not forward the Goodpaster study to the White House, but the plan did reach McGeorge

Bundy's military assistant, Col. Richard Bowman, on July 21. Observing that the study had received "no endorsement" from McNamara, Bowman described it as a "non-study" and passed it to Bundy as "background for the discussions on Vietnam."[32]

■

Thirty years afterward McNamara identified but did not seem to understand his failure to connect additional troop deployments to a strategy for ending the war on favorable terms. Citing the superficiality of his discussions with Westmoreland in Saigon, McNamara was puzzled by his inability "to [have thought] deeply and realistically" about Vietnam and his failure to have considered "alternative courses of action and their consequences." He placed a large measure of the blame on Westmoreland for not having provided answers to questions such as "what military strategy and tactics should be followed; how the Viet Cong would respond; how many casualties the United States would suffer; what responses could be expected to U.S. actions, and when they would occur."[33] But in 1965, McNamara neglected strategic thought and focused entirely on tactical changes. The defense secretary informed Westmoreland that the "main purpose" of his July 1965 trip was to receive the MACV commander's recommendations for the numbers of troops required by the end of the year, the time schedule for deployment, and "the probable requirements for additional forces next year."[34] McNamara's challenge would be to exact from Westmoreland a request consistent with the number of troops that the president was willing to approve. Before McNamara's departure McNaughton had already drafted the report that McNamara would send to the president on his return. McNaughton's deputy, Adam Yarmolinsky, recalled that McNamara's trip was "theater" designed to justify decisions already made.[35]

On July 14, as McNamara and his party departed for Saigon to discuss with Westmoreland the forthcoming troop deployments, the purpose of the use of force remained unclear. Two days after he arrived in Saigon, McNamara received a "literally eyes only" cable from his deputy, Cyrus Vance, confirming that the president intended to proceed with the deployment of thirty-four more battalions to South Vietnam because he feared that a troop deployment larger than that would "kill [the] domestic legislative program."[36] McNamara would nevertheless remain in Saigon for three more days of "consultation." Indeed, having deepened

American involvement in the war according to a pattern determined by domestic political pressures, McNamara's charge was to return with a consensus behind a list of actions consistent with the president's desire to get the Great Society package through Congress. In the early nineteenth century, Clausewitz observed that "the political object is the goal, war is the means of reaching it, and means can never be considered in isolation from their purpose."[37] The Great Society, the dominant political determinant of Johnson's military strategy, had nothing to do with the war itself. As a result the application of means continued to escalate without a vision of how military action might actually achieve the goals of the war.

On July 20 McNamara returned from Saigon and forwarded his prefabricated report to the president. Describing the objective of military force as demonstrating to the enemy "that the odds are against their winning," he concluded with an ambivalent call to arms. McNamara predicted that his proposal—if "properly integrated and executed with continuing vigor and visible determination—[stood] a good chance of achieving an acceptable outcome within a reasonable time in Vietnam." His recommendation reiterated those actions the president had already decided to support. U.S. ground force deployments would increase to thirty-four battalions or, if South Korea failed to provide nine battalions promptly, forty-three. Limitations on the air campaign would continue, and McNamara dropped actions that he had included in earlier papers, such as the mining of Haiphong Harbor.[38]

■

McNamara's trip to Saigon raised the level of congressional interest in Vietnam. While Wheeler was away with McNamara, the other chiefs met with members of the House Armed Services Committee in Chairman L. Mendel Rivers's office.[39] The representatives wanted the JCS to provide them with a comprehensive estimate of the amount of force that the war would ultimately require. If the Chiefs answered the questions directly and honestly, they might be able to foil the president's plans for "softening up" the public and the Congress upon McNamara's return from Saigon.

"Coach" Johnson would have been proud of his "team." When the representatives asked if mobilization was necessary, the officers avoided answering. Although Harold Johnson had already notified major Army commanders to prepare for a one-year mobilization of reserve units and had outlined to them a specific program for increasing the strength of the Army by sixty-three battalions, the Army chief told the committee members that he "didn't really know" what his requirement was "now or in the future." After repeated questioning Johnson replied that some 250,000 U.S. troops would be needed in Vietnam—about half the number he privately believed would be necessary to end the war on terms favorable to the United States and South Vietnam. McConnell refused to estimate the number of men the Air Force would require to satisfy the demands of the war. McDonald said that the Navy would require 40,000 more sailors, but did not state whether the increase would require mobilization of reserve forces. Although Greene believed that the committee members must have deduced from the discussion the need for mobilization, the Chiefs never made that requirement explicit. Near the end of the meeting, one of the legislators asked Greene directly how many men would be needed to win the war in Vietnam. Amid the confusing and contradictory estimates of his colleagues, however, Greene's estimate of five hundred thousand made no visible impression on the legislators.[40]

The questioning turned from troop requirements and mobilization to military action against North Vietnam. Rivers, a Democrat from South Carolina, took a nautical map of Haiphong Harbor out of a locked cabinet. Rivers and the committee's chief counsel, John R. Blandford, asked the JCS why they were not mining Haiphong Harbor and bombing fuel storage facilities in the port area: "Haven't you Chiefs recommended that this be done?" Greene deferred to McDonald and McConnell, who explained that the targets had been placed on a list but that the attack times had not been specified. McDonald said that "political factors," such as potential damage to neutral ships, had delayed them. Asked about other targets in the area, McDonald gave the same answer. Greene thought that his colleagues' statements were "not truthful" in light of repeated JCS recommendations to attack those targets and mine the harbor, but he remained silent.[41] Rivers asked Greene why SAM sites and air bases had been left untouched. Greene said that he had been "greatly concerned" about the need to hit both targets and had advocated hitting the SAM sites "from the day the first shovel had been struck into the ground to construct them."

Greene's direct response contrasted with the reticence of his colleagues. The Chiefs as a whole had been less than forthcoming. Rep. F. Edward Hébert, a Democrat from Louisiana, told them that they were "highly respected" but warned that their credibility would suffer unless they provided Congress with their honest opinions. Rivers told the Chiefs that they were "creatures of the Congress and therefore have a duty to them as well as to the Executive Branch."

Harold Johnson responded defensively, arguing that he owed allegiance principally to the president. Johnson reminded the representatives that under the National Security Act the Chiefs were "principal military advisers to the president, the National Security Council, and the Secretary of Defense." Greene told the congressmen that the Chiefs found themselves "in a very difficult position between the committee and the administration." Rep. William H. Bates, a Republican from Massachusetts, described the National Security Act as "the worst one that Congress ever passed." Greene recorded at the time that the Chiefs' evasive answers had left the committee in a "fit of frustration."

Greene experienced conflicting feelings during the consultation with the committee members. Sympathetic to his commander in chief in the April White House meetings, when LBJ seemed besieged by opponents of the U.S. role in Vietnam, Greene was nonetheless "astounded by how few of the facts regarding the situation seemed to be known" to the people's representatives. Greene's loyalty to the president and reluctance to contradict his colleagues, however, prevented him from giving the legislators his full assessment of the situation. Two hours after the meeting, he called John Blandford.

Greene told Blandford what he declined to say in the meeting. The United States, Greene said, was on the verge of a "major war" that would ultimately involve a minimum of five hundred thousand troops. The war would take at least five years, and the United States would suffer a large number of casualties. To set conditions for winning the war, the United States would have to undertake an "immediate intensification" of operations against North Vietnam and within South Vietnam. Greene had given Blandford privately the assessment that the Chiefs had failed to provide either to Congress or to the administration.[42]

With the administration deceiving the people and Congress about the depth of the American military commitment in Vietnam, the JCS were in a quandary. Although the Constitution designated the president as commander in chief of the military, each member of the JCS was sworn to "support and defend the Constitution of the United States." The Constitution charged Congress, as representatives of the people, with the responsibility to decide whether to declare war. The American people, through their representatives in Congress, were to determine whether South Vietnam's "freedom and independence" was worth the costs and risks. With the exception of Greene (and then only in private to a staff member), the Chiefs had decided to support their commander in chief by misrepresenting their own estimates of the situation in Vietnam. Greene felt keenly the tension between loyalty to the president and his responsibilities to the American people and had chosen a middle course of publicly supporting the administration while privately providing his actual views to the Congress. The Chiefs' obligations to their soldiers, airmen, sailors, and marines complicated already conflicting responsibilities. As American involvement in the war deepened, Lyndon Johnson remained determined to depict the war very differently from the way that Greene had described it.

■

Johnson would need congressional approval to mobilize reserves and to obtain additional funds to finance the war. Mobilization or a request for funds, however, would have sparked an enormous controversy over Vietnam that might have led representatives to conclude that the country could not afford both "guns and butter." Presidential aide Jack Valenti recalled that in July 1965, the president was "in the middle of the biggest legislative fight of Johnson's history."[43] Although he knew that financing the deployments that he had already decided to approve would cost approximately eight billion dollars in fiscal year 1966, the president thought it "impossible" for him to submit to Congress before January 1966 a supplementary budget request of more than three or four hundred million dollars.[44]

Intent on obscuring the cost of the war from the body that held constitutional authority over appropriations and declaring war, the president directed Vance to have the Defense Department ready to explain to Congress that no additional funds were needed until January, at which time they would "be able to come up with clear and precise figures as to what is required."[45] Separately McNamara suggested that, to avoid inflation, the president finance the war through additional taxation. Alluding to the difficulty of getting Congress to approve additional taxes for a war that had not gained enthusiastic public support, Johnson told McNamara to "get your ass up to the Hill and don't come back till you have the vote count." The president feared that a tax bill would sap the momentum behind his domestic legislation. He told McNamara, "Goddammit, Bob. . . . How many times do I have to remind you that after FDR tried to pack the Supreme Court and failed, he couldn't get Congress to pass the time of day." After finding that the votes were not there, McNamara dropped his recommendation.[46]

LBJ recognized, however, that placing limits on the use of force in time of war because of domestic political concerns would incite controversy and opposition. Valenti observed that "the last thing that Lyndon Johnson wanted was to make public his strategy about the Great Society and the war. He wasn't going to do it. There's no question that he wanted to *sotto-voce* the whole thing." On July 19 McGeorge Bundy showed the president a draft memo intended for key senators arguing that deeper U.S. involvement in Vietnam did not require additional appropriations. He included the observation that "it would create the impression that we have to have guns, not butter—and would help the enemies of the president's domestic legislative Program." Johnson ordered Bundy to "rewrite" the memo eliminating the reference to the Great Society. It was clear to Bundy that the president would "never admit" that the Great Society shaped his Vietnam decisions because "he would have thought that going around advertising that you're adjusting your public words to the nature of your legislative program suggested you didn't deserve to be in charge of the legislative program."[47]

While concern over an escalation of the war was genuine, Johnson exaggerated the danger of Chinese intervention to justify his unwillingness to ask congressional approval of measures that might jeopardize his domestic legislation. With McNamara's assistance, he contrived rationalizations that mobilization alone might provoke an escalation of the war and that a sharp congressional debate over appropriations risked sending the wrong "signal" to Hanoi about American resolve.[48]

■

Between July 21 and 27 Johnson held a series of meetings to defuse potential opposition to his Vietnam decisions. The JCS and the service secretaries met with the president on July 22. If the Chiefs found limitations on the level of force under McNamara's option unsatisfactory, the other options the president presented, "bugging out" and "maintain present force and losing slowly," were even more unpalatable to them. The president amplified his concern that if he "gave Westmoreland all he asked for" and expanded the air campaign in accord with JCS advice, China might "come in." He told the Chiefs that "there are millions of Chinese. I think they are going to put their stack in."[49] McNamara assisted the president by restricting discussion to the three alternative courses of action under consideration. As the meeting convened, he told the president that the JCS had "only a short time to review his paper" and were "unprepared to discuss the requirements for a reserve call-up or budgetary matters"—the matters about which the president was most concerned.[50]

Greene did not abide by McNamara's "ground rules." The Marine commandant began speaking softly. The president told Greene, "I don't have a hearing aid." Greene responded, "Well, Mr. President, I'll speak louder and make sure that you and everyone else in this room hears what I have to say." McNamara was visibly upset as Greene expressed frustration over limitations on military force. He urged intensifying Rolling Thunder, blockading North Vietnam, and mining Haiphong Harbor. He told the president that winning the war in South Vietnam would take five years and five hundred thousand soldiers and Marines.[51]

Ignoring Greene's estimate, the president continued to use the fear of escalation to parry JCS calls for more resolute military action. After Greene recommended the deployment of eighty thousand more Marines than Westmoreland had requested, the president asked, "Won't this cause them [China and the Soviet Union] to come in?" When Harold Johnson responded, "No, I don't think they will," the president reminded him that "MacArthur didn't think they would come in either." After reviewing his handwritten notes of July 1965, McGeorge Bundy recalled that, although the president emphasized a concern over an escalation of the war, "his unspoken object was to protect his legislative program."[52]

All the Chiefs except Greene suppressed their misgivings about the president's plans to deepen slowly American involvement in the war and focused on the global political imperative of containing Communism. McDonald observed that the United States "can't win an all-out war," but thought that a loss of international credibility that would attend a U.S. withdrawal left the United States with no choice but to send more troops. He offered weakly that the increase in the U.S. military effort would allow the United States to "do better than we're doing."[53]

There was virtually no discussion of how the additional troops would be employed or how their actions might contribute to achieving policy goals. Although Greene made one final plea for consideration of the enclave strategy, his challenge to Westmoreland's concept of seeking out and destroying the enemy sparked no debate. Wheeler made several references to the stated policy goal of maintaining "South Vietnam as free and independent," but there was no attempt to reconcile that goal with McNamara's proposal that military force should aim to achieve a stalemate in the South.

The shallowness of the discussion probably pleased LBJ. Harold Brown, who had attended the meeting as the nominee to replace Eugene Zuckert as secretary of the Air Force, recalled that the president's principal concern was to get all of his advisers "on the record" in support of his decisions.[54] At the president's request, McGeorge Bundy summarized the arguments that Defense Department officials and the JCS might face in Congress:

> For 10 years every step we have taken has been based on a previous failure. All we have done has failed and caused us to take another step which failed. As we get further into the bag, we get deeply bruised. Also we have made excessive claims we haven't been able to realize. Also, after 20 years of warning about war in Asia, we are now doing what MacArthur and others have warned against.
>
> We are about to fight a war we can't fight and win, the country we are trying to help is quitting. The failure on our own to fully realize what guerrilla war is like. We are sending conventional troops to do an unconventional job. How long — how much. Can we take casualties over five years — aren't we talking about a military solution when the solution is political. Why can't we interdict better—why are our bombings so fruitless—why can't we blockade the coast—why can't we improve our intelligence— why can't we find the VC?

Bundy had assembled an impressive overview of the arguments against intervention. The purpose of his observations, however, was not to generate discussion but to prepare the JCS and top civilian officials in the Department of Defense to defend the course on which the president had already decided.[55] At the conclusion of the meeting, LBJ told the JCS and the service secretaries that "we are going to get all kinds of criticism" and expressed his expectation that they support him in the difficult period ahead.[56]

■

Although McNamara had placed the issues of appropriations and mobilization essentially off limits, the president seemed to be preparing the Chiefs for a decision against mobilization of reserves. As in the past, Johnson played for their sympathy. He suggested that presenting the war to Americans in stark terms would make him vulnerable to congressional and public criticism. He said, "If I were to do this, mothers would come out of their pantries and take their aprons off!" He told the JCS that a full disclosure of his plans to deepen American involvement in the war would incite opposition and make him a "lonely man."[57]

Although McNamara initially favored mobilization, he told LBJ that he was "not pressing" him to make that decision.[58] McNamara's determination to give the president what he wanted soon overwhelmed his early inclination. Although he allowed the Chiefs to continue planning based on the assumption that reserves would mobilize, McNamara told the president that mobilization was unnecessary and assured Johnson that he could fight the war without it.[59]

By Friday night, July 23, it had finally become clear to the JCS that the president's domestic political priorities had overwhelmed the assumptions on which they had based Vietnam planning. Late in the evening Greene met with Nitze in the secretary of the Navy's office. Nitze told Greene that he had just received new instructions from the secretary of defense. Orders from President Johnson were to hold down the "political noise level" of escalation. Instead of the $12.7 billion that the Chiefs estimated the new deployments would cost, the administration would limit additional funding to the $1 billion already included in the 1966 Defense Appropriations Bill. Reserves would not be called up. Greene was to plan for the deployment of the First Marine Division and Air Wing to South Vietnam, and there would be no replacement for the division in the nation's strategic reserve force. Shocked, the general warned that if the First Marine Division and Air Wing were deployed, there would be no strategic reserve left in the United States for other contingencies. McNamara had anticipated Greene's objection and had told Nitze that, according to McNamara's systems analysts, the Fourth Marine Division (reserve) could be mobilized in two weeks instead of the Marine Corps planning factor of ninety days. Greene was incredulous. He told Nitze that the United States was on the "verge of escalating the South Vietnam emergency into a full-scale war and that the failure to treat it as

such was a grave error. The reserves should be called up and the full supplemental budget required should be asked of Congress."[60]

Nitze replied that the reason for keeping "the political noise level" low
was the fear of antagonizing China or the Soviet Union. Greene recognized, however, that the "real reason why this action was proposed was to
keep the political noise level down in the United States." Nitze directed
Greene to have plans ready to support the president's decision by 7:30
the next morning.[61]

In a meeting with the service secretaries and the JCS at noon on
Saturday, July 24, McNamara outlined his plan to meet Westmoreland's
request without mobilization and without asking Congress for sufficient
funding to carry it out. Mobilization, extension of tours of duty for those
already in the services, and supplemental funding would all require legislative action and were, therefore, rejected. The president would delay
all funding requests until January 1966 and then the need would be
understated by half.[62] McNamara told the Chiefs that the program was
designed to "reduce the political noise level in Communist China and
the Soviet Union." McDonald challenged him immediately, asserting
that the decision was based more on the "domestic political noise level"
than on international considerations. McNamara smiled at the admiral
and admitted that mobilization of the reserves would cause a serious
domestic debate. Quickly modifying his exaggerated concern over an
escalation of the war, McNamara insisted that such a congressional
debate would give the Communists a "wrong impression of U.S.
resolve."[63] Thirty years later McNamara admitted that the Great Society
had dominated the president's desire to conceal the cost and scale of
American intervention in Vietnam.[64]

To prevent potential opposition McNamara promised the Chiefs that
the country would take more resolute action in the future, and appealed
to service interests. As with other denials of JCS recommendations,
McNamara promised that the president would reconsider the decision
against mobilization at a later time. McNamara asked Greene whether
he would support the deployment plan if the size of Marine deployments
in 1966 increased and the ceiling on the size of the Marine Corps was
lifted. Greene, as he had in the past, went along with the administration
in exchange for decisions that benefited the Corps.[65]

Harold Johnson also went along with the president's decision, even
though he knew that the failure to mobilize was a prescription for disaster

both for his service and for the war. He also recognized that the decision to obscure the cost of the war was based on the president's desire to keep Vietnam "very, very low key" in favor of Great Society legislation. General Johnson recalled, however, that the decision left him "tongue tied." All he could do was tell McNamara that "the quality of the Army is going to erode to some degree that we can't assess now." Years afterward General Johnson asked, "'What should my role have been?' I'm a dumb soldier under civilian control. . . . I could resign, and what am I? I'm a disgruntled general for 48 hours and then I'm out of sight. Right?" Although the general thought that fighting a war while adhering to "peacetime practices" was "unconscionable" and recognized that "our self-imposed restraints exceeded by far the objectives that we sought," he did not resign, resist, or object to the president's decision. Appointed by the president to a position that he never expected to achieve, Johnson was willing to stay on and "try and fight and get the best posture that we can."[66] He was to preside over the disintegration of the Army; a disintegration that began with the president's decision against mobilization.[67] Harold Johnson's inaction haunted him for the rest of his life.

■

The president, however, expected more than acquiescence from the JCS and Wheeler in particular. He needed Wheeler's support to deceive Congress about the nature and cost of American intervention in Vietnam. The disparity between the truth and what the president was willing to tell Congress and the American people would have made Johnson's administration particularly vulnerable to the defection of an uncompromising general.

On the evening of July 27, before he made public his decision, President Johnson made one last effort to soften up his own NSC and selected members of Congress. During the NSC meeting, the president outlined five choices:

1. Use our massive power, including SAC, to bring the enemy to his knees. Less than 10% of our people urge this course of action.
2. We could get out on the grounds that we don't belong there. Not very many people feel this way about Vietnam. Most feel that our national honor is at stake and that we must keep our

commitments there. Ike, Kennedy, and I have given [a]
commitment.

3. We could keep our forces at the present level, approximately
    80,000 men, but suffer the consequences of losing additional
    territory and of accepting increased casualties. You wouldn't
    want your boy to be out there and crying for help and not get it.

4. We could ask for everything we might desire from Congress—
    money[,] authority to call up the reserves[, and] acceptance of
    the deployment of more combat battalions. This dramatic
    course of action would involve declaring a state of emergency
    and a request for several billion dollars. Many favor this course.
    However, if we do go all out in this fashion, Hanoi would be
    able to ask the Chinese Communists and the Soviets to increase
    aid and add to their existing commitment. For that reason I
    don't want to be dramatic and cause tension. I think we can get
    our people to support us without having to be provocative.

5. We have chosen to do what is necessary to meet the present
    situation, but not to be unnecessarily provocative to either the
    Russians or the Communist Chinese. We will give the
    commanders the men they say they need. We will get the
    necessary money in the new budget and will use our transfer
    authority until January. We will neither brag about what we are
    doing or thunder at the Chinese Communists and the Russians.

Johnson announced that "we will hold until January." Having portrayed
mobilization as "dramatic" and "unnecessarily provocative," he claimed
that his chosen course could make a diplomatic solution more likely.
When the president asked if anyone in the room opposed the course of
action, everyone, including General Earle Wheeler, remained silent.[68]
Lyndon Johnson would depend even more heavily on Wheeler's silence
during the meeting with the Senate and House leadership that convened
ten minutes later.

In the meeting with the senators and representatives, LBJ and
McNamara misrepresented the scale of Westmoreland's request, understated the funds they needed by approximately ten billion dollars, and
argued that mobilization, from a military perspective, was not only
unnecessary but undesirable.[69] McNamara understated by half the one
hundred thousand troops that Westmoreland had requested to arrive in

South Vietnam by the end of the year. House Republican Whip Leslie Arends asked McNamara directly, "General Westmoreland needs how much?" Stating ambiguously that "we will meet requirements," McNamara cited an "immediate need" for "thirteen battalions and 50,000 men" whom "we will ship *now*—as soon as the decision is made."[70] Although he had favored mobilization, McNamara contended that calling up the reserves would be an inefficient use of a "perishable asset." Although McNamara's cost estimate of the anticipated deployments was approximately ten to twelve billion dollars, the president claimed that "we have the money."[71] When Senate Minority Leader Dirksen told the president, "If you need the money, you ought to ask for it," Johnson expressed his desire to delay any funding requests until January—after the Great Society legislation passed—and alluded ambiguously to a "good sizable supplement" of "a few billion dollars."[72]

Even as he dramatically reduced Westmoreland's request and obscured the cost of the war, LBJ attempted to avoid potential opposition with a plea to support American troops and their commander. He told the representatives that "Westy wants help—I'm gonna give it."[73] McNamara was in top form. He sensed what the legislators wanted to hear and tried to fulfill their expectations. He lied that American troops were not engaged in combat operations and tried to allay fears that the United States was intervening on behalf of a weak client. In response to a question by House Majority Whip Hale Boggs, McNamara stated that the South Vietnamese have demonstrated a "willingness to fight" even though they were "suffering heavy casualties." Wheeler's presence lent silent support to the president's and the defense secretary's subterfuge.[74]

LBJ and McNamara succeeded. With the exception of Senator Mansfield, the only member of Congress present who had voiced opposition to American military intervention in Vietnam, all expressed support. Speaker of the House John McCormack stated that "our military men tell us we need more and we should give it to them." McCormack closed the meeting by telling LBJ that he would have "united support. This was a historic meeting. The president would have the support of all true Americans."[75] In a brief meeting with the president after the congressional leadership departed, McNamara told Johnson that he was "full of confidence" concerning their "handling" of the senators and representatives.[76]

On July 28, less than ninety minutes before he held his press conference to announce the escalation of the American effort in Vietnam, President Johnson made remarks at a Pentagon cost reduction awards ceremony. He highlighted his close relationship with McNamara:

> I am indebted to none more, and there is none that I have greater affection or admiration for than the man who ranks you all in this Department—the great Secretary of Defense, Bob McNamara. He gave up a great deal of his hobbies and his pleasures and hundreds of thousands of dollars each year, and millions of investments to come here and serve his country. He has served it faithfully and well. And if he has made mistakes, they have been mistakes of the head and not of the heart.

After he presented awards to employees of the defense establishment for their efforts to reduce costs to the government, Lyndon Johnson recognized General Wheeler in his closing remarks:

> I want to publicly thank General Wheeler, the Chairman of the Joint Chiefs of Staff, for his wise counsel during the period that I have been president. There are many honored and hallowed names on the honor roll of the Chiefs of Staff and the Chairmen of the Chiefs of Staff, but there is none that is greater or has contributed finer service or more wisdom and understanding than the man who now occupies that high office. . . . I would say that I sleep better every night when I sleep, because of General Wheeler.[77]

After honoring publicly the men who made possible his deceit and manipulation of Congress and the American people, the president left the Pentagon for the news conference.

Just after 12:30, when the television audience would be smallest, Lyndon Johnson walked into the East Room of the White House.[78] Although he understated Westmoreland's request by 75,000 troops, Johnson declared: "I have asked the Commanding General, General Westmoreland, what more he needs to meet this mounting aggression. He has told me. We will meet his needs." These deployments, the president stated, would increase troop strength from 75,000 to 125,000. Even as he explained that "additional forces will be needed later, and they will be sent as requested," Johnson again denied that forces deployed to Vietnam were already engaged in combat operations. To generate support, however, Johnson suggested that questioning his policy would be tantamount to abandoning the "men that are there." Emphasizing continuity between his administration and those of his predecessors, Johnson reassured his audience that his announcement did "not imply any change in policy whatever." He claimed that he had not exceeded his executive authority and stated that he had been forthright with Congress.

Johnson underplayed the potential costs and consequences of the war. He said that his moderate course would permit the United States to "find some solution that would substitute words for bombs." When asked whether North Vietnam would escalate its efforts to match U.S. troop deployments, the president would not "speculate on the reactions of other people." When asked how long the war might take, the president was equally unwilling to "prophesy or predict." Finally Johnson cultivated the impression that the deliberations at the end of July had been inclusive and searching. He told the people that "he [had] had lots of callers." The "past week of deliberations," Johnson said, had convinced him that mobilization was unnecessary.

■

As American involvement in Vietnam deepened, the gap between the true nature of that commitment and the president's depiction of it to the American people, the Congress, and members of his own administration widened. Lyndon Johnson, with the assistance of Robert S. McNamara and the Joint Chiefs of Staff, had set the stage for America's disaster in Vietnam.

Epilogue

The Americanization of the Vietnam War between 1963 and 1965 was the product of an unusual interaction of personalities and circumstances. The escalation of U.S. military intervention grew out of a complicated chain of events and a complex web of decisions that slowly transformed the conflict in Vietnam into an American war.

Much of the literature on Vietnam has argued that the "Cold War mentality" put such pressure on President Johnson that the Americanization of the war was inevitable.[1] The imperative to contain Communism was an important factor in Vietnam policy, but neither American entry into the war nor the manner in which the war was conducted was inevitable.[2] The United States went to war in Vietnam in a manner unique in American history. Vietnam was not forced on the United States by a tidal wave of Cold War ideology. It slunk in on cat's feet.

Between November 1963 and July 1965, LBJ made the critical decisions that took the United States into war almost without realizing it. The decisions, and the way in which he made them, profoundly affected the way the United States fought in Vietnam. Although impersonal forces, such as the ideological imperative of containing Communism, the bureaucratic structure, and institutional priorities, influenced the president's Vietnam decisions, those decisions depended primarily on his character, his motivations, and his relationships with his principal advisers.

■

Most investigations of how the United States entered the war have devoted little attention to the crucial developments which shaped LBJ's approach to Vietnam and set conditions for a gradual intervention. The first of several "turning points" in the American escalation comprised the near-contemporaneous assassinations of Ngo Dinh Diem and John F. Kennedy. The legacy of the Kennedy administration included an expanded commitment to South Vietnam as an "experiment" in countering Communist insurgencies and a deep distrust of the military that manifested itself in the appointment of officers who would prove supportive of the administration's policies. After November 1963 the United States confronted what in many ways was a new war in South Vietnam. Having deposed the government of Ngo Dinh Diem and his brother Nhu, and having supported actions that led to their deaths, Washington assumed responsibility for the new South Vietnamese leaders. Intensified Viet Cong activity added impetus to U.S. deliberations, leading Johnson and his advisers to conclude that the situation in South Vietnam demanded action beyond military advice and support. Next, in the spring of 1964, the Johnson administration adopted graduated pressure as its strategic concept for the Vietnam War. Rooted in Maxwell Taylor's national security strategy of flexible response, graduated pressure evolved over the next year, becoming the blueprint for the deepening American commitment to maintaining South Vietnam's independence. Then, in August 1964, in response to the Gulf of Tonkin incident, the United States crossed the threshold of direct American military action against North Vietnam.

The Gulf of Tonkin resolution gave the president carte blanche for escalating the war. During the ostensibly benign "holding period" from September 1964 to February 1965, LBJ was preoccupied with his domestic political agenda, and McNamara built consensus behind graduated pressure. In early 1965 the president raised U.S. intervention to a higher level again, deciding on February 9 to begin a systematic program of limited air strikes on targets in North Vietnam and, on February 26, to commit U.S. ground forces to the South. Last, in March 1965, he quietly gave U.S. ground forces the mission of "killing Viet Cong." That series of decisions, none in itself tantamount to a clearly discernable decision to go to war, nevertheless transformed America's commitment in Vietnam.

■

Viewed together, those decisions might create the impression of a deliberate determination on the part of the Johnson administration to go to war. On the contrary, the president did not want to go to war in Vietnam and was not planning to do so. Indeed, as early as May 1964, LBJ seemed to realize that an American war in Vietnam would be a costly failure. He confided to McGeorge Bundy, ". . . looks like to me that we're getting into another Korea. It just worries the hell out of me. I don't see what we can ever hope to get out of this." It was, Johnson observed, "the biggest damn mess that I ever saw. . . . It's damn easy to get into a war, but . . . it's going to be harder to ever extricate yourself if you get in."[3] Despite his recognition that the situation in Vietnam demanded that he consider alternative courses of action and make a difficult decision, LBJ sought to avoid or to postpone indefinitely an explicit choice between war and disengagement from South Vietnam. In the ensuing months, however, each decision he made moved the United States closer to war, although he seemed not to recognize that fact.

The president's fixation on short-term political goals, combined with his character and the personalities of his principal civilian and military advisers, rendered the administration incapable of dealing adequately with the complexities of the situation in Vietnam. LBJ's advisory system was structured to achieve consensus and to prevent potentially damaging leaks. Profoundly insecure and distrustful of anyone but his closest civilian advisers, the president viewed the JCS with suspicion. When the situation in Vietnam seemed to demand military action, Johnson did not turn to his military advisers to determine how to solve the problem. He turned instead to his civilian advisers to determine how to postpone a decision. The relationship between the president, the secretary of defense, and the Joint Chiefs led to the curious situation in which the nation went to war without the benefit of effective military advice from the organization having the statutory responsibility to be the nation's "principal military advisers."

∎

What Johnson feared most in 1964 was losing his chance to win the presidency in his own right. He saw Vietnam principally as a danger to that goal. After the election, he feared that an American military response to the deteriorating situation in Vietnam would jeopardize chances that his Great Society would pass through Congress. The Great Society was to be Lyndon Johnson's great domestic political legacy, and he could not tolerate the risk of its failure. McNamara would help the president first protect his electoral chances and then pass the Great Society by offering a strategy for Vietnam that appeared cheap and could be conducted with minimal public and congressional attention. McNamara's strategy of graduated pressure permitted Johnson to pursue his objective of not losing the war in Vietnam while postponing the "day of reckoning" and keeping the whole question out of public debate all the while.

McNamara was confident in his ability to satisfy the president's needs. He believed fervently that nuclear weapons and the Cold War international political environment had made traditional military experience and thinking not only irrelevant, but often dangerous for contemporary policy. Accordingly McNamara, along with systems analysts and other civilian members of his own department and the Department of State, developed his own strategy for Vietnam. Bolstered by what he regarded as a personal triumph during the Cuban missile crisis, McNamara drew heavily on that experience and applied it to Vietnam. Based on the assumption that carefully controlled and sharply limited military actions were reversible, and therefore could be carried out at minimal risk and cost, graduated pressure allowed McNamara and Johnson to avoid confronting many of the possible consequences of military action.

∎

Johnson and McNamara succeeded in creating the illusion that the decisions to attack North Vietnam were alternatives to war rather than war itself. Graduated pressure defined military action as a form of communication, the object of which was to affect the enemy's calculation of interests and dissuade him from a particular activity. Because the favored means of communication (bombing fixed installations and economic targets) were not appropriate for the mobile forces of the Viet Cong, who lacked an infrastructure and whose strength in the South was political as well as military, McNamara and his colleagues pointed to the infiltration of men and supplies into South Vietnam as proof that the source and center of the enemy's power in Vietnam lay north of the seventeenth parallel, and specifically in Hanoi. Their definition of the enemy's source of strength was derived from that strategy rather than from a critical examination of the full reality in South Vietnam—and turned out to be inaccurate.

Graduated pressure was fundamentally flawed in other ways. The strategy ignored the uncertainty of war and the unpredictable psychology of an activity that involves killing, death, and destruction. To the North Vietnamese, military action, involving as it did attacks on their forces and bombing of their territory, was not simply a means of communication. Human sacrifices in war evoke strong emotions, creating a dynamic that defies systems analysis quantification. Once the United States crossed the threshold of war against North Vietnam with covert raids and the Gulf of Tonkin "reprisals," the future course of events depended not only on decisions made in Washington but also on enemy responses and actions that were unpredictable. McNamara, however, viewed the war as another business management problem that, he assumed, would ultimately succumb to his reasoned judgment and others' rational calculations. He and his assistants thought that they could predict with great precision what amount of force applied in Vietnam would achieve the results they desired and they believed that they could control that force with great precision from halfway around the world. There were compelling contemporaneous arguments that graduated pressure would not affect Hanoi's will sufficiently to convince the North to desist from its support of the South, and that such a strategy would probably lead to an escalation of the war. Others expressed doubts about the utility of attacking North Vietnam by air to win a conflict in South Vietnam. Nevertheless, McNamara refused to consider the consequences of his recommendations and forged ahead oblivious of the human and psychological complexities of war.

■

Despite their recognition that graduated pressure was fundamentally flawed, the JCS were unable to articulate effectively either their objections or alternatives. Interservice rivalry was a significant impediment. Although differing perspectives were understandable given the Chiefs' long experience in their own services and their need to protect the interests of their services, the president's principal military advisers were obligated by law to render their best advice. The Chiefs' failure to do so, and their willingness to present single-service remedies to a complex military problem, prevented them from developing a comprehensive estimate of the situation or from thinking effectively about strategy.

When it became clear to the Chiefs that they were to have little influence on the policy-making process, they failed to confront the president with their objections to McNamara's approach to the war. Instead they attempted to work within that strategy in order to remove over time the limitations to further action. Unable to develop a strategic alternative to graduated pressure, the Chiefs became fixated on means by which the war could be conducted and pressed for an escalation of the war by degrees. They hoped that graduated pressure would evolve over time into a fundamentally different strategy, more in keeping with their belief in the necessity of greater force and its more resolute application. In so doing, they gave tacit approval to graduated pressure during the critical period in which the president escalated the war. They did not recommend the total force they believed would ultimately be required in Vietnam and accepted a strategy they knew would lead to a large but inadequate commitment of troops, for an extended period of time, with little hope for success.

■

McNamara and Lyndon Johnson were far from disappointed with the Joint Chiefs' failings. Because his priorities were domestic, Johnson had little use for military advice that recommended actions inconsistent with those priorities. McNamara and his assistants in the Department of Defense, on the other hand, were arrogant. They disparaged military advice because they thought that their intelligence and analytical methods could compensate for their lack of military experience and education. Indeed military experience seemed to them a liability because military officers took too narrow a view and based their advice on antiquated notions of war. Geopolitical and technological changes of the last fifteen years, they believed, had rendered advice based on military experience irrelevant and, in fact, dangerous. McNamara's disregard for military experience and for history left him to draw principally on his staff in the Department of Defense and led him to conclude that his only real experience with the planning and direction of military force, the Cuban missile crisis, was the most relevant analogy to Vietnam.

While they slowly deepened American military involvement in Vietnam, Johnson and McNamara pushed the Chiefs further away from the decision-making process. There was no meaningful structure through which the Chiefs could voice their views—even the chairman was not a reliable conduit. NSC meetings were strictly *pro forma* affairs in which the president endeavored to build consensus for decisions already made. Johnson continued Kennedy's practice of meeting with small groups of his most trusted advisers. Indeed he made his most important decisions at the Tuesday lunch meetings in which Rusk, McGeorge Bundy, and McNamara were the only regular participants. The president and McNamara shifted responsibility for real planning away from the JCS to ad hoc committees composed principally of civilian analysts and attorneys, whose main goal was to obtain a consensus consistent with the president's pursuit of the middle ground between disengagement and war. The products of those efforts carried the undeserved credibility of proposals that had been agreed on by all departments and were therefore hard to oppose. McNamara and Johnson endeavored to get the advice they wanted by placing conditions and qualifications on questions that they asked the Chiefs. When the Chiefs' advice was not consistent with his own recommendations, McNamara, with the aid of the chairman of the Joint Chiefs of Staff, lied in meetings of the National Security Council about the Chiefs' views.

Rather than advice McNamara and Johnson extracted from the JCS acquiescence and silent support for decisions already made. Even as they relegated the Chiefs to a peripheral position in the policy-making process, they were careful to preserve the facade of consultation to prevent the JCS from opposing the administration's policies either openly or behind the scenes. As American involvement in the war escalated, Johnson's vulnerability to disaffected senior military officers increased because he was purposely deceiving the Congress and the public about the nature of the American military effort in Vietnam. The president and the secretary of defense deliberately obscured the nature of decisions made and left undefined the limits that they envisioned on the use of force. They indicated to the Chiefs that they would take actions that they never intended to pursue. McNamara and his assistants, who considered communication the purpose of military action, kept the nature of their objective from the JCS, who viewed "winning" as the only viable goal in war. Finally, Johnson appealed directly to them, referring to himself as the "coach" and them as "his team." To dampen their calls for further action, Lyndon Johnson attempted to generate sympathy from the JCS for the great pressures that he was feeling from those who opposed escalation.

The ultimate test of the Chiefs' loyalty came in July 1965. The administration's lies to the American public had grown in magnitude as the American military effort in Vietnam escalated. The president's plan of deception depended on tacit approval or silence from the JCS. LBJ had misrepresented the mission of U.S. ground forces in Vietnam, distorted the views of the Chiefs to lend credibility to his decision against mobilization, grossly understated the numbers of troops General Westmoreland had requested, and lied to the Congress about the monetary cost of actions already approved and of those awaiting final decision. The Chiefs did not disappoint the president. In the days before the president made his duplicitous public announcement concerning Westmoreland's request, the Chiefs, with the exception of commandant of the Marine Corps Greene, withheld from congressmen their estimates of the amount of force that would be needed in Vietnam. As he had during the Gulf of Tonkin hearings, Wheeler lent his support to the president's deception of Congress. The "five silent men" on the Joint Chiefs made possible the way the United States went to war in Vietnam.[4]

■

Several factors kept the Chiefs from challenging the president's subterfuges. The professional code of the military officer prohibits him or her from engaging in political activity. Actions that could have undermined the administration's credibility and derailed its Vietnam policy could not have been undertaken lightly. The Chiefs felt loyalty to their commander in chief. The Truman-MacArthur controversy during the Korean War had warned the Chiefs about the dangers of overstepping the bounds of civilian control.[5] Loyalty to their services also weighed against opposing the president and the secretary of defense. Harold Johnson, for example, decided against resignation because he thought he had to remain in office to protect the Army's interests as best he could. Admiral McDonald and Marine Corps Commandant Greene compromised their views on Vietnam in exchange for concessions to their respective services. Greene achieved a dramatic expansion of the Marine Corps, and McDonald ensured that the Navy retained control of Pacific Command. None of the Chiefs had sworn an oath to his service, however. They had all sworn, rather, to "support and defend the Constitution of the United States."

General Greene recalled that direct requests by congressmen for his assessment put him in a difficult situation. The president was lying, and he expected the Chiefs to lie as well or, at least, to withhold the whole truth. Although the president should not have placed the Chiefs in that position, the flag officers should not have tolerated it when he had.

Because the Constitution locates civilian control of the military in Congress as well as in the executive branch, the Chiefs could not have been justified in deceiving the peoples' representatives about Vietnam. Wheeler in particular allowed his duty to the president to overwhelm his obligations under the Constitution. As cadets are taught at the United States Military Academy, the JCS relationship with the Congress is challenging and demands that military officers possess a strong character and keen intellect. While the Chiefs must present Congress with their best advice based on their professional experience and education, they must be careful not to undermine their credibility by crossing the line between advice and advocacy of service interests.[6]

Maxwell Taylor had a profound influence on the nature of the civil-military relationship during the escalation of American involvement in Vietnam. In contrast to Army Chief of Staff George C. Marshall, who, at the start of World War II, recognized the need for the JCS to suppress service parochialism to provide advice consistent with national interests, Taylor exacerbated service differences to help McNamara and Johnson keep the Chiefs divided and, thus, marginal to the policy process.[7] Taylor recommended men for appointment to the JCS who were less likely than their predecessors to challenge the direction of the administration's military policy, even when they knew that that policy was fundamentally flawed. Taylor's behavior is perhaps best explained by his close personal friendship with the Kennedy family; McNamara; and, later, Johnson. In contrast again to Marshall, who thought it important to keep a professional distance from President Franklin Roosevelt, Taylor abandoned an earlier view similar to Marshall's in favor of a belief that the JCS and the president should enjoy "an intimate, easy relationship, born of friendship and mutual regard."[8]

■

The way in which the United States went to war in the period between November 1963 and July 1965 had, not surprisingly, a profound influence on the conduct of the war and on its outcome. Because Vietnam policy decisions were made based on domestic political expediency, and because the president was intent on forging a consensus position behind what he believed was a middle policy, the administration deliberately avoided clarifying its policy objectives and postponed discussing the level of force that the president was willing to commit to the effort. Indeed, because the president was seeking domestic political consensus, members of the administration believed that ambiguity in the objectives for fighting in Vietnam was a strength rather than a weakness. Determined to prevent dissent from the JCS, the administration concealed its development of "fall-back" objectives.

Over time the maintenance of U.S. credibility quietly supplanted the stated policy objective of a free and independent South Vietnam. The principal civilian planners had determined that to guarantee American credibility, it was not necessary to win in Vietnam. That conclusion, combined with the belief that the use of force was merely another form of diplomatic communication, directed the military effort in the South at achieving stalemate rather than victory. Those charged with planning the war believed that it would be possible to preserve American credibility even if the United States armed forces withdrew from the South, after a show of force against the North and in the South in which American forces were "bloodied." After the United States became committed to war, however, and more American soldiers, airmen, and Marines had died in the conflict, it would become impossible simply to disengage and declare America's credibility intact, a fact that should have been foreseen. The Chiefs sensed the shift in objectives, but did not challenge directly the views of civilian planners in that connection. McNamara and Johnson recognized that, once committed to war, the JCS would not agree to an objective other than imposing a solution on the enemy consistent with U.S. interests. The JCS deliberately avoided clarifying the objective as well. As a result, when the United States went to war, the JCS pursued objectives different from those of the president. When the Chiefs requested permission to apply force consistent with their conception of U.S. objectives, the president and McNamara, based on their goals and domestic political constraints, rejected JCS requests, or granted them only in part. The result was that the JCS and McNamara became fixated on the means rather than on the ends, and on the manner in which the war was conducted instead of a military strategy that could connect military actions to achievable policy goals.[9]

Because forthright communication between top civilian and military officials in the Johnson administration was never developed, there was no reconciliation of McNamara's intention to limit the American military effort sharply and the Chiefs' assessment that the United States could not possibly win under such conditions. If they had attempted to reconcile those positions, they could not have helped but recognize the futility of the American war effort.

The Joint Chiefs of Staff became accomplices in the president's deception and focused on a tactical task, killing the enemy. General Westmoreland's "strategy" of attrition in South Vietnam, was, in essence, the absence of a strategy. The result was military activity (bombing North Vietnam and killing the enemy in South Vietnam) that did not aim to achieve a clearly defined objective. It was unclear how quantitative measures by which McNamara interpreted the success and failure of the use of military force were contributing to an end of the war. As American casualties mounted and the futility of the strategy became apparent, the American public lost faith in the effort. The Chiefs did not request the number of troops they believed necessary to impose a military solution in South Vietnam until after the Tet offensive in 1968.[10] By that time, however, the president was besieged by opposition to the war and was unable even to consider the request. LBJ, who had gone to such great lengths to ensure a crushing defeat over Barry Goldwater in 1964, declared that he was withdrawing from the race for his party's presidential nomination.

Johnson thought that he would be able to control the U.S. involvement in Vietnam. That belief, based on the strategy of graduated pressure and McNamara's confident assurances, proved in dramatic fashion to be false. If the president was surprised by the consequences of his decisions between November 1963 to July 1965, he should not have been so. He had disregarded the advice he did not want to hear in favor of a policy based on the pursuit of his own political fortunes and his beloved domestic programs.

■

The war in Vietnam was not lost in the field, nor was it lost on the front pages of the *New York Times* or on the college campuses. It was lost in Washington, D.C., even before Americans assumed sole responsibility for the fighting in 1965 and before they realized the country was at war;

indeed, even before the first American units were deployed. The disaster in Vietnam was not the result of impersonal forces but a uniquely human failure, the responsibility for which was shared by President Johnson and his principal military and civilian advisers. The failings were many and reinforcing: arrogance, weakness, lying in the pursuit of self-interest, and, above all, the abdication of responsibility to the American people.

Notes

PREFACE

1. On the legacies of the war, see George Herring, *America's Longest War: The United States and Vietnam, 1950–1975*, 3d ed. (New York: McGraw-Hill, 1996), pp. 299–314. See also Stanley Karnow, *Vietnam: A History*, 2d ed. (New York: Penguin Books, 1991), pp. 26–59.

2. See, for example, Phillip Caputo, *A Rumor of War* (New York: Holt, Rinehart & Winston, 1977), p. xiii.

3. Until George Herring's groundbreaking work, evaluations of the role of the Joint Chiefs of Staff (JCS) in the growing American involvement in Vietnam were impressionistic studies based largely on personal anecdotes and memories, rather than comprehensive reviews of archival sources. Herring, *LBJ and Vietnam: A Different Kind of War* (Austin: University of Texas Press, 1994). See also Bruce Palmer, *The 25 Year War* (Lexington: University of Kentucky Press, 1984), esp. pp. 17–46; Mark Perry, *Four Stars* (Boston: Houghton Mifflin, 1989), pp. 97–155; Harry Summers, Jr., *On Strategy: A Critical Analysis of the Vietnam War* (New York: Dell, 1982), esp. pp. 71–83. Exceptionally incisive is Herbert Y. Schandler, "JCS Strategic Planning and Vietnam: The Search for an Objective," in *Military Planning in the Twentieth Century*, edited by Harry R. Borowski (Washington, D.C.: U.S. Government Printing Office, 1986), pp. 295–16. Robert Buzzanco's *Masters of War: Military Dissent and Politics in the Vietnam Era* (New York: Cambridge University Press, 1996) is well-researched but often fails to consider evidence in context of the relationship between Lyndon Johnson's civilian and military advisers.

4. *Statutes at Large*, vol. 61, 253, sec. 211; vol. 61, 875, sec. 211; vol. 63, 203, sec. 1; and vol. 63, 579.

CHAPTER 1

1. *The New Frontiersmen: Profiles of the Men Around Kennedy*, edited by the *Evening Star* (Washington, D.C.: Public Affairs Press, 1961), pp. vii–viii.

2. John F. Kennedy, Inaugural Address, 20 January 1961, *Public Papers of the Presidents: John F. Kennedy, 1961* (Washington, D.C.: Government Printing Office, 1962), p. 2.

3. Ibid., p. 3.

4. Robert Lovett as quoted in Carl W. Borklund, *Men of the Pentagon: From Forrestal to McNamara* (New York: Praeger, 1966), pp. 137, 207; Arthur M. Schlesinger, Jr., *A Thousand Days* (Boston: Houghton Mifflin, 1965), pp. 131–32.

5. Borklund, *Men of the Pentagon*, pp. 207–9; Douglas Kinnard, *The Secretary of Defense: From Forrestal to McNamara* (Lexington: University of Kentucky Press, 1980), p. 77; Deborah Shapley, *Promise and Power: The Life and Times of Robert McNamara* (Boston: Little, Brown & Company, 1993), pp. 28–37; Paul Hendrickson, *The Living and the Dead: Robert McNamara and Five Lives of a Lost War* (New York: Alfred A. Knopf, 1996), pp. 98–101.

6. Kinnard, *The Secretary of Defense*, p. 77.

7. Shapley, *Promise and Power*, pp. 84–86.

8. For a description of Rusk's life, from his boyhood through his appointment as secretary of state, see Thomas J. Schoenbaum, *Waging Peace and War: Dean Rusk in the Truman, Kennedy, and Johnson Years* (New York: Simon & Schuster, 1988), chaps. 1 through 7; Theodore Sorensen, *Kennedy* (New York: Harper & Row, 1965), pp. 270–71; Kinnard, *The Secretary of Defense*, pp. 82–83; *The New Frontiersmen*, pp. 17–23; David Halberstam, *The Best and the Brightest* (New York: Random House, 1969), pp. 32–37; Joseph Kraft, *Profiles in Power* (New York: New American Library, 1966), pp. 177–84.

9. Sorensen, *Kennedy*, p. 270; Halberstam, *The Best and the Brightest*, pp. 43–46; Kraft, *Profiles in Power*, pp. 163–75. Bundy collaborated with Henry L. Stimson in *On Active Service in Peace and War* (New York: Harper and Brothers, 1947), Stimson's memoirs.

10. Halberstam, *The Best and the Brightest*, pp. 36–37; Sorensen, *Kennedy*, pp. 256, 260. Taylor observed that Kennedy preferred to conduct business with individuals who shared his outlook on life; Maxwell D. Taylor, "Defense Strategy Seminar," speech presented at the National War College, 8 July 1963, General Taylor's Speeches, Box 20, File T–415–69, Maxwell D. Taylor Papers, Special Collections Branch, National Defense University Library, for Leslie J. McNair, Washington, D.C. (hereafter cited as "Taylor Papers").

11. Taylor recalled that the NSC became "little more than a sort of registration office" for decisions that President Kennedy had already "made in the comparative privacy of the oval office." Maxwell D. Taylor, "Trends in National Security Planning," speech presented at the Naval War College, 14 March 1963, General Taylor's Speeches, Box 20, File T–415–69, Taylor Papers; William P. Bundy, unpublished manuscript, Papers of William P. Bundy, chap. 3, pp. 2–3, at the Lyndon Baines Johnson Library (hereafter cited as William Bundy, unpublished manuscript). The Lyndon Baines Johnson Library is hereafter cited as LBJ Library. Andrew J. Goodpaster, interview by author, 9 March 1993, tape recording, Washington, D.C.; Roger Hilsman, *To Move a Nation* (Garden City, N. Y.: Doubleday, 1967),

pp. 55–56. President Lyndon Johnson continued the Kennedy practice. For an insightful comparative analysis of Eisenhower's and Johnson's national security structures, see John P. Burke and Fred I. Greenstein, *How Presidents Test Reality: Decisions on Vietnam, 1954 and 1965* (New York: Russell Sage Foundation, 1989). Maxwell Taylor took a sympathetic view of the Kennedy policy process. Taylor, *Swords and Plowshares*, pp. 279–80. The Taylor quotation is from his speech "The National Security Act of 1947 and the Evolution of the DOD."

12. Gen. Victor H. Krulak, interview by author, 26 July 1993, audio tape, Point Loma, California; Andrew J. Goodpaster, interview by author, 9 March 1993; Memorandum, Colonel Ewell for General Taylor, 6 February 1962, Box 17, File T–257–69, Taylor Papers.

13. William Bundy recalled that the Bay of Pigs shook "for good what had been an almost ebullient confidence within the Administration." William Bundy, unpublished manuscript, chap. 3, p. 26. Walt Rostow confirmed Bundy's observation. Walt W. Rostow, second interview by author, 21 October 1993 (handwritten notes), Austin, Tex.

14. Trumbull Higgins, *The Perfect Failure: Kennedy, Eisenhower, and the CIA at the Bay of Pigs* (New York: W.W. Norton, 1987), pp. 61–62, 90.

15. Trumbull Higgins, *The Perfect Failure*, pp. 114–50; Sorensen, *Kennedy*, pp. 294–309; Herbert S. Parmet, *JFK: The Presidency of John F. Kennedy* (New York: Dial Press, 1983), pp. 157–79; Richard Reeves, *President Kennedy: Profile of Power* (New York: Touchstone, 1993), pp. 83–84.

16. Andrew J. Goodpaster, interview by author, 9 March 1993. Goodpaster, while serving as military assistant to President Eisenhower, was the first to present the proposal for an invasion of Cuba to the president. Goodpaster remained in the Kennedy White House for several weeks to assist in the transition between administrations. Goodpaster cited the lack of continuity between the Kennedy and Eisenhower administrations due to the new president's overhaul of the NSC structure as the primary cause of the Bay of Pigs incident. Paul Nitze observed that the Kennedy system resulted in a "perpetual state of reaction to one crisis after another rather than working toward long-term goals," and was characterized by an inability to learn from past mistakes. Paul Nitze, *From Hiroshima to Glasnost: At the Center of Decision: A Memoir* (New York: Grove Weidenfeld, 1988), p. 252.

17. Pierre Salinger, *With Kennedy* (Garden City, N.Y.: Doubleday, 1966), p. 148. Andrew J. Goodpaster, interview by author, 9 March 1993; Theodore C. Mataxis (public affairs officer for both General Lemnitzer and General Taylor from 1961 to 1964), interview by author, 19 February 1993, tape recording, Chapel Hill, N.C.; Sorensen, *Kennedy*, p. 607; Robert F. Kennedy, *Robert Kennedy, In His Own Words: The Unpublished Recollections of the Kennedy Years*, ed. Edwin O. Guthman and Jeffrey Shulman (New York: Bantam Books, 1988), p. 241; William Bundy, unpublished manuscript, chap. 3, p. 26.

18. David M. Shoup, Oral History Transcript, 7 April 1967, John F. Kennedy Library, pp. 13–23; Theodore C. Mataxis, interview by author, 19

February 1993; Curtis LeMay, "Inquiry," interview in *USA Today*, 23 July 1986, p. 9A; Thomas M. Coffey, *Iron Eagle: The Turbulent Life of General Curtis LeMay* (New York: Crown Publishers, 1986), pp. 353–56.

19. Anatoli I. Gribkov and William Y. Smith, *Operation Anadyr: U.S. and Soviet Generals Recount the Cuban Missile Crisis* (Chicago: Edition Q, 1994), p. 82.

20. Ibid., pp. 87–88.

21. Walt W. Rostow, interview by author, 21 October 1993, Austin, Tex., handwritten notes.

22. This vignette is related by Roger Hilsman in Ted Gittinger, ed., *The Johnson Years: A Vietnam Roundtable* (Austin: University of Texas Press, 1993), p. 8.

23. Gribkov and Smith, *Operation Anadyr*, pp. 87–88.

24. Walt W. Rostow, interview by author, 21 October 1993; Taylor, *Swords and Plowshares*, pp. 217–19.

25. Charles A. Stevenson, *The End of Nowhere: American Policy Toward Laos Since 1954* (Boston: Beacon Press, 1972), pp. 179, 181.

26. Walt W. Rostow, interview by author, 21 October 1993; Gribkov and Smith, *Operation Anadyr*, p. 88.

27. Moya Ann Ball, *Vietnam-on-the-Potomac* (New York: Praeger, 1992), p. 90.

28. Memorandum for Record, Telephone Conversation between General C. V. Clifton and Captain Means Johnson, 24 June 1961, in the Personal Papers of Robert S. McNamara, Record Group 200, Box 63, National Archives, Washington, D.C. (hereafter cited as McNamara Papers). President Kennedy was tormented with guilt over his decision to withdraw support for the landing force. Walt W. Rostow, interview by author, 21 October 1993.

29. For Taylor's childhood and military career, see John Taylor, *General Maxwell Taylor: The Sword and the Pen* (New York: Doubleday, 1989), pp. 11–31. See also, Maxwell Taylor, *Swords and Plowshares* (New York: W.W. Norton, 1972), chaps. 1 through 10.

30. Ridgway retired after only two of the usual four years due to his differences with Eisenhower. Lawrence Korb, *The Joint Chiefs of Staff: The First Twenty-five Years* (Bloomington: Indiana University Press, 1976), p. 39; E. Bruce Geelhoed, *Charles E. Wilson and Controversy at the Pentagon, 1953–1957* (Detroit: Wayne State University Press, 1979), pp. 121–26.

31. Maxwell Taylor, *The Uncertain Trumpet* (New York: Harper, 1959), p. 23; *Swords and Plowshares*, pp. 170–71; "The National Security Act of 1947 and the Evolution of the DOD," speech presented at the National War College, 13 February 1978, Lectures and Articles 1946–1986, Taylor Papers, pp. 5–10. On October 9, 1957, Neil McElroy replaced Charles Wilson as Secretary of Defense. Neither had much influence on the development of defense policy, and Eisenhower relied primarily on JCS chairman Adm. Arthur Radford and Secretary of State John Foster Dulles

for national security advice; Kinnard, *The Secretary of Defense*, pp. 44–71; Borklund, *Men of the Pentagon*, pp. 138–83.

32. Maxwell Taylor, "The National Security Act of 1947 and the Evolution of the DOD."

33. Herbert S. Parmet, *Eisenhower and the American Crusades* (New York: Macmillan, 1972), pp. 150–56; Fred I. Greenstein, *The Hidden-Hand Presidency: Eisenhower as Leader* (New York: Basic Books), 1982, p. 169; Samuel Huntington, *The Common Defense: Strategic Programs in National Politics* (New York: Columbia University Press, 1961), pp. 64–65; Geelhoed, *Charles E. Wilson*, pp. 16, 100–104.

34. Robert A. Divine, *Eisenhower and the Cold War* (New York: Oxford University Press, 1981), p 37.

35. For a compact summary of the New Look, see Duane Windsor, "Eisenhower's New Look Reexamined: The View from Three Decades," in Joann P. Krieg, ed., *Dwight D. Eisenhower: Soldier, President, Statesman* (New York: Greenwood Press, 1987), pp. 147–50. See also, Douglas Kinnard, *President Eisenhower and Strategy Management* (Lexington: University Press of Kentucky, 1977), pp. 14–24; Stephen E. Ambrose, *Eisenhower: The President* (New York: Simon & Schuster, 1984), pp. 171–72; Divine, *Eisenhower and the Cold War*, pp. 33–39.

36. John Foster Dulles as quoted in Kinnard, *President Eisenhower and Strategy Management*, p. 27.

37. Divine, *Eisenhower and the Cold War*, pp. 33–34; Windsor, "Eisenhower's New Look Reexamined," p. 149; Richard M. Saunders, "Military Force in the Foreign Policy of the Eisenhower Presidency," *Political Science Quarterly* 100 (Spring 1985), p. 99.

38. Taylor, *The Uncertain Trumpet*, chap. 8 passim, especially pp. 137, 146, 153.

39. Letter from John F. Kennedy to Evan Thomas, 17 December 1959, as cited in Taylor, *General Maxwell Taylor*, p. 8.

40. John F. Kennedy, "Special Message to the Congress on the Defense Budget," 28 March 1961, in John W. Gardner, ed., *To Turn the Tide* (New York: Harper Brothers, 1962), p. 59.

41. Taylor quotes in full the directive that President Kennedy signed on 26 June 1961 to establish the position in "Trends in National Security Planning." Taylor, *Swords and Plowshares*, pp. 179–81, 195–97.

42. For an account of General Taylor's childhood and career through 1958, see his autobiography, *Swords and Plowshares*, chap. 1 through 11; Maxwell D. Taylor, "The National Security Act of 1947 and the Evolution of the DOD." The quotation is from *Swords and Plowshares*, p. 170.

43. For a discussion of this dilemma, see Robert N. Ginsburgh, "The Challenge to Military Professionalism," *Foreign Affairs* 42 (January 1964), pp. 255–68. The Eisenhower quotation is from Dwight Eisenhower, *Waging Peace* (Garden City, N.Y.: Doubleday, 1956), p. 356. Taylor, "The National Security Act of 1947 and the Evolution of the DOD," p. 7; *The Uncertain Trumpet*, pp. 18–20; Korb, *The Joint Chiefs of Staff*, p. 57.

44. Andrew J. Goodpaster, "The Role of the Joint Chiefs of Staff in the National Security Structure," in Amos A. Jordan, Jr., ed., *Issues of National Security in the 1970's* (New York: Praeger, 1967), p. 222; Forrest C. Pogue, *George C. Marshall*, 4 vols. (New York: Viking Press, 1963–1987); for this point, see Volume 2, *Ordeal and Hope, 1939–1942*, pp. 283, 298–300. A debate on postwar defense organization began briefly in March of 1944 but was postponed until after the war.

45. Historical Division of the Joint Secretariat, Joint Chiefs of Staff, *Role and Functions of the Joint Chiefs of Staff: A Chronology* (Washington, D.C.: Joint Staff Historical Office, 1987), pp. 1–36; Historical Division of the Joint Secretariat, Joint Chiefs of Staff, *Organizational Development of the Joint Chiefs of Staff, 1942–1989* (Washington, D.C.: Joint Staff Historical Office, 1989), pp. 17, 21; U.S. Department of Defense, *Department of Defense Directive 5100.1: Functions of the Department of Defense and Its Major Components*, December 31, 1958, Box 17, File T–259–69, Taylor Papers. In practice the Marine Corps Commandant was given wide latitude in determining what issues related to his service. For a portion of the debate over defense organization, see U.S. Congress, Senate, Committee on Military Affairs, Hearings on S. 84 and S. 1482, 79th Congress, 2d Session, 1946.

46. The following laws codify the Joint Chiefs' major responsibilities: *Statutes at Large*, LXI, 253, sec. 211; LXI, 875, sec. 211; LXIII, 203, sec. 1; and LXIII, 579. For a summary of organizational changes in the JCS from 1942 to 1989, see Historical Division, Joint Secretariat, Joint Chiefs of Staff, *Organizational Development of the Joint Chiefs of Staff, 1942–1989*.

47. Congress, Senate, Committee on Naval Affairs, *Unification of the Armed Forces: Hearing Before the Committee on Naval Affairs*, 79th Congress, 2d Session, 1946, pp. 31–35.

48. Arleigh A. Burke, Oral History Transcript, 1973, Columbia University Oral History Project, pp. 53–56.

49. Public Law 85–599, August 6, 1958. See also, Historical Division, Joint Secretariat, Joint Chiefs of Staff, *Major Changes in the Organization of the Joint Chiefs of Staff, 1942–1969* (Washington, D.C.: Joint Staff Historical Office, 1970), p. 24. For the evolution of the Department of Defense structure between the years 1945 and 1960, see John Charles Binkley, *The Role of the Joint Chiefs of Staff in National Security Policy Making: Professionalism and Self-Perceptions, 1942–1961* (Ph.D. diss., Loyola University, Chicago, 1985). See also Goodpaster, "The Role of the Joint Chiefs of Staff in the National Security Structure," pp. 230–31.

50. Theoretically the separation between these officers and their services would mitigate service parochialism. Taylor, *The Uncertain Trumpet*, chap. 9 passim, especially pp. 175–78.

51. Memorandum for Record, Telephone Conversation between General C. V. Clifton and Captain Means Johnson, 24 June 1961, Box 63, McNamara Papers.

52. Ibid.

53. Memorandum, Colonel Ewell for General Taylor, 6 February 1962, File T–257–69, Box 17, Taylor Papers.

54. Taylor, "The National Security Act of 1947 and the Evolution of the DOD."

55. Taylor, "Trends in National Security Planning."

56. Taylor, "The National Security Act of 1947 and the Evolution of the DOD," pp. 15–16. Taylor's associates in the investigation were Attorney General Robert F. Kennedy, CIA Director Allen Dulles, and recently retired Chief of Naval Operations Adm. Arleigh Burke.

57. Taylor, "The National Security Act of 1947 and the Evolution of the DOD," pp. 15–18. See also NSAM 55, President to CJCS, 28 June 1961, as read by Maxwell D. Taylor in "Military Advice: Its Use in Government," speech delivered at the annual meeting of the Fellows of the American Bar Foundation, Chicago, February 15, 1964, in *Vital Speeches* 30, no. 11 (March 15, 1964), p. 339. See also Willard J. Webb and Ronald H. Cole, *The Chairmen of the Joint Chiefs of Staff* (Washington, D.C.: Historical Division, Joint Chiefs of Staff, 1989), p. 16; Sorensen, *Kennedy*, p. 605.

58. Taylor, *The Uncertain Trumpet*, p. 21.

59. For these contrasting earlier and later views compare Taylor, *The Uncertain Trumpet*, pp. 18–21, and *Swords and Plowshares*, p. 252.

60. Robert S. McNamara, *The Essence of Security: Reflections in Office* (New York: Harper & Row, 1968), p. x.

61. Eugene Zuckert, Oral History Transcript, 18 March 1969, sec. 1, p. 54, LBJ Library. Andrew J. Goodpaster, interview by author, 9 March 1993; Theodore C. Mataxis, interview by author, 19 February 1993.

62. Andrew J. Goodpaster, interview by author, 9 March 1993. Goodpaster described the JCS organization as "ponderous, stultified, and heavily influenced by service interests." See also Arleigh A. Burke, Oral History Interview, 18 March 1969, Columbia University Oral History Project, pp. 53–56; Henry W. Buse, Oral History Transcript, 1971, U.S. Marine Corps History and Museum Division, Marine Corps Historical Center, Washington, D.C., pp. 166–67; Taylor, *The Uncertain Trumpet*, pp. 88–129; Lawrence J. Korb, *The Joint Chiefs of Staff*, pp. 22–25.

63. Earl H. Tilford, Jr., *Setup: What the Air Force Did in Vietnam and Why* (Maxwell Air Force Base, Ala.: Air University Press, 1991), p. 284.

64. Bernard Rogers, interview by author, 12 March 1993, Washington, D.C. For tension between the Air Force and the Navy over aviation, see Memo to Air Force Chief of Staff from Lt. General David Burchinal, 2 April 1963, Folder 8, Box 134, General Curtis LeMay Papers, Special Collections Branch, Library of Congress, Washington D.C. (hereafter cited as LeMay Papers). For an Army perspective, see General H. K. Johnson, Oral History Transcript, 1972–1974, Senior Officer Debriefing Program, U.S. Army Institute for Military History, Carlisle Barracks, Pa., vol. 1, sec. 3, pp. 3–4 (hereafter cited as H. K. Johnson, Oral History Transcript). See also Norman Paul, Oral History Transcript, 21 February 1969, tape 1, pp. 20–22, LBJ

Library. For Marine Corps distrust of the Army, see Buse, Oral History Transcript, 1971, p. 168. In his oral history Army general Harold K. Johnson argued that the Marine Corps should be kept small due to its "head down and charge" mentality. For a contemporary document linking the Joint Chiefs' lack of influence to service parochialism, see Julian Ewell, Memorandum for General Taylor, Subject: Review of Staff Functions: A Look Backward and Forward, 31 January 1962, File T–257–69, Box 17, Taylor Papers.

65. In 1949 Secretary of Defense Forrestal recommended increased centralization to ameliorate interservice rivalry.

66. Presidential adviser Walt W. Rostow observed that Kennedy entrusted "extraordinary and rarely diluted" authority to McNamara. McNamara had "undisputed primacy in the Pentagon." Walt W. Rostow, *Diffusion of Power* (New York: Macmillan, 1972), p. 161. For a description of how McNamara used changes to the National Security Act of 1947 to consolidate power in the Pentagon, see Binkley, "The Role of the Joint Chiefs of Staff," p. 169.

67. Memo, Subject: Administration of the Department of Defense, undated (filed under June 1961), Box 13, McNamara Papers. Nitze became secretary of the navy.

68. Alain Enthoven, Oral History Transcript, 29 July 1970, tape 1, p. 6, LBJ Library; David Lamar McDonald, *The Reminiscences of Admiral David Lamar McDonald* (Annapolis, Md.: U.S. Naval Institute, 1976), pp. 359–61; Shoup, Oral History Transcript, 7 April 1967, JFK Library, p. 3; Theodore C. Mataxis, interview by author, 19 February 1993; Andrew J. Goodpaster, interview by author, 9 March 1993.

69. Colin S. Gray, "What RAND Hath Wrought," *Foreign Policy* 4 (Fall 1971), pp. 111–29. The Taylor quotation is from Maxwell Taylor, "Defense Strategy Seminar," speech presented at the National War College, 8 July 1963, File T–415–69, Box 20, p. 12, Taylor Papers.

70. Nitze, *From Hiroshima to Glasnost*, p. 243; Theodore C. Mataxis, interview by author, 19 February 1993; Andrew J. Goodpaster, interview by author, 9 March 1993.

71. Alain Enthoven, History Transcript, 29 July 1970, tape 1, p. 6, LBJ Library; Alain Enthoven and Wayne Smith, *How Much Is Enough: Shaping the Defense Program, 1961–1969* (New York: Harper & Row, 1971), pp. 73–116. Quotations are from pp. 73, 89, 91. For Enthoven's views on the universal applicability of systems analysis, see pp. 307–8.

72. H. K. Johnson, Oral History Transcript, 1972–1974, part 1, sec. 6, pp. 2–3; McDonald, *Reminiscences*, pp. 359–61; Shoup, Oral History Interview, 7 April 1967, JFK Library, p. 3; Theodore C. Mataxis, interview by author, 19 February 1993; Andrew J. Goodpaster, interview by author, 9 March 1993.

73. LeMay, Oral History Transcript, 28 June 1971, p. 7, LBJ Library.

74. The commandant of the Marine Corps, Gen. David Shoup, expressed frustrations similar to General LeMay's. He noted that McNamara

would question the basis for organizations that the services had "been working on for a hell of a lot of years and perfected these organizations in combat. . . . So we really questioned his audacity . . . we really gave him a low mark in that regard." Shoup, Oral History Transcript, 7 April 1967, JFK Library, p. 3. See also Harold K. Johnson, Oral History Transcript, 1972–1974, part 2, sec. 11, 1–2; Norman Paul (assistant to McNamara), Oral History Transcript, 21 February 1969, tape 2, p. 2.

75. Andrew J. Goodpaster, interview by author, 9 March 1993. For a detailed account of this bureaucratic battle, see Robert J. Art, *The TFX Decision: McNamara and the Military* (Boston: Little, Brown & Co., 1968). Shapley, *Promise and Power*, pp. 204–23.

76. On the B-70 controversy, see Curtis LeMay, *Mission with LeMay: My Story* (Garden City, N.Y.: Doubleday, 1965), pp. 4–13. See also Michael E. Brown, *Flying Blind: The Politics of the U.S. Strategic Bomber Program* (Ithaca, N.Y.: Cornell University Press, 1992), pp. 223–24. The Air Force also resisted McNamara's initiative to revise strategic nuclear targeting. Shapley, *Promise and Power*, pp. 106–11.

77. Roger Trask, *The Secretaries of Defense: A Brief History, 1947–1985* (Washington, D.C.: Office of the Secretary of Defense Historical Office, 1985), p. 29.

78. Andrew J. Goodpaster, interview by author, 9 March 1993; McDonald, *Reminiscences*, pp. 359–60.

79. Memorandum for General Taylor from Major William Y. Smith, Subject: Review of Staff Functions: A Look Backward and Forward, File T–257–69, Box 17, Taylor Papers.

80. Memorandum for General Taylor from Colonel Julian J. Ewell, 6 February 1962, File T–257–69, Box 17, Taylor Papers.

81. Memorandum for General Taylor, 16 April 1962, File T–129–69, Box 17, Taylor Papers. McNamara did not present to President Kennedy the JCS position on a proposed decrease in the Atomic Energy Commission's budget. The memo identified Alain Enthoven as a part-time member of the "club."

82. The Kennedy White House used the term "hold-overs" to describe the members of the JCS inherited from the Eisenhower administration, Sorensen, *Kennedy*, pp. 607–8; Taylor, *Swords and Plowshares*, p. 252. Walt Rostow stated that the relationship between Kennedy and the Chiefs under Chairman Lemnitzer was "a nightmare. It was just awful." Walt Rostow, Oral History Transcript, 21 March 1969, sec. 1, p. 33.

83. Lyman Lemnitzer, Oral History Interview, part 2, Lemnitzer Papers, U.S. Army Military History Institute, 4 May 1972, pp. 56–57.

84. Earle G. Wheeler, Oral History Interview, 21 August 1969, sec. 1, pp. 3–4, LBJ Library; Taylor, *Swords and Plowshares*, p. 252.

85. Theodore C. Mataxis, interview by author, 19 February 1993. Anderson had begun interviewing members of Lemnitzer's staff to determine if he would retain them after assuming the chairmanship.

86. Decker quotation is from Edward Johnson, Memorandum of Conversation, 29 April 1961, Edward C. Keefer, ed., *FRUS, 1961–1963: Laos Crisis* (Washington, D.C.: Government Printing Office, 1994), pp. 150–54.

87. Stephen F. Kenney, *Vietnam Decision-Making: A Psychological Perspective on American Foreign Policy* (Ph.D. diss., Boston University, 1978), pp. 40–42.

88. Andrew J. Goodpaster, interview by author, 9 March 1993. Theodore C. Mataxis, interview by author, 19 February 1993. Gribkov and Smith, *Operation Anadyr*, pp. 113–114.

89. Bernard W. Rogers, interview by author, 12 March 1993, Washington, D.C., tape recording; Andrew J. Goodpaster, interview by author, 9 March 1993.

90. Taylor, *The Uncertain Trumpet*, pp. 175–176; "Trends in National Security Planning," p. 15; "The National Security Act of 1947 and the Evolution of the DOD."

91. Robert S. McNamara as quoted in James G. Blight and David A. Welch, eds., *On the Brink: Americans and Soviets Reexamine the Cuban Missile Crisis* (New York: Hill & Wang, 1989), p. 51.

92. Taylor acknowledged that the influence of the JCS was low prior to his chairmanship. Taylor, *Swords and Plowshares*, p. 260; Michael Charlton and Anthony Moncrieff, eds., *Many Reasons Why: The American Involvement in Vietnam* (New York: Hill & Wang, 1978), p. 282; Coffey, *Iron Eagle*, pp. 422, 427; Buse, Oral History Transcript, 1971, pp. 174, 179, 206–7; Theodore Mataxis, interview by author, 19 February 1993.

93. Robert Divine, "Vietnam: An Episode in the Cold War," in Lloyd Gardner, ed., Vietnam: The Early Decisions (forthcoming from Austin: University of Texas Press), p. 4.

94. Karnow, *Vietnam*, p. 265.

CHAPTER 2

1. William E. Leuchtenburg, "President Kennedy and the End of the Postwar World," in Aida DiPace Donald, ed., *John F. Kennedy and the New Frontier* (New York: Hill & Wang, 1966), pp. 131–32; first published in *American Review* (Winter 1963).

2. Donald Kagan, *On the Origins of War and the Preservation of Peace* (New York: Anchor Books, 1994), pp. 488–91. Reeves, *President Kennedy*, p. 347.

3. Gribkov and Smith, *Operation Anadyr*, pp. 118, 120. The quotation is from p. 118.

4. Kagan, *On the Origins of War*, p. 493.

5. Robert Kennedy as quoted in Reeves, *President Kennedy*, p. 263.

6. Ibid., p. 366. Gribkov and Smith, *Operation Anadyr*, pp. 91–93, 113.

7. Ibid., pp. 117, 122.

8. Ibid., pp. 117–18, 123–24.

9. Ibid., pp. 123–27.

10. Graham T. Allison, *Essence of Decision: Explaining the Cuban Missile Crisis* (Boston: Little, Brown & Co., 1971), p. 57.

11. Tape Transcript, Off-the-Record Meeting on Cuba, 16 October 1962, 6:30–7:55 P.M., p. 49, Presidential Recordings Transcripts, President's Office Files, Papers of John F. Kennedy, JFK Library. Although the quality of the audio tapes is low, it is possible to sense the atmosphere of the meetings if one listens while reading the transcript.

12. Audio tape, Meeting on Cuba, 18 October 1962, Presidential Recordings, item #31.1, JFK Library.

13. Gribkov and Smith, *Operation Anadyr*, pp. 115, 135.

14. Theodore C. Mataxis, interview by author; Jeffrey G. Barlow, "President Kennedy and His Joint Chiefs of Staff" (Ph.D. diss., University of South Carolina, 1976), pp. 202–3. On Taylor's recommendation, see Gribkov and Smith, *Operation Anadyr*, p. 135.

15. Audio Tape, Meeting on Cuba, 18 October 1962, Presidential Recordings, item #31.1, JFK Library.

16. Audio Tape, Meeting with JCS on Cuba, 19 October 1962, Presidential Recordings, item #31.2, JFK Library.

17. Gribkov and Smith, *Operation Anadyr*, pp. 115, 135.

18. Tape transcript, Cuban Missile Crisis Meetings, 27 October 1962, pp. 38–39, 41, JFK Library. Reference to laughter is from the audio tape at Papers of John F. Kennedy, Presidential Papers, President's Office Files, Presidential Recordings, JFK Library.

19. Gribkov and Smith, *Operation Anadyr*, pp. 132–33.

20. Schlesinger, *A Thousand Days*, p. 831.

21. Taylor, *Swords and Plowshares*, 269; Hilsman, *To Move a Nation*, p. 205; Sorensen, *Kennedy*, pp. 692, 705; Elie Abel, *The Missile Crisis* (New York: Bantam Books, 1968), p. 83; Robert F. Kennedy, *Thirteen Days: A Memoir of the Cuban Missile Crisis* (New York: W.W. Norton, 1969), p. 36.

22. John F. Kennedy, as quoted in Benjamin C. Bradlee, *Conversations with Kennedy* (New York: W.W. Norton, 1975), p. 122. Bradlee recalled the president's "positive lack of admiration" for the Chiefs except for Maxwell Taylor, whom he called "absolutely first class."

23. Kagan, *On the Origins of War*, pp. 493–94.

24. Ibid., p. 545.

25. Ibid., p. 546

26. Ibid.

27. Gribkov and Smith, *Operation Anadyr*, p. 137.

28. Memorandum for Colonel Ewell, 1 February 1962, File T–257–69, Box 17, Taylor Papers.

29. Robert S. McNamara, interview by James G. Blight, 21 May 1987, in Blight and Welch, *On the Brink*, p. 196.

30. Robert S. McNamara, roundtable discussion of the Cuban Missile Crisis in Blight and Welch, *On the Brink*, pp. 62–64; Barlow, "President

John F. Kennedy and His Joint Chiefs of Staff," p. 213; Korb, *The Joint Chiefs of Staff*, pp. 61, 119. There remains a good bit of contention over who said what in the Flag Plot.

31. Dr. Walter S. Poole, JCS Historical Office, letter to author, 30 July 1996.

32. Sorensen, *Kennedy*, p. 708; Arthur Schlesinger, Jr., in Blight and Welch, *On the Brink*, p. 64.

33. Goodpaster, "The Role of the Joint Chiefs of Staff in the National Security Structure," p. 225. Goodpaster noted that many of these improvements were attributable to an "urge to exercise control in finer detail."

34. Gribkov and Smith, *Operation Anadyr*, pp. 136–37.

35. For a discussion of the settlement in Laos, see William P. Bundy, unpublished manuscript, chap. 4, p. 20.

36. John F. Kennedy as quoted in the *New York Times*, 7 June 1962, p. 26.

37. William Y. Smith (WYS), Memorandum for General Taylor, 31 January 1962, Box 17, File T–257–69, Taylor Papers.

38. For Ho Chi Minh's background and education, see Karnow, *Vietnam*, pp. 130–38.

39. Franklin D. Roosevelt, as quoted in Michael Hunt, *Lyndon Johnson's War: America's Cold War Crusade in Vietnam, 1945–1968* (New York: Hill and Wang, 1996), p. 6.

40. Summarized from Hunt, *Lyndon Johnson's War*, pp. 5–9. For background to the Franco-Vietminh War (1947–1954), see William J. Duiker, *The Communist Road to Power in Vietnam* (Boulder, Col.: Westview Press, 1981), pp. 57–125.

41. Herring, *America's Longest War*, pp. 11–13.

42. Bao Dai, as quoted in Karnow, *Vietnam*, p. 190.

43. "NSC Staff Study on United States Objectives and Courses of Action with Respect to Communist Aggression in Southeast Asia," 13 February 1952, in Sen. Mike Gravel, ed., *The Pentagon Papers: The Defense Department History of United States Decisionmaking on Vietnam*, vol. 1 (Boston: Beacon Press, 1971), pp. 375–81.

44. For a summary of the military's reluctance to intervene on behalf of the French, see Robert Buzzanco, *Masters of War*, pp. 41–46.

45. Karnow, *Vietnam*, pp. 213–14. Buzzanco, *Masters of War*, p. 51. For an evaluation of this decision and much of the historical literature concerning it, see George C. Herring and Richard H. Immerman, "Eisenhower, Dulles, and Dien Bien Phu: 'The Day We Didn't Go to War' Revisited," *The Journal of American History* 71 (September 1984), pp. 343–63.

46. Karnow, *Vietnam*, pp. 197–98.

47. Spector, *Advice and Support in the Early Years: The U.S. Army in Vietnam* (Washington, D.C.: U.S. Army Center of Military History, 1983), pp. 275–302.

48. Telegram, Eyes Only for Ambassador from Secretary, 5 April 1954, p. 476; Telegram, for the Undersecretary from the Secretary, 12 May 1954, p. 507; "Lansdale Team's Report on Covert Saigon Mission in 1954 and 1955," in Gravel, ed., *Pentagon Papers*, vol. 1, pp. 573–83; Herring, *America's Longest War*, pp. 43–72.

49. William J. Duiker, *Sacred War: Nationalism and Revolution in a Divided Vietnam* (New York: McGraw Hill, 1995), p. 120.

50. William Bundy, unpublished manuscript, chap. 3, p. 33; chap. 4, pp. 5, 20.

51. Reeves, *President Kennedy*, p. 280. On early Vietnam reporting, see William Prochnau, *Once upon a Distant War* (New York: Times Books, 1995), esp. pp. 210–11.

52. Duiker, *The Communist Road to Power in Vietnam*, pp. 205–6.

53. William Conrad Gibbons, *The U.S. Government and the Vietnam War: Executive and Legislative Roles and Relationships*, part 2, 1961–1964 (Princeton, N.J.: Princeton University Press, 1986), pp. 138–39. The full text of "Report of Visit of Joint Chiefs of Staff Team to South Vietnam, January 1963" can be found in the Kennedy Library, National Security File, Country File, Vietnam.

54. Cable, Lodge to Rusk, 26 August 1963, Box 1, Papers of George McT. Kahin, National Security Archive, Washington, D.C. For discussions of this period of growing disenchantment with the Diem Regime, see Gibbons, *The U.S. Government and the Vietnam War*, part 2, 144–91. William Bundy, unpublished manuscript, chap. 9.

55. William Bundy, unpublished manuscript, chapter 9, p. 3. See also Walt W. Rostow, Oral History Transcript, 21 March 1969, sec. 1, pp. 63–70, LBJ Library.

56. Telephone conversation between George Ball and Michael Forrestal, 25 August 1963, Ball Papers, Box 7, Vietnam folder 1, item #58, LBJ Library. Frederick Nolting, *From Trust to Tragedy: The Political Memoirs of Frederick Nolting, Kennedy's Ambassador to Diem's Vietnam* (New York: Praeger, 1988), pp. 123–33; Gibbons, *The U.S. Government and the Vietnam War*, part 2, pp. 148–49; Taylor, *Swords and Plowshares*, pp. 292–96; Krulak, interview by author, 26 July 1993. Deputy Secretary of Defense Roswell Gilpatric thought that the text already had the President's approval and recalled signing off on the cable the way one "countersigns a voucher." Roswell Gilpatric, Oral History Transcript, 2 November 1982, sec. 1, p. 5, LBJ Library.

57. Bromley Smith, Memorandum of Conference with the President, August 27, 1963, Subject: Vietnam; Bromley K. Smith, Memorandum of Conference with the President, September 3, 1963, Subject: Vietnam, Papers of Bromley K. Smith, Meetings on Vietnam August–November 1963 (Diem Coup), Temporary Box 16, items #36 and #63, LBJ Library. Nolting opposed the coup option. Michael Forrestal, one of Kennedy's inner circle who favored a coup, had been instrumental in removing Nolting from his

post. Gibbons, *The U.S. Government and the Vietnam War*, part 2, 135. Lodge quotation is from Historical Division of the Joint Secretariat, *The Joint Chiefs of Staff and the War in Vietnam 1960–1968*, part 1, chap. 6, p. 27.

58. Cable, Rusk to Lodge, 29 August 1963, Box 1, Kahin Papers; Cable, Eyes Only for the Secretary (Rusk) from Lodge, 2 September 1963, Box 1, Kahin Papers.

59. Cable, Eyes Only for Ambassador from Secretary, 12 September 1963, Box 1, Kahin Papers.

60. William Bundy, unpublished manuscript, chap. 9, pp. 20–25; Gravel, *The Pentagon Papers*, vol. 2, 258–62.

61. Kennedy quotation is from Telephone Conversation between the President and Ball, Ball Papers, Box 7, Vietnam folder I, item #67, LBJ Library. Cable to Lodge, 5 October 1963, Document 143, 766–67 and Cable from CIA to Lodge, 6 October 1963, Document 145, 769, Gravel, *The Pentagon Papers*, vol. 2, pp. 766–67.

62. Bromley K. Smith, Memorandum of Conference with the President, 29 October 1963–4:20 P.M., Subject: Vietnam, Temporary Box 16, Meetings on Vietnam Aug–Nov 1963 (Diem Coup), Papers of Bromley K. Smith, LBJ Library. For confirmation of Harkins's ignorance of coup plans, see Cable, Harkins to Taylor, 30 October 1963, in Gravel, *The Papers*, vol. 2, pp. 784–85.

63. Historical Division of the Joint Secretariat, *The Joint Chiefs of Staff and the War in Vietnam*, part 1, chap. 7, p. 30.

64. Ibid., p. 31.

CHAPTER 3

1. James David Barber, *The Presidential Character: Predicting Performance in the White House*, 2d ed. (Englewood Cliffs, N.J.: Prentice Hall, 1977), p. 14.

2. This account is taken from handwritten notes on legal paper, Box 50, File #T–645–71, item 15, Taylor Papers. For a less detailed account of the events of November 1, 1963, see Taylor, *Swords and Plowshares*, p. 301.

3. The general had an eye for talented officers. Two of the officers on whom he relied most heavily were Rogers and Goodpaster. Both were Rhodes scholars and held Ph.D.s in political science from Princeton University. Rogers had served previously as Taylor's aide when the general was superintendent of West Point. Goodpaster had served for five years as military assistant to President Eisenhower and remained in the Kennedy White House for several weeks to help the new president's national security team effect the transition between administrations. When Taylor became chairman of the JCS, he had Goodpaster reassigned to the Pentagon from a command in Europe. Goodpaster, interview by author, 9 March 1993; Taylor, *Swords and Plowshares*, p. 253.

4. Handwritten notes on legal paper, Box 50, File #T–645–71, item 15, Taylor Papers; Taylor, *Swords and Plowshares*, p. 301; Bernard W. Rogers, interview by author, 12 March 1993.

5. Taylor had regarded the Air Force as the protector of the "great fallacy of massive retaliation." He charged the Air Force with not fully discharging its obligations to provide close air support for the Army. He argued that the Army should be freed from Air Force "tutelage" and "have its own tactical air support and tactical air lift." Taylor, *The Uncertain Trumpet*, pp. 168–74.

6. Coffey, *Iron Eagle*, p. 43; Sorensen, *Kennedy*, p. 608; Reeves, *President Kennedy*, p. 182.

7. Maxwell D. Taylor, Oral History Interview, 18 October 1983, John F. Kennedy Library, Boston, Mass.; Theodore C. Mataxis, interview by author, 19 February 1993; Taylor, *Swords and Plowshares*, pp. 282–87.

8. LeMay, as quoted in Coffey, *Iron Eagle*, p. 423.

9. Maxwell Taylor, as quoted in Dino A. Brugioni, *Eyeball to Eyeball: The Inside Story of the Cuban Missile Crisis* (New York: Random House, 1990), p. 226.

10. Bernard W. Rogers, interview by author, 12 March 1993.

11. Shoup Oral History Transcript, JFK Library, 7 April 1967, pp. 4–5; for a brief description of Shoup's manner, see "Synopsis of Interview with Lt. Gen. William Jones," Marine Corps Historical Center, Washington Naval Yard, Washington, D.C.; Lt. Gen. Henry W. Buse, USMC (Deputy to Generals Shoup and Greene), Oral History Interview, 1986, Marine Corps Historical Center, Washington, D.C., p. 180. The quotation is from Shoup, Oral History Transcript, p. 35.

12. Contemporary observers recognized this division among the nation's professional military. See Morris Janowitz, *The Professional Soldier: A Social and Political Portrait* (Glencoe, Ill.: Free Press, 1960), pp. 272–77. Janowitz termed the competing doctrines "absolutist" and "pragmatic." The second decade of the Cold War witnessed a proliferation of studies on limited war theory. Most prominent was Robert Endicott Osgood, *Limited War: The Challenge to American Strategy* (Chicago: University of Chicago Press, 1957). See also Seymour J. Deitchman, *Limited War and Defense Policy* (Cambridge, Mass.: MIT Press, 1964).

13. Hilsman, *To Move a Nation*, p. 129. Shoup had opposed military intervention during the 1961 Laotian crisis. *FRUS, 1961–1963: Laos Crisis*, p. 170.

14. In late 1961, for example, Taylor had recommended deploying U.S. troops to South Vietnam as a show of force. He observed at the time that "the risks of backing into a major Asian war by way of South Vietnam are present but are not impressive." Cable from Taylor to Kennedy on Introduction of U.S. Troops, 1 November 1961, *The Pentagon Papers as Published by the* New York Times (New York: Quadrangle Books, 1971), p. 148.

15. Taylor, *The Uncertain Trumpet*, pp. 14–18.

16. Geelhoed, *Charles E. Wilson*, p. 125.

17. For the Navy's reaction to the removal of Anderson, see McDonald, *Reminiscences*, pp. 350, 378; quotations are from p. 378. In the same oral history, McDonald boasted of his ability to sell his programs and positions to civilian officials within the Pentagon, the administration, and the Congress. He was not averse, for example, to forging "friendships" to elicit support for the Navy's agenda. Secretary of the Navy Nitze lauded McDonald's judgment concerning the "politics of the Washington bureaucratic scene." Nitze, *From Hiroshima to Glasnost*, p. 253. See also Korb, *The Joint Chiefs of Staff*, p. 62.

18. Hanson W. Baldwin, "The McNamara Monarchy," *Saturday Evening Post*, 9 March 1963; "The Management Team," *Time*, 5 February 1965, pp. 22–33B.

19. Webb and Cole, *The Chairmen of the Joint Chiefs of Staff*, pp. 143–44.

20. Palmer, *The 25-Year War*, p. 20; Bernard W. Rogers, interview by author, 12 March 1993.

21. For Wheeler's role in the Ap Bac report, see Neil Sheehan, *A Bright Shining Lie: John Paul Vann and America in Vietnam* (New York: Random House, 1988), pp. 298–304, 341–42.

22. For JCS views on the possibility of a coup, see Harold K. Johnson, Handwritten Notes on a Meeting of the JCS, 19 August 1963, Box 126, H. K. Johnson Papers.

23. Message, Harkins to Taylor, 30 October 1963, in Gravel, *The Pentagon Papers*, vol. 2, pp. 784–85; Theodore C. Mataxis, interview by author, 19 February 1993.

24. Bernard W. Rogers, interview by author, 12 March 1993; Andrew G. Goodpaster, interview by author, 9 March 1993.

25. Taylor, *Swords and Plowshares*, p. 301; Bromley Smith, Memo of Conference with the President, 1 November 1963, 10:00 A.M., Papers of Bromley Smith, Temporary Box 16, Meetings on Vietnam Aug–Nov 1963 (Diem Coup), item #8, LBJ Library.

26. Bromley Smith, Memo of Conference with the President, 29 October 1963, Subject: Vietnam, Papers of Bromley Smith, Temporary Box 16, Meetings on Vietnam Aug–Nov 1963 (Diem Coup), item #11, LBJ Library.

27. Bromley Smith, Memo of Conference with the President, 2 November 1963, 4:30 P.M., Subject: Vietnam, Papers of Bromley Smith, Temporary Box 16, Meetings on Vietnam, Aug–Nov 1963 (Diem Coup), item #1, LBJ Library.

28. Bromley Smith, Memo of Conference with the President, 2 November 1963, 9:15 A.M., Subject: Vietnam, Papers of Bromley Smith, Temporary Box 16, Meetings on Vietnam Aug–Nov 1963 (Diem Coup), item #4, LBJ Library.

29. Ibid.

30. Gravel, *The Pentagon Papers*, vol. 3, p. 27.

31. Taylor, *Swords and Plowshares*, p. 302

32. Mataxis, interview by author, 19 February 1993; Bernard W. Rogers, interview by author, 12 March 1993; Taylor, *Swords and Plowshares*, pp. 302–3.

33. Bill Moyers's notes taken after the meeting as cited in Gittinger, *The Johnson Years*, p. 11. See also McGeorge Bundy's comments on the same page.

34. Tom Wicker, *JFK and LBJ: The Influence of Personality upon Politics* (New York: William Morrow, 1968), pp. 198, 203, 205; Gibbons, *The U.S. Government and the Vietnam War*, vol. 2, 209; Lyndon B. Johnson, *The Vantage Point* (New York: Holt, Rinehart & Winston, 1971), p. 43.

35. George Reedy, *LBJ: A Memoir* (New York: Andrews and McMeel, 1982), p. 147; Thomas Hughes in Gittinger, *The Johnson Years*, pp. 12–13.

36. Lyndon B. Johnson, Memorandum for the President, 23 May 1961, Subject: Mission to Southeast Asia, India, and Pakistan, NSF, Files of McGeorge Bundy, Box 18, Southeast Asia and the Vice President's Memo to the President, LBJ Library.

37. Before a Joint Session of Congress on 27 November, Johnson announced, "John Kennedy said, 'Let us begin,' and I say, 'Let us continue.'" Jack Valenti in Gittinger, *The Johnson Years*, p. 12. For Johnson's impressions of Rusk and McNamara, see Wicker, *JFK and LBJ*, pp. 197–98.

38. Bromley Smith, Meeting at the State Department, 31 August 1963, 11:00 A.M., Subject: Vietnam, Papers of Bromley Smith, Temporary Box 16, Meetings on Vietnam Aug–Nov 1963, LBJ Library.

39. Telephone Conversation Between President and Senator William Fulbright, 2 December 1963, 7:01 P.M., Lyndon Johnson Papers, Tapes and Transcripts of Telephone Conversations and Meetings, Box 1, LBJ Library. Robert Kennedy observed that Johnson "was against—strongly against—the coup. And so he was bitter about it." Robert F. Kennedy as quoted in Merle Miller, *Lyndon: An Oral Biography* (New York: G. P. Putnam's Sons, 1980), p. 380.

40. NSAM 273, 26 November 1963, *FRUS: Vietnam, 1963*, pp. 637–40.

41. Taylor, *Swords and Plowshares*, p. 304; Letter from General Taylor to President Johnson, 26 November 1963, Box 50, Folder 36–71D, item #2, Taylor Papers.

42. Taylor, *Swords and Plowshares*, pp. 304–5; Memorandum of Conference with the President, 29 November 1963, 10:00 A.M., Box 22, File T–236–69, Taylor Papers.

43. Memorandum of Conference with the President, 29 November 1963, 10:00 A.M., Box 22, File T–236–69, Taylor Papers.

44. Doris Kearns, *Lyndon Johnson and the American Dream* (New York: Harper & Row, 1976), p. 170. See also Miller, *Lyndon: An Oral Biography*, p. 336.

45. McGeorge Bundy, as quoted in Miller, *Lyndon, An Oral Biography*, p. 386.

46. For the president's preoccupation with loyalty, see Kearns, *Lyndon Johnson and the American Dream*, pp. 315–17; Robert F. Kennedy, *Robert Kennedy in His Own Words: The Unpublished Recollections of the Kennedy Years*, Edwin O. Guthman and Jeffrey Shulman, eds. (New York: Bantam Books, 1988), pp. 412–14; Chester Cooper, *The Lost Crusade* (New York: Dodd, Mead, 1970), p. 223; Townsend Hoopes, *The Limits of Intervention* (New York: David McKay Company, 1969), p. 31; Henry F. Graff, *The Tuesday Cabinet: Deliberation and Decision on Peace and War Under Lyndon B. Johnson* (Englewood Cliffs, N.J.: Prentice Hall, 1970), p. 6; Irving L. Janis, *Victims of Groupthink: A Psychological Study of Foreign Policy Decisions and Fiascoes* (Boston: Houghton Mifflin, 1972), p. 106; Alexander George, *Presidential Decisionmaking in Foreign Policy: The Effective Use of Information and Advice* (Boulder, Colo.: Westview Press, 1980), pp. 91, 95; Hugh Sydney, *A Very Personal Presidency: Lyndon Johnson in the White House* (New York: Atheneum, 1968), pp. 42, 70–96. Longtime Johnson aide Harry McPherson observed that many of the president's insecurities were based on very real concerns about political opposition from the Kennedy family and their allies. Harry McPherson, Oral History Transcript, 19 December 1968, tape 3, 25–29, Lyndon B. Johnson Library. Others argue that his obsession with loyalty was rooted in a deep-seated insecurity. Barber, *The Presidential Character*, pp. 78–87; Hyman L. Muslin and Thomas H. Jobe, *Lyndon Johnson, the Tragic Self: A Psychohistorical Portrait* (New York: Insight Books, 1991), pp. 84–85, 128–29, 183–200. George Herring, *LBJ and Vietnam*, p. 48.

47. Rowland Evans and Robert Novak, *Lyndon Johnson: The Exercise of Power, A Political Biography* (New York: New American Library, 1966), pp. 16, 47, 191; Carl Vinson, Oral History Transcript, 24 May 1970, LBJ Library.

48. Summarized from Robert A. Caro, *The Years of Lyndon Johnson*, vol. 2, *Means of Ascent* (New York: Alfred A. Knopf, 1990), pp. 35–53.

49. Summarized from Caro, *Means of Ascent*, pp. 35–53; quotations are from pp. 47–49.

50. Evans and Novak, *Lyndon Johnson*, pp. 16, 47, 191; Carl Vinson, Oral History Transcript, 24 May 1970, LBJ Library.

51. Evans and Novak, *Lyndon Johnson*, pp. 55–58.

52. Telephone Conversation President to Gilpatric, 23 December 1963, Lyndon Johnson Papers, Tapes and Transcripts, Box 1, item #149, LBJ Library. Longtime Johnson aide Harry McPherson recalled that Johnson "had little respect for many generals and admirals." Harry McPherson, *A Political Education: A Washington Memoir* (Boston: Houghton Mifflin, 1988), p. 118.

53. Telephone Conversations with Senator John McClellan (item #21), Congressman Carl Vinson (item #22), Congressman Bill Dawson (item #24), Senator John Stennis (item #25), and Congressman Jack Brooks (item #26), 2 December 1963, Lyndon Johnson Papers, Tapes and Transcripts of Telephone Conversations and Meetings, Box #1, December 1963 [1 of 3], LBJ Library.

54. Adam Yarmolinsky, Oral History Transcript, 13 July 1970, LBJ Library

55. The Johnson quotation is from Telephone Conversation Between the President and [Congressman] Joseph Campbell, 1 December 1963, 5:30 P.M., Lyndon Johnson Papers, Tapes and Transcripts of Telephone Conversations and Meetings, Box 1, December 1963 [1 of 3], item #10, LBJ Library.

56. Telephone Conversation Between the President and the Secretary of Defense, 10 December 1963, Lyndon Johnson Papers, Tapes and Transcripts of Telephone Conversations and Meetings, Box 1, item #109, LBJ Library.

57. President Johnson to Secretary of Defense, 12 December 1963, Lyndon Johnson Papers, Tapes and Transcripts of Telephone Conversations and Meetings, Box 1, December 1963 [3 of 3], item #140, LBJ Library.

58. Telephone Conversation between Sargent Shriver and Lyndon Johnson, 1 February 1964, 6:28 P.M., Lyndon Johnson Papers, Tapes and Transcripts of Telephone Conversations and Meetings, Box 2, item #1815, LBJ Library.

59. Taylor, *The Uncertain Trumpet*, p. 176.

60. Taylor, *Swords and Plowshares*, p. 253; Andrew G. Goodpaster, interview by author, 9 March 1993. During this interview, although Goodpaster described his increased responsibilities, he deemphasized the significance of his position.

61. Maxwell Taylor letter to McGeorge Bundy, 2 December 1963 and letter to Richard B. Russell, 9 December 1963, Box 22, File T–236–69, Taylor Papers. Later in the month Taylor wrote to the chairman of the House Armed Services Committee to thank him for his assistance in removing "the obstacles which have been in the path of General Goodpaster's confirmation."

62. Letter Curtis E. LeMay to Maxwell Taylor, 28 August 1962, and Letter George W. Anderson to Maxwell Taylor, 30 August 1962, Box 22, File T–236–69, Taylor Papers.

63. Hanson Baldwin, "Joint Chiefs Split over Move to Create New Post of Deputy to the Chairman," *New York Times*, 6 December 1963, p. 17.

64. Maxwell D. Taylor, Memorandum for Record, 6 December 1963, Subject: Discussion with the Joint Chiefs of Staff on Hanson Baldwin Article . . . , Box 22, File T–236–69. Taylor's memo confirms the accuracy of the Baldwin article. For Taylor's effort at damage control see, Maxwell Taylor, letter to Carl Vinson, 24 December 1963, Box 22, File T–236–69, Taylor Papers. Taylor's second letter to Vinson indicated that his effort to allay the congressman's concerns was successful. The first letter is unavailable in Taylor's papers.

65. "President's remarks to the Pentagon, Wednesday, Dec. 11," NSF, Agency File, Box 11, Defense Dept., vol. I [2 of 2] 11/63, item 91, LBJ Library.

66. Telegram, CINCPAC to Secretary of State, "Situation in GVN," 5 December 1963, Box 1, Kahin Papers.

67. Telegram for Lodge from the Secretary of State, 6 December 1963, National Security File—Country File—Vietnam, Box 1, Vietnam Cables vol. 1 11/63–12/63 [2 of 2], item #44; Tom Wicker, "Johnson Affirms Faith in Rusk, Asks Patience in World Affairs," New York Times, 6 December 1963, p. 10.

68. In a White House staff meeting on 10 December, McGeorge Bundy expressed exasperation over the lack of useful discussion in connection with Vietnam. Meetings often deteriorated into "gasbag" affairs in which those who knew least spoke most. William Y. Smith, Notes on Daily Meetings, 10 December 1963, Box 25, Taylor Papers.

69. A CIA memo reported the difficult relations between the two men. Harkins had told the Vietnamese generals that it was not the time to run a coup at the same time that Lodge was trying to support this effort. Telegram to Director from Embassy, 16 November 1963, President's Office Files, Countries, Vietnam Security 1963, Box 128 U, John F. Kennedy Library.

70. Historical Division of the Joint Secretariat, The Joint Chiefs of Staff and the War in Vietnam, part 1, chap. 7, pp. 9, 11.

71. Robert S. McNamara, Memo for Record, Conversation with Vice President Tho, 30 September 1963, Box 50, Folder 10–71B, item #22, Taylor Papers; Memorandum for the President from the Secretary of Defense, 2 October 1963, Subject: Report of the Taylor-McNamara Mission to South Vietnam, in Gravel, The Pentagon Papers, vol. 2, pp. 751–66.

72. Gravel, The Pentagon Papers, vol. 2, pp. 494–96.

73. Roswell Gilpatric, Oral History Transcript, 2 November 1982, LBJ Library, sec. 1, p. 12. William Bundy, unpublished manuscript, Chapter 4, p. 8.

74. William Bundy, unpublished manuscript, chap. 3, p. 3. Bundy recalled that Kennedy had been unsure about on whom to rely for Vietnam. It was "up for grabs."

75. Highlights of Discussions in Saigon, 18–20 December 1963, 21 December 1963, Box 1, Kahin Papers. McNamara, during his previous inspection tours to the beleaguered South, had applied his quantitative management techniques to the American advisory effort. During his first trip to South Vietnam in May of 1962, the Secretary of Defense exclaimed contentedly that "every quantitative measurement we have shows that we're winning this war." Robert S. McNamara as quoted by Neil Sheehan, A Bright Shining Lie (New York: Random House, 1988), p. 290. In December 1963, McNamara admitted that "the coup came when there was a downward trend which was more serious than was reported and, therefore, more serious than realized." Memo for the Record by Robert S. McNamara, 21 December 1963, in Gareth Porter, ed., Vietnam: The Definitive Documentation of Human Decisions, vol. 2 (Standfordville, N.Y.: Earl M. Coleman Enterprises, 1979), p. 233.

76. Telegram from Commander MACV(COMUSMACV) to CINCPAC, 27 December 1963, Subject: Weekly Headway Report, NSF-CF-VN, Box 1, Vietnam Cables Vol. 2, item #6, LBJ Library.

77. Robert S. McNamara, Telegram for Admiral Felt, 21 December 1963, Subject: Vietnam Infiltration, NSF-CF-Vietnam, Box 1, item #5, LBJ Library.

78. Gravel, *The Pentagon Papers*, vol. 2, pp. 150–51.

79. Coffey, *Iron Eagle*, pp. 427–28; Harold K. Johnson, JCS Meeting 181400 November 1963, Notes on Meetings of the JCS Sept-Dec 1963, Box 126, H. K. Johnson Papers. Johnson was Operations Deputy for General Wheeler until he became Army Chief of Staff in July 1964.

80. Gravel, *The Pentagon Papers*, vol. 3, p. 151.

81. Gibbons, *The U.S. Government and the Vietnam War*, vol. 2, p. 213; Gravel, *The Pentagon Papers*, vol. 2, p. 151; Michael Forrestal, Memorandum for the President, 11 December 1963, Box 1, Kahin Papers.

82. Victor H. Krulak, interview by author, 26 July 1993; Gravel, *The Pentagon Papers*, vol. 3, p. 151.

83. Coffey, *Iron Eagle*, p. 422.

84. Letter, Maxwell D. Taylor to President, 21 December 1963, Taylor Papers.

85. Robert S. McNamara as quoted in Henry L. Trewhitt, *McNamara: His Ordeal in the Pentagon* (New York: Harper & Row, 1971), p. 237.

86. For Johnson's devotion to work, see Harry McPherson, Oral History Transcript, LBJ Library, tape 2, pp. 29–32. Johnson admired the same quality in McNamara. Henry Trewhitt, *McNamara*, p. 257. For the facility with which both men misled Congress, see Telephone Conversation Between the President and the Secretary of Defense, p. 10, December 1963, Lyndon Johnson Papers, Tapes and Transcripts of Telephone Conversations and Meetings, Box 1, item #109, LBJ Library.

87. Telephone Conversation, President to McNamara, 25 December 1963, Box 1, item #160, Lyndon Johnson Papers, Tapes and Transcripts of Telephone Conversations and Meetings, LBJ Library.

88. On the intensification of the Communist effort after the Diem coup, see Duiker, *The Communist Road to Power in Vietnam*, pp. 220–23, 227–31. The situation in the province of Long An was representative of South Vietnam as a whole. See Jeffrey Race, *War Comes to Long An: Revolutionary Conflict in a Vietnamese Province* (Berkeley: University of California Press, 1972), pp. 133–34. For the percentages of the country under Viet Cong control, see William Duiker, *Sacred War: Nationalism and Revolution in a Divided Vietnam* (New York: McGraw Hill, 1995), pp. 164–65.

CHAPTER 4

1. Cyrus Vance, Oral History Transcript, 9 March 1970, sec. 3, LBJ Library, p. 11.

2. McGeorge Bundy and Jack Valenti in Gittinger, *The Johnson Years*, p. 14.

3. Public Letter to General Minh from the President, 31 December 1963, *FRUS: Vietnam, August–December 1963*, pp. 745–46.

4. Telegram, Eyes Only for Ambassador Lodge from the President, 30 December 1963, Box 1, Kahin Papers

5. Shoup, Oral History Transcript, 7 April 1967, JFK Library, p. 35; Buse, Oral History Transcript, 1971, p. 236.

6. Harold K. Johnson, Notes on JCS Meeting for 8 January 1964, 2:00 P.M., Box 126, Notes on Meetings of the Joint Chiefs of Staff Jan.–Apr. 1964, H. K. Johnson Papers; Buse, Oral History Transcript, 1971, p. 217.

7. National Security Action Memorandum 273, 26 November 1963, in Porter, ed., *Vietnam: The Definitive Documentation of Human Decisions*, vol. 2, p. 221 (emphasis added).

8. Joint Chiefs of Staff Memorandum 46–64, 22 January 1964, Subject: Vietnam and Southeast Asia, in Gravel, *The Pentagon Papers*, vol. 3, pp. 496–99. See also Historical Division of the Joint Secretariat, *The Joint Chiefs of Staff and the War in Vietnam*, part 1, chap. 8, pp. 27–31.

9. For an insightful discussion of the differences in strategic objectives between the Johnson administration and the JCS, see Herbert Y. Schandler, "America and Vietnam: The Failure of Strategy, 1964–67," in *Vietnam as History*, ed. Peter Braestrup (Washington, D.C.: University Press of America, 1984), especially pp. 23–24. The author has also benefited from conversations with Dr. Schandler.

10. Telegram from Ambassador Lodge to Secretary Rusk, 30 January, 6:00 P.M., Box 1, Kahin Papers; Telegram from Ambassador Lodge to Secretary Rusk, 31 January, 10:00 A.M., Box 1, Kahin Papers; Lyndon Baines Johnson, handwritten letter to General Khanh, 2 February 1964, Box 1, Kahin Papers.

11. Michael Forrestal, Oral History Transcript, 3 November 1969, sec. 1, LBJ Library, p. 23; McGeorge Bundy, Memorandum for the President, 4 February 1964, Subject: Your Luncheon with Secretaries Rusk and McNamara, NSF-Files of McGeorge Bundy, Box 19, Luncheons with the President, vol. 1, part 2, item #130, LBJ Library.

12. McGeorge Bundy, Memorandum for the President, 4 February 1964, Subject: Your Luncheon with Secretaries Rusk and McNamara, NSF-Files of McGeorge Bundy, Box 19, Luncheons with the President, vol. 1, part 2, item #130, LBJ Library.

13. Samuel Zaffiri, *Westmoreland: A Biography of General William C. Westmoreland* (New York: William Morrow, 1994), pp. 91, 93–95. See also, Taylor, *Swords and Plowshares*, p. 50; William C. Westmoreland, interview by author, audiotape, 27 October 1995, West Point, N.Y.

14. Andrew J. Goodpaster, interview by author, 9 March 1993.

15. McGeorge Bundy, Memorandum for the President, 4 February 1964, Subject: Your Luncheon with Secretaries Rusk and McNamara, NSF-Files of McGeorge Bundy, Box 19, Luncheons with the President, vol. 1, part 2,

item #130, LBJ Library; National Security Action Memorandum 280, 14 February 1964, NSF-NSAMs, Box 2, item 6, LBJ Library.

16. Historical Division of the Joint Secretariat, *The Joint Chiefs of Staff and the War in Vietnam*, part 1, chap. 8, p. 25.

17. Harold K. Johnson, JCS Meeting with the Sullivan Committee, 19 February 1964—2:00 P.M., Notes on Meetings of the JCS Jan.–Apr. 1964, Box 126, H. K. Johnson Papers.

18. Ibid.

19. Michael Forrestal, Oral History Transcript, 3 November 1969, sec. 1, LBJ Library, p. 27.

20. Historical Division of the Joint Secretariat, *The Joint Chiefs of Staff and the War in Vietnam*, part 1, chap. 8, pp. 26, 29.

21. Ibid., chap. 9, pp. 3–4.

22. John Johns (member of the Army staff under Army Chiefs Wheeler and Johnson), interview by author, 11 March 1993, National Defense University, Washington, D.C., audio recording. Having recently returned from Vietnam, Johns, a student at the Army Command and Staff College, challenged Greene's optimistic assessment. See also Buse, Oral History Transcript, 1971, p. 205.

23. Buse, Oral History Transcript, 1971, pp. 177–78; Rogers interview by author, 12 March 1993.

24. Telegram for the President from Lodge, 20 February 1964, Box 1, Kahin Papers.

25. Michael V. Forrestal, Memorandum for Record, 20 February 1964, Subject: South Vietnam, NSF-CF-VN, Box 2, Vietnam Memos and Miscellaneous, vol. 4 2/64–3/64, item #99, LBJ Library; Andrew J. Goodpaster, interview by author, 9 March 1993.

26. Telegram for Lodge from the President, 21 February 1964, NSF-CF-VN, Box 2, Vietnam Cables vol. 5 3/64, item #45, LBJ Library. The president concluded with, "I value these direct exchanges with you on top policy matters. We should keep them up."

27. General Goodpaster acknowledged that diffusing pressure to do more was one of the purposes of the trip but stated that its primary purpose was to find a solution to the deteriorating military situation. On Johnson's preoccupation with the election, see William Bundy, unpublished manuscript, chap. 1, p. 2; Walt Rostow, interview by author, 21 October 1993; Gittinger, *The Johnson Years*, pp. 24–25.

28. Telephone Conversation between Dean Rusk and Lyndon Johnson, 2 March 1964, 11:35 A.M., Recordings of Conversations and Meetings, Recordings of Telephone Conversations, White House Series, Tape WH6403.01, Citation #2305, LBJ Library.

29. Telephone Conversation between Robert McNamara and Lyndon Johnson, 2 March 1964, 11:00 A.M., Recordings of Conversations and Meetings, Recordings of Telephone Conversations, White House Series, Tape WH6403.01, Citation #2301, LBJ Library.

30. Johnson recounted the meeting in a taped telephone conversation with McGeorge Bundy. Telephone Conversation between McGeorge Bundy and Lyndon Johnson, 4 March 1964, 7:26 P.M., Transcripts of Telephone Conversations and Meetings, Box 3, Transcript #2347, LBJ Library.

31. Ibid.

32. Ibid. Memo for Record, 4 March 1964, "Meeting of the Joint Chiefs of Staff with the President," Box 50, File T–36–71, Taylor Papers.

33. Letter, Senator Symington to President Johnson, 12 February 1964, with cover letter to Maxwell Taylor from Jack Valenti, 18 February 1964; Taylor Draft Letter for President's Signature, undated, Box 50, File T–36–71, Taylor Papers.

34. In a February 1964 meeting on Cuba during which LeMay pressed for stronger action in the continuing effort to undermine Castro's regime, Taylor warned the JCS that their new commander in chief "dislikes split advice." Harold K. Johnson, Special JCS Meeting 08 February 1964, 10:00 A.M., Notes on Meetings of the JCS Jan.–Apr. 1964, Box 126, H. K. Johnson Papers.

35. Harold K. Johnson, Special JCS Meeting on Vietnam, 29 February, 9:00 A.M., Notes on Meetings of the JCS Jan.–Apr. 1964, Box 126, H. K. Johnson Papers.

36. Memo for Record, 4 March 1964, "Meeting of the Joint Chiefs of Staff with the President," Box 50, File T–36–71, Taylor Papers. Taylor outlined three phases of military action. Phase 1 would focus exclusively on reconnaissance over North Vietnam to make a "good case" for further military action. Phase 2 would include limited aerial attacks on selected targets and preparations to execute contingency plans that would constitute Phase 3.

37. Telephone Conversation between Dean Rusk and Lyndon Johnson, 25 February 1964, 11:40 A.M., Recordings of Conversations and Meetings, Recordings of Telephone Conversations, White House Series, Tape WH6402.21, Citation # 2190 , LBJ Library.

38. Telephone Conversation between Walt Rostow and Lyndon Johnson, 4 March 1964, 6:05 P.M., Transcripts of Telephone Conversations and Meetings, Box 3, Transcript #2346, LBJ Library. See also Walt W. Rostow, Draft Memo to the President, 25 April 1964, Box 13, Southeast Asia, Item #49a, Papers of Walt W. Rostow, LBJ Library. The memo refers to the 4 March 1964 telephone conversation. Rostow, interview by author, 21 October 1993.

39. Telephone Conversation between Frank Stanton and Lyndon Johnson, 6 February 1964, 12:31 P.M., Recordings of Conversations and Meetings, Recordings of Telephone Conversations, White House Series, Tape WH6402.07, Citation #1907, LBJ Library.

40. Telephone Conversation between Robert McNamara and Lyndon Johnson, 6 February 1964, 1:01 P.M., Recordings of Conversations and Meetings, Recordings of Telephone Conversations, White House Series, Tape WH6402.07, Citation #1912, LBJ Library.

41. Telephone Conversation between McGeorge Bundy and Lyndon Johnson, 4 March 1964, 7:26 P.M., Transcripts of Telephone Conversations and Meetings, Box 3, Transcript #2347, LBJ Library.

42. Telephone Conversation between Robert McNamara and Lyndon Johnson, 25 February 1964, 11:45 A.M., Recordings of Conversations and Meetings, Recordings of Telephone Conversations, White House Series, Tape WH6402.21, Citation #2191, LBJ Library.

43. William P. Bundy, Memorandum for Messrs. Sullivan, McNaughton, Yarmolinsky, 2 March 1964, Subject: Attached Memorandum for the President, NSF-CF-VN, Box 2, Vietnam Memos and Miscellaneous, vol. 4, 2/64–3/64, item #94, LBJ Library; William P. Bundy, Note to Members of Secretary McNamara's Trip and attached Draft Memorandum for the President, 5 March 1964, NSF-CF-VN, items #69a and #69b, LBJ Library. The final report is in Gravel, *The Pentagon Papers*, vol. 3, pp. 499–510.

44. Memorandum from the Secretary of Defense to the Members of the McNamara-Taylor Mission to Vietnam, 5 March 1964, *FRUS: Vietnam, 1964*, pp. 133–34.

45. Cover Memorandum, McGeorge Bundy to the President, 8 March 1964 NSF-CF-VN, Box 2, Vietnam Cables, vol. 5, item #69, LBJ Library; H. K. Johnson, Notes on JCS Meeting, 2 March 1964–2:00 P.M., Notes on Meetings of the JCS Jan.–Apr. 1964, Box 126, H. K. Johnson Papers.

46. Harold K. Johnson, Handwritten Notes on JCS Meeting, 13 March 1964–2:00 P M , Notes on Meetings of the JCS Jan.–Apr. 1964, Box 126, H. K. Johnson Papers.

47. Norman S. Paul, Oral History Transcript, 21 February 1969, LBJ Library, tape 1, pp. 62–65. Paul, McNamara's Assistant Secretary of Defense for Legislative Affairs, recalled that McNamara regarded intelligence and desire as the only two qualifications needed. Military experience was held in low regard relative to these attributes. McDonald, *Reminiscences*, pp. 360–61.

48. McDonald, *Reminiscences*, pp. 360–61.

49. H. K. Johnson, Notes on JCS Meeting, 2 March 1964, Box 126, Notes on Meetings of the JCS Jan.–Apr. 1964, H. K. Johnson Papers.

50. I have chosen the term "graduated pressure" because it is the term used most often at the time. Others have called McNamara's strategy graduated response, gradual response, and incrementalism.

51. The McNamara quotation is from an interview with James G. Blight, 21 May 1987, in Blight and Welch, *On the Brink*, pp. 193–94.

52. The document suggests, for example, high-level reconnaissance flights and notes that such action would be a "severe blow to the sovereignty of North Vietnam and suggests other more serious actions as in the Cuba pattern." Annex A, "U.S. Military Action Against North Viet Nam—An Analysis," Papers of Paul C. Warnke, Files of John McNaughton, Box 2, McNTN V–"Planning Pressures"–1964(1), item #5, LBJ Library.

53. See, for example, Robert McNamara, Speech Delivered at the James A. Forrestal Memorial Awards Dinner (3/64), NSF-CF-VN, Box 3, Vietnam

Cables, vol. 6, item #51, LBJ Library; Dean Rusk, Oral History Transcript, 26 September 1969, LBJ Library, interview 2, tape 1, 4–6.

54. Robert S. McNamara as quoted in Blight and Welch, *On the Brink*, p. 194; Rusk, Oral History Transcript, 26 September 1969, LBJ Library, interview 2, tape 1, p. 24.

55. Eugene Zuckert, Oral History Transcript, 18 March 1969, LBJ Library, sec. 1, p. 31.

56. Coffey, *Iron Eagle*, p. 427.

57. Letter, Arthur W. Barber to Mr. Charles Corhran (LBJ Library), 26 February 1977, Papers of Arthur W. Barber, LBJ Library.

58. Taylor, *Swords and Plowshares*, p. 310.

59. Memorandum for the President from the Secretary of Defense, 16 March 1964, in Gravel, *The Pentagon Papers*, vol. 3, pp. 499–510.

60. Historical Division of the Joint Secretariat, *The Joint Chiefs of Staff and the War in Vietnam*, part 1, chap. 9, p. 18.

61. Harold K. Johnson, Notes on JCS Meeting, 14 March–11:00 A.M., Box 126, Notes on Meetings of the JCS Jan–Apr 1964, H. K. Johnson Papers. Marine Corps general Buse described Wheeler as "apathetic." Buse, Oral History Transcript, 1971, p. 208.

62. Memorandum for the Secretary of Defense (JCSM–222–64), 14 March 1964, Box 50, File #T36–71, Taylor Papers. The referenced memo (this document has yet to be declassified) is JCSM–174–64, Subject: Vietnam, 2 March 1964.

63. The account of this meeting is from Bromley Smith, Summary Record of the National Security Council Meeting No. 524, 17 March 1964, NSF, NSC Meetings, vol. 1, tab 5, item #2, LBJ Library. Emphasis added to Maxwell Taylor's comments. Comparisons between McNamara's and Taylor's comments are made with JCS positions as recorded in Harold K. Johnson, Notes on JCS Meeting, 14 March–11:00 A.M., Box 126, Notes on Meetings of the JCS Jan.–Apr. 1964, H. K. Johnson Papers. Memorandum for the Secretary of Defense (JCSM–222–64), 14 March 1964, Box 50, File #T36–71, Taylor Papers.

64. Bromley Smith, Summary Record of the National Security Council Meeting No. 524, 17 March 1964, NSF, NSC Meetings, vol. 1, tab 5, item #2, LBJ Library (emphasis added). On McNamara's effort to dissuade Khanh from action against North Vietnam, see Telephone Conversation between Lyndon Johnson and Richard Russell, 27 May 1964, 10:55 A.M., Recordings of Conversations and Meetings, White House Series, Tape WH6405.10, Citation #3519-3521, LBJ Library.

65. William Y. Smith, Memorandum for Mr. Bundy, 17 March 1964, Subject Vietnam, NSF-CF-VN, Box 2, Vietnam Cables, vol. 5, item #59b. See also Smith's cover letter, item #59a, LBJ Library.

66. Ibid.

67. William Y. Smith, Memorandum for Mr. Bundy, 17 March 1964, Subject Vietnam, NSF-CF-VN, Box 2, Vietnam Cables, vol. 5, item #58, LBJ Library.

68. C. V. Clifton, Memorandum for Mr. Bundy, 19 March 1964, NSF, Files of C. V. Clifton, Box 1, item #11, LBJ Library.

69. Michael Forrestal, Memorandum for Mr. Bundy, 18 March 1964, NSF-CF-VN, Box 2, Vietnam Cables, vol. 5, item #59, LBJ Library.

70. Col. William Smith, author of the memos, had served on Taylor's personal staff in the White House and the Pentagon from 1961 through 1962.

71. Harold K. Johnson, Notes on JCS Meeting, 20 March 1964–2:00 P.M., Box 126, Notes on Meetings of the JCS Jan–Apr 1964, H. K. Johnson Papers.

72. Historical Division of the Joint Secretariat, *The Joint Chiefs of Staff and the War in Vietnam*, part 1, chap. 9, pp. 22–23.

73. Taylor, *The Uncertain Trumpet*, pp. 175–76; Rogers, interview by author, 12 March 1993.

74. Telephone Conversation between Robert McNamara and Lyndon Johnson, 2 March 1964, 11:00 A.M., Recordings of Conversations and Meetings, Recordings of Telephone Conversations, White House Series, Tape WH6403.01, Citation #2301, LBJ Library.

75. For a retrospective description of this division, H. K. Johnson, Oral History Transcript, 1972–1974, vol. 2, sec. 8, pp. 53–54.

76. Memorandum for the Secretary of Defense (JCSM–295–64), 9 April 1964, Box 208, Split Papers, Papers of Chairman of the Joint Chiefs of Staff Earle G. Wheeler, Record Group 220, Modern Military Branch, National Archives, Washington, D.C. (hereafter cited as Wheeler Papers); Memo for Record, "Discussion in Joint Chiefs of Staff of a Deputy COMUSMACV," Box 50, Folder 36–71, item #19, Taylor Papers. LeMay may have had a legitimate complaint. As of May 1964 the Army controlled 80 percent of the MACV staff positions and the Air Force only 10 percent. Jacob Van Staaveren, *USAF Plans and Policies in South Vietnam and Laos, 1964* (Washington, D.C.: USAF Historical Division Liaison Office, December 1965), pp. 65–68.

77. Maxwell D. Taylor, Memorandum for the Secretary of Defense (CM–1208–64), 20 February 1964, Box 22, File T–236–69, Taylor Papers; Robert S. McNamara, Memorandum for the Chairman, Joint Chiefs of Staff, 20 February 1964, Box 22, File T–236–69, Taylor Papers; McDonald, *Reminiscences*, p. 353–56. When discussing later decisions in which he failed to support the Marine Corps, Admiral McDonald said that he was simply "abiding by the rule" laid down by General Greene.

78. McDonald, *Reminiscences*, pp. 353–56, 395–96.

79. Ibid.

CHAPTER 5

1. *New York Times*, 25 April 1964, and in Gibbons, *The U.S. Government and the Vietnam War*, vol. 2, p. 249.

2. Thomas Jefferson, 19 August 1785, as quoted in Robert A. Fitton, ed., *Leadership: Quotations from the Military Tradition* (Boulder, Colo.: Westview Press, 1990), p. 297.

3. Talking Paper, Clifton's Eyes Only, 27 March 1964, National Security File, Files of C. V. Clifton, Box 1, Joint Chiefs of Staff, vol. 1, item #6a, LBJ Library. Clifton's notes in the margins (such as "done") and the fact that, one week later, Johnson acted on warnings contained in the paper indicate that Clifton gave the paper to the president.

4. Talking Paper, Clifton's Eyes Only, 27 March 1964, NSF, Files of C. V. Clifton, Box 1, Joint Chiefs of Staff, vol. 1, item #6a, LBJ Library.

5. This interpretation is consistent with George C. Herring's trenchant analysis of the JCS advisory relationship with the Johnson administration in *LBJ and Vietnam*, chap. 2, especially p. 36. See also Herring's "'Cold Blood': LBJ's Conduct of Limited War in Vietnam," *Harmon Memorial Lectures in Military History* 33, delivered to the Fourteenth Military History Symposium (Colorado Springs: United States Air Force Academy, 17 October 1990); and "Conspiracy of Silence: LBJ, the Joint Chiefs and Escalation of the War in Vietnam," in Lloyd Gardner, ed., *Vietnam: The Early Decisions*.

6. Eugene Zuckert, Oral History Transcript, 18 March 1969, LBJ Library, pp. 30–31. LeMay was in continual conflict with Secretary McNamara. Roswell Gilpatric, Oral History Transcript, 2 November 1982, LBJ Library, pp. 14–15; Roswell Gilpatric, Memorandum for the President, 20 January 1964, Subject: Post-Duty Assignment for General LeMay, NSF, Files of C. V. Clifton, Box 1, Defense-General, vol. 1, item #22, Johnson Library. The memo is interesting because of Gilpatric's disingenuousness. He wrote that the results of LeMay's survey "would be of great interest." Moreover, the general was "admirably suited" for the task. The survey would take four to six months—just long enough to keep LeMay occupied through the election (he was scheduled to retire on 30 June).

7. C. V. Clifton, Memorandum for Mr. Walter Jenkins, 28 January 1964, NSF, Files of C. V. Clifton, Box 1, Air Force, item #6, LBJ Library; Maxwell Taylor, Confidential Letter to General Lyman Lemnitzer, 14 January 1964, Box 22, File T–236–69, Taylor Papers. After Johnson decided to keep LeMay on through the election, he brought McConnell in from Europe to be the vice chief of staff of the Air Force to wait in the wings until LeMay's retirement. John P. McConnell, Oral History Transcript, 14 August 1969, LBJ Library, pp. 2–7.

8. Coffey, *Iron Eagle*, pp. 432–33.

9. Ibid., pp. 432–34. LeMay actually retired in January 1965. For LeMay's thoughts on loyalty, military professionalism, and civilian control, see Curtis E. LeMay, *Mission with LeMay: My Story* (Garden City, N.Y.: Doubleday, 1965), pp. 553–55. The quotation is from p. 554.

10. Memo, Forrestal to McGeorge Bundy, 28 April 1964, #187, "Vietnam," vol. 7, NSF-CF-VN, LBJ Library. Johnson continued to convene his inner circle throughout his presidency. Vietnam, of course, dominated the agenda. The JCS was not represented until, in 1966, congressional opinion forced the president to include Chairman Earle G. Wheeler on a regular basis. David Humphrey, "Tuesday Lunch at the Johnson White

House," *Diplomatic History* 8 (Winter 1984), pp. 88–92; W. W. Rostow, *The Diffusion of Power: An Essay in Recent History* (New York: Macmillan, 1972), p. 358. Dean Rusk remarked that Johnson and his advisers "transacted a lot of business" in these useful lunches. Dean Rusk, Oral History Transcript, 28 July 1969, sec. 1, LBJ Library, p. 23. For Tuesday lunch agendas, see NSF, Files of McGeorge Bundy, Box 19, Lunch with the President, LBJ Library.

11. Bromley Smith, Oral History Transcript, 29 July 1969, LBJ Library, sec. 2, pp. 19–20. For Johnson's preoccupation with consensus and paranoia about leaks, see also Bromley Smith, Oral History Transcript, 29 July 1969, I, p. 27, LBJ Library; Burke and Greenstein, *How Presidents Test Reality*, pp. 139, 184–85.

12. Michael Forrestal, Oral History Transcript, 3 November 1969, I, LBJ Library, p. 30. Forrestal observed that people were unable to disagree with what they felt were the president's preferences.

13. Dean Rusk, Oral History Transcript, 28 July 1969, I, LBJ Library, pp. 8–9, 22–29, 36. Rusk and McNamara established the pattern of meeting with the president together under Kennedy. Rusk recalled that "Secretary McNamara and I did not like to get into much discussion in the National Security Council or in Cabinet meetings with so many people sitting around the room. . . . We would see President Kennedy either just before or just after such a meeting where the real decision would be taken so that discussion in the National Security Council would be more restrictive and would not lend itself to leaks and distortions by people sitting around the room." Rusk referred to the luncheon group with Johnson as an "inner war cabinet." For an example of McNamara and Rusk meeting to come to a consensus position on Vietnam before meeting with the president, see William P. Bundy, unpublished manuscript, chap. 1, p. 8.

14. Walt W. Rostow, Oral History Transcript, 22 December 1968, I, p. 56, LBJ Library.

15. Harry McPherson, Oral History Transcript, 5 December 1968, session 4, tape 5, p. 33, LBJ Library; Chester Cooper, Oral History Transcript, I, p. 9, LBJ Library; George Ball, *The Past Has Another Pattern* (New York: W.W. Norton, 1982), p. 390. Ball wrote that once McNamara "made up his mind to go forward, he would push aside the most formidable impediment that might threaten to slow down or deflect him from his determined course."

16. The Chiefs made this decision immediately after reading McNamara's draft report. H. K. Johnson, Handwritten Notes on JCS Meeting, 13 March 1964—2:00 P.M., H. K. Johnson Papers.

17. "SIGMA I–64 Final Report," NSF-Agency File, Box 30, JCS War Games, vol. 1 [1], item #1, LBJ Library.

18. Ibid.

19. Memorandum for General Clifton, 6 May 1964, NSF, Files of C. V. Clifton, Box 2, Meetings with the President, vol. 1 [file 1 of 2], item #14;

Memorandum for General Clifton, 20 May 1964, NSF, Files of C. V. Clifton, Box 1, Defense General , vol. 1, item #6, LBJ Library.

20. Alexander George, *Presidential Decisionmaking in Foreign Policy: The Effective Use of Information and Advice* (Boulder, Colo.: Westview Press, 1980), p. 61.

21. Charts prepared in February 1964 in folder marked "SVN Charts," Box 33, McNamara Papers; Goodpaster, interview by author, 9 March 1993.

22. Alain Enthoven, Oral History Transcript, 27 December 1968, LBJ Library, tape 1, p. 25; tape 2, pp. 2–3, 7.

23. Henry Buse, Oral History Transcript, 1971, pp. 178–79.

24. McDonald, *Reminiscences*, p. 409.

25. H. K. Johnson, Oral History Transcript, 1972, vol. 2, sec. 11, pp. 3–4. LeMay's recollection was similar. See Coffey, *Iron Eagle*, p. 422.

26. Telegram, William Bundy to Lodge, 4 April 1964, Box 1, Kahin Papers.

27. Memo, Michael V. Forrestal to McGeorge Bundy, 16 April 1964, NSF-CF-VN, "Vietnam Planning," item #177, LBJ Library. The memo revealed Forrestal's preoccupation with keeping the effort in Vietnam "under control" until after the November election. See also Political/Military Scenarios for Pressures on DRV, Draft of 20 April 1964, item #178, LBJ Library.

28. Memo, Michael V. Forrestal to McGeorge Bundy, 16 April 1964, NSF-CF-VN, "Vietnam Planning," item #177, LBJ Library.

29. This observation is consistent with the interpretation of Herbert Y. Schandler in "JCS Strategic Planning and Vietnam: The Search for an Objective."

30. Gibbons, *The U.S. Government and the Vietnam War*, vol. 2, pp. 241–42, 244.

31. Historical Division of the Joint Secretariat, *The Joint Chiefs of Staff and the War in Vietnam*, part 1, chap. 9, pp. 35–39. The target list was later expanded to ninety-four.

32. Gravel, *The Pentagon Papers*, vol. 3, pp. 162–64; Gibbons, *The U.S. Government and the Vietnam War*, vol. 2, pp. 244–45; for an account of this and other diplomatic overtures to North Vietnam, see Wallace J. Thies, *When Governments Collide: Coercion and Diplomacy in the Vietnam Conflict, 1964–1968* (Berkeley: University of California Press, 1980).

33. William C. Westmoreland, *A Soldier Reports* (Garden City, N.Y.: Doubleday, 1976), p. 109.

34. H. K. Johnson, Notes on JCS Meeting, 24 April 1964—2:00 P.M., Notes on Meetings of the JCS, Jan. to April 64, H. K. Johnson Papers.

35. William Bundy, unpublished manuscript, chap. 1, p. 2. See also, McGeorge Bundy and Ray Cline in Gittinger, *The Johnson Years*, pp. 24–25; Kearns, *Lyndon Johnson and the American Dream*, pp. 197–198.

36. Westmoreland, *A Soldier Reports*, p. 109.

37. William C. Westmoreland, Papers of William C. Westmoreland, Box 30, Interview with Charles B. McDonald, 4 February 1973, tab A, LBJ

Library. Westmoreland recalled that due to the election, the administration wanted to "keep the war low key." He contended that the Johnson administration had "game plans directed at me and the military as well as the U.S. public" in that connection.

38. Henry Cabot Lodge, Telegram for the Secretary, Harriman, and Bundy, 4 May—3:00 P.M., Box 1, Kahin Papers. On May 2 Lodge had recommended the establishment of a U.S. naval base at Camh Ranh Bay in South Vietnam to act as a "useful trump card at a diplomatic conference." Henry Cabot Lodge, Telegram to the Secretary of State, 2 May 1964, Box 1, Kahin Papers.

39. Central Intelligence Agency Memorandum, 15 May 1964, NSF, vol. 9, Situation Report File, item #48, LBJ Library. The report characterized the situation in South Vietnam as "extremely fragile" and warned: "If the tide of deterioration has not been arrested by the end of the year, the anti-Communist position . . . is likely to become untenable."

40. At the end of April, after Secretary Rusk's visit to Saigon, Lodge instructed Harkins that he was not permitted to contact General Khanh without the ambassador's permission. Harkins fired off a letter to the ambassador in which he cited his responsibilities as MACV commander and informed Lodge that he intended simply to "keep Lodge informed" about his contacts with Khanh. Paul D. Harkins, Memorandum for Ambassador Lodge, 22 April 1964, Box 1, Kahin Papers.

41. Ambassador Lodge had already sent a telegram to Washington about the "march north fever." Memo Lodge to Rusk, 4 May 1964, Kahin Papers, Box 1.

42. Farmgate operations began in January 1962. In the first eighteen months of the program, twenty-eight U.S. airmen were killed ostensibly training South Vietnamese pilots in combat. Bromley Smith, Summary Record of National Security Council Meeting No. 532, 15 May 1964, Box 1, Kahin Papers.

43. Memo, Taylor to JCS et al., "Visit of the Secretary of Defense and Chairman, JCS, to RVN, 11–13 May," undated, Box 50, File T36–71, Taylor Papers.

44. Robert McNamara and other civilian advisers, focusing on political concerns, did not understand that there were legitimate military reasons to ask for the relaxation of restrictions. A prior incident that illustrated this difficulty occurred in Chantrea, Cambodia, in March 1964. American advisers were instructed to remain on the South Vietnamese side of the border while Vietnamese soldiers conducted raids into Cambodia. The presence of Caucasian men in an attack that killed seventeen people caused great embarrassment. In his White House office, Michael Forrestal judged the American officers' action "inexcusable" and recommended that some action "be taken to bring home to the officers involved that this kind of mistake could affect their careers." Memo, Forrestal to McGeorge Bundy, 1 April 1964, #63a, "Cambodia-Chantrea Incident," vol. 6, NSF-CF-VN, LBJ Library. Dr. Amos

A. Jordan, who served under John McNaughton in ISA, observed that these restrictions made "the senior military people have to face, Janus-like, in two directions." Dr. Amos A. Jordan as quoted in William Alexander Hamilton, "The Influence of the American Military upon Foreign Policy, 1965–1968" (Ph.D. diss., University of Nebraska, 1978), p. 76.

45. Memo, Taylor to JCS et al., "Visit of the Secretary of Defense and Chairman, JCS, to RVN, 11–13 May," undated, Box 50, File T36–71, Taylor Papers.

46. Memo, Taylor to JCS et al., "Visit of the Secretary of Defense and Chairman, JCS, to RVN, 11–13 May," undated, Box 50, File T36–71, Taylor Papers. McNamara did approve one request without hesitation. General Harkins handed him a seven-million-dollar "shopping list" for items and funds. Remembering his president's concern about the congressional examination of Harkins upon the General's return, McNamara directed John McNaughton to get written approval of the list to MACV within ten days. When McNamara and Taylor were called to testify before Congress upon their return from Vietnam, General Taylor told Congressman George Mahon, "When we left Saigon, the Secretary and I, as we always do, asked General Harkins and General Westmoreland, 'Is there anything you need you have not got?' They gave us a very short and insignificant shopping list of items which we can fill without difficulty." The general failed to mention Westmoreland's request for additional Special Forces troops, Moore's request for a relaxation of Farmgate restrictions, or Deputy Secretary Vance's requirement that any troop requests be "validated." Excerpt of testimony of General Maxwell Taylor and Secretary of Defense Robert McNamara before the Mahon Committee in the House of Representatives, undated, with cover memo for Jack Valenti, 2 June 1964, NSF-CF-VN, Box 5, Vietnam Memos, vol. 11 6/1–13/64, item #41a, LBJ Library.

47. Robert S. McNamara, Statement before the Democratic Platform Committee, 17 August 1964, Box 2, McNamara Papers.

48. Krulak, interview by author, 26 July 1993.

49. Robert S. McNamara, "Cuba Briefing Part II," 24 January 1963, Box 28, Cuban Statement Folder, McNamara Papers.

50. Compare, for example, McNamara's directive to U.S. pilots not to engage in combat with the nebulous JCS directive 6399, issued seven days later. JCS 6399 reaffirmed the policy that U.S. military personnel would not participate in combat but authorized the continued use of Farmgate aircraft to conduct "bone fide operational training missions against hostile targets." The JCS went on to stipulate that helicopter weapons "are for the protection of vehicles and passengers" and that U.S. personnel should "be exposed to combat conditions only as required." JCS 6399 as cited in Historical Division, Joint Secretariat, *Chronology of Development of Restraints and Objectives in the Air Campaign Vietnam, 1961–1966*, p. 6.

51. Enclosure E, Memo, Taylor to JCS et al., "Visit of the Secretary of Defense and Chairman, JCS, to RVN, 11–13 May," undated, Box 50, File T36–71, Taylor Papers.

52. "Error upon Error," *The Wall Street Journal*, 13 May 1964 as quoted in Gibbons, *The U.S. Government and the Vietnam War*, vol. 2, p. 248. Gibbons noted that "congressional and public criticism of U.S. policy was increasing."

53. Bromley Smith, Summary Record of National Security Council Meeting No. 532, 15 May 1964, *FRUS: Vietnam, 1964*, pp. 328–32; Andrew J. Goodpaster, interview by author, 9 March 1993. For McNamara's report upon returning from Vietnam, see "RMCN's Notes for Report to the President," 14 May 1964, NSF-CF-VN, Box 4, Vietnam Memos, vol. 9, 5/13–23/64, item #2, LBJ Library.

54. Douglas Cater in Gittinger, *The Johnson Years*, pp. 21–22; Douglas Brinkley, *Dean Acheson: The Cold War Years, 1953–1971* (New Haven, Conn.: Yale University Press, 1992), p. 239.

55. Gibbons, *The U.S. Government and the Vietnam War*, vol. 2, pp. 25455.

56. Andrew J. Goodpaster, interview by author, 9 March 1993. In a memorandum to McNamara, Forrestal recommended changes in Vietnam that would have further undercut the military commander's authority. Memo, Forrestal to McNamara, 14 February 1964, Box 1, Kahin Papers. During his first visit to Vietnam, McNaughton was the house guest of Major General and Mrs. Charles J. Timmes. When Mrs. Timmes described the complexity of the situation in South Vietnam and cautioned that despite their two and a half years in Vietnam, they "understood little of the Vietnamese culture and customs," McNaughton assured her that one can find a solution to any problem by simply dissecting it into all its elements and then piecing together the resultant formula. For the account of McNaughton's first trip to South Vietnam, see Charles J. Timmes, "The Naive Years," *Army* (May 1977), p. 40. Forrestal and McNaughton exchanged books to enhance their understanding of guerrilla warfare. Among these were a book by Roger Trinquier, *Modern Warfare: A French View of Counter-Insurgency* (New York: Praeger, 1964), and a RAND study on the Algerian war by David Galalu. Memorandum from Forrestal to McNaughton, 1 May 1964, Kahin Papers, Box 1.

57. Telephone conversation between (William) Bundy and George Ball, 22 May 1964, Papers of George W. Ball, Box 7, Vietnam I [12/9/63–12/15/64], item #42, LBJ Library. William Bundy told Ball that "there have been two sessions of the planning group and McNamara wants to get into the act." See also William Bundy, unpublished manuscript, chap. 4, p. 11.

58. The group completed a new scenario on May 23 that eliminated intermediate, unacknowledged actions against North Vietnam but retained the framework of gradually increasing pressure to convince North Vietnam to abandon its effort in the South. Gravel, *The Pentagon Papers*, vol. 3, pp. 167–68. See also Gibbons, *The U.S. Government and the Vietnam War*, vol. 2, pp. 255–56.

59. Memorandum to the President, "Basic Recommendations and Projected Course of Action on Southeast Asia," 25 May 1964, NSF-Files of

McGeorge Bundy, Box 19, Luncheons with the President, vol. 1, part 1, item #79, LBJ Library. For the next day's Tuesday lunch agenda see item #77.

60. Memorandum to the President, "Basic Recommendations and Projected Course of Action on Southeast Asia," 25 May 1964, FRUS: Vietnam, 1964, pp. 374–77.

61. Maxwell Taylor, "Highlights of Honolulu Conference," 2 June 1964, Box 50, File T–36–71, Taylor Papers.

62. Gibbons, The U.S. Government and the Vietnam War, vol. 2, pp. 261–64.

63. Maxwell Taylor, "Highlights of Honolulu Conference," 2 June 1964, Box 50, File T–36–71, Taylor Papers. Gibbons, The U.S. Government and the Vietnam War, vol. 2, pp. 261–64.

64. Maxwell D. Taylor, Memorandum for Record, 7 May 1964, Taylor Papers.

65. Telegram for McNamara from Lodge, 28 May 1964, Box 1, Kahin Papers. Apparently McNamara initiated the request for the essay.

66. William Bundy, unpublished manuscript, chap. 13, p. 21.

67. Memorandum from the Joint Chiefs of Staff to the Secretary of Defense (JCSM–471–64), 2 June 1964, FRUS: Vietnam, 1964, pp. 437–40. Taylor persuaded the Chiefs to soften the language of the original memo. For excerpts from the 30 May version, see Gravel, The Pentagon Papers, vol. 3, p. 126.

68. Historical Division of the Joint Secretariat, The Joint Chiefs of Staff and the War in Vietnam, part 1, chap. 10, p. 17.

69. Wallace Greene, Memorandum for Record, Chairman's Action on JCS Paper, 1 June 1964, Greene Papers.

70. Wallace Greene, Résumé of a Telephone Call with LTG Krulak, 1 June 1964, Greene Papers.

71. Memorandum from the Chairman of the Joint Chiefs of Staff to the Secretary of Defense, 2 June 1964, FRUS: Vietnam, 1964, pp. 436–437.

72. Memorandum from the Chairman of the Joint Chiefs of Staff to the Secretary of Defense, 5 June 1964, ibid., pp. 457–58.

73. Secretary of Defense Memorandum to CJCS, 10 June 1964, Gravel, The Pentagon Papers, vol. 3, p. 127.

74. Memorandum for Record, JCS Meeting, 3 June 1964–2:00 P.M., Greene Papers. Trying to downplay the conclusions of the conference, he told the Chiefs that McNamara, who had drafted a memo to the president, was "carrying in a mouse."

75. South Vietnam Action Program and Illustrative Military Moves Designed to Demonstrate the U.S. Intention to Prevent Further Communist Advances in Laos and South Vietnam, FRUS: Vietnam, 1964, pp. 461–64.

76. Wallace Greene, Summary of JCS and White House Actions on Emergency Situation in Laos, 6 June 1964, Greene Papers.

77. H. K. Johnson, Special JCS Meeting 6 June 1964—9:00 A.M., Box 126, Memos on Meetings of the JCS May–June 1964, H. K. Johnson Papers.

78. Wallace Greene, Summary of JCS and White House Actions on Emergency Situation in Laos, 6 June 1964, Greene Papers.

79. Ibid.

80. Michael Forrestal, Summary Record of National Security Council Meeting No. 533, 6 June 1964, NSF, NSC Meetings, vol. 2, tab 6, item #2, LBJ Library.

81. Memorandum for the Record, 10 June 1964, Meeting with the President, 7 June 1964, Laos Reconnaissance, NSF, Files of McGeorge Bundy, Meetings on SE Asia, vol. 1, item #24, LBJ Library.

82. Summary Record of the Meeting on Southeast Asia, Cabinet Room, 10 June 1964 (Without the President), NSF, Files of McGeorge Bundy, Box 18, Meetings on SE Asia, vol. 1, item #14, LBJ Library.

83. Memo McGeorge Bundy to President, 6 June 1964, "Possible Successor to Lodge," Box 1, Kahin Papers.

84. Maxwell D. Taylor, Letter to Robert S. McNamara, 1 July 1964, Box 22, File T-236-69, Taylor Papers.

85. Final Talk to Joint Staff, 2 July 1964, Box 22, File T-236-69, Taylor Papers. See also John Taylor, *General Maxwell Taylor*, p. 297.

86. John Taylor, *General Maxwell Taylor*, p. 297.

CHAPTER 6

1. Taylor, *Swords and Plowshares*, p. 252.

2. The first chairman of the JCS, General of the Army Omar Bradley, commanded a corps, an army, and an army group in Europe during World War II. Adm. Arthur Radford commanded a carrier division in the Pacific theater. Gen. Nathan Twining commanded air forces in the Pacific and Europe. General Lemnitzer commanded air defense brigades during World War II and an infantry division in the Korean War. Wheeler's background contrasted sharply with those officers' and that of his immediate predecessor, Taylor, who led a paratroop division from Normandy to Bastogne during World War II and commanded UN forces in the last months of the Korean War.

3. Webb, *The Chairmen of the Joint Chiefs of Staff*, p. 74; Biographical data on General Wheeler, Joint Staff Historical Office, Pentagon Building; "'Staff Man' in Chief," *New York Times*, 24 June 1964, p. 13. Wheeler graduated first in his class from both the Infantry Officer Advanced Course at Fort Benning, Georgia, and the U.S. Army Command and General Staff College at Fort Leavenworth, Kansas.

4. John G. Norris, "Gen. Wheeler 'Fits the Bill,'" *Washington Post*, 26 August 1962, p. E3. See also "'Staff Man' in Chief," *New York Times*, 24 June 1964, p. 13; Kinnard, *The Secretary of Defense*, p. 79.

5. The quotations (in that order) are from "The Management Team," *Time*, 5 February 1965, p. 22; "From LeMay to McConnell—A Change to

the 'New Breed,'" *Newsweek*, 4 January 1965, p. 16; Transcript of Hearings before the Department of Defense Subcommittee on Appropriations, Senate Appropriations Committee, 24 April 1963, Box 22, Taylor Papers.

6. Kinnard, *The Secretary of Defense*, p. 79.

7. Notes on Meeting with Westmoreland and the JCS, 2:00 P.M., 7 January 1964, Notes on Meetings of the JCS, Box 126, H. K. Johnson papers. For General Wheeler's sensitivity to his role in representing the administration's position before Congress, see Earle Wheeler, Oral History Transcript, sec. 1, 21 August 1969, pp. 2–3, 10–11, LBJ Library.

8. Earle Wheeler, Oral History Transcript, sec. 1, 21 August 1969, pp. 12–13, LBJ Library.

9. Andrew J. Goodpaster, interview by author, 9 March 1993.

10. John G. Norris, "Pentagon Shift Shatters JCS Rotation Precedent," *Washington Post*, 24 June 1964, p. A12.

11. Dino A. Brugioni, *Eyeball to Eyeball*, p. 290.

12. Col. William Corson as quoted in Mark Perry, *Four Stars* (Boston: Houghton Mifflin Company, 1989), p. 134.

13. General Bernard Rogers, who had been executive assistant to Generals Taylor and Wheeler, observed that, although Wheeler was the youngest officer to hold the chairmanship, the fifty-six-year-old seemed tired out when he took over. Wheeler had a heart problem and suffered from high blood pressure. Greene's operations deputy, perhaps unaware of Wheeler's physical afflictions, thought the general "apathetic." Rogers, interview by author, 12 March 1993; Henry W. Buse, Oral History Transcript, 1971, p. 208.

14. Earle Wheeler, Oral History Transcript, sec. 1, 21 August 1969, p. 5, LBJ Library.

15. Letter, President Johnson to Taylor, 2 July 1964, Box 51, Folder 161–69C, Taylor Papers.

16. Memorandum from McGeorge Bundy to the President, 25 June 1964, *FRUS: Vietnam, 1964*, p. 530.

17. In his memoirs Taylor described relations between himself, General Westmoreland, and General Wheeler as harmonious. Deference to Taylor's view was not surprising, however, given the fact that he arranged both of these officers' promotions. Certainly Westmoreland and Wheeler recognized Taylor's preponderant influence with the president. Taylor, *Swords and Plowshares*, p. 316.

18. Letter, Marshall S. Carter to Taylor, 2 July 1964, Box 51, Folder 161–69C, Taylor Papers.

19. Telegram, Rusk to Taylor, Saigon 270, 27 July 1964, NSF-CF-VN, vol. 14, LBJ Library. McGeorge Bundy sent a similar cable to Taylor on behalf of President Johnson. Telegram, President Johnson to Taylor, 10 July 1964, NSF-CF-VN, vol. 13, LBJ Library.

20. In June 1965 McGeorge Bundy told the president that it was time to change ambassadors, in part because Taylor had fulfilled his intended

purpose of acting as a symbol of Lyndon Johnson's resolve in South Vietnam. McGeorge Bundy, Memorandum for the President, 30 June 1965, NSF-NSC History, Deployment of Major Forces, Box 43, vol. 6, item #21a, LBJ Library. See also McGeorge Bundy, Handwritten Notes of Meeting, 8 June 1965, Bundy Papers, Box 1, LBJ Library.

21. Taylor, *Swords and Plowshares*, p. 316; Telegram, Taylor to Secretary of State, 7 July 1965, NSF-CF-VN, Box 6, Vietnam Cables, vol. 13 6/64–7/64, item #5, LBJ Library.

22. Telegram from the Embassy in Vietnam to the Department of State, 15 July 1964, 4:00 P.M., *FRUS: Vietnam, 1964*, pp. 547–48; Telegram from the Embassy in Vietnam to the Department of State, 15 July 1964, 9:00 P.M., ibid., pp. 548–49.

23. Memorandum from McGeorge Bundy to the President, 15 July 1964, ibid., pp. 552–53.

24. Telegram from the Embassy in Vietnam to the Department of State, 17 July 1964, 6:00 P.M., ibid., pp. 553–54; United States Military Assistance Command, Vietnam Fact Sheet, Subject: Additional Support RVN, 27 July 1964, GVN/RVNAF (July 1964), Paul L. Miles Papers, U.S. Army Military History Institute (hereafter cited as Miles Papers); Memorandum from the Secretary of State's Special Assistant for Vietnam [Michael Forrestal] to the President's Special Assistant for National Security Affairs (McGeorge Bundy), 22 July 1964, *FRUS: Vietnam, 1964*, pp. 558–59. See also Forrestal's attachment to the above memo, ibid., pp. 559–61.

25. Taylor's cable of 17 July went directly to McGeorge Bundy at the White House. See copy of the cable at NSF-CF-VN, Box 6, Vietnam Memos, vol. 14, item #119, LBJ Library.

26. JCSM–665–64, Memorandum from General Wheeler for the Secretary of Defense, Additional Support in RVN on Accelerated Basis, 4 August 1964, Box 145, Split Files, Wheeler Papers. The August 4 memo refers to the July 20 meeting.

27. Agenda for Luncheon, 21 July 1964, NSF, Files of McGeorge Bundy, Box 19, Lunch with the President [vol. 1] [part 1], item #65, LBJ Library.

28. Telegram, Rusk to Taylor, 21 July 1964, NSF-CF-VN, Box 6, Vietnam Cables, vol. 19, file 2 of 2, Item #98, LBJ Library. See also footnote to Taylor's 17 July request, *FRUS: Vietnam, 1964*, p. 554.

29. JCSM–632–64, Memorandum, Joint Chiefs of Staff for the Secretary of Defense, Extension of the U.S. Advisory Assistance, 24 July 1964, Box 145, Wheeler Papers. The Chiefs limited their approval to seven hundred manpower spaces to extend the advisory effort at the battalion and district levels.

30. JCSM–665–64, 4 August 1964, Box 145, Split Files, Wheeler Papers.

31. In the summer of 1964, the JCS were in the midst of a fractious debate over the development and employment of Army aviation. The Army argued that it needed an air arm to implement its new doctrine of "air-

mobile" warfare. American advisers had introduced troop-carrying heli-copters into South Vietnam as early as 1961. Advocates of air assault tactics believed that the ability to ferry troops rapidly between battlefields reduced dramatically the ten-to-one advantage in men that conventional wisdom deemed necessary to defeat a guerrilla force in counterinsurgency warfare. The Army developed two types of helicopters to support the new doctrine: the UH–1 ("Huey") and the H–21 ("flying banana"). The two services that already had their own land-based aircraft, the Air Force and Marine Corps, viewed the Army initiative as "illegal poaching" on their distinctive "roles and missions." Each service feared that it would have to pay for the Army's new capability with a reduction in its own force structure. Bruce Palmer, Jr., *The 25-Year War*, pp. 26–27. In a February 1964 memo to the Secretary of Defense, Taylor summarized LeMay's opinion of the Army's helicopter pro-gram, writing that LeMay "considers that no requirement exists for the pro-posed weapons systems, and that their development and procurement would lead to unnecessary duplication of the mission and capabilities of the Air Force." JCSM–106–64, 10 February 1964, Box 208, Wheeler Papers.

32. For an account of the exchange between LeMay and Johnson, see Palmer, *The 25-Year War*, pp. 27–28.

33. JCSM–665–64, Memorandum from General Wheeler for the Secretary of Defense, Additional Support in RVN on Accelerated Basis, 4 August 1964, Box 145, Split Files, Wheeler Papers.

34. Message from OSD to the American Embassy in Saigon, 23 July 1964, NSF-CF-VN, Box 6, Vietnam Cables, vol. 14, file 2 of 2, item #139, LBJ Library.

35. Telegram from the Department of State to the Embassies in Laos and South Vietnam, 26 July 1964, FRUS: *Vietnam, 1964*, pp. 574–75. On General Khanh's calls for action against North Vietnam, see Telegram from the Department of State to the Embassy in Vietnam, 24 July 1964; Telegram from the Embassy in Vietnam to the Department of State, 25 July 1964—4 P.M.; Telegram from the Embassy in Vietnam to the Department of State, 25 July 1964—5 P.M.; and Telegram from the Department of State to the Embassy in Vietnam, 25 July 1964—4:56 P.M.; FRUS: *Vietnam, 1964*, pp. 562–71.

36. Telegram from the Embassy in Vietnam to the Department of State, 27 July 1964, FRUS: *Vietnam, 1964*, pp. 582–83. For the low-level recon-naissance missions over Laos, see Gravel, *The Pentagon Papers*, vol. 3, p. 182.

37. JCSM–639–64, Memorandum from the Joint Chiefs of Staff to the Secretary of Defense, Actions Relevant to South Vietnam, 27 July 1964, FRUS: *Vietnam, 1964*, pp. 583–84. For Johnson's request see Memorandum from the Secretary of State's Special Assistant for Vietnam (Forrestal) to the Secretary of State, 31 July 1964, FRUS: *Vietnam, 1964*, p. 588.

38. JCSM–639–64, Memorandum from the Joint Chiefs of Staff to the Secretary of Defense, Actions Relevant to South Vietnam, 27 July 1964, FRUS: *Vietnam, 1964*, pp. 584–85.

39. The idea of "negative" objectives is from Mark Clodfelter's incisive analysis of air power in Vietnam, *The Limits of Air Power: The American Bombing of North Vietnam* (New York: Free Press, 1989), p. xi.

40. Memorandum from the Secretary of State's Special Assistant for Vietnam (Forrestal, who had replaced William Sullivan in that position) to the Secretary of State, 31 July 1964, *FRUS: Vietnam, 1964*, p. 588. Forrestal sent a copy of the JCS memorandum to Maxwell Taylor to use in the embassy's planning sessions.

41. Agenda for Luncheon, 14 July 1964, NSF, Files of McGeorge Bundy, Box 19, Lunch with the President [vol. 1] [part 1], item #67, LBJ Library; "Allegations from the 1964 Republican Platform," undated, Box 2, McNamara Papers; Drafts for the Democratic Platform (1964), undated, Box 2, McNamara Papers.

42. See, for example, the agendas for luncheons on 14 July, 28 July, 11 August, and 1 September in NSF, Files of McGeorge Bundy, Box 19, Lunch with the President [vol. 1] [part 1], item #s 67, 63, 61, and 55, LBJ Library.

43. This quotation and the following discussion are from W. P. Bundy and M. V. Forrestal, "Position Paper on Expanding US Action in South Vietnam to the North," 31 July 1964, NSF-CF-VN, Box 6, Vietnam Memos, vol. 14, item #205c. Bundy reproduced the document in full in his unpublished manuscript, chap. 14, pp. 10–14.

44. Jack Raymond, "More U.S. Troops Going to Vietnam to Help Regime," *New York Times*, 15 July 1964, pp. 1, 3.

45. Memorandum for the President, McGeorge Bundy, 15 July 1964, "News in Morning Papers on Troops to Vietnam," NSF-CF-VN, Box 6, Vietnam memos, vol. 13, item #17, LBJ Library.

46. Ibid.

47. Telegram, For Manning from Zorthian, 27 July 1964, Box 1, Kahin Papers.

48. Copy of AP news wire, NSF-CF-VN, Box 6, Vietnam Cables, vol. 19, item #86, LBJ Library.

49. McGeorge Bundy, Memorandum for the President, 24 July 1964, Box 1, Kahin Papers. William Bundy, unpublished manuscript, chap. 14, p. 15.

50. Marshall Green, a State Department official, recalled that the airdrops were "a fiasco. . . . A terrible disappointment." Marshall Green as quoted by Tom Wells, *The War Within: America's Battle over Vietnam* (Los Angeles: University of California Press, 1994), p. 9.

51. Edward J. Marolda and Oscar P. Fitzgerald, *The United States Navy and the Vietnam Conflict*, vol. 2, *From Military Assistance to Combat, 1959–1965* (Washington, D.C.: Naval Historical Center, 1986), pp. 335–42. On the influence of economic analysis on McNamara's enthusiasm for covert operations, see Gregory Palmer, *The McNamara Strategy and the Vietnam War* (Westport, Conn.: Greenwood Press, 1978), pp. 108–9.

52. Gravel, *The Pentagon Papers*, vol. 3, p. 183; Marolda and Fitzgerald, *The United States Navy and the Vietnam Conflict*, vol. 2, pp. 339–41.

53. Marolda and Fitzgerald, *The United States Navy and the Vietnam Conflict*, vol. 2, pp. 340–42.

54. Ibid., pp. 342–43.

55. Marolda and Fitzgerald, *The United States Navy and the Vietnam Conflict*, vol. 2, p. 410; U. S. Grant Sharp, *Strategy for Defeat* (San Rafael, Calif.: Presidio Press, 1978), p. 39; Joseph C. Goulden, *Truth Is the First Casualty: The Gulf of Tonkin Affair—Illusion and Reality* (New York: Rand McNally, 1969), pp. 124–25.

56. Summarized from Marolda and Fitzgerald, *The United States Navy and the Vietnam Conflict*, vol. 2, pp. 406–10.

57. U.S. Destroyer Attacked by North Vietnamese Patrol Boats, 3 August 1964, Meeting Notes File, Box 1, Gulf of Tonkin Incident, item #10d, LBJ Library; Message, CINCPACFLT to CNO, "Gulf of Tonkin SITREP," 2 August 1964, Box 1, Kahin Papers. Gravel, *The Pentagon Papers*, vol. 3, pp. 183–84.

58. Memorandum from the Duty Officer in the White House Situation Room to the President, 2 August 1964, *FRUS: Vietnam, 1964*, p. 590; editorial note, *FRUS: Vietnam, 1964*, pp. 590–91; Johnson, *Vantage Point*, pp. 112–13.

59. Goulden, *Truth Is the First Casualty*, pp. 23–24.

60. Ball, *The Past Has Another Pattern*, p. 379.

61. Telegram from the Chairman of the Joint Chiefs of Staff to the Commander in Chief, Pacific, 2 August 1964—12:25 P.M., *FRUS: Vietnam, 1964*, p. 591.

62. Telegram from the Embassy in Vietnam to the Department of State, Saigon, 3 August 1964—11 A.M., *FRUS: Vietnam, 1964*, pp. 593–94.

63. Telephone Conversation between Robert McNamara and George Ball, 3 August 1964—9:55 A.M., Papers of George W. Ball, Box 7, Vietnam, sec. 1 [12/9/63–12/15/64], item #7b, LBJ Library.

64. An editorial note in *FRUS: Vietnam, 1964*, pp. 597, 600, reveals that McNamara spoke to Lyndon Johnson before 11:00 A.M. on August 3. The president held an impromptu news conference at 11:30.

65. Editorial Note, *FRUS: Vietnam, 1964*, p. 597.

66. Telephone Conversation between Robert McNamara and George Ball, 3 August 1964—9:55 A.M., Papers of George W. Ball, Box 7, Vietnam, sec. 1 [12/9/63—12/15/64], item #7b, LBJ Library.

67. Telegram from the Department of State to the Embassy in Vietnam, 3 August 1964—8:49 P.M., *FRUS: Vietnam, 1964*, pp. 603–4.

68. Telephone Conversation Between George Ball and McGeorge Bundy, 3 August 1964—4:30 P.M., Papers of George W. Ball, Box 7, Vietnam, sec. 1, item #81, LBJ Library. Bundy promised Ball that he would raise this issue at the 6:25 meeting.

69. Summarized from Marolda and Fitzgerald, *The United States Navy and the Vietnam Conflict*, vol. 2, pp. 423–24. For William Bundy's comment, see his unpublished manuscript, chap. 14, p. 28.

70. Editorial note, FRUS: Vietnam, 1964, pp. 604–5; Gibbons, The U.S. Government and the Vietnam War, vol. 2, p. 289; Johnson, Vantage Point, p. 114; Alexander M. Haig, Jr., Inner Circles: How America Changed the World, A Memoir (New York: Warner Books, 1992), p. 117.

71. Gibbons, The U.S. Government and the Vietnam War, vol. 2, p. 289.

72. Bruce E. Altschuler, LBJ and the Polls (Gainesville: University of Florida Press, 1986), p. 38; John Bartlow Martin, "Election of 1964," in Arthur M. Schlesinger, Jr., ed., The History of American Presidential Elections, vol. 4 (New York: McGraw-Hill, 1971), p. 3590.

73. For the term "holding strategy" see William Bundy, unpublished manuscript, chapter 15. Altschuler, LBJ and the Polls, p. 12; Martin, "Election of 1964," pp. 3588, 3590.

74. Martin, "Election of 1964," p. 3590. See also, Kearns, Lyndon Johnson and the American Dream, p. 199.

75. Gibbons, The U.S. Government and the Vietnam War, vol. 2, p. 289; Anthony Austin, The President's War: The Story of the Tonkin Gulf Resolution and How the Nation Was Trapped in Vietnam (New York: Lippincott, 1971), p. 30.

76. Richard Russell as quoted in Kearns, Lyndon Johnson and the American Dream, p. 254.

77. Editorial note, FRUS: Vietnam, 1964, p. 605; Haig, Inner Circles, p. 117.

78. Gibbons, The U.S. Government and the Vietnam War, vol. 2, p. 289.

79. Haig, Inner Circles, pp. 118–19.

80. Editorial Note, FRUS: Vietnam, 1964, pp. 605–6.

81. Ibid., p. 607.

82. Ibid. He told LeMay that these additional actions ought to focus primarily on reinforcements, such as the deployment of B-57s into South Vietnam and of fighter-interceptors into the Philippines.

83. Ibid., pp. 607–8.

84. Bromley Smith, Summary Notes of 537th NSC Meeting, 4 August 1964—12:35 P.M., National Security File, NSC Meetings, Box 2, vol. 3, tab 19, item #2, LBJ Library. The record of the meeting is published in part in editorial note, FRUS: Vietnam, 1964, p. 608.

85. Andrew J. Goodpaster, interview by author, 9 March 1993; editorial note, FRUS: Vietnam, 1964, p. 608.

86. McGeorge Bundy, Notes on 4 August Lunch with the President, Box 1, Papers of McGeorge Bundy, LBJ Library.

87. McGeorge Bundy, Notes on 4 August Lunch with the President, Box 1, Papers of McGeorge Bundy, LBJ Library; Thomas J. Schoenbaum, Waging Peace and War: Dean Rusk in the Truman, Kennedy and Johnson Years (New York: Simon & Schuster, 1988), p. 430.

88. Editorial Note, FRUS: Vietnam, 1964, p. 609.

89. Gibbons, The U.S. Government and the Vietnam War, vol. 2, p. 290.

90. Ibid., pp. 290–91.

91. Ibid., p. 292.

92. Editorial note, *FRUS: Vietnam, 1964*, pp. 609–10. For Sharp's account of his conversation with McNamara, see Sharp, *Strategy for Defeat*, p. 44.

93. In a White House staff meeting on August 5, McGeorge Bundy, referring to the meeting with congressional leaders, remarked that "'leadership' was a funny word in this case, in that there was little congressmen could do in the way of leading in a situation in which the President's role was so primary." Memorandum for the Record of the White House Staff Meeting, 5 August 1964—8:00 A.M., *FRUS: Vietnam, 1964*, p. 632.

94. Summary Notes of the 538th Meeting of the National Security Council, Washington, 4 August 1964; 6:15 to 6:40 P.M., *FRUS: Vietnam, 1964*, pp. 611–12.

95. Ibid.

96. The following summary of the congressional leadership meeting is from Notes of the Leadership Meeting, White House, 4 August 1964—6:45 P.M., *FRUS: Vietnam, 1964*, 615–21; Gibbons, *The U.S. Government and the Vietnam War*, vol. 2, 294–295; and Notes Taken at Leadership Meeting on August 4, 1964, NSF, Meeting Notes File, Box 1, item #4, LBJ Library.

97. Haig, *Inner Circles*, p. 120.

98. Editorial Note, *FRUS: Vietnam, 1964*, p. 626.

99. Marolda and Fitzgerald, *The United States Navy and the Vietnam Conflict*, vol. 2, pp. 444–48; Karnow, *Vietnam*, p. 373.

100. Public Law 88-408.

101. Gibbons, *The U.S. Government and the Vietnam War*, vol. 2, p. 293.

102. The following account of the Senate hearing is from Goulden, *Truth Is the First Casualty*, pp. 53–67.

103. Goulden, *Truth Is the First Casualty*, p. 48.

104. Gibbons, *The U.S. Government and the Vietnam War*, vol. 2, p. 307.

105. On the misleading effects of this omission, see Gibbons, *The U.S. Government and the Vietnam War*, vol. 2, pp. 337–41. Sen. Albert Gore recalled, for example, that he had been misled into believing that U.S. ships were on routine patrol.

106. "Transcript of Secretary of Defense McNamara's News Conference Dealing with the Situation in Vietnam," *New York Times*, 7 August 1964, p. 6. See also, Goulden, *Truth Is the First Casualty*, pp. 76–77.

107. During a trip to Vietnam in 1995, McNamara finally admitted that it had been unclear whether a second attack occurred. See Tim Larimer, "On Hanoi: A Look Back at a Vietnam War Flash Point," *New York Times*, 10 November 1995, p. A3.

108. This conclusion is drawn from an examination of the hearing transcripts. See Goulden, *Truth Is the First Casualty*, pp. 53–67.

109. Altschuler, *LBJ and the Polls*, pp. 38, 40, 45.

110. William Bundy, unpublished manuscript, chap. 14, p. 50.

111. Memorandum for the Record of a Meeting, Cabinet Room, White House, Washington, 10 August 1964—12:35 P.M., *FRUS: Vietnam, 1964*, pp. 662–63.

CHAPTER 7

1. Lyndon Johnson as quoted in Herring, *LBJ and Vietnam*, p. 62.

2. Historical Division of the Joint Secretariat, *The Joint Chiefs of Staff and the War in Vietnam*, part 2, chap. 11, p. 29

3. Lyndon Johnson as quoted in *New York Times*, 6 August 1965, p 1; Maxwell Taylor, Telegram from the Embassy in Vietnam to the Department of State, 7 August 1964, *FRUS: Vietnam, 1964*, pp. 646–47.

4. State Department Chronology of the Vietnam War, p. 57, NSF-NSC Histories—Presidential Decisions—Gulf of Tonkin Attacks, vol. 1, LBJ Library. See also William Bundy, unpublished manuscript, chap. 14, p. 44.

5. Historical Division of the Joint Secretariat, *The Joint Chiefs of Staff and the War in Vietnam*, part 1, chap. 10, p. 5. See also chap. 11, p. 12. Alden K. Sibley, Memorandum for the Record by the Commanding General, U.S. Army Mobility Command, 14 August 1964, *FRUS: Vietnam, 1964*, pp. 665–66.

6. Historical Division of the Joint Secretariat, *The Joint Chiefs of Staff and the War in Vietnam*, part 2, chap. 11, p. 33; Maxwell Taylor, Telegram from the Embassy in Vietnam to the Department of State, 10 August 1964, *FRUS: Vietnam, 1964*, pp. 656–62.

7. McGeorge Bundy, Memorandum for the Record of a Meeting, ibid., pp. 662–63; McGeorge Bundy as quoted in Gittinger, *The Johnson Years*, pp. 24–25; Historical Division of the Joint Secretariat, *The Joint Chiefs of Staff and the War in Vietnam*, part 1, chap. 11, p. 12.

8. Halberstam, *The Best and the Brightest*, pp. 393–98.

9. McNamara, *In Retrospect*, p. 151.

10. William Bundy, unpublished manuscript, chap. 15, p. 2.

11. Historical Division of the Joint Secretariat, *The Joint Chiefs of Staff and the War in Vietnam*, part 2, chap. 11, p. 34. After receiving their initial guidance, Bundy coordinated a first draft with Robert McNamara and Dean Rusk on 11 August.

12. William Bundy, "Next Courses of Action in Southeast Asia," 13 August 1964, *FRUS: Vietnam, 1964*, pp. 673–79.

13. Historical Division of the Joint Secretariat, *The Joint Chiefs of Staff and the War in Vietnam*, part 1, chap. 11, p. 37; Memorandum from the Joint Chiefs of Staff to the Secretary of Defense, Subject: Next Courses of Action in Southeast Asia, 14 August 1964, *FRUS: Vietnam, 1964*, pp. 681–82.

14. Harold K. Johnson, Oral History Transcript, vol. 2, sec. 8, 1972–1974, pp. 53–54.

15. Harold K. Johnson, Notes on JCS Meeting, 8 February 1964–10:00 A.M., Box 126, Notes on Meetings of the JCS Jan–Apr 1964, H. K. Johnson Papers.

16. Historical Division of the Joint Secretariat, *The Joint Chiefs of Staff and the War in Vietnam*, part 1, chap. 12, p. 16; Memorandum from General LeMay to the Chairman of Joint Chiefs of Staff and Brief of RAND Report,

17 August 1964, NSF-CF-VN, Box 8, Vietnam Memos Vol. XVIII 9/1–15/64, items #90 and #90a, LBJ Library.

17. Historical Division of the Joint Secretariat, *The Joint Chiefs of Staff and the War in Vietnam*, part 1, chap. 12, p. 16.

18. Telegram, CINCPAC to American Ambassador Saigon, 12 August 1964, NSF-CF-VN, Box 7, Vietnam Cables, vol, 10 8/64, item #82, LBJ Library.

19. Victor H. Krulak, interview by author, 26 July 1993.

20. LTG Arthur Collins, Oral History Transcript, Senior Officer Debriefing Program, U.S. Army Institute for Military History, 1981, p. 276; Harold K. Johnson, Oral History Transcript, 1972–1973, vol. 8, pp. 53–54, and vol. 9, p. 16.

21. Maxwell Taylor, Telegram from the Embassy in Vietnam to the Department of State, 18 August 1964, *FRUS: Vietnam, 1964*, pp. 689–93.

22. Wheeler Diaries, Wheeler Papers; Historical Division of the Joint Secretariat, *The Joint Chiefs of Staff and the War in Vietnam*, part 1, chap. 12, p. 9; Memorandum from the Joint Chiefs of Staff to the Secretary of Defense, JCSM–746–64, Subject: Recommended Courses of Action—Southeast Asia, 27 August 1964, *FRUS: Vietnam, 1964*, pp. 713–17.

23. Historical Division of the Joint Secretariat, *The Joint Chiefs of Staff and the War in Vietnam*, part 1, chap. 12, p. 9.

24. Ibid., pp. 9–10; Memorandum from the Joint Chiefs of Staff to the Secretary of Defense, 27 August 1964, Subject: Recommended Courses of Action—Southeast Asia, *FRUS: Vietnam, 1964*, pp. 713–17.

25. Memorandum from the Joint Chiefs of Staff to the Secretary of Defense, 27 August 1964, Subject: Recommended Courses of Action—Southeast Asia, *FRUS: Vietnam, 1964*, pp. 713–17.

26. John T. McNaughton, Memorandum for the Secretary of Defense, Subject: Response to JCSM–729–64: Target Study—North Vietnam, 29 August 1964; in Gravel, *The Pentagon Papers*, vol. 3, pp. 555–56.

27. Ibid.

28. Historical Division of the Joint Secretariat, *The Joint Chiefs of Staff and the War in Vietnam*, part 1, chap. 12, p. 15; Bruce Palmer, Oral History Transcript, 1976, sec. 3, p. 398. Admiral McDonald told the president at the end of July 1964 that he was "more concerned with the problem of political stability in South Vietnam than the military problem." General Greene thought that McDonald was simply telling the president "what he wanted to hear." Wallace Greene, Summary of Meeting—President of the U.S. with the JCS at White House 311300 July 1964, item #36, Greene Papers.

29. Historical Division of the Joint Secretariat, *The Joint Chiefs of Staff and the War in Vietnam*, part 1, chap. 12, p. 15.

30. Ibid., pp. 15–16.

31. Ibid.; McNamara, *In Retrospect*, p. 153.

32. Harold Johnson, Oral History Transcript, 1972–1974, vol. 2, sec. 9, pp. 1–3; Harold Johnson, "Military History and the Military Leader," seminar discussion at the U.S. Army War College, Carlisle Barracks, Pennsylvania, 2 December 1971, Box 134, H. K. Johnson Papers. See also Korb, *The Joint Chiefs of Staff*, p. 44.

33. Telegram from the Embassy in Washington to the Department of State, 6 September 1964, *FRUS: Vietnam, 1964*, pp. 733–736.

34. Maxwell Taylor, Personal Diary Entry for September 7–8, Box 51, File T–163–69, Taylor Papers; Memorandum from the President's Special Assistant for National Security Affairs to the President, 8 September 1964, *FRUS: Vietnam, 1964*, pp. 746–47. The conclusion that Taylor changed his mind after speaking with the president is drawn from comparing his 6 September telegram and the "sharp debate" over the timeliness of action with Taylor's apparent reversal of his opinion during the 9 September NSC meeting. Director of Central Intelligence John McCone attended the second, but not the first meeting.

35. Memorandum from the President's Special Assistant for National Security Affairs to the President, Subject: Courses of Action for South Vietnam, 8 September 1964, *FRUS: Vietnam, 1964*, pp. 746–47; William Bundy, "Courses of Action in South Vietnam," 8 September 1964, ibid., pp. 747–49.

36. William Bundy, unpublished manuscript, chap. 15, p. 11.

37. McGeorge Bundy, Memorandum of a Meeting, 9 September 1964–11:00 A.M., *FRUS: Vietnam, 1964*, pp. 749–55.

38. McNamara, *In Retrospect*, p. 162.

39. McGeorge Bundy, Memorandum of a Meeting, September 9, 1964, 11 A.M., *FRUS: Vietnam, 1964*, pp. 749–55.

40. Senate Foreign Relations Committee Transcript, National Security File, Country File—Vietnam, Box 8, Vietnam Cables, 9/1–15/64, item #43, LBJ Library. Taylor, *Swords and Plowshares*, p. 321.

41. National Security Action Memorandum No. 314, 10 September 1964, *FRUS: Vietnam, 1964*, pp. 758–60.

42. McNamara, *In Retrospect*, p. 155; McGeorge Bundy, Memorandum of a Meeting, September 9, 1964, 11 A.M., *FRUS: Vietnam, 1964*, pp. 749–55; National Security Action Memorandum No. 314, 10 September 1964, ibid., pp. 758–60.

43. Wheeler related the first quoted conversation to his former Army vice chief of staff, Gen. Barksdale Hamlett. Barksdale Hamlett, Oral History Transcript, U.S. Army Institute of Military History, 1976, sec. 6, p. 32. The second quotation is from Wallace Greene, Memorandum for the Record, Saturday Morning, 12 September 1964, item #40, pp. 109–12, Greene Papers.

44. Carl von Clausewitz, as quoted in Peter Paret, *Clausewitz and the State: The Man, His Theories, and His Times* (Princeton, N.J.: Princeton University Press, 1985), p. 369.

45. Herring, *LBJ and Vietnam*, p. 62.

CHAPTER 8

1. McNamara, *In Retrospect*, p. 108.

2. Lyndon Johnson first approved planning for "graduated overt military pressure" on North Vietnam on March 17, 1964. See National Security Action Memorandum 288, 17 March 1964, *FRUS: Vietnam, 1964*, pp. 172–73.

3. Draft "Summary" of the Rostow Thesis prepared by OSD/ISA, 3 August 1964, Rostow Papers, Box 13, Southeast Asia, item #30, LBJ Library. The summary is published, in part, in Gravel, *The Pentagon Papers*, vol. 3, pp. 201–2.

4. Ibid.; Gravel, *The Pentagon Papers*, vol. 3, p. 190.

5. Joint War Games Agency, Joint Chiefs of Staff, "Final Report: Sigma II–64," 5 October 1964, NSF-Agency File, Box 30, item #1, p. B–1, LBJ Library (hereafter cited as "Final Report: Sigma II–64"). Lists of Participants, SIGMA II Fact Book, Wheeler Papers. SIGMA II Letters of Invitation and Responses, Wheeler Papers.

6. "Final Report: Sigma II–64," Appendix D, pp. 14–18; appendix G, p. 23, LBJ Library. SIGMA II Fact Book, Wheeler Papers.

7. SIGMA II–64 Final Report, Appendix G, p. 8, LBJ Library. SIGMA II Fact Book, Appendix D, pp. 13–15, Wheeler Papers.

8. SIGMA II–65 Final Report, Appendix G. pp. 20–21, LBJ Library.

9. "Summary," 3 August 1964, Rostow Papers, Box 13, Southeast Asia, item #30, LBJ Library.

10. Donald V. Bennett, Oral History Transcript, U.S. Army Institute for Military History, 1976, interview #7, pp. 26–27; William Bundy, unpublished manuscript, chap. 15A, pp. 2–3; George Ball, "Top Secret," p. 39.

11. William Bundy, unpublished manuscript, chap. 15, appendix, pp. 2–3.

12. Writing one year after the Gulf of Tonkin incident, Henry Kissinger described the "basic paradox of modern technology." He observed that while "power has never been greater; it has also never been less useful. In the past, the major problem of strategists was to assemble superior strength; in the contemporary period, the problem more frequently is how to discipline the available power into some relationship to objectives likely to be in dispute." He noted further that the "fear of escalation is inescapable." Henry Kissinger, ed., *Problems of National Security* (New York: Praeger, 1965), p. 5.

13. Instructions Delivered to the Canadian Embassy, 8 August 1964, Papers of Paul C. Warnke, Box 8, book 1, Department of State Material [1964], item #23a. See also George C. Herring, ed., *The Secret Diplomacy of the Vietnam War: The Negotiating Volumes of the Pentagon Papers* (Austin: University of Texas Press, 1983), pp. 33–34.

14. Letter from Chairman Khrushchev to President Johnson, 5 August 1964, *FRUS: Vietnam, 1964*, pp. 636–38. Letter from President Johnson to Chairman Khrushchev, 7 August 1964, ibid., p. 648.

15. McGeorge Bundy as quoted in William Y. Smith, Memorandum for the Record of the White House Staff Meeting, 5 August 1964, FRUS: Vietnam, 1964, p. 632; McNamara, In Retrospect, p. 160.

16. Maxwell Taylor, Telegram from the Embassy in Vietnam to the Office of the Secretary of Defense, 3 November 1964, FRUS: Vietnam, 1964, p. 884.

17. Victor H. Krulak, interview by author, 26 July 1993. Michael Forrestal wrote to Llewellyn Thompson that "we learned from the Gulf of Tonkin incident" that "it is essential that all operations involving actions in Southeast Asia be kept under some form of interdepartmental review." Michael Forrestal, Memorandum for Ambassador Llewelyn Thompson, 22 September 1964, Subject: OP 34A, NSF-CF-VN, Box 9, Vietnam Memos, vol. 18, 9/15–30/64, item #256, LBJ Library.

18. For the review process concerning OPLAN 34A operations, see Cyrus R. Vance, Memorandum for Mr. McNaughton, 30 September 1964, Gravel, The Pentagon Papers, vol. 3, p. 571. See also Historical Division of the Joint Secretariat, The Joint Chiefs of Staff and the War in Vietnam, part 1, chap. 13, p. 5.

19. Accounts of the meetings are from McGeorge Bundy, Memorandum for the Record, 20 September 1964, FRUS, Vietnam, 1964, pp. 778–81; Ball, The Past Has Another Pattern, pp. 379–80. The "flying fish" quotation is from Karnow, Vietnam, p. 390.

20. Michael Forrestal, Memorandum for John McNaughton, Subject: The Next Three Months in Indochina, 24 September 1964, NSF-CF-VN, Box 9, Vietnam Memos, vol. XVIII, 9/15–30/64, item #254a.

21. McNaughton and William Bundy often referred to their plans as "political-military scripts." John McNaughton, Plan of Action for South Vietnam, 3 September 1964, Gravel, The Pentagon Papers, vol. 3, pp. 556–59; William Bundy, unpublished manuscript, chap. 15, pp. 8–9.

22. See Palmer, The McNamara Strategy and the Vietnam War, esp. pp. 111–12.

23. Thomas C. Schelling, "Assumptions About Enemy Behavior," in Edward S. Quade, ed., Analysis for Military Decisions (Chicago: Rand McNally, 1964), esp. pp. 199–200, 216.

24. Walt W. Rostow, Memorandum for the Secretary of State, "Some Ambiguities in Southeast Asia and in Our Policy Toward That Region," 19 September 1964, FRUS: Vietnam, 1964, pp. 782–85.

25. William Bundy and John McNaughton, "Summary: Courses of Action in Southeast Asia," in Gravel, The Pentagon Papers, vol. 3, pp. 656–66; William Bundy, Memorandum for Secretary Rusk et al., Subject: Issues Raised by Papers on Southeast Asia, 24 November 1964, Papers of Paul C. Warnke, Box 8, book 4, Department of State Materials [1964], item #10, LBJ Library.

26. Andrew J. Goodpaster, interview by author, 9 March 1993.

27. Message from the Ambassador in France [Bohlen] to the President, 2 April 1964, FRUS Vietnam, 1964, pp. 216–19.

28. Telegram from the Under Secretary of State to the Department of State, 6 June 1964, ibid., pp. 464–70.

29. Ball, *The Past Has Another Pattern*, p. 378.

30. For the diplomatic initiatives rejected, see Wallace Thies, *When Governments Collide*, pp. 48–49; Maxwell Taylor, Telegram from the Embassy in Vietnam to the Department of State, August 1964, *FRUS: Vietnam, 1964*, p. 655.

31. Historical Division of the Joint Secretariat, *The Joint Chiefs of Staff and the War in Vietnam*, part 1, chap. 12, pp. 1–4. Taylor, *Swords and Plowshares*, p. 321. Telegram from the Embassy in Vietnam to the Department of State, 24 September 1964, *FRUS: Vietnam, 1964*, pp. 787–89.

32. William Colby, *Lost Victory* (Chicago: Contemporary Books, 1989), p. 173.

33. Telegram from the Embassy in Vietnam to the Department of State, 22 October 1964, *FRUS: Vietnam, 1964*, pp. 843–45; Telegram from the Embassy in Vietnam to the Department of State, 25 October 1964, ibid., pp. 845–46; Taylor, *Swords and Plowshares*, p. 323; *The Joint Chiefs of Staff and the War in Vietnam*, part 1, chap. 13, pp. 3–4.

34. On Russell's position, see Wallace Greene, Memorandum for Record, Résumé of Conversation between Commandant of the Marine Corps and Senator Russell, 26 October 1964, book 2, p. 114, Greene Papers. William Westmoreland, Telegram from the Commander, Military Assistance Command, Vietnam to the Chairman of the Joint Chiefs of Staff, 17 October 1964, *FRUS: Vietnam, 1964*, pp. 838–39; U.S.G. Sharp, Telegram to JCS Exclusive for Wheeler, 25 September 1964, in Gravel, *The Pentagon Papers*, vol. 3, pp. 569–70.

35. McGeorge Bundy, Memorandum for the Record, 20 September 1964, *FRUS: Vietnam, 1964*, pp. 778–81.

36. Record of Telephone Conversation between George Ball and McGeorge Bundy, 8 October 1964, 2:45 P.M., Ball Papers, Box 7, Vietnam, file 1, item #99, LBJ Library.

37. For Westmoreland's views see William Westmoreland, Telegram to the Chairman of the JCS, 17 October 1964, *FRUS: Vietnam, 1964*, pp. 838–39. Quotations from Ball's memorandum are cited from his article "Top Secret: The Prophecy the President Rejected," *Atlantic Monthly*, July 1972.

38. McNamara, *In Retrospect*, p. 154.

39. Editorial Note, *FRUS: Vietnam, 1964*, p. 813. See also Ball, *The Past Has Another Pattern*, pp. 383–84.

40. Memorandum of Telephone Conversation between McGeorge Bundy and George Ball, 8 October 1964, 2:45 p.m., Box 7, Vietnam I, item #99, Papers of George Ball, LBJ Library; Memorandum of Telephone Conversation between Michael Forrestal and George Ball, 8 October 1964, 2:50 P.M., Box 7, Vietnam I, item #100, Papers of George Ball, LBJ Library; Dean Rusk, oral history transcript 2, 1969, tape 1, pp. 33–34.

41. Historical Division of the Joint Secretariat, *The Joint Chiefs of Staff and the War in Vietnam*, part 1, chap. 12, pp. 37–39.

42. Ibid., pp. 37–38.

43. Ibid., pp. 39–41.

44. Ibid., pp. 41.

45. Ibid., pp. 35–36.

46. Memorandum from the Joint Chiefs of Staff to the Secretary of Defense, 27 October 1964, *FRUS: Vietnam, 1964*, pp. 847–50.

47. Ibid.

48. Appendix A, "Actions within RVN," and Appendix B, "Actions Outside the RVN," to JCSM–902–64, "Courses of Action, Southeast Asia," 27 October 1964, ibid., pp. 851–57.

49. Memorandum from the Joint Chiefs of Staff to the Secretary of Defense, 27 October 1964, ibid., pp. 847–50.

50. Ibid.

51. Memorandum from the Joint Chiefs of Staff to the Secretary of Defense, 27 October 1964, ibid., pp. 847–850. JCS quotations are from the "comments" column of Appendix B, "Actions Outside the RVN" in ibid., pp. 854–57.

52. Carl von Clausewitz, *On War*, ed. and trans. Michael Howard and Peter Paret (Princeton, N.J.: Princeton University Press, 1976), p. 585; Ball, *The Past Has Another Pattern*, p. 382.

53. Editor's note #5, Memorandum from the Joint Chiefs of Staff to the Secretary of Defense, 27 October 1964, *FRUS: Vietnam, 1964*, p. 850.

54. Maxwell Taylor, Telegram for Secretary Rusk, 3 October 1964; Dean Rusk, Telegram for Maxwell Taylor, 7 October 1964; Maxwell Taylor, Telegram to State Department, 9 October 1964; Maxwell Taylor, Telegram to State Department, 10 October 1964 in Gravel, *The Pentagon Papers*, vol. 3, pp. 576–80. The "Standing Military Committee" was later abolished in name due to objections from CINCPAC and the JCS.

55. Admiral Sharp, Telegram to JCS, "Southeast Asia Coordination," 23 October 1964, NSF-CF-VN, Vietnam Memos, vol. 20, 10/15–31/64, Box 9, item #147, LBJ Library.

56. Telegram from the Commander in Chief, Pacific to the Commander, Military Assistance Command, Vietnam, 14 August 1964, *FRUS: Vietnam, 1964*, pp. 680–81.

57. Historical Division of the Joint Secretariat, *The Joint Chiefs of Staff and the War in Vietnam*, part 1, chap. 13, p. 10.

58. Maxwell Taylor, Telegram from the Embassy in Vietnam to the Department of State, 1 November 1964–1030 A.M., *FRUS: Vietnam, 1964*, p. 873; Maxwell Taylor, Telegram from the Embassy in Vietnam to the Department of State, 1 November 1964–4 P.M., ibid., pp. 874–75.

59. Wheeler Diaries, entries for 1 and 2 November 1964, Wheeler Papers; Wallace Greene, Memorandum for Record of Actions Which Took Place on 31 October and 1 November 1964 in South Vietnam Following Viet Cong Attack on Bien Hoa Airfield, 2 November 1964, book 2, item #43, Greene Papers.

60. Wheeler Diaries, entries for 1 and 2 November 1964, Wheeler Papers; Wallace Greene, Memorandum for Record of Actions Which Took Place on 31 October and 1 November 1964 in South Vietnam Following Viet Cong Attack on Bien Hoa Airfield, 2 November 1964, book 2, item #43 (115–19), Greene Papers; Historical Division of the Joint Secretariat, *The Joint Chiefs of Staff and the War in Vietnam*, part 1, chap. 13, pp. 13–14.

61. Telegram from the Department of State to the Embassy in Vietnam, 1 November, 1964, 6:28 p.m., *FRUS: Vietnam, 1964*, pp. 876–78.

62. Telegram from the Department of State to the Embassy in Vietnam, 1 November, 1964, 6:29 P.M., ibid., pp. 878–79.

63. Louis Harris, *The Anguish of Change* (New York: Norton, 1973), pp. 23, 73. For others who reveal that the primary reason for forgoing retaliation was the president's anxiety about the election, see Theodore H. White, *The Making of the President, 1964* (New York: Atheneum, 1965), p. 257; Chester Cooper, Oral History Transcript, sec. 1, p. 6, LBJ Library; Wallace Greene, Memorandum for Record of Actions Which Took Place on 31 October and 1 November 1964 in South Vietnam Following Viet Cong Attack on Bien Hoa Airfield, 2 November 1964, book 2, item #43, Greene Papers. NSAM 314 stated that the United States "should be prepared to respond as appropriate against the DRV in the event of any attack on U.S. units . . ." NSAM 314, 10 September 1964, *FRUS: Vietnam, 1964*, pp. 758–60.

64. Telegram from the Chairman of the Joint Chiefs of Staff to the Commander in Chief, Pacific, 2 November 1964–7 p.m., *FRUS: Vietnam, 1964*, p. 881.

65. McNamara, *In Retrospect*, p. 159.

66. For McNamara's professed fear of nuclear war, see *In Retrospect*, p. 109; Wallace Greene, Summary of Meeting of JCS with SECDEF following Regular SECDEF Staff Meeting on Monday, 2 November 1964–10:55 A.M., Greene Papers.

67. Telegram from the Department of State to the Embassy in Vietnam, 1 November, 1964, 6:28 P.M., *FRUS: Vietnam, 1964*, pp. 876–78.

68. Telegram from the Embassy in Vietnam to the Office of the Secretary of Defense, 3 November 1964, ibid., pp. 882–84.

CHAPTER 9

1. Gen. Earle Wheeler, Speech to the Princeton Club, 14 January 1965, Box 126, Wheeler Papers.

2. The description of the Great Society is paraphrased from Kearns, *Lyndon Johnson and the American Dream*, pp. 210–22.

3. McGeorge Bundy, Memorandum for the President, 2 November 1964, NSF-Files of McGeorge Bundy, Box 16, "Management" file, item #10, LBJ Library; Johnson, *The Vantage Point*, p. 110; William Bundy, unpublished manuscript, chap. 1, p. 1.

4. William Bundy, unpublished manuscript, chap. 18, pp. 2–4; Cooper, *Lost Crusade*, pp. 254–55.

5. Project Outline, 3 November 1964, Papers of Paul C. Warnke, Box 8, book 2, Department of State Materials [1964], item #5a. The words emphasized were underlined by hand in the original document.

6. William Bundy, unpublished manuscript, chap. 18, pp. 2–3.

7. William P. Bundy, Memorandum, Subject: "Review of Working Drafts on Courses of Action in Southeast Asia," Papers of Paul C. Warnke, Box 8, book 3, Department of State Material [1964], item #15; Historical Division of the Joint Secretariat, *The Joint Chiefs of Staff and the War in Vietnam*, part 1, chap. 14, p. 1; William Bundy, unpublished manuscript, chap. 18, p. 9.

8. Adm. Lloyd Mustin, Memorandum for the Chairman, NSC Working Group on Southeast Asia, Subject: Comment on Draft for Part 2 of Project Outline on Courses of Action in Southeast Asia–U.S. Objectives and Stakes in SVN and SEA, 10 November 1964; and Enclosure, Subject: Comments on Draft Section 2–U.S. Objectives and Stakes in Vietnam and Southeast Asia, in Gravel, *The Pentagon Papers*, vol. 3, pp. 621–28. In a November 12 memo, the Joint Staff recommended only semantic changes to the working group's definition of the situation in Vietnam. Memorandum for NSC Working Group (Vietnam), Subject: Suggested Revisions for Section 1, "The Situation," 12 November 1964, Papers of Paul C. Warnke, Box 8, book 2, Department of State Material [1964], item #25, LBJ Library.

9. "Analysis of Option B," 13 November 1964, Papers of Paul C. Warnke, Box 8, book 2, Department of State Materials [1964], item #3, LBJ Library. "Analysis of Option B," 11 November 1964, Papers of Paul C. Warnke, Box 8, book 2, Department of State Materials [1964], item #23, LBJ Library.

10. Wheeler Private Diaries, Wheeler Papers; Andrew J. Goodpaster, interview by author, 9 March 1993. Wheeler named the "hard knock" option C Prime (C'). Memorandum from the Joint Chiefs of Staff to the secretary of defense, Subject: Courses of Action in Southeast Asia, 23 November 1964, *FRUS: Vietnam, 1964*, pp. 932–35.

11. Memorandum from the Joint Chiefs of Staff to the secretary of defense, Subject: Courses of Action in Southeast Asia, 23 November 1964, *FRUS: Vietnam, 1964*, pp. 932–35. The president had already been briefed by Rusk, McNamara, and McGeorge Bundy and had an opportunity to read an early draft of the memorandum on November 11. William Bundy, unpublished manuscript, chap. 18, p. 9.

12. Ball, *The Past Has Another Pattern*, p. 388.

13. John McNaughton, Draft Analysis of Option C, 8 November 1964, Papers of Paul C. Warnke, Box 8, book 2, Department of State Materials [1964], item #19a.

14. "Analysis of Option B" and "Analysis of Option C," 13 November 1964, Papers of Paul C. Warnke, Box 8, book 3, Department of State

Materials [1964], items #3 and 6, LBJ Library; Rowen, Memorandum for Mr. William Bundy, 23 November 1964, in Gravel, *The Pentagon Papers*, vol. 3, pp. 642–44.

15. John McNaughton, "Action for South Vietnam (3rd Draft)," 7 November 1964, NSF-CF-VN, Box 10, Vietnam Memos, vol. 21 [11/1–15/64], item #201a, LBJ Library; Forrestal, Oral History Transcript, sec. 1, p. 30; William Bundy, unpublished manuscript, chap. 18, p. 36.

16. Forrestal, Oral History Transcript, sec. 1, pp. 39–40, LBJ Library.

17. John McNaughton, "Action for South Vietnam (3rd Draft)," 7 November 1964, NSF-CF-VN, Box 10, Vietnam Memos, vol. 21 [11/1–15/64], item #201a, LBJ Library.

18. Ibid.

19. Ibid. For earlier McNaughton drafts on objectives, see John McNaughton, "Action for South Vietnam," 6 November 1964, in Gravel, *The Pentagon Papers*, vol. 3, pp. 598–99 and "Aims and Options in Southeast Asia," 13 October 1964, in Gravel, *The Pentagon Papers*, vol. 3, pp. 580–81. The first aim of the earlier memo, "to help SVN and Laos to develop as independent countries," was absent in subsequent memos.

20. John McNaughton, Analysis of Option C, 8 November 1964, in Gravel, *The Pentagon Papers*, vol. 3, pp. 610–16. The quotation is from p. 611.

21. William Bundy and John McNaughton, Summary: Courses of Action in Southeast Asia, 26 November 1964, in Gravel, *The Pentagon Papers*, vol. 3, p. 656.

22. Memorandum for the secretary of defense, Subject: Course of Action in Southeast Asia, 18 November 1964, in Gravel, *The Pentagon Papers*, vol. 3, pp. 639–40.

23. Memorandum from the Joint Chiefs of Staff to the secretary of defense, 14 November 1964, *FRUS: Vietnam, 1964*, pp. 902–906. See also Historical Division of the Joint Secretariat, *The Joint Chiefs of Staff and the War in Vietnam*, vol. 1, chap. 13, p. 26.

24. Memorandum for the Secretary of Defense, Subject: Course of Action in Southeast Asia, 18 November 1964, in Gravel, *The Pentagon Papers*, part 3, pp. 639–40.

25. Agenda for Noon Meeting with the President, 19 November 1964, NSF-Files of McGeorge Bundy, Box 18, Miscellaneous Meetings, vol. 1, item #10; Memorandum for the Record of a Meeting, White House, Washington, 19 November 1964 (Drafted by James C. Thomson on 24 November 1964), *FRUS: Vietnam, 1964*, pp. 914–16.

26. James C. Thomson, Memorandum for the Record of a Meeting, White House, Washington, 19 November 1964 (Drafted on 24 November 1964), *FRUS: Vietnam, 1964*, pp. 914–16.

27. James C. Thomson, Memorandum for the Record of a Meeting, White House, Washington, 19 November 1964 (Drafted on 24 November 1964), ibid.

28. Memorandum from the Chairman of the National Security Council Working Group to the Secretary of State, 24 November 1964, Subject: Issues Raised by Papers on Southeast Asia, ibid., pp. 938–42. Copies of the memo were also sent to McNamara, McCone, Ball, and McGeorge Bundy. Bundy's argument was apparently based, in part, on a letter with enclosures that Forrestal sent to him on 14 November. See Memorandum from Michael V. Forrestal to William Bundy, Subject: Comments on the Drafts Attached to Your Memorandum of November 13, 14 November 1964, and Memorandum for Forrestal from Thomas J. Corcoran, Subject: Option 5, 12 November 1964, Papers of Paul C. Warnke, Box 8, book 3, Department of State Materials [1964], items #9 and #9a, LBJ Library.

29. Telegram from the Commander in Chief, Pacific to the Chairman of the Joint Chiefs of Staff, 22 November 1964, FRUS: Vietnam, 1964, pp. 930–32.

30. Historical Division of the Joint Secretariat, The Joint Chiefs of Staff and the War in Vietnam, part 1, chap. 14, pp. 13–14. For a description of Westmoreland's pacification effort ("Hop Tac") and his retrospective account of this period, see William Westmoreland, A Soldier Reports, pp. 82–85, 105–106, 111–13. See also "Strategy and Policy," Westmoreland Papers, Box 30, item #4, LBJ Library.

31. Admiral Mustin reported to the working group on 14 November that a JCS "fall-back" course of action that would recommend essentially the same military program as Option C was in "an advanced state of completion." Lloyd Mustin, Memorandum for William Bundy, Subject: Additional Material for Project on Courses of Action in Southeast Asia," Papers of Paul C. Warnke, Box 8, book III, Department of State Materials [1964], item #17, LBJ Library.

32. The JCS's principal criticism of Course of Action C was that it did not determine "in advance to what degree we will commit ourselves to achieve our objectives." Memorandum from the Joint Chiefs of Staff to the secretary of defense, 23 November 1964, Subject: Courses of Action in Southeast Asia, FRUS: Vietnam, 1964, pp. 932–35. Although they remained opposed to graduated pressure, the Chiefs did not register their concerns with the president. In a JCS meeting on November 24, 1964, they had been unwilling to say that graduated pressure was worse than doing nothing. Dr. Walter Poole, Joint Staff Historical Office, letter to author, 30 July 1996.

33. Historical Division of the Joint Secretariat, The Joint Chiefs of Staff and the War in Vietnam, part 1, chap. 14, p. 9; William Bundy, Memorandum of the Meeting of the Executive Committee, 24 November 1964, FRUS: Vietnam, 1964, pp. 943–45.

34. William Bundy, unpublished manuscript, chap. 18, pp. 34–36.

35. Project Outline, 3 November 1964, Papers of Paul C. Warnke, Box 8, book 2, Department of State Materials [1964], item #5a, LBJ Library.

36. Historical Division of the Joint Secretariat, The Joint Chiefs of Staff and the War in Vietnam, part 1, chap. 13, pp. 4–8; chap. 12, pp. 26, 32–34.

37. Earle Wheeler, Memorandum for the Deputy Secretary of Defense, Subject: Operation Plan 34 A—Additional Actions 14 November 1964, NSF-CF-VN, Box 11, Vietnam Memos, vol, 23, file 1 of 2, item #102, LBJ Library.

38. See "Suggested Scenario for Controlled Escalation," undated, FRUS: Vietnam, 1964, pp. 955–57. Taylor's annotations on the accompanying original memorandum indicate that he prepared the documents in Saigon and brought them with him to Washington at the end of November 1964.

39. William Bundy, Memorandum of the Meeting of the Executive Committee, 27 November 1964, FRUS: Vietnam, 1964, pp. 958–60. Ball participated in EXCOM meetings through November 28, after which he traveled to Europe on other business. William Bundy, unpublished manuscript, chap. 19, p. 6.

40. Maxwell Taylor, "The Current Situation in Vietnam—November 1964," undated, FRUS: Vietnam, 1964, pp. 948–57. The original in Taylor Papers, T–157–69, indicates that Taylor used this paper in his Washington meetings. William Bundy, unpublished manuscript, chap. 19, p. 6.

41. Maxwell Taylor, "The Current Situation in Vietnam—November 1964," undated, FRUS: Vietnam, 1964, pp. 948–57; William Bundy, Memorandum of the Meeting of the Executive Committee, 27 November 1964, ibid., pp. 958–60. See also Historical Division of the Joint Secretariat, The Joint Chiefs of Staff and the War in Vietnam, part 1, chap. 14, pp. 16–17.

42. William Bundy, Memorandum of the Meeting of the Executive Committee, 27 November 1964, FRUS: Vietnam, 1964, pp. 958–60; William Bundy, unpublished manuscript, chap. 19, p. 7.

43. William Bundy's notes and recollection of the meeting do not mention any remarks by General Wheeler or any discussion of the Chiefs' position. William Bundy, Memorandum of the Meeting of the Executive Committee, 27 November 1964, FRUS: Vietnam, 1964, pp. 958–60; William Bundy, unpublished manuscript, chap. 19, pp. 5–8; Historical Division of the Joint Secretariat, The Joint Chiefs of Staff and the War in Vietnam, part 1, chap. 14, pp. 22–23.

44. William Bundy, Draft NSAM on Southeast Asia, Papers of Paul C. Warnke, Box 8, book IV, Department of State Materials [1964], item #3, LBJ Library; John McNaughton, "Graduated Military Pressure and Related Actions," NSF-International Meetings and Travel File, Box 28, Trip-McGeorge Bundy-Saigon, vol. 2, item #14, LBJ Library; William Bundy, unpublished manuscript, chap. 19, p. 12.

45. Historical Division of the Joint Secretariat, The Joint Chiefs of Staff and the War in Vietnam, part 1, chap. 14, pp. 26, 29. Taylor's comment is from Dr. Walter Poole, Joint Staff Historical Office, letter to author, 30 July 1996.

46. William Bundy, Memorandum for Southeast Asia Principals, 29 November 1964, Papers of Paul C. Warnke, Box 8, book 4, Department of State Materials [1964], item #3, LBJ Library; Draft NSAM on Southeast

Asia, 29 November 1964, Papers of Paul C. Warnke, Box 8, book IV, Department of State Materials [1964], item #3a, LBJ Library.

47. William Bundy, unpublished manuscript, chap. 18, pp. 31–32.

48. Historical Division of the Joint Secretariat, *The Joint Chiefs of Staff and the War in Vietnam*, part 1, chap. 14, p. 26. For the text of the excised paragraph and the other language of the November 29 draft, see William Bundy, Draft Position Paper on Southeast Asia, 29 November 1964, Gravel, *The Pentagon Papers*, vol. 3, pp. 678–83. A copy of the paper with Robert McNamara's handwritten remarks and the JCS paragraph lined through is in the Papers of Paul C. Warnke, Box 8, book 4, Department of State Materials [1964], item #3, LBJ Library. William Bundy sought to justify the decision to remove the JCS paragraph in his unpublished manuscript, chap. 18, pp. 31–32.

49. John McNaughton, Notes on a Meeting, 1 December 1964, *FRUS: Vietnam, 1964*, pp. 965–69; Historical Division of the Joint Secretariat, *The Joint Chiefs of Staff and the War in Vietnam*, part 1, chap. 14, pp. 31–33.

50. Historical Division of the Joint Secretariat, *The Joint Chiefs of Staff and the War in Vietnam*, part 1, chap. 14, p. 33.

51. John McNaughton, Notes on a Meeting, 1 December 1964, *FRUS: Vietnam, 1964*, pp. 965–69.

52. Historical Division of the Joint Secretariat, *The Joint Chiefs of Staff and the War in Vietnam*, part 1, chap. 14, pp. 33–34.

53. William Bundy, unpublished manuscript, chap. 19, pp. 14–15; Instructions from the President to the Ambassador to Vietnam, 3 December 1964, *FRUS: Vietnam, 1964*, pp. 974–78. The criteria for minimum performance are taken almost verbatim from the report that Taylor carried with him to Washington on 26 November. Maxwell Taylor, Paper Prepared by the Ambassador in Vietnam, Subject: the Current Situation in South Viet-Nam—November 1964, *FRUS: Vietnam, 1964*, pp. 948–55. The last quotation is from McGeorge Bundy, handwritten notes, 1 December 1964, Papers of McGeorge Bundy, Box 1, LBJ Library.

54. Jack Valenti as quoted in Gittinger, *A Vietnam Roundtable*, pp. 44, 66.

55. Historical Division of the Joint Secretariat, *The Joint Chiefs of Staff and the War in Vietnam*, part 1, chap. 14, pp. 35–36; State Department Chronology of the Vietnam War, NSF-NSC History-Presidential Decisions-Gulf of Tonkin Attacks August 64, vol. 1, p. 60, LBJ Library; William Bundy, unpublished manuscript, chap. 19, pp. 11–12; John McNaughton, Notes on a Meeting, 1 December 1964, *FRUS: Vietnam, 1964*, pp. 965–69. On December 7, the president sent a memo to McNamara and Rusk and McCone stressing that he considered it "a matter of highest importance that the substance of this position should not become public except as I specifically direct." Memorandum from the President to the Secretary of State, the Secretary of Defense, and the Director of Central Intelligence, 7 December 1964, *FRUS: Vietnam, 1964*, p. 984.

56. *New York Times*, 25 November 1964, p. 36.

57. Historical Division of the Joint Secretariat, *The Joint Chiefs of Staff and the War in Vietnam*, part 1, chap. 15, pp. 11–14, 18–19; Andrew J. Goodpaster, interview by author, 9 March 1993.

CHAPTER 10

1. Gen. Volney Warner, Oral History Transcript, Senior Officer Debriefing Program, 1983, U.S. Army Institute for Military History, Carlisle Barracks, Pa.

2. Ball, "Top Secret: The Prophecy the President Rejected."

3. Memorandum for Record, Subject: General Johnson's Trip to South Vietnam, December 1964, Box 34, H. K. Johnson Papers. Emphasis added.

4. Ibid.; Memorandum for Record, Subject: RVN Field Visits, Box 135, ibid. Various letters to officers visited during his trip to South Vietnam, Box 34, General Johnson's trip to South Vietnam, ibid. Harold K. Johnson, Memorandum for the Secretary of Defense, Subject: Report on Trip to Alaska, the Far East, and Southeast Asia, 2–17 December 1964, ibid.

5. Westmoreland, *A Soldier Reports*, pp. 93–94; Gravel, *Pentagon Papers*, vol. 2, pp. 342–45.

6. William Bundy, unpublished manuscript, chap. 20, p. 4.

7. Westmoreland, *A Soldier Reports*, pp. 93–94; Gravel, *The Pentagon Papers*, vol. 2, pp. 346–48. The Ky remark is from Cooper, *Lost Crusade*, p. 251.

8. Memorandum of a Conversation Between the Ambassador in Vietnam and the Commander in Chief of the Vietnamese Armed Forces, 21 December 1964, *FRUS: Vietnam, 1964*, pp. 1020–23; Telegram from the Embassy in Vietnam to the Department of State, 25 December 1964, ibid., pp. 1041–43.

9. Memorandum of a Conversation Between the Ambassador in Vietnam and the Commander in Chief of the Vietnamese Armed Forces, 21 December 1964, ibid., pp. 1020–23; Gravel, *The Pentagon Papers*, vol. 2, p. 350; Telegram from the Embassy in Vietnam to the Department of State, 25 December 1964, ibid., pp. 1041–43; Telegram from the Embassy in Vietnam to the Department of State, 23 December 1964, ibid., pp. 1031–32; Cooper, *Lost Crusade*, p. 251.

10. Historical Division of the Joint Secretariat, *The Joint Chiefs of Staff and the War in Vietnam*, part 1, chap 15, p. 19.

11. Telegram from the Embassy in Vietnam to the Department of State, 25 December 1964, *FRUS: Vietnam, 1964*, pp. 1043–44; Telegram from the Embassy in Vietnam to the Department of State, 28 December 1964, ibid., p. 1049; Cooper, *Lost Crusade*, p. 252.

12. Historical Division of the Joint Secretariat, *The Joint Chiefs of Staff and the War in Vietnam*, part 1, chap 15, pp. 21–22.

13. Paper Prepared by the President's Special Assistant for National Security Affairs, 28 December 1964, *FRUS: Vietnam, 1964*, pp. 1051–53; William Bundy, unpublished manuscript, chap. 20, pp. 11–12; Telegram from the President to the Ambassador in Vietnam, 30 December 1964, *FRUS: Vietnam, 1964*, pp. 1057–59.

14. The Rusk quotation is from a meeting with the President on 6 January 1965. See Gibbons, *The U.S. Government and the Vietnam War*, vol. 3, p. 33. Paper Prepared by the President's Special Assistant for National Security Affairs, 28 December 1964, *FRUS: Vietnam, 1964*, pp. 1051–53; William Bundy, unpublished manuscript, chap. 20, pp. 11–12.

15. Telegram from the President to the Ambassador in Vietnam, 30 December 1964, *FRUS: Vietnam, 1964*, pp. 1057–59. It seems that the president's suggestion that Taylor receive some expert assistance came from McGeorge Bundy as well. On Christmas, Bundy received a letter from Edward Lansdale who suggested that it was "about time that some of the fine do-ers among the Americans were permitted to return to Vietnam and lend their skilled help to resolving a critical situation, waiving 'personal rivalries and lesser issues.'" Memorandum from Edward G. Lansdale to the President's Special Assistant for National Security Affairs, 24 December 1964, Subject: Vietnam, *FRUS: Vietnam, 1964*, p. 1040.

16. Telegram from the President to the Ambassador in Vietnam, 30 December 1964, ibid., pp. 1057–59; Telephone Conversation between McGeorge Bundy and Lyndon Johnson, 2 March 1964, 12:35 P.M., Recordings of Telephone Conversations and Meetings, Recordings of Telephone Conversations, White House Series, tape WH6403.01, citation #2309, LBJ Library.

17. Westmoreland, *A Soldier Reports*, p. 114.

18. William Bundy, unpublished manuscript, chap 18, p. 34; Historical Division of the Joint Secretariat, *The Joint Chiefs of Staff and the War in Vietnam*, part 1, chap. 16, pp. 2–3.

19. References to ground troop deployments are present in the following document, for example: William Bundy, Memorandum for Secretary Rusk et al., Subject: Issues Raised by Papers on Southeast Asia, 24 November 1964, Papers of Paul C. Warnke, Box 8, book 4, Department of State [1964], item #10, LBJ Library. Although Option C called for the deployment of air defense units and organic security forces into South Vietnam, the paper stated that "present military planning does not envisage the introduction of substantial ground forces into SVN [South Vietnam] or Thailand in conjunction with these initial actions." William Bundy and John McNaughton, "Courses of Action in Southeast Asia," 26 November 1964, Papers of Paul C. Warnke, Box 8, Book IV, Department of State [1964], item #13, LBJ Library. For the 24 November meeting, see Gravel, *The Pentagon Papers*, vol. 3, p. 239. For the final version of the paper, see Position Paper on Southeast Asia, 2 December 1964, *FRUS: Vietnam, 1964*, pp. 969–974. For the William Bundy quotation, see William Bundy,

unpublished manuscript, chap. 18, p. 34. See also William Bundy as quoted in Gittinger, A *Vietnam Roundtable*, p. 43.

20. Robert Johnson and Paul Kattenberg, Alternative to Air Attacks on North Vietnam: Proposals for Use of U.S. Ground Forces in Support of Diplomacy in Vietnam, 30 November 1964, Papers of Paul C. Warnke, Box 8, Book IV, State Department [1964], Item #4a, LBJ Library.

21. Robert Johnson and Paul Kattenberg, Alternative to Air Attacks on North Vietnam: Proposals for Use of U.S. Ground Forces in Support of Diplomacy in Vietnam, 30 November 1964, Papers of Paul C. Warnke, Box 8, Book IV, State Department [1964], Item #4a, LBJ Library; Memorandum from the Chairman of the Policy Planning Council to the Secretary of Defense, 16 November 1964, Subject: Military Dispositions and Political Signals, *FRUS: Vietnam, 1964*, pp. 906–909.

22. Historical Division of the Joint Secretariat, *The Joint Chiefs of Staff and the War in Vietnam*, part 2, chap 17, pp. 1–3.

23. Taylor, *Swords and Plowshares*, 327. For Taylor's suggestion that a "pulmotor treatment might become necessary," see Maxwell Taylor, Telegram from the Embassy in Vietnam to the Department of State, 10 November 1964, *FRUS: Vietnam, 1964*, pp. 899–900.

24. Maxwell Taylor, Telegram for the President, 6 January 1965, NSF-International Meetings and Travel File, Box 29, Trip-McGeorge Bundy to Saigon, Vol. III 2/4/65 [1 of 2], Item #16, LBJ Library.

25. Ibid.

26. Ibid.

27. Ibid.

28. McGeorge Bundy, handwritten notes of a meeting, 6 January 1965, Papers of McGeorge Bundy, Box 1, LBJ Library.

29. Lyndon Johnson, Telegram for Maxwell Taylor, 7 January 1965, NSF-NSC History-Deployment of Major Forces to Vietnam, Box 40, Vol. I tabs 1–10, Item #10a, LBJ Library.

30. John McNaughton, Draft-Observations Re South Vietnam, 4 January 1965, Gravel, *Pentagon Papers*, vol. 3, pp. 683–684; William Bundy, Memorandum for the Secretary, Subject: Notes on the South Vietnamese Situation and Alternatives, 6 January 1965, Gravel, *Pentagon Papers*, vol. 3, pp. 684–686; William Bundy, unpublished manuscript, chap 20, pp. 19–23.

31. Gibbons, *The U.S. Government and the Vietnam War*, vol. 3, p. 33; Robert F. Kennedy, Letter to Maxwell Taylor, received in Saigon on 8 February 1965, Taylor Papers, Box 50, Item #11.

32. McGeorge Bundy, Memorandum for the President, 4 January 1965, NSF-NSC History-Deployment of U.S. Forces, Box 40, Vol. I tabs 1–10, Item #6, LBJ Library; Lyndon Johnson, Memorandum for the Secretary of Defense, 7 January 1965, NSF-Agency File, Box 11, Defense Vol. II 1–65, Item #28, LBJ Library; "Can the U.S. Win in Vietnam?", *U.S. News and World Report*, 11 January 1965, pp. 44–52.

33. Chester Cooper, Memorandum for McGeorge Bundy, 22 January

1965, and Telegram From American Embassy London to Secretary of State, 18 January 1965. Both documents are at NSF-CF-VN, Box 12, Vietnam Memos Vol. XXVI 1/10–31/65 [1 of 2], Item #'s 159 and 159a.

34. McNamara, *In Retrospect*, p. 165.

35. Historical Division of the Joint Secretariat, *The Joint Chiefs of Staff and the War in Vietnam*, part 2, chap 15, pp. 22–24.

36. Ibid., vol. 2, chap 17, pp. 12–14; Telegram to the Joint Chiefs of Staff from the Commander in Chief, Pacific, 26 January 1965, NSF-CF-VN, Box 12, Vietnam Cables Vol. XXVI [1/10–31/65], Item #21, LBJ Library; Telegram to the Commander in Chief, Pacific from the Joint Chiefs of Staff, 27 January 1965, NSF-CF-VN, Box 12, Vietnam Cables Vol. XXVI [1/10–31/65], Item #26, LBJ Library; R.C.B. [Richard C. Bowman], Memorandum for McGeorge Bundy, 5 January 1965, Subject: Southeast Asia Operations, NSF-CF-VN, Box 12, Vietnam Cables Vol. XXV [12/26/64–1/9/65], item # 155, LBJ Library.

37. Henry Raymont, "Saigon Buddhists Stone U.S. Library," *New York Times*, 23 January 1965, pp. 1, 3; Seymour Topping, "Monks in Vietnam Assail U.S. Envoy; Library is Raided," *New York Times*, 23 January 1965, pp. 1–2; *The Joint Chiefs of Staff and the War in Vietnam*, part 2, chap 17, p. 12.

38. Telegram from LTG Richard Meyer to Westmoreland, 14 January 1965, Policy/Strategy File, Miles Papers; Frank Osmonski, interview by Charles B. McDonald, Box 31, item # 3, Westmoreland Papers; John McNaughton, Observations Re South Vietnam, in Gravel, *The Pentagon Papers*, vol. 3, pp. 683–84.

39. Seymour Topping, "2 Saigon Leaders Chide U.S. on Role," *New York Times*, 22 January 1965, p. 3; Charles Mohr, "Johnson Briefs Congress Chiefs on World Events," *New York Times*, 22 January 1965, pp. 1, 3.

40. For a summary of this meeting and the nature of public and Congressional opinion at the time, see Gibbons, *The U.S. Government and the Vietnam War*, vol. 3, pp. 36–43.

41. Bromley K. Smith, Notes on the Meeting of 22 January 1965, NSF, Files of McGeorge Bundy, Box 18, Miscellaneous Meetings File, vol. 1, item #6. The date on this memorandum is incorrect. The meeting actually occurred on January 21. See Charles Mohr, "Johnson Briefs Congress Chiefs on World Events," *New York Times*, 22 January 1965, pp. 1, 3.

42. Ibid.

43. Message from Arthur Sylvester (Assistant Secretary of Defense for Public Affairs) to CINCPAC, 23 January 1965, NSF-CF-VN, Box 12, Vietnam Cables, vol. 26, item #17.

44. McNamara, *In Retrospect*, pp. 166–68; John McNaughton, Observations Re South Vietnam After Khanh's "Re-Coup," Gravel, *Pentagon Papers*, vol. 3, pp. 686–87. McNaughton's memo includes notes taken during a discussion with McNamara. McGeorge Bundy as quoted in Gittinger, *A Vietnam Roundtable*, pp. 47–49; Gibbons, *The U.S. Government and the Vietnam War*, vol. 3, pp. 46–47.

45. McGeorge Bundy, Memorandum for the President, 27 January 1965, NSF-NSC History-Deployment of Major Forces to Vietnam, Box 40, vol. 1, tabs 1–10, item #22.

46. Ibid.; William Bundy, unpublished manuscript, chap. 22, p. 4.

47. Gibbons, *The U.S. Government and the Vietnam War*, vol. 3, p. 51. Emphasis is in McGeorge Bundy's original handwritten notes of the January 27 meeting with the president.

48. Historical Division of the Joint Secretariat, *The Joint Chiefs of Staff and the War in Vietnam*, part 2, chap 17, p. 14–15; McGeorge Bundy as quoted in Karnow, *Vietnam*, p. 426. On avoiding congressional criticism, see Gibbons, *The U.S. Government and the Vietnam War*, vol. 3, pp. 52–53.

49. Historical Division of the Joint Secretariat, *The Joint Chiefs of Staff and the War in Vietnam*, part 2, chap. 17, pp. 16–17.

50. Gibbons, *The U.S. Government and the Vietnam War*, p. 51. Although Taylor resisted Bundy's trip, he had first suggested that Bundy travel to Saigon on 6 January 1965. Telegram from Maxwell Taylor for the President, 6 January 1965, NSF-CF-VN, box 40, Deployment of Major U.S. Forces, vol. 1, tabs 1–10; Cooper, Oral History Transcript, sec. 1, p. 9, LBJ Library.

51. Cooper, Oral History Transcript, sec. 1, pp. 10–15; Cooper, *The Lost Crusade*, p. 258; Andrew J. Goodpaster, interview by author, 9 March 1993.

52. On 24 July 1964, Michael Forrestal sent Bundy a memo comparing the numbers of soldiers killed in action in Vietnam during the Kennedy and Johnson presidencies with the number of traffic accident "casualties" in Washington. Michael Forrestal, Memorandum for McGeorge Bundy, 24 July 1964, NSF-CF-VN, Box 6, Vietnam Memos, vol. 14, LBJ Library. In May 1963 Bundy suggested that Vice President Johnson make a speech on Vietnam. He stated that "seventy-two Americans have been killed there" and suggested that "you could wrap the flag around that sum." Telcon between McGeorge Bundy and George Ball, Box 7, Vietnam, file 1, item #40, Ball Papers, LBJ Library.

53. Andrew J. Goodpaster, interview by author, 9 March 1993; William Westmoreland, interview by Charles B. McDonald, 3 February 1973, Box 30, Westmoreland Papers, LBJ Library. See also Westmoreland, *A Soldier Reports*, p. 115.

54. Cooper, *Lost Crusade*, pp. 259–60.

CHAPTER 11

1. Earle Wheeler, Speech to the Inter-American Defense College, 23 March 1965, Box 126, Wheeler Papers.

2. Arthur S. Collins, Oral History Transcript, 1981, p. 309, U.S. Army Military History Institute, Carlisle Barracks, Pa.

3. Marolda and Fitzgerald, *The United States Navy and the Vietnam Conflict*, vol. 2, pp. 496–97.

4. McGeorge Bundy, Memorandum for the President, 7 February 1965, NSF-CF-VN, Box 13, Vietnam Memos, vol. 27, item #118, LBJ Library. On Bundy's coordination of his report with Taylor, see Westmoreland, A *Soldier Reports*, p. 116.

5. John McNaughton, "Graduated Military Pressure and Related Actions (Option C)," 30 November 1964, NSF-CF-VN, Box 11, Vietnam Memos, vol. 23 12/1–18/64 [file 1 of 2], item #155a, LBJ Library; McGeorge Bundy, "A Policy of Sustained Reprisal," in Gravel, *The Pentagon Papers*, vol. 3, pp. 687–91.

6. McGeorge Bundy, "A Policy of Sustained Reprisal," 7 February 1965, in Gravel, *The Pentagon Papers*, vol. 3, pp. 687–91.

7. Ibid.

8. McGeorge Bundy as quoted in Gittinger, A *Vietnam Roundtable*, pp. 59–60.

9. Lyndon Johnson, Telegram for Maxwell Taylor, 8 February 1965, NSF-NSC History-Deployment of Major Forces, Box 40, vol. 1, tabs 11–41, item #65, LBJ Library. McGeorge Bundy recalled: "Was President Johnson's way of discussing his Vietnam decisions shaped by his strong desire to keep the track open for the most extraordinary legislative program of the twentieth century in a single year? Yes. And would he admit it? No." Jack Valenti made the same general observation. McGeorge Bundy and Jack Valenti as quoted in Gittenger, A *Vietnam Roundtable*, pp. 65–66; See also Gibbons, *The U.S. Government and the Vietnam War*, vol. 3, pp. 115–16.

10. Historical Division of the Joint Secretariat, *The Joint Chiefs of Staff and the War in Vietnam*, part 2, chapter 18, pp. 5–6.

11. McGeorge Bundy, "A Policy of Sustained Reprisal," 7 February 1965, Gravel, *The Pentagon Papers*, vol. 3, pp. 687–91.

12. Bromley Smith, Summary Notes of 546th NSC Meeting, 7 February 1965, NSF-Meeting Notes File, Box 1, LBJ Library.

13. Ibid.

14. Bromley Smith, Summary Notes NSC Meeting No. 548, 10 February 1965, NSF-Meeting Notes File, Box 1, LBJ Library.

15. Summary Record of National Security Council Meeting No. 548, 10 February 1965, NSF-NSC Meetings File, Box 7, vol. 3, tab 30, item #2, LBJ Library.

16. Marolda and Fitzgerald, *The United States Navy and the Vietnam Conflict*, vol. 2, pp. 498–500.

17. Historical Division of the Joint Secretariat, *The Joint Chiefs of Staff and the War in Vietnam*, part 2, chap. 17, p. 23; Marolda and Fitzgerald, *The United States Navy and the Vietnam Conflict*, vol. 2, p. 500.

18. Historical Division of the Joint Secretariat, *The Joint Chiefs of Staff and the War in Vietnam*, part 2, chapter 17, p. 23.

19. Ibid., chap. 18, p. 15.

20. "From LeMay to McConnell—A Change to the 'New Breed,'" *Newsweek*, 4 January 1965, p. 16; "To the Top," *Time*, 1 January 1965, pp.

29–30; "The Management Team," *Time*, 5 February 1965, pp. 22–23A.

21. Maxwell Taylor, Confidential Letter to General Lyman Lemnitzer, 14 January 1964, Box 22, File T–236–69, Taylor Papers; John P. McConnell, Oral History Transcript, 14 August 1969, LBJ Library, pp. 2–7.

22. On McConnell's view of his role as Chief of Staff, see John McConnell, "Some Reflections on a Tour of Duty," *Air University Review* 21, no. 6 (Sept.–Oct. 1969), p. 4. Emphasis in original.

23. John P. McConnell, Oral History Transcript, 14 August 1969, LBJ Library, pp. 2–7.

24. Harold K. Johnson, Oral History Transcript, Senior Officer Debriefing Program, vol. 1, tape 2, p. 13.

25. Historical Division of the Joint Secretariat, *The Joint Chiefs of Staff and the War in Vietnam*, part 2, chap. 17, p. 16; chap. 18, p. 6.

26. Andrew J. Goodpaster, interview by author, 9 March 1993; Bruce Palmer in John Schlight, ed., *Second Indochina War Symposium* (Washington, D.C.: U.S. Army Center of Military History, 1986), p. 154.

27. Partial Record of February 8, 1965, meeting with the president by a group that met before NSC meeting, NSF-NSC Meetings File, Box 1, vol. 3 tab 29, 8 February 1965, item #3, LBJ Library.

28. McNamara suggested that there might be "leeway" in the president's desire to impose sharp limitations on the air campaign. Historical Division of the Joint Secretariat, *The Joint Chiefs of Staff and the War in Vietnam*, part 2, chap. 18, pp. 6, 15.

29. For the JCS position, see ibid., p. 8; Palmer quotations are from Schlight, *Second Indochina War Symposium*, p. 154. See also Palmer, *The 25-Year War*, pp. 34–35.

30. Historical Division of the Joint Secretariat, *The Joint Chiefs of Staff and the War in Vietnam*, part 2, chap. 17, p. 16; chap. 18, p. 6.

31. Ibid., chap. 18, p. 7; Gravel, *The Pentagon Papers*, vol. 3, pp. 318–20.

32. McNamara, *In Retrospect*, p. 174.

33. Historical Division of the Joint Secretariat, *The Joint Chiefs of Staff and the War in Vietnam*, part 2, chap. 18, pp. 6, 9.

34. Ibid., pp. 11–14.

35. Maxwell Taylor, Telegram to the Secretary of State, 14 February 1965, NSF-NSC History-Deployment, Box 40, vol. 1, item #10, LBJ Library.

36. Gibbons, *The U.S. Government and the Vietnam War*, vol. 3, pp. 45, 55; Central Intelligence Agency, Intelligence Memorandum, 25 February 1965, NSF-CF-VN, Box 14, Vietnam Memos, vol. 29, item #145, LBJ Library; Historical Division of the Joint Secretariat, *The Joint Chiefs of Staff and the War in Vietnam*, part 2, chap. 17, p. 8; U. Alexis Johnson, *The Right Hand of Power* (Englewood Cliffs, N.J.: Prentice-Hall, 1984), pp. 418–19.

37. Johnson, *The Right Hand of Power*, p. 421.

38. Ibid., pp. 422–25.

39. Ibid.

40. Maxwell Taylor, handwritten notes used in addressing Internal Security Council, 26 February 1965, Taylor Papers, Diary File, item #22; Gibbons, *The U.S. Government and the Vietnam War*, vol. 3, pp. 113–14.

41. Duiker, *Sacred War*, pp. 170–71; Jack Langguth, "Week in Vietnam Costliest of War for the Two Sides," *New York Times*, 18 February 1965, p. 10; Historical Division of the Joint Secretariat, *The Joint Chiefs of Staff and the War in Vietnam*, part 2, chap. 17, p. 3.

42. Gibbons, *The U.S. Government and the Vietnam War*, vol. 3, p. 85.

43. Central Intelligence Agency, "Individuals and Cliques in South Vietnam," 25 February 1965, NSF-CF-VN, Box 14, Vietnam Memos, vol. 29, item #145, LBJ Library.

44. Gibbons, *The U.S. Government and the Vietnam War*, vol. 3, p. 114, Taylor cable to State Department; William C. Westmoreland, interview by Charles B. MacDonald, 10 April 1973, Westmoreland Papers, Box 30, item #4, LBJ Library.

45. Maxwell Taylor, Paper Prepared by the President's Military Representative, 3 November 1961, *FRUS: Vietnam, 1961*, pp. 479–81.

46. John Taylor, *The Sword and the Pen*, p. 328.

47. U. Alexis Johnson, *The Right Hand of Power*, p. 427.

48. William Westmoreland, Interview by Paul Miles, 10 April 1971, Miles Papers, Interview File, p. 9.

49. Bruce Palmer, "U.S. Intelligence and Vietnam," *Studies in Intelligence*, vol. 28 (special issue, 1984), pp. 34–35.

50. Historical Division of the Joint Secretariat, *The Joint Chiefs of Staff and the War in Vietnam*, part 3, chap. 19, pp. 1–2.

51. Maxwell Taylor, Telegram to the Joint Chiefs of Staff, 22 February 1965, *FRUS: Vietnam, 1965*, pp. 347–49; Johnson, *The Right Hand of Power*, pp. 427–28.

52. Maxwell Taylor, Telegram to the Joint Chiefs of Staff, *FRUS: Vietnam, January–June 1965*, pp. 347–49.

53. Dean Rusk, Telegram from the Department of State to the Embassy in Vietnam, 26 February 1965, ibid., p, 376. Telegram from the Chairman of the Joint Chiefs of Staff to the Commander in Chief, Pacific, 27 February 1965, pp. 380–81. Gibbons, *The U.S. Government and the Vietnam War*, vol. 3, p. 123.

54. U. Alexis Johnson, *The Right Hand of Power*, pp. 427–28; Westmoreland, *A Soldier Reports*, p. 123; Taylor, *Swords and Plowshares*, p. 338; William C. Westmoreland, Interview by Charles B. MacDonald, 10 April 1973; Message from Westmoreland to CINCPAC, 22 February 1965, NSF-NSC Histories-Deployment of Major U.S. Forces to Vietnam, Box 40, vol. 2, item #15a, LBJ Library.

55. Memorandum from the Joint Chiefs of Staff to the Secretary of Defense, 11 February 1965, *FRUS: Vietnam, January–June 1965*, pp. 240–43. Message from JCS to CINCPAC, 12 February 1965, NSF-NSC Histories-Deployment of Major U.S. Forces to Vietnam, Box 40, vol. 1, item #90, LBJ Library.

56. Ibid.

57. Message from CINCPAC to the JCS, Deployment of MEB to Danang, 24 February 1965, NSF-NSC Histories-Deployment, Box 40, vol. 2, item #23a, LBJ Library.

58. Message from JCS to CINCPAC and MACV, 27 February 1965, NSF-NSC Histories-Deployment, Box 40, LBJ Library.

59. Telegram from Rusk to Taylor, 26 February 1965, NSF-NSC Histories-Deployment, Box 40, vol. 2, item #28a, LBJ Library.

60. Historical Division of the Joint Secretariat, The Joint Chiefs of Staff and the War in Vietnam, part 2, chap. 18, pp. 15–16. Apparently in support of Westmoreland's and Wheeler's concerns, Eisenhower told LBJ on February 17 that "centralization is the refuge of fear" and urged him to "trust" the military to conduct operations against North Vietnam. Andrew Goodpaster, Memorandum of a Meeting with President Johnson, 17 February 1965, FRUS: Vietnam, January-June 1965, p. 376.

61. Historical Division of the Joint Secretariat, The Joint Chiefs of Staff and the War in Vietnam, part 2, chap. 18, pp. 16–17.

62. Marolda and Fitzgerald, The United States Navy and the Vietnam Conflict, vol. 2, p. 505.

63. On the confusion surrounding expectations for and conceptions of the air campaign, see William Bundy as quoted in Gittinger, ed., The Johnson Years, p. 54; Cooper, Oral History Transcript, I, p. 16; Gibbons, The U.S. Government and the Vietnam War, vol. 3, pp. 68, 88, 118–19; Historical Division of the Joint Secretariat, The Joint Chiefs of Staff and the War in Vietnam, part 3, chapter 18, pp. 11, 19. See also, Clodfelter, Limits of Air Power, pp. 75–76; Tilford, Crosswinds, p. 71.

64. Gibbons, The U.S. Government and the Vietnam War, vol. 2, pp. 87–90; Ball, The Past Has Another Pattern, pp. 390–92.

65. Gibbons, The U.S. Government and the Vietnam War, vol. 3, pp. 87–90; Ball, The Past Has Another Pattern, pp. 390–92.

66. Gibbons, The U.S. Government and the Vietnam War, vol. 3, pp. 89–90; Maxwell Taylor, Telegram for Dean Rusk, NSF-CF-VN, Box 14 Vietnam Memos Vol 29 [2/20–28/65], item 150a, LBJ Library; Maxwell Taylor, Telegram for Dean Rusk, 15 February 1965, NSF-NSC-Histories, Deployment, Box 40, vol. 1, item #106, LBJ Library. The final quotation is from Dean Rusk, as quoted in William Bundy, unpublished manuscript, chapter 22B, p. 23.

67. Telephone Conversation between George Ball and McGeorge Bundy, 13 February 1965, 11:30 A.M., Papers of George W. Ball, Box 7, Vietnam I [1/3/65–5/24/65], item #36; NSAM 288, 17 March 1964, FRUS: Vietnam, 1964, pp. 172–73. NSAM 288 approved the objective in Vietnam as written in McNamara's March 16 Memorandum to the President. Memorandum from the Secretary of Defense to the President, 16 March 1964, FRUS: Vietnam, 1964, p. 154; Ball, The Past Has Another Pattern, pp. 390, 504–5, n. 8.

68. John McNaughton, Memorandum for McGeorge Bundy, 10 March 1965, "Action for South Vietnam," in Gibbons, *The U.S. Government and the Vietnam War*, vol., pp. 157–58. For the full document, see NSF-CF-VN, Box 14, Vietnam Memos vol. 30, item #131, LBJ Library.

69. Ibid.

70. Telegram from General Earle Wheeler to General William Westmoreland, 17 February 1965, Miles Papers, Policy/Strategy 16–20 February 65; NSAM 288, 17 March 1964, *FRUS: Vietnam, 1964*, pp. 172–73. The Army staff continued to plan with NSAM 288 in mind. Department of the Army, Office of the Deputy Chief of Staff for Military Operations, "A Program for the Pacification and Long-Term Development of South Vietnam(Pr?OVN)," March 1966, p. 11, Pentagon Library.

71. Historical Division of the Joint Secretariat, *The Joint Chiefs of Staff and the War in Vietnam*, part 2, chap. 18, pp. 11, 19.

72. Ibid., p. 19; Maxwell Taylor, Telegram for the Secretary of State, 8 March 1965, Westmoreland Papers, Box 5, #14 (History Backup) file I, item #50, LBJ Library.

73. Chester Cooper, Notes on National Security Council Meeting, 18 February 1965, NSF-NSC Meetings, Box 2, vol. 3, tab 31, item #2, LBJ Library. See also, Charles Mohr, "Johnson Asserts U.S. Will Persist in Vietnam Policy," 18 February 1965, *New York Times*, pp. 1, 10. On the connection between Vietnam and the Great Society, see Kearns, *Lyndon Johnson and the American Dream*, pp. 309–10. For Johnson's continued preoccupation with unity, see Telephone Conversation between George Reedy and George Ball, 12 February 1965, Ball Papers, Box 7, Vietnam I [1/5/65–5/24/65], item #35, LBJ Library. On February 11 the president's closest advisers were preparing for a cabinet meeting on Vietnam. When George Ball asked McGeorge Bundy how the meeting was to be "handled," Bundy replied that "it should be more candid than the sessions with the Congress." See also Telephone Conversation between George Ball and McGeorge Bundy, 11 February 1965, Papers of George Ball, Box 7, Vietnam I [1/5/65–5/24/65], item #33, LBJ Library. Before a meeting with the NSC on March 26, McGeorge Bundy advised the president that "the group, although carefully selected, will be quite large, and I doubt if in this group you will wish to go beyond the line you have taken with the Governors and in your Cabinet statement yesterday." McGeorge Bundy, Memorandum for the President, 26 March 1965, NSF-CF-NSC Meetings, Box 1, vol. 3, tab 32, item #4, LBJ Library.

74. Ball, *The Past Has Another Pattern*, p. 391; Tad Szulc, "Vietnam Policy Statement is Expected in Washington," *New York Times*, 15 February 1965, pp. 1, 3; Telephone conversation between Lyndon Johnson and George Ball, 15 February 1965, Papers of George Ball, Box 7, Vietnam I [1/5/65–5/24/65], item #38, LBJ Library. For Johnson's concern over possible opposition to his Vietnam policy in the Senate, see McGeorge Bundy, handwritten notes of meetings with the President, 15 February and 18 February 1965, Papers of McGeorge Bundy, Box 1, LBJ Library.

75. Telephone conversation between Lyndon Johnson and George Ball, 15 February 1965, Papers of George Ball, Box 7, Vietnam I [1/5/65–5/24/65], item #38, LBJ Library.

76. McGeorge Bundy, Memorandum to the President, 16 February 1965, NSF-NSC Histories-Deployment of Major Forces, Box 40, vol. 1, tabs 42–60, item #116, LBJ Library.

77. Lyndon Johnson, Remarks to the National Industrial Conference Board, 17 February 1965, *Public Papers of the Presidents of the United States: Lyndon B. Johnson, 1965*, book 1 (Washington, D.C.: U.S. Government Printing Office, 1966), p. 205.

78. Charles Mohr, "Johnson Asserts U.S. Will Persist in Vietnam Policy," *New York Times*, 18 February 1965, pp. 1, 10.

79. Lyndon Johnson, Remarks to the National Industrial Conference Board, 17 February 1965, *Public Papers of the Presidents of the United States: Lyndon B. Johnson, 1965*, book 1, p. 205; Mohr, "Johnson Asserts U.S. Will Persist in Vietnam Policy."

80. Hubert Humphrey, Memorandum for the President, 15 February 1965, in Hubert Humphrey, *The Education of a Public Man* (New York: Doubleday, 1979), pp. 320–24. See also Thomas Hughes as quoted in Gittinger, *A Vietnam Roundtable*, pp. 51–52.

81. In his 1995 memoir McNamara contended that "our government lacked experts for us to consult to compensate for our ignorance" of Southeast Asia (McNamara, *In Retrospect*, p. 32). Whether or not "experts" were available, however, was irrelevant. President Johnson limited himself to his small circle of devotees and was determined to stifle rather than encourage debate over Vietnam. Humphrey, *Education of a Public Man*, p. 325; Thomas Hughes and McGeorge Bundy as quoted in Gittinger, *A Vietnam Roundtable*, pp. 51–52; Ball, *The Past Has Another Pattern*, p. 390. For an example of coordination before a meeting with the President, see Telephone Conversation between William Bundy and George Ball, 18 February 1965, Papers of George Ball, Box 7, Vietnam I, item #44, LBJ Library.

CHAPTER 12

1. Hans J. Morganthau, "War with China?" *The New Republic*, 3 April 1965, p. 11.

2. McNamara, *In Retrospect*, p. 206.

3. "News Summary and Index," *New York Times*, 1 March 1965, p. 1; Tad Szulc, "More Marines Due for Vietnam Duty," *New York Times*, 2 March 1965, pp. 1, 2.

4. Telegram from McNamara to Westmoreland, 2 March 1965, Westmoreland Papers, Box 5, #14 (History Backup), item #19, LBJ Library.

5. Wallace Greene, Memorandum for the Record, Developments in South Vietnam, 2 March 1965, Greene Papers.

6. Gibbons, *The U.S. Government and the Vietnam War*, vol. 3, p. 149.

7. Wallace Greene, Memorandum for the Record, Developments in South Vietnam, 2 March 1965, Greene Papers; Vincent Demma, unpublished paper, "Suggestions for the Use of Ground Forces, June 1964–March 1965," U.S. Army Center of Military History, Washington, D.C.

8. Harold K. Johnson as quoted in Gibbons, *The U.S. Government and the Vietnam War*, vol. 3, pp. 149–50.

9. In a meeting with the highest-ranking members of his team, General Johnson, referring to McNaughton's memo, stated that LBJ "took out a bit on bribery; he didn't want it to show in a Pearl Harbor investigation." Johnson also deleted a proposal for the use of nonlethal chemical and biological weapons. Harold K. Johnson, Informal Discussion, 7 March 1965, Box 35, Trips and Visits, General Johnson's Trip to South Vietnam in March 1965, H. K. Johnson Papers. Gibbons, *The U.S. Government and the Vietnam War*, vol. 3, pp. 149–53; Harold K. Johnson, Memorandum for the assistant secretary of defense, International and Security Affairs, Subject: Survey of the Military Situation in Vietnam, March 1965 (exact date illegible), Box 135, H. K. Johnson Papers.

10. Harold K. Johnson, Informal Discussion, 7 March 1965, Box 35, H. K. Johnson Papers, Trips and Visits, General Johnson's Trip to South Vietnam in March 1965, Schedule of Events, undated; Memorandum from Westmoreland to Johnson, Subject: Items for Discussion, Box 35, Trips and Visits, General Johnson's Trip to South Vietnam in March 1965, ibid.; William Westmoreland, Interview with Charles B. McDonald, 2 April 1973, Papers of William C. Westmoreland, Box 30, item #33, LBJ Library. See also Gibbons, *The U.S. Government and the Vietnam War*, vol. 3, pp. 159–61.

11. Telegram from Maxwell Taylor to Dean Rusk, NSF-CF-VN, Box 14, Vietnam Cables, vol. 30, item #22, LBJ Library; Historical Division of the Joint Secretariat, *The Joint Chiefs of Staff and the War in Vietnam*, part 3, chap. 19, pp. 7–8.

12. Andrew Krepinevich, *The Army and Vietnam* (Baltimore, Md.: Johns Hopkins University Press, 1986), p. 140; Gibbons, *The U.S. Government and the Vietnam War*, vol. 3, pp. 159–61; Westmoreland, *A Soldier Reports*, p. 128.

13. Palmer, *The 25-Year War*, pp. 38–40; Vincent Demma, "Suggestions for the Use of Ground Forces, June 1964–March 1965."

14. Gibbons, *The U.S. Government and the Vietnam War*, vol. 3, p. 160; Historical Division of the Joint Secretariat, Historical Division of the Joint Secretariat, *The Joint Chiefs of Staff and the War in Vietnam*, part 2, chap. 19, pp. 7–8; chap. 22, p. 4.

15. Harold K. Johnson, "Report on Survey of Military Situation in Vietnam," 14 March 1965, and Johnson Report Outline, NSF-CF-VN, General Johnson Report, items #1a and #4a, LBJ Library. For Taylor's view expressed to Johnson, Telegram from Maxwell Taylor to Dean Rusk, 7 March 1965, NSF-CF-VN, Box 14, Vietnam Cables, item #22, LBJ Library.

16. Historical Division of the Joint Secretariat, *The Joint Chiefs of Staff and the War in Vietnam*, part 2, chap. 19, pp. 9–10; Harold K. Johnson, Johnson Report Outline, NSF-CF-VN, General Johnson Report, items #1a and #4a, LBJ Library.

17. Gibbons, *The U.S. Government and the Vietnam War*, pp. 160, 163.

18. Telegram from Westmoreland to Wheeler and Sharp, Subject: Employment of U.S. Aircraft in South Vietnam, 6 March 1965, NSF-CF-VN, Box 14, Vietnam Cables, vol. 30, item #76, LBJ Library; Earle Wheeler, Memorandum for the Secretary of Defense, Subject: Constraint Against Hot Pursuit of Viet Cong Across Cambodian Border, 6 March 1965; Earle Wheeler, Memorandum for the secretary of defense, Subject: Elimination of Restrictions on Use of US Aircraft, 6 March 1965; Earle Wheeler, Memorandum for the Secretary of Defense, Subject: FARMGATE Restrictions in the Republic of Vietnam, NSF-CF-VN, Box 193, JCS Memos, vol. 1 [2 of 2], items #23, #25, and #29, LBJ Library. See also Wheeler Papers, Box 145. Memorandum for McGeorge Bundy, Subject: Military Issues, 9 March 1965, NSF-CF-VN, Box 14, Vietnam Cables, item #120. On JCS recognition of the trend, see Historical Division of the Joint Secretariat, *The Joint Chiefs of Staff and the War in Vietnam*, part 2, chap. 18, p. 19.

19. Gibbons, *The U.S. Government and the Vietnam War*, pp. 154–57; McGeorge Bundy, handwritten meeting notes, 10 March 1965, Papers of McGeorge Bundy, Box 1, LBJ Library; McGeorge Bundy, as quoted in Gittinger, *The Johnson Years*, p. 53.

20. Gravel, *The Pentagon Papers*, vol. 3, p. 406; Wallace Greene, Memorandum for the Record, 19 March 1965, Greene Papers; Gibbons, *The U.S. Government and the Vietnam War*, vol. 3, pp. 165–66. Wheeler Diary, 15 March 1965, Wheeler Papers.

21. Earle Wheeler as quoted in Historical Division of the Joint Secretariat, *The Joint Chiefs of Staff and the War in Vietnam*, part 2, chap. 19, p. 11.

22. Ibid., chap. 19, pp. 11–13, 21.

23. Ibid., pp. 22–23.

24. Tilford, *Crosswinds*, p. 71.

25. Historical Division of the Joint Secretariat, *The Joint Chiefs of Staff and the War in Vietnam*, part 2, chap. 18, pp. 21–24.

26. Ibid., pp. 20–21.

27. Wallace Greene, Memorandum for Record: Navy Policy Council Meeting, 19 March 1965, Greene Papers.

28. Earle Wheeler, Memorandum for the Secretary of Defense (JCS 1008–65), 20 March 1965, Greene Papers; Historical Division of the Joint Secretariat, *The Joint Chiefs of Staff and the War in Vietnam*, part 2, chap. 19, pp. 13–14.

29. Historical Division of the Joint Secretariat, *The Joint Chiefs of Staff and the War in Vietnam*, part 2, chap. 19, p. 11; William Westmoreland,

interview by Charles McDonald, 10 April 1973, Westmoreland Papers, Box 30, LBJ Library; William C. Westmoreland, interview by author, 27 October 1995.

30. Historical Division of the Joint Secretariat, *The Joint Chiefs of Staff and the War in Vietnam*, part 2, chap. 19, p. 11.

31. Maxwell Taylor, Telegram for Dean Rusk, 18 March 1965, Papers of William C. Gibbons, Box 1, State Department Documents, item #4, LBJ Library; William C. Westmoreland, interview by Paul Miles, 10 October 1970, Miles Papers; William C. Westmoreland, interview by author, 27 October 1995.

32. Earle Wheeler, Telegram for General Westmoreland and Admiral Sharp, 20 March 1965, Westmoreland Papers, Box 5, #13 (History Backup) 2 21 JAN–28 FEB 65, item #109, LBJ Library. Document is misdated (by hand) February instead of March 1965. Another copy is in Greene Papers.

33. McGeorge Bundy as quoted in Gibbons, *The U.S. Government and the Vietnam War*, vol. 3, pp. 153, 191.

34. Historical Division of the Joint Secretariat, *The Joint Chiefs of Staff and the War in Vietnam*, part 2, chap. 19, pp. 16–17; Gibbons, *The U.S. Government and the Vietnam War*, vol. 3, pp. 174–78.

35. Robert S. McNamara as quoted in Gibbons, *The U.S. Government and the Vietnam War*, vol. 3, p. 195.

36. Historical Division of the Joint Secretariat, *The Joint Chiefs of Staff and the War in Vietnam*, part 2, chap. 18, p. 25.

37. For a discussion of the State Department white paper, see William Bundy, unpublished manuscript, chap. 22B, pp. 36–39.

38. *Public Papers of the President: Lyndon B. Johnson, 1965*, vol. 1, pp. 364–72.

39. McGeorge Bundy, handwritten notes, 1 April 1965, Papers of McGeorge Bundy, Box 1, LBJ Library.

40. Ibid.

41. Ibid.; Historical Division of the Joint Secretariat, *The Joint Chiefs of Staff and the War in Vietnam*, part 2, chap. 21, p. 3.

42. John McCone, Memorandum for the Secretary of State *et al*, NSF-CF-VN, Box 16, Vietnam Memos, vol. 32 [file 2 of 2], item #231d, LBJ Library.

43. Gibbons, *The U.S. Government and the Vietnam War*, vol. 3, pp. 200–201. On McCone's disenchantment and resignation, see Ray S. Cline, *Secrets, Spies, and Scholars: Blueprint of the Essential CIA* (Washington, D.C.: Acropolis Books, 1976) pp. 199–201, 210–11. John Ranelagh, *The Agency: The Rise and Decline of the CIA* (New York: Simon & Schuster, 1986) pp. 422–23.

44. Author unknown, Memorandum for the Record, 6 April 1965, Westmoreland Papers, #15 (History Backup) file I, item #11, LBJ Library. See also, Leonard Unger, Memorandum for the Record, 3 April 1965, ibid. For Bundy's quotation to the president, see McGeorge Bundy,

Memorandum for the president, 6 March 1965, NSF-CF-VN, Box 15, Vietnam Memos (A), vol. 31 [2 of 2], item #204, LBJ Library.

45. George Ball, Memorandum of Telephone Conversation with the president, 6 March 1965, Ball Papers, Box 6, Presidential Telcons, item #9, LBJ Library.

46. Gibbons, *The U.S. Government and the Vietnam War*, vol. 3, pp. 205–208.

47. *Public Papers of the Presidents: Lyndon B. Johnson, 1965*, Statement by the President on Viet-Nam, 25 March 1965, p. 130.

48. W. Averell Harriman, Memorandum for McGeorge Bundy with Attachment, 1 April 1965, NSF-Files of McGeorge Bundy, Box 17, SE Asia Regional Development, items #1 and #1a, LBJ Library.

49. *Public Papers of the Presidents: Lyndon B. Johnson, 1965*, Address at Johns Hopkins University: "Peace Without Conquest," 7 April 1965, pp. 394–99. The last quotation is from McGeorge Bundy, handwritten notes on Agenda for Luncheon Meeting, 6 April 1965, Files of McGeorge Bundy, Box 19, Lunch with the president [vol. 1] [part 1], item #45, LBJ Library.

50. *Public Papers of the Presidents: Lyndon B. Johnson, 1965*, address at Johns Hopkins University: "Peace Without Conquest," 7 April 1965, pp. 394–99.

51. Duiker, *Sacred War*, pp. 172–74.

52. John Kenneth Galbraith as quoted in Gibbons, *The U.S. Government and the Vietnam War*, vol. 3, pp. 218ff.

53. Thirty years later McNamara recognized the failure to take a long-term view of the problem in Vietnam. See *In Retrospect*, p. 182.

54. Excerpts from Admiral Taylor's report are in Marolda and Fitzgerald, *The United States Navy and the Vietnam Conflict*, vol. 2, p. 486. On the Marine Corps study, see William C. Westmoreland, interview with Charles B. McDonald, 12 March 1973, Westmoreland Papers, Box 31, tab B, LBJ Library. Andrew J. Goodpaster, interview by author, 9 March 1993.

CHAPTER 13

1. McDonald, *Reminiscences*, pp. 390, 393.

2. Historical Division of the Joint Secretariat, *The Joint Chiefs of Staff and the War in Vietnam*, part 2, chap. 21, pp. 1–5.

3. Telegram from the Joint Chiefs of Staff to CINCPAC, 6 April 1965, Box 52-D, item #4, Taylor Papers. Historical Division of the Joint Secretariat, *The Joint Chiefs of Staff and the War in Vietnam*, part 2, chap. 21, pp. 1–5, chap. 18, p. 25.

4. NSAM 328, 6 April 1965, Wheeler Papers. For Rusk's desire to "describe the mission as defensive," see Memorandum for the Record, Minutes of Meeting on 3 April 1965, Westmoreland Papers, #15 (History Backup), item #11, LBJ Library. On the President's desire to obscure his

policy decisions, see also McGeorge Bundy, Memorandum for the Secretaries of State and Defense, 10 April 1965, NSF-Agency File, Box 11, Defense Department, vol. 2, item #9, LBJ Library.

5. William Bundy, unpublished manuscript, chap. 24, pp. 13–14; Brian VanDeMark, *Into the Quagmire: Lyndon Johnson and the Escalation of the Vietnam War* (New York: Oxford University Press, 1991), pp. 119–20, 124; Gibbons, *The U.S. Government and the Vietnam War*, vol. 3, p. 212.

6. *Public Papers of the Presidents: Lyndon B. Johnson, 1965*, vol. 1, p. 396.

7. Wallace Greene, Memorandum for Record, Conference with the President 081530–1730 April 1965, 17 April 1965, Greene Papers.

8. Historical Division of the Joint Secretariat, *The Joint Chiefs of Staff and the War in Vietnam*, part 2, chap. 18, p. 25.

9. The account of this meeting is from Wallace Greene, Memorandum for Record, Conference with the President 081530–1730 April 1965, Greene Papers.

10. This and the remainder of the account of this meeting is from Wallace Greene, Memorandum for Record, Conference with the President 081530–1730 April 1965, 17 April 1965, Greene Papers.

11. Ibid.

12. Ibid.

13. The "middle ground" quotation is from Sen. Frank Church in 1969 as quoted in Gibbons, *The U.S. Government and the Vietnam War*, vol. 3, p. 220.

14. On April 8 a deployment conference convened at CINCPAC headquarters in Honolulu. Its purpose was to respond to McNamara's request for a time-phased deployment schedule for approximately twenty thousand logistic support troops and three divisions. The plan, forwarded to the JCS on April 10, called for the arrival of initial units in coastal enclaves to secure vital U.S. installations and support South Vietnamese Armed Forces operations. After U.S. forces established the enclaves, they would conduct offensive operations from them. Subsequent units would secure inland bases and areas. Finally U.S. units would conduct offensive operations inland, concentrating on the Central Highlands. Historical Division of the Joint Secretariat, *The Joint Chiefs of Staff and the War in Vietnam*, part 2, chap. 21, pp. 6–8. See also Appendix A to JCSM–288–65, Subject: Concept for the Logistic Actions Required to Support Expedited Introduction of Additional Forces into Southeast Asia, 17 April 1965, Box 182, Wheeler Papers. Robert S. McNamara, testimony before the Senate Foreign Relations Committee, 7 April 1965, as quoted in Gibbons, *The U.S. Government and the Vietnam War*, vol. 3, pp. 214–15.

15. Gibbons, *The U.S. Government and the Vietnam War*, vol. 3, pp. 212–14.

16. When Taylor returned to Saigon after his trip to Washington, he told Westmoreland of congressional anxiety over the possible deployment

of division-size American units. William Westmoreland, Telegram to CINCPAC et al., Subject: Additional Deployments and Command Concepts, 11 April 1965, Westmoreland Papers, Box 5, #15 History Backup I, item #31, LBJ Library.

17. William Westmoreland, Telegram to CINCPAC et. al., Subject: Additional Deployments and Command Concepts, 11 April 1965, Westmoreland Papers, Box 5, #15 History Backup I, item #31, LBJ Library. See also Historical Division of the Joint Secretariat, The Joint Chiefs of Staff and the War in Vietnam, part 2, chap. 21, p. 7.

18. The following account of the April 13 meeting is from Wallace Greene, Memorandum for Record, Subject: Joint Chiefs Luncheon and Conference with the President at the White House, 13 April 1965, Greene Papers.

19. McGeorge Bundy, Handwritten Notes of Meeting, 13 April 1965, Papers of McGeorge Bundy, Box 1, LBJ Library.

20. Wallace Greene, Memorandum for Record, Subject: Joint Chiefs Luncheon and Conference with the President at the White House, 13 April 1965, Greene Papers.

21. Ibid.

22. Gibbons, The U.S. Government and the Vietnam War, vol. 3, p. 226.

23. Telegram from the JCS to CINCPAC, 17 April 1965, NSF-CF-VN, Box 16, Vietnam Cables, vol. 32 [file 2 of 2], item #153, LBJ Library.

24. William Bundy, unpublished manuscript, chap. 24, pp. 13–14; VanDeMark, Into the Quagmire, pp. 119–20, 124; Gibbons, The U.S. Government and the Vietnam War, vol. 3, pp. 212.

25. Sen. Michael Mansfield, who opposed the bombing, appeared amenable to the deployment of ground troops in enclaves along the coast of South Vietnam. Gibbons, The U.S. Government and the Vietnam War, vol. 3, p. 207.

26. Marine Corps Memorandum for the Joint Chiefs of Staff, Subject: Proposed U.S. Courses of Action to Implement Policy as Enunciated in the President's Speech of 7 April 1965, 8 April 1965, Greene Papers; Wallace Greene, Memorandum for Record, Subject: Joint Chiefs Luncheon and Conference with the President at the White House, 13 April 1965, Greene Papers.

27. Wallace Greene, Memorandum for Record, Subject: Joint Chiefs Luncheon and Conference with the President at the White House, 13 April 1965, ibid.

28. Ibid.

29. Ibid.

30. Telegram from the JCS to CINCPAC, 14 April 1965, Taylor Papers, Box 52, File D.

31. Earle Wheeler, Telegram to William C. Westmoreland, 11 April 1965, Miles Papers.

32. Gibbons, The U.S. Government and the Vietnam War, vol. 3, p. 235.

CHAPTER 14

1. Sen. Frank Church in 1969, as quoted in Gibbons, *The U.S. Government and the Vietnam War*, vol. 3, p. 220.

2. Maxwell Taylor, Telegram for the Secretary of State, 14 April 1965, 4:42 A.M., NSF-CF-VN, Box 16, Vietnam Cables, vol. 32 [file 1 of 2], item #30, LBJ Library.

3. Maxwell Taylor, Telegram for the Secretary of State, 14 April 1965, 7:47 A.M., ibid.

4. McGeorge Bundy, Memorandum for the President, NSF-NSC History-Deployment of Major U.S. Forces, Box 41, vol. 3, item #24a, ibid. Emphasis in original.

5. McGeorge Bundy, Memorandum for the President, 14 April 1965, NSF-NSC History-Deployment of Major U.S. Forces, ibid.

6. Joint State and Defense Message to American Embassy Saigon, 15 April 1965, NSF-CF-VN, Box 16, Vietnam Cables, vol. 32 [file 2 of 2], item #157, ibid.

7. Maxwell Taylor, Telegram to the Secretary of State, 17 April 1965, 3:10 A.M., ibid.

8. Gibbons, *The U.S. Government and the Vietnam War*, vol. 3, pp. 228–29.

9. Claudia Alta Taylor Johnson, *White House Diary* (New York: Holt, Rinehart & Winston, 1970), pp. 257–61.

10. William Bundy, unpublished manuscript, chap. 24, pp. 13–14.

11. Gibbons, *The U.S. Government and the Vietnam War*, vol. 3, p. 222.

12. *Public Papers of the Presidents: Lyndon B. Johnson, 1965*, vol. 1, pp. 428–29.

13. Gibbons, *The U.S. Government and the War in Vietnam*, vol. 3, pp. 228–29.

14. Appendix to Memorandum for the Secretary of Defense, undated, Subject: US Deployments to the Republic of Vietnam, NSF-CF-VN, Box 16, Vietnam Memos, vol. 32 [file 1 of 2], item #20B, LBJ Library. See also Historical Division of the Joint Secretariat, *The Joint Chiefs of Staff and the War in Vietnam*, part 2, chap. 21, pp. 13–14.

15. Robert S. McNamara, Memorandum for the President, 21 April 1965, NSF-CF-VN, Box 16, Vietnam Memos, vol. 3, item #103a, LBJ Library. See also Gibbons, *The U.S. Government and the Vietnam War*, vol. 3, pp. 231–32. McNamara's memorandum was based on the minutes of the meeting taken by John McNaughton. See Minutes of April 20, 1965, Honolulu Meeting, Westmoreland Papers, Box 5, #15 (History Backup) II, item #78, LBJ Library. For McCone's notes, see Memorandum for the Record, *FRUS: Vietnam, January-June 1965*, pp. 578–81.

16. Historical Division of the Joint Secretariat, *The Joint Chiefs of Staff and the War in Vietnam*, part 2, chap. 21, 16–17. McNamara, *In Retrospect*, p. 183.

17. Westmoreland, *A Soldier Reports*, p. 132.

18. Sharp, *Strategy for Defeat*, p. 80.

19. Ibid. For Maxwell Taylor's recollection of the JCS position, see *Swords and Plowshares*, pp. 342–43.

20. Ball, *Past Has Another Pattern*, p. 393.

21. Gibbons, *The U.S. Government and the Vietnam War*, vol. 3, p. 232.

22. Historical Division of the Joint Secretariat, *The Joint Chiefs of Staff and the War in Vietnam*, part 2, chap. 23, p. 1.

23. Sharp, *Strategy for Defeat*, p. 79. See also, William Bundy, unpublished manuscript, chap. 25, pp. 4–6.

24. McNamara, *In Retrospect*, p. 182.

25. Gibbons, *The U.S. Government and the Vietnam War*, vol. 3, pp. 233–34.

26. Ibid., p. 234.

27. Historical Division of the Joint Secretariat, *The Joint Chiefs of Staff and the War in Vietnam*, part 2, chap. 23, p. 1; Gibbons, *The U.S. Government and the Vietnam War*, vol. 3, p. 234; McNamara, *In Retrospect*, p. 183.

28. Duiker, *Sacred War*, pp. 172, 175; Phillip B. Davidson, *Vietnam at War* (Novato, Calif.: Presidio Press, 1988), p. 348.

29. Lyndon Johnson as quoted in VanDeMark, *Into the Quagmire*, p. 133.

30. William Bundy, unpublished manuscript, chap. 24, p. 17; chap. 25, p. 18.

31. *Public Papers of the Presidents: Lyndon B. Johnson, 1965*, vol. 1, p. 494.

32. Ibid., pp. 495, 498.

33. William Bundy, unpublished manuscript, chap. 25, p. 19.

34. VanDeMark, *Into the Quagmire*, p. 134.

35. Gibbons, *The U.S. Government and the Vietnam War*, vol. 3, p. 250.

36. John McNaughton, Possible Pause Scenario, 25 April 1965, Warnke Papers, Box 1, McNaughton I Drafts 1965 (4), item #66, LBJ Library.

37. William Raborn, letter to the President, 28 April 1965, NSF-CF-VN, Box 17, Vietnam Memos, vol. 34, file 1 of 2, item #282a, LBJ Library.

38. Lyndon Johnson, Telegram for Maxwell Taylor, 10 May 1965, NSF-NSC History-Deployment of Major U.S. Forces, Box 41, vol. 4, item #6a, LBJ Library.

39. William Bundy, unpublished manuscript, chap. 24, pp. 18–19; VanDeMark, *Into the Quagmire*, pp. 136–37.

40. McGeorge Bundy, Memorandum for Secretary Rusk et al., 11 May 1965, NSF-NSC History-Deployment of Major U.S. Forces, Box 41, vol. 4, item #7a, LBJ Library.

41. Andrew J. Goodpaster, Memorandum for Record, Subject: Meeting with General Eisenhower, 13 May 1965, NSF-Name File, Box #3, President Eisenhower [file 2 of 2], item #30a, ibid.

42. VanDeMark, *Into the Quagmire*, p. 139.

43. Jack Valenti, Meeting Notes, 16 May 1965, NSF-Meeting Notes File, Box 1, item #18, LBJ Library.

44. Ibid.; Historical Division of the Joint Secretariat, *The Joint Chiefs of Staff and the War in Vietnam*, part 2, chap. 26, p. 4.

45. Historical Division of the Joint Secretariat, *The Joint Chiefs of Staff and the War in Vietnam*, part 2, chap. 25, pp. 7–8.

46. Clodfelter, *The Limits of Air Power*, pp. 40–44.

47. Historical Division of the Joint Secretariat, *The Joint Chiefs of Staff and the War in Vietnam*, part 2, chap. 25, pp. 11–12.

48. Meeting with the President, 23 June 1965, NSF-NSC History-Deployment of Major Forces, vol. 5, item #60b, LBJ Library.

49. Historical Division of the Joint Secretariat, *The Joint Chiefs of Staff and the War in Vietnam*, part 2, chap. 25, pp. 9–11, 13–16.

50. William Raborn, Letter to Lyndon Johnson, 8 May 1965, NSF-NSC History-Deployment of Major Forces, Box 41, vol. 4, item #3b, LBJ Library.

51. Bruce Palmer, "U.S. Intelligence and Vietnam," p. 35.

52. Clark Clifford, Letter to Lyndon Johnson, 17 May 1965, NSF-NSC History-Deployment of Major Forces, Box 41, vol. 4, item #3a, LBJ Library.

53. Gibbons, *The U.S. Government and the Vietnam War*, vol. 3, p. 259.

54. Davidson, *Vietnam at War*, p. 348.

55. VanDeMark, *Into the Quagmire*, pp. 145–47.

56. Memorandum of Telephone Conversation between George Ball and William Bundy, 4 June 1965, Ball Papers, Box 7, Vietnam II, item #8, LBJ Library.

57. William Bundy, unpublished manuscript, chap. 26, pp. 3–4.

58. McGeorge Bundy, handwritten notes on meeting, 5 June 1965, Papers of McGeorge Bundy, Box 1, LBJ Library.

59. The account of this meeting is taken from the following sources: William Bundy, unpublished manuscript, chap. 26, pp. 3–6; McGeorge Bundy, handwritten notes on meeting, 5 June 1965, Papers of McGeorge Bundy, Box 1, LBJ Library.

60. Gibbons, *The U.S. Government and the Vietnam War*, vol. 3, p. 277.

61. William Westmoreland, Telegram to CINCPAC, 7 June 1965, Miles Papers, Policy/Strategy File; Gibbons, *The U.S. Government and the Vietnam War*, vol. 3, p. 277; Westmoreland, *A Soldier Reports*, p. 140.

62. Statements Concerning Mission of U.S. Combat Forces in Vietnam, undated, NSF-CF-VN, Box 18, Vietnam Memos (B), vol. 35, item #285a, LBJ Library; U. Alexis Johnson, Telegram for the Secretary of State, 7 June 1965, NSF-CF-VN, Box 18, Vietnam Cables, vol. 35, item #98, ibid.; Telegram from American Embassy in Saigon to Secretary of State, 20 May 1965, NSF-CF-VN, Box 17, Vietnam Cables, vol. 34, item #84, ibid.

63. Gibbons, *The U.S. Government and the Vietnam War*, vol. 3, pp. 278–79.

64. News Conference, 9 June 1965, NSF-NSC History-Deployment of Major Forces, Box 41, vol. 4, item #53a, LBJ Library.

65. William Westmoreland, Telegram to CINCPAC, 12 June 1965, NSF-NSC History-Deployment of Major Forces, Box 42, Vietnam vol. 5, item #14a, ibid. See also U. Alexis Johnson, Telegram for the Secretary of State, 7 June 1965, NSF-CF-VN, Box 18, Vietnam Cables, vol. 35, item #78, ibid.

66. William Westmoreland, Telegram to CINCPAC, 12 June 1965, NSF-NSC History-Deployment of Major Forces, Box 42, Vietnam vol. 5, item #14a, ibid.; Ulysses S. Sharp, Telegram to General Westmoreland, 13 June 1965, NSF-CF-VN, Box 18, Vietnam Cables (B) vol. 35, item #237, ibid.

67. For Bundy's desire that Taylor leave soonest, see McGeorge Bundy, Memorandum for the President, 30 June 1965, NSF-NSC History, Deployment of Major Forces, Box 43, vol. 6, item #21a, ibid. Memorandum of Telephone Conversation between George Ball and McGeorge Bundy, 31 May 1965, Ball Papers, Box 7, Vietnam II, item #5, ibid. See also McGeorge Bundy, Handwritten Notes of Meeting, 8 June 1965, Bundy Papers, Box 1, ibid.

68. Gibbons, The U.S. Government and the Vietnam War, vol. 3, p. 279.

69. For a summary of the enclave concept, see Davidson, Vietnam at War, pp. 346–47. Wallace Greene, Memorandum for Record, 8 June Trip to South Vietnam, Greene Papers.

70. William Bundy, unpublished manuscript, chap. 26, pp. 8–9.

71. McGeorge Bundy, Handwritten Notes, 10 June 1965, Papers of McGeorge Bundy, Box 1, LBJ Library.

72. Ibid.

73. William Bundy, unpublished manuscript, chap. 26, p. 11.

74. McGeorge Bundy, handwritten notes, 10 June 1965, Papers of McGeorge Bundy, Box 1, LBJ Library. The Mansfield memorandum is reprinted in part in Gibbons, The U.S. Government and the Vietnam War, vol. 3, p. 276.

75. Gibbons, The U.S. Government and the Vietnam War, vol. 3, pp. 288–89.

76. William Bundy, unpublished manuscript, chap. 26, pp. 13–14.

77. McGeorge Bundy, Handwritten Notes, 10 June 1965, Papers of McGeorge Bundy, Box 1, LBJ Library.

78. Telephone Conversation between Robert McNamara and Lyndon Johnson as quoted in McNamara, In Retrospect, p. 189.

79. William Bundy, unpublished manuscript, chap. 26, p. 15A; Gibbons, The U.S. Government and the Vietnam War, vol. 3, p. 292.

80. Bromley Smith, Summary Notes of 552nd NSC Meeting, 11 June 1965, NSF-NSC Meetings File, Box 1, vol. 3, item #2, LBJ Library.

81. Ibid.

82. Ibid.

83. Ibid.

84. William Bundy, unpublished manuscript, chap. 26, p. 15A.

85. Davidson, *Vietnam at War*, pp. 348–49.

86. Telephone Conversation between Robert McNamara and Lyndon Johnson as cited in McNamara, *In Retrospect*, p. 189.

87. Telephone Conversation between Lyndon Johnson and George Ball, 14 June 1965, Ball Papers, Box 6, Presidential Telcons, item #14, LBJ Library.

88. George Ball, Memorandum for the President, 18 June 1965, NSF-NSC History-Deployment of Major U.S. Forces, Box 42, vol. 5, tabs 314–25, item #48a, ibid.

89. Gibbons, *The U.S. Government and the Vietnam War*, vol. 3, p. 317.

90. Memorandum from the Joint Chiefs of Staff to the Secretary of Defense, Subject: Deployments to South Vietnam, 18 June 1965, Box 182, Wheeler Papers.

91. William C. Westmoreland, Telegram to U.S.G. Sharp and Earle Wheeler, 24 June 1965, Policy/Strategy for Vietnam, Miles Papers.

92. McGeorge Bundy, Handwritten Notes, 21 June 1965, Papers of McGeorge Bundy, Box 1, LBJ Library.

93. McNamara, *In Retrospect*, pp. 191, 195.

CHAPTER 15

1. Harold K. Johnson, Oral History Transcript, 1972–1974, II, sec. 9, pp. 22–23.

2. Gibbons, *The U.S. Government and the Vietnam War*, vol. 3, p. 327.

3. For Ball's original memo, see George Ball, Memorandum for the Secretary of State et al., 28 June 1965, Warnke Papers, Box 1, McNaughton I Drafts 1964 (4), item #60a, LBJ Library.

4. Gibbons, *The U.S. Government and the Vietnam War*, vol. 3, pp. 326–27.

5. On July 2, McGeorge Bundy described Ball's revised paper as "dangerous." Ibid., p. 342.

6. Ibid., pp. 319–20.

7. Wallace Greene, Memorandum for Record on the Situation in Vietnam, 28 June 1965, Greene Papers.

8. Telephone Conversations between McGeorge Bundy and George Ball, 28 June 1965, 9:45 A.M. and 2:00 P.M., Ball Papers, Box 7, Vietnam 2, items #36 and #37, LBJ Library. Bundy informed Ball that McNamara lied to Wheeler to keep the JCS Chairman from attending the crucial meeting during which the president's advisers coordinated the Ball and McNamara drafts.

9. Robert McNamara, Memorandum for the President, Subject: Program of Expanded Military and Political Moves with Respect to Vietnam, 26 June 1965, NSF-NSC History-Deployment of Major U.S. Forces, Box 43, vol. 6, item #13b, ibid.

10. Gibbons, *The U.S. Government and the Vietnam War*, vol. 3, pp. 327–28.

11. McGeorge Bundy, Memorandum for the Secretary of Defense, 30 June 1965, NSF-NSC History-Deployment of Major U.S. Forces, vol. 6, tabs 341–56, item #13a, LBJ Library.

12. McGeorge Bundy, Memorandum for the President, 1 July 1965, NSF-NSC History-Deployment of Major Forces, Box 43, vol. 6, item #32a, ibid.

13. Gibbons, *The U.S. Government and the Vietnam War*, vol. 3, p. 327; William Bundy, unpublished manuscript, chap. 26, p. 26.

14. McGeorge Bundy, Memorandum for the President, 1 July 1965, NSF-NSC History-Deployment of Major Forces, Box 43, vol. 6, item #32a, LBJ Library.

15. McGeorge Bundy, Handwritten Notes of Meeting, 29 June 1965, Papers of McGeorge Bundy, Box 1, ibid.

16. Joint State/Defense Message, Subject: Deployment of USMC Forces, 1 July 1965, NSF-NSC History-Deployment of Major Forces, Box 43, vol. 6, item #30a, ibid.; Maxwell Taylor, Telegram to the Secretary of State, 1 July 1965, NSF-NSC History-Deployment of Major Forces, Box 43, vol. 6, item #26a, ibid.

17. Gibbons, *The U.S. Government and the Vietnam War*, vol. 3, pp. 342–43, 345.

18. For Greene's views on the enclave strategy, see Wallace Greene, Memorandum for Record, 8 June 1965, Greene Papers. Greene recorded his conversation with Wheeler in Wallace Greene, Memorandum for Record on the Situation in Vietnam, 28 June 1965, Greene Papers.

19. Wallace Greene, Memorandum for Record, 28 June 1965, ibid.

20. Harold K. Johnson, Oral History Transcript, 1973, pp. 8–9; Edwin H. Simmons, Interview by Author, 8 July 1993.

21. Wallace Greene, Memorandum for Record, Subject: Escalation of Effort in South Vietnam, 10 July 1965, Greene Papers.

22. Ibid.

23. Wallace Greene, Handwritten Notes, 12 July 1965, ibid.; Gibbons, *The U.S. Government and the Vietnam War*, vol. 3, p. 359.

24. Telephone Conversation between Robert McNamara and Lyndon Johnson as cited in McNamara, *In Retrospect*, p. 189.

25. Gibbons, *The U.S. Government and the Vietnam War*, vol. 3, p. 356.

26. Ibid., p. 357.

27. John McNaughton, Memorandum for General Goodpaster, 2 July 1965, in Gravel, *The Pentagon Papers*, vol. 4, pp. 291–93.

28. Gibbons, *The U.S. Government and the Vietnam War*, vol. 3, p. 364.

29. John McNaughton, Memorandum for General Goodpaster, 2 July 1965, in Gravel, *The Pentagon Papers*, vol. 4, pp. 291–93.

30. Summary of the Report of the JCS and the Ad Hoc Study Group, "Intensification of the Military Operations in South Vietnam, Concept and

Appraisal," in Gibbons, *The U.S. Government and the Vietnam War*, vol. 3, p. 469.

31. Andrew J. Goodpaster, Interview by Author, 9 March 1993.

32. R. C. Bowman, Memorandum for McGeorge Bundy, Subject: Goodpaster Study on Vietnam, 21 July 1965, NSF-CF-VN, Box 20, Vietnam Memos, vol. 37, 7/65 [file 1 of 2], item #413, LBJ Library.

33. McNamara, *In Retrospect*, pp. 189, 203.

34. Robert S. McNamara, Telegram to the U.S. Embassy in Saigon, 7 July 1965, NSF-NSC History-Deployment of Major Forces, Box 43, vol. 6, item #38b, LBJ Library.

35. Gibbons, *The U.S. Government and the Vietnam War*, vol. 3, p. 369.

36. Ibid., p. 381.

37. Clausewitz, *On War*, p. 87.

38. Robert S. McNamara, Memorandum for the President, Subject: Recommendations of additional deployments to Vietnam, 20 July 1965, NSF-NSC History-Deployment of Major Forces, Box 43, vol. 6, item #56a, LBJ Library.

39. The account of that meeting is from Wallace Greene, Memorandum for Record, Subject: First Meeting of the Joint Chiefs of Staff with the Policy Subcommittee of the House Armed Services Committee, 15 July 1965, Greene Papers.

40. Ibid.

41. Ibid.

42. Ibid.

43. Jack Valenti as quoted in Gittinger, *A Vietnam Roundtable*, p. 72. See also William Bundy, unpublished manuscript, chap. 27, p. 14.

44. Gibbons, *The U.S. Government and the Vietnam War*, vol. 3, p. 381.

45. Vance informed McNamara that the plans to hide from Congress the cost of the president's decisions were limited to himself, McGeorge Bundy, Department of Defense Comptroller Charles Hitch, and Assistant Secretary of Defense for Installations and Logistics Paul R. Ignatius. Gibbons, *The U.S. Government and the Vietnam War*, vol. 3, p. 381.

46. McNamara, *In Retrospect*, p. 205.

47. Jack Valenti as quoted in Gittinger, *A Vietnam Roundtable*, p. 66; McGeorge Bundy, Memorandum for the President, Subject: The Reasons for Avoiding a Billion Dollar Appropriation in Vietnam, 19 July 1965, NSF-NSC History-Deployment of Major Forces, Box 43, vol. 6, item #53a, LBJ Library; McGeorge Bundy as quoted in Gittinger, *A Vietnam Roundtable*, p. 65.

48. McGeorge Bundy, Memorandum Prepared on November 2, 1968, from Notes Dated July 27, 1965 at 6:00 P.M., NSF-Notes on Meeting File, Box 1, Meetings July 1965, item #24a, LBJ Library. Although at the time he dutifully deceived the JCS and members of Congress concerning the president's reluctance to request mobilization or funds that he knew were necessary for the war effort, McNamara, thirty years later, admitted that the presi-

dent "was protecting his Great Society programs." McNamara, *In Retrospect*, p. 205. In July 1965 intelligence reports indicated that China would not intervene unless it was attacked directly. William Bundy, unpublished manuscript, chap. 28, p. 3. See also, Gibbons, *The U.S. Government and the Vietnam War*, vol. 3, pp. 461–62. A July 23 CIA estimate concluded that China would only intervene if the United States invaded North Vietnam or attacked air bases in China. The CIA predicted that the Chinese would conclude that troop deployments consistent with Westmoreland's full request would only postpone and worsen the eventual U.S. defeat.

49. Jack Valenti, Notes on Meeting, 22 July 1965, NSF-Meeting Notes File, Box 1, July 21–27 1965, Meetings on Vietnam, item #119a, LBJ Library.

50. Wallace Greene, Record of Conference on Southeast Asia held at White House, 22 July 1965, Greene Papers.

51. Ibid.

52. Jack Valenti, Notes on Meeting, 22 July 1965, NSF-Meeting Notes File, Box 1, July 21–27 1965 Meetings on Vietnam, item #119a, LBJ Library; McGeorge Bundy, Memorandum Prepared on November 2, 1965, from Notes Dated July 27, 1965 at 6:00 P.M., NSF-Notes on Meeting File, Box 1, Meetings July 1965, item #24a, LBJ Library.

53. Jack Valenti, Notes on Meeting, 22 July 1965, NSF-Meeting Notes File, Box 1, July 21–27 1965 Meetings on Vietnam, item #119a, ibid.

54. Harold Brown, Oral History Transcript, p. 12, ibid.

55. Jack Valenti, Notes on Meeting, 22 July 1965, NSF-Meeting Notes File, Box 1, July 21–27 1965 Meetings on Vietnam, item #119a, ibid.

56. Wallace Greene, Record of Conference on Southeast Asia held at White House, 22 July 1965, Greene Papers.

57. Ibid.

58. Telephone Conversation between McNamara and the President, 14 July 1965, 6:15 P.M., Tape 6507.02, PNO 22, PR, LBJ Library. The conversation is transcribed in McNamara, *In Retrospect*, p. 201.

59. McNamara worked closely with Johnson on the mobilization question to the exclusion of all other advisers. McGeorge Bundy as quoted in Gittinger, *A Vietnam Roundtable*, pp. 60, 69. For the plan that McNamara developed to meet Westmoreland's request without mobilization, see Robert McNamara, Plan vol. 3, NSF-NSC History-Deployment of Major Forces, Box 43, vol. 7, item #12a, LBJ Library.

60. Wallace Greene, Memorandum for Record, Subject: Developing Situation in Vietnam, 24 July 1965, Greene Papers.

61. Ibid.

62. Robert McNamara, Plan vol. 3, 24 July 1965, NSF-NSC History-Deployment of Major Forces, Box 43, vol. 7, item #12c, LBJ Library.

63. Wallace Greene, Memorandum for Record, Subject: Developing Situation in Vietnam, 24 July 1965, Greene Papers.

64. McNamara, *In Retrospect*, p. 205.

65. Wallace Greene, Memorandum for Record, Subject: Developing Situation in Vietnam, 24 July 1965, Greene Papers.

66. Harold K. Johnson, Oral History Transcript, 1973, LBJ Library, pp. 6, 12–13, 16–18, 30.

67. Ronald H. Spector, "The Vietnam War and the Army's Self-Image," in Schlight, *Second Indochina War Symposium*, pp. 169–85.

68. This account is a composite of two sets of notes on the meeting. See Jack Valenti, Notes on National Security Council Meeting, 27 July 1965, NSF-Meeting Notes File, Box 1, [July 21–27, 1965 Meetings on Vietnam], item #119e, LBJ Library; Bromley Smith, Subject: Deployment of Major Forces to Vietnam—July 1965, undated, NSF-NSC History-Deployment of Major Forces, Box 40, July '65, vol. 1, item #1, ibid.

69. For a list of those who attended the meeting and a summary of the meeting, see VanDeMark, *Into the Quagmire*, pp. 208–10.

70. McGeorge Bundy, Handwritten Notes on Joint Leadership Meeting, 27 July 1965, Papers of McGeorge Bundy, Box 1, LBJ Library.

71. Jack Valenti, Notes on congressional Leadership Meeting, 27 July 1965, NSF-Meeting Notes File, Box 1, [July 21–27, 1965 Meetings on Vietnam], item #119f, LBJ Library.

72. McGeorge Bundy, Handwritten Notes on Joint Leadership Meeting, 27 July 1965, Papers of McGeorge Bundy, Box 1, ibid.

73. McGeorge Bundy, Memorandum Prepared on November 2, 1968, from Notes Dated July 27, 1965 at 6:00 P.M., NSF-Notes on Meeting File, Box 1, Meetings July 1965, item #24a, ibid.

74. Compare Jack Valenti's Notes on the NSC Meeting and the Meeting with the congressional Leadership, 27 July 1965, NSF-Meeting Notes File, Box 1, [July 21–27, 1965 Meetings on Vietnam], items #119e and #119f, ibid. On July 11 Maxwell Taylor sent to the State and Defense Departments a cable in which he reported a high desertion rate, poor morale, inadequate training, and "low ARVN battle worthiness." Maxwell Taylor, Telegram for the Secretary of State, 11 July 1965, Box 51, T–160–69H, Taylor Papers.

75. McGeorge Bundy, Memorandum Prepared on November 2, 1968, from Notes Dated July 27, 1965 at 6:00 P.M., NSF-Notes on Meeting File, Box 1, Meetings July 1965, item #24a, ibid.

76. McGeorge Bundy, Handwritten Notes on Joint Leadership Meeting, 27 July 1965, Papers of McGeorge Bundy, Box 1, ibid.

77. Lyndon Johnson, Remarks at the Department of Defense Cost Reduction Awards Ceremony, 28 July 1965, *Public Papers of the Presidents: Lyndon B. Johnson, 1965*, vol. 2, p. 793.

78. The following is from Lyndon Johnson, The President's News Conference of July 28, 1965, *Public Papers of the Presidents: Lyndon B. Johnson, 1965*, vol. 2, pp. 794–803.

EPILOGUE

1. George Herring's now classic study of American involvement in Vietnam provides the most lucid statement of this interpretation. "U.S. involvement in Vietnam was not primarily a result of errors of judgment or of the personality quirks of the policymakers, although these things existed in abundance. It was a logical, if not inevitable outgrowth of a world view and a policy—the policy of containment—which Americans in and out of government accepted without serious question for more than two decades." Herring, *America's Longest War*, p. xi. See also Brian VanDeMark, *Into the Quagmire*, especially pp. vii–viii and 215–16. In his presidential address to the Society for Historians of American Foreign Relations, historian and LBJ biographer Robert Dallek argued that "it is difficult to imagine" LBJ and his advisers doing anything other than transforming Vietnam into an American war. See Robert Dallek, "Lyndon Johnson and Vietnam," *Diplomatic History* 20 (Spring 1996): esp. pp. 147–49. For the most compelling treatment of "inexorable Cold War logic" and its role in Lyndon Johnson's escalation of the war, see Michael Hunt, *Lyndon Johnson's War*. See also Robert Divine, "Vietnam: An Episode in the Cold War."

2. Journalist Stanley Karnow came to a similar conclusion in *Vietnam*. The issue is also addressed in Fred Logevall's study of the international context of the Americanization of the war and the efforts to promote a negotiated settlement (forthcoming from Berkeley: University of California Press).

3. Telephone Conversation between Lyndon Johnson and McGeorge Bundy, 27 May 1964, 11:24 A.M., Recordings of Conversations and Meetings, White House Series, Tape WH6405.10, Citation #3522, LBJ Library. See also Telephone Conversation between Lyndon Johnson and Richard Russell, 27 May 1964, 10:55 A.M., Recordings of Conversations and Meetings, White House Series, Tape WH6405.10, Citation #3519–3521, LBJ Library.

4. Herring, *LBJ and Vietnam*, p. 54. By 1967, some of the more junior officers in the Pentagon had begun to refer to the Joint Chiefs of Staff as the "five silent men."

5. Ibid., pp. 38, 40–41, 49.

6. This idea is taken from a course on the history of American civil-military relations taught by Col. Charles F. Brower IV at the United States Military Academy at West Point.

7. Forrest Pogue, *George C. Marshall*, vol. 2, *Ordeal and Hope, 1939–1942* (New York: Viking Press, 1966), p. 372.

8. Ibid., vol. 1, *Education of a General, 1860–1939* (New York: Viking Press, 1963), pp. 323–24. Taylor, *Swords and Plowshares*, p. 252.

9. On the ambiguity of the military strategy for Vietnam, see Palmer, *25-Year War*, pp. 45–46; Andrew Krepinevich, *Army and Vietnam*, p. 161; Clodfelter, *Limits of Air Power*, pp. 74–76. The Army staff did not complete the development of a comprehensive strategy for the war until March 1966. Planners continued to base their effort on the policy objective stated in

NSAM 288, "a free and independent, non-communist South Vietnam." See Office of the Deputy Chief of Staff for Military Operations, "A Program for the Pacification and Long-Term Development of South Vietnam" (PROVN), U.S. Army Center for Military History, Washington, D.C., p. 1.

10. Even then, the JCS could not demonstrate that the additional 206,000 men requested would be decisive. Herring, *LBJ and Vietnam*, p. 179.

Selected Bibliography

MANUSCRIPT SOURCES

JOINT HISTORY OFFICE, THE PENTAGON, WASHINGTON, D.C.

Biographical Files.

Historical Division of the Joint Secretariat. *Chronology of Development of Restraints and Objectives in the Air Campaign Vietnam, 1961–1966.* 1966.

Historical Division of the Joint Secretariat. *Cross-Border Operations Southeast Asia, 1964–1968.* 7 August 1973.

Historical Division of the Joint Secretariat. *The Joint Chiefs of Staff and the War in Vietnam, 1960–1968.* Parts 1 and 2 (1960–66). 1970.

JOHN F. KENNEDY PRESIDENTIAL LIBRARY, BOSTON, MASS.

Oral Histories

Taylor, Maxwell D., 18 October 1983

Shoup, David M., 7 April 1967

Papers of John F. Kennedy

Presidential Papers, President's Office Files, Presidential Recordings; Presidential Recordings Transcripts

LIBRARY OF CONGRESS, SPECIAL COLLECTIONS BRANCH, WASHINGTON, D.C.

Papers of General Curtis LeMay

LYNDON BAINES JOHNSON PRESIDENTIAL LIBRARY, AUSTIN, TEXAS

National Security File (NSF)

Agency File, Defense Department

Agency File, JCS War Games

Agency File, Joint Chiefs of Staff

Country File, Vietnam

Files of C. V. Clifton

Files of McGeorge Bundy

International Travel and Meetings File

Memos to the President

Name File: Colonel Bowman Memos, Cooper Memos, President Dwight D. Eisenhower, Forrestal Memos, Senator Fulbright, Colonel Ginsburgh Memos, Komer Memos, Vietnam—Mansfield Memo and Reply, and Thomson Memos

National Security Action Memoranda

National Security Council Histories: Gulf of Tonkin Incident, Deployment of Major U.S. Forces to Vietnam, July 1965

National Security Council Meetings

Situation Report File

Papers of George W. Ball

Papers of Arthur Barber

Papers of Edwin E. Boise

Papers of McGeorge Bundy

Papers of William P. Bundy

Papers of Henry Fowler

Papers of William C. Gibbons

Papers of Lyndon B. Johnson, President, 1963–1969: Tapes and Transcripts of Telephone Conversations and Meetings

Papers of Walt W. Rostow

Papers of Bromley Smith

Papers of Paul C. Warnke

Papers of William C. Westmoreland

White House Central Files (WHCF)

Declassified and Sanitized Documents from Unprocessed Files

Meeting Notes File, Vice Presidential Security Files

Oral Histories

Brown, Harold, 17 January 1969

Bundy, William P., 26 May 1969, 29 May 1969, and 2 June 1969

Christian, George E., 11 November 1968 and 17 September 1979

Cooper, Chester, 9 July 1969

Enthoven, Alain, 27 December 1968

Forrestal, Michael V., 3 November 1969

Foster, John S., 3 December 1968

Gilpatric, Roswell L., 2 November 1982

Goodpaster, Andrew J., 21 June 1971

Humphrey, Hubert H., 17 August 1971

Humphrey, Hubert H., 20 June 1977 and 21 August 1977

Jordan, William H., Jr., 8 December 1974

Lansdale, Edward G., 5 June 1981

LeMay, Curtis E., 28 June 1971

McCone, John A., 19 August 1970

McConnell, John P., 14 August 1969 and 28 August 1969

McPherson, Harry, December 1968

Neustadt, Richard E., undated (transcript given to library on 15 August 1972)

Paul, Norman S., 21 February 1969

Resor, Stanley, 16 November 1968

Rostow, Walt W., 22 December 1968 and 21 March 1969

Rusk, Dean, 28 July 1969, 26 September 1969, 2 January 1970, and 8 March 1970

Sharp, Ulysses S., eleven sessions between 20 September 1969 and 7 June 1970

Smith, Bromley, 29 July 1969 and 25 September 1969

Stennis, John, 17 June 1972

Taylor, Maxwell D., 9 January 1969, 10 February 1969, 1 June 1981 and 14 September 1981

Udall, Stewart L., 18 April 1969

Valenti, Jack, 14 June 1969, 18 October 1969, 19 February 1971, 3 March 1971, and 12 July 1972

Vance, Cyrus, 3 November 1969, 29 December 1969 and 9 March 1970

Vinson, Carl, 24 May 1970

Walt, Lewis W., 24 January 1969

Warnke, Paul, 8 January 1969, 15 January 1969, and 17 January 1969

Westmoreland, William C., 25 July 1969 and 2 August 1969

Wheeler, Earle G., 21 August 1969 and 7 May 1970

Yarmolinsky, Adam, 13 July 1970, 21 October 1980, and 22 October 1980

Zuckert, Eugene M., 18 March 1969

NATIONAL ARCHIVES—MODERN MILITARY BRANCH, WASHINGTON, D.C. AND SUITLAND, MD.

Papers of Robert S. McNamara

Papers of General Earle G. Wheeler

NATIONAL DEFENSE UNIVERSITY LIBRARY, WASHINGTON, D.C.

Papers of General Maxwell D. Taylor

NATIONAL SECURITY ARCHIVE, WASHINGTON, D.C.

Papers of George M. Kahin

Southeast Asia Collection

Vietnam Collection

United States Army Military History Institute, Carlisle Barracks, Pennsylvania

Papers of General Harold K. Johnson

Papers of General Lyman Lemnitzer

Papers of Colonel Paul Miles

Oral Histories

Collins, Arthur S., 1981

Hamlett, Barksdale, 1976

Johnson, Harold K., 1972–74

Lemnitzer, Lyman, 1972

Taylor, Maxwell D., 1973

United States Navy Historical Office, Washington, D.C.

McDonald, David Lamar. *The Reminiscences of Admiral David Lamar McDonald U.S. Navy (Retired)*. Annapolis, Md. U.S. Naval Institute, 1976.

Papers of Admiral David L. McDonald

United States Marine Corps Historical Center, Washington, D.C.

Papers of General Wallace M. Greene

David Shoup Biographical File

Oral Histories

Buse, Henry W., Jr., 1971

Chapman, Leonard F., Jr., 17 January 1979

Jones, William, undated (synopsis only)

Shoup, David M., 1972

GOVERNMENT DOCUMENTS AND
DOCUMENTARY COLLECTIONS

Eisenhower, Dwight D. *Public Papers of the Presidents of the United States: Dwight D. Eisenhower, 1960–1961*. Washington, D.C.: U.S. Government Printing Office, 1961.

Gravel, Mike, Sen., ed. *The Pentagon Papers: The Defense Department History of the Vietnam War*. 5 vols. Boston: Beacon Press, 1971.

Johnson, Lyndon B. *Public Papers of the Presidents: Lyndon B. Johnson, 1964*. Washington, D.C.: U.S. Government Printing Office, 1965.

Johnson, Lyndon B. *Public Papers of the Presidents: Lyndon B. Johnson, 1965*. 2 vols. Washington, D.C.: U.S. Government Printing Office, 1965–66.

Kennedy, John F. *Public Papers of the Presidents: John F. Kennedy*. Washington, D.C.: U.S. Government Printing Office, 1963.

U.S. Department of State. *Foreign Relations of the United States, 1961–1963*. Vol. 1, *Vietnam 1961*; vol. 2, *Vietnam 1962*; vol. 3, *Vietnam January–August 1963*; vol. 4, *Vietnam August–December 1963*. Washington, D.C.: United States Government Printing Office, 1988–91.

———. *Foreign Relations of the United States, 1964–1968*. Vol. 1, *Vietnam 1964*; vol. 2, *Vietnam: January–June 1965*. Washington, D.C.: U.S. Government Printing Office, 1992–96.

———. *Foreign Relations of the United States, 1961–1963*. Vol. 24, *Laos Crisis*. Washington, D.C.: U.S. Government Printing Office, 1994.

INTERVIEWS BY AUTHOR

Goodpaster, Andrew J. 9 March 1993, Washington, D.C. Tape recording.

Johns, John. 11 March 1993, Washington, D.C. Tape recording.

Krulak, Victor H. 26 July 1993, Point Loma, Calif. Tape recording.

Mataxis, Theodore C. 19 February 1993, Chapel Hill, N.C. Tape recording.

Rogers, Bernard W. 12 March 1993, Washington, D.C. Tape recording.

Rostow, Walt W. 13 July 1993, Austin, Tex. Tape recording.

Rostow, Walt W. 21 October 1993, Austin, Tex. Handwritten notes.

Schandler, Herbert Y. 11 March 1993, Washington, D.C. Handwritten notes.

Simmons, Edwin. 8 July 1993, Washington, D.C. Handwritten notes.

Westmoreland, William C. 27 October 1995, West Point, N.Y. Tape recording.

PRIMARY SOURCE BOOKS

Acheson, Dean. *Present at the Creation*. New York: W.W. Norton and Company, 1969.

Allyn, Bruce J., James G. Blight, and David A. Welch, eds. *Back to the Brink: Proceedings of the Moscow Conference on the Cuban Missile Crisis, January 27–28, 1989*. CSIA Occasional Paper no. 9. Lanham, Md.: University Press of America, 1992.

Ball, George W. *The Past Has Another Pattern*. New York: W.W. Norton and Company, 1982.

Blight, James G., and David A. Welch, eds. *On the Brink: Americans and Soviets Reexamine the Cuban Missile Crisis*. New York: Hill & Wang, 1989.

Clifford, Clark. *Counsel to the President: A Memoir*. New York: Random House, 1991.

Cline, Ray S. *Secrets, Spies, and Scholars: Blueprint of the Essential CIA*. Washington, D.C.: Acropolis Books, 1976.

Colby, William. *Lost Victory*. Chicago: Contemporary Books, 1989.

Cooper, Chester. *The Lost Crusade*. New York: Dodd, Mead, 1970.

Diem, Bui. *In the Jaws of History*. Boston: Houghton Mifflin, 1987.

Eisenhower, Dwight David. *Waging Peace*. Garden City, N.Y.: Doubleday, 1956.

Enthoven, Alain, and Wayne K. Smith. *How Much Is Enough?* New York: Harper & Row, 1971.

Gittinger, Ted, ed. *The Johnson Years: A Vietnam Roundtable*. Austin, Tex.: Lyndon Baines Johnson Library, 1993.

Haig, Alexander M., Jr. *Inner Circles: How America Changed the World, A Memoir*. New York: Warner Books, 1992.

Harris, Louis. *The Anguish of Change*. New York: Norton, 1973.

Hilsman, Roger. *To Move a Nation*. Garden City, N.Y.: Doubleday, 1967.

Hoopes, Townsend. *The Limits of Intervention*. New York: David McKay, 1969.

Humphrey, Hubert. *The Education of a Public Man*. Garden City, N.Y.: Doubleday, 1979.

Johnson, Claudia Alta Taylor. *A White House Diary*. New York: Holt, Rinehart & Winston, 1970.

Johnson, Lyndon B. *The Vantage Point: Perspectives on the Presidency, 1963–1969*. New York: Holt, Rinehart & Winston, 1971.

Johnson, U. Alexis. *The Right Hand of Power*. Englewood Cliffs, N.J.: Prentice-Hall, 1984.

Kennedy, Robert F. *Robert Kennedy in His Own Words: The Unpublished Recollections of the Kennedy Years*. Edited by Edwin O. Guthman and Jeffrey Shulman. New York: Bantam Books, 1988.

————. *Thirteen Days: A Memoir of the Cuban Missile Crisis*. New York: W.W. Norton, 1969.

Lansdale, Edward. *In the Midst of Wars: An American's Mission to Southeast Asia*. New York: Harper & Row, 1972.

LeMay, Curtis E. *America Is in Danger*. New York: Harper & Row, 1968.

————. *Mission with LeMay*. Garden City, N.Y.: Doubleday, 1965.

Lodge, Henry Cabot. *The Storm Has Many Eyes*. New York: W.W. Norton and Company, 1973.

McNamara, Robert S. *The Essence of Security: Reflections in Office*. New York: Harper & Row, 1968.

————. *In Retrospect: The Tragedy and Lessons of Vietnam*. New York: Times Books, 1995.

Miller, Merle. *Lyndon: An Oral Biography*. New York: G. P. Putnam's Sons, 1980.

Nitze, Paul. *From Hiroshima to Glasnost: At the Center of Decision: A Memoir*. New York: Grove Weidenfeld, 1988.

Nolting, Frederick. *From Trust to Tragedy: The Political Memoirs of Frederick Nolting, Kennedy's Ambassador to Diem's Vietnam*. New York: Praeger, 1988.

Palmer, Bruce, Jr. *The 25-Year War: America's Military Role in Vietnam*. Lexington: University Press of Kentucky, 1984.

Rostow, Walt W. *The Diffusion of Power*. New York: MacMillan, 1972.

Rusk, Dean. *As I Saw It*. New York: W.W. Norton and Company, 1990.

Sharp, Ulysses S. G. *Strategy for Defeat: Vietnam in Retrospect*. San Rafael, Calif.: Presidio Press, 1978.

Taylor, Maxwell D. *Swords and Plowshares*. New York: W.W. Norton and Company, 1972.

————. *The Uncertain Trumpet*. New York: Harper, 1959.

Walt, Lewis W. *Strange War, Strange Strategy: A General's Report on Vietnam*. New York: Funk and Wagnalls, 1970.

Westmoreland, William C. *A Soldier Reports*. New York: Dell, 1976.

SECONDARY SOURCE BOOKS

Altschuler, Bruce E. *LBJ and the Polls*. Gainesville: University of Florida Press, 1986.

Ambrose, Stephen E. *Eisenhower*. Vol. 2, *The President*. New York: Simon & Schuster, 1984.

Art, Robert J. *The TFX Decision: McNamara and the Military*. Boston: Little, Brown & Company, 1968.

Ball, Moya Ann. *Vietnam-on-the-Potomac*. New York: Praeger, 1992.

Baral, Jaya Krishna. *The Pentagon and the Making of U.S. Foreign Policy: A Case Study of Vietnam, 1960–1968*. New Delhi, India: Radiant Publishers, 1978.

Barrett, David M. *Uncertain Warriors: Lyndon Johnson and His Vietnam Advisors*. Lawrence: University of Kansas Press, 1993.

Berman, Larry Lyndon. *Planning a Tragedy: The Americanization of the War in Vietnam*. New York: W.W. Norton and Company, 1982.

———. *Lyndon Johnson's War: The Road to Stalemate in Vietnam*. New York: W.W. Norton and Company, 1989.

Blaufarb, Douglas S. *The Counterinsurgency Era: U.S. Doctrine and Performance, 1950 to the Present*. New York: Free Press, 1977.

Blight, James G. *The Shattered Crystal Ball: Fear and Learning in the Cuban Missile Crisis*. Savage, Md.: Rowan and Littlefield, 1990.

Borklund, Carl W. *Men of the Pentagon: From Forrestal to McNamara*. New York: Praeger, 1966.

———. *The Department of Defense*. New York: Praeger, 1968.

Borowski, Harry R., ed. *Military Planning in the Twentieth Century*. Washington, D.C.: Office of Air Force History, 1986.

Braestrup, Peter. *Vietnam as History*. Washington, D.C.: University Press of America, 1984.

Brinkley, Douglas. *Dean Acheson: The Cold War Years, 1953–71*. New Haven, Conn.: Yale University Press, 1991.

Brugioni, Dino A. *Eyeball to Eyeball: The Inside Story of the Cuban Missile Crisis*. New York: Random House, 1990.

Burke, John P., and Fred I. Greenstein. *How Presidents Test Reality: Decisions on Vietnam, 1954 and 1965*. New York: Russell Sage Foundation, 1989.

Buzzanco, Robert. *Masters of War: Military Dissent and Politics in the Vietnam Era*. New York: Cambridge University Press, 1996.

Caro, Robert A. *The Years of Lyndon Johnson*. Vol. 1, *The Path to Power*. New York, Alfred A. Knopf, 1982.

————. *The Years of Lyndon Johnson*. Vol. 2, *Means of Ascent*. New York: Alfred A. Knopf, 1990.

Clarke, Jeffrey J. *Advice and Support: The Final Years, 1965–1973*. Washington, D.C.: U.S. Army Center of Military History, United States Army, 1988.

Clausewitz, Carl von. *On War*. Edited and translated by Michael Howard and Peter Paret. Princeton, N.J.: Princeton University Press, 1976.

Clodfelter, Mark. *The Limits of Air Power: The American Bombing of North Vietnam*. New York: Free Press, 1989.

Coffey, Thomas M. *Iron Eagle: The Turbulent Life of General Curtis LeMay*. New York: Crown Publishers, 1986.

Davidson, Phillip B. *Vietnam at War: The History, 1946–1975*. Novato, Calif.: Presidio Press, 1988.

DiLeo, David L. *George Ball, Vietnam and the Rethinking of Containment*. Chapel Hill: University of North Carolina Press, 1991.

Divine, Robert A. *Eisenhower and the Cold War*. New York: Oxford University Press, 1981.

————. ed. *Exploring the Johnson Years*. Austin: University of Texas Press, 1981.

————. *Foreign Policy and Presidential Elections, 1952–1960*. New York: New Viewpoints, 1974.

Duiker, William J. *The Communist Road to Power in Vietnam*. Boulder, Colo.: Westview Press, 1981.

————. *Sacred War: Nationalism and Revolution in a Divided Vietnam*. New York: McGraw Hill, 1995.

Evans, Rowland and Robert Novak. *Lyndon Johnson: The Exercise of Power*. New York: The New American Library, 1966.

Gardner, Lloyd. *Pay Any Price: Lyndon Johnson and the Wars for Vietnam*. Chicago: Ivan R. Dee, 1995.

————. ed. *Vietnam: The Early Decisions*. Austin: University of Texas Press, forthcoming.

Garthoff, Raymond L. *Reflections on the Cuban Missile Crisis*. Washington, D.C.: Brookings Institution, 1989.

Gelb, Leslie H., and Richard K. Betts. *The Irony of Vietnam: The System Worked*. Washington, D.C.: Brookings Institution, 1979.

George, Alexander. *Presidential Decisionmaking in Foreign Policy: The Effective Use of Information and Advice*. Boulder, Colo.: Westview, 1980.

George, Alexander; David K. Hall, and William E. Simons. *The Limits of Coercive Diplomacy*. Boston: Little Brown & Company, 1971.

Gibbons, William Conrad. *The U.S. Government and the Vietnam War: Executive and Legislative Roles and Relationships*. 4 vols. Princeton, N.J.: Princeton University Press, 1986–95.

Goulden, Joseph C. *Truth is the First Casualty: The Gulf of Tonkin Affair— Illusion and Reality*. New York: Rand McNally, 1969.

Gribkov, Anatoli I. and William Y. Smith. *Operation Anadyr: US and Soviet Generals Recount the Cuban Missile Crisis*. Chicago: Edition q, 1994.

Halberstam, David. *The Best and the Brightest*. New York: Random House, 1969.

Hendrickson, Paul. *The Living and the Dead: Robert McNamara and Five Lives of a Lost War*. New York: Alfred A. Knopf, 1996.

Henggeler, Paul R. *In His Steps: Lyndon Johnson and the Kennedy Mystique*. Chicago: Ivan R. Dee, 1991.

Herring, George C. *America's Longest War: The United States and Vietnam, 1950–1975*. 3rd ed., New York: Alfred A. Knopf, 1996.

Herring, George C. *LBJ and Vietnam: A Different Kind of War*. Austin: University of Texas Press, 1994.

Herring, George C., ed. *The Secret Diplomacy of the Vietnam War: The Negotiating Volumes of the Pentagon Papers*. Austin: University of Texas Press, 1983.

Hewes, James E. *From Root to McNamara: Army Organization and Administration, 1900–1963*. Washington, D.C.: U.S. Government Printing Office, 1975.

Higgins, Trumbull. *The Perfect Failure: Kennedy, Eisenhower, and the CIA at the Bay of Pigs*. New York: W.W. Norton and Comany, 1987.

Historical Division of the Joint Secretariat. *The Joint Chiefs of Staff and the War in Vietnam*. Part 1, *History of the Indochina Incident, 1940–1954*. Wilmington, Del.: Michael Glazier, 1982.

Hunt, Michael. *Lyndon Johnson's War: America's Cold War Crusade in Vietnam, 1945-1968*. New York: Hill & Wang, 1996.

Isaacson, Walter, and Evan Thomas. *The Wise Men: Six Friends and the World They Made*. New York: Simon & Schuster, 1986.

Janis, Irving. *Victims of Groupthink: A Psychological Study of Foreign Policy Decisions and Fiascoes*. Boston: Houghton Mifflin, 1972.

Kagan, Donald. *On the Origins of War and the Preservation of Peace*. New York: Anchor Books, 1994.

Karnow, Stanley. *Vietnam: A History*. 2nd. ed. New York: Penguin Books, 1991.

Kaufmann, William W. *The McNamara Strategy*. New York: Harper & Row, 1964.

Kearns, Doris. *Lyndon Johnson and the American Dream*. New York: Harper & Row, 1976.

Kinnard, Douglas. *President Eisenhower and Strategy Management: A Study in Defense Politics*. Lexington: University Press of Kentucky, 1977.

———. *The War Managers*. Wayne, N.J.: Avery Publishing Group, 1985.

———. *The Certain Trumpet: Maxwell Taylor and the American Experience in Vietnam*. New York: Brassey's, 1991.

———. *The Secretary of Defense*. Lexington: University of Kentucky Press, 1980.

Korb, Lawrence. *The Joint Chiefs of Staff: The First Twenty-Five Years*. Bloomington: Indiana University Press, 1976.

Krepinevich, Andrew F., Jr. *The Army and Vietnam*. Baltimore, Md.: Johns Hopkins University Press, 1986.

Krieg, Joann P., ed. *Dwight Eisenhower: Soldier, President, Statesman*. New York: Greenwood Press, 1987.

Marolda, Edward J., and Oscar P. Fitzgerald, *The United States Navy and the Vietnam Conflict*. Vol. 2, *From Military Assistance to Combat, 1959–1965*. Washington, D.C.: Naval Historical Center, 1986.

Palmer, Gregory. *The McNamara Strategy and the Vietnam War*. Westport, Conn.: Greenwood Press, 1978.

Paret, Peter. *Clausewitz and the State: The Man, His Theories, and His Times*. Princeton, N.J.: Princeton University Press, 1985.

Parmet, Herbert S. *JFK: The Presidency of John F. Kennedy*. New York: Dial Press, 1983.

———. *Jack: The Struggles of John F. Kennedy*. New York: The Dial Press, 1980.

———. *Eisenhower and the American Crusades*. New York: Macmillan, 1972.

Perry, Mark. *Four Stars*. Boston: Houghton Mifflin, 1989.

Pogue, Forrest C. *George C. Marshall*. Vol. 1., *Education of a General, 1880–1939*; vol. 2, *Ordeal and Hope, 1939–1942*; vol. 3, *Organizer of Victory, 1943–1945*; vol. 4, *Statesman, 1945–1949*. New York: Viking, 1963–80.

Prochnau, William. *Once Upon a Distant War*. New York: Times Books, 1995.

Quade, E. S., ed., *Analysis for Military Decisions*. Chicago: Rand McNally, 1964.

Race, Jeffrey. *War Comes to Long An: Revolutionary Conflict in a Vietnamese Province*. Berkeley: University of California Press, 1972.

Ranelagh, John. *The Agency: The Rise and Decline of the CIA*. New York: Simon & Schuster, 1986.

Reeves, Richard. *President Kennedy: Profile of Power*. New York: Touchstone, 1993.

Reeves, Thomas C., ed. *John F. Kennedy: The Man, The Politician, The President*. Melbourne, Fla.: Krieger, 1990.

Schandler, Herbert Y. *The Unmaking of a President: Lyndon Johnson and Vietnam*. Princeton: Princeton University Press, 1977.

Schlesinger, Arthur M., Jr., ed. *History of American Presidential Elections, 1789–1968*. 4 vols. New York: Chelsea House, 1971.

———. *A Thousand Days*. Boston: Houghton Mifflin, 1965.

Schlight, John, ed. *Second Indochina War Symposium: Papers and Commentary*. Washington, D.C.: U.S. Army Center of Military History, 1986.

Schoenbaum, Thomas J. *Waging Peace and War: Dean Rusk in the Truman, Kennedy and Johnson Years*. New York: Simon & Schuster, 1988.

Shapley, Deborah. *Promise and Power: The Life and Times of Robert McNamara*. Boston: Little Brown, 1993.

Sheehan, Neil. *A Bright Shining Lie: John Paul Vann and America in Vietnam*. New York: Random House, 1988.

Sorensen, Theodore C. *Kennedy*. 2nd ed. New York: Harper & Row, 1988.

Spector, Ronald. *Advice and Support: The Early Years: The U.S. Army in Vietnam*. Washington, D.C.: U.S. Army Center of Military History, 1983.

Stevenson, Charles A. *The End of Nowhere: American Policy Toward Laos Since 1954*. Boston: Beacon Press, 1973.

Summers, Harry G. *On Strategy: A Critical Analysis of the Vietnam War*. New York: Dell, 1982.

Taylor, John M. *General Maxwell Taylor: The Sword and the Pen*. New York: Doubleday, 1985.

Thies, Wallace J. *When Governments Collide: Coercion and Diplomacy in the Vietnam Conflict, 1964–1968*. Berkeley, Calif.: University of California Press, 1980.

Thompson, James Clay. *Rolling Thunder: Understanding Policy and Program Failure*. Chapel Hill: University of North Carolina Press, 1980.

Tilford, Earl H. *Setup: What the Air Force Did in Vietnam and Why*. Maxwell Air Force Base, Ala.: Air University Press, 1991.

Trewhitt, Henry L. *McNamara: His Ordeal in the Pentagon*. New York: Harper & Row, 1971.

VanDeMark, Brian. *Into the Quagmire: Lyndon Johnson and the Escalation of the Vietnam War*. New York: Oxford University Press, 1991.

Zaffiri, Samuel. *Westmoreland: A Biography of General William C. Westmoreland*. New York: Morrow, 1994.

ARTICLES

Ball, George W. "Top Secret: The Prophecy the President Rejected." *Atlantic* 230 (July 1972), pp. 35–49.

Barrett, David M. "The Mythology Surrounding Lyndon Johnson, His Advisors, and the 1965 Decision to Escalate the Vietnam War." *Political Science Quarterly* 103 (Winter 1988–89), pp. 637–63.

Berman, Larry. "Coming to Grips with Lyndon Johnson's War." *Diplomatic History* 17 (Fall 1993), pp. 519–38.

Brodie, Bernard. "Why We Were So Wrong." *Foreign Policy* 5 (Winter 1971–72), pp. 151–62.

Brower, Charles F. "Strategic Reassessment in Vietnam: The Westmoreland 'Alternative Strategy' of 1967–1968." *Naval War College Review* 44 (Spring 1991), pp. 20–51.

Bundy, William P. "The Path to Vietnam: Ten Decisions." *Orbis* (Fall 1967), pp. 647–63.

Buzzanco, Robert. "U.S. Military Opposition to Vietnam, 1950–1954." *Diplomatic History* 17 (Spring 1993), pp. 201–22.

Clifford, Clark M. "A Viet Nam Reappraisal: The Personal History of One Man's View and How It Evolved." *Foreign Affairs* 47 (Summer 1969), pp. 601–22.

Davidson, Michael W. "Senior Officers and Vietnam Policymaking." *Parameters* 16 (Spring 1986), pp. 55–62.

Divine, Robert A. "Vietnam Reconsidered." *Diplomatic History* 12 (Winter 1988), pp. 79–94.

Ginsburgh, Robert N. "The Challenge to Military Professionalism," *Foreign Affairs* 42 (January 1964), 255–68.

Gray, Colin S. "What RAND Hath Wrought." *Foreign Policy* 4 (Fall 1971), pp. 111–29.

Greenstein, Fred I., and John P. Burke. "The Dynamics of Presidential Reality Testing: Evidence From Two Vietnam Decisions." *Political Science Quarterly* 104 (Winter 1989–90), pp. 557–80.

Halperin, Morton H. "The President and the Military." *Foreign Affairs* 50 (January 1972), pp. 310–24.

Hamilton, William A. "The Decline and Fall of the Joint Chiefs of Staff," *US Naval War College Review* (April 1972), pp. 36–58.

Herring, George C., and Richard H. Immerman. "Eisenhower, Dulles, and Dien Bien Phu: 'The Day We Didn't Go to War' Revisited." *Journal of American History* 71 (September 1984), pp. 343–63.

Humphrey, David C. "Tuesday Lunch at the Johnson White House: A Preliminary Assessment." *Diplomatic History* 8 (Winter 1984), 81–101.

Janis, Irving. "Groupthink." *Psychology Today* (November 1971), pp. 43–44, 46, 74–76.

Johnson, Harold K. "The Army Chief of Staff on Military Strategy in Vietnam." *Army Digest*, 23 April 1968, pp. 6–9.

Kearns, Doris. "Lyndon Johnson's Political Personality." *Political Science Quarterly* 91 (Fall 1976), pp. 385–410.

McConnell, John. "Some Reflections on a Tour of Duty,." *Air University Review* 20, no. 6 (September-October 1969), pp. 2–11.

McFetridge, Charles D. "Foreign Policy and Military Strategy: The Civil-Military Equation." *Military Review* 66 (April 1986), pp. 22–30.

McKitrick, Jeffrey S. "The JCS: Evolutionary or Revolutionary Reform?" *Parameters* 16 (Spring 1986), pp. 63–75.

Muslin, Hyman, and Thomas Jobe. "The Tragic Self of Lyndon Johnson and the Dilemma of Leadership." *Psychohistory Review* 15 (Spring 1987), pp. 69–119.

Palmer, Bruce. "U.S. Intelligence and Vietnam." *Studies in Intelligence* 28 (1984), Special Edition.

Tatum, Lawrence B. "The Joint Chiefs of Staff and Defense Policy Formulation." *Air University Review* (May-June, 1966), pp. 40–44.

Trachtenberg, Marc. "Strategic Thought in America, 1952–1966." *Political Science Quarterly* 104 (Summer 1989), pp. 301–34.

Taylor, Maxwell D. "Military Advice—Its Use in Government." *Vital Speeches*, March 18, 1964, pp. 336–39.

"Post-Vietnam Role of the Military In Foreign Policy." *Air University Review*. 19 (September-October, 1968), pp. 50–58.

"Security Will Not Wait." *Foreign Affairs* 39 (January 1961), pp. 174–84.

THESES AND UNPUBLISHED PAPERS

Barlow, Jeffrey Graham. "President John F. Kennedy and His Joint Chiefs of Staff." Ph.D. diss., University of South Carolina, 1981.

Binkley, John Charles. "The Role of the Joint Chiefs of Staff in National Security Policy Making: Professionalism and Self-Perceptions, 1942–1961." Ph.D. diss., Loyola University, Chicago, 1985.

Bundy, William. Unpublished manuscript, Papers of William P. Bundy, LBJ Library.

Demma, Vincent. "Suggestions for the Use of Ground Forces, June 1964–March 1965." U.S. Army Center of Military History, Washington, D.C.

Hamilton, W. Alexander. "The Influence of the American Military Upon United States Foreign Policy, 1965–1968," Ph.D. diss., University of Nebraska, 1978.

Kenney, Stephen F. "Vietnam Decision-Making: A Psychological Perspective on American Foreign Policy." Ph.D. diss., Boston University, 1978.

NEWSPAPERS AND PERIODICALS

Business Week

Harper's

The New Republic

Newsweek

New York Times

Saturday Evening Post

Time

U.S. News & World Report

Wall Street Journal

Washington Post

Index

Johnson, Robert H., 180, 203
Johnson, U. Alexis, 26, 208, 228, 230, 252
Joint Chiefs of Staff (JCS)
  administrative system, 17–18, 74
  advice on covert activity, 59
  advice on warfare in Vietnam and "hard knock" approach, 43, 63–65, 68–80, 85–87, 92, 94, 100–3, 137–39, 141, 142–50, 159–60, 166, 168–71, 176, 182, 186, 187, 191, 192–93, 209–10, 261
  appointment of chairman, policy on, 108
  and Bay of Pigs, 5–7, 16, 22, 24, 27
  and Congressional responsibility, 331
  "Courses of Action in Southeast Asia," 180–89
  and Cuban invasion plans, 25, 27–28
  deceptions and lies to, 92–93, 94, 101–2, 176, 192, 298, 301
  and deployment of troops, 210, 217–18, 262–64, 269, 300–22
  Diem coup, opposition to, 45–46, 66
  and Eisenhower, 5, 12–13
  formation of, 13–14
  and Gulf of Tonkin incident, 127–36
  and graduated pressure doctrine, 64, 70, 72–76, 78, 79, 81, 92–93, 99, 100–3, 116, 147, 154, 177–78, 185–89, 207–8, 238, 247, 273, 327–28
  interservice rivalries/divisiveness, 14, 18, 21, 23, 81–83, 113–14, 142–43, 152–54, 168, 217–18, 225, 249, 255, 272, 304, 327
  and Johnson, 5, 49–50, 54, 63–65, 67–68, 85–89, 94, 113, 175, 187–88, 244, 261, 264–65, 284, 313–19
  and Kennedy, 5–23, 43, 46
  and Laos, 7–8
  loss of presidential access/influence, 54–56, 65, 67, 85–89, 90–92, 98–103, 111, 113, 114, 115–17, 139, 147–48, 151–154, 186, 189, 192, 208–9, 222, 225, 285–86, 303, 328–29
  loyalties, conflicting, 311–12, 329–33
  and McNamara, 64, 71–87, 90–91, 98–99, 147, 151, 168, 175–76, 185–87, 208–9, 222, 249–50, 285–86, 295–96, 298, 301–22, 328, 329
  memoranda on escalation, 247
  and ordering action in Vietnam, 160–62, 222, 233–34

philosophies of members, 44–45, 64, 103–4
silence and consensus of, 167, 178, 181–82, 191–92, 196, 217–18, 225–26, 243, 247, 261, 298, 317–18, 319, 329
targets recommended, 93, 127, 147, 158, 173, 186, 192, 214, 221, 222, 226, 238, 286
and Taylor, 14–17, 21, 22, 27–28, 42–45, 76–79, 85, 87–88, 94, 97, 101–3, 115–17, 278
war games, 89–91, 155–58
and Wheeler chairmanship, 108–10, 116, 225–26
withdrawal memo, 175–76

Kattenberg, Paul, 203
Katzenbach, Nicholas, 294, 295
Keating, Kenneth, 24
Kennedy, Jacqueline, 105
Kennedy, John F.
  appointments, 2–4, 22, 31, 43
  approach to decision-making and administration, 4–5, 6, 15, 21, 23, 39
  assassination, 47
  Bay of Pigs, 5–7, 8, 11, 16, 22, 23, 24, 25
  and Berlin Wall, 23, 31
  and Bundy, 3–4, 15–16
  Castro, personal antipathy toward, 25
  Cuban missile crisis, 24–31
  decision to withdraw one thousand advisers from Vietnam, 40
  and Department of Defense/Pentagon, 2, 5, 23
  and Diem coup, 38–41, 46
  election of, 1–2
  and the JCS, 5–23, 28, 43, 46
  Laotian crisis, 7–8, 22, 23, 32
  and LeMay, 43
  and McNamara, 2–4, 15, 17–22
  military policy, 10–11, 32, 43, 109
  and NSC dismantlement, 4–5, 6
  personality and style, 15–16
  and Rusk, 3–4
  and Soviets, 8, 30, 43
  speech to West Point graduating class, 1962, 32
  and Taylor, 8–17, 21–22, 105, 109
  and Vietnam, 22, 23, 32, 37–41, 324
Kennedy, Robert
  and Castro assassination attempts, 25
  and Cuban missile crisis, 26, 28

McNamara, Robert (*cont.*)
  and Johnson, 47–49, 53–54, 60–63, 66,
    69, 74–84, 88, 89, 90–91, 123, 126,
    206, 209, 212–14, 240, 255, 269–70,
    278–79, 281, 284, 293, 295–96,
    312–13, 316, 321, 326
  and mobilization, 316–22
  opposition to Air Force bomber
    development, 81
  philosophy on military, 2, 96, 328
  and strategic planning/systems analysis,
    29–30, 41, 72–73, 91, 155, 163, 223,
    326–27
  and Taylor, 22–23, 47, 76–79, 254,
    278–79
  Vietnam policy, 58–61, 62–63, 72, 73,
    75–79, 80, 81, 83, 84, 85, 89, 96–97,
    100, 107, 120, 154, 166–67, 212–14,
    221–22, 231, 253–54, 280–81, 285,
    289, 293, 298, 300–301, 306–8,
    326–27
  Vietnam visits, 57–58, 69, 71, 75,
    95–97, 308–9
  and war games, 156
  and Whiz Kids, 2, 18–21, 24
McNaughton, John, 18–19, 71–72, 74,
    196, 237, 255, 278, 295
  aims memo, 236–37
  "Courses of Action in Southeast Asia,"
    180–89
  defeat, planning for, 219, 237
  "Graduated Military Pressure and
    Related Actions," 191
  and issuing orders, 161–62
  Vietnam policy making by, 98–99,
    114–15, 147–48, 151, 160, 163, 190,
    206–7, 286, 289, 301, 306, 308
  Vietnam trips, 214–16, 245–48
  and war games, 156
media
  banning of, 211
  criticism of Johnson Vietnam policy, 97
  deceptions/lies to, 100, 104, 117–19,
    195, 211–12
  leaks, 239–40, 244, 266, 290
  need for support from, 128
  reporting of events in Vietnam, 210
Meeker, Leonard, 294
Military Assistance and Advisory Group
  (MAAG), 36
Military Assistance Command, Vietnam
  (MACV), 38, 66, 87, 95, 96, 100,
  110, 112, 187
Moore, Joseph H., 95

Morgenthau, Hans, 243
Morse, Wayne, 133–34, 152, 214, 272
Moyers, Bill, 174, 293
Munich Agreement, 1938, 146, 248
Mustin, Lloyd, 180, 181, 182

National Security Action Memorandum
  (NSAM) 55, 16, 105
National Security Action Memorandum
  (NSAM) 273, 16, 64
National Security Action Memorandum
  (NSAM) 288, 99, 236
National Security Action Memorandum
  (NSAM) 314, 153, 155, 161
National Security Act of 1947, 4, 13, 311
National Security Council (NSC), 13
  and Eisenhower, 4
  Executive Committee (EXCOM),
    26–27
  and JCS, 5
  and Kennedy, 4
negotiations/diplomacy, 283–85, 288,
  289–90
  and bombing campaign, 234, 235–36,
    258
  and Canada, 159
  and graduated pressure policy, 94, 155,
    160, 164
New Frontiersmen, 4, 5, 21, 23. *See also*
  Kennedy, John F., appointments
New York Times, 240, 333
  articles on widening war, 239, 244
  editorials, 195, 291
  Johnson and senators, Jan 21, 1965, 211
Ngo Dinh Diem, 35–41, 42, 45, 46, 66, 324
Ngo Dinh Khoi, 35
Ngo Dinh Nhu, 35, 38, 39, 42, 45, 46, 324
Nguyen Cao Ky, 119, 199, 200, 228, 288
Nguyen Khanh, 65, 75, 78, 95, 115,
  139–40, 151, 152, 164–65, 199, 215,
  227–29
Nguyen Xuan Oanh, 227
Nha Trang, 231
Nitze, Paul, 18, 19, 26, 81, 140, 316–17
Nixon, Richard M., 1
Nolting, Frederick, 38–39
Norstad, Lauris, 22
North Atlantic Treaty Organization
  (NATO), 22, 103
North Vietnam
  advances into South/build up, 262–63,
    281
  air strikes against, 107, 161, 217–20,
    234, 238, 299

About the Author

H. R. McMaster is the Fouad and Michelle Ajami Senior Fellow at the Hoover Institution at Stanford University. He is also the Susan and Bernard Liautaud Fellow at the Freeman Spogli Institute and Lecturer at the Stanford Graduate School of Business. He serves as chairman of the advisory board of the Center for Military and Political Power at the Foundation for Defense of Democracy and the Japan Chair at the Hudson Institute. A native of Philadelphia, H.R. graduated from the United States Military Academy in 1984. He served as a U.S. Army officer for thirty-four years and retired as a lieutenant general in 2018. He remained on active duty while serving as the twenty-sixth assistant to the president for national security affairs. He taught history at West Point and holds a PhD in history from the University of North Carolina at Chapel Hill.

H. R. McMaster, author of *Dereliction of Duty*, was chosen by the Air Force Association as the 1998 recipient of the Gill Robb Wislon Award—the highest award presented annually by the association in the field of Arts and Letters. The citation reads "For his insight and courage in authoring *Dereliction of Duty*, a book that has been extraordinary, if not unprecedented, in the degree of attention, credibility and influence it has achieved among military leaders and professionals. Major McMaster's diligent research and quality analysis of how and why the United States entered the Vietnam War is perhaps the most important book on a military subject to be published in years."

Dereliction of Duty also received the New York Military Affairs Symposium's 1997 Award for Outstanding Book on Military History.